The Iraq War Encyclopedia

The Iraq War Encyclopedia

Thomas R. Mockaitis, Editor

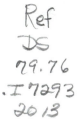
 ABC-CLIO

Santa Barbara, California • Denver, Colorado • Oxford, England

Copyright 2013 by ABC-CLIO, LLC

All rights reserved. No part of this publication may be reproduced, stored in a retrieval system, or transmitted, in any form or by any means, electronic, mechanical, photocopying, recording, or otherwise, except for the inclusion of brief quotations in a review, without prior permission in writing from the publisher.

Library of Congress Cataloging-in-Publication Data

The Iraq War encyclopedia / Thomas R. Mockaitis, Editor.
    pages cm
  Includes bibliographical references and index.
    ISBN 978–0–313–38062–4 (hard copy : alk. paper) — ISBN 978–0–313–38063–1 (ebook)
  1. Iraq War, 2003–2011—Encyclopedias. I. Mockaitis, Thomas R., 1955– editor.
  DS79.76.I7293   2013
  956.7044′303—dc23   2013008479

ISBN: 978–0–313–38062–4
EISBN: 978–0–313–38063–1

17 16 15 14 13   1 2 3 4 5

This book is also available on the World Wide Web as an eBook.
Visit www.abc-clio.com for details.

ABC-CLIO, LLC
130 Cremona Drive, P.O. Box 1911
Santa Barbara, California 93116-1911

This book is printed on acid-free paper ∞

Manufactured in the United States of America

To the Newest Members of My Family:

Jill Gamer Mockaitis
Samantha Gilchrist Mockaitis

Contents

List of Entries

Preface

The Iraq War was a watershed in modern U.S. military history. The army that invaded Iraq in March 2003 differed markedly from the one that left the country in December 2011. The invading army's equipment, organization, and doctrine belonged to the era of the Cold War for which it had been redesigned in 1970s. Built around heavy armored divisions equipped with M-1A Abrams tanks, it had been created to fight the Warsaw Pact in Germany's Fulda Gap. Traumatized by the experience of Vietnam, that army wanted nothing to do with unconventional operations, which it gladly delegated to the Special Forces. Forced to engage in unwanted peace operations during the 1990s, it welcomed the election of a president who promised to eschew further adventures in nation building. Counterinsurgency (COIN) was the dirtiest word in its lexicon. The last war it wanted to fight was the one it got in the Tigris-Euphrates Valley.

During the next eight years that army went through a profound transformation. Faced with a growing insurgency, it produced its first new COIN manual since the Vietnam War. It reorganized its cumbersome conventional divisions into smaller more flexible units that could be assembled into brigade combat teams tailored to specific tasks. A new generation of junior officers and senior noncommissioned officers (NCOs) gained combat experience that far exceeded that of the generals who commanded them. Fortunately, those generals had the good sense to delegate responsibility to the young men and women in the field. A new strategy called the Anbar Awakening turned the tide of the insurgency as Americans trained Iraqi forces to handle their own security.

The story of the Iraq War has been told and retold over the past decade by the men and women who fought there, by the reporters who covered the conflict, and by the analysts who tried to make sense of events. The process of analysis has, however, only begun. Much about the war has become clearer in the past couple of years; more will come into focus in the years and decades ahead. The process of understanding has been furthered by the many researchers and writers who have contributed to a growing body of literature on the subject. This volume of essays hopes to add to that literature by providing a comprehensive overview of the war, valuable to scholars but comprehensible to ordinary readers. Its authors come from a variety of disciplines, each bringing a unique perspective to the topic about which he or she writes. I hope that as much as it informs contemporary readers it will also inspire future analysts to delve more deeply into each of the topics it addresses and so further our understanding of this important conflict.

Overview

The Iraq War was a decade in the making. The neoconservatives who entered the White House with George W. Bush had long considered eliminating President Saddam Hussein to be unfinished business from the 1991 Gulf War. In his debate with Vice President Al Gore, then governor Bush complained that the Iraqi dictator remained in power despite his defiance of numerous United Nations (UN) resolutions. As a new president put in office by the most controversial election in recent memory, however, he could not hope to take the United States to war with Iraq without some pretext. Containment kept Hussein in check, and as long as he posed no immediate threat to his neighbors, it would be difficult to garner sufficient public and political support for removing him from power. The September 11, 2001, terrorist attacks changed the situation dramatically. Although few people believed that the Iraqi dictator had anything to do with al-Qaeda, arguments for removing him became much easier to sell in the paranoia of the post–September 11 world. The administration had first to deal with the Taliban, but within a year of liberating Kabul they turned their attention to Baghdad.

The White House played up a dubious terrorist threat posed by Iraq. Intelligence reports that have since been discredited raised the unlikely specter of a nuclear-armed Saddam Hussein. When critics challenged this conclusion, the administration warned of Iraq's alleged chemical and biological weapons programs, which, it claimed, might fall into the hands of terrorists. This threat too seemed dubious, so at the end of the day Washington invaded Iraq to liberate its people from tyranny and reinvent their country as a bastion of democracy in the Middle East.

Like so many leaders before him, President Bush promised the American people that the war would be short. The ensuing conflict, in fact, lasted eight long years and cost the lives of more than 4,000 U.S. servicemen and women as well as untold billions of taxpayer dollars. The Iraqi dead have yet to be counted. The conflict unfolded in roughly four phases. From March to May 2003 coalition forces launched a conventional invasion of Iraq. During the spring and summer of that year the United States and its allies faced a growing insurgency that increased in intensity through June of 2007. The surge strategy and the Anbar Awakening took the next two years to defeat the insurgency. From then until the withdrawal in December 2011 U.S. and coalition forces concentrated on training Iraq's army and police in preparation for the transition to complete autonomy.

Planning for invasion presumed a swift march to Baghdad followed by a brief period of transition to democracy and a prompt withdrawal of American troops. Because he did not wish to engage in a protracted nation-building operation requiring a large occupation force, Secretary of Defense Donald Rumsfeld kept the invasion force as small possible. Fewer than 150,000 troops made up the invasion force, more than enough to defeat Saddam Hussein's hollow military, but not nearly enough to occupy and stabilize a country the size of Iraq. The Pentagon also sorely neglected planning for phase four stability operations, which they did not want to undertake.

As anticipated, the U.S. Army and Marine Corps supported by British troops easily defeated the Iraqi military following a brief but intense air campaign dubbed "shock and awe." As they advanced toward Baghdad, however, Iraqi Army units did not surrender en masse or return to barracks as requested. Many units simply melted away, their soldiers going home with their small arms. U.S. forces also encountered organized guerrillas, the Fedayeen Saddam, trained and equipped by the dictator to impede the invasion. Unemployed soldiers and the regime's trained partisans would be a major source of insurgent recruitment during the occupation. This danger did not become immediately clear until much later. On April 5, 2003, U.S. forces entered Baghdad; two days later the British took Basra; and a week after that the Pentagon declared an end to major ground operations. On May 1 President Bush landed on the deck of the U.S.S. *Abraham Lincoln* and gave his famous "mission accomplished" speech.

During the spring and summer of 2003 discontent among the Iraqi people intensified. Far from being prepared to run the country once Saddam was gone, the Iraqi government collapsed. Widespread looting and lawlessness resulted from the power vacuum. Iraq's already weakened infrastructure broke down completely in many areas. High unemployment exacerbated by L. Paul Bremer III's de-Baathification and demobilization orders fueled resentment by dismissing without pay thousands of party officials and military personnel. At the same time a long oppressed Shia majority asserted itself against the Sunni minority. The Kurds in northern Iraq had even less love for the government in Baghdad, having suffered brutal repression by Hussein, including a poison gas attack in the 1980s. The U.S.-led coalition lacked the requisite number of troops, the experience, and the training to police a country of 26 million people. To make matters worse, foreign mujahideen entered the country to fight the invaders. The country slid rapidly and inexorably into a toxic a blend of insurgency, civil war, and terrorism.

The United States took a long time to identify the problem and even longer to develop an appropriate strategy for dealing with it. For most of the first year in Iraq, the White House insisted that regime holdouts were responsible for the escalating violence. In keeping with this mistaken conclusion, U.S. forces concentrated on rounding up regime leaders, the famous deck of cards with pictures of the fugitives. The futility of this approach soon became clear. On December 13, 2003, they captured Saddam Hussein. His arrest, trial, and execution had no effect on the insurgency, which continued to grow. Far from withdrawing troops, Washington had to deploy more of them along with thousands of private contractors to provide security and rebuild the country.

In 2006 the situation began to change, though few at the time recognized it. That year the Pentagon released its first new counterinsurgency manual since the Vietnam War. On the ground, American units began working with Sunni sheiks to rid the country of the hated mujahideen, particularly the forces of al-Qaeda in the Land of the Two Rivers (generally called al-Qaeda in Iraq). These measures notwithstanding, *The Report of the Iraq Study Group* released in the fall of 2006 painted a grim picture of the situation in Iraq. In response to this study President Bush announced a "surge" of some 30,000 combat troops to defeat the insurgency. In January 2007 he appointed General David Petraeus to command coalition land forces in Iraq. As commander of the 101st Airborne Division north of Baghdad, Petraeus had enjoyed considerable success countering the insurgents. He was also involved in producing the new counterinsurgency manual.

By early 2009 the United States had decisively turned the corner on the insurgency. U.S. advisers could now devote the bulk of their effort to preparing Iraqi forces to assume full responsibility for the security of their country. In February 2009 newly elected president Barack Obama announced that combat operations in Iraq would end by August 31, 2010. The Pentagon withdrew units specifically designated for combat by the stipulated withdrawal date. By agreement with the Iraqi government, the remaining U.S. forces were to be withdrawn by December 18, 2011. Iraqi prime minister Nuri al-Maliki and President Obama wanted to extend the deadline, but the idea met with too much opposition to be implemented. Iraq remains a fragile state but, contrary to worst-case fears, the country has not degenerated into renewed civil war. The complex political system created by its new constitution allows provinces and regions sufficient autonomy to allay the fears of ethnic persecution. The United States continues to provide aid and support to the Baghdad government, and maintains a large military presence in the Persian Gulf that could intervene should the security situation in the country deteriorate.

While it is difficult to assess the consequences of such a recent conflict, some conclusions can be drawn. The war lasted much longer and cost considerably more in blood and treasure than the White House anticipated. According to the Department of Defense, 4,485 servicemen and women lost their lives in Iraq.[1] Estimates of civilian deaths related to the war range from 111,000 to over 121,000.[2] The economic cost of the war was also high. The Congressional Budget Office put the total spent at $806 billion, while President Obama maintains the war cost over $1 trillion.[3] The indirect costs of the war are harder to gauge but no less significant. The money spent on the war, which the Bush administration kept out of the budget during its time in office, contributed significantly to the burgeoning U.S. national debt. Removing Saddam Hussein from power eliminated the threat he posed to his neighbors, but it also eliminated the principal means of holding Iran in check. It will be years before the balance of power in the region is restored.

The impact of the war on the U.S. military continues to unfold. The re-election of President Obama in November 2012 will prevent the expansion of conventional forces promised by the Republicans. At the same time the administration has already begun the "pivot to Asia" designed to counter Chinese dominance of the region. These factors suggest that the U.S. military will continue to evolve as a hybrid force, more capable of waging war across the conflict spectrum than it was in 2003. There will be more Special Operations forces and more unmanned aircraft. These changes derive in part from experience gained in Iraq and should make America's armed forces better suited to the contingencies of the contemporary world.

Notes

1. Iraq War Casualty Database, available at http://nrcdata.ap.org/casualties/default.aspx?user name=casualty&password=2005battle, accessed December 24, 2012.

2. Iraq Body Count, available at http://www .iraqbodycount.org/, accessed December 24, 2012.

3. Daniel Kurtzleben, "What did the Iraq War cost? More than you think?," *USA News*, December 15, 2011, available at http://www.usnews .com/news/articles/2011/12/15/what-did-the-iraq -war-cost-more-than-you-think, accessed December 24, 2012.

Causes of the Iraq War

In the year and half between the September 11, 2001, terrorist attacks and the invasion of Iraq, President George W. Bush argued persistently for war. The president and administrative officials trotted out an array of justifications for war. Some of their reasons had been presented before, but the terrorist attacks on Washington, DC, and New York City gave them new urgency. The claim that Saddam Hussein possessed weapons of mass destruction (WMD) and ties to terrorist organizations to which he might give these weapons persuaded an American public fearful of another attack that something had to be done about the brutal dictator. Persuasive though this argument ultimately proved, it hid a more complex reality. A mix of ideological and pragmatic motives lay behind the decision to invade Iraq. By themselves or even together, they probably would not have been compelling enough to persuade the American people that war could not be avoided. Only the terrorist argument could do that, but many experts believe that September 11 provided a pretext for a war the administration had wanted some time before.

U.S. Foreign Policy and the Middle East

During the second half of the 20th century, Iraq figured prominently in American foreign policy toward a crucial but volatile region of the world. That policy rested on three pillars. The United States wished to make certain that it and its European allies would have unfettered access to Middle Eastern oil. Western vulnerability to a cut-off or even a reduction of supply became painfully clear during the oil embargo following the Yom Kippur (Ramadan) War of October 1973. Americans experienced rising prices and gas rationing for the first time since World War II. Security for the state of Israel was the second pillar of American policy. With its technological superiority and nuclear arsenal, the Jewish state had proven a match for any combination of Arab countries in every war since 1948. The Yom Kippur War, however, had demonstrated Israel's vulnerability. Only a massive infusion of American military aid made a victory over Syria and Egypt possible without resort to nuclear weapons. Israel's reliability as an ally, coupled with a strong Zionist lobby in the United States, has assured it American support. Preventing any country from dominating the region formed the final pillar of U.S. Middle Eastern policy.

Iraq figured prominently in achieving these broad goals. Second only to Saudi Arabia in known oil reserves, it could affect both the price and supply of oil. It was one of only two states large enough to dominate the region, and it could threaten Israel, particularly if it acquired nuclear weapons. Iraq's importance in the balance of power equation became abundantly clear following the 1979 Islamic revolution in Iran. Deprived of its longtime ally, the Shah of Iran, and concerned about Iranian belligerence following the American hostage crisis, the Ronald Reagan administration reached a rapprochement with Hussein and armed him to wage war against Iran. The Iran-Iraq War (1980–1988) sapped the strength of both nations and ended in a bloody stalemate.

By the end of the 1980s Hussein had outlived his usefulness and become a liability. The Israelis had never trusted him. In June 1981 they conducted a surprise attack to destroy a nuclear reactor in Baghdad for fear that it would produce weapons-grade uranium. Hussein's use of poison gas against Iraqi Kurds in 1988 led to widespread international condemnation. While these factors made the United States leery of the Iraqi dictator, they did not justify military action against him. That situation would change in August 1991.

The Persian Gulf War

On August 2, 1991, Iraqi forces invaded the small wealthy Persian Gulf state of Kuwait. Hussein accused the emirate of slant drilling into Iraqi oil fields. Perhaps because of miscommunication by acting ambassador April Glaspie, he believed that the United States would not act to reverse his fait accompli. Allowing the invasion to go unchallenged, however, would leave the brutal dictator in a position to threaten Saudi Arabia and dominate the Persian Gulf. The George H. W. Bush administration amassed a coalition of 500,000 troops and drove the Iraqis from Kuwait in February 1991.

The president's aim had always been limited to driving the Iraqis from Kuwait.

However, wartime rhetoric escalated to the point that Bush called upon Kurds and Shiite Muslims to rise against the dictator. Unfortunately, they took him at his word, only to be slaughtered when expected U.S. support never materialized. For some members of the administration, especially Secretary of Defense Dick Cheney, the Persian Gulf War would be seen as an incomplete victory, a job that needed to be finished by removing Hussein from power.

In the decade following the Persian Gulf War, however, the United States pursued a policy of containment against Iraq. No-fly zones over the northern and southern regions of the country gave persecuted ethnic groups some protection. Occasional airstrikes kept Hussein in check, and an embargo prevented him from rearming. Weapons inspectors sought to prevent him from gaining WMD until he expelled them. Hussein retained a firm grasp on power, but for the foreseeable future at least, he threatened none of his neighbors. American forces in the Persian Gulf would make sure of that.

Neoconservatism

National interest tempered by pragmatism drives foreign policy far more than does ideology. This fact explains why foreign policy changes little from one administration to the next. Under certain circumstances, however, ideology can exercise considerable influence. Such a situation occurred at the end of the Cold War. Convinced that the West, led by the United States, had won this titanic ideological struggle, a group of intellectuals and policy makers proclaimed what Francis Fukuyama dubbed "the end of history." Western liberal democracy represented the highest and final state of political development. All that remained was for it to permeate the globe. This philosophy spawned an ideological movement called neoconservatism.

While many neocons had no political agenda, others advocated a more aggressive foreign policy to promote American values as well as American interests. The Project for a New American Century, a neoconservative think tank supported by many future members of the George W. Bush administration, was such a group. In 1998 several of its members, including Donald Rumsfeld and Paul Wolfowitz, sent a letter to President Bill Clinton calling for the removal of Hussein. For the neocons and the Bush administration, Iraq was to be a demonstration model, a bastion of democracy that would provide an example for the entire region. A year before the September 11 attacks, Bush, then the governor of Texas, chastised Vice President Al Gore for leaving Hussein in power, clearly suggesting that were he elected, this situation would change.

The WMD Argument

Whether the neocons supported it or not, containment worked. Two no-fly zones, a robust U.S. presence in the Persian Gulf, and sanctions prevented Hussein from threatening any of his neighbors. A newly elected U.S. president would not be able to make a case for invading Iraq, never mind one who had won a highly controversial election by a narrow electoral college margin while losing the popular vote. Barring a dramatic change in circumstances, Bush would have a hard time making a case for invading Iraq. But September 11 provided an opportunity for an invasion that might not otherwise have occurred. The climate of fear following the terrorist attacks made it much easier to persuade the American public that even the possibility of Hussein possessing WMD he might pass to terrorists was unacceptable.

Following the successful operation against the Taliban government in Afghanistan, President Bush and members of his administration launched a concerted and persistent campaign to persuade Congress and the American people of the need to invade Iraq. In his 2002 State of the Union address, Bush identified Iraq as part of an "axis of evil" supporting terrorism around the world. His advisers revived interest in Hussein's nuclear weapons program, which most experts believed had been moribund since the end of the Persian Gulf War. Much of the evidence they presented was so suspect that the United Nations (UN), the North Atlantic Treaty Organization (NATO), and many of America's allies refused to support the war. Even the failure of the UN Monitoring, Verification and Inspection Commission (UNMOVIC), which reentered Iraq in November 2002 to find convincing evidence of an Iraqi nuclear program, did not dissuade the Bush administration from its determination to invade Iraq.

Regime Change

For Congress and the American people, the threat of Hussein possessing WMD, however remote, was sufficient to justify war. The Bush administration still found it useful to put an altruistic gloss on the invasion, albeit one it believed. By the time the first bombs fell on Baghdad, liberating Iraqis from the tyranny of Hussein had become the mission dubbed Operation IRAQI FREEDOM. Not surprisingly, the name resonated with the philosophy of the neocons. Iraq would be an island of liberal democracy in a sea of Middle Eastern despotism. Bush's desire for regime change, voiced in the presidential debate with Gore, could now be achieved. Whether the invaders actually found WMD would be irrelevant if the mission succeeded.

Consequences of the Iraq War

For the United States, the Iraq War ended in December 2011 when the last U.S. forces left the country. Any conclusions about the consequences of such a recent event must be tentative. There can be little doubt, however, that the conflict has already had a profound impact on regional security, which will probably increase over time. It also changed the nature and stability of the Iraqi state in ways that have yet to be fully realized. Eight years of war also affected the United States itself. The economic and security implications of the conflict continue to unfold. Whether the struggle was worth its cost in blood and treasure will be debated for years to come.

Iraq and Regional Security

Any threat Iraq posed to its neighbors has been removed for the foreseeable future. Iraqi forces not destroyed during the invasion were disbanded during the occupation. The army and police that replaced them have been retooled to deal primarily with internal security. The cost of rebuilding the country will leave little revenue left to create a military capable of offensive action, even if the international community would tolerate such bellicosity. At this time and without U.S. assistance, Iraq probably could not even defend itself from foreign aggression. The new government in Baghdad certainly has no weapons of mass destruction (WMD) program.

However desirable removing the threat posed by Saddam Hussein may have been, it has had one undesirable consequence. Iraq was the only regional power with the population and resources to hold Iran in check. Since the 1950s the United States has played the two off one another. Weakening Iraq has enhanced the threat posed by Iran. While the United States got bogged down in a protracted insurgency, fueled in part by clandestine Iranian aid to Shiite insurgents, Tehran was much freer to develop its nuclear program than it might otherwise have been. With no Arab state capable or willing to challenge Iran, the United States and Israel must do so alone. Preemptive military action by either could have serious consequences, not least of which might be an oil shortage and a spike in prices. At some point in the future, Iraq may regain its stature as a regional power, but that possibility does nothing to counter the immediate threat posed by Iran.

A Fragile State

An invasion followed by eight years of internal conflict has, of course, profoundly changed Iraq. Far from the easy victory the Bush administration promised, the war created a power vacuum filled first by lawlessness and then by an intractable insurgency. The resulting destruction of property and infrastructure, coupled with unemployment that topped 60 percent, caused the standard of living in Iraq to plummet. Resentment of Americans fueled the insurgency. The conflict further damaged infrastructure and delayed recovery. The country is still struggling to rebuild and regain its prewar standard of living.

Operation IRAQI FREEDOM did deliver on its promise to remove Hussein from power and replace his brutal regime with a democratic one. Iraqi democracy is, however, still on shaky ground. Because simple majority rule does not work in an ethnically divided state, the U.S.-led coalition facilitated creation of a complex system of proportional representation and regional autonomy. These arrangements prevented Iraq from disintegrating into three separate states as many feared at the height of the insurgency. The coalition led by Nuri al-Maliki continues to govern more or less effectively, but ethnic tensions persist. Internal divisions threaten to keep the Iraqi state weak for years to come.

The U.S. Army

The U.S. Army entered Iraq with the same aversion to insurgency it had harbored since the end of the Vietnam War. National security strategy eschewed direct involvement in counterinsurgency (COIN) campaigns, preferring to provide aid for internal defense, which could be handled by Special Forces. Regular soldiers received little education and training for unconventional war. The forces that invaded Iraq in 2003 did so with equipment and doctrine developed during the late 1970s. The best in the world at conventional war, these soldiers were woefully unprepared for internal security operations.

Fortunately, they adapted quickly. The army and marines wrote a new counterinsurgency manual that embraced the lessons of past campaigns and the experiences of Iraq and Afghanistan. Soldiers from armed units and even office clerks found themselves patrolling the streets of Baghdad and Fallujah. By the time of the Anbar Awakening, they had become as adept at COIN as at they were a conventional war-fighting. They had also adopted new equipment and undergone reorganization from traditional divisions into flexible brigade combat teams far more capable of handling an array of threats across the conflict spectrum.

With the end of direct American involvement and the winding down of the mission in Afghanistan, the U.S. Army will almost certainly contract. As it does, a healthy debate over its proper role in the 21st century will continue. This debate will occur amid a climate of fiscal conservatism and isolationism, as Americans have grown tired, for the time being at least, of foreign adventures. Under these circumstances, the army might be expected to revert to the conventional mentality of the post-Vietnam era. The absence of a Central European battlefront, however, makes such a decision unlikely. With no major war on the horizon, the U.S. military must continue to train and plan for a host of contingency operations from mid-level conventional conflict through counterinsurgency.

Counting the Cost

Whether its long-term consequences will be for good or ill, Iraq has been an expensive war. A report by the Congressional Research Service published in March 2011 put defense expenditures for the conflict at $806 billion. Indirect costs, including reconstruction, could easily push the total to well over a trillion dollars. Funding the war drove up the national debt and contributed significantly to deficit spending. The financial cost of the war must, therefore, be borne by Americans for years to come.

Although far lower than in previous wars, the human cost has been considerable. The U.S. military alone sustained 4,287 killed and 30,182 wounded. Improved medical care allowed perhaps three times as many wounded to survive than had done so in previous wars. Many of these wounded, however, suffered severe trauma and will need special care for the rest of their lives. In addition to American and other coalition service personnel, more than 100,000 Iraqi civilians have died from war-related violence since 2003, most of them killed by other Iraqis.

Whether any possible gain from the war is worth its cost in blood and treasure is both an academic and a moral question. Defenders of the war will argue that many more people might have suffered and died had Hussein continued to rule. Critics will point out that the policy of containment was working and that since Hussein had a weakened military and no WMD, he threatened no one. The final assessment of the war, if indeed there is one, may depend on how Iraq turns out in the long run.

MIDDLE EAST

Black Sea

Caspian Sea

40°N

TURKEY

Mosul

Euphrates R.

Tigris R.

Tehran

CYPRUS

Nicosia

SYRIA

LEBANON

Damascus

Beirut

Baghdad

ISRAEL

Tel Aviv

IRAQ

IRAN

Amman

Nasiriyah

Jerusalem

JORDAN

Basra

SINAI

Rafha

KUWAIT

Cairo

Hafar al-Batin

Kuwait

Ras al-Mishab

Persian
Gulf

BAHRAIN

Sharjah

EGYPT

Nile R.

Jubail

Ras Tanura

QATAR

Dubai

Dammam

Doha

Abu
Dhabi

Gulf of Oman

Medina

Red Sea

Riyadh

UNITED ARAB
EMIRATES

Muscat

Mecca

SAUDI

ARABIA

Masirah

20°N

OMAN

SUDAN

YEMEN

ERITREA

Sanaa

Arabian
Sea

DJIBOUTI

ETHIOPIA

SOMALIA

0   50   100 mi

0   50   100 km

30°E

40°E

50°E

60°E

KAZAKHSTAN

RUSSIA

Black Sea

Caspian Sea

UZBEKISTAN

GEORGIA

40°N

ARMENIA AZERBAIJAN

TURKMENISTAN

TURKEY

AFGHANISTAN

CYPRUS

SYRIA

LEBANON

I R A N

Mediterranean Sea

IRAQ

ISRAEL

30°N

JORDAN

PAKISTAN

KUWAIT

EGYPT

BAHRAIN

Persian Gulf

QATAR

UNITED ARAB EMIRATES

Arabian Sea

S A U D I

A R A B I A

OMAN

Red Sea

20°N

SUDAN

ERITREA

YEMEN

INDIAN

OCEAN

DJIBOUTI

Elevation (in feet)
10,000 +
7,000–10,000
5,000–7,000
2,000–5,000
1,000–2,000
500–1,000
0–500
Below sea level

SOMALIA

ETHIOPIA

0   100   200 mi
0   100   200 km

40°E

50°E

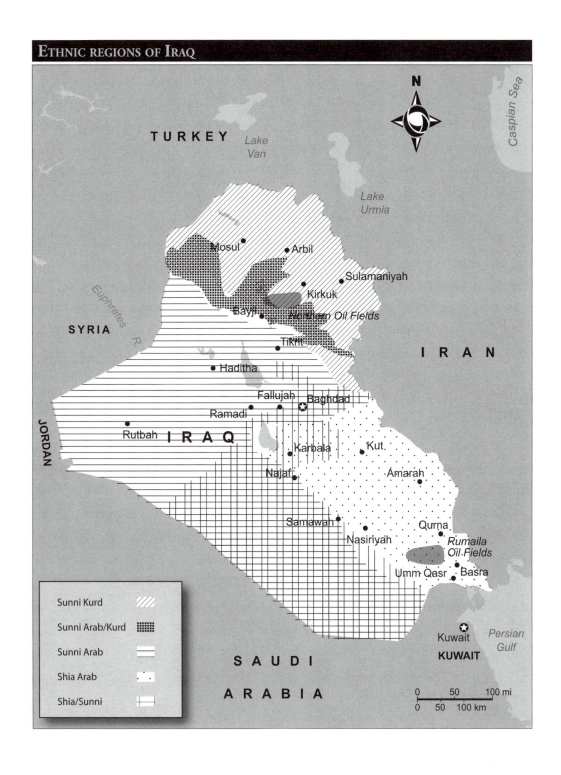

ETHNIC REGIONS OF IRAQ

N

TURKEY

Lake Van

Lake Urmia

Caspian Sea

SYRIA

Euphrates R.

• Mosul

• Arbil

• Sulamaniyah

Kirkuk

Bayji • Kurdish Oil Fields

• Tikrit

IRAN

• Haditha

Fallujah • Baghdad

Ramadi •

Rutbah • IRAQ

• Karbala

• Kut.

Najaf •

• Amarah

JORDAN

Samawah •

• Qurna

Nasiriyah •

Rumaila Oil Fields

Umm Qasr • • Basra

Kuwait

KUWAIT

Persian Gulf

SAUDI

ARABIA

Sunni Kurd	
Sunni Arab/Kurd	
Sunni Arab	
Shia Arab	
Shia/Sunni	

0   50   100 mi
0   50   100 km

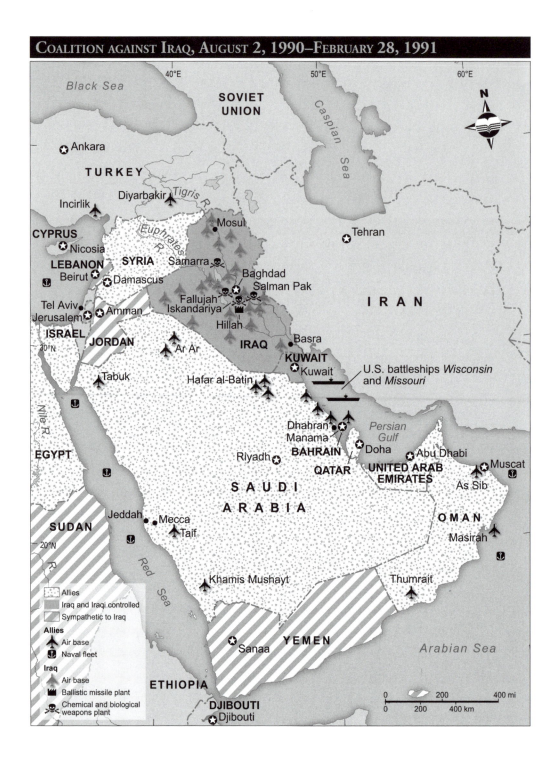

Black Sea

SOVIET UNION

Caspian Sea

Ankara

TURKEY

Diyarbakir Tigris R.

Incirlik

CYPRUS

Nicosia

LEBANON

Beirut

SYRIA

Euphrates R.

Damascus

Mosul

Samarra

Baghdad

Salman Pak

Tehran

IRAN

Tel Aviv

Jerusalem

Amman

ISRAEL

JORDAN

Fallujah

Iskandariya

Hillah

Ar Ar

Tabuk

Hafar al-Batin

IRAQ

Basra

KUWAIT

Kuwait

U.S. battleships Wisconsin and Missouri

Dhahran

Manama

BAHRAIN

Persian Gulf

Doha

Abu Dhabi

Muscat

Riyadh

QATAR

UNITED ARAB EMIRATES

As Sib

EGYPT

SAUDI

ARABIA

OMAN

Nile R.

Jeddah

Mecca

Taif

SUDAN

Masirah

Red Sea

Khamis Mushayt

Thumrait

Allies
Iraq and Iraqi controlled
Sympathetic to Iraq

Allies
Air base
Naval fleet

Iraq
Air base
Ballistic missile plant
Chemical and biological weapons plant

YEMEN

Arabian Sea

Sanaa

ETHIOPIA

DJIBOUTI

Djibouti

0   200   400 mi
0   200   400 km

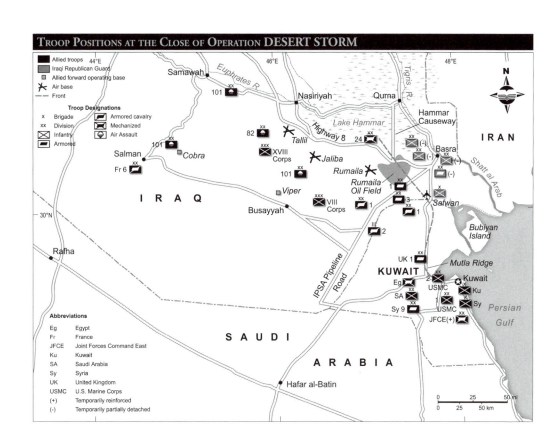

Troop Positions at the Close of Operation DESERT STORM

Legend:
- Allied troops
- Iraqi Republican Guard
- Allied forward operating base
- Air base
- Front

Troop Designations:
- x Brigade
- xx Division
- Infantry
- Armored
- Armored cavalry
- Mechanized
- Air Assault

Abbreviations
Eg	Egypt
Fr	France
JFCE	Joint Forces Command East
Ku	Kuwait
SA	Saudi Arabia
Sy	Syria
UK	United Kingdom
USMC	U.S. Marine Corps
(+)	Temporarily reinforced
(-)	Temporarily partially detached

DISPOSITION OF FORCES ON THE EVE OF THE 2003 IRAQ WAR

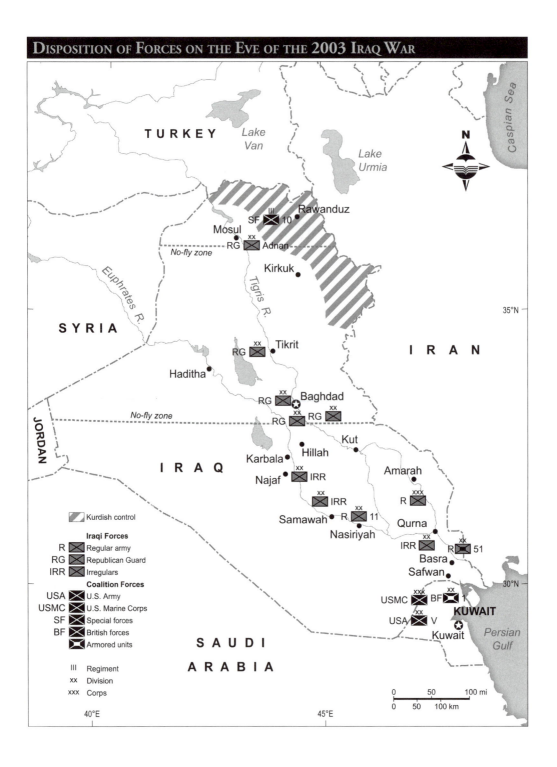

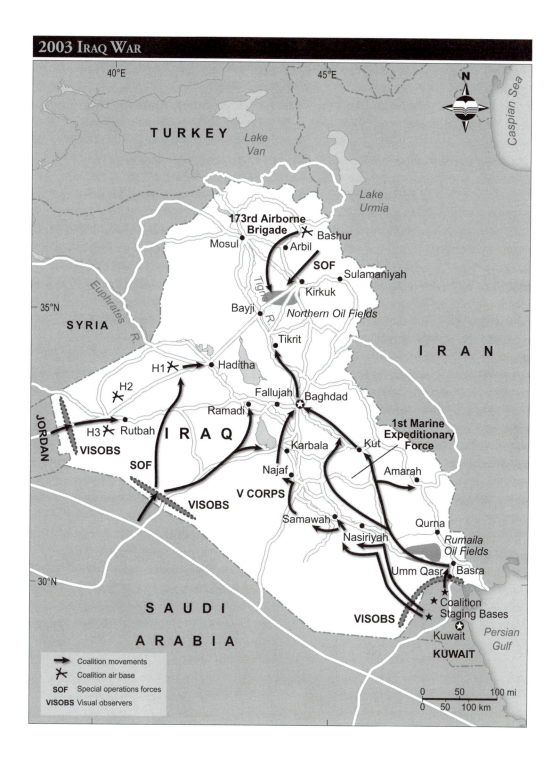

2003 IRAQ WAR

TURKEY

Lake Van

Lake Urmia

Caspian Sea

173rd Airborne Brigade

Bashur

Mosul

Arbil

SOF

Sulamaniyah

Kirkuk

Bayji

Northern Oil Fields

SYRIA

Tikrit

IRAN

H1

Haditha

H2

Fallujah

Baghdad

JORDAN

H3

Rutbah

VISOBS

Ramadi

IRAQ

Karbala

Kut

1st Marine Expeditionary Force

Amarah

SOF

Najaf

VISOBS

V CORPS

Samawah

Qurna

Rumaila Oil Fields

Nasiriyah

Umm Qasr

Basra

VISOBS

★ Coalition Staging Bases

SAUDI

ARABIA

Kuwait

Persian Gulf

KUWAIT

→ Coalition movements
✈ Coalition air base
SOF Special operations forces
VISOBS Visual observers

Euphrates R.

Tigris R.

0   50   100 mi
0   50   100 km

40°E   45°E   35°N   30°N

IRAQ SECURITY PICTURE

Centers of insurgency
(Islamic or nationalist)

Former regime elements

Moqtad militia

A

Abu Ghraib

Prison facility located about 20 miles west of the Iraqi capital, Baghdad. Known during the regime of Saddam Hussein as an infamous place of torture and execution, Abu Ghraib prison later drew international attention when photographs of inmate abuse and reports of torture at the hands of coalition troops were made public in 2004.

Abu Ghraib, officially called the Baghdad Central Confinement Facility (BCCF) under the Hussein regime, was built by British contractors hired by the Iraqi government in the 1960s. Covering an area of about one square mile, the prison housed five different types of prisoners during the Hussein regime: those with long sentences, those with short sentences, those imprisoned for capital crimes, those imprisoned for so-called special offenses, and foreign detainees. Cells, which are about 51 square feet in area, held as many as 40 people each.

During the Iran-Iraq War (1980–1988), the Iraqi Baathist regime used the facility to imprison political dissidents and members of ethnic or religious groups seen as threats to the central government. In particular, hundreds of Arab and Kurdish Shiites and Iraqis of Iranian heritage were arrested and housed in the BCCF; torture and executions became routine. One of the tactics used by prison guards was feeding shredded plastic to inmates, and it has been speculated that prisoners were used as guinea pigs for Hussein's biological and chemical weapons. Although the Iraqi government kept its actions within the complex secret from Iraqi citizens and the international community alike, Amnesty International reported several specific incidents, including the 1996 execution of hundreds of political dissidents and the 1998 execution of many people who had been involved in the 1991 Shiite revolt. The prison, which contained thousands of inmates who were completely cut off from outside communication and held without conviction, was also used to house coalition prisoners of war during the Persian Gulf War.

With the 2003 U.S.-led Iraq War and subsequent fall of the Hussein government in Iraq, coalition troops took control of Abu Ghraib prison. The U.S. military used the complex for holding Iraqi insurgents and terrorists accused of attacks against the United States' interests, although by 2004 it had released several hundred prisoners and shared use of the facility with the Iraqi government. Because of the disarray in the Iraqi criminal system, many common criminals uninvolved in the war were held at the facility as well. Abu Ghraib became a household name in April 2004, when the television program *60 Minutes II* aired photographs of prisoner abuse at the hands of coalition troops. Just two days later, the photographs were posted online with Seymour Hersch's article in the *New Yorker* magazine. The photos, which showed prisoners wearing black hoods, attached to wires with which they were threatened with electrocution, and placed in humiliating sexual positions, sparked worldwide outrage and calls

Cell block in Abu Ghraib prison, Iraq. (U.S. Department of Defense)

for the investigation and conviction of the military personnel involved.

The abuse was immediately decried by U.S. president George W. Bush and by Defense Secretary Donald Rumsfeld, who (on May 7, 2004) took responsibility for the acts that had occurred during his tenure. The Pentagon, which had been investigating reports of abuse since 2003, launched a further investigation into the acts documented by the photographs. Previously, detainee abuse had been investigated by U.S. Army major general Antonio Taguba, who had been given digital images of the abuse by Sergeant Joseph Darby in January 2004. Major General Taguba concluded in his 53-page report that U.S. military personnel had violated international law. More than a dozen U.S. soldiers and officers were removed from the prison as a result of the internal investigation.

More details emerged following the *60 Minutes II* broadcast. Photographs that the U.S. government would not allow to be released earlier were circulated in 2006. Most importantly, it appeared that the senior U.S. military officer, Lieutenant General Ricardo Sanchez, had authorized treatment "close to" torture, such as the use of military dogs, temperature extremes, and sensory and sleep deprivation, making it more difficult to determine whether the perpetrators or their commanders were primarily responsible for creating the environment that led to the abuses. However, in addition to charging certain troops and contractors with torture, the United States made an effort to reduce the number of detainees— estimated at 7,000 prior to the scandal's outbreak—by several thousand. However, many argued that the measures taken were not harsh enough to fit the crime, and some demanded Rumsfeld's resignation.

In August 2004, a military panel confirmed 44 cases of prisoner abuse at the facility and identified 23 soldiers as being responsible. The so-called ringleader of the operation, Army Specialist Charles Graner, was convicted and sentenced to 10 years in prison in January 2005. Meanwhile, Abu Ghraib was twice attacked by insurgents attempting to undermine U.S. security at the facility and set prisoners free. In September 2006, the United States handed over control of Abu Ghraib to the Iraqi government.

Jessica Britt

See also: Bush, George Walker; Rumsfeld, Donald Henry; Sanchez, Ricardo S.

Further Reading

Danner, Mark. *Torture and Truth: America, Abu Ghraib, and the War on Terror.* New York: New York Review Books, 2004.

Graveline, Christopher, and Michael Clemens. *The Secrets of Abu Ghraib Revealed.* Dulles, VA: Potomac Books, 2010.

Greenberg, Karen J., and Joshua L. Dratel, eds. *The Torture Papers: The Road to Abu Ghraib.* Cambridge: Cambridge University Press, 2005.

Strasser, Steven, ed. *The Abu Ghraib Investigations: The Official Independent Panel and Pentagon Reports on the Shocking Prisoner Abuse in Iraq.* New York: PublicAffairs, 2004.

Air Defenses in Iraq, Iraq War

Before the U.S.-led invasion of Iraq in March 2003, the Iraqi air defense system was a major concern for coalition planners. The system included elements of the defenses used in the 1991 Persian Gulf War, during which 39 coalition aircraft were downed. Overall, however, the Iraqi air defenses proved to be largely ineffectual in the Persian Gulf War, and the coalition achieved rapid and complete air supremacy. The Iraqi air defense system was badly degraded by damage in 1991, an ongoing arms embargo, and continued sporadic attacks by U.S. and British aircraft over more than a decade of enforcing the no-fly zones.

Following the 1991 Persian Gulf War, the arms embargo on Iraq made it difficult for Saddam Hussein to replace weapons that had been destroyed in the fighting or had become outmoded. Iraq's air defenses continued to be based on the Soviet model, with radar and observers providing information to a central command in real time. The central commanders were then able to determine the best mix of surface-to-air missiles (SAMs), antiaircraft artillery (AAA), and fighter aircraft to deal with the threat. The system was known as Kari, French for "Iraq," spelled backwards. The system employed technology from the 1980s and had been developed by French companies. Computers and equipment came from both European and Soviet sources.

Iraq's central National Air Defense operations center was located in central Baghdad. It received data from four independent Sector Operations Centers (SOCs), which covered different parts of Iraq. The first sector, headquartered at Taji Military Camp in northern Baghdad, covered central and eastern Iraq, as well as the capital. This SOC controlled most of the SAMs and AAA. Prior to 2003, many weapons had been removed from other parts of Iraq and concentrated in the capital area. The region included the most sensitive targets, such as presidential palaces and factories where weapons of mass destruction could be produced. The SOC also controlled many individual radar sites and an electronic countermeasures unit.

The second SOC covered western Iraq, including the Jordanian and Syrian border. The third SOC was headquartered near Talil Airbase and covered southern Iraq. This SOC was most often in action against allied aircraft covering the southern no-fly zone. The fourth SOC was based near

Kirkuk and covered the northern part of the country. Its SAM batteries engaged aircraft in the northern no-fly zone.

A separate SOC was also established during the 1990s in Baghdad. It was controlled by the Republican Guard and was armed with some of the most modern SAMs available. Other lightweight SAMs were employed by Republican Guard and regular Iraqi Army units, and were not integrated into the Kari system. Instead, these weapons were individually aimed and posed a deadly threat to coalition aircraft, especially those flying at low altitudes and relatively slow speeds. These weapons shot down a number of allied helicopters during the March 2003 invasion.

Most radar used by the Iraqis had been supplied by the Soviets, although some French, Italian, and Chinese radars had been integrated into the system. Different sets included such surveillance radars as the Soviet P-15 "Flat Face" (NATO designation) and P-15M(2) "Squat Eye," and the French Thompson-CSF Volex, which were not mobile. Other radars included target tracking and guidance radars, which were usually mounted on vans or trailers and could be moved to avoid coalition targeting. Some jamming and electronic countermeasure equipment was also available, along with thermal imaging telescopes and laser rangefinders that coalition countermeasures could not block. Even so, most of the equipment in 2003 was the same that had been in place in 1991.

Most of the SAMs available to Saddam Hussein's forces were introduced during the 1950s and 1960s. Some SA-2s and SA-3s were built by Iraqi factories, but most sources of missile replacement were cut off after the Persian Gulf War in 1991. More recent area defense SAMs included the SA-6, SA-8, SA-9, SA-13, and a few French-made Roland VIIs. While some had been upgraded since 1991, most remained obsolete. The SAMs were supplemented by over 4,000 antiaircraft guns ranging in size from 12.7 (millimeter) mm to 57 mm. Fighter aircraft from the Iraqi Air Force played little role in Iraq's air defenses.

During the 1991 Persian Gulf War, the coalition had attacked Kari's communications nodes. Since then, the Iraqis had improved communications with greater use of optical fiber links, along with continued use of underground bunkers to protect command and communication nodes.

Following the Persian Gulf War, the United States, Great Britain, and France established no-fly zones in southern and northern Iraq. Fighter planes patrolled these areas to prevent Iraqi aircraft from attacking Kurd and Shiite dissidents. After losing several fighters to the allies in 1992 and 1993, the Iraqi Air Force no longer sent aircraft to challenge the patrols. However, the Iraqi Air Defense Command periodically harassed allied patrols with SAM attacks, especially after Operation DESERT FOX in 1998. For the next five years, Iraq's radar and missile sites targeted allied aircraft and tried to shoot them down. In response, allied aircraft were allowed to respond with missiles and bombs. When the Iraqis learned to position their SAMs in population centers, the allies responded with attacks on fixed air defense installations, such as radar sites or communication centers.

Denied access to new technology, the Iraqis developed tactics to improve their chances against allied aircraft. By observing Serbian tactics in Kosovo that brought down several U.S. aircraft, they learned how to quickly turn radars on and off to prevent allied countermeasures from locking on, while still allowing a quick launch by SAMs. The Iraqis also improved their use of decoys and hidden deployment of weapons. More incidents of Iraq launching missiles and using radar to lock onto allied aircraft were reported after 1998.

Saddam encouraged attacks on allied aircraft by offering $5,000 to any unit that shot down a U.S. aircraft and $2,500 to any soldier who captured a downed pilot. In response, however, the allies began to target air defense targets in the no-fly zones more intensively, especially from late 2001 to early 2003. Although the number of Iraqi provocations declined, the number of air attacks on air defense sites increased dramatically during that time. In September 2002, for example, a raid by over 100 U.S. aircraft on air defense sites in western Iraq was not intended to protect aircraft patrolling the no-fly zone. Instead, it opened the way for U.S. Special Forces to fly from Jordan into northern Iraq. By the time U.S. and British forces moved into Iraq on March 20, 2003, Iraqi air defenses had already been seriously degraded.

The allies took Iraqi air defenses seriously during Operation Iraqi Freedom. The main targets of the early air strikes were the command centers in Baghdad. Tactics were similar to those used in 1991. To weaken air defenses at little risk to pilots, stealth aircraft and cruise missiles made up the first wave. Extensive use of drones forced the Iraqis to turn on their radars, allowing allied aircraft to destroy them. Although the Iraqis fired over 1,660 radar-guided SAMs during the invasion, they failed to down any allied aircraft. Another 1,224 AAA "incidents" involving centrally controlled Iraqi batteries were reported by the allies, with no effect as well. A complete lack of involvement by Iraqi fighters pleasantly surprised the allies. Most Iraqi Air Force aircraft were hidden in residential or agricultural areas to prevent their destruction. After the first few days of the operation, strategic air defenses declined in activity. Allied suppression missions and the lack of SAMs had done their job.

The most effective Iraqi air defenses during the war were the individually aimed SAMs and AAA. These weapons were locally controlled and were most effective against low-altitude targets. On March 24, 2003 for example, the U.S. Army 11th Aviation Brigade attacked the Republican Guard Medina mechanized division deep behind Iraqi lines. One McDonnell Douglas/Boeing AH-64D Apache was shot down, and 33 were so badly shot up that they were rendered unserviceable for some time. A total of seven U.S. aircraft were shot down by locally controlled Iraqi air defenses.

In the end, Iraq's air defenses in 2003 were far too obsolete and limited to prevent the allies from striking at targets that they were determined to hit. Even so, however, the Iraqi defenses in certain areas, such as around Baghdad, were so dense that they continued to pose a threat to low-flying allied aircraft until the collapse of Saddam Hussein's regime. All of the aircraft lost to Iraqi defenses were helicopters or ground attack aircraft, indicating that determined Iraqi defenders remained dangerous.

Tim J. Watts

See also: Hussein, Saddam; Iraqi Freedom, Operation, Air Campaign

Further Reading

Cordesman, Anthony H. *The Iraq War: Strategy, Tactics, and Military Lessons.* Westport, CT: Praeger, 2003.

Keegan, John. *The Iraq War: The Military Offensive, from Victory in 21 Days to the Insurgent Aftermath.* New York: Vintage, 2005.

Ripley, Tim. *Air War Iraq.* Barnsley, UK: Pen and Sword, 2004.

Air-Land Battle Doctrine

In the development of military doctrine, victory in war is usually followed by a period of complacency and stagnation, while defeat spurs a period of critical self-examination and robust internal debate that often leads to dramatic doctrinal innovations. This was true for the United States following the Vietnam War. For the U.S. military, the trauma of the loss in Vietnam was compounded by the unexpected lethality of modern weapons witnessed in the short but violent 1973 Yom Kippur (Ramadan) War. That in turn led to an increasing recognition that the North Atlantic Treaty Organization (NATO) could not rely on battlefield nuclear weapons to offset the overwhelming numerical advantage of the Warsaw Pact in any future war on the European continent.

Working through the problem, U.S. military thinkers identified two types of wars that the United States could face in the future: a heavy mechanized war in Europe or a light infantry war in some other part of the world. Although the mechanized war in Europe was the least likely scenario, it was also the most dangerous. U.S. military doctrine had to be revised to allow the nation to defeat its strongest and most dangerous enemy.

Initially, the sights of the U.S. military were fixed at the tactical level—"Win the first battle"—with little consideration beyond that. There also was recognition that the next major conflict would be a "come as you are war." Under the direct guidance of General William E. DePuy, the first commander of the newly established U.S. Army Training and Doctrine Command (TRADOC), the initial expression of this doctrinal rethinking was the 1976 edition of *FM 100-5, Operations*. The new manual introduced the notion of active defense, a highly questionable substitute for the tested defensive concepts of mobile defense and defense in-depth. In focusing on the lethality of modern weapons, the new doctrine stressed the effects of firepower by devoting the preponderance of space to a discussion of its effects. The new *FM 100-5* did not ignore maneuver, but it did relegate that element of combat power to the mere function of movement to deliver firepower rather than gain positional advantage.

The 1976 edition of *FM 100-5* was wildly controversial even before it had been fully distributed to the field. The critics of DePuy's doctrine rejected it as too mechanical, too dogmatic, and too mathematically deterministic. Nonetheless, DePuy's efforts were a major contribution to the post–Vietnam War U.S. Army because for the first time in many years, officers were again thinking and writing about doctrine. The resulting debate fueled a renaissance in U.S. military thinking.

The immediate reactions to the 1976 edition resulted in the notion of follow-on forces attack (FOFA), which in turn led to recognition of the operational depth of the battlefield. That led directly to the final acceptance by the American military and NATO of the concept of the operational level of war, as distinct from the tactical or the strategic. The Soviets had formally recognized this level of warfare as early as the 1920s and had aggressively worked to define and expand the theory of operational art ever since. The West had long rejected the concept as little more than yet another crackpot element of Marxist thinking, but the Soviets had been right all along on this point.

The principal guiding force behind the development of Air-Land Battle Doctrine was General Donn A. Starry, who assumed command of TRADOC in July 1977. Working directly under Starry, Major General

Donald R. Morelli, TRADOC's deputy chief of staff of doctrine, closely supervised the team of doctrine writers, which included Lieutenant Colonels Leonard D. Holder, Huba Wass de Czega, and Richard Hart Sinnerich. Classical German military thought had a great deal of influence on the development of the new doctrine. Even in the 1976 edition of *FM 100-5*, General DePuy had instructed the doctrine writers to study carefully the current capstone doctrinal manual of the West German Bundeswehr. That manual, *HDv 100/100, Truppenführung* (Command and Control in Battle), was based closely on the manual of the same name first introduced in 1932 with which the German Army fought World War II. Through the influence of the German manual, such standard German doctrinal concepts as *Auftragstaktik* (mission orders) and *Schwerpunkt* (center of gravity) became firmly embedded in U.S. military thinking. Another major influence that was specifically mentioned in that edition was Basil Liddell Hart's book *Strategy*, one of the most important books written about the indirect approach in warfare.

The 1982 edition of *FM 100-5* marked the U.S. military's first formal recognition of the operational level of war and introduced the concepts of airland battle and deep battle. Air-Land Battle Doctrine took a nonlinear view of combat. It enlarged the battlefield area, stressing unified air and ground operations throughout the theater. It recognized the nonquantifiable elements of combat power and restressed that maneuver was as important as firepower. Most significantly, the doctrine emphasized the human element of war, "courageous, well-trained soldiers and skillful, effective leaders." An undercurrent to this last theme, of course, was the fact that the United States had only recently abolished conscription and was then in the process of building an all-volunteer professional army. The Air-Land Battle Doctrine identified the keys to success in war, which included indirect approaches, speed and violence, flexibility and reliance on the initiative of junior leaders, rapid decision making, clearly defined objectives and operational concepts, a clearly designated main effort, and deep attack.

Depth was one of the keys. A commander had to fight and synchronize three simultaneous battles: close, deep, and rear. The deep battle, of course, would be the enemy's rear battle, and vice versa. A well-coordinated attack deep in an enemy's rear area might in fact prove decisive. This marked the first recognition in U.S. military doctrine that the battle might not necessarily be decided along the line of contact.

One of the most controversial features of the 1976 edition of *FM 100-5* had been the elimination of the venerable Principles of War, first adopted by the U.S. Army in the early 1920s. The 1982 edition restored the Principles of War but then went one step further by introducing the Four Tenets of Air-Land Battle: initiative, depth, agility, and synchronization. Initiative is the ability to set the terms of the battle by action and was identified as the greatest advantage in war. Depth has components of time, space, and resources. Agility is the ability to act faster to exploit the weakness and frustrate the plans of an enemy. Synchronization ensures that no effort will be wasted, either initially or as operations develop.

Some critics complained that the Four Tenets of AirLand Battle were unnecessary additions to the Principles of War or were ultimately an attempt to replace them. But as other analysts pointed out, the Four Tenets were for the most part combinations of two or more of the Principles of War. Synchronization, for example, combined economy of force and unity of effort. Initiative combined offensive, maneuver, and surprise.

The 1982 *FM 100-5* was a major milestone in U.S. military thought, but it was far from a perfect document. After its release to the field, the debate continued, and the doctrine writers continued to refine it. The 1986 edition of *FM 100-5* contained no significant changes or innovations, but it presented a far better discussion of the doctrine and corrected some of the minor errors in the 1982 edition. Some errors still remained, however. The 1986 edition used the German concept of *Schwerpunkt* interchangeably as either the center of gravity or the decisive point. As defined originally by 19th-century Prussian military strategist Carl von Clausewitz, however, the center of gravity and the decisive point (*Entscheidungsstelle*) were two distinct and separate concepts. The confusion was not corrected until the 1993 edition of *FM 100-5*, which stated clearly that "Decisive points are not centers of gravity, they are the keys to getting at the centers of gravity."

NATO never fully embraced the Air-Land Battle Doctrine and ironically neither did the U.S. Air Force. In any event, the new doctrine never had to be used in an actual war against the Warsaw Pact on the plains of Northern Europe. AirLand Battle, however, greatly concerned the Soviets and was just one more element of pressure in the 1980s that eventually contributed to the collapse of the Soviet Union. The overwhelmingly successful prosecution of the Persian Gulf War (Operation DESERT STORM) in 1991 was based on the 1986 edition of *FM 100-5*, which was arguably the single best official articulation of U.S. war-fighting doctrine ever published.

The 1993 edition of *FM 100-5* actually shifted the emphasis away from operations

and conventional war fighting toward strategy and operations other than war (OOTW). Even the term "Air-Land Battle" was dropped in favor of "Army Operations," but that was more the result of bureaucratic infighting between the U.S. Army and the U.S. Air Force. A new edition of *FM 100-5* in 1998 was supposed to shift the emphasis back to the operational art, but the final coordinating draft caused considerable internal controversy. The new manual was finally issued in June 2001, under a new numbering system, as *FM 3-0 Operations*. Although the term "AirLand Battle" is no longer officially in use, the U.S. Army continues to train and operate in accordance with its principles, and its precepts were used again in the initial invasion of Iraq in 2003 during Operation IRAQI FREEDOM.

David T. Zabecki

See also: IRAQI FREEDOM, Operation

Further Reading

Naveh, Shimon. *In Pursuit of Military Excellence: The Evolution of Operational Theory*. London: Frank Cass, 1997.

Romjue, John L. *From Active Defense to Air-Land Battle: The Development of Army Doctrine, 1973–1982*. Fort Monroe, VA: United States Army Training and Doctrine Command, 1984.

Zabecki, David T., and Bruce Condell, eds. and trans. *Truppenführung: On the German Art of War*. Boulder, CO: Lynne Rienner, 2001.

Allawi, Iyad

Iraqi politician and prime minister of Iraq's appointed interim government that assumed the governance of Iraq on June 28, 2004; he held the premiership until April 7, 2005. Iyad Allawi was born into a well-to-do family in Baghdad on May 31, 1944. His father and uncle were physicians. His father was also a member of Iraq's parliament, and his grandfather had participated in the negotiations that granted Iraq its independence in 1932. His mother was Lebanese. The family had long-standing commercial and political ties to both the British and the Americans.

Allawi graduated from the American Jesuit's Baghdad College, an intermediate- and senior-level preparatory school, and entered the Baghdad University College of Medicine in 1961, the same year he joined the Baath Party, met future Iraqi dictator Saddam Hussein, and became active in the Iraqi National Students' Union. Allawi organized strikes and other activities against the government of Abd al-Karim Qasim. On February 8, 1963, Qasim was overthrown in a Baathist coup, which resulted in General Ahmad Hassan al-Bakr becoming prime minister. Allawi was eventually placed in charge of the central security office at the presidential palace and was given the nickname of the Palace Doctor.

Although unproven, there are charges that Allawi participated in intense interrogations and torture that led to the deaths of trade union officials, students, and political leaders. Allawi was arrested on these charges, but he was released after Bakr intervened. Allawi participated in the July 17, 1968, coup that made Bakr president and excluded all but Baathists from government positions. Bakr then pressured the minister of health, Ezzat Mustafa, to expedite Allawi's graduation from the college of medicine.

Opposition to Allawi grew within the government, and he was sent to Beirut in 1971 before moving to London in 1972 to head the Baath National Students Union and to pursue advanced medical studies. Allawi left the Baath Party in 1975 and supposedly began working for MI6, the British foreign intelligence service. In 1976 he earned a

Iraqi prime minister Iyad Allawi, shown here attending a meeting of the European Union (EU) in Brussels, on November 5, 2004. Allawi was critical of the EU over its lack of support for the U.S.-led coalition in the Iraq War. (Council of the European Union)

masters of science in medicine from London University. Allawi's name was placed on an assassination list in 1978 after Iraqi president Saddam Hussein failed to convince him to rejoin the Baathists. In February 1978 Allawi and his wife were attacked by an ax-bearing intruder in their Surrey home but escaped serious injury. Allawi earned a doctorate in medicine in 1979 from London University before being certified as a neurologist in 1982.

In 1979 Allawi began gathering alienated former Iraqi Baathists together into a group that grew into a Hussein opposition party. It was formalized in December 1990 as the Iraqi National Accord (INA). The INA received backing from Britain, the United States, Jordan, Saudi Arabia, and Turkey. It fomented dissent among the disaffected in Iraq and committed acts of terror and sabotage in that country in an attempt to bring down the Hussein regime. Allawi and the INA were recruited by the U.S. Central Intelligence Agency (CIA) after the 1991 Persian Gulf War and were paid $5 million in 1995 and $6 million in 1996. The CIA supported the INA's 1996 failed military coup, code-named DBACHILLES, which led to the execution of many Iraqis and to the confiscation or destruction of approximately $250 million of Allawi family assets.

The INA and Allawi gathered intelligence to establish the alleged existence of weapons of mass destruction (WMD) in Iraq that formed the core of the MI6 dossier released in September 2002. This dossier formed a major part of the rationale for the 2003 U.S.- and British-led coalition invasion of Iraq in March 2003. On July 13, 2003, Allawi was appointed by Coalition Provisional Authority administrator L. Paul Bremer to the 25-member Iraqi Governing Council (IGC), where he served as minister of defense and assumed the rotating presidency for October 2003. He resigned as head of the IGC security committee in April 2004 over alleged concerns about U.S. tactics used to subdue the 2004 Fallujah insurgency.

The coalition-led IGC transferred authority to the Iraqi Interim Government, with Allawi as the appointed interim prime minister, on June 28, 2004. During his tenure in this position, he created a domestic spy agency named the General Security Directorate to counter the Iraqi insurgency, closed the Iraqi office of the television network Al Jazeera, attempted to marginalize radical Shiite cleric Muqtada al-Sadr and his militia, and assumed the power to declare martial law. Allawi tried to draw Baathists who had not committed criminal acts during Hussein's rule into the government and considered pardoning insurgents who surrendered their weapons. Allawi stepped down as

premier on April 7, 2005, the day the Islamic Dawa Party leader Ibrahim al-Jafari was elected to lead the transitional Iraqi National Assembly.

Allawi's INA won just 25 seats in the December 2005 elections to establish the permanent Iraqi National Assembly. This placed the party a distant third in the assembly, with only 14 percent of the vote. In 2007 the INA boycotted the Iraqi government altogether, and Allawi refused to take a cabinet position in it. He retains his dual British citizenship, and his wife and children reside in the United Kingdom for security reasons. In January 2009 Allawi excoriated the George W. Bush administration for its mismanagement of the Iraq War since 2003 and criticized Bush for his insistence on elections and democratic institutions in Iraq before first having achieved stability. Allawi was also highly critical of the Iraqi government led by Nuri al-Maliki.

Richard M. Edwards

See also: Bremer, L. Paul, III; Maliki, Nuri Muhammed Kamil Hasan al-

Further Reading

Allawi, Ali A. *The Occupation of Iraq: Winning the War, Losing the Peace*. New Haven, CT: Yale University Press, 2007.

Keegan, John. *The Iraq War: The Military Offensive, from Victory in 21 Days to the Insurgent Aftermath*. New York: Vintage, 2005.

Polk, William R. *Understanding Iraq: The Whole Sweep of Iraqi History, from Genghis Khan's Mongols to the Ottoman Turks to the British Mandate to the American Occupation*. New York: Harper Perennial, 2006.

al-Qaeda in Iraq

Al-Qaeda in Iraq (al-Qa'ida fi Bilad al-Rafhidayn, AQI) is a violent Sunni jihadist organization that has taken root in Iraq

Jordanian-born terrorist mastermind Abu Musab al-Zarqawi is seen in these undated photos. The photo at left was released in Amman, Jordan, December 14, 2002. The photo at right was released by the Department of State in September 2004. Zarqawi was killed in an airstrike in an isolated house about 30 miles north of Bagdad on June 7, 2006. (AP Photo/File)

since the 2003 Anglo-American–led invasion of that nation. The U.S. government has characterized AQI, sometimes referred to as al-Qaeda in Mesopotamia, as the most deadly Sunni jihadist insurgent in Iraq. Other sources and experts argue that this designation is exaggerated, as the group is merely one of more than 40 similar organizations, and that the claim was made symbolically to rationalize the idea that coalition forces are fighting terrorism in Iraq and thus should not withdraw precipitously.

Opponents of the continuing U.S. presence in Iraq have argued that the 2003 invasion sparked the growth of Salafi Jihadism and suicide terrorism in Iraq, and its export to other parts of the Islamic world. AQI first formed following the invasion and

toppling of the Iraq regime, under the name Jama'at al-Tawhid wa-l Jihad (Group of Monotheism and Jihad) under Abu Musab al-Zarqawi.

Zarqawi fought in Afghanistan in the 1980s and 1990s, and upon traveling to Jordan he organized a group called Bayt al-Imam with the noted Islamist ideologue Abu Muhammad al-Maqdisi (Muhammad Tahir al-Barqawi) and other veterans of the war in Afghanistan. Zarqawi was arrested and imprisoned but was released in 1999. Returning again to Afghanistan and setting up camp in Herat, he reportedly took charge of certain Islamist factions in Kurdistan, from there moving into Iraq and sometimes Syria. Once Mullah Krekar, the leader of the Kurdish group Islamist Ansar al-Islam, was deported to the Netherlands in 2003, certain sources claim that Zarqawi led some 600 Arab fighters in Syria.

Tawhid wa-l Jihad was blamed for, or took credit for, numerous attacks, including bombings of the Jordanian embassy, the Canal Hotel that killed 23 at the United Nations (UN) headquarters, and the Imam Ali mosque in Najaf. It is also credited with the killing of Italian paramilitary police and civilians at Nasiriyah and numerous suicide attacks that continued through 2005. The group also seized hostages and beheaded them. A video of the savage execution of U.S. businessman Nicholas Berg, murdered in Iraq on May 7, 2004, reportedly by Zarqawi himself, was followed by other killings of civilians.

The group has targeted Iraqi governmental and military personnel and police because of their cooperation with the U.S. occupying force. AQI's recruitment videos have highlighted American attacks and home searches of defenseless Iraqis, and they promise martyrdom. Estimates of the number of AQI members have ranged from 850 to several thousand. Also under dispute have been the numbers of foreign fighters in relation to Iraqi fighters. Foreign fighters' roles were first emphasized, but it became clear that a much higher percentage (probably 90 percent) of fighters were Iraqi: members of the Salafist Jihadist, or quasinationalist jihadist, groups.

In October 2004, Zarqawi's group issued a statement acknowledging the leadership of al-Qaeda under Osama bin Laden and adopted the name al-Qa'ida fi Bilad al-Rafidayn. The Iraqi city of Fallujah, in western Anbar Province, became an AQI stronghold. U.S. forces twice tried to capture the city, first in the prematurely terminated Operation VIGILANT RESOLVE from April 4 to May 1, 2004. The Fallujah Guard then controlled the city. U.S. military and Iraqi forces conquered the city in Operation PHANTOM FURY (code-named Operation FAJR) during November 7 through December 23, 2004, in extremely bloody fighting.

Zarqawi formed relationships with other Salafist Jihadist organizations, announcing an umbrella group, the Mujahideen Shura Council, in 2006. After Zarqawi was reportedly at a safe house in June 2006, the new AQI leader, Abu Ayyub al-Masri, announced a new coalition, the Islamic State of Iraq, that included the Mujahideen Shura Council.

Al-Qaeda, along with other Sunni Salafist and nationalist groups, strongly resisted Iraqi and coalition forces in Baghdad, Ramadi, and Baqubah and continued staging very damaging attacks into 2007. However, by mid-2008, U.S. commanders claimed dominance over these areas. Nevertheless, AQI was acknowledged to still be operative southeast of Baghdad in Jabour, Mosul, Samarra, Hawijah, and Miqdadiyah. The United States believes that AQI's diminished presence is attributable to the Anbar Awakening, which enlisted numerous tribes, including some former AQI members, to fight al-Qaeda. The Americans further believe that AQI has been diminished because of the troop-surge strategy that began in early 2007. Until his death in 2011 bin Laden urged the mujahideen to unify in the face of these setbacks.

AQI has strongly influenced other jihadist groups and actors, particularly through its Internet presence. In sparking intersectarian strife in Iraq, the group has also damaged Iraqi postwar reconstruction and has tapped into the intolerance of many Salafi groups and voices as well as other Sunni Iraqis and Sunni Muslims outside of Iraq who have been threatened by the emergence of Shia political parties and institutions that had suffered under the Baathist regime under Saddam Hussein.

Sherifa Zuhur

See also: al-Qaeda in Iraq; Salafism

Further Reading

Associated Press. "In Motley Array of Iraqi Foes, Why Does U.S. Spotlight al-Qaida?" *International Herald Tribune*, June 8, 2007.

Brisard, Jean-Charles, in collaboration with Damien Martinez. *Zarqawi: The New Face of al-Qaeda*. New York: Other Press, 2005.

Burns, John, and Melissa Rubin. "U.S. Arming Sunnis in Iraq to Battle Old Qaeda Allies." *New York Times*, June 11, 2007.

Congressional Research Service, Report to Congress. *Iraq: Post-Saddam Governance and Security, September 6, 2007*. Washington, DC: U.S. Government Printing Office, 2007.

Anbar Awakening

A U.S. operation to obtain or regain the loyalties of Sunni Arab tribes of Anbar Province, Iraq, that began in the provincial capital of Ramadi in September 2006. Tribal sheikhs who had been marginalized, or who sought revenge against al-Qaeda in Iraq (AQI) began cooperating with U.S. forces to root out the AQI network from the province. The Anbar Awakening restored a degree of order to a region that appeared on the verge of slipping irrevocably under insurgent control. It is credited as being a major factor in the diminution of violence in Iraq, which began in earnest in 2007.

That the Sunni tribes of Anbar would serve as the catalyst for such a transformative development was a carefully planned movement based on sentiments expressed by U.S. ambassador Zalmay Khalilzad and General David Petraeus as well as others that the Sunni population must be granted a stake in the outcome. However, the province's recent engagement in violent opposition to the U.S.

-led coalition and differences with the new Iraqi government were obstacles to be surmounted. Anbar is the largest of Iraq's 18 provinces and has a predominantly Sunni population. It became a hotspot of insurgent activity following the fall of Baghdad in 2003. Disaffected sheikhs and their tribal followers gravitated to the insurgency, driven by anger at seeing their lands occupied by foreign soldiers, resentment over the loss of jobs and prestige, and distrust of the new Shiite-dominated political order, among other things. The porous border that Anbar shared with Syria at the far western end of the province also provided an easy point of entry for fighters from other nations, who filtered into Fallujah, Ramadi, and the smaller population centers along the upper Euphrates River. Many joined the organization founded by Jordanian extremist Abu Musab al-Zarqawi, which evolved into the AQI.

Tribal insurgents had formed an alliance of convenience with AQI jihadists in Anbar, and the AQI itself was actually an overwhelmingly Iraqi, not foreign, organization. By the middle of 2006, the insurgency had grown so strong that Anbar outpaced even Baghdad in terms of the number of violent incidents, with 30–40 attacks occurring daily in the province. Conditions in Ramadi were particularly grim: public services were negligible, and the Iraqi security presence was almost nonexistent, enabling insurgent fighters to operate freely in most sections of the city. A classified assessment completed by the U.S. Marine Corps in August 2006 concluded that the province was all but lost to the insurgency.

Yet the AQI laid the groundwork for its own demise by demanding control of the insurgency and reducing Anbar's tribal chiefs to subordinate status. AQI operatives punished in brutal fashion any who opposed them, with bombings and murders that targeted not only

Sheikh Sattar, founder of al-Anbar Awakening, arrives for a meeting with tribal leaders of Iraq's Anbar province in the provincial capital of Ramadi, 115 kilometers (70 miles) west of Baghdad on August 16, 2007. They promised to "work together against terrorism, militias and al-Qaida until they're uprooted from the country." The chieftains also urged all blocs and political parties to put the nation above their private interests. (AP Photo)

the sheikhs, but also their family members and supporters. The vicious tactics used by the AQI to cow the tribes also alienated them and opened up a rift within the insurgency. In what in retrospect can be seen as a precursor to the Anbar Awakening movement, several tribes around Ramadi in January 2006 formed the al-Anbar People's Council, a breakaway group that sought to distance itself from the AQI while continuing to resist the coalition. The council collapsed soon thereafter after seven of its members were assassinated and a suicide bomber killed dozens at a police recruiting event.

The demise of the al-Anbar People's Council demonstrated that the Ramadi tribes lacked the strength and cohesion to stand up against the AQI on their own. A few months later, the sheikhs gained a powerful new benefactor when Colonel Sean MacFarland arrived with the U.S. Army's 1st Brigade Combat Team to take charge of Ramadi's security. MacFarland and his brigade had deployed first in January 2006 to Tal Afar, the city in northern Iraq that had been pacified the previous year by Colonel H. R. McMaster in what was widely hailed as a textbook counterinsurgency operation. Moving to Ramadi in June 2006, MacFarland was determined to apply some of the same counterinsurgency practices that had proven so effective at Tal Afar.

As one of the first steps in his plan to win back the city, MacFarland launched an outreach program aimed at gaining the trust and support of Ramadi's leaders. Among the earliest to respond was a charismatic young sheikh of relatively junior stature named Abd al-Sattar Buzaigh al-Rishawi. His record was far from clean, however: he was reputed to be a smuggler and highway bandit who had cooperated with the AQI in the past. More recently, however, he had lost his father and three brothers to the AQI's campaign of terror against the tribes, so he was receptive to U.S. overtures. With Sattar's help in gathering recruits, MacFarland was able to begin the process of rebuilding Ramadi's embattled police force, which numbered only about 400 at the beginning of his tour. The sheikh also assisted with MacFarland's efforts to persuade other tribal leaders to shift their allegiance from the AQI to the coalition.

Sattar expanded his opposition to the AQI into a full-fledged movement after AQI agents bombed one of the new Iraqi police stations that had been set up in the city and murdered the sheikh whose tribesmen were staffing the post. In response, Sattar convened a meeting of over 50 sheikhs and MacFarland at Sattar's home on September 9, 2006. At the gathering, Sattar announced the launch of the Anbar Awakening, an alliance of tribes dedicated to expelling the AQI from the region. Initially, only a handful of tribes signed on to the movement. However, over the next few months, the movement acquired new converts in and around Ramadi once those related to Sattar saw that MacFarland was committed to using his troops to protect tribes that rejected the AQI. The U.S. commander also supported the tribes' efforts to defend themselves through the organization of armed tribal auxiliary groups, later known as Concerned Local Citizens or Sons of Iraq. MacFarland arranged for militia members to receive training and ensured that as many as possible were incorporated into the Iraqi police force. By the end of 2006, some 4,000 recruits had been added to police ranks.

The AQI did not allow itself to be swept aside by the Anbar Awakening movement without a fight. Violence levels in Anbar peaked in October 2006 and remained high through March 2007. But the movement acquired its own momentum, spreading from Ramadi and gaining adherents in Fallujah and other parts of the province throughout 2007. Insurgent activity dropped sharply after March, a trend that reflected not only the diminishing strength of the AQI, but also the fact that once sheikhs joined the Anbar Awakening, they directed their followers to cease all attacks on U.S. troops. Sattar himself was killed in a bombing outside his Ramadi home on September 13, 2007, a mere 10 days after he had met with President George W. Bush at a military base in Anbar. Nonetheless, Sattar's death did not reverse or slow the progress in the province, nor did it diminish local support for the Awakening Councils and their militia off-shoots, which had sprouted up in Sunni areas outside of Anbar.

On September 1, 2008, Anbar completed its own remarkable turnaround from the most volatile region in Iraq to a more stable environment, and security for the province was officially transferred to the Iraqi government.

Growing tensions between the Awakening Councils and the government over late pay and lack of jobs led in March 2009 to an uprising in the Sunni-dominated Fahdil section of Baghdad and the disarmament by Iraqi and U.S. troops of the Awakening Council there. The government retained a number of members of the Fahdi Council but subsequently announced that the 150 members of the council would be offered jobs in the Iraqi security forces.

Jeff Seiken

See also: al-Qaeda in Iraq; Iraqi Insurgency; Petraeus, David Howell; Terrorism

Further Reading

Lubin, Andrew. "Ramadi: From the Caliphate to Capitalism." *Proceedings* 134 (April 2008): 54–61.

McCary, John A. "The Anbar Awakening: An Alliance of Incentives." *Washington Quarterly* 32 (January 2009): 43–59.

Smith, Major Niel, and Colonel Sean MacFarland. "Anbar Awakens: The Tipping Point." *Military Review* (March–April 2008): 41–52.

West, Bing. *The Strongest Tribe: War, Politics, and the Endgame in Iraq*. New York: Random House, 2008.

Ansar al-Islam

A radical Kurdish Islamist separatist movement formed in 2001 in northern Iraq (Kurdistan). The U.S. government has held that the group was founded by Mullah Krekar, with assistance and funds from al-Qaeda leader Osama bin Laden. The complicated history of Ansar al-Islam (Supporters of Islam) dates back to the Islamic Movement in Kurdistan (IMK), formed in 1987 of various factions, some of whom had trained and fought in Afghanistan. Some others apparently returned to Kurdistan after the fall of the Taliban in late 2001, which was the basis of U.S. arguments that the group had links to al-Qaeda, a claim also made by its enemies in the larger Kurdish factions.

The IMK fought with the Popular Union of Kurdistan (PUK) and eventually had to retreat to the Iranian border before returning to its base in Halabja. In 2001 the group splintered, and various new groupings formed the Jund al-Islam in September of that year, declaring jihad on those Kurdish parties that had left the Islamic path. The PUK fought Jund al-Islam, which dissolved and renamed itself Ansar al-Islam in December 2001 under the leadership of Amir Mullah Krekar, also known as Najmuddin Faraj Ahmad. Since then, however, Krekar has been living in Norway and has faced various indictments and deferred deportation for supporting terrorism.

While still operating under the name of Jund al-Islam, Ansar al-Islam tried to quash non-Islamic practices. It banned music, television, and alcohol; imposed the veil on women and beards on men; closed schools and employment to women; and tried to force a minority religious group called the Ahl al-Haqq to convert and then drove its members out of their villages. Ansar al-Islam also cracked down on the Naqshabandi Sufis. The group also pursued individuals, and some were held and tortured. The group's strict Salafi stance makes it akin to various Sunni nationalist resistance groups that developed after 2003 and accentuates its differences with the principal Kurdish political factions.

The struggle between the PUK and Ansar al-Islam has also involved human rights violations, the assassination of the governor of Arbil, and fighting that has continued for years. In December 2002 Ansar al-Islam forces took two PUK outposts and killed about 50 people; more than half of these reportedly died after they had surrendered. On the other hand, Ansar al-Islam prisoners have been mistreated by the PUK.

When the invasion of Iraq occurred in March 2003, Ansar al-Islam mounted various small attacks and carried out actions against those it called "collaborators" with the Americans, including civilians. The

Najmuddin Faraj Ahmad, also known as Mullah Krekar, founder of the Iraqi Kurd Islamist group Ansar al-Islam. He was found not guilty of "inciting terrorism" but sentenced two years and ten months in prison for issuing threats and intimidating witnesses. (Daniel Sannum-Lauten/AFP/Getty Images)

group carried out a much larger attack during 2004, when its suicide bombers attacked the PUK and Kurdistan Democratic Party (KDP) headquarters and killed 109 people, among them the KDP's deputy prime minister, Sami Abd al-Rahman. In 2005 Ansar al-Islam assassinated an aide to Grand Ayatollah Sayyid Ali Husayn al-Sistan, Sheikh Mahmud al-Madayini, in Baghdad.

In 2003 fighters from Ansar al-Islam joined with other Sunni Salafi fighters in the central region of Iraq, forming Jamaat Ansar al-Sunna (formerly Jaysh Ansar al-Sunna). But the Ansar al-Islam elements returned to their earlier name in 2007. Also in 2007, the Ansar al-Sunna, along with Ansar al-Islam, the Islamic Army of Iraq, and the Army of the Mujahideen, formed a new grouping called the Jihad and Reformation Front. In any event, it remains unclear what links Ansar al-Islam has to al-Qaeda in Iraq, and there is some evidence to suggest that it might have received aid from Iran. The group continues to battle more secularist Kurdish groups, and in March 2009 it kidnapped and beheaded three Kurdish truck driver hostages to punish them for cooperating with the Americans.

Sherifa Zuhur

See also: al-Qaeda in Iraq; Kurdistan Democratic Party

Further Reading

"Ansar al-Islam in Iraqi Kurdistan." Human Rights Watch Backgrounder, www.hrw.org/legacy/backgrounder/mena/ansarbk020503.htm.

Stansfield, Gareth R. V. *Iraqi Kurdistan: Political Development and Emergent Democracy.* New York: Routledge, 2003.

Wong, Edward. "The Reach of War: Violence, Militants Show the Beheading of 3 Kurdish Hostages." *New York Times*, March 22, 2009.

Antiaircraft Missiles, Iraqi

Air defense missiles have constituted the most significant component of Iraq's integrated air defense system during its three major conflicts since 1980. Iraq used radar-guided surface-to-air missiles (SAMs) for medium- to high-altitude and area air defense and shoulder-fired infrared-guided SAMs for tactical air defense and to complement its antiaircraft artillery systems. Since the most common tactic to evade radar-guided SAMs involved a high-speed roll and dive to lower altitudes, the integration of guns, missiles, and fighter aircraft into a layered defense in-depth theoretically provided an almost impenetrable barrier to air attack. Aircraft that successfully avoided radar-guided SAMs found themselves flying through a gauntlet of intense antiaircraft fire supplemented by infrared-guided SAMs, the intensity of which increased as the attacking aircraft approached their target. Those that made it past the target pulled up into the sights of waiting fighter aircraft. Fighters escorting the attack aircraft had to penetrate the same gauntlet to engage enemy interceptors.

Although it did not lead to high scores among the defending pilots, it was a system that inflicted heavy losses on U.S. aircraft over North Vietnam in the 1960s. The United States and its coalition allies learned from that conflict, however, and possessed the electronic warfare equipment and weapons to defeat the system during Operations DESERT STORM and IRAQI FREEDOM.

Most Iraqi air defense missiles were Soviet-built, with the venerable SA-2 Guideline (the missile and radar designations are those of the North Atlantic Treaty Organization [NATO]) and its supporting Fan Song radar being the oldest and longest-ranged weapon in service. Developed in the 1950s, the SA-2, with a range of 27 nautical miles, enjoyed great success during the Vietnam War but was at best obsolete by 1990. Although it could engage aircraft operating at altitudes of up to 89,000 feet, its radar was easily defeated, and only a highly trained crew could employ its electro-optical guidance and electronic counter-countermeasures features effectively. Also, its minimum range of 4–5 nautical miles and its minimum altitude of 3,280 feet made it all but useless against low-flying targets. The SA-3 Goa was newer and longer ranged. Introduced in Soviet service in 1963, the Goa, with a range of 22 nautical miles, used the Flat Face radar for guidance. It had an operational engagement ceiling of 59,000 feet and enjoyed better tactical mobility than the SA-2. The SA-2 and SA-3 were deployed around major Iraqi cities.

Iraq also deployed a wide range of Soviet mobile SAM systems, including the SA-6 Gainful, SA-9 Gaskin, and SA-12. Of these, the Gainful was the best known, having inflicted heavy losses on the Israeli Air Force when first employed during the October 1973 Yom Kippur (Ramadan) War. Mounted on a tracked chassis, the Gainful was a medium-ranged SAM supported by a robust Straight Flush fire-control radar that was difficult to deceive. Introduced into Soviet service in 1970, the SA-6 deployed in four transporter-erector-launcher (TEL) batteries supported by a single fire-control radar. The missile has a maximum range of 13.2 nautical miles and an operational engagement ceiling of 39,000 feet.

The SA-9 Gaskin was a much shorter-ranged SAM mounted on a wheeled vehicle that carried two pairs of ready-to-fire missiles. The Gaskin was infrared-guided (IR), but unlike most IR missiles, it could engage an incoming target unless the sun obscured the aircraft. Normally deployed in proximity to the ZSU-23/4 mobile antiaircraft gun, the SA-9 dated from 1966 and had a maximum range of 4.4 nautical miles and a ceiling of 20,000 feet. The SA-9 had little impact on allied air operations in either of the Persian Gulf conflicts.

The newest mobile SAM in the Iraqi inventory was the short-ranged radar-guided SA-8 Gecko. Carried in six-missile canisters mounted atop a wheeled transporter-erector-launcher-and-radar (TELAR), the SA-8 was employed with Iraqi Army units in the field. Its six-wheeled TELAR was amphibious and was equipped with a frequency agile fire-control radar and alternate electro-optical guidance that made it particularly difficult to defeat electronically. Its normal engagement range was 1.1–5 nautical miles against targets flying between 100 and 16,500 feet. The most common tactics employed against the SA-8 were using antiradiation missiles against its radar or flying above its engagement envelope.

The remaining SAMs in Iraqi service were man portable. Of these, the Soviet-built IR-guided SA-7 Grail, SA-14 Gremlin, SA-16 Gimlet, and SA-18 Grouse were the most numerous. The SA-7 was the shortest ranged, reaching out only about 10,000 feet and effective only against slow-moving targets flying away at altitudes below 4,000 feet. The SA-14 was an improvement on the SA-7, providing greater range (3.7 nautical miles) and a limited capability for head-on engagements. The SA-16 incorporated an identification-friend-or-foe (IFF) feature and a more effective IR counter-countermeasures capability. The SA-18 was a simplified and more reliable improvement

of the SA-16. The Gimlet and Grouse can engage a target from any aspect; they have a maximum range of 3.1 miles and a ceiling of 15,700 feet. Their performance is comparable to the U.S. FIM-92A Stinger.

The last SAM in Iraqi service was the French-built Roland. The Iraqis used the Roland for airfield defense. The radar-guided Roland had a maximum operational range of 5 nautical miles and an engagement ceiling of 17,100 feet. Its rapid acceleration and high speed made it an ideal air defense weapon. However, in the hands of inexperienced or poorly trained operators, it proved vulnerable to jamming and other electronic countermeasures. Also, the Iraqi missile crews had to operate the system from exposed positions, making them vulnerable to enemy attack, a factor that inhibited the weapon's effectiveness.

Coalition superiority in terms of both numbers and technology as well as superior tactics all but negated Iraq's integrated air defense system. Its SAMs achieved only limited success in the few opportunities that the air campaign presented to them. Allied air defense suppression systems, anti-radiation missiles, and well-orchestrated electronic countermeasure operations blinded Iraqi radars, destroyed their command and control systems and communications networks, and inflicted heavy losses on SAM batteries. Although Iraq nominally possessed a modern integrated air defense system, its weapons, sensors, and communications networks were outdated, and its operators were poorly trained for war against a well-trained opponent equipped with third- and fourth-generation aircraft and precision-guided weapons.

Carl Schuster

See also: Iraqi Freedom, Operation, Air Campaign

Further Reading

Blake, Bernard, ed. *Jane's Weapons Systems, 1988–89 (Jane's Land-Based Air Defence)*. London: Jane's, 1988.

Cooper, Toni, and Farzad Bishop. *Iran-Iraq War in the Air: 1980–1988*. Atglen, PA: Schiffer Military History, 2000.

General Accounting Office. *Operation Desert Storm: Evaluation of the Air War; Report to Congress*. Washington, DC: U.S. Government Printing Office, 1996.

Hallion, Richard P. *Storm over Iraq: Air Power and the Gulf War*. Washington, DC: Smithsonian Institution Press, 1997.

Lynch, Kristin. *Supporting Air and Space Expeditionary Forces: Lessons from Operation Iraqi Freedom*. Washington, DC: RAND Corporation, 2004.

Antitank Weapons

Because of the large number of tanks and armored vehicles that saw service in both the Persian Gulf War and the Iraq War, antitank weapons played a critical role. Although initially equipped with large numbers of Soviet- and Russian-designed tanks and other weapons, the Iraqi Army managed to knock out only a small handful of U.S. tanks. In the Iraq War, U.S. forces lost 9 tanks to friendly fire and 2 to mines, and 13 were damaged by various forms of Iraqi antitank fire (5 of those were severely damaged). Crew casualties from Iraqi fire were 1 killed and 13 wounded. In both wars the Iraqi Air Force played virtually no role, so whatever rotary and fixed-wing antitank aircraft they may have had in their inventory were largely irrelevant. The primary Iraqi antitank weapons were limited to antitank guided missiles (ATGMs) and shoulder-fired infantry weapons. In Afghanistan the Taliban had no armored vehicles, and their antitank weapons were limited primarily to shoulder-fired infantry weapons, recoilless rifles, and mines. The majority of the weapons considered here, therefore, are U.S. systems.

Despite their armor and armament, tanks and other armored vehicles are not invulnerable. They can be defeated by land mines, aircraft, artillery, other tanks, rockets, guided missiles, and a wide range of infantry weapons. The various categories of tank kills are a function of the damage done to the tank combined with the tactical situation. A mobility kill, called an M-kill in current U.S. doctrine, occurs when the tank's power train or running gear have been damaged to the point where the tank cannot move. The tank may still be able to fire its weapons, but its inability to maneuver severely degrades its combat value. A firepower kill, called an F-kill, occurs when the tank's main gun or its fire-control optics and electronics have been severely damaged. A catastrophic kill, called a K-kill, occurs when the tank completely loses its ability to operate. It can neither move nor fire. A K-kill usually means that the tank has been totally destroyed and often also means that the tank crew has been killed.

Whether fired by artillery, aircraft, another tank, or infantry weapons, the warheads of all antitank rounds are classified as either kinetic energy or chemical energy. Most main battle tanks are capable of firing both types of rounds through their main guns. The three basic types of chemical energy (i.e., explosive) warheads are high explosive (HE), high-explosive antitank (HEAT), and high-explosive plastic (HEP).

Tanks can be defeated by a blast from conventional HEs, but only if the charge is large enough and close enough. HE projectiles delivered by artillery or air require a direct or very close hit, which usually exceeds the circular probable error of all but the most advanced precision-guided munitions (PGMs).

The most common and effective chemical energy projectile, the HEAT round, has a shaped-charge warhead that relies on the Munroe Effect to burn a hole through the tank's armor in the form of an expanding cone. What actually kills the tank crew is the semimolten armor of their own tank. HEAT round detonations can also set off fuel and ammunition fires as well as secondary explosions.

HEP rounds, also called high-explosive squash head (HESH) rounds, carry a charge of plastic explosive that upon impact spreads over the outer surface of the armor before detonating. Unlike a HEAT round, the HEP round does actually penetrate the tank's armor. When the HEP charge explodes, it knocks off chunks of armor of a corresponding size, called spall, inside the tank, causing havoc for the crew and the internal components. HEP rounds are generally ineffective against most modern tanks because the internal compartments are equipped with spall liners, protecting the crew, ammunition, fuel, and equipment.

Nonexploding kinetic energy rounds are very heavy and dense, and they are fired at an extremely high velocity. The most common is some form of sabot round in which an outer casing falls away as soon as the round leaves the gun's muzzle. On impact the sabot punches its way through the target's armor. The effect inside the tank is usually even more catastrophic than that caused by a HEAT round. Tungsten and depleted uranium are two heavy and dense materials widely employed as sabots.

Because kinetic energy rounds require a flat line-of-sight trajectory and an extremely high velocity, they must be fired from a gun as opposed to a howitzer and from a very heavy platform. Thus, only tanks and antitank artillery can fire sabot rounds. The area of a tank most vulnerable to a sabot round is at the slip ring, where the turret joins the main hull. Smaller nonsabot kinetic energy rounds are fired from rotary or fixed-wing aircraft armed with special antitank machine guns that deliver a high volume of fire to defeat the target's armor, usually from above, where the armor is the weakest.

Chemical energy rounds do not require a heavy launching platform and are thus ideal for infantry antitank weapons, which include rocket launchers, recoilless rifles, and antitank guided missiles (ATGMs). The best way to defeat a HEAT warhead is to cause it to detonate prematurely, which will prevent the Munroe Effect from forming properly on the outer skin of the tank's armor. Something as simple as a mesh outer screen mounted on the side of a tank with a few inches of standoff distance will cause that premature detonation. Reactive explosive armor, also called appliqué armor, mounted on the tank's integral armor is also relatively effective against HEAT rounds but not at all effective against sabot rounds. Each element of reactive armor contains a small explosive charge that detonates when it is hit, causing the impacting HEAT round to detonate prematurely and spoiling the Munroe Effect. Finally, the sloped surfaces of the tank's armor can cause the HEAT round to deflect, which also spoils the Munroe Effect. Sloped armor surfaces can also deflect sabot rounds in certain instances.

Although common in World War II, purpose-built antitank artillery fell into disuse in the years following 1945. By the 1960s the Soviet Union, West Germany, and Sweden were among the few remaining countries still building antitank artillery. Most armies came to regard the tank itself as the premier, but certainly not the only, antitank weapon.

The antitank rifle first entered service in World War I. Today it is known as the anti-material (antimatériel or equipment) rifle. Essentially a large-caliber high-velocity rifle firing special armor-piercing ammunition, it is designed to operate against enemy equipment such as thin-skinned and lightly armored vehicles. The weapon may also be used for long-range sniping. Antimaterial rifles are often favored by special operations military units.

The U.S. Army Browning M-2 .50-caliber machine gun, which can be fired in single-shot mode, fits in this category. The Austrian Steyr 25-millimeter (mm) antimaterial rifle, with a claimed effective range of 1.2 miles, features both a muzzle brake and a hydro-pneumatic sleeve to reduce recoil. It has a bipod, and the weapon can be broken down for ease of transport by its crew. Among other such weapons is the South African Mechem NTW-20. This 20-mm bolt-action rifle features a three-round side-mounted box magazine. There is also a 14.5-mm model. To reduce recoil, the NTW-20 uses a hydraulic double-action damper along with a double baffle muzzle brake. Among other such weapons are the U.S. Armalite AR-50 and Barretta M-82A1, both of which fire the 12.7-mm NATO (.50-caliber) round; the British Accuracy International AW50F, firing the 12.7-mm NATO (.50-caliber) round; the Hungarian Gerpard M-1(B) and M-2(B) 12.7-mm rifles, which with an interchangeable barrel can also fire the .50-caliber round; and the Russian KSVK 12.7-mm rifle. A number of these or similar weapons have been used in various Middle Eastern wars.

In the years following the Vietnam War, both the Americans and the Soviets developed special antitank machine guns for attack aircraft. Although the kinetic energy rounds fired by such weapons are far lighter than the sabot rounds fired from tanks, the high rate of fire from the machine guns produces multiple impacts in a concentrated area on the target that literally chews into the tank's armor. Attacking from above, the aircraft target the top of the tank, where the armor is generally the thinnest.

Entering service in 1977, the American GAU-8/A Avenger is a 30-mm seven-barrel electrically driven Gatling gun. It fires both armor-piercing incendiary (API) and high-explosive incendiary rounds, usually in a four-to-one mix. The API round weighs a little less than one pound and carries a depleted uranium penetrator. The GAU-8/A has a cyclic rate of fire of 3,900 rounds per minute. The Russian GSh-6-30 30-mm aircraft automatic cannon is a very similar weapon, except that it is gas operated rather than electrically driven. Entering service in 1998, the U.S. M-230 Chain Gun also fires a 30-mm antitank round. Having only a single barrel, its rate of fire is only 625 rounds per minute, but it is considerably lighter than the GAU-8/A.

Purpose-built antitank mines first appeared in the last years of World War I and figured prominently during World War II. Most modern antitank mines use an HE charge to produce M-kills by blowing off the tread or damaging the road wheels. Some mines are designed to produce K-kills by attacking the underside of the tank, where the armor is thin. Although sometimes command detonated by either wire or remote control, most use pressure or magnetically triggered detonators that react to vehicles but not ground personnel.

The improvised explosive device (IED) is a variation on the antitank mine that has produced a high percentage of U.S. and allied casualties during the Iraq War since 2003 and increasingly in Afghanistan. An IED is any locally fabricated explosive charge coupled with a detonating mechanism. Deadly to personnel, most IEDs initially could damage only unarmored and lightly armored vehicles. If the base explosive charge was large enough—for example, an artillery projectile buried in the road—the resulting explosion could do serious damage to a tank. In recent years, however, IEDs have become more sophisticated, especially with the appearance of explosively formed penetrators (EFPs). The EFP works on the same principle as the shaped charge, effectively transforming the IED from a simple HE to a HEAT weapon. An EFP has a cylindrical-shaped charge capped by a concave metal disk pointed inward. When detonated, the metal disk, often made of copper, becomes a bolt of molten metal that can penetrate the armor on most vehicles in Iraq. An IED with an EFP is difficult to detect and counter because it is effective at standoff distances up to 164 feet.

Recoilless rifles and recoilless guns (smoothbore) were developed during World War II primarily as antitank weapons. Firing HE and HEAT projectiles similar to conventional artillery, a recoilless rifle is essentially a long tube, similar to a modern rocket launcher. Unlike the latter, however, the recoilless rifle has a breech mechanism. Also unlike conventional artillery, that breech has large exit vents, and the ammunition shell casings are perforated. When fired, almost all of the propellant blast escapes from the rear of the weapon. The resulting forward inertial force, however, is still sufficient to launch the projectile. The neutralization of almost all recoil eliminates the need for a standard gun carriage and a recoil system. Although most recoilless rifles are fired from some sort of vehicle or ground mount, some of the smaller calibers can be shoulder fired in the same manner as an infantry rocket launcher.

Recoilless rifles were widely used in Korea and Vietnam, but they were phased out of service in most armies as antitank rockets and guided missiles became more sophisticated from the 1970s on. Nonetheless, Taliban forces in Afghanistan have used a number of recoilless rifles, most of them captured from Soviet forces in the 1980s. The most common is the 82-mm B-10, which first entered service in 1950. Although it has a maximum range of 2.7 miles, its maximum effective range is only 1,640 feet. The most modern of the Taliban's recoilless antitank weapons is the 73-mm SPG-9. Designed initially for Soviet airborne units and entering service in 1962, it has a maximum effective range of 2,624 feet.

The first effective shoulder-fired infantry antitank weapons were free-flight rockets with HEAT warheads, entering service during World War II. All subsequent antitank rocket systems are derived from two basic designs, both introduced in 1942. The German Panzerfaust was an inexpensive single-shot lightweight weapon that could be fired by one man. The Panzerfaust consisted of a very simple small-diameter disposable launcher preloaded with a three-foot-long finned projectile with an oversized warhead that extended outside of the muzzle of the launching tube. The hollow tube concentrated the escaping gasses away from the gunner and made the firing recoilless. Pulling the trigger ignited a small charge of black powder inside the tube, driving the projectile toward its target. The projectile exploded on impact. The Panzerfaust was the prototype upon which the subsequent Soviet/Russian family of rocket-propelled grenade (RPG) antitank weapons was based.

The first U.S. antitank rocket was the 2.36-inch bazooka, which consisted of a rocket and launcher operated by a two-man crew of gunner and loader. The launcher was a reloadable aluminum tube with a shoulder stock and a hand grip that contained a trigger assembly with an electric generator. When the gunner squeezed the trigger, it generated an electric current through the wires to ignite the solid fuel in the rocket. Unlike the Panzerfaust, the entire antitank rocket was launched from inside the bazooka's firing tube. The Germans reverse-engineered captured bazookas to produce the significantly up-gunned 88-mm Panzerschreck. Except for the RPG family of weapons, the bazooka is the prototype for all other modern shoulder-fired infantry antitank rockets.

The Soviet RPG-7 is one of the most widely produced shoulder-fired infantry antitank weapons in the world. It is one of the principal weapons of choice of Afghan and Iraqi insurgents. It is also widely used by Afghan and Iraqi police and military forces loyal to the national governments. First entering service in 1961 and used extensively by the Viet Cong and the North Vietnamese Army against U.S. armored vehicles in Vietnam, the RPG-7 consists of a steel launching tube 40 mm in diameter and 37 inches long. Depending on the exact type of projectile, the protruding warhead can be anything from 83 mm to 105 mm. Most RPG-7 ammunition has a range up to 2,952 feet, and the most effective warhead has a tandem HEAT charge capable of penetrating 600 mm to 700 mm of rolled homogeneous armor (RHA).

The only shoulder-fired free-flight rocket antitank weapon used by U.S. forces today is the Swedish-built AT-4. Similar in operating principle to the World War II–era bazooka, the AT-4 fires an 84-mm projectile with a HEAT warhead to a maximum effective range of 984 feet. The resulting blast can penetrate up to 400 mm of RHA. Unlike the earlier bazooka, the AT-4 is not reloadable. The launcher and projectile are manufactured and issued as a single unit of ammunition. The entire system weighs 14.75 pounds.

ATGMs first started to appear in the late 1960s and represented a vast improvement on the early unguided antitank rockets. ATGMs vary widely in size and type, from individual shoulder-fired missiles to crew-served missiles and to those launched from ground vehicles and from aircraft. Unlike unguided systems, missiles have the great advantage of standoff capability.

First-generation guided missiles were manually controlled during flight. Once the missile was fired, the gunner guided it to the target by means of a joystick or similar device. Second-generation antitank missiles required only that the gunner keep the sight on the target. Guidance commands for the missile were transmitted either by radio or by wire. Third-generation antitank missiles operate by laser painting or marking of the target on a nose-mounted TV camera. They are known as fire-and-forget missiles.

Antitank missiles generally carry a hollow-charge or shaped-charge HEAT warhead. Tandem warhead missiles are designed specifically to defeat reactive or spaced vehicle armor, while top-attack antitank missiles are designed to strike from above against the more lightly armored tops of tanks and armored fighting vehicles (AFVs).

The 9K11 Malyutka, known by its NATO designation as the AT-3 Sagger, was the Soviet Union's first man-portable ATGM and probably the most extensively produced ATGM in history. It was widely used by Iraqi forces in both the Persian Gulf War and the Iraq War. Entering service in September 1963, it was the standard model for all subsequent first-generation ATGMs. Some 25,000 Saggers were produced yearly by the Soviet Union alone in the 1960s and

1970s. It was also manufactured by other Soviet bloc countries as well as the People's Republic of China. The Sagger has been widely exported to the Middle East, including Afghanistan, Algeria, Egypt, Iran, Iraq, Libya, and Syria. Guided to its target by means of a joy stick and wire, the Sagger has a launch weight of some 24 pounds with a warhead of 5.5 pounds. It has a minimum range of 1,640 feet and a maximum range of 1.8 miles. At maximum range, it takes the missile about 30 seconds to reach its target. The Sagger can be fired from a portable suitcase launcher; from armored vehicles, such as the Soviet BMP-1 or BRDM-2; or from attack helicopters, including the Mi-2, Mi-8, and Mi-24.

The U.S.-made BGM-71 tube-launched optically tracked wire-guided (TOW) missile is a second-generation ATGM. TOWs were first produced by Hughes Aircraft Company and are now produced by Raytheon Systems Company. More than 500,000 TOWs have been manufactured, and they are employed by more than 45 nations. The TOW is designed to attack tanks, AFVs, bunkers, and fortifications. First entering service in 1970, the TOW underwent a number of modifications, the most recent of which is the TOW-2B of 1991. The first use of the TOW in combat came in May 1972 during the Vietnam War. It also saw wartime service with the Israeli Army against Syrian forces and in the Iran-Iraq War (1980–1988). The TOW-2B first saw combat in 2003 during the Iraq War.

The TOW-2B missile weighs 49.8 pounds (64 pounds with carrier) and has an explosive filler of some 6.9 pounds. The missile is 5.8 inches in diameter and is 48 inches in length. It has a minimum range of 213 feet and a maximum range of 2.3 miles. TOW missiles can be ground fired from a tripod by a crew of four or, more usually, from both wheeled and tracked vehicles, including the

M-1/M-3 Bradley, the M-966 HMMWV, and the M-1134 Stryker. TOWs also are mounted on attack helicopters. The missile operates on command line-of-sight guidance. The gunner uses a sight to locate the target and, once the missile is fired, continues to track the target through the sight, with guidance commands transmitted along two wires that spool from the back of the missile. The TOW-2B attacks the target from the top, and its double warheads explode downward when the missile is just above the target. A bunker-buster variant is designed to defeat bunkers, field fortifications, and buildings.

The Soviet Union's second-generation man-portable 9K111 Fagot (NATO designation AT-4 Spigot) ATGM entered service in 1972. Designed to replace the Sagger, the Spigot has a minimum range of 246 feet and a maximum range of 1.5 miles in a flight time of 11 seconds. Fired from a ground-mount folding tripod, the entire system in firing configuration weighs some 74 pounds, with the missile itself weighing 25.3 pounds and the warhead 5.5 pounds.

The M-47 Dragon was a U.S. antitank infantry weapon that was fired from the gunner's shoulder but stabilized in front by a ground bipod. First fielded in 1975, it was used in the 1991 Persian Gulf War and was retired from service in the late 1990s. The improved Dragon II entered service in 1985, and the Super-Dragon entered service in 1990. At one time the Dragons were supplied to Iran, and the Iraqis captured some Dragons during the Iran-Iraq War and put them into service. The 140-mm wire-guided missile carried a HEAT warhead capable of penetrating 450 mm of RHA and defeating Soviet T-55, T-62, and T-72 tanks. The Dragon's maximum effective range was 3,280 feet. The launcher itself was expendable, but the sights could be removed after firing and reused. The

Dragon's most significant drawback was that its tracking system required the gunner to remain kneeling and exposed to enemy fire while tracking the missile to the target.

The Dragon was replaced by the man-portable FGM-148 Javelin, a third-generation system. A joint venture of Texas Instruments (now Raytheon Missile Systems) of Dallas, Texas, and Lockheed Martin Electronics and Missiles (now Missiles and Fire Control) of Orlando, Florida, the Javelin entered service with the U.S. Army and U.S. Marine Corps in 1996. Designed for a two-man crew, the Javelin has a minimum range of 246 feet and a maximum effective range of 1.5 miles, more than twice that of the M-47 Dragon.

The Javelin system consists of a missile in a disposable launch tube, a reusable command launch unit (CLU) with triggering mechanism, an integrated day/night sighting device, and target-acquisition electronics. The missile weighs 49.5 pounds and is 5 feet 9 inches in length. Fins deploy when the missile is launched. The Javelin employs a small thermal imaging TV camera and sophisticated computer guidance system in its seeker section. To fire the missile, the gunner places a cursor over the selected target. The CLU then sends a lock-on-before-launch signal to the missile. The missile's infrared guidance system and onboard processing guide it after launch. The Javelin is designed for top attack and has a dual 8.5-pound warhead capable of defeating all known armor. U.S. forces have used the Javelin in both Afghanistan and Iraq since 2003, and British forces also fielded the Javelin in 2005.

The AGM-65 Maverick was a U.S. air-to-ground missile designed to destroy not only armored vehicles, but also ships, air defense and artillery emplacements, and logistics nodes. Entering service in 1972, the missile weighs between 462 and 670 pounds, depending on the warhead. The 125-pound shaped-charge warhead has a point-detonating fuse, and the 300-pound high-explosive penetrator has a delay-action fuse. The missile itself has a maximum effective range of 17 miles. The missile has an onboard infrared television camera with which the aircraft pilot or weapons systems officer locks onto the target before firing. Once launched, the Maverick tracks its target automatically, making it a fire-and-forget system. Fired primarily from fixed-wing aircraft, the Maverick was used extensively in both the Persian Gulf War and the Iraq War.

The AGM-114 Hellfire entered service in 1984. It was designed specifically as an antitank weapon, primarily for launch from attack helicopters, although it can be fired from some fixed-wing attack aircraft and can even be ground launched. The missile weighs 106 pounds, including the 20-pound warhead. It has a maximum effective range of 4.9 miles. The initial versions of the Hellfire were laser guided, but the more recent variants have been radar guided. The Hellfire has been used in the Persian Gulf War, the Afghanistan War, and the Iraq War. Between 2001 and 2007 U.S. forces have fired more that 6,000 Hellfires in combat.

Although direct-firing antitank artillery guns have been phased out of service by most armies since the 1950s, the increasing technical sophistication of artillery ammunition has given a new antitank role to indirect-firing field artillery. Most U.S. antitank field artillery rounds are 155 mm and are fired by either the M-198 towed howitzer or the M-109 family of self-propelled howitzers. Special antitank warheads also exist for the M-270 multiple launch rocket system (MLRS) and the army tactical missile system (ATACMS), which use the same self-propelled launcher system as the MLRS. The most current version of the M-109 howitzer, the Paladin M-109A6, entered service in 1999 and fires to a maximum range of 13.6 miles. The United States used the M-109A6 in the Iraq War, and the U.S., British, Egyptian, and Saudi armies all used earlier versions of the M-109 in the Persian Gulf War. The M-270 MLRS, which entered service in 1983, was developed jointly by the United States, Britain, Germany, and France. It fires 12 free-flight rockets to a maximum range of 26.1 miles. The MLRS launcher also can fire two MGM-140 ATACMS at a time. Operational in January 1991 and first fired in combat during the Persian Gulf War, the guided missiles have a range of 102 miles.

The improved conventional munitions (ICM) artillery round entered service for the U.S. 105-mm howitzer in 1961 and was first fired in combat in the Vietnam War. The projectile was a cargo-carrying round that burst in the air over the target, dispersing a number of unguided antipersonnel submunitions. In common terms, the ICM was an artillery version of a cluster bomb. In the early 1970s the United States developed a projectile for the 155-mm howitzer that carried submunitions designed to work against either personnel or tanks. Called a dual-purpose ICM (DPICM), the M-483 155-mm projectile carries 88 submunitions capable of penetrating 65 mm of RHA. Each M-42 or M-46 bomblet carries a HEAT shaped charge designed to attack a tank's relatively thin top armor. The DPICM warhead for the MLRS rocket carries 644 M-77 submunitions, each capable of penetrating 100 mm of RHA. The ATACMS MGM-140 missile warhead carried 950 M-74 submunitions that are classified as antipersonnel/antimaterial (APAM). They are effective against thin-skinned tactical vehicles but not against armored vehicles. The most significant drawback to DPICMs is the 2–5 percent dud rate of the submunitions, which has caused unintended casualties as friendly forces have moved into a target area after the firing. During the 1991 Persian Gulf War, DPICMs acquired the nickname "Steel Rain."

Like DPICM artillery ammunition, family of scatterable mines (FASCAM) rounds are also cargo-carrying projectiles that burst in the air above the target area and disperse unguided submunitions. FASCAM rounds can be emplaced remotely, deep in an enemy's rear, by either field artillery or aircraft. FASCAM projectiles were initially developed for both the 155-mm and 8-inch howitzers and carried either antipersonnel mines (called area denial munitions [ADAMs]) or antitank mines (called remote antiarmor mines [RAAMs]). The 8-inch howitzer was retired from the U.S. arsenal after the Persian Gulf War. The 155-mm M-741 projectile carries nine M-73 antitank mines, which are preset to self-destruct 48 hours after they have been emplaced. The M-741 projectile carries nine M-70 antitank mines, with a preset self-destruct time of four hours.

Unlike many antitank mines, the FASCAM RAAMs are designed to achieve a K-kill rather than just an M-kill. Each 3.75-pound M-70 and M-73 mine contains slightly more than one pound of RDX (cyclonite) explosive. When the mine is detonated by its magnetically induced fuse, a two-sided Miznay-Shardin plate creates a self-forging fragment that becomes a superdense molten slug that punches through the tank's relatively thin underarmor. The principle is similar to that of the explosively formed penetrators used in some IEDs. The first artillery-delivered FASCAM minefield in combat was fired by the 5th Battalion, 11th Marines, during the Battle of Khafji (January 29 to February 1, 1991).

The first PGM for field artillery weapons was the American M-712 Copperhead, a 155-mm fin-stabilized terminally guided projectile specifically designed to engage tanks and other hardened targets. In order for the Copperhead round to hit a tank directly, an observer must have the target under observation and be close enough to "paint" it with a laser-designator during the terminal leg of the projectile's trajectory. This requires that the round be below cloud cover long enough for it to lock on to the target and have sufficient time to maneuver to impact. The observer can be either a forward observer on the ground or an aerial in a helicopter. Unmanned aerial vehicles (UAVs) equipped with television cameras and laser designators can also be used to guide the Copperhead round to its target. The Copperhead was fired in combat for the first time during the Persian Gulf War.

The U.S. sense and destroy armor (SADARM) system is based in a cargo-carrying artillery round similar to the DPICM projectile except that it carries smart submunitions. The 155-mm M-898 round carries two submunitions that are released 3,280 feet above the target area. Specially designed parachutes slow the descent of the submunition and cause it to swing in a circle. As it descends, its millimeter wave radar and infrared telescope sensors sweep the area below about 492 feet in diameter. When the sensors acquire a target, the explosive charge triggers at the right time, sending an explosively formed penetrator through the top armor of the tank. SADARM rounds were fired in combat for the first time during the Iraq War. The divisional artillery of the U.S. 3rd Infantry Division fired 108 rounds and achieved 48 vehicle kills.

Purpose-built ground attack aircraft first appeared in the final year of World War I, and during World War II the British, Soviets, and Germans all developed fixed-wing aircraft specifically designed to attack tanks. During the Vietnam War the United States first started using helicopters in a ground-attack role, and during North Vietnam's 1972 Easter Offensives U.S. helicopters firing TOW missiles attacked tanks for the first time.

The first U.S. purpose-designed attack helicopter was the AH-1 Cobra, which entered service in 1967. The U.S. Army retired the Cobra in 1999, but the U.S. Marine Corps still flies the AH-1W Super Cobra, which can mount an antitank armament of eight TOW or eight Hellfire missiles. The U.S. Army's AH-64 Apache entered service in 1983 and saw significant service in the Persian Gulf War. It has also seen significant service in the Afghanistan War and the Iraq War. Specifically designed as a tank killer, the AH-64's primary armament is the M-230 Chain Gun. Depending on its specific mission, each AH-64 can carry up to 16 Hellfire antitank missiles and 1,200 rounds of 30-mm ammunition.

A number of U.S. fixed-wing ground-support aircraft are capable of carrying anti-tank armament, but like the AH-64 Apache, the A-10 Thunderbolt II, universally known as the Wart-hog, was specifically designed as a tank killer. Its primary armament is the GAU-8/A Gatling gun, which weighs 4,029 pounds and accounts for some 16 percent of the aircraft's unladen weight. The A-10 carries 1,174 rounds of 30-mm ammunition. When configured for a specific antitank mission, the A-10 can carry four AGM-65 Maverick missiles.

Unmanned aerial vehicles (UAVs) were initially designed as reconnaissance platforms. Their sophisticated onboard sensor systems and long dwell times over target areas made them critically valuable assets in finding enemy tanks. But some UAVs also have sufficient lift to carry 106-pound AGM-114 Hellfire missiles in addition to their sensor packages. Although not originally designed as attack platforms, both the MQ-1B Predator and the MQ-9 Reaper have carried and successfully launched Hellfires.

David T. Zabecki and Spencer C. Tucker

See also: Iraq, Army; IRAQI FREEDOM, Operation; IRAQI FREEDOM, Operation, Ground Campaign

Further Reading

Gander, Terry J. *Anti-Tank Weapons*. Marlborough, UK: Crowood, 2000.

Gander, Terry J. *The Bazooka: Hand-Held Hollow-Charge Anti-Tank Weapons*. London: PRC Publishing, 1998.

Ripley, Tim. *Tank Warfare*. Drexel Hill, PA: Casemate, 2003.

Weeks, John S. *Men against Tanks: A History of Anti-Tank Warfare*. New York: Mason/ Charter, 1975.

Armored Warfare, Persian Gulf and Iraq Wars

The U.S. Army's overwhelming success against Soviet-equipped Iraqi divisions during the 1991 Persian Gulf War marked the culmination of a long-developed doctrine of armored warfare, the hallmarks of which were speed, maneuverability, and high technology. With a few notable exceptions, U.S. armored doctrine following the Korean War (1950–1953) anticipated set-piece battles to defend the plains of Central Europe from a Soviet incursion. In the 1970s, catalyzed by the effectiveness of wire-guided antitank weapons used during the 1973 Yom Kippur (Ramadan) War and the burgeoning requirement to modernize and compete against new Warsaw Pact tanks, the U.S. armor community prepared to fully modernize its equipment, training, and doctrine. By 1982 the army had fielded the turbine-powered M-1 Abrams main battle tank; established a state-of-the-art desert training facility at Fort Irwin, California; and published the newly developed Air-Land Battle Doctrine.

The 1991 Persian Gulf War (Operation DESERT STORM) served as a crucible to test the new doctrine. In particular, AirLand Battle focused on deep-attack offense to extend operational commanders' view of the modern battlefield in both distance and time. It viewed deep attack, the concept of engaging an enemy in close and rear actions simultaneously, as an indispensable requirement in defeating follow-on echelons in Europe. AirLand Battle also focused on the importance of maneuverability and close coordination with heavy forces. Armored combined-arms teams became the key instruments of combat power: the M-1 and M-1A1 Abrams main battle tank would be supported by mechanized infantry, self-propelled artillery, and mechanized combat engineers. Additionally, AirLand Battle emphasized the importance of initiative, adapting the German Army's principle of Auftragstaktik (mission tactics). Under this principle, American commanders were to continue to press an enemy on the offensive, even in the absence of higher orders, to take advantage of developing tactical situations.

U.S. armored units effectively employed AirLand Battle against the Iraqi Army in 1991. In the opening salvo of the war, an aerial bombing campaign that began in January and lasted more than a month attempted to destroy Iraqi command and control facilities and follow-on echelon forces. Armor units, supported by mechanized infantry, engineers, and coordinated indirect artillery fire, decisively destroyed Iraqi units during four days of offensive operations in February 1991. Massed coalition units conducted a frontal attack across the eastern edge of the Iraq-Saudi border while heavy elements of VII Corps engaged in a deep attack from the west, encircling rear and escaping Iraqi units in a maneuver later nicknamed the Hail Mary. The M-1A1's advanced thermal targeting systems, capable of destroying targets at long ranges while on the move, provided mass firepower and shock effect.

The Battle of 73 Easting well exemplified armored employment of AirLand Battle concepts in the Persian Gulf War. On February 26, 1991, the 2nd Armored Cavalry Regiment, a reconnaissance element of the U.S. Army VII Corps, had been directed to find and fix elements of the Iraqi Tawakalnah Armored Division and halt at 70 Easting (a Global Positioning System [GPS] coordinate). Eagle Troop of the 2nd Armored Cavalry Regiment, commanded by Captain H. R. McMaster, was comprised primarily of M-1A1 tanks and M3 Bradley Fighting Vehicles. As the force reached 70 Easting during a late afternoon sandstorm and rainstorm, thermal targeting systems allowed it to identify an enemy battalion strong point visible about 1.8 miles away (73 Easting).

Despite earlier orders to hold his force's position, McMaster acted independently, aggressively attacking the Iraqi battalion while maintaining the elements of mass, surprise, and speed. Eagle Troop's tank platoons led the charge, supported by Bradley Fighting Vehicles to the rear. M-1A1 targeting systems decimated the Iraqi force while on the move, fixing and eventually destroying the battalion at 73 Easting. Bradley Fighting Vehicles then cleared dismounted

infantry and assisted in holding off a counterattack.

In 1993 the U.S. Army developed a revised doctrine known as Full-Dimensional Operations to anticipate post–Cold War challenges and incorporate lessons learned from the Persian Gulf War. In it, the army attempted to enlarge the doctrinal scope of Air-Land Battle by including a section on operations other than war, introducing joint terms, and expanding its scope to encapsulate strategic operations. The doctrine acted as the foundational document during peacekeeping operations in Bosnia and Kosovo and during the next eight years of the army's transformation.

As part of the armor community's force modernization, M-1A2 tanks and other vehicles were retrofitted with new digital battle command systems to increase situational awareness on the battlefield. However, the difficulties in deploying Task Force Hawk in the early days of the Kosovo conflict made clear the difficulty of deploying heavy Cold War equipment. Under the leadership of U.S. Army chief of staff general Eric Shinseki, the army established an immediate ready force in Europe and attempted to decrease reliance on tanks by establishing a lighter objective force capable of quick deployment using Stryker wheeled vehicles via Stryker Brigades. Commensurate with these objectives, in 2001 the army published a revised doctrine known as Full-Spectrum Operations, which provided the foundation for rapid deployment in response to global threats and sustained military campaigns, and it revealed the growing importance of stability and support operations. This doctrine also anticipated that adaptive enemies would seek asymmetric advantages and attempt to pull troops into urban combat.

Strategic doctrine used during the Iraq War (Operation Iraqi Freedom) can be divided into two primary periods: the initial

2003 attack lasting from March 20 to May 1, 2003, and subsequent full-spectrum operations thereafter. While the operational strategy used in the 1991 Persian Gulf War can be described as overwhelming force, the 2003 action constituted overmatching power. Under the touted umbrella of shock and awe, U.S. planners intended to overwhelm Iraqi military and government systems by conducting the main ground and air offensive at the same time rather than preparing objectives with a lengthy preinvasion air campaign. Thus, Iraqis were placed on the horns of a multipronged dilemma, defending against rear and forward attacks while maintaining command and control.

To counter the significantly fewer armored vehicles and soldiers employed during the 2003 invasion, U.S. commanders increased combat power by augmented use of special operations forces, speed in movement, and electronic reconnaissance to precisely identify and target enemy locations. Rather than seizing and holding the entire theater, coalition units intended initially only to control key terrain and supply lines as armored U.S. Army V Corps units conducted a blitzkrieg-type movement to Baghdad.

Doctrinally, V Corps, commanded by Lieutenant General William Scott Wallace, adhered to conventional AirLand Battle tenets in executing its initial offensive operations in Iraq. Although the total number of coalition troops employed in 2003 was significantly smaller than in 1991, as directed by AirLand Battle principles, helicopter and artillery units engaged the enemy simultaneously in close and rear actions by conducting deep-strike attacks, while combined-arms units conducted offensive operations using fire and maneuver to seize Baghdad. This proven conventional doctrine allowed V Corps units to occupy Baghdad and remove the Baathist regime from power in just three weeks.

Under the army's 2001 Full-Spectrum Operations doctrine, coalition forces were capable of transitioning smoothly from combat to stability and support operations. Although army planners realized that the operation's posthostility phase would entail a rolling transition to stability and support operations, the coalition force's numbers were insufficient when compared historically with similar postconflict scenarios, including recent deployments in Bosnia and Kosovo. As sectarian and insurgent violence increased over the ensuing years, coalition troops were forced to counter asymmetric warfare to oppose amplified guerrilla and decentralized attacks. Increasingly, armored units were forced to fight in urban terrain alongside infantry and engineer units.

Actions to quell the 2004 Shia uprisings in Sadr City provide an example of armored employment within the Full-Spectrum Operations doctrine. In this suburban district of Baghdad, U.S. armored units negotiated the gridlike pattern of streets using a box pattern and moved slowly up streets, with weapon systems focused outside of the box. This formation created an artificial set of interior lines, allowing tanks and Bradleys to take advantage of independent thermal viewers to identify targets. Tankers moved with their hatches closed to prevent casualties from enemy sniper fire and removed unnecessary equipment from the top of the tanks to allow Bradleys to kill targets who attempted to climb onto the tanks. As insurgents increasingly used more powerful improvised explosive devices (IEDs) against coalition forces, tanks led the box formation to reduce casualties.

Commensurate with Full-Spectrum Operations, armored units in Iraq faced a wide variety of missions, including route clearance, reconnaissance and surveillance patrols, traffic control points, and raids. To enhance the Abrams's survivability and lethality in urban environments, Tank Urban Survivability Kits were fielded to add reactive armor tiles to counter antiarmor weapons, armored gun shields, and a tank infantry phone to communicate with ground troops. Despite disadvantages in urban terrain, including the Abrams's inability to elevate weapons far enough to fire at upper floors of buildings from close range and their vulnerability to light and medium antiarmor weapons when not supported by light infantry, tanks provided decisive support and protection throughout the spectrum of operations in Iraq.

William E. Fork

See also: Air-Land Battle Doctrine; Iraq, Army; IRAQI FREEDOM, Operation, Ground Campaign

Further Reading

Biddle, Stephen. "Victory Misunderstood: What the Gulf War Tells Us about the Future of Conflict." *International Security* 21, no. 2 (Fall 1996): 139–79.

Blackwell, James A. "Professionalism and Army Doctrine: A Losing Battle?" In *The Future of the Army Profession*, edited by Don M. Snider and Lloyd J. Matthews, 325–48. Boston: McGraw-Hill, 2005.

Bourque, Stephen A. "Hundred-Hour Thunderbolt: Armor in the Gulf War." In *Camp Colt to Desert Storm: The History of U.S. Armored Forces*, edited by George F. Hofmann and Donn A. Starry, 497–530. Lexington: University Press of Kentucky, 1999.

Chiarell, Peter, Patrick Michaelis, and Geoffrey Norman. "Armor in Urban Terrain: The Critical Enabler." *Armor* (June–October 2004): 7–9.

DeRosa, John P. J. "Platoons of Action: An Armor Task Force's Response to Full-Spectrum Operations in Iraq." *Armor* (November–December 2005): 7–12.

Fontenot, Gregory et al. *On Point: The United States Army in Iraqi Freedom*. Annapolis, MD: Naval Institute Press, 2005.

MacGregor, Douglas. *Warrior's Rage: The Great Tank Battle of 73 Easting*. Annapolis, MD: Naval Institute Press, 2009.

Murray, Williamson, and Robert H. Scales Jr. *The Iraq War: A Military History*. Cambridge, MA: Belknap, 2005.

Scales, Robert H. *Certain Victory: The U.S. Army in the Gulf War*. Washington, DC: Brassey's, 1994.

Swain, Richard M. "AirLand Battle." In *Camp Colt to Desert Storm: The History of U.S. Armored Forces*, edited by George F. Hofmann and Donn A. Starry, 360–402. Lexington: University Press of Kentucky, 1999.

Tucker, Terry. "Heavy Armor: The Core of Urban Combat." *Armor* (May–June 2005): 4, 49.

ARROWHEAD RIPPER, Operation

Multi-National Force–Iraq (MNF-I) assault against al-Qaeda in Iraq and other insurgents in and around the Iraqi city of Baquba from June 19 to August 19, 2007. Baquba is located about 30 miles northeast of Baghdad. As a result of the Baghdad Security Plan developed in early 2007 and the U.S. troop surge that accompanied it, al-Qaeda in Iraq and other Sunni forces withdrew from some areas of Baghdad and began operating in Diyala Province.

The insurgents, who belonged to the Khalf al-Mutayibin group, established a strong presence in Diyala Province and especially in Baquba, a city of some half-million people. They made it the capital of their self-proclaimed Islamic State of Iraq. Al-Qaeda was determined to create havoc for the newly formed government of Iraq and to kill coalition troops who were attempting to gain control of the province.

On June 19, 2007, ARROWHEAD RIPPER, an operation north of Baghdad to clear the region of al-Qaeda militants, was launched with 10,000 U.S. soldiers, along with more than 1,000 Iraqi police and Iraqi military personnel. Three U.S. brigades participated in the opening days of ARROWHEAD RIPPER: the 1st Cavalry Division's 3rd Brigade Combat Team, commanded by Colonel David Sutherland; the 2nd Infantry Division's 4th Stryker Brigade Combat Team, commanded by Colonel John Lehr; and the 2nd Infantry Division's 3rd Stryker Brigade Combat Team, commanded by Colonel Steven Townsend.

For security reasons, Iraqi leaders were not included in the initial planning of ARROWHEAD RIPPER, but as the operation progressed, the Iraqi 2nd Brigade and 5th Iraqi Army Division played sizable roles. By the operation's end, the Iraqi 5th Army Division had particularly distinguished itself.

The operation began with a night air assault by Colonel Townsend's 3rd Stryker Brigade Combat Team, which led the effort to clear Baquba. As the operation unfolded, it quickly became apparent that al-Qaeda units, estimated to number more than 1,000 fighters, had dug in to stay. However, news sources reported that the leadership had fled in advance of the operation. In addition to Iraqi security forces (army and police), groups of "concerned citizens"—also referred to as Iraqi police volunteers—cooperated with U.S. military personnel and Iraqi security forces in rooting out insurgents. The citizens' movement hoped to restore a measure of peace to the war-torn region. It was instrumental in finding and exposing the safe houses where al-Qaeda militants were hiding.

Fighting was fierce throughout Diyala Province, but especially in Baquba, where al-Qaeda had essentially taken control of the city. Multinational troops, going house to house to capture or kill al-Qaeda insurgents, met heavy resistance in the early stages of the battle. As troops entered neighborhoods, they found schools, businesses, and homes booby-trapped with homemade improvised explosive devices (IEDs). The heaviest fighting during the operation occurred within the first four weeks.

American commanders had always believed that al-Qaeda was its own worst enemy, particularly in the way that it treated the locals. Thus, American leaders had anticipated help from citizens in the province, and when these citizens began to pass information as to the whereabouts of insurgents, it was clear that they were ready for al-Qaeda and its operatives to leave their province.

An important goal of ARROWHEAD RIPPER was to prevent insurgents fleeing Baquba from escaping and reorganizing elsewhere. Therefore, the attacking forces set up a series of blocking posts to the northwest of Baquba in the Khalis corridor and south of the city near Khan Bani Saad to deny insurgents passage through these areas.

Coalition and Iraqi forces also conducted operations to disrupt enemy lines of communication and deny al-Qaeda any areas of safe haven. Following the initial push that cleared Baquba of insurgents, coalition forces began to reposition and destroy al-Qaeda positions northeast of Baquba in the Diyala River Valley. In spite of their attempts to contain al-Qaeda forces inside the area to prevent them from reorganizing elsewhere, many of the insurgents escaped capture and fled.

During the operation, which ended on August 19, the al-Qaeda leader in Baquba was killed, along with more than 100 other insurgents. An additional 424 suspected insurgents were taken prisoner. A total of 129 weapons caches were captured or destroyed and some 250 IEDs were found and rendered inoperable, including 38 booby-trapped houses, which the military refers to as house-borne IEDs, and 12 vehicle-borne IEDs. Coalition casualties included 18 Americans killed and 12 wounded; 7 Iraqi army personnel killed and 15 wounded; 2 allied Iraqi militiamen killed; and 3 Iraqi police killed. Civilian casualties in the province were not accurately recorded, but an estimated 350 were killed and many more were wounded. However, it was unclear if civilian casualties were a direct result of Multi-National Force–Iraq military actions or al-Qaeda members simply killing civilians who had helped their enemies.

One reason for the success of the operation was the newly formed Diyala Operations Center, established to coordinate coalition activities in the province. Through it, coalition forces, local police, the Iraqi military, and citizen informants sympathetic to the U.S. military were all linked to one headquarters location. This enabled planners and leaders of the operation to react quickly to any situation, a scenario that the insurgents had not anticipated.

The surge in U.S. troop strength in Iraq combined with operations such as ARROW-HEAD RIPPER forced al-Qaeda insurgents out of the cities of the Diyala Valley and broke their ability to sustain day-to-day attacks on coalition troops in the area. Success was also achieved in enabling government ministries to provide fundamental goods and services such as food, fuel, and displaced-persons services to Diyala Province. This enabled the local and national Iraqi governments to show that they could provide for their people and thus raised confidence in government authorities.

The U.S. troop surge begun in early 2007, and operations such as ARROWHEAD RIPPER had great success in the Diyala Valley, with normal life beginning to reemerge by the end of the offensive. Schools, hospitals, and businesses were reopened in the relatively safer environment that came about as a result of the operation.

Randy Jack Taylor

See also: al-Qaeda in Iraq; Iraqi Insurgency

Further Reading

Bensahel, Nora. *After Saddam: Prewar Planning and the Occupation of Iraq.* Skokie, IL: RAND Corporation, 2008.

Miller, Debra A. *The Middle East.* Detroit: Greenhaven, 2007.

Radcliffe, Woodrow S. *The Strategic Surge in Iraq: Pretense or Plan for Success?* USAWC Strategy Research Project. Carlisle Barracks, PA: U.S. Army War College, 2007.

Simon, Steven, and Council on Foreign Relations. *After the Surge: The Case for U.S. Military Disengagement from Iraq.* New York: Council on Foreign Relations, 2007.

Simons, G. L. *Iraq Endgame? Surge, Suffering and the Politics of Denial.* London: Politico's, 2008.

Woodward, Bob. *The War Within: A Secret White House History, 2006–2008.* New York: Simon and Schuster, 2008.

"Axis of Evil"

Term coined by President George W. Bush in his January 29, 2002, State of the Union address to describe regimes that sponsor terrorism. Specifically, he identified the axis as consisting of Iran, Iraq, and North Korea, all of which he believed threatened the security of the United States. Conceived by presidential speechwriter David Frum, the phrase "axis of evil" was originally intended to justify the invasion of Iraq, but it came to be used by political neoconservatives to criticize Secretary of State Colin Powell's position on the Bush

Doctrine. That doctrine, arising after the September 11, 2001, terror attacks, modified U.S. military policy to allow for a preemptive war against terrorists, unilateral military action against rogue states, and U.S. measures to remain the sole military superpower in the world.

The origin of the phrase "axis of evil" can be traced to December 2001, when head speechwriter Mike Gerson tasked David Frum with articulating the case for ousting the government of Saddam Hussein in a few sentences, which were to be included in the 2002 State of the Union address. Frum originally intended to use the phrase "axis of hatred" but changed it to "axis of evil" to match the "theological" tone adopted by President Bush after September 11, 2001. Expecting his speech to be edited, Frum was surprised when his "axis of evil" was actually included, and the text of the speech was read nearly verbatim by President Bush, a controversial move that was seen in some quarters to be dangerously undiplomatic. Certainly, that speech, and particularly the term "axis of evil," was not well received in many of the world's capitals.

The usage of the phrase "axis of evil" was ultimately meant to suggest links between terrorists and nations that, according to neoconservatives, threatened the United States and its allies. Criteria for inclusion in the axis of evil were that the included nations be "rogue states," or that they allegedly support terrorist groups seeking to attack the United States or its allies, potentially with weapons of mass destruction.

President Bush's 2002 speech shocked people in many nations, but it was also viewed with considerable trepidation by the United States' stalwart allies. Not surprisingly, Iraqi president Saddam Hussein mocked and dismissed the talk as needless bluster. Tehran's fundamentalist regime

U.S. president George W. Bush delivers his first State of the Union address to a joint session of Congress at the U.S. Capitol Building in Washington, D.C., on January 29, 2002. In his speech, Bush outlined his plan to fight the Global War on Terror and characterized the nations of Iran, Iraq, and North Korea as forming an "axis of evil." (AP/Wide World Photos)

sharply denounced its inclusion in the axis of evil. North Korean spokesmen bitterly rebuked Bush and his speech, vowing that any aggression toward North Korea would be met with withering military counterforce. In the longer term, Bush's incendiary language may have had the opposite effect intended; it likely induced Pyongyang and Tehran to be even less compliant with international rules of behavior.

Keith A. Leitich

See also: Bush, George Walker; Hussein, Saddam

Further Reading

Cha, Victor D. "Korea's Place in the Axis." *Foreign Affairs* 81, no. 3 (May/June 2002): 79–92.

Frum, David. *The Right Man: The Surprise Presidency of George W. Bush.* New York: Random House, 2003.

Woodward, Bob. *Bush at War.* New York: Simon and Schuster, 2002.

Aziz, Tariq

Iraqi foreign minister (1983–1991) and deputy prime minister (1979–2003). Tariq Aziz was born on April 1, 1936, into a Chaldean Catholic family in Tell Kaif, Iraq. Originally named Michael Yuhanna, Aziz was the only Christian in a position of power during Saddam Hussein's 34-year dictatorship. While in college, he changed his name to Tariq Aziz, which means "glorious past," in order to avoid hostility regarding his religious heritage.

In 1957 Aziz joined the Baath Party and worked with Saddam Hussein to generate propaganda against the pro-Western Iraqi monarchy. After receiving his bachelor's degree in English literature in 1958 from the Baghdad College of Fine Arts, Aziz continued to produce Baath Party propaganda in addition to working as a journalist. From 1963 to 1966, Aziz was both editor in chief of the Baath Party's newspaper, *al-Thawra* (The Revolution), and director of the Arab Baath Socialist Party's press office in Damascus, Syria. When the British-imposed Hashimite monarchy came to an end in 1958, the Baath Party continued to seek power in Iraq. After an unsuccessful coup in 1963, the party finally gained power in 1968.

From 1974 to 1977 Aziz served as a member of the Regional Command, the Baath Party's highest governing unit.

Tariq Aziz became deputy prime minister of Iraq in 1979 and held that post until the fall of the Saddam Hussein government in the 2003 Iraq War. Although acquitted of other charges, in March 2009, Aziz was sentenced to 15 years in prison for his role in the executions of 42 merchants found guilty of profiteering in 1992. (AP/Wide World Photos)

In 1979, Iraqi dictator Saddam Hussein named him deputy prime minister. His primary role was to explain and justify Iraq's policies to global audiences. With his effective communication skills, Aziz became known around the world for his eloquent diplomatic discourses.

In 1980 Aziz was wounded in an assassination attempt initiated by the Iranian-backed Shiite fundamentalist group al-Dawa Islamiyyah (the Islamic Call). Members of the group threw a grenade at him in downtown Baghdad, killing several Iraqis in the process. The attack was one of several that Saddam Hussein blamed on the Iranian government, which was part of his justification for his

September 1980 invasion of Iran that produced the Iran-Iraq War (1980–1988).

In 1984, just a year after being named foreign minister, Aziz secured the restoration of diplomatic relations with the United States after a 17-year interruption. The United States had chosen to support Iraq as a buffer to Iran's Islamic fundamentalist extremism.

When Iraq invaded Kuwait in August 1990, Aziz ardently supported the military action. He stated that the invasion was justified because of Kuwait's cheating on oil production quotas, which was driving down the price of oil, and because of Kuwait's alleged slant-drilling into Iraqi oil fields. During the subsequent Persian Gulf War (1991), Aziz enjoyed a substantial international profile and was seen by the media as the chief Iraqi spokesperson. After the war, Aziz took on more responsibility as deputy prime minister, which forced him to relinquish the foreign ministry portfolio. Nevertheless, he retained a high profile in the government. Aziz monitored the Iraqi media. In this position, Aziz also conducted Iraq's negotiations with United Nations (UN) weapons inspectors.

In his public remarks, Aziz blamed the United States, rather than the United Nations, for the economic sanctions that followed the Persian Gulf War, believing that they were implemented as a result of U.S. domestic policies. In 1997 he supported the expulsion of U.S. citizens from Iraq who were working for the UN Special Commission.

In February 2003 as tensions over Iraq's alleged illegal weapons programs were about to boil over into war, Aziz spoke with Pope John Paul II about the Iraqi government's desire to cooperate with the international community, notably on disarmament. In response, the pope insisted that Iraq respect and give concrete commitments to abide by UN Security Council resolutions. The Iraqis did not heed the advice. On March 19, 2003, at the beginning of the Anglo-American–led invasion of Iraq, there were reports that Aziz had been killed. They were proven false when Aziz later held a press conference. He surrendered to coalition forces on April 24, 2003.

Aziz, who is charged with crimes against humanity in connection with the murder of hundreds of Kurds in 1982, testified as a defense witness before the Iraq Special Tribunal set up by the Iraq Interim Government in May 2006. He testified that the crackdown against the Kurds had been fully justified because of attacks against him and others in the regime. He also reiterated his loyalty to his old comrade Saddam Hussein.

Aziz is imprisoned at Camp Cropper in western Baghdad. On March 11, 2009, he was sentenced to 15 years in prison for his role in the 1992 summary executions of 42 merchants accused of fixing food prices.

Charlene T. Overturf

See also: Baath Party; Hussein, Saddam

Further Reading

Farouk-Sluglett, Marion, and Peter Sluglett. *Iraq since 1958: From Revolution to Dictatorship*. London: I. B. Tauris, 2001.

MacKey, Sandra. *The Reckoning: Iraq and the Legacy of Saddam Hussein*. New York: Norton, 2002.

B

B-2 Spirit

A multipurpose U.S. heavy bomber with stealth technology capable of deploying both conventional and nuclear weapons. The B-2 was designed specifically for penetrating air defense networks and disrupting command and control facilities. The Northrop Grumman B-2 Spirit stealth bomber played a vital role in delivering initial strikes during Operations ENDURING FREEDOM in Afghanistan (October 2001) and IRAQI FREEDOM (March 2003).

After flight testing at Edwards Air Force Base, California, the B-2 first saw combat action during the Kosovo War in 1999. Given its astronomical price tag of $1.2 billion per aircraft, the Pentagon has strictly limited its employment. Featuring a range of 6,000 nautical miles without refueling, the B-2 can reach any point around the globe within hours. Featuring a revolutionary "flying wing" construction designed to reduce radar cross-section, this Air Force platform has proven to be practically undetectable by radar in combat to date. Since its initial deployment, a new substance, known as alternate high-frequency material (AHFM), has been added to the plane to further enhance the radar-absorbent coating of its control surfaces. Engine intakes and exhausts are positioned low to the surface to minimize thermal detection. Designed ostensibly for daylight raids as well as night bombings, the B-2 is painted with a bluish-gray antireflective paint that reduces optical visibility.

The bomber is aerodynamically unstable and thus requires the use of a quadruple-redundant, fly-by-wire (FBW) system powered by a General Electric (GE) flight control computer. The aircraft flies with a crew of two (pilot in the left seat and mission commander on the right), and all of its weapons are internally housed. The B-2 can carry up to 40,000 pounds of munitions, including conventional or nuclear weapons, precision-guided ordnance, gravity bombs, and a variety of maritime weapons. Two separate weapons bays are located in the center of the plane outfitted with a rotary launcher and two bomb-rack assemblies. Among the bombs compatible with the aircraft are the B61-11 earth-penetrating nuclear bomb; the B83 free-fall nuclear bomb; and the AGM-129 advanced cruise missile with a range of roughly 1,500 miles.

The military's Joint Direct Attack Munition (JDAM) missiles can also be deployed aboard a B-2 with the capacity expanded from 16 to 80 with the installation of new bomb racks in 2009. The aircraft can accommodate two massive ordnance penetrators (MOPs), which at 5,300 pounds apiece are potent weapons for eliminating hardened, buried targets with conventional explosives. The latest upgrade to the B-2 provided a generic weapons interface system (GWIS) that enables the aircraft to carry up to four different types of ordnance so that both stand-off strikes and direct attack munitions assaults are possible. Work has also begun on creating the means to engage moving targets. The B-2 is equipped with countermeasures and a J band multipurpose radar with terrain-following and terrain-avoidance modes. Also, Northrop Grumman received a contract in 2007 to develop an extremely high frequency (EHF) satellite communications capability and computer upgrade for the B-2.

The B-2 is 69 feet long with a wingspan of 172 feet. The aircraft is 17 feet in height, with landing gear, and weighs 158,000 pounds; its maximum allowable takeoff weight is 336,500 pounds. It is powered by four General Electric nonafterburning jet engines capable of achieving a maximum air speed of 604 miles per hour (mph). The B-2 has an operational ceiling of 50,000 feet.

The B-2's high operational ceiling has allowed it to maintain high sortie reliability rates. During the first three days of Operation ENDURING FREEDOM, six B-2s flew from Whiteman Air Force Base, Missouri, to Afghanistan to complete the longest nonstop military aviation mission in history. They joined with Boeing B-52 Strato-fortress bombers and Lockheed F-117 Nighthawk stealth ground attack aircraft to strike military training facilities, surface-to-air missile (SAM) sites, troop staging areas, and al-Qaeda infrastructure targets.

With the advent of a transportable hangar system, the B-2 was deployed to forward locations for the first time during Operation IRAQI FREEDOM in 2003. During that war, about 60 percent of the B-2s flew out of Whiteman, while the remainder operated from the island of Diego Garcia in the Indian Ocean. On the evening of March 21, 2003, the inauguration of the shock-and-awe aerial campaign against Iraq, six B-2 sorties were assessed as having eliminated 92 targets. The extensive use of precision-guided weapons obviated the need for the sort of carpet bombing and elimination of civilian infrastructure (such as power stations) that had attracted much negative publicity during the 1991 Persian Gulf War. More

than 1.5 million pounds of munitions were released by B-2 aircraft over Iraq, and the bomber was declared at full operational capability by December 2003.

To date, no B-2 has been shot down in the course of combat. In February 2008, one B-2 bomber crashed shortly after takeoff from Anderson Air Force Base, Guam. Investigations revealed moisture in the port transducer units that caused faulty information to be relayed to the air data system. Preventive maintenance has been developed to address the problem. This accident left 20 B-2 bombers in the U.S. arsenal.

Critics of the aircraft continue to note its very high cost, difficulty in reacting to pop-up threats, relatively slow speed, and often clumsy maneuverability. While new construction of a successor is unlikely in the near future, the B-2 bomber (with ongoing upgrades) remains in the vanguard of U.S. operational planning.

Jeffrey D. Bass

See also: Air-Land Battle Doctrine; IRAQI FREEDOM, Operation, Air Campaign

Further Reading

Donald, David. *Black Jets: The Development and Operation of America's Most Secret Warplane.* Westport, CT: AIRtime Publishing, 2004.

Sweetman, Bill. *Northrop B-2 Stealth Bomber: The Complete History, Technology, and Operational Development of the Stealth Bomber.* St. Paul, MN: MBI Publishing, 1992.

Veronico, Nicholas, and Jim Dunn. *21st Century U.S. Air Power.* St. Paul, MN: MBI Publishing, 2004.

Baath Party

Political party that currently dominates Syria and that was the leading party in Iraq from 1968 to the end of Saddam Hussein's

Hafiz al-Asad, president of Syria from 1971 until his death in 2000. Assad ruled Syria with an iron hand and was a key figure in Middle East politics. (Courtesy: Embassy of the Syrian Arab Republic)

regime in 2003. The Baath Party (Hizb al-Baath al-Arabi al-Ishtiraki) also had branches in Lebanon, Jordan, the Sudan, Yemen, Mauritania, and Bahrain, and it enjoys support from some Palestinians. The Arabic word "Baath" means "renaissance" or "resurrection." The party's fundamental principles have been Arab unity and freedom from imperialist control for all Arab states, personal freedom for Arab citizens, and support for Arab culture. The party also supported Arab socialist policies intended to eliminate feudalism but not private property. The Arab Socialist Baath Party of Syria explains its ideology as "national (Pan-Arab), socialist, popular and revolutionary," and its founding charter and constitution identifies its commitment to the "Arab Nation, the Arab homeland, the Arab citizen, the Arab people's authority over their own land and the freedom of the Arab people."

The Arab Baath Party, as it was originally called, grew out of an ideological and political movement that began in Damascus, Syria, in 1940 with the goal of revitalizing the Arab nation and society. Syrian intellectuals Michel Aflaq, a Greek Orthodox Christian; Salah al-Din al-Bitar, a Sunni Muslim who studied at the Sorbonne in the early 1930s; and Zaki al-Arsuzi were the principal founders of the Baath movement and party. The Arab Baath Party accepted Arabs of all religious backgrounds and ethnic groups.

The first Arab Baath Party Congress was held on April 4–6, 1947. Abd al-Rahman al-Damin and Abd al-Khaliq al-Khudayri attended that congress and upon their return to Iraq founded a branch of the party there. This branch evolved into a small group of about 50 individuals, mainly friends and associates of Fuad al-Rikabi, who took control of the group in 1951. The Baathists in Iraq joined with other organizations that were in opposition to the monarchy. Baathism spread more slowly in Iraq than in Syria, with its candidates losing out to Communists in many elections in the 1960s.

Meanwhile in Syria, in 1954 Aflaq and Bitar joined forces with Akram al-Hawrani, a populist leader who headed the Socialist Party. They adopted the name Arab Socialist Baath Party. The Baath Party found its greatest strength in Syria and Iraq, although it had branches all over the Arab world.

The Baath Party came to power first in Iraq and then in Syria in coups d'état in 1963. The coup in Iraq did not last out the year, however, during which time 10,000 leftists, Marxists, and communists were killed, 5,000 of whom were from the Iraqi Communist Party. Three years later, the Syrian and Iraqi parties split. Each was subsequently plagued by factionalism. Some disputes occurred as a result of Syria's union with Egypt in the United Arab Republic (UAR); others concerned a possible union of Syria and Iraq or ties with the Soviet Union and local Communist parties, as well as the Syrian Socialist Nationalist Party (SSNP) in Syria.

Rivalries between different factions of the Syrian Baath Party led to an interparty coup in 1966 followed by another one four years later that brought General Hafiz al-Asad to power. He headed a pragmatic faction that gained control of the military in contrast to a "progressive" faction that had pushed a more pervasive socialism and nationalizations as well as a harder line regionally. Asad remained in office until his death in 2000. His son, Bashar al-Asad, assumed leadership of the Syrian Baath Party upon the death of his father.

Saddam Hussein joined the Iraqi Baath Party at the age of 21 in 1956 and steadily rose in the party's ranks, first as a consequence of the Iraqi Revolution of 1958 and then as an assassin in the U.S.-backed plot to do away with President Abd al-Karim Qasim. Later, after the Baath Party had regained power in a 1968 coup, Hussein served as vice-chairman of the Revolutionary Command Council and later as president and secretary-general of the Baath Party.

The Baath parties of Iraq and Syria operated in associations in schools, communities, and the army, and had workers' and women's associations, such as the General Association of Iraqi Women (al-Ittihad al-amm li-nisa al-Iraq). While the party ostensibly sought to expand membership to comprise a "mass party," in fact, membership was tightly controlled. Nonetheless, party members wielded considerable power. Average Syrians and Iraqis could hardly conclude any official business without the intercession of a party member. In the military and in academia, it was nearly impossible to advance or be promoted without being a party member. In Iraq, the party claimed 1.5 million members, or about 10 percent of the country's population in the late 1980s; however, only about 30,000 were bona fide party cadres. In Syria, Asad opened up membership so that by 1987, it was at about 50,000 people, and there were also some 200,000 probationary party members.

The Baath parties of both countries did not tolerate political challenges of any other group or party. They strongly opposed the Islamist movements that arose in each nation. Despite the dictatorial nature of the Iraqi governments in this period, one notable accomplishment, in part facilitated through the party, was the serious effort to modernize the economy and society by promoting literacy, education, and gender equality. As a result, by the 1970s, Iraq had a fairly high level of education. Hussein's disastrous war with Iran and then his invasion of Kuwait, which prompted war with the United States and a coalition of states, had a profoundly negative impact on the country and its economy.

The U.S.-led invasion of Iraq in March 2003 and the overthrow of Saddam Hussein led to an immediate ban of the Baath Party, the so-called de-Baathification, under U.S. and coalition occupation forces. Iraqis also attacked Baath Party offices all over the country. Some critics of the U.S. occupation policies in Iraq claim that U.S. administrator Paul Bremer's decision, approved by Washington, to bar all Baathists from government posts hopelessly hamstrung the government and fueled the Iraqi insurgency, which included some bitter and disenfranchised Baathists. Iraqi prime minister Nuri al-Maliki is still enforcing a ban on the Baath Party and has extended rehiring only to those who can show they were forced to join the party. A related controversy emerged over the transfer of the Baath Party records to the Hoover Institution at Stanford University via an agreement with the Iraq Memory Foundation and with permission of Maliki. The seizure of these documents (which could reveal the precise status of connections with the party) has been protested by, among others, the director of the Iraq National Library and Archive and the acting Iraqi minister of culture.

In Syria, the Baath Party has had a great impact. Changes in landholding and commercial policies in the 1960s displaced earlier elites, but suppression of the Sunni merchants and Islamists led, even after the Hama massacre, to an Islamist revival that challenged Baath Party primacy. Although President Bashar al-Asad promised democratic reforms in 2005, not much change has occurred. Asad's recent cooperation with the United States makes it less likely that he will be removed in favor of an alternative Baathist leader.

In Lebanon, Bahrain, and other countries, the Baath Party retains a small presence. In Lebanon, it held two seats in Parliament in the 1990s, and the Iraqi branch also had a link to a group within the Palestinian Fatah organization. The Sudanese Baath Party operates underground as part of the opposition to the Sudanese regime and publishes a journal, *al-Hadaf.*

Stefan Brooks and Sherifa Zuhur

See also: Bremer, L. Paul, III; Hussein, Saddam; Maliki, Nuri Muhammed Kamil Hasan al-

Further Reading

Batatu, Hanna. *Old Social Classes and New Revolutionary Movements of Iraq.* London: Al-Saqi Books, 2000.

Committee against Represssion and for Democratic Rights in Iraq, ed. *Saddam's Iraq: Revolution or Reaction?* London: Zed Books, 1986.

Devlin, John F. *The Ba'th Party: A History from Its Origins to 1966.* Stanford, CA: Hoover Institution Press, 1976.

Heydemann, Steven. *Authoritarianism in Syria: Institutions and Social Conflict, 1948–1970.* Ithaca, NY: Cornell University Press, 1999.

Hinnebusch, Raymond. *Syria: Revolution from Above.* Florence, NY: Routledge, 2001.

Ismael, Jacqueline S., and Shireen T. Ismael. "Gender and State in Iraq." In *Gender and Citizenship in the Middle East,* edited by Suad Joseph, 185–211. Syracuse, NY: Syracuse University Press, 2000.

Sallam, Qasim. *Al-Baath wal Watan Al-Arabi* [The Baath and the Arab Homeland]. Paris: EMA, 1980.

Tripp, Charles. *A History of Iraq.* Cambridge: Cambridge University Press, 2007.

Van Dam, Nikolaos. *The Struggle for Power in Syria: Sectarianism, Regionalism and Tribalism in Politics.* London: I. B. Tauris, 1979.

Badr Organization

Paramilitary wing of the Supreme Islamic Iraqi Council (SIIC), also referred to as the Supreme Islamic Council in Iraq, that was known for decades as the Supreme Council for the Islamic Revolution in Iraq (SCIRI), a Shia political party founded in Tehran, Iran, in November 1982 by Iraqi exiles led by Ayatollah Muhammad Baqir al-Hakim. The Badr Organization (Faylaq Badr), which is also commonly referred to as the

Badr Corps, the Badr Brigade(s), and the Badr Army, was named after the Battle of Badr, fought between the Prophet Muhammad and the first Muslims against a larger and more well-equipped armed force commanded by his Meccan opponents. The Badr Organization is led by Hadi al-Amiri, a high-ranking SIIC official and an ally of its political leaders, Abd al-Aziz al-Hakim and his son, Sayyid Ammar al-Hakim. Abd al-Aziz is the youngest brother of Muhammad Baqr, who was assassinated by a massive car bombing probably carried out by the organization headed by the Jordanian Abu Musab al-Zarqawi (1966–2006) and a son of Grand Ayatollah Sayyid Muhsin al-Hakim (1889–1970), the most influential and widely followed Shia religious leader in Iraq from 1955 until his death.

The Badr Organization's origins lay in armed units, numbering several thousand men at most, made up of Iraqi Arab exiles trained and equipped with assistance from the Iranian government. These units were named after Ayatollah Sayyid Muhammad Baqir al-Sadr (1935–1980), a prominent Iraqi Arab Shia religious scholar and opposition leader who was executed by the ruling Iraqi Baath Party along with his sister, Amina bint Haydar al-Sadr (also known as Bint al-Huda), in April 1980. Both Muhammad Baqr and Abd al-Aziz al-Hakim were students of Baqir al-Sadr, who was a student of their father, Muhsin al-Hakim. The two brothers along with their other brother, Muhammad Mahdi, were early members of the Islamic Dawa Party (Hizb al-Dawa al-Islamiyya), which was originally founded by Shia religious scholars (*ulama*) in the southern Iraqi shrine city of Najaf.

The Iranian Revolutionary Guard Corps (IRGC), an armed force dedicated to the protection and preservation of the Iranian revolutionary system, was the key source of training and military equipment for the SCIRI's paramilitary wing. This militia was renamed after the Battle of Badr (1982–1983) during the Iran-Iraq War. Badr drew its membership from the tens of thousands of Iraqi Arabs, the majority of them Shia political activists and anti-Baath operatives, who fled to Iran in the late 1970s and 1980s, particularly following the execution of Ayatollah Muhammad Baqir al-Sadr and his sister in April 1980.

After the start of the Iran-Iraq War (1980–1988) following Iraq's invasion of western Iran in September 1980, Badr also recruited members from among Iraqi prisoners of war because many Iraqi soldiers were Shia conscripts who had neither love nor loyalty for Iraqi president Saddam Hussein. Prisoners of war who wished to join Badr were first required to repent for their membership in the Iraqi Army because it was regarded as an instrument not of the Iraqi nation but of the Iraqi Baath Party. Abd al-Aziz al-Hakim served as Badr's commander from its founding in 1982 and 1983 until he and his brother Muhammad Baqr returned to Iraq in May 2003 following the collapse of the Iraqi Baathist regime in the wake of the U.S.- and British-led invasion of the country. Despite its Iraqi identity and membership, Badr's leadership was split between Iraqi Arabs such as Abd al-Aziz al-Hakim and IRGC officers, who were largely responsible for the military training of Badr's recruits. Badr included infantry, armored, artillery, antiaircraft, and commando units and maintained ties to activists and small units in Iraq.

The Badr Organization was actively involved in the Iran-Iraq War, primarily in northern Iraq (Iraqi Kurdistan). Following the capture of Haj Omran, villages in northeastern Iraq, by Iranian forces in 1983, Badr units were stationed there, and Muhammad

Baqr al-Hakim visited them and prayed on what was termed "freed Iraqi soil." The participation of Badr paramilitary fighters on the side of the Iranians during the war was not welcomed by all Iraqi Shia and was widely criticized by some of SCIRI's political rivals in the Iraqi Shia community.

Badr also carried out bombings and attacks on Iraqi Baath officials and offices during the 1980s and 1990s, and it sent units across the Iran-Iraq border in March and April 1991 to aid the uprisings in southern and northern Iraq among the Shia and Kurdish populations. These uprisings, encouraged by the U.S. government, were brutally crushed by Baath security forces and the Republican Guard after the United States refused to aid the rebels. The United States was reportedly fearful of empowering Iraq's Shia population, heeding alarmist talk from their Sunni Arab allies and reacting warily to the appearance of Badr fighters in southern Iraq, many of whom carried portraits of Iran's late revolutionary leader, Grand Ayatollah Ruhollah Khomeini, and banners calling for the formation of an Islamic republic in Iraq.

Following the collapse of the Iraqi Baath government in April 2003, the SCIRI and Badr leaderships returned to Iraq from exile, mainly from Iran, in May 2003. Muhammad Baqir al-Hakim was welcomed in southern Iraq by tens of thousands of his supporters. According to the Hakims and SIIC/Badr officials, the Badr Organization fielded some 10,000 paramilitary fighters upon their return to Iraq. Abd al-Aziz al-Hakim subsequently claimed that Badr, in addition to its regular fighters, could call upon tens of thousands of other reservists, although this claim seems to be highly exaggerated.

The United Iraqi Alliance (UIA), a loose coalition of mainly Shia political parties, was swept into power in the December 2005 national elections. The SCIRI and the Islamic Dawa Party were the two dominant political parties in the UIA. Bayan Jabr, a SCIRI official, was selected by Abd al-Aziz al-Hakim to head the Iraqi Ministry of the Interior in the 2005 and 2006 transitional government. Jabr oversaw the infiltration of the Iraqi security forces, police, and special commando units, all of which fall under the Interior Ministry. Badr members, both inside and outside of the national security forces, have engaged in gun battles with rival Shia parties, particularly the Sadr Movement led by Muqtada al-Sadr, and in a series of operations in Basra and other southern Iraqi cities and towns in the spring and summer of 2008, which were aimed at weakening the Sadr Movement's political and paramilitary structure in southern Iraq before the 2009 elections. Badr members have also been blamed for carrying out sectarian killings and ethnic cleansing of Sunni Arabs in southern and central Iraq as well as in the capital city of Baghdad.

Christopher Paul Anzalone

See also: Sadr, Muqtada al-

Further Reading

Jabar, Faleh A. *The Shi'ite Movement in Iraq.* London: Saqi Books, 2003.

Marr, Phebe. "Democracy in the Rough." *Current History* (January 2006): 27–33.

Samii, A. William. "Shia Political Alternatives in Postwar Iraq." *Middle East Policy* 10 (May 2003): 93–101.

Baghdad

The capital city of Iraq. Baghdad, established in 762 CE by Abbasid caliph al-Mansur, straddles the Tigris River and its tributary, the Diyala. The city is located at

33°18′ north latitude and 44°36′ east longitude in east-central Iraq. The city sits some 130 feet above sea level. Baghdad's climate typically consists of hot, dry summers and cool winters. With a 2003 population of 5.772 million people, Baghdad was the second-largest city in Southwest Asia (behind Tehran, Iran) and the second-largest city in the Arab world (behind Cairo, Egypt). For comparison, the next two largest cities in Iraq—Mosul and Basra—were estimated in 2003 at 1.74 million and 1.338 million people, respectively. The population of Baghdad constitutes about one-fifth of the country's people. The name "Baghdad" also refers to the small province that surrounds the city, one of 18 in Iraq. Iraq's capital city is ethnically Arab, with small Kurdish and Turcoman minorities.

Baghdad is the center of Iraq's power infrastructure, with power lines webbing outward in all directions. During the 1991 Persian Gulf War, this power infrastructure was severely damaged by the U.S.-led coalition's air strikes against the city in retaliation for Iraq's August 1990 annexation of Kuwait. Baghdad is also the air, road, and railroad center of Iraq, including Baghdad International Airport, several major highways, two primary railroads, two key oil pipelines, and one major gas pipeline. Baghdad is Iraq's foremost center of oil refining, food-processing plants, textile mills, tanneries and leather production, cement companies, metal-product manufacturers, and tobacco processing. The local economy is augmented by way of Baghdad's famous bazaars that showcase jewelry, utensils, rugs, cloth, leather, and felt.

Until the Anglo-American–led invasion of Iraq in March 2003, military installations in the area included air bases, barracks, bunkers, the Iraqi Air Force headquarters, the Republican Guard headquarters, and the Ministry of Defense. Key political buildings included various presidential palaces, the National Assembly, and the Baath Party headquarters. Baghdad is also home to three universities: the University of Baghdad, the University of Technology, and al-Mustansiriyah University.

Notable historical structures include the Abbasid Palace (1179 CE), the ruins of Bab al-Wastani, the Central Gate of Baghdad, and the Mirjan Mosque (1358 CE). The archaeological site of Ctesiphon is to the south, while the attractive domed mosque of Kazinayn is just to the north.

Portions of Baghdad were heavily damaged during the Persian Gulf War of 1991. Transportation, communication, sanitation, and power-generating centers were all affected to varying degrees. President George H. W. Bush halted coalition troops, however, and they never were allowed to proceed to Baghdad, a controversial decision that left Iraqi dictator Saddam Hussein in power.

In the war's aftermath Hussein, now far weaker militarily and economically, attempted to rebuild Baghdad. But the extent of the damage, international economic sanctions, and Hussein's own spending priorities meant that this proceeded only in piecemeal fashion. Spending on Hussein's palaces and on projects glorifying the regime and Hussein himself continued unabated, however.

In March and early April 2003, Baghdad was bombed heavily during the 2003 Iraq War (Operation IRAQI FREEDOM). By April 10, coalition forces had taken the city, and the widely televised toppling of Hussein's statue in Firdaws Square signaled the end of his oppressive regime. Baghdad saw more damage in the extensive looting immediately following the city's fall.

The conquerors soon established a Coalition Provisional Authority in a three-square-mile area (known as the Green Zone) in central Baghdad from which it governed the nation. Democratic elections commenced in 2004, and a new constitution was drafted. However, Baghdad experienced significant violence from both terrorist actions and Sunni-on-Shia sectarian violence. With Baghdad spiraling out of control with massive car bombings and scattered random executions and with the coalition military effort in Iraq seemingly in jeopardy, in January 2007 President George W. Bush authorized an increase of more than 20,000 troops in Baghdad to restore order. By the fourth quarter of 2007, Bush's troop surge had brought a reduction in violence in Baghdad, following the cordoning off of neighborhoods and sectarian designations of formerly mixed neighborhoods. The trend since then has been toward a gradual diminution in sectarian- and terrorist-inspired violence. Nevertheless, the city still remains a dangerous place in certain sectors, and periodic car and truck bombings continue to occur. Reconstruction efforts until 2008 had been modest because of the earlier unrest in the city, but there are signs that privately funded rebuilding projects are gathering momentum.

Dylan A. Cyr and Paul G. Pierpaoli Jr.

See also: Coalition Provisional Authority; Hussein, Saddam; Iraqi Freedom, Operation; Iraqi Insurgency

Further Reading

Cohen, Saul B., ed. *The Columbia Gazetteer of the World*, Vol. 1. New York: Columbia University Press, 1998.

Pax, Salam. *The Baghdad Blog*. London: Grove Atlantic, 2003.

The World Guide: An Alternative Reference to Countries of Our Planet, 2003/2004. Oxford, UK: New Internationalist Publications, 2003.

Baghdad, Battle for

Climactic battle of the 2003 Anglo-American invasion of Iraq that ended with the fall of the Iraqi capital and the collapse of Saddam Hussein's government. American planners before the war operated under the assumption that removing Hussein from power would very likely require some kind of ground attack on Baghdad. What everyone, from President George W. Bush on down, wanted to avoid, however, was grueling urban warfare that would devastate the city and lead to heavy casualties on all sides, the civilian populace included. To avoid being drawn into a costly city fight, the U.S. Army developed a plan to isolate Baghdad first, with the 3rd Infantry Division encircling the city from the west and the I Marine Expeditionary Force enveloping it from the east. Once a rough cordon had been established around Baghdad, the Americans intended to employ a combination of air strikes, armored and mechanized infantry raids, special forces incursions, and other small-scale operations to whittle away at the city's defenses and Baath Party control of the government, ideally reducing one or both to the breaking point.

The army never got the opportunity to test its operational concept for taking Baghdad, however, as the plan was scrapped once elements of the 3rd Infantry Division reached the outskirts of Baghdad just a little over two weeks into the campaign. By April 4, 2003, the division had secured two of the three objectives on its half of the cordon west of the Tigris River: Saddam International Airport (Operation Lions) and the crucial highway junction just south of the city (Operation Saints). The third area (Operation Titans) controlled the roads heading northwest out of Baghdad and remained in Iraqi

U.S. marines on a foot patrol in Baghdad prepare to rush a house believed to contain a weapons cache, April 18, 2003. (U.S. Department of Defense)

hands. Meanwhile, the 1st Marine Division, which had a more difficult approach to the capital through the populated center of the country, was involved in fierce fighting with Republican Guard armor, Iraqi militia, and foreign irregulars and had yet to reach either of the two objectives on its side of the Tigris. Rather than wait for the encirclement of Baghdad to be completed, the 3rd Infantry Division commander, Major General Buford Blount, decided to begin probing the city's defenses immediately.

The recent battles on the approach to the city suggested to Blount that Iraqi resistance was beginning to crumble, while the latest intelligence reports indicated that Baghdad was not the heavily fortified, stoutly defended deathtrap that some were expecting. In fact, the opposite proved to be true, as Hussein's paranoia had played directly into American hands. His fears of a coup had prevented him from undertaking

military preparations of any kind in Baghdad, and he had entrusted defense of the capital to a relatively small cadre of loyal troops—the three brigades of the Special Republican Guard—supported by the irregulars known as Fedayeen Saddam.

Blount launched his first foray into Baghdad on April 5, sending an armored battalion from the 2nd Brigade Combat Team on a thunder run (or reconnaissance in-force) from the SAINTS area into the city center and then out to the airport. The column of 29 Abrams tanks, 14 Bradley fighting vehicles, and assorted other vehicles met with a hail of small-arms fire, rocket-propelled grenades, and mortar fire from the many hundreds of Iraqi fighters who took up positions along its route. A lucky shot from a rocket-propelled grenade disabled one of the American tanks, and it had to be abandoned. Otherwise, the thickly armored Abrams and Bradleys were able to withstand multiple hits, and while the crews were exhausted at the end of the 140-minute-long mission, the vehicles themselves needed only minor repairs before again being ready for action.

The outcome of the April 5 thunder run confirmed Blount's suspicion that Baghdad's defenses were brittle. While the members of the 2nd Brigade Combat Team battalion received a day to catch their breath, Blount employed the 3rd Brigade Combat Team to tighten his grip on the city perimeter. On April 6 the brigade advanced to take control of objective Titans, an area that included the Highway 1 bridge across the Tigris, a crucial point of entry and exit from the capital. This move triggered an intense battle with Iraqi tanks and infantry seeking to regain control of the crossing. The Iraqi attack began on the evening of April 6 and continued into the next morning before it was finally broken up by a combination of concentrated artillery fire, direct fire, and low-level strafing attacks by Fairchild-Republic A-10 Thunderbolts flying close air support.

The conclusion of the battle for the Tigris bridge to the northwest coincided with the launching of the second thunder run. Intended to be a limited raid much like the first, the April 7 thunder run developed into something altogether different, an armored strike into the heart of downtown Baghdad. Colonel Dave Perkins, the commander of the 2nd Brigade Combat Team, took all three of his maneuver battalions on the mission. Blount and his superiors up the chain of command expected Perkins to pull back to the city's edge at the end of the thunder run. Instead, Perkins made the daring decision to lead his two armored battalions into the center of Baghdad and remain there. The battalions met with strong resistance on their drive into the city and afterward had to fend off repeated attacks by small bands of Iraqi fighters once they established their defensive perimeters in the downtown area. But it was the trailing infantry battalion, assigned the vital task of protecting the brigade's supply line into Baghdad, that found itself engaged in some of the heaviest and most desperate fighting. The battalion was assailed not only by Republican Guard and Fedayeen Saddam troops, but also by hundreds of Syrian volunteers who had arrived in Iraq only days earlier. Despite some tense moments, the battalion kept the roadway open so that supply vehicles could reach the units parked downtown.

The thunder run of April 7 struck the decisive blow in the Battle for Baghdad. On the same day, the marines breached the Iraqi defenses along the Diyala River and began their advance into east Baghdad. Fighting continued on April 8, especially in the downtown area and in the 3rd Brigade Combat Team's sector at Titans. By April 9, however, resistance within the city had become generally disorganized and sporadic as increasing numbers of Iraqi fighters put down their weapons and melted into the general populace. The Baathist regime also dissolved, and some governing officials returned home. Others, most notably Saddam Hussein and his two sons, Uday and Qusay, slipped out of the capital and sought refuge elsewhere, leaving Baghdad to troops of the U.S. Army and the U.S. Marine Corps. Baghdad was considered secured by April 10.

Casualty figures are not terribly reliable, but it is believed that the coalition suffered 34 dead and at least 250 wounded. Iraqi dead have been given as 2,300 killed but were undoubtedly higher. There is no estimate of Iraqi wounded.

Jeff Seiken

See also: Baghdad; Iraqi Freedom, Operation, Air Campaign; Iraqi Freedom, Operation,

Ground Campaign; Hussein, Qusay; Hussein, Uday

Further Reading

Fontenot, Gregory et al. *On Point: The United States Army in Iraqi Freedom.* Annapolis, MD: Naval Institute Press, 2005.

Gordon, Michael R., and General Bernard E. Trainor. *Cobra II: The Inside Story of the Invasion and Occupation of Iraq.* New York: Pantheon Books, 2006.

Zucchino, David. *Thunder Run: The Armored Strike to Capture Baghdad.* New York: Grove, 2004.

Basra

Major Iraqi port city. Basra (or al-Basra), Iraq's main port, is located on the Shatt al-Arab waterway near the Persian Gulf (75 miles distant). With a present approximate population of 2.59 million, Basra is also Iraq's second-largest city and the capital of the Basra Governorate. Because of its geographically and economically strategic location, Basra has played an important role in a number of conflicts.

In 636 Arab tribesmen who made up the armies of Emir Umar ibn al-Khattab formally established Basra. While fighting Sassanid forces, Muslim commander Utba ibn Ghazwan set up camp on the site of an old Persian settlement known as Vahestabad Ardasir, which ultimately became Basra. The name Al-Basrah, which means "the over-watcher," was given to the settlement because it served as a military stronghold against the Sassanid Empire. Basra served as a cultural center under Caliph Harun al-Rashid but eventually declined in influence with the fall of the Abbasid caliphate. Possession of Basra was long contested by both the Persians and the Turks because of its agricultural production and important geo-strategic locale.

Basra and its environs hold significant petroleum resources, and the oil refinery at Basra has a daily production rate of approximately 140,000 barrels. Agricultural commodities also represent an important component to Basra's economy. Products such as millet, wheat, barley, dates, and corn are produced in the area's rich soil. Livestock are also an important part of the agricultural sector here. Basra's population is mainly of the Jafari Shia sect, but there are also many Sunni Muslims and some Christians. A pre-Islamic Gnostic sect known as the Mandaeans, who were based in the area formerly called Suk al-Shaykh, also contribute to Basra's population.

During World War I, the British occupied Basra and thoroughly modernized its port facilities. After the war, the construction of a rail line linking Basra to Baghdad and the establishment of a modern harbor made the city all the more important. In World War II, much of the military equipment and supplies sent to the Soviet Union by its Western allies via the Lend-Lease program moved through Basra.

Because of its location on the Shatt al-Arab waterway, Basra became a primary target for Iranian forces during the long and bloody Iran-Iraq War (1980–1988). The port at Basra also sustained heavy damage from bombing by coalition forces during the Persian Gulf War (Operation Desert Storm) in 1991.

During the Persian Gulf War, a serious revolt against Iraqi dictator Saddam Hussein occurred in Basra, which was quelled by Iraqi military forces with much bloodshed. In 1999 a second revolt against the Hussein regime led to mass executions in the city. After this second uprising, the Iraqi government purposely diverted most of the country's sea-based commerce to Umm Qasr. Human rights abuses at Basra were among the many charges against Hussein that were considered by the Iraq Special Tribunal, which was established following the start of the 2003 Iraq War (Operation IRAQI FREEDOM) to try the former dictator for war crimes and crimes against humanity. He was eventually found guilty and executed in December 2006.

At the commencement of Operation IRAQI FREEDOM in March 2003, taking Basra was the first and primary goal for coalition troops during the 2003 Iraqi invasion. After a bruising battle, on April 7, 2003, British forces, led by the 7th Armored Brigade, took control of Basra. Nevertheless, from March to May 2003, Basra and its surrounding areas witnessed much of the heaviest combat in the war between Anglo-American–led coalition forces and Iraqi fighters. After the fighting stopped, the Multi-National Division under British command engaged in security and stabilization missions in the Basra Governorate and surrounding areas. Despite these pacification efforts, in mid-2006 Basra saw several violent confrontations between secular Iraqis and Shiite Muslims in the area.

In September 2007 the British troops occupying Basra were withdrawn to the city's airport, part of a plan to gradually return occupied areas of Iraq to Iraqi control. In December 2007 British troops withdrew entirely from Basra, including the airport. After receiving control of Basra, the Iraqi government stated that the city remained relatively stable and that violence has decreased in intensity and frequency.

Charlene T. Overturf

See also: Basra, Battle for; Hussein, Saddam; IRAQI FREEDOM, Operation; United Kingdom, Army, Iraq War

Further Reading

Abbott, Delbert N. *Courage and Cowardice: The Liberation of Kuwait and the Rape of Basra.* Lincoln, NE: iUniverse, 2005.

Lyman, Robert, and Howard Gerrard. *Iraq 1941: The Battles for Basra, Habbaniya, Fallujah and Baghdad.* New York: Osprey, 2006.

Visser, Reidar. *Basra, the Failed Gulf State: Separatism and Nationalism in Southern Iraq.* Somerset, NJ: Transaction Publishers, 2006.

Basra, Battle for

Battle fought between British and Iraqi forces during the Iraq War of 2003 at the Iraqi city of Basra (Basrah) in southeastern Iraq near the Shatt al-Arab waterway and the Persian Gulf. The battle began on March 23 and ended with the British capture of the city on April 7. At Basra, the British pursued a strategy considerably different from that followed by their American coalition partners during the invasion of Iraq. While this British strategy sharply limited loss of life, it also allowed many Iraqi soldiers and officials to escape and fight in the subsequent insurgency.

During the opening days of the Iraq War, British forces, supported by U.S. marines and offshore coalition naval units, seized the Faw peninsula and the deep-water port of Umm Qasr. British forces then took over occupation of the Rumaylah oil fields from American units that were needed elsewhere. The next major task for the British then became the capture of Basra, Iraq's second-largest city and its principal port, with an estimated population of more than 1.25 million people.

To achieve the capture of Basra, the British deployed the 1st Armored Division commanded by Major General Robin Brims. Iraqi forces in the city were commanded by General Ali Hassan al-Majid, otherwise known as Chemical Ali for his role in the Iraqi nerve gas attack on the Kurdish town

Iraqi civilians fleeing the city of Basra in southern Iraq during Operation IRAQI FREEDOM, March 28, 2003. (AP/Wide World Photos)

of Halabja in 1988. Ali commanded a mixed force of Iraqi regulars and Baathist militia.

Brims decided upon a unique strategy for the taking of Basra, which would limit civilian deaths and mitigate physical damage to the city's buildings and infrastructure. The population of the city was made up primarily of anti–Saddam Hussein Shia. Basra had suffered greatly during President Hussein's suppression of the 1991 southern Shia rebellion that had followed the 1991 Persian Gulf War. Brims did not want to destroy the city and did not want to inflict needless casualties on the civilian population and thereby turn its people against the coalition.

Brims thus ordered the 1st Armored Division to surround Basra beginning on March 23, but he did not place the city under siege. He allowed anyone who wanted to leave Basra to do so, hoping to encourage desertion among Iraqi conscripts, which did

occur. Brims also avoided the use of indirect artillery fire against Iraqi positions in Basra, thereby minimizing civilian casualties. Ali's strategy was to draw the British into battle in the narrow city streets of Basra where the British advantage in armor would be nullified, but Brims refused to engage in street fighting.

Frustrated, the Iraqis attempted to provoke the British into launching a major attack on the city. Ali sent out a column of Soviet-built T-55 tanks to attack the British on the evening of March 26. However, the T-55s were outranged by the 120-millimeter (mm) guns of the British Challenger tanks of the Royal Scots Dragoon Guards, resulting in the destruction of 15 T-55s without loss to the British.

On March 31 British reconnaissance, intelligence, and sniper teams began infiltrating the city, gathering intelligence, sniping at Iraqi officers and Baathist officials, making contact with anti-Hussein resistance circles, and directing artillery and air strikes. Beginning in early April, the British initiated a series of devastating yet limited raids against Iraqi positions using Warrior armored vehicles equipped with 30-mm cannons and capable of speeds of more than 50 miles per hour (mph).

On April 5 an American F-16 fighter-bomber dropped two satellite-guided Joint Direct Attack Munition (JDAM) bombs on a building thought to be Chemical Ali's headquarters. The building was destroyed, and initially Ali was reported killed. Ali in fact survived the bombing and was not captured until after the war, but reports of his death were widely believed by Iraqi defenders, whose morale plummeted.

A probe by the British into northern Basra on the morning of April 6 proved highly successful. Brims decided that the time had come to move into Basra in force. At 11:00 a.m. on April 6, he ordered British troops into the city. Despite heavy fighting, most of the city was under British control by nightfall. The British suffered only three soldiers killed. Some additional fighting continued the next day, but by the evening of April 7 the battle was officially over, and Basra was secure.

Because the British were not assigned the task of assaulting Baghdad and overthrowing Hussein's regime and because they were facing a population that they believed was sympathetic, the British could adopt a strategy at Basra that differed markedly from the strategy followed by the Americans in their drive to Baghdad. Loss of life was minimized, and further damage to the city's infrastructure was avoided. However, many of the Baathists who were allowed to escape from Basra must have certainly joined the postwar Sunni insurgency. Basra also experienced a wave of immediate postwar looting and violence similar to what took place in Baghdad.

Paul William Doerr

See also: Basra; Iraqi Freedom, Operation, Ground Campaign; United Kingdom, Army, Iraq War

Further Reading

Gordon, Michael R., and General Bernard E. Trainor. *Cobra II: The Inside Story of the Invasion and Occupation of Iraq*. New York: Pantheon Books, 2006.

Keegan, John. *The Iraq War: The Military Offensive, from Victory in 21 Days to the Insurgent Aftermath*. New York: Vintage, 2005.

Biological Weapons and Warfare

Biological weapons are forms of natural organisms that are used as weapons or modified versions of germs or toxins to kill or harm people or animals. The first type of biological weapon includes diseases such as anthrax or smallpox, while the second category includes toxins or poisons such as ricin or aflatoxin. Along with nuclear and chemical arms, biological weapons are considered to be weapons of mass destruction (WMD).

Israel's advanced nuclear program prompted several Arab states to initiate biological weapons programs as a means to counter the Israeli nuclear arsenal. The proliferation of WMD, including biological weapons, is one of the most serious security issues in the Middle East.

By the early 1970s, several Arab states had established biological weapons programs as a means to balance Israel's nuclear arsenal as they concurrently sought to develop their own nuclear and chemical weapons programs. Biological weapons were attractive to many states because they were perceived as being less expensive and easier to manufacture. Biological agents could also be developed far more quickly than nuclear or chemical programs.

The Middle Eastern country with the oldest biological weapons program is Israel. During the Israeli-Arab War (1948–1949), there were charges that Israeli units infected Arab wells with malaria and typhoid. Following independence, a biological weapons unit was created. Israel's program was designed to develop both offensive and defensive capabilities, and its successful nuclear program overshadowed its chemical and biological efforts. In the 2000s, Israel's biological and chemical weapons programs were increasingly focused on counterproliferation in the region and efforts to prevent bioterrorism.

Egypt began a wide-scale biological program in the 1960s and recruited European scientists to advance the program. By 1972 Egypt had an offensive biological weapons capability, a fact later confirmed by President Anwar Sadat in public addresses. In 1972 Egypt signed the Biological Weapons Convention (which bans the use of these arms) but did not ratify the convention. Among the Arab states, Egypt went on to develop one of the most comprehensive biological weapons programs, including anthrax, cholera, plague, botulism, and possibly smallpox. These agents were weaponized in such a fashion that they could be delivered in missile warheads. Beginning in the late 1990s, Egypt began working with the United States to develop more effective biological weapons defenses, ranging from decontamination plants to national contingency planning to stockpiles of personal gas masks.

Following the Yom Kippur (Ramadan) War of October 1973, evidence emerged from captured documents and equipment that Syria had a highly developed WMD program that included biological weapons such as anthrax, botulinum, and ricin. Syria's program proceeded with aid and products from Chinese and European firms. In the 1990s Western intelligence agencies identified the town of Cerin as the center of Syria's biological weapons program. Toward the end of the decade, Syria also launched an effort to acquire missiles capable of delivering biological warheads into Israeli territory. Syria also developed a robust chemical weapons program. Syria's military planners hoped that their biological and chemical arsenals would deter Israel from using its nuclear weapons in the event of a conflict. For Israel and the United States, Syria's biological weapons program is especially troublesome because of the country's sponsorship of anti-Israeli groups such as Hezbollah and the fear that these weapons might be shared with terrorists.

Libya attempted to develop a broad WMD program in the 1970s that included biological weapons. However, international sanctions prevented that nation from acquiring significant biological arms. Instead, its program remained mainly at the research level. In 2003 Libyan leader Muammar Qaddafi renounced WMD and pledged that his country would dismantle its WMD programs as part of a larger strategy to improve relations with the United States and Europe.

In 1974 the Iraqi government officially launched a biological weapons program, and within a year the country established facilities for research and development of biological agents. Through the 1970s and 1980s Iraq obtained cultures and biological agents from Western governments and firms through both legitimate and illicit means. Among the biological weapons that Iraq obtained were anthrax, salmonella, and botulinum. By 1983, Iraq began stockpiling biological warheads and accelerated its program, including efforts to develop new types of weapons.

During 1987 and 1988 Saddam Hussein's regime employed biological weapons against Iraq's Kurdish minority. There have been charges that this activity included rotavirus, a major killer of the young in developing countries. Iraq reportedly invested heavily in a rotavirus biological warfare program. Used either by itself or with other biological agents, rotavirus would produce major deaths and illness among children and infants.

Large-scale Iraqi production of anthrax and aflatoxin began in 1989, and that same year Iraqi scientists initiated field tests of biological weapons. In 1990 Iraq stockpiled some 200 bombs and 100 missiles capable of delivering biological agents.

Under the terms of the cease-fire that ended the 1991 Persian Gulf War, Iraq began destroying its biological weapons capability. Also in 1991, Iraq ratified the Biological Weapons Convention. United Nations (UN) weapons inspectors were granted limited access to biological weapons facilities and were able to verify the extent of the program and confirm that some materials had been destroyed. The belief by President George W. Bush's administration that Hussein's regime had not complied with UN resolutions to destroy its WMD programs was a major justification for the U.S.-led invasion in 2003. Following the occupation of Iraq, however, U.S. and international inspectors were unable to find any hidden WMD.

The Iranian military worked with the United States during the 1960s and 1970s to develop defensive strategies against biological weapons. Iran signed the Biological Weapons Convention in 1972 and ratified it a year later. Following the Iranian Revolution in 1979, however, the country began a secret biological weapons program. The Iraqi use of chemical weapons in the war between the two countries from 1980 to 1988 accelerated the Iranian program. Throughout the 1980s and 1990s, Iranian agents and representatives attempted to acquire biological agents both legally and illicitly. The country also hired large numbers of scientists and experts on WMD from the former Soviet Union. As a result, Iran has been able to develop small amounts of biological weapons. Iran has also developed the missile capabilities to deliver WMD to Israeli territory.

Tom Lansford

See also: Bush, George Walker; Hussein, Saddam; UN Weapons Inspectors; Weapons of Mass Destruction

Further Reading

Cordesman, Anthony. *Iran's Developing Military Capabilities*. Washington, DC: CSIS, 2005.

Guillemin, Jeanne. *Biological Weapons: From the Invention of State-Sponsored Programs to Contemporary Bioterrorism*. New York: Columbia University Press, 2005.

Walker, William. *Weapons of Mass Destruction and International Order*. New York: Oxford University Press, 2004.

Zubay, Geoffrey et al. *Agents of Bioterrorism: Pathogens and Their Weaponization*. New York: Columbia University Press, 2005.

Blackwater

Private U.S.-based security firm involved in military security operations in Afghanistan and Iraq. Blackwater USA (known as Blackwater Worldwide since October 2007) is one of a number of private security firms hired by the U.S. government to aid in security operations in Afghanistan and Iraq. The company was founded in 1997 by Erik D. Prince, a former Navy SEAL, wealthy heir to an auto parts fortune, and staunch supporter of the Republican Party. He serves as the firm's chief executive officer (CEO). The firm was named for the brackish swampy waters surrounding its 6,000-plus acre headquarters and training facilities located in northeastern North Carolina's Dismal Swamp.

Details of the privately held company are shrouded in mystery, and the precise number of paid employees is not publicly known. A good number of its employees are not U.S. citizens. Blackwater also trains upwards of 40,000 people per year in military and security tactics, interdiction, and counterinsurgency operations. Many of its trainees are military, law enforcement, or civilian government employees, mostly American, but foreign government employees are also trained at its facilities. Blackwater claims that its training facilities are the largest of their kind in the world. Nearly 90 percent of the company's revenues are derived from government contracts, two-thirds of which are no-bid contracts. It is estimated that since 2002 Blackwater has garnered U.S. government contracts in excess of $1 billion.

Following the successful ouster of the Taliban regime in Afghanistan in late 2001, Blackwater was among the first firms to be hired by the U.S. government to aid in security and law enforcement operations there. In 2003 after coalition forces ousted the regime of Iraqi president Saddam Hussein, Blackwater began extensive operations in the war-ravaged country. Its first major operation there included a $21 million no-bid contract to provide security services for the Coalition Provisional Authority and its chief, L. Paul Bremer. Since then, Blackwater has received contracts for several hundred million dollars more to provide a wide array of security and paramilitary services in Iraq. Some critics—including a number of congressional representatives and senators—took issue with the centrality of Blackwater in Iraq, arguing that its founder's connections to the Republican Party had helped it garner huge no-bid contracts.

Although such information has not been positively verified by either Blackwater or the U.S. government, it is believed that at least 30,000 private security contractors are in Iraq; some estimates claim as many as 100,000. Of that number, a majority are employees or subcontractors of Blackwater. The State Department and the Pentagon, which have both negotiated lucrative contracts with Blackwater, contend that neither one could function in Iraq without resorting to the use of private security firms. Indeed, the use of such contractors has helped keep down the need for even greater numbers of U.S. troops in Iraq and Afghanistan. After Hurricane Katrina smashed the U.S. Gulf Coast in 2005, the U.S. government contracted with Blackwater to provide security, law enforcement, and humanitarian services in southern Louisiana and Mississippi.

In the course of the Iraqi insurgency that began in 2003, numerous Blackwater employees have been injured or killed in ambushes, attacks, and suicide bombings. Because of the instability in Iraq and the oftentimes chaotic circumstances, some Blackwater personnel have found themselves in circumstances in which they felt threatened and had to protect themselves by force. This has led to numerous cases in which they have been criticized, terminated, or worse for their actions. Because they are not members of the U.S. military, they often fall into a gray area, which can elicit demands for retribution either by the U.S. government or Iraqi officials.

Loose oversight of Blackwater's operations has led to several serious cases of alleged abuse on the part of Blackwater employees. One of the most infamous examples of this occurred in Baghdad on September 16, 2007. While escorting a diplomatic convoy through the streets of the city, a well-armed security detail comprised of Blackwater and Iraqi police mistakenly opened fire on a civilian car that it claimed had not obeyed instructions to stop. Once the gunfire began, other forces in the area opened fired. When the shooting stopped, 17 Iraqi civilians lay dead, including all of the car's occupants. Included among the dead was a young couple with their infant child. At first there were wildly diverging accounts of what happened, and Blackwater contended that the car contained a suicide bomber who had detonated an explosive device, which was entirely untrue. The Iraqi government, however, faulted Blackwater for the incident, and U.S. Army officials backed up the Iraqi claims. Later reports state that the Blackwater guards fired on the vehicle with no provocation.

The Baghdad shootings caused an uproar in both Iraq and the United States. The Iraqi government suspended Blackwater's Iraqi operations and demanded that Blackwater be banned from the country. It also sought to try the shooters in an Iraqi court. Because some of the guards involved were not Americans and the others were working for the U.S. State Department, they were not subject to criminal prosecution. In the U.S. Congress, angry lawmakers demanded a full accounting of the incident and sought more detailed information on Blackwater and its security operations.

To make matters worse, just a few days after the shootings federal prosecutors announced that they were investigating allegations that some Blackwater personnel had illegally imported weapons into Iraq that were then being supplied to the Kurdistan Workers' Party, which has been designated by the United States as a terrorist organization.

These incendiary allegations prompted a formal congressional inquiry, and in October 2007 Erik Prince, Blackwater's CEO, was compelled to testify in front of the House Committee on Oversight and Government Reform. Prince did neither himself nor his company much good when he stonewalled the committee and told them that Blackwater's financial information was beyond the purview of the government. He later retracted this statement, saying that such information would be provided upon a "written request." Blackwater then struggled under a pall of suspicion, and multiple investigations were soon under way involving the incident in Iraq, incidents in Afghanistan, and the allegations of illegal weapons smuggling by company employees. In the meantime, Congress considered legislation that would significantly tighten government control and oversight of private contractors, especially those involved in sensitive areas such as military security.

In February 2009 Blackwater officials announced that the company would now operate under the name Xe, noting that the new name reflected a "change in company focus away from the business of providing private security." There is no meaning in the new name, which was decided upon after a year-long internal search.

In June 2009 the Central Intelligence Agency (CIA) disclosed to Congress that in 2004 it had hired members of Blackwater as part of a secret effort to locate and assassinate top al-Qaeda operatives. Reportedly Blackwater employees assisted with planning, training, and surveillance, but no members of al-Qaeda were captured or killed by them.

Paul G. Pierpaoli Jr.

See also: Bremer, L. Paul, III; Coalition Provisional Authority

Further Reading

Buzzell, Colby. *My War: Killing Time in Iraq.* New York: Putnam, 2005.

Engbrecht, Shawn. *America's Covert Warriors: Inside the World of Private Military Contractors.* Dulles, VA: Potomac Books, 2010.

U.S. Congress. *Private Security Firms: Standards, Cooperation, and Coordination on the Battlefield; Congressional Hearing.* Darby, PA: Diane Publishing, 2007.

Blix, Hans

Swedish diplomat, head of the United Nations (UN) International Atomic Energy Agency (IAEA) from 1981 to 1997, and head of the UN weapons inspection program in Iraq during the run-up to the 2003 Iraq War. Born in Uppsala, Sweden, on June 28, 1928, Hans Blix earned a degree in international law from the University of Stockholm in 1959 and also pursued studies at Trinity Hall, Cambridge University, from which he earned a doctorate in law. He was appointed associate professor of international law at the University of Stockholm in 1960.

Blix soon abandoned his academic career to pursue his passion for international politics. Between 1962 and 1978 he represented Sweden at the Disarmament Conference in Geneva, and from 1961 to 1981 he was a member of the Swedish delegation to the UN. In 1978 and 1979 he served as Swedish foreign minister in the government of the ruling Liberal Party.

In 1981 Blix was appointed to head the IAEA, a position he held until 1997. One of the major issues confronting the IAEA during Blix's tenure was monitoring the nuclear weapons program of the Iraqi

Hans Blix, the executive chairman of the new UN Monitoring, Verification and Inspection Commission for Iraq. (Associated Press)

regime of Saddam Hussein. Although Blix made several inspection visits to the Iraqi nuclear reactor at Osiraq before it was destroyed by an Israeli air strike in June 1981, the IAEA failed to discover the Iraqi clandestine nuclear weapons program initiated during the 1970s. The full extent of the Iraqi nuclear program was discovered only during the 1991 Persian Gulf War, and Blix was forced to acknowledge that the Iraqis had misled the IAEA. Following the loss of credibility for the IAEA, Blix tendered his resignation.

Less than three years later in 2000, however, UN secretary-general Kofi Annan lured the veteran diplomat out of retirement to head the United Nations Monitoring,

Verification and Inspection Commission (UNMOVIC), a body assigned the responsibility of monitoring Iraqi weapons program following the Persian Gulf War. Because of Blix's perceived failures as head of the IAEA, Washington opposed the appointment.

Blix now attempted to build a diplomatic consensus for avoiding war and assuring the world that Iraq was compliant with UN resolutions regarding weapons development. Be that as it may, he chastised Saddam Hussein for playing "cat and mouse" games with weapons inspectors and seemed to realize that his inspectors were not getting the full story from Iraq. Blix nevertheless believed that UNMOVIC's monitoring of Iraq's weapons program could be employed to foster Iraqi disarmament. Critics in the George W. Bush administration, who seemed anxious for any pretense to wage war against Iraq, asserted that Blix was not sufficiently aggressive in searching for weapons of mass destruction (WMD).

Following the invasion of Iraq by the United States and Great Britain in March 2003, Blix expressed considerable reservations regarding the war, asserting that the Bush administration had exaggerated the threat of WMD in order to bolster its case for regime change in Iraq. In June 2003 Blix left UNMOVIC to chair the Weapons of Mass Destruction Commission, an independent body based in Stockholm. Blix elaborated on his criticisms of the rush to war in Iraq and the spurious intelligence reports upon which it was based in his 2004 memoir *Disarming Iraq*.

Ron Briley

See also: Hussein, Saddam; UN Monitoring, Verification and Inspection Commission; UN Security Council Resolution 1284; UN Weapons Inspectors; Weapons of Mass Destruction

Further Reading

Blix, Hans. *Disarming Iraq*. New York: Pantheon, 2004.

Williams, Ian. "Frustrated Neocons: Former U.N. Weapons Head Blix Assesses Year of War on Iraq." *Report on Middle East Affairs* 23 (May 1, 2004): 30–38.

BMP-1 Series Infantry Fighting Vehicles

The BMP series of infantry fighting vehicles (IFVs) represented a revolutionary shift in doctrinal thinking not only for the Soviet military, but also for other nations, including the United States. Prior to introduction of the BMP series in 1966, the predominant thinking about the use of mechanized infantry on the battlefield was that of the battlefield taxi, whereby the troops were moved to the combat area and then dismounted to fight on foot. The BMP dramatically changed this picture. While other nations such as the Federal Republic of Germany (West Germany) were working on their own IFVs, the BMP was the first to be fielded in any quantity.

Soviet doctrine in the 1950s was shifting to that of a nuclear battlefield, and to have infantry typically fighting on foot was a serious liability. The BMP was specifically designed with the nuclear battlefield in mind. The production model was armed with a 73-millimeter (mm) smoothbore gun that fired projectiles similar to those used in the handheld RPG-7 antitank launcher along with a rail to mount the new AT-3 Sagger 9M14M Malyutka wire-guided antitank missile (ATGM). The driver and vehicle commander were placed in tandem in the left-front of the hull, while the gunner for the 73-mm gun and AT-3 was alone in the small turret basket. The infantry squad

A Soviet-made BMP-1, infantry fighting vehicle, riding near the village of Chagatai in Takhar province, northern Afghanistan, on November 12, 2001, the day after this vehicle came under Taliban fire in which two French radio reporters and a German magazine journalist were killed. The brown areas under the vehicle tower are left by the sand-covered blood of the killed journalists. The three were believed to be the first foreign journalists killed in Afghanistan since the October 7 beginning of American airstrikes in support of the northern alliance. (AP Photo/Sergei Grits)

of eight men sat in the rear, four on each side back-to-back and each with a firing port and vision block to allow them to fight from within the vehicle.

BMPs saw combat service in the October 1973 Yom Kippur (Ramadan) War as well as action in southern Lebanon in 1982 and the Iran-Iraq War of the 1980s. In the latter, BMPs were used by both sides. Crews liked the BMP's speed and maneuverability but discovered that the Sagger ATGM was virtually useless when fired from within the vehicle, mostly due to the inability of inexperienced gunners to guide the missile onto the target. Infantry also found it difficult to engage targets with any effectiveness from inside the vehicle. As a consequence, tactics began to develop that appeared to be a return to the battlefield taxi role of previous carrier designs.

The lessons learned from the Yom Kippur War led to an overhaul of the BMP design, culminating in the BMP-2 and BMP-3. As the Soviets continued to improve and modify the design, remaining BMP-1s were shipped off to client states such as Iraq. Thus, it was the BMP-1, constantly upgraded and modified, that continued to see the lion's share of combat service in Middle Eastern wars. The Iraqis also received an unknown quantity of BMP-2s equipped with a 23-mm autocannon and the AT-4 Fagot 9M111 ATGM.

During the 1991 Persian Gulf War, coalition forces encountered a strange oddity. For years, British, French, and American tank and infantry personnel had engaged targets meant to look like Soviet tanks and infantry vehicles. Coalition forces were deployed along with Egyptian and Syrian units, equipped with large numbers of

BMPs, and that created some initial confusion regarding vehicle identification, as it was sometimes hard to distinguish friendly BMPs from Iraqi vehicles. When the campaign began, it was deemed critical to keep forces properly organized and separated to limit allied fratricide. Combat units did engage BMPs only on limited occasions, as these were largely grouped with the Iraqi Republican Guard divisions that generally avoided serious ground action. When coalition forces did manage to engage BMPs, they typically found them integrated with T-72 or T-62 Soviet-made tanks in combined arms company and battalion-sized groups. Some BMPs of the Medina Armored Division were destroyed by tankers from Colonel Montgomery Meigs's 2nd Brigade, 1st Armored Division, on February 27, 1991, but it would be the destruction of the Tawakalna Mechanized Division that saw one of the greatest losses of Iraqi BMPs in any one area.

The Tawakalna Mechanized Division was equipped with 220 T-72 tanks and more than 280 BMPs. It regularly trained in task-oriented battalion formations, and thus whenever tanks were encountered, BMPs were alongside. A typical formation was composed of between 30 and 40 T-72 tanks and 12 BMP IFVs, with the infantry dug in around the vehicles. However, Soviet equipment was designed mostly for massed attack formations, not for flexible defensive tactics in small formations. The division was spread out over a large area and was hit by the concentrated power of the U.S. VII Corps, commanded by Lieutenant General Frederick Franks Jr. On February 26 in the Battle of 73 Easting, M1-A1 Abrams tanks and M3 Bradleys of the 2nd Armored Cavalry Regiment under Colonel Leonard Holder engaged and destroyed 37 T-72s and their escorting BMPs in a matter of six minutes, all in a swirling sandstorm at a range of more than 2,200 yards.

During the Iraq War of 2003 (Operation IRAQI FREEDOM), U.S. Army tanks and helicopters engaged some BMPs, again in mixed combined arms formations with tanks. Advancing elements of the 3rd Infantry Division encountered small combined arms groups attached to larger formations of Iraqi infantry during their drive north to Baghdad. On April 4, 2003, just south of the city at a crossroads marked "Objective Saints" on battle maps, American forces destroyed several dozen BMP-1s and BMP-2s that were part of the Medina Armored Division. The Iraqi forces had bravely resisted, and at one point a platoon of BMP-2s had engaged the advancing Americans with accurate fire from their 30-mm cannon before they were destroyed by tankers of the 4-64 Armored Battalion. Later, as American columns pushed into Baghdad, BMPs individually and in pairs attempted to ambush the Americans from the numerous narrow alleys of the city. As the Battle for Baghdad came to a close, there were numerous Iraqi tanks and BMPs littering the roadways. Unfortunately, precise loss statistics for the BMPs are not readily available for either the Persian Gulf War or the Iraq War of 2003. However, in the case of the former the losses may have been as high as 200.

Even though the BMP was outclassed by U.S. tanks and infantry vehicles as well as those of other Western nations, when used by smaller armies against comparable foes it proved itself an effective vehicle, as attested to by the Iraqi experience during the Iran-Iraq War. Therefore, BMPs of various configurations will likely be encountered on Middle Eastern battlefields into the foreseeable future.

Specifications of the BMP-1 are as follows:

Armament: 1 73-mm 2A28 smoothbore gun with a rate of fire of 7–8 rounds per minute; 1 coaxial 7.62-mm machine gun

Main Gun Ammunition: 40 Rounds

Armor: 23-mm maximum

Crew/Passengers: 3, with 8 infantry

Weight: 13.28 tons

Length: 22 feet 2 inches

Width: 9 feet 8 inches

Height: 7 feet 1 inch

Engine: V-6 diesel; 300 horsepower at 2,000 revolutions per minute

Speed: Road, 45 miles per hour

Range: 340 miles

Russell G. Rodgers

See also: Iraq, Army; Iraqi Freedom, Operation, Ground Campaign

Further Reading

Bourque, Stephen A. *Jayhawk! The VII Corps in the Persian Gulf War.* Washington, DC: Department of the Army, 2002.

Fontenot, Gregory et al. *On Point: The United States Army in Iraqi Freedom.* Annapolis, MD: Naval Institute Press, 2005.

Foss, Christopher, ed. *Jane's Armour and Artillery, 2007–2008.* Coulsdon Surrey, UK: Jane's Information Group, 2007.

Gordon, Michael R., and General Bernard E. Trainor. *The Generals' War: The Inside Story of the Conflict in the Gulf.* New York: Little, Brown, 1995.

Hull, Andrew W., David R. Markov, and Steven J. Zaloga. *Soviet/Russian Armor and Artillery Design Practices: 1945 to Present.* Darlington, MD: Darlington, 1999.

Scales, Robert H. *Certain Victory: The U.S. Army in the Gulf War.* Washington, DC: Brassey's, 1994.

Zaloga, Steven J. *BMP Infantry Combat Vehicle.* New Territories, Hong Kong: Concord, 1990.

Bombs, Cluster

Small explosive submunitions, or bomblets, dropped from aircraft or fired by artillery that are designed to detonate prior to, on, or after impact. In the 1930s munitions experts in the Soviet Union developed early versions of cluster bomb technology. However, it was the Germans who first used cluster bombs operationally in World War II during the Battle of Britain in 1940. Called butterfly bombs by the Germans, their usage was not widespread because they were difficult to produce and were very fragile aboard aircraft. Despite these limitations, both British firefighters and civilians viewed butterfly bombs as extremely dangerous because, unlike most cluster bombs, they did not explode upon impact but instead detonated later under the slightest vibration.

Cluster bombs quickly grew in popularity and are now produced in many countries thanks to their versatility on the battlefield. The United States first used cluster bombs in the Korean War (1950–1953) as an antipersonnel weapon. Since then, the U.S. military has employed cluster munitions in Laos, Cambodia, Vietnam, Iraq, Kosovo, and Afghanistan. During Operation Desert Storm, the U.S. Air Force used the weapon extensively, dropping a total of 34,000 cluster bombs. U.S. warplanes dropped an estimated 1,100 cluster bombs during the North Atlantic Treaty Organization's 1999 Operation Allied Force in Kosovo, deploying roughly 222,200 submunitions. Fighter pilots flying the A-10 Thunderbolt II attack aircraft in Kosovo preferred using cluster bombs because they enabled them to neutralize targets without using precision-guided ordnance.

Cluster bombs remain a primary weapon among world military arsenals because of their wide variety of battlefield applications. Relatively inexpensive to make, cluster munitions offer a wide array of options in combat. They can be fired from the ground or dropped from the sky and afford numerous methods for delivery and employment. Ground-based deployments include the firing of cluster munitions with artillery or rocket launchers. Aircraft, meanwhile, are able to drop cluster munitions in a bomb-shaped container, or cluster bomb unit (CBU), that breaks open at a predetermined height, scattering hundreds of bomblets over a wide area. Either delivery method results in an effective weapon when used against personnel or armor. Cluster bombs are also frequently used on runways, electrical facilities, munitions dumps, and parked aircraft. Within the U.S. military, all four service branches use various forms of cluster munitions.

There are many different types of cluster munitions. Some versions of cluster bombs are meant to be incendiary, while others are used as fragmentation bombs, designed to explode and scatter deadly pieces of metal in all directions.

Antitank versions of cluster munitions contain shaped-charge bomblets designed to penetrate armor more effectively. Sometimes the bomblets can be small mines that are intended to function like regular land mines upon landing. Different types of submunitions may also be used together to increase lethality. These weapons, called combined effects munitions (CEM), may implement incendiary, fragmentation, and armor-piercing bomblets in one dispenser to maximize the level of damage against different enemy targets located in the same vicinity.

The most controversial type of cluster bomb involves the air-dropped mines meant to immobilize enemy movements and act as an area denial weapon. These versions are designed to land softly and detonate only when the internal battery runs out, when the internal self-destruct timer runs out, or when they are disturbed in any way. Mine-laying cluster bombs proved relatively effective when used against Scud missile launchers during Operation Desert Storm in 1991. At the same time, these types of cluster bombs can cause many deaths and serious injuries to unsuspecting civilians who may run across them. A small percentage of the bomblets do not explode or detonate as planned.

Mines deployed by cluster bombs pose a greater long-term threat to civilians living in a war zone. Roughly 1–10 percent of cluster submunitions do not explode on impact, becoming deadly to any nonmilitary personnel who may stumble upon them. Thousands of such civilian casualties have been reported in Iraq, Kosovo, Afghanistan, Lebanon, and Israel.

Following Operation Allied Force in Kosovo, in 1999 the U.S. Department of Defense estimated that there were 11,110 unexploded bomblets that caused an estimated 500 civilian deaths. Additionally, an estimated 1.2 million to 1.5 million unexploded submunitions still remained in Iraq after Operation Desert Storm, claiming more than 4,000 civilian casualties.

While cluster munitions have caused controversy in many conflicts, their use in the summer 2006 war between Israel and Hezbollah was especially controversial. After the brief conflict, an estimated 1 million unexploded cluster bomb submunitions littered southern Lebanon and northern

Israel. Thousands of artillery rounds carrying cluster munitions were fired between the two combatants, according to the United Nations (UN) Mine Action Coordination Center. Human rights organizations have accused both belligerents of deliberately targeting civilians during the conflict, as many of the bomblets fell into villages and towns where civilians were living. Human rights organizations also reported more than 1,600 deaths in Kuwait and Iraq stemming from unexploded submunitions dropped during the 1991 Persian Gulf War. Examples such as these have given rise to increased efforts to outlaw cluster bombs internationally.

Following the 1991 Persian Gulf War, the U.S. Defense Department reviewed its use of cluster munitions in an attempt to minimize collateral damage and reduce the noncombatant casualty rate. Thanks to the inaccuracy of certain types of cluster munitions, such as the CBU-87 used during Operation DESERT STORM, the U.S. Defense Department established a goal of reducing the dud rate among cluster submunitions to less than 1 percent by 2001.

In the mid-1990s the U.S. Air Force began experimenting with wind corrected munitions dispensers (WCMDs) in a further effort to reduce the noncombatant death rate. WCMD features include directional aerodynamic fins and an internal navigation system that adjusts for wind variations after its release. Additionally, cluster bombs such as the CBU-105 have dispensers loaded with smart bomblets, which are designed to self-destruct if they do not hit their target. As an additional safety measure, these smart bomblets are designed to deactivate within minutes if they do not explode upon impact.

The U.S. military has also experimented with a new version of cluster munitions, substituting thousands of specially designed darts or ordinary nails, for bomblets. When dropped from an aircraft or fired from the ground, these cluster munitions employ thousands of small nail-like pieces of metal that can destroy personnel and other soft targets. This method eliminates the possibility of duds, as there are no explosive submunitions that could cause harm to an unsuspecting civilian.

During Operation IRAQI FREEDOM American forces made wide use of cluster bombs, much to the consternation of international human rights groups. It is estimated that in the opening weeks of the war, some 13,000 cluster munitions were employed in Iraq, and despite their careful use, the bombs caused considerable civilian deaths and casualties. Some human rights watch groups have alleged that as many as 240,000 cluster bombs have been used in Iraq since March 2003, a number that cannot be verified because the Defense Department does not provide such figures. In Operation IRAQI FREEDOM the United States also used the CBU-105 smart-guided cluster bomb, which was dropped from B-52 bombers. Cluster bombs were also employed during Operation ENDURING FREEDOM in Afghanistan. The collateral damage caused by these munitions raised international concern and may have unwittingly precipitated a backlash against U.S. operations there among many Afghan citizens.

After successful efforts to ban antipersonnel mines, many countries initiated efforts to implement policies curbing the use of cluster bombs or advocating their complete elimination. In February 2007 Norway invited interested countries to Oslo and began to push for an international ban on cluster bombs. More than 45 countries participated in the discussions and agreed to meet again in February 2008. Once again led by Norway, more than 80 countries signed the Wellington Declaration at the

Cluster Munitions Conference in New Zealand. This meeting committed the participating countries to solving the humanitarian problems created by cluster bombs and their unexploded ordnance.

Continuing on in the goal of banning cluster munitions altogether, 111 countries met in Dublin, Ireland, in May 2008 and agreed on a treaty banning certain types of cluster munitions. Furthermore, the signatories agreed to eliminate stockpiled cluster ordnance by 2016. Signatories also promised not to develop, produce, use, obtain, stockpile, or transfer additional cluster munitions. British prime minister Gordon Brown was among the many diplomats calling for a total ban on the use of cluster bombs. However, representatives from the world's largest producers of cluster bombs, which include the United States, Russia, and the People's Republic of China, did not attend. Diplomats from Israel, India, and Pakistan raised objections about a total ban.

In lieu of an outright ban on cluster bombs, the UN and human rights organizations have begun new efforts to minimize damage to noncombatants. Education emphasizing the dangers associated with unexploded cluster bomb submunitions is being distributed to civilians living in war-torn areas around the world. The United States has opposed the ban because of the extreme utility of these weapons, preferring instead to improve the safety measures in cluster bomb technology.

Matthew Basler

See also: Iraqi Freedom, Operation, Air Campaign; U.S. Air Force, Iraq War

Further Reading

Bailey, Jonathan B. A. *Field Artillery and Firepower*. Annapolis, MD: Naval Institute Press, 2004.

Bond, Horatio, ed. *Fire and the Air War*. Boston: National Fire Protection Association, 1946.

Conway, Simon. "Banning Bomblets." *The World Today* 64, no. 5 (May 2008): 13–15.

Haave, Christopher E., and Phil M. Haun, eds. *A-10s over Kosovo: The Victory of Airpower over a Fielded Army as Told by the Airmen Who Fought in Operation Allied Force*. Maxwell Air Force Base, AL: Air University Press, 2003.

Hammick, Denise. "NZ Conference Paves Way for Cluster Munitions Treaty." *Jane's Defense Weekly* 45, no. 10 (March 5, 2008): 7.

Hogg, Ian V. *Artillery 2000*. London: Arms and Armour Press, 1990.

Lennox, Duncan, ed. *Jane's Air-Launched Weapons*. Alexandria, VA: Jane's Information Group–Sentinel House, 1999.

Bombs, Precision-Guided

Precision-guided munitions, commonly called smart bombs, are bombs that have integral guidance systems that compensate for environmental interference and poor aim and that ensure the bomb's accurate emplacement against the target. They differ from dumb or iron bombs in that they have an internal guidance system and a related power source. Typically, a modern smart bomb has a circular probable error of 20–94 feet. But even a highly trained pilot operating in an optimal environment can, at best, reliably place a dumb bomb within 300 feet of the aim point. Most modern smart bomb systems rely on a computer-based guidance system that accepts a target designated by the aircraft's pilot or weapons officer, or a forward air or ground controller and guides the bomb onto it. The target's identification and designation are derived from electro-optical, infrared, or radar imaging. However, a growing number of guidance systems guide the bomb onto the target's geographic location using the target's and bomb's Global Positioning System (GPS) respective location. The bomb reverts to inertial guidance if the GPS link is lost. GPS-guided bombs are employed against fixed targets, while the others can be used against moving targets or those in which a specific entry point (e.g., ventilation shaft) is required.

The Germans employed the first guided bombs during World War II. The German Fritz bombs were radio-controlled bombs that the plane's bombardier glided into the target using a joy stick. He tracked the bomb's path via a flare in the bomb's rear. The Americans also employed a television-based guided bomb called the Azon bomb in 1945 and continued to pursue bomb-guidance systems after the war. The resulting AGM-62 Walleye relied on a TV camera installed in the bomb's nose that transmitted the target's image back to the aircraft's weapons officer. He steered the bomb to the target by keeping the aim in the TV cross-hairs. The early Walleyes required so much operator attention, however, that they were primarily employed from crewed aircraft such as the navy's A-6 Intruder.

In 1968 during the Vietnam War, the U.S. Air Force introduced the Bolt-117, the first laser-guided bomb. These early bombs guided onto the reflected beam of a laser designator that illuminated the target. The early versions had to be illuminated by a second aircraft in the target area. By 1972 this system had given way to an automatic laser-tracking illuminator that enabled the bombing aircraft to illuminate the target as it withdrew. However, these early laser-based systems were vulnerable to smoke and poor visibility, which interfered with the laser beam.

By the late 1970s the United States introduced improved laser, infrared, and electro-optical target-designation systems. Israel acquired some of these weapons and used them in strike missions over Lebanon in the mid-1980s, but the first significant large-scale use of smart bombs came in 1991, when the United States led a United Nations (UN) coalition to drive Iraqi troops out of Kuwait (Operation DESERT STORM). In that war, U.S. aircraft used precision weapons in approximately 20 percent of their strike missions over Iraq. They were employed primarily against high-priority targets located within population areas or in circumstances where the target's first-strike destruction had to be guaranteed (Scud surface-to-surface missile launchers, for example).

The lessons learned from that war drove U.S. development of the Joint Direct Attack Munition (JDAM), Joint Standoff Weapon (JSOW), and GPS-based bomb-guidance systems. During Operation ENDURING FREEDOM (2001), more than 80 percent of the bombs dropped were smart bombs, and a similar percentage marked the air missions over Iraq in Operation IRAQI FREEDOM (2003).

Precision weapons will continue to gain ground in the years ahead as the world takes an increasingly harsh view of collateral damage and casualties inflicted on civilians. The introduction of cost-effective retrofit guidance kits has enabled many countries to convert their dumb bombs into smart bombs at little expense. Israel and most of the Arab frontline states are now acquiring guidance kits for their bomb arsenals. However, blast effects remain a problem regardless of the weapon's precision. For example, the Palestinian terrorists' strategic placement of their facilities within apartment blocks and housing areas has driven Israel away from the use of bombs. Israel increasingly employs short-range tactical missiles with small warheads (less than 30 kilograms) against terrorist targets in the occupied territories and southern Lebanon. Still, smart bombs will figure prominently in any future Middle Eastern conflict.

Carl Schuster

See also: IRAQI FREEDOM, Operation, Air Campaign; U.S. Air Force, Iraq War

Further Reading

Allen, Charles. *Thunder and Lightning: The RAF in the Gulf; Personal Experiences of War.* London: Her Majesty's Stationery Office, 1991.

Drendei, Lou. *Air War Desert Storm.* London: Squadron Signal Publications, 1994.

Frieden, David R. *Principles of Naval Weapons Systems.* Annapolis, MD: Naval Institute Press, 1985.

Pollack, Kenneth M. *Arabs at War: Military Effectiveness, 1948–1991.* Lincoln: University of Nebraska Press, 2002.

Werrell, Kenneth P. *Chasing the Silver Bullet: U.S. Air Force Weapons Development from Vietnam to Desert Storm.* Washington, DC: Smithsonian Institution Scholarly Press, 2003.

Winnefeld, James A., Preston Niblack, and Dana J. Johnson. *A League of Airmen: U.S. Air Power in the Gulf War.* Santa Monica, CA: RAND Corporation, 1994.

Yenne, Bill. *Secret Weapons of the Cold War.* New York: Berkley Publishing, 2005.

Bradley Fighting Vehicle

Lightly armored tracked infantry and cavalry fighting vehicle. In 1975 the U.S. Army requested proposals for an armored mechanized vehicle to carry infantry on the battlefield for combined arms operations with the new M-1 Abrams tank. The new vehicle would gradually replace the M-113 armored personnel carrier, which the army did not believe could keep up with the new tank.

The Food Machinery Corporation, later United Defense and then BAE Systems, produced the XM-723 prototype in 1975, which differed slightly from the actual production models. It was an armored tracked vehicle with a 20-millimeter (mm) gun and a 7.62-mm machine gun in a turret. It had a crew of three and could carry eight infantrymen. A tracked vehicle with six road wheels, the original Bradley was 21.5 feet long, 11.75 feet wide, and 8 feet 5 inches tall. Its 22.58 tons were moved by a 500-horsepower Cummins V-8 diesel, and it had a top speed of 41 miles per hour (mph) with a range of 300 miles. It was capable of crossing water at a speed of 4 mph. Aluminum and spaced-laminated armor protected the hull.

The Bradley program evolved into the development of two vehicles, which in 1981 were named Bradley Fighting Vehicles and are produced by BAE Systems Land and Armaments. The M-2 is the infantry fighting vehicle, while the M-3 is designated as a cavalry fighting vehicle. The M-2 Bradley carries a crew of three—commander, driver, and gunner—as well as six infantry. The M-3 transports two cavalry scouts and additional radios and ammunition. Crew size remains unchanged at three. The interiors of the two models differed, and the only exterior differences were gun ports to allow the infantry to fire shoulder weapons from inside the M2.

Some Bradley production models began an upgrade to the M-2 and M-3 A2 models, which had engines capable of producing 600 horsepower and a stronger drive wheel that allowed a top speed of 45 mph. Internal armor and improved ammunition storage were also added in production.

Both models differed from the XM-723, as their upgraded turrets mounted a 25-mm

A Bradley fighting vehicle provides security as soldiers of the U.S. Army's 3rd Infantry Division conduct a joint clearing operation with local Abna'a Al Iraq (Sons of Iraq) through a group of small villages south of Salman Pak, Iraq, on February 16, 2008. (U.S. Department of Defense)

Bushmaster chain gun and a 7.62-mm machine gun. The main gun automatically fired armor-piercing or high-explosive rounds as selected by the gunner, who could also select single or multiple shots for each fire mission. The bushmaster has a range of 1.2 miles. The vehicle could attack heavy armor with TOW (tube-launched, optically tracked, wire-guided) missile rounds, although it could not do so on the move but rather only after stopping for more than a minute and activating a collapsible launcher. Developers believed that the range of the TOW, 2.25 miles, and its ability to destroy any current armored vehicle with a missile that approached the speed of sound outweighed this drawback. The M-2 and M-3 also had smoke grenade launchers for concealment as well as the ability to generate their own smokescreen on the move.

These models have a length of 21 feet 2 inches, a width of 10.5 feet, a height of 9.75 feet, and a weight of 25–33 tons, depending on the weight of additional armor for the A2 models.

The reduction in the number of infantrymen to six in the M-2 was controversial because of the impact on the force structure, but solid performance in the 1991 Persian Gulf War proved the viability of the reduced squad number. The U.S. Army's first order for the Bradley was in 1979 when 100 were to be produced, with subsequent orders for 600 yearly. By 1995, the army had received delivery of 6,375 vehicles, with 400 more produced for Saudi Arabia. About 2,200 Bradleys deployed for the 1991 Persian Gulf War, of which 1,619 were in maneuver units, with the rest at division level, in theater reserve, or declared excess.

Before the Persian Gulf War, work had already begun on upgrading the Bradleys, first to the A2 and then the A3 models. The A2 Bradleys had additional armor, which increased the weight to 30 tons and then an additional 3 tons with add-on tile armor. A 600-horsepower engine compensated for the additional weight.

Because of the threat of Iraqi tanks, the army rushed 692 A2s to the theater during Operation DESERT SHIELD in 1990, and by the time DESERT STORM began in early 1991, about half of the Bradleys involved were A2s. The Bradleys performed well during DESERT STORM. They had a reliability of 90 percent during the land war in spite of the fact that they traveled from 60 to 180 miles during the 100-hour land war. Twenty were destroyed, all but 3 from friendly fire, and only 12 were damaged, 4 of which were repaired quickly. The Bradleys kept pace with the Abrams tanks and accounted for more destroyed enemy armored vehicles than did the Abrams.

The conflict did reveal problems with the Bradleys, however. These led to further refinements, resulting in the A3 model. Improvements included a position navigation system with GPS receiver. Coupled with sophisticated digital electronics and communications, the Bradley is now able to function in real time as an integral part of the combined arms team of tanks, attack helicopters, and other weapons systems. Better sights and a laser-range finder along with other digital upgrades allow for enhanced command and control as well as more lethal and reliable fire control. Upgrades to the identification of friend and foe (IFF) systems reduce the problem of friendly fire. Some crew functions were automated, and the vehicle's speed in reverse increased to match that of the tanks.

The vehicle armor was also improved, with the requirement to resist up to 30-mm rounds and the introduction of reactive armor. The TOW missile system was changed to add a hydraulic lift for the launchers, and the range finder allowed the system to fire on the move. The wear and tear of operating in a desert environment also required changes to various components to reduce damage from sand and dust. These changes have since been tested in Operation IRAQI FREEDOM, launched in March 2003 to topple the rule of Saddam Hussein.

The Bradleys were an integral part of the mechanized infantry brigades in both the infantry and armored divisions deployed. The 100-hour ground war of DESERT STORM gave credence to the projection of a short conflict once the Iraqi capital was taken. That did not happen, however, and the conflict continues, thanks to a strong insurgency that began in earnest in 2004. Bradleys continued to be deployed, with units rotating to and from Iraq for 12- to 15-month deployments. By April 2006, some 50 Bradleys had been lost in combat, along with 20 Abrams tanks, 20 Stryker wheeled combat vehicles (deployed with some mechanized infantry units), and 20 M-113s, which continued to play a role in the conflict. The Bradleys performed well, but this conflict yielded many lessons learned, which will figure in further development of U.S. military forces.

Among these lessons is the impact of sustained combat on both soldiers and matériel. Armored vehicles in the combat area operate at a tempo up to six times that in peacetime, with Abrams tanks driving 5,000 miles per year as opposed to 800 in peacetime. In spite of this, the army maintained an equipment readiness rate of 90 percent three years into the war in Iraq. Operation DESERT

STORM validated the effectiveness of U.S. forces against a well-armed enemy in conventional unit-on-unit engagements. The conflict has also allowed evaluation of the tracked Bradley compared to the wheeled Stryker armored infantry vehicle in terrain that varies from desert sand to mountains and includes operations in large cities. More important will be the lessons learned from fighting militant insurgents who operate in a hit-and-run manner that includes use of improvised explosives capable of destroying armored vehicles.

As with the M-113 armored fighting vehicle, which is still in the inventory, the Bradley has been used as a platform for many functions. These include an air defense vehicle with Stinger rockets, an electronic fighting vehicle system, a fire-support team vehicle, an ambulance, and a platform for the stingray countermeasure system that detects enemy fire-control systems and destroys them with a laser transmitter. The multiple rocket launch system (MLRS) is based on the Bradley chassis.

Daniel E. Spector

See also: IRAQI FREEDOM, Operation, Ground Campaign; U.S. Army, Iraq War

Further Reading

Cordesman, Anthony H., and Abraham R. Wagner. *The Lessons of Modern War*, Vol. 4, *The Gulf War*. Boulder, CO: Westview, 1996.

Hogg, Ian V. *The Greenhill Armoured Fighting Vehicles Data Book*. London: Greenhill Books, 2002.

Scales, Robert H. *United States Army in the Gulf War: Certain Victory*. Washington, DC: U.S. Army, 1993.

Thompson, Loren B., Lawrence J. Korb, and Caroline P. Wadhams. *Army Equipment after Iraq*. Arlington, VA: Lexington Institute, Center for American Progress, 2006.

Bremer, L. Paul, III

U.S. diplomat, career U.S. State Department official, and administrator of the Coalition Provisional Authority in Iraq (2003–2004). Lewis Paul "Jerry" Bremer was born in Hartford, Connecticut, on September 30, 1941. He received a BA from Yale University in 1963 and an MBA from Harvard University in 1966. Later that same year, he joined the Foreign Service and began his lengthy career as a diplomat.

Bremer's tenure with the State Department featured posts as an assistant to National Security Advisor and then Secretary of State Henry Kissinger (1972–1976), ambassador to the Netherlands (1983), and ambassador-at-large for counterterrorism (1986). In 1981 Secretary of State Alexander Haig named Bremer executive secretary of the State Department, where he directed the country's round-the-clock crisis management and emergency response center.

In 2002 in the aftermath of the September 11, 2001, terrorist attacks, Bremer was appointed to the Homeland Security Advisory Council. Considered an expert on terrorism, Bremer spent much of his career advocating a stronger U.S. position against states that sponsor or harbor terrorists.

After Iraqi forces were defeated in the March to May 2003 war, on May 6, 2003, President George W. Bush named Bremer U.S. presidential envoy in Iraq. In this role, Bremer became the top executive authority in Iraq as the administrator of the Coalition Provisional Authority. He was tasked with overseeing the beginning of the transition from the U.S.-led military coalition governing Iraq to Iraqi self-governance. Bremer was brought in to replace retired U.S. Army general Jay Garner, who had been put in place only two weeks earlier. Bremer's job,

American Lewis Paul Bremer was director of reconstruction and humanitarian assistance in postwar Iraq (2003–2004). Among his controversial decisions accepted by the Bush administration was disbanding the Iraqi Army. (U.S. Department of Defense)

which began just five days after Bush declared that major combat operations were completed, was to serve as the top civilian leader of Iraq until such time that the nation was stable enough to govern itself.

Garner's leadership has been generally praised but was not without its problems. Under Garner's watch, looting of commercial and government buildings was rampant, including the alleged theft of priceless archaeological treasures from Iraqi museums. Iraqi citizens also faced growing problems with failing infrastructure and burgeoning street violence.

Bremer's first move was to increase the number and visibility of U.S. military police in Baghdad while making the reconstruction of the Iraqi police force a high priority. Bremer also pushed to speed up the rebuilding of Iraq's infrastructure and to make certain that government workers were being paid. Despite his efforts, however, violence—both sectarian and by insurgents—continued to mount, and Iraqis were becoming increasingly frustrated with the U.S.-led coalition. Bremer was also forced to postpone establishing an Iraqi-led transitional government.

Bremer is given credit for making some critically important decisions in his role as envoy. Among these were the removal of all restrictions against freedom of assembly, the suspension of the death penalty, and the establishment of a central criminal court. However, many were critical of some of Bremer's decisions, particularly his decision to disband the Iraqi Army and to remove members of Saddam Hussein's Baath Party from critical government positions. Bremer responds to his critics that there was, in truth, no Iraqi Army left for him to dissolve, as that task had already been accomplished by the war. He also claims that his Baath Party purge was directed at only the top 3 percent of the party leadership. During his tenure, Bremer was also the target of numerous failed assassination attempts. At one point, al-Qaeda leader Osama bin Laden placed a bounty of 10,000 grams of gold on the ambassador's head.

Despite the violence and the assassination attempts, Bremer was able to achieve many of his goals. On July 13, 2003, the Iraqi Interim Governing Council, chosen from prominent Iraqis, was approved. On March 8, 2004, the interim constitution was signed after being approved by the governing council. Then, on June 28, 2004, the U.S.-led coalition formally transferred limited sovereignty to the interim government. In a move that surprised many, Bremer left Iraq the same day. After his departure, U.S. ambassador to Iraq John Negroponte became the highest-ranking U.S. civilian in Iraq.

After leaving Iraq, Bremer embarked on several speaking tours and coauthored a book, *My Year in Iraq*, published in 2006. He is currently serving as chairman of the advisory board for Global Secure Corporation, a firm that deals with homeland security issues.

Keith Murphy

See also: Coalition Provisional Authority; Garner, Jay Montgomery

Further Reading

Bremer, L. Paul, ed. *Countering the Changing Threat of International Terrorism: Report from the National Commission on Terrorism*. Darby, PA: Diane Publishing, 2000.

Bremer, L. Paul, with Malcolm McConnell. *My Year in Iraq: The Struggle to Build a Future of Hope*. New York: Simon and Schuster, 2006.

Ricks, Thomas E. *Fiasco: The American Military Adventure in Iraq*. New York: Penguin, 2006.

Scheuer, Michael. *Imperial Hubris: Why the West Is Losing the War on Terror*. Washington, DC: Potomac Books, 2004.

Brown, James Gordon

British Labour Party politician and chancellor of the exchequer (1997–2007) who succeeded Tony Blair as prime minister on June 27, 2007. James Gordon Brown was born on February 20, 1951, in Glasgow, Scotland, but grew up in Kirkcaldy. His father was a minister in the Church of Scotland. The younger Brown attended an accelerated program at Kirkcaldy High School and entered the University of Edinburgh at the age of 16. He studied history, eventually earning a doctorate in 1982. While a student, Brown served as rector and chair of the University Court. He briefly worked as a lecturer at Edinburgh and then taught politics at Glasgow College of Technology. Brown subsequently worked as a journalist and editor for Scottish Television between 1980 and 1983.

Brown first ran for Parliament in 1979 but lost to Michael Ancram. In 1983 Brown ran again and was elected to represent Dunfermline East (boundary changes later renamed this constituency Kirkcaldy and Cowdenbeath). He was also named chair of the Labour Party's Scottish Council. In the House of Commons, Brown shared an office with fellow Labourite Tony Blair, who was elected that year to represent Sedgefield. The two young, energetic politicians became fast friends, and their careers would be closely linked during their rise through government. Considered two leading modernizers, Brown and Blair set out to change the Labour Party. In 1987 Brown became the Labour Party's shadow chief secretary to the treasury, then controlled by the Conservative Party government. He served in that position until 1989, when he became shadow trade and industry secretary. He remained there until becoming opposition spokesperson on treasury and economic affairs (shadow chancellor) in 1992.

Brown reportedly wanted to run for the position of Labour Party leader in 1994, but he stood aside for Blair, who was elected that November. In 1997 the two achieved their goal of placing the Labour Party back in control after 18 years in the opposition. Rumors have since suggested that a deal between the two put Brown in charge of economic policy while Blair assumed the premiership, although that has never been confirmed. In May 1997 Brown was appointed chancellor of the exchequer, the equivalent of the U.S. treasury secretary. As chancellor, Brown presided over a long period of economic growth. He made the Bank of England independent and froze spending for two years. He controversially established five economic criteria that had to be met before allowing the public vote on joining the European Monetary Union. His methods were often called ruthless, but no one could argue with his record of high employment and low inflation.

By 2007 Brown was the longest-serving chancellor of the exchequer in modern British history. As Blair's popularity declined because of his support of the U.S.-led Iraq War, Brown appeared poised to assume the premiership. Indeed, Brown was the leading contender when Blair announced in May 2007 that he would step down on June 27. Brown formally announced his bid for leadership of the Labour Party on May 11, facing no opposition. He became prime minister on June 27 with the approval of Queen Elizabeth II.

Observers noted that Brown would not be a radical departure from Blair and the New Labour movement. However, he began to transfer several prime ministerial powers to Parliament and even some parliamentary powers to the general public. In the early days of his leadership, he faced an attempted terrorist attack on the airport in Glasgow and was praised for his handling of the incident. Although Brown pledged to address such issues as health care and housing during his leadership, he said that terrorism and the war in Iraq would remain at the forefront.

Although it was widely perceived that Brown was less enthusiastic about the Iraq War than Blair, Brown publicly remained staunchly loyal to the George W. Bush administration and the conflict in Iraq.

At the same time, the prime minister has begun to draw down troops in Iraq, and he has more recently stated that he is becoming increasingly concerned about the Afghanistan War. The close relationship between London and Washington was reiterated in the very early days of the Barack Obama administration, especially by Secretary of State Hillary Clinton. Beginning in the last quarter of 2008, the Brown government became enveloped in the financial meltdown that began on Wall Street, and by early 2009 the British economy was mired in deep recession.

Melissa Stallings

See also: Clinton, Hillary Rodham

Further Reading

Beckett, Francis. *Gordon Brown: Past, Present and Future*. London: Haus, 2007.

Bower, Tom. *Gordon Brown*. New York: Harper Perennial, 2005.

Routledge, Paul. *Gordon Brown: The Biography*. New York: Simon and Schuster, 1998.

Serfaty, Simon. *Architects of Delusion: Europe, America, and the Iraq War*. Philadelphia: University of Pennsylvania Press, 2008.

Bush, George Walker

Republican Party politician, governor of Texas (1995–2001), and president of the United States (2001–2009). George Walker Bush was born in New Haven, Connecticut, on July 6, 1946, and grew up in Midland and Houston, Texas. He is the son of George H. W. Bush, president of the United States from 1989 to 1993.

The younger Bush graduated from the exclusive Phillips Academy in Andover, Massachusetts, and from Yale University in 1968. He volunteered for the Texas Air

National Guard after graduation and became a pilot, although questions later surfaced about his actual service. He earned an MBA from Harvard University in 1975 and returned to Texas, founding Arbusto Energy Company in 1977. He then served as a key staffer during his father's 1988 presidential campaign and later became one of the owners of the Texas Rangers baseball team.

In 1994, Bush was elected governor of Texas. As governor, he worked with the Democratic-dominated legislature to reduce state control and taxes. In 1996 he won reelection, by which time he had earned a reputation as an honest broker who could govern in a bipartisan manner.

In 2000, having set records for fundraising and having campaigned as a "compassionate conservative," Bush easily won the 2000 Republican nomination for the presidency of the United States. His platform included tax cuts, improved schools, Social Security reform, and increased military spending. On foreign policy issues, he downplayed his obvious lack of experience but eschewed foreign intervention and nation-building.

The U.S. presidential election of November 2000 was one of the most contentious in American history. The Democratic candidate, Vice President Al Gore, won a slim majority of the popular vote, but the electoral vote was in doubt. Confusion centered on Florida. Eventually, after weeks of recounts and court injunctions, the issue reached the U.S. Supreme Court. On December 12, 2000, a deeply divided court halted the recount in Florida, virtually declaring Bush the winner. For many Americans, Bush was an illegitimate and unelected president.

As president, Bush secured a large tax cut in hopes that this would spur the economy, and he pushed forward Social Security reform. He and the Republican-controlled

George W. Bush, son of President George H. W. Bush, was president of the United States between 2001 and 2009. His largely unilateral approach to foreign policy and decision to invade Iraq in 2003 and undertake the mission with inadequate troop resources have been widely criticized. (U.S. Department of Defense)

Congress also enacted a tax rebate for millions of Americans in the late summer and early autumn of 2001. That same year, with prodding from the White House, Congress passed the No Child Left Behind Act, a standards-based reform measure designed to build more accountability into public education. Although the measure won broad bipartisan support, it later was criticized for being too narrowly conceived and incapable of accounting for differences in the way children learn. Many also came to believe that the mandate was not properly funded, especially in poorer school districts. In 2003 Bush was successful in passing a prescription drug act for U.S. citizens over the age of 65, but the measure ended up being far more expensive than originally forecast. Many also criticized the plan for being too complicated and offering too many options.

Bush sent many mixed messages about his commitment to environmental issues. Although he seemed to support the Kyoto Protocol dealing with climate change and global warming while campaigning in 2000, once in office Bush withdrew American support for the pact, citing conflicting scientific evidence on global warming. He also stated that the protocol could hurt the U.S. economy and American industry because neither India nor China had signed on to the agreement. His rejection of the Kyoto Protocol angered many environmentalists and other nations of the world that had already embraced the accord. This in fact was the first of many policy decisions that caused consternation in the international community. Throughout its first term, the Bush administration repeatedly downplayed the extent of global warming and the role human activities play in it. In its second term, it seemed more accepting of the science on global warming but took few steps to mitigate it. In 2002 Bush did sign legislation mandating the cleanup of the Great Lakes, but he also supported limited drilling for oil in Alaska's Arctic National Wildlife Refuge, which is anathema to environmentalists and conservationists.

The course of Bush's presidency was forever changed on September 11, 2001, when 19 hijackers associated with the al-Qaeda terrorist organization seized commercial airliners and crashed them into the World Trade Center and the Pentagon. The attacks killed nearly 2,700 Americans and 316 foreign nationals. Over the next few days, Bush visited the scenes of the attacks, reassuring the public and promising to bring those responsible to justice. The catastrophe of September 11 seemed to bring legitimacy and purpose to Bush's presidency, although it tilted the economy further into recession.

On September 20, 2001, Bush appeared before Congress and accused al-Qaeda of carrying out the attacks. He warned the American people that they faced a lengthy war against terrorism. He also demanded that the Taliban government of Afghanistan surrender members of al-Qaeda in their country or face retribution. When the Taliban failed to comply, U.S. and British forces began a bombing campaign on October 7. Initially, the United States enjoyed broad international support for the War on Terror and its campaign to oust the Taliban from Afghanistan. Indigenous Northern Alliance forces, with heavy American support—chiefly in the form of air strikes—handily defeated the Taliban and by November 2001 had captured the capital of Kabul. Taliban resistance continued thereafter, but the multinational coalition was nevertheless able to establish a new government in Afghanistan.

The Bush administration also sought to improve national security in the wake of September 11. A new Department of Homeland Security was created to coordinate all agencies that could track and defeat terrorists. In October 2001, at the behest of the Bush administration, Congress passed the so-called Patriot Act, giving the federal government sweeping powers to fight the War on Terror. Many Americans were uncomfortable with this legislation and feared that it might undermine American freedom and civil liberties.

In 2002 the Bush administration turned its attentions toward Iraq. Intelligence reports suggested that Iraqi dictator Saddam Hussein was continuing to pursue weapons of mass destruction (WMD). When Bush demanded that he comply with United

Nations (UN) resolutions seeking inspection of certain facilities, Hussein refused. Unfortunately, some of the intelligence dealing with Iraqi intentions and capabilities was faulty, and some have argued that the Bush White House pressured the Central Intelligence Agency (CIA) and other intelligence services to interpret their findings in a way that would support armed conflict with Iraq. Still others claim that the White House and Pentagon misled themselves and the public by reading into the intelligence reports more than what was actually there. By the end of 2002, the Bush administration had formulated a new policy of preemptive warfare (the Bush Doctrine) to destroy regimes that intended to harm the United States before they were able to do so.

In October 2002 Bush secured from Congress a bipartisan authorization to use military force against Iraq if necessary. Many in Congress had believed that all means of international diplomacy and economic sanctions would be exhausted before the United States undertook military action against the Iraqis. Such was not the case, however, for the White House seemed intent on war.

By the beginning of 2003 a military buildup against Iraq was already taking place. However, Bush's efforts to create a broad multinational coalition failed to achieve the success of the Persian Gulf War coalition against Iraq in 1991. Nearly all of the forces were American or British, and the United Nations failed to sanction military action against Iraq, as it had done in 1990. The virtually unilateral U.S. approach to the situation in Iraq greatly angered much of the international community, even U.S. allies. Such longtime partners as France and Germany refused to sanction American actions in Iraq, and relations with those nations suffered accordingly. To much of the world, the Bush Doctrine smacked of heavy-handed intimidation and hubris that simply circumvented international law whenever the Americans believed unilateral action to be necessary.

Military operations commenced on March 19, 2001, and Baghdad fell on April 9. At that point, organized resistance was minimal, but manpower resources, while sufficient to topple Hussein, were clearly insufficient to maintain the peace. Rioting and looting soon broke out, and weapons stockpiles were pillaged by insurgents. Religious and ethnic tensions came to the fore between Sunnis, Shias, and Kurds. Far more American troops were killed trying to keep order in Iraq than had died in the overthrow of the regime.

Although Bush won reelection in November 2004 in large part because of his tough stance on the so-called War on Terror, support for the war in Iraq gradually waned, the consequence of mounting American military and Iraqi civilian dead, reports of American atrocities committed in Iraq, the war's vast expense, revelations that the White House trumped up or knowingly used questionable intelligence about Iraqi WMD, and general mismanagement of the war effort. Meanwhile, large budget deficits and trade imbalances piled up. Clearly, the failure to find WMD in Iraq undercut the stated reason for the attack, although Bush then claimed that the war was about overthrowing an evil dictatorship and bringing democracy to Iraq, a statement that was diametrically opposed to his insistence during the 2000 campaign that the United States should not undertake nation-building operations using the U.S. military.

The Bush administration was at first ambivalent toward the Arab-Israeli conflict, but with violence escalating, in August 2001 at the urging of Crown Prince Abdullah of

Saudi Arabia, Bush issued a letter supporting the concept of a Palestinian state. September 11 and ensuing events in Iraq soon took precedence, however. Bush and his advisers realized that Arab support of, or at least acquiescence to, his Iraq policies would be more likely if a peace process were under way.

On June 24, 2002, Bush publicly called for a two-state solution. He failed to outline specific steps but supported a process in which each side would meet certain criteria before moving to the next step. The result was called the Road Map to Peace. Bush agreed to work with the European Union (EU), the United Nations, and Russia in developing it. This so-called Quartet developed a series of steps intended to provide assurances for each side but did not involve the Israelis or Palestinians in its development.

The Road Map to Peace was unveiled in March 2003, just before the invasion of Iraq, but no details were announced. In June of that year Bush arranged a summit conference at Aqaba, Jordan, involving Prime Minister Ariel Sharon of Israel and Prime Minister Mahmoud Abbas of the Palestinian National Authority (PNA). Progress on the plan stalled. The Bush administration's push for elections in the Palestinian-controlled West Bank backfired in January 2006 when these were won by the radical Hamas organization, which has called for the destruction of Israel and has continued to harass Israelis with random rocket attacks from Gaza and the West Bank. The peace process then ground to a halt. The Bush administration, faced with mounting American public dissatisfaction over the continuing American troop presence in Iraq, concentrated on that issue to the exclusion of virtually all other foreign developments.

Meanwhile, Bush suffered stunning setbacks at home. The White House was roundly denounced for its poor handling of relief efforts following Hurricane Katrina in the autumn of 2005 in which hundreds died in Louisiana and along the Gulf Coast. In the November 2006 midterm elections, Republicans lost both houses of Congress, and Bush was forced to fire Secretary of Defense Donald Rumsfeld, whose tenure had been rife with controversy. Many Americans placed the onus of blame for the Iraq debacle on his shoulders. The year before, Secretary of State Colin L. Powell had resigned because of sharp differences he had with the White House's foreign policy; he has since publicly regretted being taken in by faulty pre–Iraq War intelligence. By early 2007 Bush was besieged by bad news: plummeting approval ratings, a war gone bad in Iraq with no end in sight, and incipient signs that massive budget deficits fanned by Bush's spending and failure to veto appropriation bills were beginning to undermine the economy.

In January 2007, amid increasing calls for the United States to pull out of Iraq, Bush decided on just the opposite tack. His administration implemented a troop surge strategy that placed as many as 40,000 more U.S. soldiers on the ground in Iraq. Within six months, the surge strategy seemed to be paying dividends, and violence in Iraq was down. At the same time, however, a growing Taliban insurgency in Afghanistan was threatening to undo many of the gains made there since 2001. Many critics, including a number of Republicans, argued that Bush's Iraq policies had needlessly diluted the U.S. effort in Afghanistan. But Bush was hard-pressed to send significantly more troops to Afghanistan because the military was already badly overstretched.

In the meantime, the White House's controversial policy of indefinitely detaining non-U.S. terror suspects, most of whom were being held at the Guantánamo Bay Detainment Camp in Cuba, drew the ire of many in the United States and the international community. Although most of the detainees were supposed to be tried in secret military tribunals, few were ever brought to trial. Some observers have alleged abuse and mistreatment at Guantánamo, which further eroded the United States' standing in the world. More recently, several U.S. courts have weighed in on the detainees' status and have ordered that they be tried or released. In June 2008, the U.S. Supreme Court ruled that terror detainees were subject to certain rights under the U.S. Constitution. Even more controversial has been the use of "coercive interrogation techniques" on terror suspects and other enemy combatants. A euphemism for torture, this has included waterboarding, which goes against prescribed international norms for the treatment of prisoners of war. The Bush administration at first insisted that it had not authorized coercive interrogation, but when evidence to the contrary surfaced, the administration claimed that waterboarding had been used on some suspects. The White House, and especially Vice President Dick Cheney, however, attempted to assert that the technique did not constitute torture.

Not all the news on the international scene was bad, however. After the departure of such neoconservatives as Rumsfeld and Deputy Secretary of Defense Paul Wolfowitz, Bush's foreign policy became more pragmatic and less dogmatic. Secretary of State Condoleezza Rice worked diligently to try to repair the United States' standing in the world, and she met with some success by the end of the administration. President Bush's 2003 Emergency Plan for AIDS Relief, a multibillion dollar aid package to African nations hit hard by the AIDS epidemic, drew much praise in the United States and abroad.

By 2008 Bush's approval ratings were as low as for any U.S. president in modern history. In the autumn the U.S. economy went into a virtual free fall, precipitated by a spectacular series of bank, insurance, and investment house failures, necessitating a massive government bailout worth more than $800 billion. Other corporate bailouts followed as more and more businesses teetered on the brink of insolvency. Unemployment began to rise dramatically in the fourth quarter of 2008, and consumer spending all but collapsed. The only bright note was a precipitous drop in the price of oil and gas, which had risen to dizzying heights in July 2008. Bush, a formal oil man, and Vice President Cheney, who had also been in petroleum-related business, were excoriated for the run-up in energy prices, which certainly made the economic downturn even more severe. By the time Bush left office in January 2009, the nation was facing the worst economic downturn in at least 35 years.

Tim J. Watts and Paul G. Pierpaoli Jr.

See also: "Axis of Evil"; Bush Doctrine; Cheney, Richard Bruce; Iraqi Freedom, Operation; Rumsfeld, Donald Henry; Weapons of Mass Destruction; Wolfowitz, Paul Dundes

Further Reading

Bruni, Frank. *Ambling into History: The Unlikely Odyssey of George W. Bush.* New York: HarperCollins, 2002.

Daalder, Ivo H., and James M. Lindsay. *America Unbound: The Bush Revolution in Foreign Policy.* Washington, DC: Brookings Institute, 2003.

Schweizer, Peter. *The Bushes: Portrait of a Dynasty.* New York: Doubleday, 2004.

Singer, Peter. *The President of Good and Evil: The Ethics of George W. Bush*. New York: Dutton, 2004.

Woodward, Bob. *Bush at War*. New York: Simon and Schuster, 2002.

Woodward, Bob. *Plan of Attack*. New York: Simon and Schuster, 2004.

Woodward, Bob. *State of Denial: Bush at War, Part III*. New York: Simon and Schuster, 2006.

Woodward, Bob. *The War Within: A Secret White House History, 2006–2008*. New York: Simon and Schuster, 2008.

Bush Doctrine

Foreign/national security policy articulated by President George W. Bush in a series of speeches following the September 11, 2001, terrorist attacks on the United States. The Bush Doctrine identified three threats against U.S. interests: terrorist organizations, weak states that harbor and assist such terrorist organizations, and so-called rogue states. The centerpiece of the Bush Doctrine was that the United States had the right to use preemptory military force against any state that was seen as hostile or that made moves to acquire weapons of mass destruction, be they nuclear, biological, or chemical. In addition, the United States would "make no distinction between the terrorists who commit these acts and those who harbor them."

The Bush Doctrine represented a major shift in American foreign policy from the policies of deterrence and containment that characterized the Cold War and the brief period between the collapse of the Soviet Union in 1991 and the beginning of his presidency in 2001. This new foreign policy and security strategy emphasized the strategic doctrine of preemption. The right of self-defense would be extended to use of preemptive attacks against potential enemies, attacking them before they were deemed capable of launching strikes against the United States. Under the doctrine, furthermore, the United States reserved the right to pursue unilateral military action if multilateral solutions could not be found. The Bush Doctrine also represented the realities of international politics in the post–Cold War period; that is, that the United States was the sole superpower and that it aimed to ensure American hegemony.

A secondary goal of the Bush Doctrine was the promotion of freedom and democracy around the world, a precept that dates to at least the days of President Woodrow Wilson. In his speech to the graduating class at West Point on June 1, 2002, Bush declared that "America has no empire to extend or utopia to establish. We wish for others only what we wish for ourselves—safety from violence, the rewards of liberty, and the hope for a better life."

The immediate application of the Bush Doctrine was the invasion of Afghanistan in early October 2001 (Operation ENDURING FREEDOM). Although the Taliban-controlled government of Afghanistan offered to hand over al-Qaeda leader Osama bin Laden if it was shown tangible proof that he was responsible for the September 11 attacks and also offered to extradite bin Laden to Pakistan, where he would be tried under Islamic law, its refusal to extradite him to the United States with no preconditions was considered justification for the invasion.

The administration also applied the Bush Doctrine as justification for the Iraq War, beginning in March 2003 (Operation IRAQI FREEDOM). The Bush administration did not wish to wait for conclusive proof of Saddam Hussein's weapons of mass destruction (WMD), so in a series of speeches, administration officials laid out the argument for invading Iraq. To wait any longer was to run the risk of having Hussein employ or transfer the alleged WMD. Thus, despite the lack of any evidence of an operational relationship between Iraq and al-Qaeda, the United States, supported by Britain and a few other nations, launched an invasion of Iraq.

The use of the Bush Doctrine as justification for the invasion of Iraq led to increasing friction between the United States and its allies, as the Bush Doctrine repudiated the core idea of the United Nations (UN) Charter. The charter prohibits any use of international force that is not undertaken in self-defense after the occurrence of an armed attack across an international boundary or pursuant to a decision by the UN Security Council. Even more vexing, the distinct limitations and pitfalls of the Bush Doctrine were abundantly evident in the inability of the United States to quell sectarian violence and political turmoil in Iraq. The doctrine did not place parameters on the extent of American commitments, and it viewed the consequences of preemptory military strikes as a mere afterthought.

Keith A. Leitich

See also: Bush, George Walker; Iraqi Freedom, Operation; Weapons of Mass Destruction

Further Reading

Buckley, Mary E., and Robert Singh. *The Bush Doctrine and the War on Terrorism: Global Responses, Global Consequences*. London: Routledge, 2006.

Dolan, Chris J. *In War We Trust: The Bush Doctrine and the Pursuit of Just War*. Burlington, VT: Ashgate, 2005.

Gurtov, Melvin. *Superpower on Crusade: The Bush Doctrine in U.S. Foreign Policy*. Boulder, CO: Lynne Rienner, 2006.

Heisbourg, François. "Work in Progress: The Bush Doctrine and Its Consequences." *Washington Quarterly* 6, no. 22 (Spring 2003): 75–88.

Jervis, Robert. *American Foreign Policy in a New Era*. New York: Routledge, 2005.

Schlesinger, Arthur M. *War and the American Presidency*. New York: Norton, 2004.

C

Central Intelligence Agency

Primary civilian government agency charged with carrying out intelligence and espionage activities for the United States. The Central Intelligence Agency (CIA), created by the National Security Act of 1947, exercises primary responsibility for intelligence collection and analysis but also for the conduct of covert actions.

The agency is the direct successor of the World War II Office of Strategic Services (OSS). In January 1946, President Harry S. Truman signed an executive order forming a Central Intelligence Group (CIG) patterned after the OSS, and on July 16, 1947, Truman signed the National Security Act, replacing the CIG with the new CIA as an independent agency within the executive branch. The CIA was to advise the National Security Council (NSC) on intelligence matters and make recommendations regarding coordination of intelligence activities. Although the original intent was only to authorize espionage, broad interpretation of the act's provisions led to authorization of covert operations. The director of central intelligence (DCI) was charged with reporting on intelligence activities to the president and Congress.

Known to insiders as "the Agency" or "the Company," the CIA played a key role in the overthrow of allegedly radical governments in Iran in 1953 and Guatemala in 1954. It was also active in assisting the Philippine government in crushing the Hukbalahap uprising; in Southeast Asia, especially in Laos, it operated Air America to funnel U.S. aid to anticommunist forces. Notable failures included the Bay of Pigs fiasco in Cuba in April 1961 and attempts to assassinate or discredit Cuban leader Fidel Castro. The CIA played an important role in the 1962 Cuban Missile Crisis, and its agents penetrated key governmental agencies in the Soviet Union. The CIA-sponsored Phoenix Program in Vietnam for the assassination of communist operatives engendered considerable controversy, as did its role in helping to oust Chilean president Salvador Allende in 1973. The CIA's involvement in assassination plots and domestic spying led to the creation of the President's Intelligence Oversight Board, as well as an Intelligence Committee in each house of Congress. The CIA failed to predict the 1979 revolution overthrowing the Shah of Iran, Mohammad Reza Shah Pahlavi. It provided important assistance to Afghan rebels following the Soviet invasion of that country. It also took part in the secret sale of arms to Iran arranged with the hostage release and funneling of the proceeds to Contra rebels fighting Nicaragua's leftist Sandinista government, the so-called Iran-Contra Affair. This activity led Congress in 1991 to pass a new oversight law to prevent a reoccurrence. The CIA did provide useful intelligence on the threat posed by Iraq to neighboring Kuwait, but it was caught off guard by the actual August 1990 invasion.

The sudden collapse of the Soviet Union beginning with the failed coup attempt against Mikhail Gorbachev in August 1991

President George W. Bush, right, and Central Intelligence Agency (CIA) director George Tenet pose in the main entrance of agency headquarters in Langley, Virginia, on March 20, 2001. (AP/Wide World Photos)

came as a complete surprise to the agency. Although the CIA had warned that terrorists might attempt to seize control of civilian airliners and fly them into buildings, it failed to provide timely intelligence that might have prevented the September 11, 2001, terrorist attacks against the World Trade Center in New York City and the Pentagon in Washington, DC.

In December 2004 President George W. Bush signed the Intelligence Reform and Terrorism Prevention Act. That legislation abolished the positions of director of central intelligence (DCI) and deputy director of central intelligence (DDCI) and created the positions of director of the Central Intelligence Agency (D/CIA) and director

of national intelligence (DNI), which took over some of the responsibilities that had been formerly handled by the CIA. These reforms were in response to the lapses of intelligence over the preceding years, including the September 11, 2001, attacks; bogus reports of weapons of mass destruction (WMD) in Iraq; and other incidents that called into question CIA credibility and effectiveness.

The D/CIA is nominated by the president and approved by the U.S. Senate. Working with numerous staffs, the D/CIA is responsible for managing the operations, staff, and budget of the CIA. The D/CIA also oversees the National Human Source Intelligence division (HUMINT) and interacts with the Department of Homeland Security (DHS) to monitor terrorist and extremist activities within the United States. The CIA is organized into four primary directorates: the National Clandestine Service, the Directorate of Intelligence, the Directorate of Science and Technology, and the Directorate of Support. All four directorates are supposed to work together to collect, analyze, and distribute intelligence that is deemed necessary to protect national security.

In 1999 CIA director George Tenet developed plans to deal with the al-Qaeda terrorist organization, which was headquartered in Afghanistan. The CIA was soon involved in sending flights over Afghanistan with drones to gather intelligence information on the terrorist training camps there. Following the terror attacks on September 11, 2001, the CIA came under great pressure regarding its previous efforts to combat terrorism, which in turn prompted the 2004 changes described earlier in this essay to America's intelligence-gathering apparatus.

The CIA has also received considerable criticism for its role in the Iraq War. Indeed, the agency was blamed, rightly or wrongly, for the assertion that Iraq possessed WMD, which was a key factor in the 2003 decision to invade the country. As it turned out, no WMD were found, and public support for the war fell quickly after this was made public. Because the George W. Bush administration used the threat of WMD as a justification for the war, the CIA's reputation was badly tarnished. As the war in Iraq continued, more information regarding early CIA involvement was released. Since then, numerous people have come forward claiming that a large percentage of CIA officials did not support what the agency was claiming about WMD in Iraq. Many claim the CIA was pressured by the Bush administration to produce reports with intelligence

that the administration wanted the CIA to find and not necessarily the actual intelligence collected. More recently, the CIA has come under sharp criticism for its connection to the torturing of terrorist suspects, especially the controversial technique of waterboarding. Harsh interrogation techniques were officially authorized by top CIA officials (and approved by Vice President Richard "Dick" Cheney and President George W. Bush).

Arthur M. Holst

See also: IRAQI FREEDOM, Operation; Weapons of Mass Destruction

Further Reading

Blum, William, Larry Bleidner, and Peter Scott. *Killing Hope: U.S. Military and CIA Interventions since World War II*. Monroe, ME: Common Courage, 1995.

Jeffreys-Jones, Rhodri. *The CIA and American Democracy*. New Haven, CT: Yale University Press, 1998.

Kessler, Ronald. *Inside the CIA: Revealing the Secrets of the World's Most Powerful Spy Agency*. New York: Pocket Books, 1994.

Prados, John. *Presidents' Secret Wars: CIA and Pentagon Covert Operations from World War II through the Persian Gulf*. Chicago: Ivan R. Dee, 1996.

Theoharis, Athan, ed. *The Central Intelligence Agency: Security under Scrutiny*. Westport, CT: Greenwood, 2006.

Chalabi, Ahmed Abd al-Hadi

Prominent Iraqi dissident and founder and leader of the U.S.-funded Iraqi National Congress (INC) from 1992 to 1999. Born on October 30, 1944, in Baghdad, Iraq, Ahmed Abd al-Hadi Chalabi, a liberal Shiite Muslim, was a member of one of Iraq's wealthiest and most influential families. Prior to the 1958 revolution that overthrew the Iraqi monarchy, Chalabi's father, a prominent banker, was president of the Senate and an adviser to King Faisal II.

Although the entire royal family and many of its supporters were murdered by the revolutionaries, Chalabi's family managed to escape into exile, living primarily in England and the United States. Chalabi earned a BS in mathematics from the Massachusetts Institute of Technology in 1965. In 1969 he obtained a PhD in mathematics from the University of Chicago and subsequently taught mathematics at the American University in Beirut until 1977.

In 1977 Chalabi relocated to Jordan, where he established the Petra Bank. Within two years Petra Bank had become the second-largest bank in Jordan. In 1989, Jordanian Central Bank governor Mohammad Said Nabulsi ordered the 20 banks operating in Jordan to deposit 30 percent of their foreign exchange holdings with the Central Bank. When Petra Bank refused to comply with the order, the Jordanian government launched an investigation of the bank's holdings, which revealed that most of the bank's stated assets in fact did not exist. Chalabi then fled to the United Kingdom. Although Chalabi later claimed that the entire situation was the result of Iraqi dictator Saddam Hussein's chicanery, the Jordanian government was forced to pay $200 million to depositors to avert the complete collapse of the Jordanian banking system. In 1992 the Jordanian government sentenced Chalabi in absentia to 22 years in prison for bank fraud. Chalabi continues to proclaim his innocence in the affair.

In 1991, immediately following the Persian Gulf War, Chalabi began lobbying influential members of the U.S. Congress, the Central Intelligence Agency (CIA), and the Pentagon for funding to sponsor a coup against Saddam Hussein's government. In 1992 he formed the Iraqi National Congress. Between 1992 and 2004, Chalabi and the Iraqi National Congress received more than $30 million from U.S. government sources.

Many within the CIA and the U.S. State Department eventually became suspicious of Chalabi's ability to deliver on promises made concerning the opposition, and they attacked his veracity. But his close ties with former defense secretary and then-vice president Dick Cheney and Deputy Secretary of Defense Paul Wolfowitz enabled Chalabi to continue to receive funding until the eve of the 2003 Anglo-American invasion of Iraq. In 1999, Chalabi broke with the INC and established the National Congress Coalition, a group that considered itself a less Islamist alternative to other Iraqi opposition groups. During the U.S. occupation of Iraq, Chalabi served as one of the deputy prime ministers in Ibrahim al-Jafari's cabinet.

When it had become patently clear that there were no weapons of mass destruction (WMD) in Iraq, the existence of which had been a major pretext of the 2003 war, the George W. Bush administration became more concerned about its connections with Chalabi. The information that he had been giving the administration since at least mid-2001 was either falsified or unintentionally erroneous. Be that as it may, Chalabi steadfastly stood by the top-secret reports, much of the information in which pointed to an illicit Iraqi program to build nuclear, chemical, and biological weapons. It is surprising that the Bush administration would have given so much credence to Chalabi's assertions, unless it was because they supported the administration's own conclusions.

On May 20, 2004, U.S. and Iraqi forces raided Chalabi's residence to determine the extent of his duplicity in his dealings with American officials. Charges were briefly drawn up against him, but these were later dropped. Nevertheless, in November 2005, Chalabi flew to Washington, DC, to meet with high-level Bush administration officials.

From December 2005 to January 2006, Chalabi was Iraq's oil minister, and in April 2005 he was appointed deputy prime minister, a post he held from May 2005 to May 2006. In the December 15, 2005, elections, Chalabi suffered a humiliating defeat in his quest to become Iraqi prime minister. Allegations that Chalabi was bolstering his relations with Iranians and supposedly passed secret information to them in 2004 further tarnished his reputation in Washington. Paradoxically, his reputation in Iraq was troubled by his close relationship with the Americans.

Chalabi continues to lead the National Congress Coalition. In October 2007 Iraqi prime minister Nuri al-Maliki appointed Chalabi to head the Iraq Services Committee, a group that brings together eight government service ministries and several Baghdad municipal agencies that are at the forefront of the recovery and modernization effort in postwar Iraq. By all indications, Chalabi has performed effectively in this position.

Michael R. Hall

See also: Central Intelligence Agency

Further Reading

Fox, Robert. *Peace and War in Iraq, 2003–2005*. Barnsley, UK: Leo Cooper, 2005.

Packer, George. *The Assassins' Gate: America in Iraq*. New York: Farrar, Straus and Giroux, 2005.

Ricks, Thomas E. *Fiasco: The American Military Adventure in Iraq*. New York: Penguin, 2006.

Chemical Weapons and Warfare

Chemical weapons use the toxic effects from synthetic or natural substances to kill or incapacitate enemy forces. Chemical weapons range from such riot control agents as tear gas and pepper spray, which cause short-term incapacitation, to lethal nerve agents such as tabun and sarin, which can kill humans with only a miniscule exposure. The use of living organisms, such as bacteria, viruses, or spores, is classified not as chemical warfare but as biological warfare. However, certain chemical weapons such as ricin and botulinum toxins use products created from living organisms.

Chemical weapons are typically described by the effects they have on victims. The major classes of chemical weapons are nerve agents, blood agents, vesicants, pulmonary agents, cytotoxic proteins, lachrymatory agents, and incapacitating agents. Nerve agents quickly break down neuron-transmitting synapses, resulting in the paralysis of major organs and quick death. Blood agents cause massive internal bleeding or prevent cells from using oxygen, leading to anaerobic respiration, seizures, and death. Vesicants, also known as blistering agents, burn skin and respiratory systems, either of which can be fatal. Pulmonary agents suffocate victims by flooding the respiratory system. Cytotoxic agents prevent protein synthesis, leading to the failure of one or more organs. Lachrymatory agents cause immediate eye irritation or blindness, although the effects are deliberately temporary. Incapacitating agents, also temporary, cause effects similar to drug intoxication.

The most important characteristics of an effective chemical weapon are its ability to be delivered accurately and its ability to persist as a danger to enemy troops. Throughout history, delivery methods for chemical weapons have evolved from simple dispersion, often by releasing a gas into the wind, to artillery shells or missile warheads containing chemical agents and to aerodynamic dispersal from aircraft. Since

World War II, binary chemical weapons have been developed that contain two substances that are harmless by themselves but when combined form a weapons-grade chemical agent.

Primitive chemical weapons were used as early as the Stone Age, when hunter-gatherer societies used poison-tipped weapons for hunting. Sources of poisons included animal venoms and vegetable toxins. Undoubtedly, poison-tipped weapons were also used in intertribal warfare. Ancient writings describe efforts to poison water systems to halt invading armies. Chinese texts from approximately 1000 BCE describe methods to create and disperse poisonous smoke in war. Ancient Spartan and Athenian armies both used chemical weapons by the fifth century BCE. The Roman Army, however, considered the use of poisons abhorrent, and Roman jurists condemned enemies for poisoning water supplies. With the dawn of the gunpowder era, besieging armies launched incendiary devices and poisonous projectiles into enemy fortifications. By the 19th century, inventors in Britain and the United States proposed the development of artillery shells containing toxic gasses.

During World War I (1914–1918), more chemical weapons were used than during any other war in history. At the Second Battle of Ypres (April 22, 1915), German troops opened canisters of chlorine gas and waited for the wind to push the gas into Allied trenches. Soon both sides were using artillery shells to deliver chemical attacks, incorporating a wide variety of chemical agents.

Although they caused a great deal of panic and disruption on the battlefield and caused more than 1 million mostly nonlethal casualties in World War I, chemical weapons were never decisive by themselves. The chemical weapons of the period were relatively weak by modern standards, and no

A U.S. soldier training in protective clothing designed to guard against biological and chemical weapons, in Saudi Arabia during Operation Desert Shield in 1990. (Peter Turnley/Corbis)

army of the time had developed nerve agents. Although early gas masks and other countermeasures were relatively primitive, they did neutralize the chemical effects to some degree. The Germans, under the artillery genius Colonel Georg Bruchmüller, came the closest to achieving decisive breakthroughs with chemical weapons during the 1918 offensives, but the German Army did not have the operational mobility to exploit the tactical advantage.

During World War II (1939–1945) chemical weapons were used in a few isolated instances, although both the Axis and the Allies had developed large arsenals of extremely toxic agents. Both sides feared retaliation by the enemy, and neither chose to use its massive stockpiles of chemical weapons.

In the Middle East, the first modern large-scale use of lethal chemical agents occurred during the Iran-Iraq War (1980–1988). Early in the war, Iraq dropped bombs containing mustard agent and tabun on Iranian troops, causing 100,000 casualties including 20,000 deaths. Iraq accused Iran of having used chemical weapons first, but the allegations were never confirmed by United Nations (UN) investigators. Near the end of the war, the Iraqi government used chemical weapons against rebellious Kurdish Iraqi citizens.

During the 1991 Persian Gulf War Iraq was accused of launching Scud missiles with chemical warheads against Israel, although no traces of chemical weapons were found. Iraq did not strike the attacking coalition forces with chemical weapons. One possibility is that the Iraqis feared that the coalition would retaliate with its own chemical weapons or perhaps even tactical nuclear weapons. A more likely possibility, however, is that the Iraqis never had the planning and coordination time necessary to employ chemical weapons. Virtually every successful use of chemical weapons in the 20th century was in an offensive operation, where the attacker had the initiative and necessary time to plan and tightly control the use of such weapons and their effects. Being on the defensive from the start, the Iraqis never had that flexibility.

Chemical weapons in the hands of terrorist groups pose a significant potential threat. On March 20, 1995, Aum Shinrikyo, a Japanese apocalyptic cult, released sarin gas on a Tokyo subway, killing 12 commuters and injuring more than 5,000. In 2002 the terrorist organization al-Qaeda released a videotape purportedly showing the deaths of dogs from a nerve agent. Al-Qaeda has repeatedly announced its intention to obtain chemical, biological, and nuclear weapons.

There have been many attempts to prohibit the development and use of chemical weapons. In 1874 the Brussels Declaration outlawed the use of poison in warfare. The 1900 Hague Conference banned projectiles carrying poisonous gasses, as did the Washington Arms Conference Treaty of 1922 and the Geneva Protocol of 1929. None of the prohibitions proved sufficient to eradicate chemical warfare, however. The most recent effort to eliminate chemical weapons was the multilateral Chemical Weapons Convention (CWC) of 1993. The CWC came into effect in 1997 and prohibited the production and use of chemical weapons. Numerous nations known to maintain or suspected of maintaining chemical weapons stockpiles refused to sign or abide by the treaty, including several in the Middle East. Egypt, Libya, and Syria, all known to possess chemical weapons, each refused to sign the CWC, although Libya acceded to the treaty in early 2004 and has vowed to dismantle its chemical weapons program.

Israel, long known to possess a sophisticated chemical weapons capability, signed the CWC but never ratified the agreement. Iran signed and ratified the CWC but refused to prove that it had destroyed known stockpiles of chemical weapons and does not allow international inspectors to examine its facilities.

In future Middle Eastern conflicts, chemical weapons are far less likely to be used in terrorist attacks than in large-scale military operations. Chemical weapons are not easy to use. They are difficult and awkward to store, transport, and handle; their use requires detailed and expensive planning and lead times; once they are released, their effects are difficult to predict and control; and one's own troops require specialized equipment and extensive training to operate in a chemical environment.

Possession of chemical weapons formed part of the case the United States made accusing Saddam Hussein of possessing WMD he might give to terrorists. He had used chemical weapons during the Iran-Iraq War and against the Kurdish population in northern Iraq. Many experts feared that he might deploy such weapons against coalition troops during Operation IRAQI FREEDOM. Few U.S. combat troops had adequate protection against chemical weapons. However, this threat never materialized.

Paul Joseph Springer

See also: Weapons of Mass Destruction

Further Reading

Butler, Richard. *The Greatest Threat: Iraq, Weapons of Mass Destruction and the Growing Crisis in Global Security.* New York: PublicAffairs, 2000.

Morel, Benoit, and Kyle Olson. *Shadows and Substance: The Chemical Weapons Convention.* Boulder, CO: Westview, 1993.

Solomon, Brian. *Chemical and Biological Warfare.* New York: H. W. Wilson, 1999.

Torr, James D. *Weapons of Mass Destruction: Opposing Viewpoints.* San Diego: Greenhaven, 2005.

Tucker, Jonathan B. *War of Nerves: Chemical Warfare from World War I to Al-Qaeda.* New York: Pantheon, 2006.

Cheney, Richard Bruce

Politician, businessman, secretary of defense (1989–1993), and vice president (2001–2009). Richard Bruce "Dick" Cheney was born on January 30, 1941, in Lincoln, Nebraska. He grew up in Casper, Wyoming, and was educated at the University of Wyoming, earning a BA in 1965 and an MA in political science in 1966. He completed advanced graduate study there and was a PhD candidate in 1968.

Cheney acquired his first governmental position in 1969 when he became the special assistant to the director of the Office of Economic Opportunity. He served as a White House staff assistant in 1970 and 1971, and as assistant director of the Cost of Living Council from 1971 to 1973. He briefly worked in the private sector as the vice president of an investment advisory firm. In 1974 he returned to government service as President Gerald R. Ford's deputy assistant. In 1975 Ford appointed Cheney as White House chief of staff.

In 1978, Cheney was elected to the U.S. House of Representatives, where he served six terms. He was elected House minority whip in December 1988. Cheney was known for his conservative votes: he opposed gun control, environmental laws, and funding for Head Start.

Republican Richard Cheney served as secretary of defense during the 1991 Persian Gulf War. A highly controversial yet powerful vice president of the United States between 2001 and 2009, he was a prime mover behind the decision to invade Iraq in 2003. (White House)

Cheney became secretary of defense on March 21, 1989, in the George H. W. Bush administration. In this position, Cheney significantly reduced U.S. military budgets and canceled several major weapons programs. In addition, in the wake of the Cold War he was deeply involved in the politically volatile task of reducing the size of the American military force throughout the world. Cheney also recommended closing or reducing in size many U.S. military installations, despite intense criticism from elected officials whose districts would be adversely impacted by the closures.

As secretary of defense, Cheney also provided strong leadership in several international military engagements, including the December 1989 Panama invasion and the humanitarian mission to Somalia in early 1992. It was Cheney who secured the appointment of General Colin Powell as chairman of the Joint Chiefs of Staff in 1989.

Cheney's most difficult military challenge came during the 1991 Persian Gulf War. He secured Saudi permission to begin a military buildup there that would include a United Nations (UN) international coalition of troops. The buildup proceeded in the autumn of 1990 as Operation DESERT SHIELD. When economic sanctions and other measures failed to remove the Iraqis from Kuwait, the Persian Gulf War commenced with Operation DESERT STORM on January 16, 1991. A five-week air offensive was followed by the movement of ground forces into Kuwait and Iraq on February 24, 1991. Within four days the UN coalition had liberated Kuwait. Cheney continued as secretary of defense until January 20, 1993, when Democrat Bill Clinton took office.

Upon leaving the Pentagon, Cheney joined the American Enterprise Institute as a senior fellow. He also became president and chief executive officer of the Halliburton Company in October 1995 and chairman of its board in February 2000.

Only months later Republican presidential candidate George W. Bush chose Cheney as his vice presidential running mate. After a hard-fought campaign, the Bush-Cheney ticket won the White House in December 2000, although only after a court fight and having lost the popular vote.

Arguably one of the more powerful vice presidents in U.S. history, Cheney endured much criticism for his hawkish views (he is believed to have strongly promoted the 2003 Iraq War) and his connections to the oil industry (Halliburton won several contracts for work in postwar Iraq). He also raised eyebrows by refusing to make public the records of the national energy task force he established to form the administration's energy initiatives.

Many people who knew Cheney personally have asserted that he became a changed man after the September 11 terrorist attacks. He became, they say, far more secretive, more hawkish than ever before, and, some say, even paranoid, seeing terrorists everywhere. As one of the principal promoters of the U.S. invasion of Iraq (Operation IRAQI FREEDOM), which began in March 2003, Cheney was well placed to receive the burden of criticism when the war began to go badly in 2004. As the subsequent Iraqi insurgency increased in size, scope, and violence, Cheney's popularity plummeted. Following the 2006 midterm elections, which caused the Republicans to lose control of Congress principally because of the war in Iraq, Cheney took a far lower profile. When his fellow neoconservative Donald Rumsfeld, the secretary of defense, resigned in the election's aftermath, Cheney was increasingly perceived as a liability to the Bush White House, which was under intense pressure to change course in Iraq or quit it altogether.

Cheney did not help his approval ratings when he accidentally shot a friend during a hunting trip in February 2006 and the information was slow to be released. Even more damaging to Cheney was the indictment and conviction of his chief of staff, I. Lewis "Scooter" Libby, for his involvement in the Valerie Plame Wilson–Joseph Wilson CIA leak case. Some alleged that it was Cheney who first leaked the classified information to Libby and perhaps others, who in turn leaked it to the press. Cheney continued to keep a remarkably low profile. Beginning in 2007 a small group of Democrats in the House attempted to introduce impeachment proceedings against Cheney, but such efforts did not make it out of committee.

Paul G. Pierpaoli Jr.

See also: Bush, George Walker; Iraqi Freedom, Operation; Libby, I. Lewis; Rumsfeld, Donald Henry; Wilson, Joseph Carter, IV; Wilson, Valerie Plame

Further Reading

Nichols, John. *The Rise and Rise of Richard B. Cheney: Unlocking the Mysteries of the Most Powerful Vice President in American History.* New York: New Press, 2005.

Woodward, Bob. *Bush at War.* New York: Simon and Schuster, 2002.

Woodward, Bob. *Plan of Attack.* New York: Simon and Schuster, 2004.

Woodward, Bob. *State of Denial: Bush at War, Part III.* New York: Simon and Schuster, 2006.

Chirac, Jacques René

French politician who served as mayor of Paris (1977–1995), premier (1974–1976, 1986–1988), and president (1995–2007). Jacques René Chirac was born on November 29, 1932, in Paris to a middle-class Roman Catholic family. He attended the Lycées Carnot and Louis le Grand, and both the Institut d'Études Politiques de Paris and the École Nationale d'Administration. Upon graduation from the latter in 1959, Chirac embarked on a civil service career. In 1962 he became Premier Georges Pompidou's chief of staff. In 1967 Chirac was elected to the French National Assembly as a center-right Gaullist. He then held a series of important governmental posts, including state secretary of the economy (1968–1971), minister of agriculture and rural development (1972–1974), and minister of the interior (1974).

Throughout this period, Chirac was more aligned with Pompidou than with the

Portrait of Jacques Chirac, president of France between 1995 and 2007. In foreign affairs, Chirac sought to restrain American hegemony and maintain French autonomy; he also promoted greater European integration. (Courtesy: Embassy of France; photo by Bettina Rheims)

Gaullists but nevertheless was among the inner sanctum of Gaullist political circles. When Valéry Giscard d'Estaing was elected president in 1974, Chirac became premier, helping reconcile the Gaullist leadership to more social spending. In 1974 and 1975 Premier Chirac met with Iraqi leader Saddam Hussein to promote the interests of French businesses and oil companies in Iraq. Given the ties between the two nations, which were further advanced by Chirac, French companies sold the components necessary for the Iraqi nuclear reactor at Osiraq that was destroyed in an Israeli air strike in 1981. In the aftermath of the 1991 Persian Gulf War, documents seized suggested that the Iraqis had intended to use the facility as a means of constructing nuclear weapons.

Chirac resigned as premier in 1976, no longer able to bridge the gap between Giscard's policies and the more conservative Gaullists. In 1977 Chirac was elected mayor of Paris, a position he held until 1995 concurrently with the premiership. In 1981 he challenged d'Estaing for the conservative leadership, which may have contributed to socialist leader François Mitterrand's victory in the 1981 presidential election. As French patience with socialist economic prescriptions wore thin in 1986, the Right took control of the National Assembly, and Chirac again became premier.

In 1988 Chirac lost the presidential election to Mitterrand. This prompted Chirac to resign his post as premier, and some people began to write his political epitaph. Chirac was undeterred, however, and continued to set his sights on the presidency, announcing in 1993 that he had no desire to become premier in another government. He finally achieved the presidency in 1995, leading a center-right coalition that promised tax cuts and continued social spending. Chirac proved to be relatively popular, and he won reelection in 2002.

Domestically, Chirac's policies centered on job creation, tax cuts, and trimming government spending, certainly the hallmarks of modern conservative thinking. However, government-mandated austerity programs and the trimming of the very generous French welfare state created considerable friction with the Left and centrist parties and precipitated a series of major labor strikes. The Chirac government also endured its share of scandals, and in the president's second term challenges from the Far Right (such as Jean-Marie Le Pen's National Front party) and immigration issues that touched off nationwide rioting took up much of his administration's attention.

In foreign affairs, Chirac pursued a traditional Gaullist course by attempting to create a multipolar world capable of restraining American hegemony and maintaining French autonomy. However, he has differed from Gaullist foreign policy in his pursuit of greater European integration, generally along a French-German axis. In 1995 he created a national and international stir when he went forward with a nuclear test in French Polynesia, only to vow the next year that France would never again test a nuclear device. Chirac was a staunch proponent of the Constitution of the European Union (EU), and many viewed its defeat by referendum in France in 2005 as a personal failure for him.

Chirac was one of the first foreign leaders to condemn the September 11, 2001, terrorist attacks on the United States, and he offered French support. He also advocated invoking the North Atlantic Treaty Organization (NATO) charter, which stipulates that an attack on one signatory is an attack on them all. Chirac supported the U.S.-led effort to topple the Taliban regime in Afghanistan in 2001 and 2002, and France provided a small troop contingent as part of the NATO effort there. In January 2006 Chirac publicly warned would-be terrorists that France was able and willing to retaliate with tactical nuclear weapons for any large-scale terrorist attack on his country.

Yet for all his antiterrorist rhetoric and his early support of the George W. Bush administration, Chirac refused to support the preemptory attack on Iraq that began in March 2003. In this stance he was joined by the leaders of Germany, now France's closest ally. France, which had long maintained commercial ties to Iraq, along with many other nations opposed the U.S. proposals to invade Iraq in 2003. Within the United Nations (UN), France favored a two-step process. One resolution would have required further inspections of Iraq's weapons program, while the second resolution would have been required to authorize the use of force in the case of a breach of trust. The Americans, meanwhile, worded the first resolution such that war would be a necessary means of restoring stability.

Chirac adamantly opposed the Iraqi invasion, believing that there was not yet adequate justification to go to war. He was, however, supportive of reconstruction efforts in Iraq. Chirac was also supportive of Saudi proposals to forestall the war by allowing Saddam Hussein to be exiled. Thus, Russia, the People's Republic of China (PRC), Germany, and France all issued statements calling for further inspections rather than war. Chirac also attempted to extend the weapons inspections for another 30 days, but the Americans chose to proceed.

Differences within Europe on Iraq disrupted one of the main pillars of the EU: a common foreign and security policy. This saw France and Germany heading a Europeanist bloc that acted with Russia and China on the UN Security Council to constrain

the United States, while Great Britain, Italy, and many of the newer East European nations within the EU backed a more Atlanticist position that supported the United States in its war policy.

After deciding not to seek a third term as president, Chirac left office in May 2007. In retirement, he took up residence in a palatial apartment on the Quai Voltaire in Paris and joined the Constitutional Council of France, the nation's highest constitutional body. The council is charged with supervising national elections and referenda and upholding the statutes of the 1958 constitution.

Michael K. Beauchamp and
Paul G. Pierpaoli Jr.

See also: Bush, George Walker; Iraqi Freedom, Operation

Further Reading

Madelin, Philippe. *Jacques Chirac: Une Biographie* [Jacques Chirac: A Biogrpahy]. Paris: Flammarion, 2002.

Wright, Gordon. *France in Modern Times.* New York: Norton, 2002.

Clinton, Hillary Rodham

Attorney, former first lady (1993–2001), U.S. senator (2001–2009), presidential candidate (2008), and secretary of state (2009–2013). Hillary Diane Rodham was born on October 26, 1947, in Chicago and was raised in Park Ridge, a prosperous Chicago suburb. Her family was staunchly Republican, and during the 1964 presidential campaign, while still a high school student, she actively campaigned for Republican nominee Barry Goldwater. She entered Wellesley College in 1965, and by 1968 she had become disenchanted with Republican politics and the Vietnam War. By 1968 she supported the Democratic antiwar presidential candidate

Hillary Rodham Clinton, the wife of former president Bill Clinton, was the U.S. senator from New York between 2001 and 2009. In 2009, Clinton became the secretary of state in the Barack Obama administration. (U.S. Senate)

Eugene McCarthy; the following year she graduated with a degree in political science.

Rodham enrolled at Yale Law School, where she met fellow student Bill Clinton, whom she would later marry. Graduating in 1973, she took a position with a child-advocacy group. The next year she served as a staff attorney for the House Committee on the Judiciary during the Watergate Scandal that caused President Richard Nixon to resign in 1974. In 1975 she wed Bill Clinton.

In 1976 Bill Clinton launched his political career when he was elected attorney general of Arkansas. The next year Hillary Clinton joined the Rose Law Firm, the premier legal firm in Arkansas, where she specialized in intellectual property law and continued pro-bono child advocacy legal work. Bill Clinton became governor of Arkansas

in January 1979, the same year that Hillary Clinton became a full partner in the Rose Law Firm, the first woman to achieve such status. In 1981 Bill Clinton lost a reelection bid but was reelected in 1982; Hillary Clinton was again the first lady of Arkansas, an informal post that she would hold until her husband became president in January 1993. She continued her legal work and was active on several boards, including those of Arkansas-based Walmart as well as Lafarge and TCBY.

Taking a leave of absence from the Rose Law Firm to help her husband campaign for the presidency in 1992, Clinton proved to be a formidable campaigner, repeatedly weathering allegations that her husband had engaged in extramarital affairs. After Bill Clinton upset incumbent president George H. W. Bush in the November 1992 elections, Hillary Clinton became first lady in January 1993. She was an activist first lady, certainly more so than any of her immediate predecessors. Some pundits likened her to Eleanor Roosevelt, but it quickly became clear that Clinton would be a far more influential first lady than even Roosevelt.

Hillary Clinton's role in White House policy making was derided by the right wing of the Republican Party, and even some mainstream Democrats openly questioned her central role in decision making. In 1993 her husband named her chairperson of the Task Force on National Health Care Reform, a move that in retrospect was probably not a wise idea. Many questioned Hillary Clinton's motives, and the secrecy in which she conducted much of the task force's business only added to the public's skepticism. In the end, her health care plan was deemed too bureaucratic and too burdensome for business. The plan died in the Congress and became a major campaign boon to the Republicans in the 1994 elections, which saw the Democrats lose their control of Congress. Despite the setback, Clinton actively promoted certain national legislation, including the State Children's Health Insurance Program in 1997. She traveled widely, ultimately visiting 79 nations.

Clinton was at the epicenter of the fruitless Whitewater investigation, a Republican-inspired inquiry into a decade-old land deal in which the Clintons had been involved in Arkansas. As such, she became the only first lady to be subpoenaed by a federal grand jury. Although years of probing and $50 million of taxpayers' money went into the Whitewater inquiry, neither Clinton was found to have engaged in any illegal activity. Unfortunately, however, Whitewater revealed a sexual dalliance between Bill Clinton and a White House intern, Monica Lewinsky, that mortified Hillary Clinton and led to the president's impeachment in December 1998. While Mrs. Clinton's allegation that the persecution of her and her husband was the result of a "vast right-wing conspiracy" may have been hyperbole, there can be little doubt that the Clintons were subjected to endlessly harsh scrutiny and criticism, particularly by Republicans and other detractors.

In 2000 the Clintons purchased a home in New York, and Hillary Clinton ran for the state's senatorial seat that was being vacated by retiring U.S. senator Daniel Patrick Moynihan. Clinton was at first running against popular New York City mayor Rudolph Giuliani, and many believed that her chances of winning were not good. But after Giuliani dropped out of the race because of health problems, Clinton—now running against Rick Lazio, a relatively unknown congressman—was virtually assured a win. Clinton won the election by an impressive 12-point margin and took office in January 2001.

During her first term Clinton maintained a relatively low profile but garnered high marks for her intellect, excellent grasp of issues, and willingness to work in a bipartisan manner. Following the September 11, 2001, terror attacks on the United States, Clinton strongly backed the George W. Bush administration's response, including Operation ENDURING FREEDOM in Afghanistan and the 2001 Patriot Act. In October 2002 Clinton voted with the majority to grant the Bush administration authority to wage war in Iraq to enforce United Nations (UN) resolutions should diplomacy fail. She did not support an amendment that would have required another congressional resolution to invade Iraq. Meanwhile, Clinton visited both Afghanistan and Iraq to gauge the effectiveness of the U.S. war efforts there.

By 2005, already planning a run for the presidency in 2008, Clinton began to publicly criticize the Iraq war effort, noting the growing insurgency and the absence of firm plans to either extricate the United States from Iraq or quash the insurgents. She was careful to state, however, that a precipitous withdrawal was unwise if not dangerous, a position that chagrined many antiwar Democrats. Clinton did not back any of the Bush tax cuts, viewing them as economic grenades that would derail the economy, nor did she vote for Bush's two Supreme Court nominees, John Roberts and Samuel Alito.

In November 2006 Clinton, now quite popular with New York voters, won a landslide reelection. In early 2007 she began transferring leftover funds from her Senate race to her presidential campaign. On January 20, 2007, she announced her intention to form an exploratory committee for the 2008 presidential contest. That same year, she refused to support the Bush administration's troop surge in Iraq and backed unsuccessful legislation that would have forced the president to withdraw troops from Iraq based on a predetermined time line. Forced to deal with her affirmative vote for the Iraq War, Clinton now had to explain that she probably would have voted against the 2002 resolution had she been privy to accurate and reliable intelligence. Her position change left many wondering why she had taken so long to come to such a conclusion.

By the autumn of 2007 Clinton seemed the person to beat amid a large Democratic presidential field. Following a mediocre performance in a debate in October, Clinton's momentum began to slip. After placing third in the January 2008 Iowa caucus, Clinton's campaign began to slowly unravel as Senator Barack Obama made significant inroads with Democratic voters. After waging a well-run and valiant campaign, Clinton finally dropped out of the race on June 7, 2008, and endorsed Obama's candidacy. In 2009 Obama nominated Clinton as secretary of state, and she was subsequently confirmed in that position by the Senate. After assuming the office, she widely traveled the globe and was particularly active in initiatives to repair U.S. relations with Western Europe and Russia that had deteriorated since the 2003 invasion of Iraq.

Paul G. Pierpaoli Jr.

See also: Bush, George Walker; IRAQI FREEDOM, Operation

Further Reading

Bernstein, Carl. *A Woman in Charge: The Life of Hillary Rodham Clinton*. New York: Knopf, 2007.

Clinton, Hillary Rodham. *Living History*. New York: Simon and Schuster, 2003.

Coalition Provisional Authority

Established in May 2003, the Coalition Provisional Authority (CPA) was the head

diplomatic office for the coalition occupation of Iraq. It was both an international body and an office of the U.S. government. Paul Bremer, head of the CPA, would become associated with two of the most noteworthy actions of the early occupation, the de-Baathification policy and the decision to dissolve the Iraqi military. These two events spurred the insurgency in Iraq and affected the occupation throughout the rest of the conflict. The CPA existed until June 28, 2004, when Iraq became a fully sovereign nation after the authority's dissolution.

The CPA replaced the Office of Reconstruction and Humanitarian Assistance (OHRA), headed by Jay Garner. The CPA had the approval of the United Nations (UN) Security Council through its resolutions 1483 and 1511 that recognized the occupation authority of both the United States and Britain. These resolutions made the CPA the official organization in charge of administering the occupation. Under U.S. law the CPA derived its authority from the Emergency Supplemental Appropriations Act for Defense and for the Reconstruction of Iraq and Afghanistan, which was passed in 2003. This meant that the CPA had both international and U.S. authorization to create and implement policies to direct the actions of American and international forces in Iraq.

The CPA had direct oversight over many domestic departments, including the directors of oil policy, civil affairs policy, economic policy, regional operations, security affairs, and communications. In addition, the CPA had a general counsel compromised of a military staff, operations support group, executive secretariat, strategic policy office, and financial oversight group. It also had its own intelligence organization. Ambassador Bremer had authority over the chair of the

International Coordination Council, the body that organized humanitarian assistance from nongovernmental organizations and the United Nations.

One problem with the organization of the CPA was the lack of direct control over military forces in Iraq. Although Ambassador Bremer was the senior U.S. civilian in the nation, he did not have any direct military authority. He could not order military forces to focus on any particular region or conduct any specific type of mission. He could coordinate or communicate his requirements and although he was the head U.S. and international official in Iraq, he had no command authority. This meant that the CPA had difficulty achieving one of its four fundamental objectives, which were security, governance, economic, and essential services.

Iraqis did participate in the CPA, albeit in a limited fashion. The Iraqi Governing Council (IGC) acted as an advisory body to the CPA. It could not veto legislation and, initially, functioned as more of a pro forma approval body. A point of concern was that Bremer's policies carried the full weight of law inside Iraq; this caused much frustration in the IGC. However, as the CPA's administration in Iraq continued, the IGC grew more confident and began to demand more input and authority over policies and laws considered by the CPA. This led to a deterioration of the CPA's efficiency but a rise in Iraqi sovereignty.

The first actions of the CPA included changes in the nation's currency, dissolution of the military, and elimination of Baath Party officials from most government posts. The two most problematic policies, the dissolution of the military and the de-Baathification policy, did not go through any Iraqi legislative process. The de-Baathification and dissolution of the

military policies were the most far-reaching of the CPA policies and had serious second and third order effects on the future of the occupation mission in Iraq.

The decision to destroy the Baath Party came on May 16, 2003. This order was the first Bremer gave as head of the organization. The actual decision to remove party officials from government posts and destroy the Baath Party came from Washington. Douglas Fieth, head of the Department of Defense Office of Special Plans, drafted the policy. Supporters of the policy included Iraqi exiles, Shia groups, and Kurds inside Iraq. For these groups, the Baath Party represented the worst of the Saddam regime and was inextricably linked to the horror of his rule.

When Bremer announced the policy, he included a caveat that his office could issue exemptions. Many Sunnis feared that de-Baathification would turn into a sectarian program to remove Sunnis from government posts and other positions of influence. The de-Baathification policy also overlooked the reality of life in Iraq and the power of the Baath Party. Many Iraqis under Saddam had to join the party in order to keep their jobs, earn promotions in government service, or get hired for certain government positions. Although Bremer's authority allowed him to offer exemptions, this would prove difficult. If he were too lenient, the policy would not have the desired effect. If he were too hard, he would alienate many of the Sunnis in the country and drive them away from participation in a new Iraq.

The dissolution of the Iraqi military was the second of Bremer's most influential decisions. This policy immediately left approximately 400,000 people unemployed. It also discounted the almost cult-like status that the Iraqi military had in the culture of Iraq. The military was the body that protected the nation from Iran and protected the Arab world from the threat of Persian invasion. Under Saddam the military was a force that unified the people of Iraq. Dissolving this organization was a blow not only to the almost half a million soldiers employed by it, but also the identity of Iraq as a nation.

The CPA was short lived; it ended its existence in June 2004 with the resumption of Iraqi sovereignty. Its two major policy decisions, the dissolution of the military and de-Baathification, set the stage for the growing insurgency by alienating many Sunnis from the new government, which Shias controlled. It accomplished its stated mission by turning over authority to an Iraqi government in the middle of 2004. However, it did not leave the new government of Iraq a smooth path forward as it struggled to deal with the budding insurgency and growing sectarian strife.

Gates Brown

See also: Baath Party; Bremer, L. Paul, III; Hussein, Saddam

Further Reading

Allawi, Ali. *The Occupation of Iraq: Winning the War.* New Haven, CT: Yale University Press, 2007.

Bensahel, Nora. *After Saddam: Prewar Planning and the Occupation of Iraq.* Santa Monica, CA: RAND Arroyo Center, 2008.

Sanchez, Ricardo, and Donald Philips. *Wiser in Battle: A Soldier's Story.* New York: Harper Collins, 2008.

Coercive Interrogation

Methods of interrogation meant to compel a person to behave in an involuntary way or reveal information by use of threat, intimidation, or physical force or abuse. In particular, coercive interrogation has been used during the U.S. Middle Eastern wars to obtain information from prisoners, especially those being held as terrorists. Coercive interrogation has been labeled by numerous individuals and organizations as inhumane torture and war crimes that violate international law. In addition, coercive interrogation has been criticized by many for being ineffective; critics contend that it leads to false confessions.

There are various techniques of interrogation that can be described as coercive, including, sleep deprivation, food deprivation, ceaseless noise, sexual abuse, forced nakedness, cultural humiliation, exposure to extreme cold, prolonged isolation, painful postures, beating, and waterboarding. Waterboarding, a highly controversial interrogation method, involves positioning a victim on his or her back, with the head in a downward position, while pouring water over the face and head. Soon, as water enters the nasal passages and mouth, the victim believes that drowning is imminent. Waterboarding is a favored interrogation technique because it leaves no visible marks on the victim and can be very effective in extracting confessions.

During the 1991 Persian Gulf War, records indicate that the U.S. military generally abided by international law concerning treatment of civilian and military detainees. However, there is ample evidence that Iraqis tortured American prisoners of war (POWs) by employing numerous coercive interrogation techniques. Coercive interrogation became a much larger issue during the George W. Bush administration after the Global War on Terror began in 2001. Although many international agreements signed by the United States forbid torture, President Bush, Vice President Richard Cheney, and the administration supported the use of coercive interrogation in the

Global War on Terror, the Afghanistan War, and the Iraq War. After the September 11, 2001, terrorist attacks on the United States, the Bush administration acknowledged a need for new interrogation techniques.

Shortly after the September 11 attacks, the Bush administration worked to gain support for coercive interrogation techniques and began to change the definition of torture to better suit its needs. Numerous senior officials believed that the Central Intelligence Agency (CIA) had to employ coercive interrogation techniques to deal with al-Qaeda suspects and other terrorists. The administration then began to devise arguments for going against prevailing prescriptions vis-à-vis torture. First, Bush believed that as commander in chief he could use the inherent powers given to him in the U.S. Constitution to stretch U.S. policy to best protect the citizens of the United States. The administration argued repeatedly that terrorism is a major threat that cannot be fought with conventional means. Also, the White House repeatedly stated that coercive interrogation is not torture in the strict sense of the word. Most legal scholars on the subject disagree with this assessment.

Beginning in 2004 accounts surfaced of Iraqi prisoners being abused by U.S. soldiers in the Abu Ghraib Prison in Iraq. Pictures showing U.S. military personnel abusing and violating prisoners by various means proved highly incendiary. Some methods used included urinating on prisoners, punching prisoners excessively, pouring phosphoric acid on prisoners, rape, forcing prisoners to strip nude and attaching electrodes to their genitals, and photographing prisoners in compromising positions to humiliate them. Eventually, 17 soldiers and officers were removed from duty because of the Abu Ghraib scandal; some eventually faced criminal charges and trial.

The situation was compounded when the CIA was accused of having destroyed evidence of the torture of civilian detainees in 2005. There were apparently two videotapes (subsequently destroyed) that contained images of al-Qaeda suspects being tortured. By 2007 the CIA admitted to some use of coercive interrogation. However, the agency admitted that this had happened rarely and that techniques such as waterboarding were used fewer than five times. In a television interview in December 2008, Vice President Cheney admitted that he had supported the use of water-boarding. More allegations of CIA-sponsored torture surfaced, but the Bush administration stuck to its support of coercive interrogation techniques, asserting that they were not cruel and unusual, and therefore did not constitute torture. Nevertheless, under considerable pressure, Bush signed an executive order in July 2007 forbidding the use of torture against terror suspects; it did not, however, specifically ban waterboarding.

In early 2008 waterboarding was again a hot topic as Congress considered an antitorture bill designed largely to limit the CIA's use of coercive interrogation. The bill, which was passed in February 2008, would have forced the CIA to abide by the rules found in the *Army Field Manual on Interrogation* (FM 34-52). The manual forbids the use of physical force and includes a list of approved interrogation methods; waterboarding is not among them.

Arizona senator John McCain, who had been brutally tortured as a POW during the Vietnam War and had already engaged in a war of words with the Bush White House over the use of torture, voted against the bill. McCain, in defending his vote, argued that the CIA should have the ability to use techniques that are not listed in the *Army Field Manual on Interrogation*. He argued that other available techniques are effective, and not cruel and unusual. He continued to claim, however, that waterboarding is torture and illegal. Bush vetoed the February 2008 bill, and its proponents did not have the requisite votes to override it.

Arthur M. Holst

See also: Abu Ghraib; Bush, George Walker; Central Intelligence Agency

Further Reading

Bellamy, Alex J. "No Pain, No Gain? Torture and Ethics in the War on Terror." *International Affairs* 82 (2006): 121–148.

Dershowitz, Alan M. *Is There a Right to Remain Silent? Coercive Interrogation and the Fifth Amendment after 9/11.* Oxford: Oxford University Press, 2008.

Guiora, Amos N. *Constitutional Limits on Coercive Interrogation.* New York: Oxford University Press, 2008.

Posner, Eric A., and Adrian Vermeule. *Terror in the Balance? Security, Liberty, and the Courts.* New York: Oxford University Press, 2007.

Containment Policy

Key U.S. foreign policy strategy during the Cold War that was also applied in the Middle East. It is impossible to understand the origins and course of the Cold War without comprehending the policy, or doctrine, of containment. The concept can be traced back to February 1946 when George F. Kennan, deputy head of the U.S. mission in Moscow, sent an 8,000-word telegram to Secretary of State James F. Byrnes. In the message, dubbed the "Long Telegram," Kennan provided both an analysis of Soviet behavior and a diplomatic strategy to deal with Moscow. Arguing that "at the bottom of the Kremlin's neurotic view of world affairs is the instinctive Russian sense of insecurity," Kennan went on to suggest that Soviet leader Joseph Stalin required a hostile international environment to legitimize his autocratic rule. Kennan also asserted that the Marxist-Leninist ideology upon which Stalin had built his regime contained elements of a messianism that envisioned the spread of Soviet influence and conflict with capitalism. The only way to stop the communist contagion, Kennan opined, was to strengthen Western institutions, apply appropriate counterforce when needed, and wait for the Soviet system to either implode under its own weight or sufficiently mellow so that it could be rationally bargained with. In short, the Soviets were to be contained. Kennan, however, was not at all specific as to how containment was to be achieved.

Although U.S. policy toward the Soviets had already begun to take on elements of containment, Kennan's missive struck like a lightning bolt in Washington. Indeed, Secretary of the Navy James Forrestal immediately took note of the telegram and used it as further justification for his own hard-line views of the Soviet Union. Kennan returned to Washington something of a hero to anti-Soviet hawks in the Harry Truman administration and became the first director of the U.S. State Department's policy planning staff. Kennan served in that capacity from April 1947 to December 1949.

In the meantime, the containment policy continued to gain traction. The first public invocation of the strategy came in March 1947. Concerned about the communist insurgency in the Greek civil war and instability in neighboring Turkey, Truman addressed a joint session of Congress, ostensibly to request aid money for Greece and Turkey. Clearly echoing Kennan's Long Telegram, Truman stated in what became known as the Truman Doctrine that we must "support free peoples who are resisting attempted subjugation by armed minorities or by outside pressures." The United States had now taken on the responsibility of helping any nation fighting against communism.

Next came the June 1947 announcement of the Marshall Plan (of which Kennan was the chief architect). The Marshall Plan aimed at fostering European reconstruction. But it was also a program clearly aimed at containing Soviet influence and keeping it out of Western Europe. In July 1947 Kennan anonymously wrote an article for the influential journal *Foreign Affairs*. Dubbed the "X" article for its supposed anonymity, it went even further than Kennan's earlier telegram. Using somewhat alarmist language, Kennan asserted that U.S. policy toward the Soviets must be a "patient but firm vigilant containment of Russian expansive tendencies." The "X" article gave full voice to containment, although Kennan would soon argue that policy makers had unnecessarily militarized the idea.

In November 1948 Truman approved a top-secret memo (NSC-20/4) from the National Security Council (NSC) that made the containment of Soviet influence a key precept of American foreign policy. The formation of the North Atlantic Treaty Organization (NATO) in April 1949 further entrenched containment. But up until 1950 containment was largely limited to economic and institutional mechanisms. The Korean War changed that forever. In April 1950 the NSC produced what is considered one of the seminal documents of the early Cold War. This report, known as NSC-68, was a call to arms. It presented in stark terms the low level of U.S. military capabilities while playing up Soviet motives and capabilities. The NSC claimed 1954 to be the "year of maximum danger," a time during which the Soviet Union would possess sufficient nuclear and conventional military capacity to launch a catastrophic strike against the United States. The only way to avoid such a possibility was to embark on a massive rearmament program. Truman shelved the project because the political environment would not have tolerated such an expensive program.

After the Korean War began in June 1950, however, the political climate had indeed changed. Truman approved NSC-68 in September, and the nation undertook a massive and permanent mobilization, allowing it to react to crises anywhere in the world. Containment was now fully militarized and would remain so (although defense budgets would wax and wane) until the end of the Cold War. Containment not only produced a permanent and large military establishment—not to mention a constantly expanding nuclear arsenal—but also informed policy makers' thinking toward all type of foreign threats. Indeed, the domino theory, a corollary of sorts to containment, can be traced to the Truman years, although it became de rigueur under Dwight Eisenhower and his immediate successors. Concerned that communist insurgencies in Indochina would result in a domino effect in which one nation after the other would fall to what was incorrectly assumed to be a monolithic communist empire controlled by Moscow, U.S. policy makers decided to hold the line in Vietnam. Ultimately, this thinking helped bring the long and tortuous debacle of the Vietnam War. The domino theory was also applied in other areas where communist advances were feared, including Africa, Central and South America, and the Middle East.

As the U.S. containment policy matured, critics from both sides of the political spectrum attacked it. Many on the Left, epitomized by Franklin D. Roosevelt's former vice president, Henry Wallace, attacked the policy from a moral standpoint, arguing that the United States was acting hypocritically by seeking to impose a stringent moral code on the Soviet Union that America itself often did not live up to. In effect, Wallace argued that the United States was not good enough to hold the Soviet Union to a standard of behavior that the United States was unwilling to apply to its own actions. Critics on the Far Right were just as vocal but argued that containment did not go far enough in rolling back communist global gains. Merely containing the spread of communism, many on the Right claimed, was a totally defensive measure that gave tacit acceptance by Washington of the status quo. Those espousing this position demanded that the United States instead take offensive action to roll back communism, regardless of the risks involved. Even somewhat more moderate critics, such as Walter Lippman, criticized the containment policy, predicting that the vast expenditure of economic and military resources that must be committed in the attempt to contain communism everywhere in the world would only weaken the United States more than it would harm the Soviet Union. Although these various arguments against containment waxed and waned during the nearly half century of the Cold War, they never completely disappeared.

During the 1970s as détente between the United States and the Soviet Union flourished and with the aftermath of the Vietnam War still fresh in Americans' minds, containment appeared less attractive. During President Ronald Reagan's tenure in office (1981–1989), containment was virtually abandoned. In its place was the belief that the Soviet Union should be defeated rather than merely contained. Reagan attempted to do this by engaging the United States in a major military buildup, announcing his controversial Strategic Defense Initiative (SDI) and signaling his intention to employ American nuclear might against any Soviet advance. The theory behind the approach was that the United States would force the Soviets into bankruptcy by forcing them to keep up with U.S. military advances. In the end the Soviet Union did fall, although it is inaccurate and overly simplistic to suggest that Reagan's policies alone caused the collapse. The Soviet system had within it the seeds of its own destruction. Kennan made that clear 50 years ago. And since Truman's time, every president employed all or part of containment to hasten the demise of the Soviet Union.

While not specifically formulated for the Middle East, the containment policy nevertheless informed U.S. policy in the region. Indeed, between the late 1940s and the end of the Cold War in 1991, the United States built alliances with various Middle Eastern nations in an attempt to check or contain Soviet influence in the region. An example of this was the Baghdad Pact, a treaty of mutual cooperation and mutual defense among the nations of Turkey, Iraq, Pakistan, Iran, and Great Britain agreed to in February 1955. Also known as the Central Treaty Organization (CENTO) or the Middle East Treaty Organization (METO), it was part of a wider effort by the United States and the West in general to establish regional alliances to contain the spread of Soviet influence.

Until the 1979 Iranian Revolution, Iran was the strongest Middle Eastern U.S. ally and the recipient of hundreds of millions of U.S. dollars in aid and military hardware. Saudi Arabia and Israel have also been longtime U.S. allies in the region. The Carter Doctrine, enunciated in January 1980 by President Jimmy Carter, was a direct offshoot of containment. The doctrine held that the United States would employ military force if needed to forestall any threats to shipping or oil supplies in the region. Carter's declaration came at a time in which the Cold War had once more become active and détente had all but collapsed. The Soviets had just invaded Afghanistan, and it was quite clear that Carter was putting the Kremlin on notice that the United States would not permit further Soviet encroachments into the Middle East.

From the end of the Persian Gulf War to the 2003 invasion, the United States pursued a containment policy toward Iraq. No-fly zones in the north and south of the country protected ethnic groups from persecution by Saddam Hussein. International sanctions kept up pressure on his regime. While none of these measures seriously undermined his power within Iraq, they did limit his ability to threaten his neighbors. In the 2000 presidential election, then-governor George W. Bush campaigned against such a policy, arguing Saddam should be removed from power.

Paul G. Pierpaoli Jr.

See also: Bush, George Walker

Further Reading

Acheson, Dean. *Present at the Creation: My Years at the State Department.* New York: Norton, 1969.

Gaddis, John Lewis. *Strategies of Containment: A Critical Appraisal of Postwar American National Security Policy.* New York: Oxford University Press, 1982.

Gaddis, John Lewis. *We Now Know: Rethinking Cold War History.* New York: Oxford University Press, 1997.

Hixson, Walter. *George F. Kennan: Cold War Iconoclast.* New York: Columbia University Press, 1989.

Lafeber, Walter. *America, Russia and the Cold War, 1945–2002.* Updated 9th ed. New York: McGraw-Hill, 2004.

Yergin, Daniel H. *Shattered Peace: The Origins of the Cold War.* New York: Penguin, 1990.

Conway, James Terry

U.S. Marine Corps officer, veteran of Operations DESERT STORM and IRAQI FREEDOM, and the 34th commandant of the U.S. Marine Corps since November 2006. James Terry Conway was born in Walnut Ridge, Arkansas, on December 26, 1947. His family moved back and forth between St. Louis, Missouri, and Walnut Ridge before finally settling in St. Louis in 1958. Conway graduated from Southeast Missouri State University in 1969 and was commissioned a second lieutenant in the U.S. Marine Corps in 1970. His first duty station was Camp Pendleton, California. He then served aboard the aircraft carrier *Kitty Hawk.* Conway next served in the 2nd Marine Regiment and as operations officer for the 31st Marine Amphibious Unit with sea duty in the western Pacific and in operations off the coast of Beirut, Lebanon, in 1983. Returning to the United States, he was for two years senior aide to the chairman of the Joint Chiefs of Staff (JCS). After completing further U.S. Marine Corps schooling in 1990, Conway took command of the 3rd Battalion, 2nd Marines. The next year he commanded the Battalion Landing Team during its eight-month deployment to Southwest Asia as a diversionary unit during Operation DESERT STORM.

In 1993 Conway assumed command of the Marine Basic School at Quantico, Virginia. He was promoted to brigadier general in December 1995. Conway's next assignment was to the JCS. In 1998 he served as president of the Marine Corps University at Quantico. Advanced to major general in 2000, he served as commander of the 1st Marine Division and

Commandant of the Marine Corps General James T. Conway briefs the press on current Marine deployments at the Pentagon, in Arlington, Virginia, on December 15, 2009. (AP Photo/Dept. of Defense, Master Sgt. Jerry Morrison)

was deputy commanding general of Marine Forces Central. In 2002 he was promoted to lieutenant general and assumed command of the I Marine Expeditionary Force, serving two combat tours in Operation IRAQI FREEDOM. In Iraq, Conway's 60,000 men included not only U.S. Marines, but also U.S. Army troops, U.S. Navy personnel, and British Special Forces. His I Marine Expeditionary Force was among the first U.S. forces to enter Baghdad in March 2003 and also formed a key component in Operation VIGILANT RESOLVE in the First Battle of Fallujah in Iraq from April 4 to May 1, 2004.

Conway was advanced to the rank of full general and assumed his current post as commandant of the U.S. Marine Corps on November 13, 2006. Upon assuming his post, he stated that he hoped to provide the nation with a U.S. Marine Corps fully prepared to meet any contingency in keeping with his motto, "Be most ready when the nation is least ready." He also set out to improve the quality of life for marines and their families and to reinstill the core values and warrior ethics that have served the U.S. Marine Corps so well in past conflicts.

Randy Jack Taylor

See also: IRAQI FREEDOM, Operation

Further Reading

Anderson, Jon Lee. *The Fall of Baghdad*. New York: Penguin, 2004.

Brady, James. *Why Marines Fight*. New York: Thomas Dunne Books/St. Martin's, 2007.

Franks, Tommy, with Malcolm McConnell. *American Soldier*. New York: Regan Books, 2004.

Keegan, John. *The Iraq War: The Military Offensive, from Victory in 21 Days to the Insurgent Aftermath*. New York: Vintage, 2005.

Reynolds, Nicholas E. *Basrah, Baghdad, and Beyond: The U.S. Marine Corps in the Second Iraq War*. Annapolis, MD: Naval Institute Press, 2005.

West, Bing, and Ray L. Smith. *The March Up: Taking Baghdad with the 1st Marine Division*. New York: Bantam, 2003.

Counterinsurgency

A warfare strategy employed to defeat an organized rebellion or revolutionary movement aimed at bringing down and replacing established governmental authority. Among the more confusing terms relating to the practice of warfare, the term "counterinsurgency" implies both the purpose of military operations and methods selected. U.S. interest in counterinsurgency soared in 2005 as it became increasingly apparent that an insurgency was gravely undermining the efforts of the United States and its allies to establish a new regime in Iraq after the 2003 Anglo-American–led invasion and occupation. To a lesser degree, a revived Taliban movement has also hindered U.S. progress in nation-building in Afghanistan, and counterinsurgency tactics are being employed there as well.

Understanding the term "counterinsurgency" requires an appreciation of its logical opposite, insurgency. Counterinsurgency originated as a conceptual response to the spread of insurgencies, particularly as carried out by anticolonialist or communist movements during the Cold War from the late 1940s to the 1980s. Insurgents typically lacked key sources of power, such as financial wealth, a professional military, or advanced weaponry, that were available to established regimes or governments. Consequently, insurgents adopted asymmetric tactics and strategies that focused on avoidance of direct combat until such time as governmental power had been gravely weakened. Instead, skillful insurgents blended an array of methods including propaganda, attacks on public institutions and infrastructure, the creation of secret support networks, and use of unconventional or guerrilla combat tactics. By these means, insurgents could whittle away at the strength of existing regimes or occupying powers while slowly increasing their own capabilities.

U.S. interest in counterinsurgency, sometimes referred to as counterrevolutionary warfare, grew during the Vietnam War. Efforts to defeat the Viet Cong guerrillas in South Vietnam were considered important but more often than not took a backseat to the conduct of conventional military operations against the People's Army of Vietnam (PAVN, North Vietnamese Army). With the American withdrawal from Vietnam in 1973, however, the U.S. military resumed focusing on conventional war, and the study of counterinsurgency by the U.S. Army waned. Even with the end of the Cold War in 1991, the U.S. military did not regard the study of counterinsurgency as equally important to the mastery of conventional combat.

To many, Operation DESERT STORM in Iraq in 1991 justified the American focus on conventional combat. The Persian Gulf War provided an awesome demonstration of U.S. military proficiency and technology. Indeed, American dominance was so compelling that it may have dissuaded future potential opponents from attempting to challenge American might on any conventional battlefield. One result of this was perhaps to encourage adversaries to attack U.S. interests by asymmetric means, such as guerrilla insurgency tactics or terror. There was also a growing perception among enemies of the United States that American politicians and military leaders were extremely uncomfortable in situations in which they could not bring superior conventional military power to bear. The deaths of 18 U.S. Army soldiers on October 3 and 4, 1993, during a raid against a renegade warlord in Somalia may have been the exception that proved the rule. Largely a product of events in Somalia, Bill Clinton's casualty-averse posture of U.S. forces in subsequent peacekeeping missions in Haiti, Bosnia, and Kosovo during the 1990s tended to reinforce the view that Americans were reluctant to suffer any casualties in scenarios short of unconstrained conventional combat.

The startling terror attacks on U.S. soil on September 11, 2001, led to a swift reorientation in American military thinking. The immediate American response was to strike against the Taliban regime in Afghanistan that had provided refuge for al-Qaeda terrorists claiming responsibility for the attacks. Informed by its own support for the mujahideen guerrilla resistance to the Soviet occupation of Afghanistan during the 1980s, the United States decided to rely as much as possible on small teams of special operations forces, which would support allied indigenous forces with cutting-edge technologies, rather than on massed conventional forces. The fall of the Taliban regime within three months now placed American forces in the position of stabilizing a fledgling regime under Hamid Karzai.

Very soon the tools of counterinsurgency would prove most relevant in Afghanistan against surviving remnants of the Taliban that found sanctuary along the Pakistani frontier. One important measure taken was the creation and deployment of Provincial Reconstruction Teams (PRTs) beginning in 2003. These combined a small number of military specialists with representatives of various U.S. or other foreign governmental agencies possessing expertise in diplomacy, policing, agriculture, and other fields relevant to the process of fostering security and development. Found to be effective in Afghanistan in extending governmental reach to remote areas, the concept soon found application in Iraq as well.

In the meantime, the invasion of Iraq in March 2003, while initially marking another triumph of conventional operations, did not result in a smooth transition to a stable civilian government. Indeed, coalition forces in Iraq soon faced a formidable counterinsurgency challenge for which neither military nor civilian officials had fully prepared. In fact, many critics maintain that the early failure to establish public order, restore services, and identify local partners provided the insurgency, which Iraqis term "the resistance," with an interval of chaos that enabled it to organize and grow. Since Iraqi politics had consistently shown wave after wave of resistance, purges, and new coups, such a challenge could reasonably have been expected. Sectarian leaders and their militias began to assert influence, and al-Qaeda fighters infiltrated key provinces in anticipation of a new struggle to come.

By 2005 spreading ethnic and religious violence in Iraq resulted in the deaths of many civilians as well as local governmental and security personnel. Suicide bombings as well as the remote detonation of improvised explosive devices (IEDs) became signature tactics of the Iraqi insurgency. Furthermore, repeated attacks on United Nations (UN) personnel and foreign relief workers caused a virtual suspension of outside aid to the Iraqi people.

Recognition of the need to focus on counterinsurgency methods led to a vitally significant effort to publish a military doctrinal manual on the subject. An initial indicator of the official shift in U.S. military thinking was the release of Department of Defense Directive 3000-05 on November 28, 2005, which specifically acknowledged responsibility for planning and carrying out so-called support and stability operations essential to any counterinsurgency campaign. Under the leadership of Lieutenant General David Petraeus during his tenure as commander, Combined Arms Center, and commandant of the U.S. Army Command and General Staff College at Fort Leavenworth, Kansas, in 2006 and 2007, a team of writers and practitioners with experience in Iraq and Afghanistan undertook a crash project to draft, revise, and publish the new manual.

In his opening address to the Combat Studies Institute Military History Symposium on August 8, 2006, Petraeus set forth several points of emphasis of the soon-to-be-published U.S. Army Field Manual 3-24 (also known as U.S. Marine Warfighting Publication No. 3-33.5), titled *Counterinsurgency*. Asserting that T. E. Lawrence (of Arabia) had figured out the essentials of counterinsurgency during World War I, Petraeus contended that any prospect of success depended upon identifying capable local leaders, providing them necessary assistance without doing the hard work for them, fostering the development of public institutions, forming a partnership with existing security forces, and maintaining a flexible and patient outlook. In other words, counterinsurgency would require far more of military leaders than the performance of traditional and familiar combat tasks. Petraeus himself had practiced these principles in Iraq, where in late 2004 he served

as the first commander of the Multi-National Security Transition Command–Iraq, which focused on the training of local personnel to become civilian and military leaders in Iraq.

Officially released in December 2006, *Counterinsurgency* attracted great attention in the press and conveyed the impression that the military was not stuck in an outmoded mind-set. Rather, U.S. Army and U.S. Marine Corps leaders on the ground in Afghanistan and Iraq became increasingly adaptive and creative in the search for improved solutions to the problem of combating insurgency where nation building was still very much in progress. *Counterinsurgency* devoted a majority of its eight chapters and five appendices to tasks other than war fighting. Lengthy sections also related to ethics, civilian and military cooperation, cultural analysis, linguistic support, the law of war, and ethical considerations.

Of course, the U.S. Army and the U.S. Marine Corps had not ignored the principles of counterinsurgency before the new doctrine was published. However, publication signaled to the American public and the U.S. Congress that the military was wholly committed to the implementation of counterinsurgency principles. Since the end of 2007, it would appear that the implementation of this new counterinsurgency doctrine was beginning to bear fruit, as there was a sizable diminution in violence in most parts of Iraq beginning in the fourth quarter of the year.

Robert F. Baumann

See also: Iraqi Insurgency

Further Reading

Keegan, John. *The Iraq War: The Military Offensive, from Victory in 21 Days to the Insurgent Aftermath*. New York: Vintage, 2005.

Kitson, Frank. *Low Intensity Operations: Subversion, Insurgency and Peacekeeping.* London: Faber and Faber, 1971.

Nagl, John A. *Learning to Eat Soup with a Knife: Counterinsurgency Lessons from Malaya and Vietnam.* Chicago: University of Chicago Press, 2005.

Counterterrorism Strategy, U.S.

A general approach toward the struggle against terrorism that involves the selection, distribution, and application of all resources and means available to achieve the desired aims (i.e., the prevention and/or eradication of terrorism). A successful counterterrorism strategy must target the vital dimensions of terrorism; address its current and prospective trends; reflect its rapidly changing nature, complexity, and flexibility; and employ a wide array of military, political, economic, social, ideological, cultural, law enforcement, and other means in often intermingled offensive and defensive efforts.

Terrorist activity, especially from Islamic extremists based in the Middle East, has in recent years demonstrated significantly increasing diversity and complexity. There is a wide range of participants with a diverse set of motivations, goals, structures, and strategies. Despite the destruction of the al-Qaeda sanctuaries in Afghanistan after the September 11, 2001, terror attacks, this global terrorist clearinghouse network continues to operate and, utilizing global information technology, continues to recruit and train supporters, share experiences, coordinate activities of various widely dispersed terrorist cells, and advance its ideological and strategic goals. These include the eradication of Western influence and presence in the region and the overthrow of existing regimes that accommodate the Western powers.

More structured than al-Qaeda, Hezbollah, headquartered in Lebanon, retains some potential for regional and even overseas terrorist activity but currently is concentrating its efforts on securing additional political influence within Lebanon and is not engaging in violence within Lebanon against Lebanese. The Palestinian terrorist organization Islamic Jihad has continued sporadic terrorist activities, mainly within the framework of the Israeli-Palestinian confrontation. Syria and Iran view support for organizations such as Hamas and Hezbollah as a means to promote their own national interests and ambitions in the region.

The successful expansion of transnational terrorism, according to American analysis under President George W. Bush, owes much to the emergence of so-called failed states such as Afghanistan, where such terrorism was able to prosper, virtually unchecked, due to the combination of political and social disintegration, fierce civil strife, and a lack of interest and support from the international community. The concept of a failed state is, however, disputed in the region, where underdevelopment and incomplete political control are commonplace. According to the Western ideas about transnational terrorists, the latter use the paramount anarchy in the failed states as well as weak governmental control over some portions of territory to obtain safe haven and to set up their training camps and communication centers, exploiting the remains of local infrastructure. In the late 1990s al-Qaeda managed to secure a close alliance with the Taliban in Afghanistan. The Taliban, after being driven from power in Afghanistan in 2001, has managed to reestablish itself in certain areas, including the remote Afghanistan-Pakistan border.

Any effective counterterrorism strategy must also take into account new developments in strategy and tactics of the terrorist actors. The terrorists have constantly tried to acquire more lethal weapons. This is particularly true with respect to weapons of mass destruction (WMD). Until 2001 al-Qaeda, using sanctuaries in Afghanistan, planned to launch chemical or biological attacks on U.S. and European targets. In addition to the continuous pursuit of more deadly weapons, the terrorists persistently employ suicide bombings to increase the lethality of their attacks.

Terrorist leaders have also demonstrated their ability to adjust to changing conditions. The decentralized, loose organizational structure of al-Qaeda allowed it to continue to operate even after the loss of Afghanistan in 2001. This has been amply demonstrated in its terrorist attacks in Yemen, Tunisia, Saudi Arabia, Jordan, and Kuwait as well as in Istanbul, Madrid, and London. The U.S. government had argued that al-Qaeda operated a network that recruited and operated in the Muslim communities of Britain, Spain, France, Germany, Italy, Spain, the Netherlands, and Belgium. Current thinking, however, sees al-Qaeda more as an inspiration to and clearinghouse for local groups who are autonomous of it. By active participation in the Iraqi insurgency since 2003, the terrorist networks have also acquired experience in urban warfare and enhanced their skills in ambush tactics, assassinations, and kidnappings.

The profound transformation, both in the scale and the complexity of operations that terrorists could undertake, allowed powerful, well-organized, and devoted groups and associations as well as smaller ones to evade state powers and to obtain global-reach capability. These terrorists are able to endanger the international security profoundly. Because the terrorist challenge amounts to a new form of warfare, successful counterterrorism strategy must

constantly realign itself with the developments of the threats. Conventional military force has played a strong role in the struggle against alleged terrorism, as the long history of Israeli military campaigns against the Palestine Liberation Organization (PLO), the Israeli-Hezbollah War of 2006, and the Gaza War of 2009 demonstrate. Israel's strategy of heavy punishment of a neighboring state for permitting and/or abetting terrorism, while inflicting disproportionate loss of life and property damage, does not seem to have ended terrorist activity, which its proponents regard as rightful and necessary resistance, and has led to serious criticism of the Jewish state, even from its traditional allies.

Special operations forces play an important role in the struggle against terrorism. While capable of a global reach, military operations against terrorists need to be pinpointed and limited in scale to avoid civilian and collateral damage. This is particularly important because of the inability or reluctance of particular governments to attack the terrorist leadership and cells directly. Special operations transcend national boundaries and reflect the transnational character of the struggle against terrorism. The Israeli experience of deep-penetration commando raids and targeted assassinations of terrorist leaders reveals the ability of special operations to undermine the morale and disrupt activities of terrorist organizations and to violate state sovereignty as well as the terms of truces concluded with the enemy, although there are limits to what special operations can accomplish. Primarily, these special operations have angered the local population, making the resistance, or terrorism, that much more difficult to uproot.

Conventional military approaches retain their importance in dealing with state-sponsored terrorism, namely to wage wars against nations and achieve regime change, surely denying safe haven for the terrorists. At the same time, as the U.S.-led campaigns in Afghanistan after 2001 and Iraq after 2003 demonstrated, even victorious conventional campaigns can be complicated by ensuing insurgencies, which demand much greater flexibility on the part of the military. Here again, special operations come into play.

While the achievement of a decisive military victory remains elusive because of the dispersed and decentralized organizational structure of modern terrorism and while the use of military means resembles an endless war of attrition, the readiness to apply overwhelming and destructive military force can work to some extent. As recent changes in the policies of the Palestinian National Authority (PNA) and Libya suggest, providing governmental bodies with enticements to stop terrorist activities can also work to curb terrorist activity. These include economic, territorial, and governing incentives.

Diplomacy is another essential tool in fighting terrorism. International cooperation is vital in collecting information on terrorist cells, which includes tracking and disrupting financial transactions, recruitment, and propaganda activities of the terrorists. It is also of paramount importance in seeking to isolate regimes that sponsor terrorism.

Intelligence gathering is essential in any successful counterterrorist strategy. Simply gathering the information is not sufficient; it must be properly disseminated and coordinated within government agencies. The failure of the U.S. intelligence community to provide early warning about the September 11 terrorist attacks demonstrates this all too clearly.

Defensive efforts within the framework of counterterrorism strategy focus predominantly on homeland security and encompass enhanced border security. This includes monitoring and protecting likely terrorist targets (transportation, communication systems, and other elements of infrastructure as well as high-profile objects and places of significant concentration of populations) using intelligence, law enforcement, and military means. While Israel over the years has dealt with existential threats by developing comprehensive, integrated, and highly effective systems of territorial defense, the United States and European countries remain vulnerable to terrorist attacks because of porous borders and/or the ability of the Islamic terrorists to strike from inside, mobilizing militants from the Muslim diaspora, particularly in Western Europe. While the Western democracies' domestic counterterrorism strategies have improved vastly since September 11, 2001, they still remain deficient compared to those of Israel.

Comprehensive and multifaceted counterterrorism strategies must also involve political efforts to mobilize domestic support, social and cultural efforts to resist extremist propaganda efforts, and a determination to resolve problems and issues that terrorists often use for their own advantage. This is perhaps the most challenging aspect of any successful counterterrorism strategy. Political activities should include the resolving regional disputes, especially the Israeli-Palestinian issue; advancing economic development; addressing economic inequality and poverty; and promoting democracy, high-quality governance, and the rule of law.

Peter J. Rainow

See also: Bush, George Walker; Iraqi Insurgency; Weapons of Mass Destruction

Further Reading

Berntsen, Garry. *Human Intelligence, Counterterrorism, and National Leadership: A Practical Guide.* Washington, DC: Potomac Books, 2008.

Davis, Paul K. *Deterrence and Influence on Counterterrorism: A Component in the War on al-Qaeda*. Santa Monica, CA: RAND Corporation, 2002.

Forrest, James J. F. *Countering Terrorism and Insurgency in the 21st Century*. 3 vols. Westport, CT: Praeger Security International, 2007.

Freedman, George. *America's Secret War: Inside the Worldwide Struggle between America and Its Enemies*. New York: Broadway Books, 2004.

Guiora, Amos N. *Global Perspectives on Counterterrorism*. New York: Aspen Publishers, 2007.

Rubin, Barry, and Judith Colp Rubin, eds. *Anti-American Terrorism and the Middle East*. New York: Oxford University Press, 2002.

Cultural Imperialism, U.S.

The term "cultural imperialism" refers to the process of imposing cultural values onto another culture or entity, often for the purposes of assimilation and political domination or long-term economic ties. It is also seen in policies that assume that the cultural values of the dominant country are the norm, while those of another culture are deviant, traditional, or less desirable. The ambiguity in defining this term in relation to the Middle East stems from the highly politicized attitudes of the West toward the Middle East, coupled with an almost total ignorance of the region's cultures. A similar Middle Eastern lack of sustained contact with and knowledge of the United States and distrust of its political motives in the region exists, as well as a long-standing embrace and defense of traditionalism.

Imperialism implies the extension of power over another entity for exploitative purposes. Typically, this term is used in reference to empires, colonies, nations, and states. Culture generally refers to patterns of human activities and symbolic expressions. So while imperialism takes the forms of military hostilities, political dominance, or economic leverage, cultural imperialism is a more subtle process achieved mainly through symbolism, language, education, and meaning via consumer products, civil institutions, and the media.

Since at least the turn of the 20th century, some have labeled the United States a cultural hegemon that practices the transmittal of cultural imperialism through both government-sponsored means as well as private enterprise. Indeed, the concept of American exceptionalism, the idea that the U.S. democratic political system represents not only the best of all systems but should stand as an example, a "shining city on a hill" for other countries to emulate, dates back to the founding of the Republic. Much of this American attitude was embodied in President Woodrow Wilson's Fourteen Points, his plan to remake the post–World War I world by calling for self-determination of peoples and representative institutions. Nationalists throughout the Middle East embraced Wilson's program. At the same time, they saw no need to give up their own cultures.

Most Middle Eastern populations, while they had had little contact with Americans, had experienced extensive cultural imperialism accompanied by political manipulation at the hands of French, British, Italian, and other European nations. Thus in the case of Egypt, everything that was native Egyptian, or *baladi*, was degraded, whereas that which was foreign—of Turko-Circassion origin or Levantine, French, or British—was prized. Those who embraced the occupying foreigners and their cultures secured special legal and economic privileges through the capitulatory treaties.

The impact of Western cultural influences in the Middle East accelerated rapidly after World War II with the advent of modern communication and transportation technologies that figuratively shrank the world. The sheer size and dominance of the U.S. economy in the decades after World War II ensured that American cultural values would spill into all corners of the globe, mainly through the media and consumerism. In the Middle East, as in other parts of the Third World, this influence mostly impacted the upper elites, but it also coincided with new governmental policies and national pride in indigenous language, customs, traditions, and the arts. Many countries in the region sought to overcome disadvantageous balances of trade, which accompanied colonial suppression of native industries. Many people saw and wanted American products, and they tried to buy them whenever possible. However, these came with heavy tariffs, as certain governments, such as Egypt until 1974 and Syria, applied protective policies so as to bolster indigenous industries and agricultural products. Western foods and customs of eating more protein-rich foods such as red meat and chicken often displaced local consumption patterns as Western-style one-stop supermarkets replaced traditional markets.

As far as social culture was concerned, the worlds of the Middle East and the United States and other Western nations were at polar opposites. Many in the Middle East did not understand or wish to replicate American individualism and societal independence, a tradition in which people live at great distances from their relatives, may marry or not as they choose, have relationships outside of marriage without censure, and are not expected to care for their parents in old age.

Many young people in the Middle East, however, embraced American popular culture, products, and business methods. In a number of countries, the United States Information Service offered English classes and general programs about the United States and American culture, which were very popular. At the same time, however, Arab populations were in general critical of U.S. Middle Eastern foreign policy that appeared to offer unconditional support to Israel or that, even though principally intended to counter Soviet influence in the region during the Cold War, seemed intended to secure American dominance in the region.

In the 1970s the rise of more militant Islamist movements and groups coincided with economic changes that saw a greater influx of imported consumer goods, such as cars and electronic items, from the West, which not all could afford. Conservative and new Islamist groups were specifically critical of the way their nations' elites and youth aped Western styles and overspent to acquire the latest products. Many were highly suspicious of U.S. motives and saw American culture as antithetical to their own basic values.

This theme was the subject of a book in prerevolutionary Iran by Jalal-e Ahmad, which identified *gharbzadeghi*, or Westoxification, as a primary problem. Islamists elsewhere complained of women dressing in Western styles, and Islamic businesses and banks responded to consumers' desire to spend where they would not be contributing to usury.

U.S. cultural imperialism in the Middle East has been most evident in political campaigns and efforts to influence Islamic beliefs and societies since both the September 11, 2001, terrorist attacks against the United States and the commencement of the Iraq War of 2003. It has manifested itself in a battle "to win the hearts and minds" of the Muslim world, specifically in Iraq and Afghanistan, but also to pressure the broader Islamic world to refrain from and reject militant Islamic policies. In this, the so-called Global War on Terror was used as a vehicle for promoting American culture in the region that had given birth to the September 11 terrorists. The basic logic of U.S. cultural imperialism followed that if American values could be brought to bear in radical Islamic societies, then potential terrorists would not hate America.

The official campaigns that involved winning hearts and minds claimed that the United States invaded Iraq in 2003 to overthrow an evil dictator and establish democracy there. However, it was clear to most people in the Middle East that this was a war of choice, waged for other reasons, and many believed that securing Iraq's oil industry was a primary reason.

Americans had promoted democracy, although not its attendant cultural aspects, in a region historically dominated by authoritarian rulers and repressive regimes. However, in the case of key allies, U.S. foreign policy in the region had often downplayed democratization in favor of stability. Thus, the United States had not promoted democracy in Saudi Arabia, nor did it insist that the Shah of Iran democratize or that the Egyptian and Syrian governments do so.

The Middle East was bombarded in the years following 2001 with Western critiques of its culture and deeply held religious beliefs. Such messages of cultural superiority were ill timed, coming as they did after decades of programs aimed to build pride in national and religious identity.

Various U.S. organizations engaged in "information warfare," "information campaigns," or "information operations" and understood that such programs could be the strongest weapons in the Global War on Terror. The processes of this cultural imperialism are manifested primarily through media outlets, with the basic goal of the United States being to expunge the enemy's civil and governmental media, replacing it with its own. For example, Iraqi radio and television stations were one of the first U.S. targets at the beginning of the March 2003 invasion. Iraqis laughed at many of these programs because they had extensive experience with official propaganda under Hussein's regime. The bright side was a mushrooming of many smaller news publications, even though many have been censored.

There were various tangible applications of what results in cultural imperialism by several branches of the U.S. government. The Public Diplomacy and Public Affairs Office conceived of promoting positive images of the United States to the Arab/Muslim world after September 11. The Office of Global Communications was also created immediately after September 11 by the White House to synchronize official opinion among various organizations like the Central Intelligence Agency (CIA), the Department of Defense, and the State Department. The Advertising Council of America, a World War II creation, formulated positive television advertisements for the White House. As per military operations, press agencies called Coalition Information Centers were created in November 2001 by the U.S. government to ensure that official opinions were aired during Operation Enduring Freedom in Afghanistan.

During the Iraq War, coalition air forces dropped leaflets with the intention of warning civilians of upcoming military dangers or to threaten Iraqi military forces of the dire consequences of resisting. The U.S. Department of Defense converted all Iraqi television stations into the al-Iraqiyya Network, while the State Department created a satellite and cable network, known as 911, for promoting American-friendly programming. Many other organizations also performed information operations funded annually by the federal government.

A more extensive example of an American information operation can be seen through Radio Sawa (Sawa meaning "together"). This station broadcasts in FM and medium-wave frequencies, day and night, to Middle Eastern and North African countries. It replaced the Voice of America in the region, which was never as popular as the BBC radio service. It took advantage of new rules that permitted establishment of private FM radio stations; in the past, all were state controlled. Syria and Saudi Arabia have not yet liberalized their radio station practices.

Listeners can also tune in to Radio Sawa via the Internet. Its stations are located in Washington, DC, and Dubai, United Arab Emirates (UAE). In addition, Radio Sawa has several news centers in the region. The broadcast language is Arabic, and the content consists of information and entertainment programs friendly to American culture. It broadcasts a strange mix of Arabic, American, and Spanish music. It is a service of U.S. International Broadcasting, which is organized, managed, and funded by the Broadcasting Board of Governors, an agency of the State Department under the supervision of the U.S. Congress. The station is meant to counterbalance the frequently anti-American Arabic news organizations. However, its impact is minimal in much of the region, where, like the decidedly unpopular American-created Alhurra (al-Hurra) television satellite channel, it is regarded as a propaganda outlet. Actually, far more popular than Radio Sawa are

many smaller radio stations, some of which focus on Arabic musical heritage and now broadcast hard-to-find recordings, more popular types of music, or controversial news programs.

Despite American efforts, positive Arab sentiments toward the United States decreased with exposure to information warfare. Prior to the attacks of September 11, 2001, the Arab world was already resentful of American financial and moral support of Israel. However, immediately after Third World, most moderate Arabs expressed genuine sympathy for American suffering and support for the Global War on Terror. This did not last long, however, as antipathy toward the United States skyrocketed in the wake of the 2003 Iraq War and the occupation and pacification campaign there. In the absence of a United Nations (UN) resolution calling for armed intervention in Iraq, many in the Arab world viewed the U.S.-led war as illegal, and the mere existence of Iraq's large oil reserves created skepticism toward the motives behind the American-led invasion amid U.S. calls for democracy and freedom. When no weapons of mass destruction (WMD) were discovered in Iraq, many Muslims became even more cynical of U.S. motives. In Iraq, impatience with the continuing presence of American troops has also served to disillusion many who initially welcomed the action.

Many Arabs feared that the U.S. attempt to shape Iraq into a democracy would merely be the opening step in a U.S. effort to transform the entire region. Indeed, some U.S. officials, such as Paul Wolfowitz, had long asserted this to be a U.S. objective. People in the region do not object to democracy, but rather to a pseudo-democracy set up by a foreign government by military means that imposes a particular set of foreign policies on the new government.

Many of the new political leaders in Iraq support the imposition of Islamic law, rather than the Iraqi civil code. Indeed, the Iraqi constitution sets out the role of Islamic law in Iraq. With the intensely Islamist atmosphere in Afghanistan and Pakistan, many American programs, products, and movies are highly controversial and are banned by Islamist conservatives throughout the region. Tying the creation of markets to democratization tends to confuse the issue of cultural imperialism in the Middle East.

Americans tend to believe in the universality of their goods, ideas, and culture, and that, deep within every Iraqi or Afghan, there is an American waiting to leap out. This is not the case.

Dylan A. Cyr and Sherifa Zuhur

See also: Central Intelligence Agency; IRAQI FREEDOM, Operation

Further Reading

Eckes, Alfred, and Thomas Zeiler. *Globalization and the American Century.* Cambridge: Cambridge University Press, 2003.

Harding, Jim. *After Iraq: War, Imperialism and Democracy.* Black Point, Nova Scotia: Fernwood, 2004.

Said, Edward. *Culture and Imperialism.* New York: Knopf, 1999.

Schiller, Herbert. *Communication and Cultural Domination.* New York: M. E. Sharpe, 1976.

Tatham, Steve. *Losing Arab Hearts and Minds: The Coalition, Al-Jazeera and Muslim Public Opinion.* London: Hurst, 2006.

D

Defense Intelligence Agency

Formally established at the direction of Secretary of Defense Robert McNamara on October 1, 1961, the Defense Intelligence Agency (DIA) is the leading intelligence agency for the Department of Defense. The DIA is directly responsible for meeting the intelligence requirements of the secretary of defense, the Joint Chiefs of Staff (JCS), and each of the Combatant Commands. Prior to the agency's establishment, each of the military services collected and analyzed its own intelligence separately and disseminated the intelligence to its own service chiefs, components, and the Unified and Specific Commands (now called Combatant Commands).

The Defense Reorganization Act of 1958, which gave birth to the DIA, sought to reduce the duplication and uncoordinated efforts that derived from those separate efforts. It also hoped to provide integrated intelligence analysis and support to the JCS and secretary of defense. The DIA acquired the mandate for all aspects and phases of the Defense Department's intelligence production except those intelligence-collection platforms and activities specifically assigned to the individual military services.

The 1962 Cuban Missile Crisis was the first major test for the DIA. That crisis was followed almost immediately by the Berlin Crisis. For a new agency, the DIA performed surprisingly well in both instances.

The Vietnam War saw the DIA become the primary authority and coordinating agency for military intelligence related to facilities and infrastructure. In the late 1970s the DIA also became the coordinating agency for any Defense Department relationships with foreign military intelligence organizations. By the 1980s the DIA became the Defense Department's coordinating agency for national collection assets as well as its spokesman before Congress on budgeting and national intelligence production priorities.

Driven by the lessons learned from the Persian Gulf War (Operation DESERT STORM, 1991), the DIA's authority and mission expanded in consonance with America's increasing integration of its military forces into a joint structure and operations. Combatant Command intelligence centers now report their production requirements to and acquire their operating funds from the DIA. Although dissenting intelligence analysis is included in the DIA's coordinated national intelligence assessments, the DIA's assessment has become the dominant one.

The September 11, 2001, terror attacks on the United States perpetrated by al-Qaeda and the sequella from these have placed a spotlight on the DIA and its activities. The September 11 Commission, charged with evaluating America's response to the September 11 attacks, was critical of the DIA's inability to thwart them and called into question its ability to effectively compile and disseminate intelligence information to prevent another such terrorist attack.

Similarly, the DIA has been criticized by the Weapons of Mass Destruction (WMDs) Commission for its role in the faulty

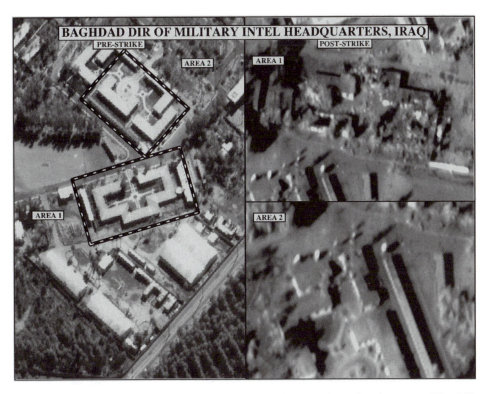

BAGHDAD DIR OF MILITARY INTEL HEADQUARTERS, IRAQ

A Defense Intelligence Agency (DIA) photograph of Iraqi military headquarters. The DIA is the primary producer of strategic intelligence within the Department of Defense. (U.S. Department of Defense)

intelligence surrounding Iraq's alleged WMD program prior to the Anglo-American invasion of Iraq in March 2003. The George W. Bush administration was later embarrassed when no WMD were found in Iraq. Their presence had been one of the key reasons for the invasion. Indeed, both commissions cited the DIA's failure to use open-source and human intelligence sources effectively. In all fairness, however, other intelligence agencies were criticized in similar fashion. The intelligence-gathering reforms based on the commission's recommendations began in 2005 but may not be fully implemented until the end of the decade. In 2005 a new cabinet-level intelligence position was created: director of national intelligence. The director serves as the president's chief intelligence adviser and also serves as principal adviser to the National Security Council and the Department of Homeland Security. As such, the post calls upon the director to coordinate information from the DIA and other intelligence-gathering agencies.

Carl Schuster

See also: Intelligence; Weapons of Mass Destruction

Further Reading

Richelson, Jeffrey T. *The U.S. Intelligence Community.* 4th ed. Boulder, CO: Westview, 1999.

Roberts, Pat, ed. *Report on U.S. Intelligence Community's Prewar Intelligence Assessments on Iraq: Conclusions.* Washington, DC: Diane Publishing, 2004.

21st Century Complete Guide to American Intelligence Agencies. Washington, DC: U.S. Government Printing Office, 2002.

Delta Force

U.S. Army counterterrorism unit. The 1st Special Forces Operational Detachment–Delta (Airborne), officially known as the Combat Applications Group (CAG) and known commonly to the general public as Delta Force, is a Special Operations force of the U.S. Army Special Operations Command (USASOC).

Although the force has diverse capabilities, Delta Force's main task is counterterrorism. Delta Force is widely known for its activities during Operations DESERT SHIELD and DESERT STORM in the Persian Gulf War (1990–1991), Operation RESTORE HOPE (1993) in Somalia, Operation ENDURING FREEDOM (2001), and the U.S.-led Iraqi invasion in March 2003 (Operation IRAQI FREEDOM). It is modeled on other elite counterterrorism forces worldwide, such as the British Special Air Service (SAS), the Australian Special Air Service Regiment (SASR), the Israeli Sayeret Matkal, and Germany's GSG-9.

Delta Force was established in 1977 in response to numerous terrorist incidents that occurred in the 1970s. Its first commander was Colonel Charles Beckwith. From its inception, Delta Force was heavily influenced by the British SAS, a result of Colonel Beckwith's year-long exchange tour with that unit.

The force is organized into three operating squadrons (A, B, and C), which are subdivided into small groups known as troops. Each troop specializes in either HALO (high-altitude low-opening parachute insertion), HAHO (high-altitude high-opening parachute insertion), or scuba (self-contained underwater breathing apparatus) insertion.

The troops can be further divided into smaller units as needed. Delta Force maintains support units that handle selection and training, logistics, finance, and the unit's medical requirements. Within these units is a vital technical unit responsible for maintaining covert eavesdropping equipment.

The Department of Defense doggedly protects detailed information about Delta Force and publicly refuses to comment on specifics about the unit. Delta Force is able to deploy anywhere in the world with 18 hours' notice. Delta Force capabilities include airborne operations; direct action operations; raids; infiltrating and exfiltrating by sea, air, or land; intelligence collection; recovery of personnel and special equipment; and support of general purpose forces.

Delta Force recruits its members solely from the U.S. Army, usually from the army Special Forces, specifically the Green Berets and Rangers. Headquartered in a remote facility at Fort Bragg, North Carolina, Delta Force's compound holds numerous shooting facilities, both for close-range and longer-range sniping; a dive tank, an Olympic size swimming pool; a climbing wall; and a model of an airliner.

Delta Force operatives are granted an enormous amount of flexibility and autonomy. They do not maintain a general uniformed presence and usually wear civilian clothing while on or off duty at Fort Bragg in order to conceal their identity. Hair styles and facial hair are also allowed to grow to civilian standards to allow for greater anonymity. In addition, Delta Force soldiers carry highly customized weapons. While the unit's weapon of choice is the M4 carbine, operatives often carry foreign weapon systems that are used by the enemy in the area of operation. This allows them to remain inconspicuous and to employ the ammunition from slain enemy fighters if necessary.

While Delta Force specializes in counter-terrorism operations, it also engages in hostage rescue. For example, the unit took part in Operation EAGLE CLAW, the failed attempt to rescue the American hostages from the U.S. embassy in Iran in April 1980. The mission failed when a severe sandstorm clogged engine intakes on several U.S. helicopters, forcing them to abort the mission and leaving too few helicopters to successfully complete it. The mission ended in disaster when one of the remaining helicopters and a Lockheed C-130 Hercules transport plane had a midair collision that killed 8 servicemen. After the failure of EAGLE CLAW, the U.S. Army established the 160th Special Operations Aviation Regiment to specialize in the type of air support necessary for special operations.

At the beginning of Operation DESERT STORM in 1991, Delta Force was deployed to the Persian Gulf to serve as bodyguards for senior army officials and to work with British SAS units to search for and destroy mobile Scud missile launchers in Iraq's northern deserts. The primary mission for both the SAS and Delta Force, however, was to locate and designate targets for destruction by coalition warplanes. This contributed immensely to the quick and relatively painless victory of coalition forces in the Persian Gulf War.

Delta Force was also involved in Operation GOTHIC SERPENT in Somalia. That operation led to the Battle of Mogadishu and was later detailed in Mark Bowden's *Black Hawk Down: A Story of Modern War* (1999). In 2001 the unit also played an important role in overthrowing the Taliban regime in Afghanistan in Operation ENDURING FREEDOM, the U.S. military response to the September 11, 2001, terrorist attacks. Two years later Delta Force played a vital role in Operation IRAQI FREEDOM, the Anglo-American operation to oust Iraqi dictator Saddam Hussein from power. Accompanied by Navy SEALS from DEVGRU (the U.S. Navy Special Warfare Development Group), the unit entered Baghdad in advance of the attack to build networks of informants while eavesdropping on and sabotaging Iraqi communication lines.

Charlene T. Overturf

See also: IRAQI FREEDOM, Operation

Further Reading

Beckwith, Charlie A., and Donald Knox. *Delta Force: The Army's Elite Counterterrorist Unit*. New York: Avon, 2000.

Bowden, Mark. *Black Hawk Down: A Story of Modern War*. 1st ed. New York: Atlantic Monthly Press, 1999.

Haney, Eric. *Inside Delta Force: The Story of America's Elite Counterterrorist Unit*. New York: Dell, 2003.

Democratization and the Global War on Terror

The link between democratization and the Global War on Terror has been one of the most controversial elements of post–September 11, 2001, U.S. foreign policy. However, democratization has also been a consistent plank of U.S. foreign policy, especially in the Middle East, although it is more often stated than fully supported. Democratization is the complex process whereby a democracy replaces a non-democratic political regime or pluralism is increased. Free elections for government control, the participation of a legal opposition or multiple parties, the application of equal rights, and the extension of liberal rules of citizenship and laws are typically considered minimum requirements of democratization. In turn, the term "Global War on Terror" may take either of two meanings. First, it may refer to a general state of conflict against violent radicalism, broadly defined. In this sense, the George W. Bush administration contends that democratization is the key to winning the Global War on Terror, especially in the Middle East. Second, the term "Global War on Terror" may refer to a bundle of unilateralist and often forceful security strategies initiated by the United States after the September 11 terror attacks. This interpretation of the Global War on Terror is also closely associated with an assertive promotion of democracy, including by military imposition, as seen in the U.S.-led invasions of Afghanistan (2001) and Iraq (2003). This essay focuses on the second meaning of the term "Global War on Terror."

The notion that democratization enhances national and global security is deeply rooted in the study of international relations as well as U.S. foreign policy. The liberal (sometimes called idealist) approach to international relations views nondemocratic governments as a primary cause of war. Eighteenth-century German philosopher Immanuel Kant proposed that "perpetual peace" requires an alliance of liberal states. Such governments, he reasoned, need the consent of citizens who are averse to the risks of war. In 1917 President Woodrow Wilson justified the U.S. intervention in World War I by condemning traditional balance-of-power politics as the undemocratic "old and evil order" that pushed nations toward war. Future world peace, Wilson asserted, must be founded upon political liberty. When he spelled out U.S. war aims in his Fourteen Points speech of January 8, 1918, Wilson made an international organization of nations one of them. The representatives at the Paris Peace Conference of 1919 set up the League of Nations called for by Wilson, and its

covenant was very much along the lines he proposed. While the U.S. Senate failed to ratify the treaty that would have brought U.S. membership in the League of Nations—and indeed the United States never joined that organization—liberal Wilsonian internationalism continues to influence U.S. foreign policy. President Franklin Roosevelt was a firm believer in Wilsonian principles and continued this approach. Roosevelt was an ardent champion of the successor to the League of Nations, the United Nations (UN), which came into being after World War II.

In recent years scholars have turned to historical evidence to test whether democracies are indeed more pacific than undemocratic regimes. Proponents of the democratic peace theory argue that similar liberal institutions, cultures, laws, and linked economies make democracies especially unwilling to fight each other. Consequently, Michael Doyle argues that liberal democracies have reached a separate peace among themselves, although they remain insecure and conflict-prone toward nations that are not democratic.

Liberal theorists therefore expect that an increase in the number of democracies will expand existing zones of the democratic peace. Not all agree, however, on the full implications to the world system. For example, John Owen argues that a peaceful union of liberal countries would still need nondemocratic states against which to define themselves.

Many notable scholars, particularly those working in the dominant realist tradition of international relations, vigorously dispute the premises of democratic peace theory. They maintain, for example, that the theory neglects how peace among Western democracies during the Cold War was induced by a shared Soviet threat. Moreover, Edward

Mansfield and Jack Snyder conclude that emerging democracies are historically more, not less, war-prone than other states.

Such criticisms aside, democratic peace theory's impact on U.S. policy makers since the 1980s is hard to exaggerate. Proponents, including both Republican and Democratic presidents, presented the 1989 fall of the Berlin Wall, the 1991 collapse of the Soviet Union, and a roughly concurrent rise in the global number of democracies as bellwethers of a freer, more secure international order. Political theorist Francis Fukuyama's famous thesis on the emergence of Western liberal democracy (*The End of History and the Last Man*) as "the final form of government" captured liberalism's optimistic, even triumphal, spirit at the start of the post–Cold War era.

Complicating the picture, however, was the distinctive neoconservative political philosophy that also gained influence in the 1980s, especially within the Republican Party. With the Soviet collapse, neoconservatives contend that the proper role of the United States as the sole remaining superpower is to forge and maintain a benevolent world order. Neoconservatives share liberals' confidence that democracies do not fight each other, but they depart from traditional liberalism by arguing that the United States should shun reliance on international organizations—including the UN, toward which they have much antipathy—in promoting democracy overseas. Rather, the United States should be willing to use unilateral force if necessary to bring democracy to steadfastly nondemocratic states and regions.

Significantly, a public letter from associates of the neoconservative think tank Project for the New American Century urged President William J. Clinton to consider removing Iraqi dictator Saddam Hussein militarily more than three years before the 2001 terror attacks. The 1998 letter was signed by numerous individuals who would go on to occupy top foreign and national security policy posts in the first and second George W. Bush administrations, including Secretary of Defense Donald Rumsfeld, Deputy Secretary of Defense Paul Wolfowitz, Undersecretary of Defense for Policy Douglas Feith, and U.S. representative to the UN John Bolton.

Neoconservative influence became most pronounced after September 11, which the Bush administration framed as an attack on liberal democracy around the world. Shortly after the invasion of Afghanistan, neoconservative speechwriter David J. Frum coined the phrase "Axis of Evil" to describe undemocratic Iran, Iraq, and North Korea for the president's January 2002 State of the Union address. This address was widely seen as setting the stage for further U.S. military action overseas. Other aspects of the Global War on Terror strategy reflect neoconservative precepts, including the Bush Doctrine of preemptive war, the decision to invade Iraq despite strong international and UN opposition, the belief that a lack of democracy in the Middle East fosters terrorism, and the argument that democratization justifies military action.

The ideas of Israeli politician and former Soviet dissident Natan Sharansky also align with neoconservative priorities. In 2005 President Bush praised Sharansky's recent work, which argues that the United States must lead the drive for democratization, as "a great book" that validated his own policies. However, observers note a decline in the more forceful aspects of the administration's prodemocracy rhetoric after Egyptian Islamists made notable gains in 2005 parliamentary elections and the armed Hamas movement won the Palestinian parliamentary elections of January 2006.

Policy makers continue to debate both the desirability of an alliance of democracies and the U.S. role in promoting democracy abroad. Critics of the current strategy linking democratization to national security and the Global War on Terror reflect a number of ideological and theoretical approaches and include former Bush administration officials. They can be divided into three major camps, with frequent overlap. One camp emphasizes pragmatism and feasibility. These critics see efforts to propel democracy via military invasion and occupation as unworkable, fed by false analogies to post–World War II Germany and Japan. They may also judge the strategy counterproductive, arguing that it heightens anti-Americanism and hurts the legitimacy of local prodemocracy groups in target countries. A second camp is rooted in ethical or nationalistic concerns. While some critics label the democratization strategy hypocritical in light of close American ties to Saudi Arabia and other undemocratic states, others assert that neoconservatives in the Bush administration have crafted a Global War on Terror strategy that privileges Israeli over U.S. security concerns. A third camp argues that the Global War on Terror is a veiled and fundamentally antidemocratic attempt to enhance U.S. power in regions rich in important natural resources, such as oil.

The difficulty of installing stable, workable, and effective governments in Afghanistan and Iraq offer a prime example of the problems associated with linking democratization to the Global War on Terror. In nations that have no history of democratic organizations, imposing democracy—even by use of force—is rife with difficulties and contradictions. Furthermore, in nations in which the economic system was either nonexistent (such as Afghanistan) or badly damaged (such as Iraq), the cultivation of democracy is not as important as survival for the great majority of the citizenry. Democracy and widespread poverty and economic and social inequalities do not often go together very well.

Ranjit Singh

See also: "Axis of Evil"; Bush, George Walker; Feith, Douglas; Rumsfeld, Donald Henry

Further Reading

Doyle, Michael W. "Liberalism and World Politics." *American Political Science Review* 80 (December 1986): 1151–1169.

Fukuyama, Francis. *The End of History and the Last Man.* New York: Free Press, 1992.

Kant, Immanuel. *Perpetual Peace, and Other Essays on Politics, History, and Morals.* Translated by Ted Humphrey. Indianapolis: Hackett, 1983.

Mansfield, Edward D., and Jack Snyder. *Electing to Fight: Why Emerging Democracies Go to War.* Cambridge, MA: MIT Press, 2005.

Owen, John M., IV. *Liberal Peace, Liberal War: American Politics and International Security.* Ithaca, NY: Cornell University Press, 1997.

Sharansky, Natan, and Ron Dermer. *The Case for Democracy: The Power of Freedom to Overcome Tyranny and Terror.* New York: PublicAffairs, 2004.

Woodward, Bob. *State of Denial: Bush at War, Part III.* New York: Simon and Schuster, 2006.

DESERT CROSSING, OPLAN

A plan developed in June 1999 to stabilize Iraq in the event of the death or overthrow of Iraqi president Saddam Hussein. Following the liberation of Kuwait in 1991 during Operation DESERT STORM, the United States adopted a Middle East policy based, in part, on dual containment. Dual containment sought to restrain both further adventurism by Iraq and Iran's exportation of its Islamic fundamentalist revolution. With respect to Iraq, Hussein's actions and threats in the years immediately after the Persian Gulf War prompted the United States and its allies to react at least annually with several options—from low-end shows of force to the four-day intensive bombing campaign of December 1998 known as Operation DESERT FOX. For seven years, the Iraqi part of dual containment consisted of a cycle of provocation and response.

Late in 1998 U.S. national security advisor Samuel R. "Sandy" Berger stated in a speech that the United States would eventually remove Hussein from power and would do so with force if necessary. That speech effectively replaced dual containment with a policy of containing Iran while preparing for Iraqi regime change at a time and place of U.S. choosing. Following the speech, commentators and pundits focused on what it meant and how regime change might be accomplished.

The impact on the U.S. Central Command (CENTCOM) was somewhat different. One of the U.S. regional combatant commands, CENTCOM was responsible for U.S. military peacetime operations as well as combat operations in a geographic area that encompasses most of the Middle East, including Iraq.

In CENTCOM'S daily planning directorate staff meeting following the Berger speech, an epiphany of sorts occurred. The question that the planners believed should have been considered long before was what would happen to Iraq absent Hussein (for any number of reasons, including a coup, an accident, or regime-replacement operations) and consequently what would be the command's responsibilities in a potentially unstable situation. Key concerns were how

unstable would Iraq be after two decades of centralized repression and what kind of response would be required to reestablish stability and prevent the potential crisis from spreading beyond Iraq's borders. Thus began a planning effort that resulted in a planning document or operation plan (OPLAN). An OPLAN provides broad concepts of operations versus operational detail. CENTCOM's effort in this regard came to be code-named DESERT CROSSING.

As DESERT CROSSING was developed over the next few months, it became evident that a true interagency response would be required. Intelligence estimates indicated that a post-Hussein Iraq would indeed be highly and dangerously unstable. Probable scenarios included ethnic strife fueled by the emergence of the majority Shia population and disenfranchisement of the ruling but minority Sunnis, retribution against the Sunni Baath Party, and efforts to secure autonomy or even independence by the Kurds in the north. Other possibilities included the emergence of one or more Hussein-like strongmen, interference by outside entities, fierce competition among players within each of the three major Iraqi groups, and the expansion of a separate Kurdish state into Turkey and Iran. Stabilization would require not only military and police forces to provide security, but also the application of numerous instruments of international power, including diplomacy; humanitarian, financial, and technical assistance; facilitation of a rational Iraqi political process; and coordination of the contributions that could be made by nongovernmental organizations (NGOs).

While CENTCOM planners could lay down broad concepts, the best product would result from an interagency effort. CENTCOM leaders believed that the most efficient approach would be a two- to three-day tabletop simulation to test the planners' assumptions and concepts. The resulting DESERT CROSSING seminar, held during June 28 through 30, 1999, brought together senior officials from the State Department, the Defense Department, the National Security Council, the Central Intelligence Agency, and senior officers from the Joint Staff, the CENTOM staff, and the army, navy, air force, and marine commands subordinate to Central Command.

The seminar participants were organized into four groups: two replicated the U.S. interagency process, one represented Iraq, and one represented the international community. The two U.S. groups acted as the principals' committee (cabinet-level officials providing direct advice to the president) and deputies' committee (principals' deputies charged with considering alternative courses of action and making recommendations to the principals). Each of the four groups was presented with information that they would be likely to have in a real-world scenario and was asked to evaluate their options given the ideas contained in the draft OPLAN.

The simulation proved highly successful in developing valuable insights that helped to refine the plan. The key points considered included triggering events that would require U.S. and international intervention; reactions by neighboring states and what should be done about them; the assembling and maintenance of a military coalition; humanitarian concerns involved in an invasion of Iraq; the disposition of the Iraqi military postinvasion; the avoidance of a fragmented Iraq; the synchronization of humanitarian, military, and civilian activities in a postwar environment; and the development of an exit strategy.

The seminar exercise reached the following goals: the end result should be a stable, unified Iraq with effective governance in place and a military capable of defending Iraq's borders but not threatening to Iraq's neighbors; Turkish and Iranian interests must be understood, addressed, and managed, primarily through effective diplomacy; an international coalition would best be built around humanitarian considerations and a stable outcome; NGOs must be included; military and police forces would be required in large numbers to achieve and maintain the long-term broad-based security; and the actual interagency process, in accordance with standing presidential directives, should commence immediately to plan for the eventuality of regime change in Iraq.

OPLAN DESERT CROSSING was modified and refined as a result of the seminar. A planned follow-on seminar did not occur, however, and the revised plan was shelved to be used as a starting point should real-world events dictate an Iraqi invasion or regime change. When Operation IRAQI FREEDOM commenced in March 2003, DESERT CROSSING was largely ignored and was not utilized in the George W. Bush administration's planning.

John Sigler

See also: Bush, George Walker; IRAQI FREEDOM, Operation

Further Reading

Byman, Daniel, and Matthew C. Waxman. *Confronting Iraq: U.S. Policy and the Use of Force since the Gulf War.* Santa Monica, CA: RAND Corporation, 2002.

Clancy, Tom, with Anthony Zinni and Tony Kolz. *Battle Ready.* New York: Putnam, 2004.

Ricks, Thomas E. *Fiasco: The American Military Adventure in Iraq.* New York: Penguin, 2006.

E

Explosive Reactive Armor

Explosive reactive armor (ERA) is a common form of add-on armor employed in many armored fighting vehicles (AFVs) such as tanks. AFVs utilize an armor casing to protect the crew and the machinery against strikes from enemy antitank weapons. The antitank weapons, in turn, work by piercing the armor and killing the crew or damaging hardware and software. ERA is effective only against chemical energy antiarmor weapons such as high-explosive antitank (HEAT) rounds. ERA is not effective against kinetic energy weapons such as sabot rounds.

In the late 1970s the Israel Defense Forces (IDF) developed the new ERA technology to protect AFVs. The concept underlying ERA was accidently discovered in 1967 and 1968 by a German researcher, Manfred Held, who was then working in Israel. Held and his team conducted tests by firing shells at wrecked tanks left over from the 1967 Six-Day War. They noticed that tanks that still contained live ordnance exploded and that this explosion could disrupt the penetration of a shaped charge. This insight led to the manufacture of ERA.

ERA utilizes add-on protection modules, called tiles, made from thin metal plates layered around a sloped explosive sheath. The sheath explodes when it senses the impact of an explosive charge such as a HEAT projectile. By creating its own explosion, the HEAT warhead detonates prematurely, which prevents the plasma jet of molten metal from the shell penetrating into the crew compartment of the AFV. Explosive reactive armor is most effective against HEAT rounds. Once used, an ERA tile has to be replaced.

The early ERA models effectively defended tanks and other AFVs from single strikes. However, after they performed their task, the explosive sheath was spent, leaving the AFV vulnerable to another shell in the same location. More recent reactive armor uses a combination of energetic and passive materials to withstand multiple strikes. These modern designs employ smaller tiles and more complex shapes to offer optimal plate slopes to counter potential threats, including missile warheads, exploding shells, and rocket-propelled grenades (RPGs).

In early 1991 technicians installed ERA on the nose and glacis plate of Challenger 1, the main battle tank of the British Army. Likewise, the U.S. Army Materiel Command applied reactive armor plates to the U.S. Marine Corps M60-series tanks. Since that time, modern AFVs such as the Abrams M-1A2, the British Challenger 1 and 2, and a variety of Russian tanks have all demonstrated excellent protection by using ERA.

New generations of antitank guided missiles continue to pose a threat. In addition, in urban combat such as that which occurred in the Iraq War after 2003, enemy infantry armed with RPGs fired from multiple directions at close range have the potential to overwhelm the target's ERA. One downside to the use of ERA is the potential to harm nearby friendly troops. In times past, infantry soldiers commonly used tanks as a means of transport. They would even ride on the tanks as they entered combat. ERA-equipped tanks made this practice too dangerous.

During the 1991 Persian Gulf War, the Iraqi military fielded almost 6,000 main battle tanks ranging from the obsolete T-55 to the modern T-72. Iraqi tanks lacked ERA. The main Iraqi battle tank, the T-72, had reactive armor but not ERA.

Development of ERA technology has continued. Advanced versions of ERA were based on better understanding of the science associated with ERA systems, and they utilized lower masses of explosives. These considerations have had significant implications on the logistics, storage, and handling of AFVs and protection systems without a reduction in the protection levels. Future ERA models are likely to employ so-called smart armor concepts that will integrate sensors and microprocessors embedded into the armor. These devices will sense the location, type, velocity, and diameter of the projectile or jet and will trigger smaller explosive elements precisely tailored to defeat a specific penetrator.

James Arnold

See also: Iraqi Freedom, Operation

Further Reading

Dunnigan, James F., and Austin Bay. *From Shield to Storm: High-Tech Weapons, Military Strategy, and Coalition Warfare in the Persian Gulf.* New York: William Morrow, 1992.

Hutchison, Kevin Don. *Operation Desert Shield/Desert Storm: Chronology and Fact Book.* Westport, CT: Greenwood, 1995.

Jane's Armour and Artillery, 1990–1991. London: Jane's Information Group, 1990.

Jane's Armour and Artillery, 2001–2002. London: Jane's Information Group, 2001.

F

Fallujah

City located in central Iraq, within the so-called Sunni Triangle, and a center of insurgency activity after the March 2003 Anglo-American–led invasion of Iraq. On the eve of the Iraq War, Fallujah had a population of approximately 440,000 people, the great majority of whom were Sunni Muslims. The city is located along the Euphrates River about 42 miles to the west of the capital city of Baghdad. The city consisted of more than 2,000 city blocks laid out in regular grid fashion. A typical block grid featured tenements and two-story concrete houses surrounded by courtyard walls and divided by narrow alleyways. Highway 10, a two-lane road that runs through the city, becomes a four-lane throughway in the city's center.

The area encompassing Fallujah has been inhabited for many centuries, and its history can be traced back at least as far as the reign of the Babylonian king Hammurabai, during 1780–1750 BCE. After the Babylonian captivity of the Jews and beginning in around 219 CE, the area encompassed by Fallujah became a center of Jewish learning and scholarship that included many Jewish academies. This lasted until around 1050. The city was a crossroads during the many centuries of Ottoman rule.

Following World War I the British established a mandate over the area of Iraq. With a rise of Iraqi nationalism, in April 1941, during World War II, there was a coup that brought Rashid Ali al-Gaylani

to power. He formed a cabinet that contained a number of individuals with Axis connections. Encouraged by hints of Axis aid, Gaylani refused to honor a 1930 treaty that allowed British troops to be transported from Basra across Iraq. The Iraqi government also positioned troops and artillery around British bases in Iraq. In the ensuing fighting, British troops defeated the Iraqi Army near Fallujah.

In 1947 the city had just 10,000 inhabitants, but it grew exponentially in the decades to follow because of Iraq's growing oil wealth, Fallujah's strategic position along the Euphrates, and Iraqi dictator Saddam Hussein's program designed to make it a centerpiece of his power base beyond Baghdad. Many Sunnis from the city held positions within the government, and the ruling Baath Party claimed many important ties to Fallujah. The city came to be highly industrialized under Hussein's rule, although westward-running Highway 1, a four-lane divided superhighway, bypassed the city and caused the city to decline in strategic importance by the early 2000s. Fallujah retained its political importance thanks to the many senior Baath Party members from the area.

During the 1991 Persian Gulf War, bridges spanning the Euphrates River in Fallujah were targeted by coalition aircraft. In the process several markets were hit, resulting in substantial civilian casualties. As many as 200 Iraqi civilians may have been killed in these bombing raids.

During the initial stages of Operation IRAQI FREEDOM, Fallujah remained largely

Members of the U.S. Navy assigned to a mobile construction battalion patrol a Fallujah street one day before the January 30, 2005, national elections in Iraq. (U.S. Navy)

unaffected by the fighting because Iraqi troops who had garrisoned the city fled, leaving considerable military equipment behind. However, as the war progressed and Hussein's regime was toppled, Fallujah was struck by a spasm of violence and looting, with individuals sacking military storage areas, stores, hospitals, and restaurants. To make matters worse, Hussein had released all political prisoners held in the nearby Abu Ghraib Prison, which flooded the area with an assortment of bitter political exiles and criminals who delighted in the anarchy of Fallujah in the spring and summer of 2003. Inhabitants fled the city by the thousands, leaving behind the remnants of their lives and livelihoods. A large percentage of the male population of Fallujah was unemployed, and they proved to be a major source of recruits for the Iraqi insurgency movement. The Iraqis of Fallujah perceived themselves as having

lost the status they had enjoyed under Hussein and believed that they had little to gain in a new governmental system dominated by his former enemies.

In April 2003 U.S. occupation forces finally attempted to exert control over the city, but by then the major damage had already been done, and the city was increasingly anti-American. Sunni rebels had soon taken root in Fallujah, as had foreign insurgents allied with al-Qaeda. Operation VIGILANT RESOLVE (the First Battle of Fallujah), launched in April 2004 by U.S. forces, failed to wrest the city from the insurgents. During November and December 2004 U.S. and Iraqi security forces launched Operation PHANTOM FURY (the Second Battle of Fallujah), a large and bloody affair that caused the insurgents to flee the city. However, the coalition and Iraqi forces had to conduct yet another operation in Fallujah in June 2007.

Since then Fallujah's population has trickled back into the city, but they have returned to a disaster zone. Half of the city's housing was destroyed, much of its infrastructure lay in ruins or disrepair, and city services were absent. Reconstruction has advanced slowly, and it is estimated that almost 150,000 refugees still reside in massive tent cities on the outskirts of Fallujah. In 2009 the Iraqi government estimated the population of the city at 350,000, but Fallujah struggles to return to normalcy.

Paul G. Pierpaoli Jr.

See also: Fallujah, First Battle of; Fallujah, Second Battle of; IRAQI FREEDOM, Operation

Further Reading

Buzzell, Colby. *My War: Killing Time in Iraq.* New York: Putnam, 2005.

Keegan, John. *The Iraq War: The Military Offensive, from Victory in 21 Days to the Insurgent Aftermath.* New York: Vintage, 2005.

Ricks, Thomas E. *Fiasco: The American Military Adventure in Iraq.* New York: Penguin, 2006.

Fallujah, First Battle of

A U.S. offensive, the principal goal of which was to retake the Iraqi city of Fallujah after insurgents had seized control of it. Codenamed VIGILANT RESOLVE, it occurred between April 4 and May 1, 2004. Sunni insurgents, including al-Qaeda fighters, had steadily destabilized Anbar Province in Iraq in the aftermath of the 2003 U.S.-led invasion. Fallujah, located some 42 miles west of Baghdad in the so-called Sunni Triangle, emerged as a focal point for anticoalition attacks. The town was dominated by Salafist groups who were extremely suspicious of all outsiders, particularly foreigners; family and clan ties dominated personal relationships. The collapse of Iraqi president Saddam Hussein's regime had left some 70,000 male inhabitants in the city unemployed, providing a major source of recruits for the Iraqi insurgency movement.

Growing violence in Fallujah in March 2004 led the U.S. military to withdraw forces from the city and conduct only armed patrols. On March 31 insurgents ambushed four contractors working for Blackwater USA, a private contracting company that provided security personnel to the Coalition Provisional Authority (CPA). The insurgents dragged the bodies through the streets and then hanged them from a bridge. Television cameras transmitted the grisly images around the world, prompting a strong response to offset the perception that coalition forces had lost control of the area.

In an effort to regain control of the city and the surrounding province, the U.S. military launched a series of operations against suspected insurgent groups and their bases. The lead unit was the I Marine Expeditionary Force (I MEF), which had been deployed to Anbar in March. The ground forces were supported by coalition aircraft and helicopter units. U.S. lieutenant general James Conway had overall command of the operation. On April 4 some 2,200 marines surrounded Fallujah. They blockaded the main roads in and out of the city in an effort to allow only civilians to escape the fighting. The commanders on the ground believed that the marines should remain outside of the city because they lacked the troops to effectively control the area and the population; nevertheless, they were ordered to seize the city.

In the opening days of the operation, U.S. forces conducted air strikes on suspected targets and undertook limited incursions into Fallujah, including a strike to take control of its main radio station. At least one-quarter of the civilian population fled the city as insurgents used homes, schools, and mosques to attack the marines, who responded with devastating firepower that often produced high collateral damage and civilian casualties.

Within the city there were an estimated 15,000–20,000 insurgent fighters divided among more than a dozen insurgent groups of various origins. Some were former members of Hussein's security forces. They were armed with a variety of weapons, including light arms, rocket-propelled grenades (RPGs), mortars, and improvised explosive devices (IEDs). The insurgents used guerrilla tactics against the marines, including ambushes, mortar attacks, and mines and IEDs. Sniper fire was common throughout the operation. U.S. forces responded with artillery and air strikes, including the use of heavily armed Lockheed AC-130 gunships. Support from Bell AH-1W Super Cobra attack helicopters, however, was limited because of significant ground fire. Meanwhile, the marines attempted to secure neighborhoods one or two blocks at a time using air support and tanks.

There were problems coordinating movements in the dense urban environment, especially because maps were not standardized between the various units. Meanwhile, many of the remaining Iraqi security forces within the city either joined the insurgents or simply fled their posts. After three days of intense fighting, the marines had secured only about one-quarter of Fallujah.

In response to the escalating violence, the failure of the marines to make significant progress in the city, growing pressure from Iraqi political leaders, and increasing domestic pressure on the George W. Bush administration that was largely the result of media coverage, the U.S.-led CPA ordered a unilateral cease-fire on April 9 and initiated negotiations with the insurgent groups. The marines allowed humanitarian aid into the city; however, in spite of the cease-fire, sporadic fighting continued. Throughout the negotiations, it was decided that the United States would turn over security for the city to a newly formed ad hoc Iraqi militia force, the Fallujah Brigade. The United States agreed to provide arms and equipment for the brigade, which included former soldiers and police officers of the Hussein regime.

On May 1 U.S. forces completely withdrew from Fallujah, but they maintained a presence outside of the city at an observation base. More than 700 Iraqis had been killed in the fighting (the majority of these, perhaps as many as 600, were civilians), while 27 U.S. marines were killed and 90 were wounded.

The Fallujah Brigade failed to maintain security and began to disintegrate during the summer of 2004. Many of its members joined or rejoined the insurgency, and the military announced that Abu Musab al-Zarqawi, the leader of al-Qaeda in Iraq, was headquartered in Fallujah. The coalition undertook a second campaign in Fallujah in the autumn of 2004, code-named Operation PHANTOM FURY.

Tom Lansford

See also: al-Qaeda in Iraq; Fallujah; Fallujah, Second Battle of

Further Reading

Afong, Milo. *Hogs in the Shadows: Combat Stories from Marine Snipers in Iraq*. New York: Berkley, 2007.

Cockburn, Patrick. *The Occupation: War and Resistance in Iraq*. New York: Verso, 2007.

O'Donnell, Patrick K. *We Were One: Shoulder to Shoulder with the Marines Who Took Fallujah*. New York: Da Capo, 2007.

West, Bing. *No True Glory: A Frontline Account of the Battle for Fallujah*. New York: Bantam, 2006.

Fallujah, Second Battle of

Major battle fought in and around the city of Fallujah, some 42 miles west of Baghdad, between U.S., Iraqi, and British forces and Iraqi insurgents (chiefly al-Qaeda in Iraq but also other militias). Following the decision to halt the coalition assault on Fallujah in Operation VIGILANT RESOLVE (the First Battle of Fallujah) during April and May 2004, the U.S. marines had withdrawn from the city and turned over security to the so-called Fallujah Brigade, an ad hoc force of local men who had formerly served in the Iraqi Army. The Fallujah Brigade failed dismally in this task, giving the insurgents another chance to claim victory and attract additional recruits. During the summer and autumn months, the Fallujah police turned a blind eye as the insurgents fortified positions inside Fallujah and stockpiled supplies. The Iraqi interim government, formed on June 28, 2004, then requested new efforts to capture and secure Fallujah.

In preparation for the ground assault, coalition artillery and aircraft began selective strikes on the city on October 30, 2004. Coalition ground forces (American, Iraqi, and British) cut off electric power to the city on November 5 and distributed leaflets warning people to stay in their homes and not use their cars. This was a response to insurgent suicide bombers who had been detonating cars packed with explosives. On November 7 the Iraqi government announced a 60-day state of emergency throughout most of Iraq. Because of all these warnings, between 75 and 90 percent of Fallujah's civilian population abandoned the city before the coalition ground offensive began. Many of them fled to Syria, where they remain as refugees.

The Americans initially labeled the assault Operation PHANTOM FURY. Iraqi prime minister Iyad Allawi, however, renamed it AL-FAJR

A U.S. marine at an observation post in Fallujah, Iraq, during Operation NEW DAWN, on November 10, 2004. (U.S. Army)

(New Dawn). The operation's main objective was to demonstrate the ability of the Iraqi government to control its own territory, thereby bolstering its prestige. The American military focused on the important secondary objective of killing as many insurgents as possible while keeping coalition casualties low. About 10,000 American soldiers and marines, and 2,000 Iraqi troops participated in Operation AL-FAJR. Some Royal Marines also took part. The American forces involved had considerable experience in urban combat.

The assault plan called for a concentration of forces north of Fallujah. Spearheaded by the army's heavy armor, army and marine units would attack due south along precisely defined sectors. The infantry would methodically clear buildings, leaving the trailing Iraqi forces to search for insurgents and assault the city's 200 mosques, which coalition tacticians suspected would be used as defensive insurgent strong points. Intelligence estimates suggested that some 3,000 insurgents defended the city, one-fifth of whom were foreign jihadists. Intelligence estimates also predicted fanatical resistance.

Ground operations associated with the Second Battle of Fallujah commenced on November 7, 2004, when an Iraqi commando unit and the Marine 3rd Light Armored Reconnaissance Battalion conducted a preliminary assault. The objective was to secure the Fallujah General Hospital to the west of the city and capture two bridges over the Euphrates River, thereby isolating the insurgent forces inside the city. This preliminary assault was successful, allowing the main assault to commence after dark the following evening. The American military chose this time because it knew that its various night-vision devices would provide it a tactical advantage over the insurgents. Four marine infantry and two army mechanized battalions attacked in the first wave. M-1A2 Abrams tanks and M-2A3 Bradley infantry fighting vehicles provided mobile firepower for which the insurgents had no answer. The M-1A2 Abrams tanks exhibited the ability to absorb enormous punishment and keep operating. The speed and shock of the massed armor overwhelmed the insurgents, enabling the American soldiers to drive deep into Fallujah. Iraqi forces also performed surprisingly well. After four days of operations, coalition forces had secured about half the city.

By November 11 the methodical American advance had driven most of the insurgents into the southern part of Fallujah. Three days of intense street fighting ensued, during which time the Americans reached the southern limits of the city. On November 15 the Americans reversed direction and attacked north to eliminate any insurgents who had been missed in the first pass and to search more thoroughly for insurgent weapons and supplies. For this part of the operation, the ground forces broke down into squad-sized elements to conduct their searches. By November 16 American commanders judged Fallujah secured, although the operation would not end officially until December 23, by which time many residents had been allowed to return to their homes.

U.S. casualties in the Second Battle of Fallujah were 95 killed and 560 wounded; Iraqi Army losses were 11 killed and 43 wounded. Insurgent losses were estimated at between 1,200 and 2,000 killed, with another 1,000–1,500 captured. The disparity in the casualties indicated the extent of the coalition's tactical advantage. Indeed, post-battle army and marine assessments lauded the tremendous tactical skill in urban warfare displayed by American forces.

However, the intense house-to-house fighting had caused the destruction of an estimated 20 percent of the city's buildings, while another 60 percent of the city's structures were damaged. The tremendous damage, including that to 60 mosques, enraged Iraq's Sunni minority. Widespread civilian demonstrations and increased insurgent attacks followed the Second Battle of Fallujah. Although the 2005 Iraqi elections were held on schedule, Sunni participation was very low, partially because of the Sunnis' sense of grievance over the destruction in Fallujah.

James Arnold

See also: al-Qaeda in Iraq; Fallujah; Fallujah, First Battle of

Further Reading

Ballard, John R. *Fighting for Fallujah: A New Dawn for Iraq*. Westport, CT: Praeger Security International, 2006.

Bellavia, David. *House to House: An Epic Memoir of War*. New York: Free Press, 2007.

Gott, Kendall D., ed. *Eyewitness to War: The U.S. Army in Operation Al Fajr; An Oral History*. 2 vols. Fort Leavenworth, KS: Combat Studies Institute Press, 2006.

Fatwa

The fatwa (singular, *responsa*) or fatawa (plural, *responsae*) is a question and answer process referred to in the Qur'an (4:127, 176) that began in early Islam as a means to impart knowledge about theology, philosophy, hadith, legal theory, religious duties, and, later and more specifically, sharia (Islamic law). Fatawa may deal with a much broader series of subjects than did the Islamic courts, and a fatwa, unlike a court ruling, is not binding. The reason it is not binding is that in a court, a *qadi* (judge) is concerned with evidentiary matters and may actually investigate these and hear two sides to an argument, but a cleric or authority issuing a fatwa is responding instead to just one party should the question involve a dispute.

In modern times a fatwa is usually defined as a legal opinion given by someone with expertise in Islamic law. However, so long as a person mentions the sources he uses in a legal opinion, other Muslim authorities or figures may issue fatwa. A modern fatwa usually responds to a question about an action, form of behavior, or practice that classifies it as being obligatory, forbidden, permitted, recommended, or reprehensible. Traditionally, a fatwa could be issued by a Muslim scholar knowledgeable about both the subject and the theories of jurisprudence. These persons might be part of or independent from the court systems. However, other persons might issue fatawa as well. Muslim governments typically designated a chief mufti, who was in the role of the sheikh of Islam in the Ottoman Empire.

In the colonial period the Islamic madrasahs (*madaris* is the Arabic plural), which can mean either simply a school or a higher institute of Islamic education, began in some cases to include a fatwa-issuing office, a *dar al-ifta*. Muslim governments continued efforts to control and limit the issuing of fatawa, as in the Higher Council of Ulama or the Permanent Council for Scientific Research and Legal Opinions in Saudi Arabia or the Council of Islamic Ideology in Pakistan. However, many Muslim authorities—from lesser-trained sheikhs to political figures to legal specialists classified as *fuqaha* (specialists in jurisprudence), mujtahids, and muftis—issue fatawa. Some are no more than a short response to the inquiry, whereas others are recorded, published, or circulated along with explanations.

For many reasons, including the development of differing legal schools within Islam and the history of opinions concerning religious requirements as opposed to mere duties, fatawa may conflict with each other. For example, the legal opinions concerning women's inheritance under Jafari, or Twelver Shia law, and those given by a Hanafi Sunni jurist would differ. At times, even councils of jurists from a single sect may issue a complex opinion with, for instance, each indicating his agreement with or reservations about different implications or subquestions of a fatwa.

Muslim countries today may govern with civil laws that are partially dependent on principles of Islamic law or are derived in part from Ottoman law. When matters of civil legal reform are discussed, then the opinions of religious authorities might be consulted. A fatwa may also be issued by popular figures outside of the venue of civil authorities. Other countries, however, operate on the basis of uncodified Islamic law. At the supranational level, there is no single authoritative person or body that can settle conflicting issues or declare binding fatawa in Islamic law (as the pope and the Vatican issue religious decrees for Roman Catholicism).

In 1933 clerics in Iraq issued a fatwa that called for a boycott of all Zionist-made products. In 2004 the very popular Egyptian Sunni Muslim cleric and scholar Yusuf al-Qaradawi declared a fatwa that similarly called for a boycott of goods manufactured in Israel or the United States.

Other much-disputed questions have concerned the necessary resistance of Palestinians to Israeli rule or the actual status of Palestine and the status of Iraqi resistance to coalition forces. Many fatawa were issued earlier to confront foreign occupation in Muslim lands, in Morocco, Egypt, Syria, Iraq, Iran, and elsewhere. Modern responses that affect the right to wage jihad (holy war) concern the land's status (dar al-Islam) as an Islamic territory. That is the generally agreed status of Iraq and of Palestine because of the presence of the holy sites at the al-Aqsa Mosque complex from which the Prophet Muhammad experienced the Miraj and the Isra (the Night Journey and the Ascent to Heaven, respectively), as well as other holy sites in Palestine. Because the country is an Islamic land and yet many Palestinian Muslims cannot visit their holy sites or practice their religion and have had their lands and properties seized, some fatawa assert that jihad is, in this context, an individual duty incumbent on Muslims. Divergent fatawa identify the country, now Israel, as *dar al-kufr*, a land of unbelief (somewhat like India under British rule) from which Muslims should flee, as in a highly disputed fatwa by Sheikh Muhammad Nasir al-Din al-Albani. While Palestinian Islamic Jihad issued a lengthy fatwa in 1989 that legitimated suicide attacks by Palestinians in the context of jihad, no leading clerics actually signed this document. It could be countered by a statement by the grand mufti of Saudi Arabia, made on April 21, 2001, that Islam forbids suicide attacks and is referred to as if it were a formal fatwa. On the other hand, Sheikh Qaradawi issued a fatwa in 2002 that said women could engage in martyrdom operations in conditions when jihad is an individual duty.

Paul G. Pierpaoli Jr. and Sherifa Zuhur

See also: Shia Islam; Sunni Islam

Further Reading

Coulson, Noel J. *A History of Islamic Law.* Edinburgh, UK: Edinburgh University Press, 1994.

Esposito, John L. *Islam: The Straight Path.* New York: Oxford University Press, 1991.

Messick, Brinkley. *The Calligraphic State: Textual Domination and History in a Muslim Society.* Berkeley: University of California Press, 1993.

Peters, Rudolph. *Islam and Colonialism: The Doctrine of Jihad in Modern History.* The Hague: Brill, 1979.

Faw Peninsula

Strategically important peninsula located in southeastern Iraq, adjacent to the Persian Gulf. The Faw (Fao) peninsula lies to the south and east of Basra, Iraq's principal port and second-largest metropolis, and west of the Iranian city of Abadan. The peninsula separates Iraq from Iran and lies to the immediate west of the critical Shatt al-Arab waterway, which is Iraq's only access to the sea and only seagoing route to the port at Basra. Control of the Faw peninsula has thus been strategically essential to Iraq, as loss of control there likely means being cut off from access to the Persian Gulf.

The Faw peninsula is also important because it has been home to some of Iraq's biggest oil installations, including refineries. The country's two principal terminals for oil tankers—Khor al-Amayya and Mina al-Bakr—are also located here. The only significant population center on the peninsula is Umm Qasr, the base of former Iraqi dictator Saddam Hussein's navy.

The Faw peninsula was a center of attention during the Iran-Iraq War (1980–1988) and was the site of several pitched battles, as both nations struggled to control the Shatt al-Arab waterway. In February 1986 Iranian forces were able to overwhelm the poorly trained Iraqi forces charged with guarding the peninsula. Despite desperate fighting and even in the face of numerous offensives, the Iraqis were unable to dislodge the Iranians from the area. The Iranians were then able to threaten Basra and Umm Qasr and use the Faw peninsula as a base from which to launch missiles into Iraq, into naval and merchant assets in the Persian Gulf, and into Kuwait, which was backing Iraq in the war. In April 1988 the Iraqis launched a new and determined effort to dislodge the Iranians from the peninsula. With almost 100,000 troops, heavy artillery, and aerial bombing that included chemical weapons, the Iraqis finally drove the Iranians out after a 35-hour offensive.

In the lead-up to the 1991 Persian Gulf War, the Faw peninsula and Shatt al-Arab waterway became a bone of contention between Iraq and Kuwait, as both nations jockeyed to control access to Umm Qasr as well as two small adjacent islands. Hussein used the dispute as part of his justification for the August 1990 Iraqi invasion of Kuwait. When Operation Desert Storm began in January 1991, coalition air forces heavily bombed the Faw peninsula, wiping out much of Iraq's naval assets and oil facilities. Although no significant ground actions occurred there, Iraqi shipping was closed down by the bombardment, meaning that Iraq was cut off from any seaborne trade or resupply efforts.

During Operation Iraqi Freedom, which began in March 2003, American and British plans called for the immediate seizure and occupation of the Faw peninsula to deny Iraq access to the Persian Gulf and to open Umm Qasr and Basra to humanitarian and military resupply missions. Military planners also hoped to secure the peninsula before Iraqi troops could damage or destroy its oil facilities.

The coalition attack on Umm Qasr, led by U.S. and British marines and Polish special land forces, began on March 21, 2003, but ran into unexpectedly heavy Iraqi resistance. After four days of sporadically heavy fighting, however, Umm Qasr and the Faw peninsula had been largely secured, and the adjacent waterway had been cleared of Iraqi mines. Pockets of Iraqi resistance endured in the "old city" of Umm Qasr until March 29, when the entire peninsula had essentially been occupied and secured. Almost immediately coalition forces opened the port at Umm Qasr, which then became the primary entrepôt for humanitarian and civilian aid to Iraq.

Paul G. Pierpaoli Jr.

See also: Iraqi Freedom, Operation; Umm Qasr

Further Reading

Keegan, John. *The Iraq War: The Military Offensive, from Victory in 21 Days to the Insurgent Aftermath*. New York: Vintage, 2005.

Tripp, Charles. *A History of Iraq*. Cambridge: Cambridge University Press, 2007.

Fayyad, Muhammad Ishaq al-

One of the five grand ayatollahs who make up the *marjaiyya* (the highest level of Shiite clerics), the informal council of Iraq's senior resident Twelver Shia religious scholars, of Najaf. He has frequently served as the council's representative public voice in post-2003 invasion of Iraq. Born in 1930 in a small village in the Afghan province of Ghazni to a family of farmers, Muhammad Ishaq al-Fayyad is an ethnic Hazara, a Dari-speaking people who reside in Afghanistan and parts of Iran and northwestern Pakistan. Despite this the grand ayatollah is fluent in Arabic, although Western reporters and scholars who have met him say that he speaks it with a distinct Dari Afghan accent. He is widely considered to be one of the most influential members of the marjaiyya (meaning those

who can be emulated, or followed, as spiritual guides) and is also one of the most publicly engaged, arguably even more so than Grand Ayatollah Ali al-Husayni al-Sistani, Iraq's most senior Shia scholar.

Fayyad, like many young Muslims from religious families, began his informal religious studies early, at the age of 5, learning the Qur'an from the village mullah, the local religious scholar. According to some reports, Fayyad and his family moved to Najaf when he was 10 years old. As he grew older he began studying other subjects, including the Arabic language and grammar, rhetoric, logic, Islamic philosophy, *ahadith* (traditions of the Prophet Muhammad and the 12 Shiite imams), and Islamic jurisprudence. He ultimately pursued his studies under the supervision of Grand Ayatollah Abu al-Qasim al-Khoi, one of Iraq's senior resident Shia scholars during the 1970s and the most senior during the 1980s until his death in 1992.

According to accounts from individuals close to both Fayyad and Khoi, the former excelled at his studies and is widely acknowledged to have been one of the latter's best students. Some reports hold that Fayyad was, in fact, Khoi's best student and now is the most senior member of the marjaiyya, but he did not seek to chair the council because scholars who are not Iraqi or Iranian have little chance of gaining followers among Arabs and Iranians, who make up the majority of the world's Shia. In 1992 when the *marjaiyya* was left without a chair after Khoi's death, Fayyad, along with the council's other members, supported Sistani for the position.

Following the March 2003 invasion and subsequent occupation of Iraq by the United States and Great Britain, aided by a relatively small coalition of other countries, Fayyad proved to be the most willing to engage with the Americans and British. Unlike Sistani, he has met occasionally with U.S. and British officials, both diplomatic and military, in order to relay the position of the marjaiyya. Fayyad has stated that Iraqi law must take into account Islamic religious law, particularly with regard to social and family issues. He has spoken out strongly against forced secularization of Iraqi society and has argued that there can be no absolute separation of the state from religion. However, like Sistani, Fayyad has also rejected the implementation of an Iranian-style governmental model for Iraq, one based on Grand Ayatollah Ruhollah Khomeini's concept of *wilayat al-faqih*, the governance of the supreme religious jurist in the absence of the twelfth imam, Muhammad al-Mahdi, whom Twelver Shias believe went into a mystical "hiding" or occultation in the 10th century and who will return at a time appointed by God.

Thus, Fayyad has gone on record as being opposed to clerical rule in Iraq, although he does believe that the *ulama* (Muslim religious scholars) should exercise some influence over Iraqi society, specifically ensuring the protection of Muslim moral and social values. According to a December 2007 report from the Associated Press, Fayyad was supervising the seminary studies of Muqtada al-Sadr, the populist Iraqi Shia leader and head of the Sadr Movement, although Fayyad and the marjaiyya do not approve of Sadr's approach toward politics and have pressured him to clamp down on his more militant followers.

The marjaiyya backed the United Iraqi Alliance (UIA), a loose coalition of mainly Shiite Arab political parties that includes the Supreme Islamic Iraqi Council (SIIC) and the Party of Islamic Call (Hizb al-Dawa al-Islamiyya), in the January 2005 interim elections and the December 2005 formal elections. Despite their early support, Fayyad and his council colleagues reportedly became increasingly critical of the UIA's performance, particularly the combative political sectarianism of the SIIC (then known as the Supreme Council for the Islamic Revolution in Iraq, or SCIRI) and the Islamic Dawa Party. The marjaiyya, through senior spokespeople for the various members, let it be known in the latter half of 2008 that it would not back any slate of candidates and would instead urge its followers to vote for the party or parties that had the best plan for improving the situation in Iraq.

Christopher Paul Anzalone

See also: Shia Islam; Sistani, Sayyid Ali Husayn al-

Further Reading

Cole, Juan R. I. *The Ayatollahs and Democracy in Iraq*. ISIM Paper 7. Leiden, Netherlands: Amsterdam University Press and the International Institute for the Study of Islam in the Modern World, 2006.

Hendawi, Hamza, and Qassim Abdul-Zahra. "Iraq's Maverick Cleric Hits the Books." *Associated Press*, December 13, 2007.

Khalaji, Mehdi. *Religious Authority in Iraq and the Election*. Policy Watch #1063. Washington, DC: Washington Institute for Near East Policy, 2005.

Nasr, Seyyed Vali Reza. "Iraq: The First Arab Shia State." *Missouri Review* 29, no. 2 (2006): 132–53.

Visser, Reidar. *Shi'i Separatism in Iraq: Internet Reverie or Real Constitutional Challenge?* Oslo, Norway: Norwegian Institute of International Affairs, 2005.

Fedayeen

Term used to refer to various (usually Muslim) groups or civilians who have engaged in either armed struggle or guerrilla tactics against foreign armies. The term "fedayeen" is the English transliteration of the term *fida'iyuna*, which is the plural of the Arabic word meaning "one who is ready to sacrifice his life" (*fida'i*) and referred historically to different types of Muslim fighters, including Muslim forces waging war on the borders; freedom fighters; Egyptians who fought against the British in the Suez Canal Zone, culminating in a popular uprising in October 1951; Palestinians who waged attacks against Israelis from the 1950s until the present (including fighters of Christian background); Iranian guerrillas opposed to Mohammad Reza Shah Pahlavi's regime in the 1970s; Armenian fighters in Nagarno-Karabakh (also Christian); and a force loyal to Iraqi dictator Saddam Hussein (the Fedayeen Saddam) during the Iraq War that began in 2003.

Following the rejection by Jewish and Arab leaders of the 1947 United Nations (UN) partition plan that would have created a Palestinian state in the West Bank and the Gaza Strip and the resulting declaration of the State of Israel the following year, Palestinian refugees were driven from their homes and flooded into the areas surrounding the new Jewish state. Anti-Israel activity became prevalent, particularly in West Bank and Gaza Strip areas. Supported by money and arms from a number of Arab states, Palestinians carried out attacks against Israeli military forces and also Israeli settlers, and in 1951 the raids became more organized. These fighters were referred to as fedayeen since they were an irregular rather than a government force. The fighters created bases in Egypt, Jordan, and Lebanon, with Egyptian intelligence training and arming many of them. Between 1951 and 1956 the fedayeen orchestrated hundreds of raids along the Israeli border, killing an estimated 400 Israelis and injuring 900 others.

The fedayeen operated primarily out of Jordan and Lebanon, causing these countries to bear the brunt of the retaliation campaigns carried out by the Israel Defense Forces (IDF) and paramilitary groups. Fedayeen attacks and subsequent retaliations were significant factors in the outbreak of hostilities during the 1956 Suez Crisis. The fedayeen also launched attacks into Israel from the Jordanian-controlled territory of the West Bank. The fighters included those associated with the Palestine Liberation Organization (PLO), the Popular Front for the Liberation of Palestine (PFLP), and various other militant groups.

King Hussein of Jordan was initially supportive of the groups, but by 1970 he deemed their presence detrimental to Jordan and a threat to his own political power. Although based in refugee camps, the fedayeen were able to obtain arms and financial support from other Arab countries and therefore clashed with Jordanian government troops who attempted to disarm them beginning in 1968. The civil war that erupted in 1970 during what has been called Black September saw the eventual defeat and removal of the fedayeen from Jordanian soil.

The fedayeen were forced to recognize Jordanian sovereignty via an October 13, 1970, agreement between PLO leader Yasser Arafat and King Hussein. Although PLO members often participated in commando raids, the PLO denied playing a role in several terrorist attacks. After being ousted from Jordan, the PLO and the fedayeen relocated to Lebanon, where they continued to stage attacks on Israel. At present, the terms *fida'iyuna* and *fida'iyin* are still used by many Arabs for Palestinian militants, and the Arabs see the militants as freedom fighters who struggle for the return (*awda*) of their lands and property in Palestine.

Fidayan-e Islam (in Farsi there is an "e"; in Arabic there is none) was the name taken by a radical Islamist group opposed to the reign of Mohammad Reza Shah Pahlavi of Iran beginning in the 1940s. Between 1971 and 1983 these Iranian fedayeen carried out numerous attacks, including political assassinations, against people supportive of the Pahlavi regime. The same name was adopted by a radical group in Islamabad, Pakistan. The freedom fighter term was also given to a group created by ousted Iraqi leader Saddam Hussein. The Fedayeen Saddam was so-named to associate the force with patriotic self-sacrifice and anti-imperialism. Initially led by Hussein's son Uday in 1995, the group's leadership was handed over to his other son, Qusay, when it was discovered that Uday was diverting Iranian weaponry to the group. Many of them became part of the Iraqi resistance, or *muqawamah*, who following the March 2003 U.S.- and British-led invasion used rocket-propelled grenades, machine guns, and mortars to attack coalition forces, forces of the new Iraqi government, and Sadrists. In January 2007 the group recognized Izzat Ibrahim al-Duri as the rightful leader of Iraq and secretary-general of the Iraqi Baath Party following the execution of Saddam Hussein.

Jessica Britt and Sherifa Zuhur

See also: Hussein, Qusay; Hussein, Saddam; Hussein, Uday; Iraqi Freedom, Operation

Further Reading

Abdullah, Daud. *A History of Palestinian Resistance*. Leicester, UK: Al-Aqsa Publishers, 2005.

Khoury, Elias. *Gate of the Sun*. Translated by Humphrey Davies from *Bab al-Shams*. New York: St. Martin's, 2006.

Laqueur, Walter, and Barry Rubin, eds. *The Israel-Arab Reader: A Documentary History of the Middle East Conflict*. London: Penguin, 2001.

Nafez, Nazzal, and Laila A. Nafez. *Historical Dictionary of Palestine*. Lanham, MD: Scarecrow, 1997.

O'Neill, Bard E. *Revolutionary Warfare in the Middle East: The Israelis vs. the Fedayeen*. Boulder, CO: Paladin, 1974.

Rubin, Barry. *Revolution until Victory? The Politics and History of the PLO*. Cambridge, MA: Harvard University Press, 1996.

Feith, Douglas

Attorney, foreign and military policy expert, noted neoconservative, and undersecretary of defense for policy (2001–2005). Born on July 16, 1953, in Philadelphia, Douglas Feith attended Harvard University, earning a BA degree in 1975. In 1978 he earned a law degree from Georgetown University. While in law school, Feith interned at the Arms Control and Disarmament Agency, where he met Fred Iklé, John Lehman, and Paul Wolfowitz. After graduation Feith practiced law in Washington, DC, and wrote articles on foreign policy. As Feith grew older, he developed positions on foreign policy that would eventually identify him as a neoconservative who believed in the use of force as a vital instrument of national policy.

Feith entered government service in 1981 during the Ronald Reagan administration, working on Middle East issues for the National Security Council. Feith then transferred to the Department of Defense as special counsel for Assistant Secretary of Defense Richard Perle and later served as deputy assistant secretary of defense for negotiations from March 1984 to September 1986. After that Feith left government to form a law firm, Feith & Zell, P.C., which he managed

Douglas Feith, former U.S. undersecretary of defense, at a press conference at the U.S. Embassy in Kabul, Afghanistan, in September 2002. Feith and his staff were subsequently accused of developing dubious intelligence linking Iraqi leader Saddam Hussein and al-Qaeda as a justification for launching the Iraq War. (AP/World Wide Photos)

until 2001, although he continued to write and speak on international affairs.

In April 2001 President George W. Bush nominated Feith as undersecretary of defense for policy. Confirmed in July 2001, Feith held that position until August 2005. His tenure would prove to be highly controversial. At the Pentagon, Feith's position was advisory; he was not within the military chain of command, yet his office held approval authority over numerous procedures. He was the number three civilian in the Pentagon, next to Secretary of Defense Donald Rumsfeld and Deputy Secretary of Defense Paul Wolfowitz.

As undersecretary, Feith became associated with three projects that, although well known, did not bear fruit. First, he hoped to engage America's opponents in the Global War on Terror in a battle of ideas. In the late autumn of 2001 Feith supported the development of the Office of Strategic Influence (OSI), a division of the Department of Defense that would seek to counter propaganda sympathetic to terrorist groups such as al-Qaeda through psychological campaigns. The clandestine nature of the OSI and a lack of oversight forced Rumsfeld to close it down in February 2002.

Second, Feith advocated arming a force of Iraqi exiles to accompany the U.S. invasion of Iraq in 2003. According to Feith, the idea was not well received in the Pentagon, the State Department, or the Central Intelligence Agency (CIA). Third, before Operation IRAQI FREEDOM began, Feith and his staff developed a plan for the creation of an Iraqi Interim Authority (IIA), which would have allowed for joint American-Iraqi control of Iraq after the defeat of Saddam Hussein's regime, as a prelude to a new Iraqi government. This plan was nixed by U.S. administrator in Iraq L. Paul Bremer in the autumn of 2003.

During his time at the Pentagon, Feith became a lightning rod for criticism of the Bush administration's conduct of the Global War on Terror and the Iraq War. He has been blamed for a myriad of policy miscues in Afghanistan and Iraq, and some have accused him of pursuing policies that led to the highly damaging Abu Ghraib prison scandal in 2004. Former vice president Al Gore called for Feith's resignation in a speech at New York University on May 26, 2004.

In various press accounts, Feith has been accused of setting up a secret intelligence cell designed to manipulate the prewar intelligence on Iraq to build a case for war.

Feith's account of events in his memoirs differs considerably, however. He presented the Policy Counter Terrorism Evaluation Group, which evaluated prewar intelligence, as a small group of staffers tasked with summarizing the vast amounts of intelligence that had crossed his desk. Far from being a cadre of Republican political operatives, he argued, the small staff included Chris Carney, a naval officer and university professor who won a seat in Congress in 2006 as a Democrat.

In addition, Feith was accused of attempting to politicize intelligence and to find and publish evidence of links between Iraq and al-Qaeda that did not exist. In his memoirs, Feith states that he tasked career intelligence analyst Christina Shelton with reviewing intelligence on Iraqi–al-Qaeda connections and that she developed a view that was critical of the methods by which CIA analysts examined that intelligence. A subsequent Senate Intelligence Committee investigation concluded that staffers of the Office of the Undersecretary of Defense for Policy did not, in fact, pressure intelligence analysts into changing their product. However, intelligence and military analysts as well as other policy experts and media were either concerned by the scrutiny of or influenced by Rumsfeld's and Feith's office, and this did in fact affect their products.

In August 2005, with both Rumsfeld and Wolfowitz gone and discredited and the Bush administration's war and national security policy under attack from both Democrats and Republicans, Feith tendered his resignation and left government service. In 2006 he took a position at Georgetown University as visiting professor and distinguished practitioner in national security policy. His contract at Georgetown was not renewed in 2008. Also in 2006 Feith published his memoirs, *War and Decision:*

Inside the Pentagon at the Dawn of the War on Terrorism, which offered a sustained defense of his reputation and an explanation of the decisions that he made while serving in government. The book hardly appeased his legion of critics and detractors, however, and Feith now operates on the margins of policy, but his ideas still retain influence.

Mitchell McNaylor

See also: Bremer, L. Paul, III; Bush, George Walker; IRAQI FREEDOM, Operation; Rumsfeld, Donald Henry; Wolfowitz, Paul Dundes

Further Reading

Feith, Douglas. *War and Decision: Inside the Pentagon at the Dawn of the War on Terrorism*. New York: Harper, 2008.

U.S. Senate. *Report of the Select Committee on Intelligence on the U.S. Intelligence Community's Prewar Assessments on Iraq*. Washington, DC: U.S. Government Printing Office, 2004.

Woodward, Bob. *State of Denial: Bush at War, Part III*. New York: Simon and Schuster, 2006.

Franks, Tommy Ray

U.S. Army general. Tommy Ray Franks was born in Wynnewood, Oklahoma, on June 17, 1945. After studying briefly at the University of Texas, Franks joined the U.S. Army in 1965 and went into the artillery. He served in Vietnam, where he was wounded three times. He again attended the University of Texas but dropped out and rejoined the army after being placed on academic probation. Franks later earned a master's degree in public administration at Shippensburg University (1985). He also graduated from the Armed Forces Staff College in 1967, and in 1972 he attended the Field Artillery Center at Fort Sill, Oklahoma.

As commander of the U.S. Central Command, Army general Tommy Franks led the successful military efforts that toppled the Taliban in Afghanistan in 2001 and overthrew Saddam Hussein in Iraq in 2003. (U.S. Department of Defense)

From 1976 to 1977 Franks attended the Armed Forces Staff College in Norfolk, Virginia, and in 1984 and 1985 he attended the U.S. Army War College at Carlisle Barracks, Pennsylvania. He advanced through the ranks, and by the time of Operation Desert Storm in 1991 he was serving as an assistant division commander of the 1st Calvary Division. Franks was appointed brigadier general in July 1991 and major general in April 1994. From 1994 to 1995 he was assistant chief of staff for combined forces in Korea. Franks was advanced to lieutenant general in May 1997 and to general in July 2006.

After the September 11, 2001, terrorist attacks on the United States, Franks was named U.S. commander of the successful Operation Enduring Freedom to topple the Taliban in Afghanistan. In early 2003 he took command of Central Command (CENTCOM) for Operation Iraqi Freedom, the invasion of Iraq that began in March 2003.

Franks was a principal author of the war plans for the ground element of the invasion of Iraq and was an advocate of the lighter, more rapid mechanized forces that performed so well during the ground campaign. Franks designed a plan for the 125,000 U.S., 45,000 British, 2,000 Australian, 400 Czech and Slovak, and 200 Polish troops under his command. His plan involved five ground thrusts into Iraq, with two main thrusts—one by the I Marine Expeditionary Force up the Tigris River and one through the western desert and up the Euphrates by the army's 3rd Armored Division.

The plan allowed for great flexibility, and even though CENTCOM advertised a shock-and-awe bombing campaign, in fact there was never any such intention. Franks's plans called for a near-simultaneous ground and air assault. When missiles struck Iraqi president Saddam Hussein's compound on March 19, 2003, ground forces moved into Iraq. Franks emphasized speed, bypassing cities and Iraqi strong points. Contrary to media reports that coalition forces were "bogged down" and had not occupied many cities, Franks maintained that this was by design: CENTCOM did not want the Iraqis to see the method and tactics by which coalition forces planned to take Baghdad demonstrated in advance in Basra or Najaf.

Franks's campaign was an unqualified success, going farther, faster, and with fewer casualties than any other comparable military campaign in history. This reflects what Franks calls "full-spectrum" war, in which troops not only engage the enemy's military forces, but also perform simultaneous attacks on computer/information facilities, the banking/monetary structure, and public morale.

During the campaign, American forces operated in true "joint" operations, wherein different service branches spoke directly to units in other service branches. The plans also featured true "combined arms" operations in which air, sea, and land assets were simultaneously employed by commanders in the field to defeat the enemy.

Although sources suggest that Secretary of Defense Donald Rumsfeld offered Franks the post of army chief of staff when the ground war ended in late April 2003, Franks wanted to leave the army to pursue other interests. He retired in late May 2003 and subsequently wrote his memoir, *American Soldier* (2004). Franks's departure was fortuitous for him, as he left Iraq prior to the start of the Iraqi insurgency and thus avoided most of the criticism that it engendered. In retirement, Franks started his own consulting firm that deals in disaster recovery operations. He also sits on the boards of several large corporations.

Larry Schweikart

See also: IRAQI FREEDOM, Operation; Rumsfeld, Donald Henry

Further Reading

Cordesman, Anthony H. *The Iraq War: Strategy, Tactics, and Military Lessons.* Westport, CT: Praeger, 2003.

Fontenot, Gregory et al. *On Point: The United States Army in Iraqi Freedom.* Annapolis, MD: Naval Institute Press, 2005.

Franks, Tommy, with Malcolm McConnell. *American Soldier.* New York: Regan Books, 2004.

Murray, Williamson, and Robert H. Scales Jr. *The Iraq War: A Military History.* Cambridge, MA: Belknap, 2005.

Woodward, Bob. *Plan of Attack.* New York: Simon and Schuster, 2004.

Garner, Jay Montgomery

U.S. Army general who, after retirement from active duty, in 2003 served as the first civilian director of the Office for Reconstruction and Humanitarian Assistance (ORHA) for Iraq. Jay Montgomery Garner was born on April 15, 1938, in Arcadia, Florida. After service in the U.S. Marine Corps, he earned a degree in history from Florida State University and secured a commission in the army. He later earned a master's degree from Shippensburg University in Pennsylvania.

Garner rose steadily through the ranks, holding a series of commands in the United States and in Germany, and rising to major general by the time of the Persian Gulf War (Operation DESERT STORM) in 1991. Garner helped develop the Patriot antimissile system and oversaw the deployment of Patriot batteries in Saudi Arabia and Israel during the Persian Gulf War. Garner subsequently managed efforts to improve the Patriot systems and to finalize and deploy the joint U.S.-Israeli Arrow theater antiballistic missile systems. He also worked with Israel, Kuwait, and Saudi Arabia on the sale of the Patriot system. Garner next commanded Operation PROVIDE COMFORT, the coalition effort to provide humanitarian assistance to Kurds in northern Iraq. He directed international forces that included U.S., British, French, and Italian troops in the delivery of food, medicine, and other supplies, and in efforts to prevent reprisals by Iraqi government forces. Garner was subsequently named to command the U.S. Space and Strategic Defense Command.

Garner retired in 1997 as a lieutenant general and assistant vice chief of staff of the army. In September 1997 he was named president of SY Technology, a defense contractor, and he served on a variety of advisory boards on security issues, including the Commission to Assess United States National Security Space Management and Organization.

In March 2003 Garner was named head of ORHA for the Coalition Provisional Authority of Iraq, to coincide with Operation IRAQI FREEDOM and the allied postwar occupation. In this post, Garner was the senior civilian official during the initial period after the overthrow of Saddam Hussein in April 2003. He reported directly to the U.S. military commander in Iraq, General Tommy Franks. Garner's previous service in the region and work during Operation PROVIDE COMFORT made him an attractive candidate for the position, and the George W. Bush administration hoped that he would be able to integrate civilian and military occupation efforts in Iraq.

Garner's occupation strategy emphasized a quick turnover of appropriate authority to the Iraqis and a withdrawal of U.S. and coalition forces to protected bases outside of major urban areas. He also advocated early elections to create an interim Iraqi government with widespread popular legitimacy. Senior defense officials opposed his plans, however, and argued that too rapid a withdrawal of coalition forces would create a power vacuum and might lead to increased sectarian strife. U.S. officials also sought to ensure that former political and military officials linked to Saddam's Baath Party would be purged from their positions (a policy known as de-Baathification). Meanwhile, Garner's status as a former general and his close ties to Secretary of Defense Donald Rumsfeld undermined his ability to work with nongovernmental organizations and non-U.S. officials. Both groups saw him as an indication that the United States was not committed to democratic reform in Iraq.

Garner was confronted with a range of challenges. There was a growing insurgency being waged by Saddam loyalists and foreign fighters, and the country's infrastructure was in worse condition than anticipated as a result of the international sanctions of the 1990s, coalition military action, and a scorched-earth policy carried out by the former regime to deny assets to the invading forces. As a result, Garner was unable to restore basic services in a timely manner.

After initially dismissing the nation's security forces, Garner recalled police officers and initiated a new recruitment and screening process to expedite both the return of former police officers without close ties to the regime and the hiring of new officers. This was part of a broader effort to counter growing lawlessness in major cities, such as Baghdad. Garner also made the initial Iraqi appointments to various ministries as part of the foundation of a transitional government.

Garner was critical of the failure of the United Nations (UN) to immediately end sanctions on Iraq, and he called for the world body to act quickly to facilitate economic redevelopment and the rebuilding of the country's oil-producing infrastructure. Nevertheless, the blunt and plainspoken Garner faced increasing criticism for the deteriorating conditions in Iraq. He was replaced on May 11, 2003, by career diplomat L. Paul Bremer, who reported directly to Rumsfeld instead of to the coalition's military commander. Most members of Garner's senior

Former U.S. Army general Jay Garner, who was named by U.S. president George W. Bush as director of the Office of Reconstruction and Humanitarian Assistance in Iraq following the overthrow of Saddam Hussein. (U.S. Department of Defense)

staff were also replaced. Garner returned to the United States to work in the defense industry. He has remained largely silent on his short and tumultuous tenure in Iraq.

Tom Lansford

See also: Bremer, L. Paul, III; Coalition Provisional Authority

Further Reading

Allawi, Ali A. *The Occupation of Iraq: Winning the War, Losing the Peace.* New Haven, CT: Yale University Press, 2007.

Bremer, L. Paul, with Malcolm McConnell. *My Year in Iraq: The Struggle to Build a Future of Hope.* New York: Simon and Schuster, 2006.

Gates, Robert Michael

U.S. Air Force officer, president of Texas A&M University, director of the Central Intelligence Agency (CIA), and secretary of defense from 2006 to 2011. Robert Michael Gates was born in Wichita, Kansas, on September 25, 1943. He graduated in 1965 from the College of William and Mary with a bachelor's degree in history, then earned a master's degree in history from Indiana University in 1966, and a PhD in Russian and Soviet history from Georgetown University in 1974.

Gates served as an officer in the U.S. Air Force's Strategic Air Command (1967–1969) before joining the CIA in 1969 as an intelligence analyst, a post he held until 1974. He was on the staff of the National

Former Central Intelligence Agency director Robert Gates replaced the controversial Donald Rumsfeld as U.S. secretary of defense in 2006. New president Barack Obama kept Gates in the post. (U.S. Department of Defense)

Security Council (NSC) from 1974 to 1979, before returning to the CIA as director of the Strategic Evaluation Center in 1979. Gates rose through the ranks to become the director of central intelligence (DCI)/deputy director of central intelligence (DDCI) Executive Staff (1981), deputy director for intelligence (DDI) (1982), and deputy director of Central Intelligence (1986–1989).

Nominated to become director of the CIA in 1987, he withdrew his nomination when it appeared that his connection with the Iran-Contra Affair might hamper his Senate confirmation. He then served as deputy assistant to the president for National Security Affairs (March–August 1989) and as assistant to the president and deputy national security adviser from August 1989 to November 1991.

The Iran-Contra Affair erupted in 1987 when it was revealed that members of President Ronald Reagan's administration had sold weapons to Iran and illegally diverted the funds to the Nicaraguan Contras, the rightist anti-Sandinista rebels. Gates's political enemies assumed that he was guilty because of his senior status at the CIA, but an exhaustive investigation by an independent counsel determined that Gates had done nothing illegal, and on September 3, 1991, the investigating committee stated that Gates's involvement in the scandal did not warrant prosecution. The independent counsel's final 1993 report came to the same conclusion. In May 1991 President George H. W. Bush renominated Gates to head the CIA, and the Senate confirmed Gates on November 5, 1991.

Gates retired from the CIA in 1993 and entered academia. He also served as a member of the Board of Visitors of the University of Oklahoma International Programs Center and as an endowment fund trustee for William and Mary. In 1999 he became the interim dean of the George Bush School of

Government and Public Service at Texas A&M University, and in 2002 he became president of Texas A&M University, a post he held until 2006.

Gates remained active in public service during his presidency, co-chairing in January 2004 a Council on Foreign Relations task force on U.S.-Iran relations, which suggested that the United States engage Iran diplomatically concerning that nation's pursuit of nuclear weapons. Gates was a member of the Iraq Study Group (also known as the Baker-Hamilton Commission; March 15, 2006–December 6, 2006), a bipartisan commission charged with studying the Iraq War, when he was nominated to succeed the controversial and discredited Donald Rumsfeld as defense secretary. Gates assumed the post on December 18, 2006.

In addition to the challenges of the Iraq War, Gates was faced in February 2007 with a scandal concerning inadequate and neglectful care of returning veterans by Walter Reed Army Medical Center. In response, he removed both Secretary of the Army Francis J. Harvey and Army Surgeon General Kevin C. Kiley from their posts. Gates further tightened his control of the Pentagon when he did not recommend the renomination of U.S. Marine Corps general Peter Pace as chairman of the Joint Chiefs of Staff (JCS) that June. Pace would have certainly faced tough questioning by Congress. It was also Gates's job to implement the so-called troop surge initiated by Bush in January 2007.

In March 2008 Gates accepted the resignation of Admiral William Joseph "Fox" Fallon, commander of the U.S. Central Command (CENTCOM), a departure that was due in part to the controversy surrounding an article by Thomas P. M. Barnett titled "The Man between War and Peace," published in

Esquire magazine on March 11, 2008. The article asserted policy disagreements between Fallon and the Bush administration on the prosecution of the war in Iraq and potential conflict with Iran over that nation's nuclear arms program. Gates rejected any suggestion that Fallon's resignation indicated a U.S. willingness to attack Iran in order to stop its nuclear weapons development.

Unlike his abrasive predecessor, Gates brought an era of calm and focus to the Pentagon and has appeared far more willing to engage in discussion and compromise over matters of defense and military policy. In April 2009 Gates proposed a major reorientation in the U.S. defense budget, which would entail deep cuts in more traditional programs that provide for conventional warfare with such major military powers as Russia and China, and shift assets to those programs that would aid in fighting the insurgencies in both Iraq and Afghanistan. Among his proposed cuts were missile defense, the army's Future Combat Systems, navy shipbuilding, new presidential helicopters, and a new communications satellite system. Gates would delay development of a new air force bomber and order only four additional F-22 fighters for a total of 197, while purchasing as many as 513 of the less expensive F-35 strike fighters over the next five years. Purchases of large navy ships would be delayed. At the same time, the new budget would provide for a sharp increase in funding for surveillance and intelligence-gathering equipment, to include the Predator-class unmanned aerial vehicles, and increase manpower in the army to include special forces and the Marine Corps. These decisions triggered major debate in Congress over defense spending and priorities. In December 2009 Gates was the first senior U.S. official to visit Afghanistan after President Barack Obama announced his intention to deploy 30,000 additional military personnel to that country.

Richard M. Edwards

See also: Central Intelligence Agency; Iraq Study Group; Obama, Barack Hussein, II; Rumsfeld, Donald Henry

Further Reading

Barnett, Thomas P. M. "The Man between War and Peace." *Esquire*, March 11, 2008, 1–4.

Gates, Robert M. *From the Shadows: The Ultimate Insider's Story of Five Presidents and How They Won the Cold War.* New York: Simon and Schuster, 1996.

Gates, Robert M. *Understanding the New U.S. Defense Policy through the Speeches of Robert M. Gates, Secretary of Defense.* Rockville, MD: Arc Manor, 2008.

Oliphant, Thomas. *Utter Incompetents: Ego and Ideology in the Age of Bush.* New York: Thomas Dunne Books, 2007.

Golden Mosque Bombing

The Askariya shrine, also known as that Golden Dome mosque, in Samarra, Iraq is one of Shi'a Islam's most holy sites. The mosque holds the tombs of two ninth-century Shia imams, Hassan al-Askari and Muhammad al-Mahdi. On February 22, 2006, terrorists tied to al-Qaeda in Iraq bombed the mosque, destroying the golden dome as well the imams' tombs. This unleashed a series of reprisal attacks on Sunnis in the Samarra area. The bombing of the mosque was the beginning of a sectarian clash in Iraq that contributed to the increased violence that precipitated the U.S. military's Surge Strategy in 2007.

No one died because of the actual attack. However, the day of the bombing Shia and Sunni groups fought in Samarra. This sectarian fighting killed 20 people. The violence then spread through Iraq. The following day over 100 people died in clashes, including several Sunni clerics. This began the most violent period of sectarian violence during the war in Iraq.

The shrine, built in 944, is one of Shia Islam's holiest sites. In addition to housing two of Shia Islam's imams, it was also the place where the hidden imam, a messianic figure in the Shia branch, left his followers in the ninth century. The golden dome, built in 1905, contains over 70,000 golden tiles. It represents the importance of the shrine to the Shia branch of Islam. Many faithful believe the hidden imam will return to the mosque and emerge from the crypt underneath the blue mosque that is next to the shrine. These religious figures and their association with the shrine and its adjacent mosque make this site key to Shia faith and identity. It remains a place of pilgrimage and a vital part of Iraqi Shia culture.

The terrorists who destroyed the dome disguised themselves in Iraqi military uniforms. They entered the shrine and subdued the guards. Then the al-Qaeda in Iraq operatives placed explosives on the dome. The resulting explosion demolished the iconic feature of the shrine, the golden dome.

The eight al-Qaeda in Iraq terrorists who executed the attack on February 22 succeeded in their goal of instigating sectarian strife throughout Iraq. Although the violence began in Samarra with the burning of Sunni businesses, it soon engulfed the entire nation. By the end of 2006 over 10,000 Iraqis had died as a result of the sectarian violence that began in Samarra. This violence was part of the reason for President Bush's decision to increase the number of American troops in the surge of 2007.

This bombing, with its subsequent conflict, sparked the rise in violence in Iraq through 2007. It showed the fragile nature of the relative peace that was in place in early 2006. The Sunni al-Qaeda in Iraq terrorists' attack struck a key aspect of Shia identity. The Shia responded with attacks on Sunnis. These retaliations drove the two groups further apart, resulting in mass violence and complicating hopes of a relatively quick American withdrawal from Iraq.

Gates Brown

See also: al-Qaeda in Iraq; Shia Islam; Surge, U.S. Troop Deployment, Iraq War

Further Reading

Hammer, Joshua. "Samarra Rises." *Smithsonian* 39, no. 10 (January 2009): 28–37.

Worth, Robert. "Blast Destroys Shrine in Iraq, Setting Off Sectarian Fury." *New York Times*, February 22, 2006, http://www.nytimes.com/2006/02/22/international/middleeast/22cnd-iraq.html.

Goldwater-Nichols Defense Reorganization Act

Congressional act, formally known as the Department of Defense Reform Act of 1986, designed to enhance the ability of the U.S. Armed Services to operate more effectively in joint operations. This act, named for its lead sponsors Senator Barry M. Goldwater (R-Ariz.) and Congressman William "Bill" Nichols (D-Ala.), was designed to address lingering problems associated with compromises made in the crafting of the National Security Act of 1947, which established the Department of Defense structure. Congressional sponsors and defense reform advocates had pushed for the changes to address problem areas generated by bureaucratic inefficiencies and interservice competition, as well as issues that had been identified in prior combat operations, ranging from the Korean War to Operation URGENT FURY (the U.S. invasion of Grenada

in 1983). The primary objectives of the Goldwater-Nichols Act were to strengthen civilian authority, improve the military advice provided to senior civilian leaders, reduce the effects of service parochialism and interservice rivalry, enhance the role of the chairman of the Joint Chiefs of Staff (JCS) and the Joint Staff, and improve the operational authority of the commanders in chief (CINCs) of the unified combatant commands.

The Goldwater-Nichols Act strengthened the authority of the secretary of defense and made the chair of the JCS the "principal military adviser" to the president, secretary of defense, and National Security Council (NSC). Previously, under a system requiring unanimity, the JCS had provided collective recommendations, which were often watered-down compromises made among the service chiefs. Prior to the passage of Goldwater-Nichols, any service chief, to protect the parochial interests of his own service, could block a Joint Staff action. The new act established the chair as the final approval authority for all Joint Staff actions, allowing the chair to override any service objections. Although the chair and the individual service chiefs remained outside the formal operational chain of command (which flows from the president, through the secretary of defense, directly to the combatant commanders in the field), the reforms allowed the president and the defense secretary to pass operational orders to the combatant commanders, including both the geographic theater joint commanders and the functional joint command commanders through the JCS chair.

The act also established a vice chairman position for the JCS and revised the Joint Staff responsibilities to clarify and enhance the staff's role in the planning and decision-making process. Goldwater-Nichols also adjusted the defense personnel system to encourage service in joint organizations and to require that senior officers have career experiences and professional education that provide a joint perspective in their leadership roles. Additionally, the act clarified and enhanced the roles of the CINCs. At the time the act was passed, the JCS chairman was Admiral William J. Crowe Jr., although the first chairman to be appointed under the new structure was General Colin L. Powell. The effects of Goldwater-Nichols were clearly evident in the conduct of Operation DESERT SHIELD and Operation DESERT STORM, in 1990 and 1991 respectively, in response to the Iraqi invasion of Kuwait. During the conflict, General Powell played a key role in the national leadership as the principal military adviser. Additionally, President George H. W. Bush and Secretary of Defense Dick Cheney used Powell as the primary conduit for orders flowing to the theater CINC, General H. Norman Schwarzkopf. Schwarzkopf also found it useful to pass information back through the JCS chairman, as well as to report directly to the defense secretary and the president.

Within the theater itself, Schwarzkopf fully exploited the Goldwater-Nichols authority and the emphasis on joint efforts to create a highly effective joint and coalition force structure and to conduct a well-coordinated joint campaign for the liberation of Kuwait. Operation DESERT STORM was viewed by many analysts as a validation of the wisdom of the reforms implemented by the Goldwater-Nichols Act. In October 2002 Secretary of Defense Donald Rumsfeld directed that the functional and regional CINCs be referred to as "combat commanders" or "commanders," arguing that there can be but one commander in chief—namely the president of the United States. During U.S. military operations in Afghanistan in 2001

(Operation ENDURING FREEDOM) and Iraq in 2003 (Operation IRAQI FREEDOM), the wisdom of Goldwater-Nichols was once again clearly evident, as both operations were conducted with a great deal of efficiency and joint effort.

Jerome V. Martin

See also: IRAQI FREEDOM, Operation

Further Reading

Lederman, Gordon Nathaniel. *Reorganizing the Joint Chiefs of Staff: The Goldwater-Nichols Act of 1986.* College Station: Texas A&M University Press, 2002.

Locher, James R. *Victory on the Potomac: The Goldwater-Nichols Act Unifies the Pentagon.* College Station: Texas A&M University Press, 2002.

Guantánamo Bay Detainment Camp

Detainment camp operated by the U.S. government to hold enemy combatants taken prisoner during the Global War on Terror, which began in late 2001 after the September 11, 2001, terror attacks against the United States. The Guantánamo Bay Detainment Camp is situated on the Guantánamo Bay Naval Base, operated by the United States in southeastern Cuba. The base is an area of 45 square miles that has been formally occupied by the United States since 1903, a result of the 1898 Spanish-American War. The original intent of the base was to serve as a coaling station for the U.S. Navy. A subsequent lease was signed on July 2, 1906, on the same terms. A new lease was negotiated between the Cuban and U.S. governments in 1934.

Shortly after the 1959 Cuban Revolution, the Castro government demanded that the Guantánamo Bay area be returned to Cuban sovereignty, but the U.S. government refused,

A detainee is led by military police to be interrogated by military officials at Camp X-Ray at the U.S. Naval Base at Guantánamo Bay, Cuba, on February 6, 2002. There are 158 al-Qaeda and Taliban prisoners being held at Camp X-Ray. (AP Photo/Lynne Sladky)

citing that the lease required the agreement of both parties to the modification or abrogation of the agreement. Since then, the United States has continued to send a check to the Cuban government for the lease amount every year, but the Cuban government has steadfastly refused to cash them.

During its invasion of Afghanistan that began in October 2001, the U.S. military captured a large number of al-Qaeda fighters and other insurgents. The George W. Bush administration determined that those captured were enemy combatants, not prisoners of war.

This decision came after lawyers from the White House, the Pentagon, and the Justice Department issued a series of secret memorandums that maintained that the prisoners had no rights under federal law or the Geneva Conventions. In this ruling, enemy combatants could be held indefinitely without charges. A number of conservative lawyers in the Justice Department's Office of Legal Counsel (OLC) provided the legal opinions for this decision. The Bush administration issued this decision on January 22, 2002.

Finally, after considering several sites to hold these prisoners, the U.S. military decided to build a prison at Guantánamo Bay, Cuba, the Guantánamo Bay Detention Camp. Camp X-Ray was the first facility, and the first 110 prisoners arrived there on January 11, 2002. They were held in wire cages. Later Camp Delta was constructed, but neither camp was up to standards for prison inmates in the United States. At their peak, the camps held 680 prisoners.

The Bush administration selected Guantánamo Bay for a specific reason.

If the prisoners were held on U.S. soil, then they might claim access to legal representation and American courts. Guantánamo Bay fell under a unique legal situation because the land is leased from Cuba and thus is not technically American soil. Furthermore, because the United States has no diplomatic relationship with Cuba, the prisoners had no access to the Cuban legal system. There the prisoners reside in legal limbo with few if any legal rights.

The detainment camp is run by the U.S. military. At the beginning, command responsibility for the base was divided between Major General Michael Dunlavey, an army reservist, and Brigadier General Rick Baccus, of the Rhode Island National Guard. Dunlavey maintained a hard-line attitude toward the detainees, but Baccus was more concerned about their possible mistreatment. They often quarreled over interrogation techniques and other issues. This situation changed when U.S. Army major general Geoffrey Miller replaced them and established a unitary command at Guantánamo in November 2003.

Miller had no experience running a prison camp, and he was soon criticized for allowing harsh interrogation techniques that included the controversial waterboarding technique, which the Bush administration insisted was not torture. Later Miller was transferred to Iraq, where he took over responsibility for military prisons there.

After Camp Delta was built, the detainees lived in better but still restrictive conditions. At Camp X-Ray, the original camp, the detainees lived behind razor wire in cells open to the elements and with buckets in place of toilets. At Camp Delta the detainees were held in trailer-like structures made from old shipping containers that had been cut in half lengthwise, with the two pieces stuck together end to end. Cells were small,

six feet eight inches by eight feet, with metal beds fixed to the steel mesh walls. Toilets were squatting-style flush on the floor, and sinks were low to the ground so that detainees could wash their feet before Muslim prayer. There was no air conditioning for the detainees, only a ventilation system that was supposed to be turned on at 85 degrees but rarely was. Later a medium-security facility opened up, and it gave much greater freedom and better living conditions to the detainees.

The Bush administration gave the Central Intelligence Agency (CIA) responsibility for interrogations. Because these enemy combatants had no legal standing in American courts, they were treated as merely sources of intelligence. President Bush had determined this stance after deciding that al-Qaeda was a national security issue, not a law enforcement issue. Consequently, the Federal Bureau of Investigation (FBI) was completely left out of the loop. But this did not mean that the FBI gave up on questioning prisoners. For various reasons, FBI personnel did interrogate detainees on occasion.

To encourage cooperation, levels of treatment for detainees were determined by the degree of a detainee's cooperation. Level one was for cooperating prisoners, and they received special privileges. Level two included more moderately cooperative detainees, and they received a few privileges, such as a drinking cup and access to the library. Level three was for detainees who absolutely refused to cooperate. They were given only the basics: a blanket, a prayer mat and cap, a Qur'an, and a toothbrush.

The CIA ultimately determined that the most important al-Qaeda prisoners should not be held at the Guantánamo Bay Detention Camp. There were simply too many American officials from too many agencies trying to interrogate the prisoners.

Moreover, it was too public. CIA leaders wanted a secret location where there would be no interference in the interrogations. Several secret interrogation sites were then set up in friendly countries where the CIA could do what they wanted without interference.

Soon after prisoners had been transferred to the Guantánamo Bay Detention Camp, reports began to surface about mistreatment, which caused considerable consternation abroad. In the late spring of 2002, a CIA analyst visited the camp and was aghast at the treatment of the prisoners. Because he spoke Arabic, he was able to talk to the detainees. In his report the analyst claimed that half of the detainees did not belong there. This report traveled throughout the Bush administration, but no action was taken. The American public was still upset over the September 11 attacks, and public reports about mistreatment of those held at Guantánamo Bay garnered little sympathy.

The Bush administration decided in the summer of 2006 to transfer the top captured al-Qaeda leaders to the Guantánamo Bay Detention Camp. In September 2006 the transfer of these 14 detainees was complete. Then beginning in March 2007, court proceedings were begun to determine their status. In the most important case, that of Khalid Sheikh Muhammed, the accused made a total confession of all his activities both in and outside al-Qaeda. However, his confessions were elicited through torture and physical abuse. Among these were planning for the September 11 attacks and the execution of U.S. journalist Daniel Pearl. Muhammed's justification was that he was at war against the United States. Proceedings against the other detainees continued in the spring of 2007.

Meanwhile, growing public criticism in the United States and elsewhere about the status of the detainees led to a series of court cases in the United States in 2007 and 2008 that tried to establish a legal basis for them. Finally, in June 2008 the U.S. Supreme Court ruled that Guantánamo detainees were indeed subject to protection under the U.S. Constitution. By that time the situation in Cuba had become a public relations fiasco for the Bush administration. In October 2008 a federal judge ordered the release of five Algerians being held at Guantánamo because the government had shown insufficient evidence for their continued incarceration. More detainees were likely to be reevaluated, which would result in their potential release or a trial. Experts have recommended exactly such a process, which they termed R2T2: (1) review, (2) release or transfer, and (3) try. In January 2009 President Barack Obama firmly declared that his administration would close the prison at Guantánamo but conceded that doing so presented unique challenges and would take some time. Since 2008, discussions have taken place with other countries that have agreed to take prisoners. Some have already been released to other countries, where they are incarcerated.

Stephen E. Atkins

See also: Abu Ghraib; Central Intelligence Agency; Democratization and the Global War on Terror

Further Reading

Epstein, Edward. "Guantanamo Is a Miniature America." *San Francisco Chronicle*, January 20, 2002, A6.

Hansen, Jonathan M. "Making the Law in Cuba." *New York Times*, April 20, 2004, A19.

Hersh, Seymour. *Chain of Command: The Road from 9/11 to Abu Ghraib.* New York: HarperCollins, 2004.

Mendelsohn, Sarah E. *Closing Guantanamo: From Bumper Sticker to Blueprint.* Washington, DC: Center for Security and International Studies, 2008.

Saar, Erik, and Viveca Novak. *Inside the Wire: A Military Intelligence Soldier's Eyewitness Account of Life at Guantanamo.* New York: Penguin, 2005.

Yee, John. *War by Other Means: An Insider's Account of the War on Terror.* New York: Atlantic Monthly, 2006.

H

Haass, Richard Nathan

Foreign policy expert, prolific author, and national security/foreign policy official in the George H. W. Bush and George W. Bush administrations. Richard Nathan Haass was born in Brooklyn, New York, on July 28, 1951. He received his BA degree from Oberlin College (Ohio) in 1973. Selected as a Rhodes Scholar, he continued his education at Oxford University, from which he ultimately earned both a master's and a doctoral degree. Haass subsequently held a series of academic posts at Hamilton College and the John F. Kennedy School of Government at Harvard University. He also served as vice president and director of foreign policy studies at the Brookings Institute and held posts with the prestigious Carnegie Endowment for International Peace and the International Institute for Strategic Studies. Although Haass's interests and research are wide reaching, most of it deals with foreign policy and national security issues. By the end of the 1980s he had become especially interested in the Middle East.

Haass began his government service in 1979 as an analyst for the Department of Defense, a post he held until 1980. Concomitantly, he was a legislative aide for the U.S. Senate. In 1981 he began serving in the U.S. State Department, where he remained until 1985. By 1989 Haass had earned a reputation as a thoughtful yet cautious foreign policy adviser. That year he began serving as a special assistant to President George H. W. Bush as senior director for Near East and East Asian Affairs on the National Security Council (NSC). As such, Haass was deeply involved in the policy decisions surrounding Operations DESERT SHIELD and DESERT STORM. Indeed, he helped facilitate the Bush administration's success in cobbling together an impressive international coalition that ultimately defeated Iraq in 1991 and reversed that nation's occupation of Kuwait. In 1991 Haass was given the Presidential Citizens Medal for his work before and during the Persian Gulf War. Haass resigned his post in 1993 at the end of Bush's term in office.

When President George W. Bush took office in January 2001, Haass was appointed the State Department's director of policy planning, arguably the most influential foreign policy post next to that of secretary of state. Haass's main role during this time was to act as Secretary of State Colin L. Powell's chief adviser. Remaining in this post until June 2003, Haass had a significant role in the U.S. reaction to the September 11, 2001, terror attacks; the subsequent war in Afghanistan (Operation ENDURING FREEDOM); and the lead-up to war with Iraq in March 2003. Perhaps reflecting Powell's caution and skepticism toward the implementation of a second war with Iraq, Haass was not seen as a war hawk, at least not in the same league as neoconservatives such as Deputy Secretary of Defense Paul Wolfowitz, Secretary of Defense Donald Rumsfeld, or Vice President Richard (Dick) Cheney. While Powell's more cautious stance was cast aside in the months leading up to the war, Haass nevertheless remained publicly loyal to Bush's foreign policy.

For a brief time Haass served as policy coordinator for U.S. policy in Afghanistan after the fall of the Taliban regime there. He also served as special U.S. envoy to the Northern Ireland peace process, succeeding Senator George Mitchell. In late 2003 Haass chose to step down from government service and was awarded the Distinguished Honor Award from the U.S. Department of State. In July 2003 he accepted the post of president of the Council on Foreign Relations (CFR), and upon his departure from government he dedicated all of his efforts to the CFR. The CFR is a nonpartisan independent think tank and publisher dedicated to studying and articulating the foreign policies of the United States and other nations of the world. The author of 12 books, Haass lives in New York City.

Paul G. Pierpaoli Jr.

See also: Bush, George Walker; Cheney, Richard Bruce; Feith, Douglas; Iraqi Freedom, Operation; Rumsfeld, Donald Henry

Further Reading

DeYoung, Karen. *Soldier: The Life of Colin Powell.* New York: Knopf, 2006.

Haass, Richard. *The Opportunity: America's Moment to Alter History's Course.* New York: Public-Affairs, 2006.

Haass, Richard. *War of Necessity, War of Choice: A Memoir of Two Iraq Wars.* New York: Simon and Schuster, 2009.

Haditha, Battle of

Military engagement during August 1 through 4, 2005, between U.S. marines and Iraqi insurgents belonging to Ansar al-Sunnah, a militant Salafi group operating in and around Haditha, Iraq. Haditha is a city of some 100,000 people located in Anbar Province in western Iraq about 150 miles to the northwest of Baghdad. The city's population is mainly Sunni Muslim.

The battle was precipitated when a large force of insurgents ambushed a six-man marine sniper unit on August 1; all six marines died in the ensuing fight. The rebels videotaped part of the attack, which included footage allegedly showing one badly injured marine being killed. On August 3 the marines, along with a small contingent of Iraqi security forces, decided to launch a retaliatory strike against Ansar al-Sunnah, dubbed Operation QUICK STRIKE. Those involved included about 1,000 personnel from Regimental Combat Team 2.

The operation commenced with a ground assault against insurgent positions southwest of Haditha; this was augmented by four Bell AH-1 Super Cobra attack helicopters. U.S. officials reported at least 40 insurgents killed during this engagement. The next day, August 4, insurgents used a large roadside bomb to destroy a marine amphibious vehicle; 15 of the 16 marines inside it were killed, along with a civilian interpreter. Meanwhile, the marines had conducted a raid on a house suspected of harboring insurgents outside Haditha. In so doing, they discovered a large weapons cache containing small arms and improvised explosive devices (IEDs), and they detained seven insurgents for questioning. Later, six of the men admitted to having ambushed and killed the six marines on August 1.

After the roadside bombing, coalition forces decided to regroup for a more concerted attack on Haditha itself, which would come in early September. In total, the marines suffered 21 killed; insurgent losses were estimated at 400.

On September 5, 2005, the 3rd Battalion, 1st Marines, launched a full-scale assault against Haditha, expecting heavy resistance. The resistance did not materialize, however, and the marines took the entire city in four days with minimal insurgent activity. The operation uncovered more than 1,000 weapons caches and resulted in the detention of an additional 400 militants. Four marines were casualties. In early 2006 eight Iraqis suspected of involvement in the initial attack on the marine snipers were tried by an Iraqi court, found guilty, and executed.

Paul G. Pierpaoli Jr.

See also: Iraqi Insurgency

Further Reading

Hashim, Ammed S. *Insurgency and Counter-Insurgency in Iraq.* Ithaca, NY: Cornell University Press, 2006.

Tracy, Patrick. *Street Fight in Iraq: What It's Really Like Over There.* Tucson: University of Arizona Press, 2006.

Haditha Incident

The alleged murder of 24 Iraqi civilians in Haditha, in Anbar Province, on November 19, 2005, by U.S. marines of the 1st Squad, 3rd Platoon, K Company, 3rd Battalion, 1st Marine Regiment, 1st Marine Division. The incident gained international notoriety when it eventually became public knowledge, fueling critics' attacks on the conduct of the U.S.-led coalition's counterinsurgency operations in Iraq and raising charges that the U.S. Marine Corps had initially attempted to cover up the killings before reporters broke the story. Domestic and international pressure to investigate the incident fully and to prosecute those involved gained increasing momentum, as public knowledge of the Haditha Incident in early 2006 coincided with other allegations of unnecessary violence against Iraqi

civilians by U.S. military personnel during military operations elsewhere in the country. Strong criticism of the incident and the U.S. Marine Corps' handling of its aftermath by congressional opponents of the George W. Bush administration was led by U.S. congressman John Murtha (D-Pa.). Murtha's status as a former marine combat veteran of the Vietnam War has frequently made him the Democrats' point man in attacks on the Bush administration's handling of the Global War on Terror. Murtha was subsequently sued by one of the alleged marine participants in the Haditha killing. Although several marine participants were eventually brought up on criminal charges for their roles in the incident, none has been convicted of a capital crime.

In November 2005 Anbar Province was one of the most dangerous places in Iraq, the heart of the Iraqi insurgency. The murders are alleged to have been in retaliation for the death of U.S. Marine Corps lance corporal Miguel Terrazas and the wounding of two other marines on November 19 after a four-vehicle U.S. convoy triggered the detonation of an improvised explosive device (IED) and came under attack by small-arms fire.

The U.S. Marine Corps initially reported that 15 civilians had been killed by the bomb's blast and that 8 or 9 insurgents had also been killed in the ensuing firefight. However, reports by Iraqi eyewitnesses to the incident, statements by local Iraqi officials, and video shots of the dead civilians in the city morgue and at the houses where the killings occurred contradicted the initial U.S. military version of events. Some of the Iraqi eyewitness reports were particularly compelling, such as testimony by a young girl who said she saw marines shoot her father while he was praying. The vividness and detail of Iraqi eyewitness reports gave substantial credibility to their claims,

Two Iraqis examine the charred side of a home a day or two after the Haditha Incident of November 19, 2005. (AP/Wide World Photos)

making it virtually impossible for U.S. military authorities to ignore them. The Iraqi claims contradicting the official military report prompted *Time* magazine to publish a story alleging that the marines deliberately killed 24 Iraqi civilians, including women and 6 children.

Although *Newsmax* questioned *Time*'s sources for the story, claiming that the dead were known insurgent propagandists and insurgent-friendly Haditha residents, based on the *Time* report and the international outcry it generated, on February 24, 2006, the U.S. military initiated an investigation. Led by U.S. Army major general Eldon Bargewell, the investigation was charged with determining how the incident was reported through the chain of command. On March 9 a criminal investigation was also launched, led by the Naval Criminal Investigative

Services (NCIS) to determine if the marines deliberately targeted and killed Iraqi civilians. As *Newsweek* stated in a report on the Haditha Incident dated October 9, 2007, "the sinister reality of insurgents' hiding among civilians in Iraq has complicated the case" and was one of the main obstacles military investigators faced in trying to determine if any Iraqi civilians were deliberately killed.

Marines on patrol in Haditha initially reported that 1 marine and 15 Iraqi civilians had been killed from an IED, whereupon insurgents opened fire on the marines, who proceeded to kill the 8 or 9 alleged insurgents. The U.S. Marine Corps then subsequently reported that the 15 Iraqi civilians had instead been accidentally killed as marines cleared four nearby houses in front of the road where the IED had exploded and in which they believed the insurgents were firing from and/or hiding in. According to Iraqi accounts, however, after the IED explosion, the incensed marines went on a rampage, set up a roadblock, and first killed 4 Iraqi students and a taxi driver who were all unarmed and surrendering to the marines at the time. The marines then stormed the four nearby houses and killed numerous people (accounts vary as to the exact number), including perhaps as many as 5 women and 6 children. Details beyond that remain sketchy and changeable.

On April 9, 2007, one marine, Sergeant Sanick De La Cruz, was granted immunity from prosecution for unpremeditated murder in exchange for his testimony. He testified on May 9, 2007, that he and others, including his squad leader, Staff Sergeant Frank Wuterich, killed the four Iraqi students and the driver of a white taxi who were attempting to surrender. De La Cruz further testified that Wuterich then told the men under his command, including De La Cruz, to lie about the killings. According to De La Cruz, the five Iraqis, including the driver, had been ordered out of a taxi by Wuterich and himself after the marines had put up a roadblock following the ambush of the convoy.

Other marines, however, reported that shortly after the explosion of the IED they noticed a white unmarked car full of "military-aged men" arrive and then stop near the bombing site. Suspecting the men of being insurgents or having remotely detonated the IED, Wuterich and De La Cruz ordered the five men to stop and surrender, but instead they ran; they were all shot and killed. As reinforcements arrived, the marines began taking small-arms fire from several locations on either side of their convoy, and while taking cover they identified at least one shooter in the vicinity of a nearby house. Lieutenant William Kallop ordered Wuterich and an ad hoc team to treat the buildings as hostile and to "clear" them. They forced entry and shot a man on a flight of stairs and then shot another when he made a movement toward a closet. The marines say that they heard the sound of an AK-47 bolt slamming, so they threw grenades into a nearby room and fired; they killed five occupants, with two others wounded by grenade fragments and bullets. Wuterich and his men pursued what they suspected were insurgents running into an adjacent house. They led the assault with grenades and gunfire, in the process killing another man. Unknown to the marines, two women and six children were in a back room. Seven were killed. It was a chaotic and fast-moving action conducted in the dark in close-range quarters, causing accounts to diverge on the precise chronology and exact sequence of events.

After the firefight ended around 9:30 p.m., the marines noted men suspected of scouting for another attack peering behind the wall of a third house. A marine team, including Wuterich and Lance Corporal Justin Sharratt, stormed the house to find women and children inside (who were not harmed). They moved to a fourth house off a courtyard and killed two men inside who were wielding AK-47s, along with two others.

Thirty minutes after the house clearing, an intelligence unit arrived to question the marines involved in the operation. Shortly after the IED explosion, an unmanned aerial vehicle (UAV) flew over the blast area and for the rest of the day transmitted views of the scene to the company command headquarters and also the to battalion, regimental, and divisional headquarters. *Newsmax* reported that the UAV recorded marines sweeping the four houses for suspected insurgents and also showed four insurgents fleeing the neighborhood in a car and joining up with other insurgents. Based on Staff

Sergeant Wuterich's account that in the first house he cleared he observed a back door ajar and believed that the insurgents had fled to another nearby house, it is possible that the four fleeing insurgents seen by the UAV were the same ones who left through the back door of the first house that Wuterich and other marines were clearing. The UAV followed both groups of insurgents as they returned to their safe house, which was bombed around 6:00 p.m. and then stormed by a squad from K Company.

On December 21, 2006, in accordance with U.S. Marine Corps legal procedures, criminal charges were brought against eight marines for war crimes in the Haditha killings. Four enlisted marines (including Wuterich) were accused of 13 counts of unpremeditated murder, and four officers were charged with covering up their subordinates' alleged misdeeds by failing to report and investigate properly the deaths of the Iraqis. In 2007 the charges against three of the four enlisted marines were dismissed, and by the summer of 2008 the charges against three of the officers were dismissed; the other was found not guilty by court-martial. Kallop was never charged with a crime.

On June 17, 2008, military judge Colonel Steve Folsom dismissed all charges against Lieutenant Colonel Jeffrey R. Chessani, the most senior officer to face charges, because the officer overseeing the Haditha investigation, Lieutenant General James Mattis, had been improperly influenced by legal investigator Colonel John Ewers, who was a witness to the case and later became a legal adviser to Mattis. The judge ruled that Ewers should not have been allowed to attend meetings and discussions with Mattis because Ewers's participation prejudiced and tainted the decision to charge and prosecute Chessani, who was accused of failing

to report the incident and investigate the alleged killing of civilians by marines under his command. The U.S. Marine Corps has appealed the ruling to the Navy and Marine Court of Criminal Appeals, postponing indefinitely Chessani's case.

Of the eight marines originally charged on December 21, 2006, Staff Sergeant Frank D. Wuterich, the platoon sergeant implicated in the Haditha killings, has been convicted of wrong doing. He was initially charged with multiple counts of murder, but after a hearing the charges were reduced to nine counts of voluntary manslaughter. His court-martial, however, has been indefinitely postponed to allow prosecutors time to appeal a judge's decision to throw out a subpoena for unaired footage from a CBS *60 Minutes* program interview with Wuterich. Military prosecutors argued that the additional footage shows that Wuterich may have admitted to his role in the killings. In addition, the dismissal of all charges against Chessani has implications for Wuterich's case because Colonel Ewers also investigated Wuterich's case before becoming a legal adviser to Mattis, who recommended prosecuting Wuterich. Wuterich reached a plea agreement with prosecutors. On January 23, 2012, he pled guilty to one count of negligent dereliction of duty in return for the other charges against him being dropped. He forfeited two-thirds of his pay for three months and was reduced to the rank of private. He served no jail time.

Wuterich insists his unit followed the rules of engagement and did not purposefully attack civilians, and that his squad entered the houses to suppress insurgent fire and pursue gunmen who had opened fire on them. He further asserts that the civilian deaths occurred during the sweep of nearby homes in which fragmentation grenades and clearing fire were used before entering the houses. Wuterich also said that his unit never attempted to cover up the incident and immediately reported that civilians had been killed in Haditha.

The Department of Defense has said that the rules of engagement in effect at Haditha prohibited unprovoked attacks on civilians, but this of course assumes that the marines knew that the homes were populated by civilians. In addition, marines are trained as a matter of combat survival to suppress enemy fire with overwhelming force, including the tossing of grenades into a room before entering. The lead investigator of the Haditha incident has confirmed that some training the marines received conflicted with their rules of engagement and led them to believe that if fired upon from a house, they could clear it with grenades and gunfire without determining whether civilians were inside.

The Haditha Incident stands as a classic example of the profound difficulties and the immense potential for human tragedy encountered by conventional military forces engaged in combating an insurgency in which the insurgents' very survival depends on blending in with—and often becoming indistinguishable from—the local civilian population. Indeed, even when conventional forces win a tactical battle against insurgents, they risk incurring a more important strategic loss when they kill civilians (intentionally or accidentally) in the process. Inevitably, conventional forces conducting counterinsurgency operations are confronted by an unavoidable double standard: while being held strictly accountable to observing all of the internationally accepted laws of war, they must fight an enemy whose tactics principally rely on terror and indiscriminate killing of civilians and combatants alike. The very thought that al-Qaeda or other terrorist group leadership would conduct war crimes investigations for atrocities committed by its members as the U.S. Marine Corps has done in the wake of the Haditha Incident seems absurd; atrocities are the insurgents' main tactic, not aberrations occurring during the heat of battle. The Haditha Incident also emphasizes that a conventional counterinsurgency force's major actions and policies must be in place to prevent or at least limit civilian deaths: effective training, strict discipline and individual accountability, rigidly enforced rules of engagement, and competent leaders at every level of command who remain totally involved in the conduct of all combat operations. Not even one of these critical elements can be lacking or ignored, as that raises the risk of a repeat of such incidents as that which occurred at Haditha. When an atrocity occurs or is even suspected to have taken place, it must be rigorously investigated and, whenever warranted, vigorously prosecuted. A cover-up (or even the appearance of one) not only denies justice to the victims but, in a practical military sense, is also ultimately counterproductive.

Stefan Brooks

See also: Abu Ghraib; Guantánamo Bay Detainment Camp

Further Reading

Brennan, Phil. "New Evidence Emerges in Haditha Case." *Newsmax*, June 26, 2006.

Ephron, Dan. "Haditha Unraveled." *Newsweek*, October 29, 2007.

McGirk, Tim. "Collateral Damage or Civilian Massacre at Haditha." *Time*, March 19, 2006.

"What Happened at Haditha." Editorial. *Wall Street Journal*, October 19, 2007.

White, Josh. "Marine Says Rules Were Followed." *Washington Post*, June 11, 2006.

Hakim, Abd al-Aziz al-

A mid-level Iraqi Arab Shia cleric and former leader of the Supreme Islamic Council of Iraq, Abd al-Aziz al-Hakim was born sometime in 1950 in the southern Iraqi city of Najaf, a descendant of the Prophet Muhammad and the fourth caliph, Ali ibn Abi Talib. Hakim is a hujjat al-Islam (literally "proof of Islam") and the lower-level ranking of cleric, not a *mujtahid*. More importantly, he is the current leader of the Supreme Islamic Iraqi Council (SIIC), one of the two largest Iraqi Shia political parties, a position he inherited upon the assassination of his brother, Ayatollah Muhammad Baqir al-Hakim, who was killed by a massive car bomb in Najaf in August 2003.

Abd al-Aziz's father was Grand Ayatollah Sayyid Muhsin al-Hakim (1889–1970), the preeminent Shia religious scholar and authority in Iraq from 1955 until his death in 1970. The family has deep roots in Iraq as one of the premier Arab Shia scholarly families based in Najaf, where Imam Ali's shrine is located, although the family originally came from the Jabal Amil in southern Lebanon. Abd al-Aziz's brother, Sayyid Muhammad Mahdi (1940?–1988), another activist, was assassinated in Khartoum, Sudan, most likely on the orders of Iraqi president Saddam Hussein. All three of the Hakim brothers studied religious subjects under both their father and then Ayatollah Sayyid Muhammad Baqir al-Sadr (1935–1980), one of their father's leading students and an activist scholar who was one of the intellectual founders of the Islamic Dawa Party (Hizb al-Da'wah al-Islamiyya), Iraq's other large Shia political party.

Abd al-Aziz's earliest social and political activism occurred in tandem with his father and older brothers, all of whom were

Abd al-Aziz al-Hakim, leader of the Supreme Council for the Islamic Revolution in Iraq, casts his vote in Baghdad on January 30, 2005. (U.S. Department of Defense)

actively opposed to the growing influence of the Iraqi Communist Party (ICP) among segments of Shia youth during the 1950s and 1960s. Grand Ayatollah Hakim was an outspoken critic of communism, and he passed a juridical opinion (fatwa) against membership in the ICP in February 1960. He was also instrumental in the formation and support of the Jamaat al-Ulama (Society of Religious Scholars), a coalition of religious scholars (*ulama*) opposed to the growing influence of the ICP and other Iraqi secular political parties. Due to his age, Abd al-Aziz was not actively involved in the Jamaat al-Ulama and the earlier stages of the Islamic Dawa Party, although his brothers were.

Following the Iraqi invasion of Iran in September 1980 and the outbreak of the Iran-Iraq War (1980–1988), when Hussein issued orders calling for the execution of members of the Dawa Party, Abd al-Aziz and his brother Muhammad Baqir left Iraq for Iran along with thousands of other Iraqi Shias, many of them political activists. The Iraqi government claimed that it might face traitorous actions by Iraq's long-disenfranchised Shia Arab majority. Ayatollah Baqir al-Sadr had been executed along with his sister, Amina bint Haydar al-Sadr (also known as Bint al-Huda), in April 1980.

In November 1982 Baqir al-Hakim announced the formation of the Supreme Council for the Islamic Revolution in Iraq (SCIRI), which initially was an umbrella organization that brought together officials from the various Iraqi exiled opposition movements, although it eventually became its own political party as other groups broke away over policy and ideological disputes. SCIRI's leadership was based in Tehran, and it was more heavily influenced by Iranian individuals and political competition than the Dawa Party. In 1982 and 1983 SCIRI's paramilitary wing, the Badr Organization, was founded under Abd al-Aziz's leadership. Badr was made up of recruits from among the Iraqi exile community living in Iran as well as Iraqi Shia prisoners of war, who received training and equipment from the Iranian Revolutionary Guard Corps on the instructions of Grand Ayatollah Ruhollah Khomeini, Iran's revolutionary leader. On the eve of the U.S.- and British-led invasion of Iraq in March 2003, Badr reportedly fielded 10,000–15,000 fighters, with a core elite group of several thousand fighters.

Abd al-Aziz and Muhammad Baqir returned to Iraq on May 12, 2003, making their way to the southern Iraqi port city of Basra, where the ayatollah gave a rousing speech in front of an estimated 100,000 Iraqi supporters in the main soccer stadium, rejecting U.S. postwar domination of the country. The Hakims were soon joined by thousands of SCIRI members and Badr fighters who flooded into southern Iraq. Following his brother's assassination on August 29, 2003, Abd al-Aziz assumed control of the SCIRI, which several years later was renamed the Supreme Iraqi Islamic Council (SIIC). He has maintained a close relationship with the U.S. government. In fact, he was the favorite of various American figures to succeed Ibrahim al-Jafari, perhaps due to his English skills and demeanor, but he was not as popular with Iraqis, as was demonstrated at the polls. During Abd al-Aziz's tenure as party chief, then-SCIRI achieved a key electoral victory in December 2005 as part of the United Iraqi Alliance, a loose coalition of primarily Shia political parties that, together with the Kurdish political list, dominates Iraqi politics today. In the past, he has supported attempts to create a decentralized federal system. He has vocally supported the creation of an autonomous Shia region in southern and central Iraq, a move that has been repeatedly opposed by other Shiite parties such as Fadhila and by Sunni Arab politicians and Tayyar al-Sadr (Sadr Movement), the sociopolitical faction led by Muqtada al-Sadr.

Badr officials and fighters are heavily represented in the Iraqi state security forces and important ministries, including the Ministry of the Interior. They were blamed for summarily arresting, kidnapping, torturing, and murdering Sunni Arabs (many of whom were also political rivals) and random civilians off of the streets, particularly in mixed Sunni-Shia neighborhoods, which they sought to cleanse of Sunni Arabs. The SIIC leadership denies involvement in such attacks despite strong evidence to the contrary.

Beginning in 2004 and reaching its apogee in the spring of 2008, Badr fighters, many of them while in their capacity as Iraqi state security, engaged in running street battles with the Sadrists over political power, reportedly seeking to weaken them before the 2009 municipal elections. Heavy fighting under the direction of the official Iraqi state, backed by Prime Minister Nuri al-Maliki and the U.S. military, took place between SIIC-dominated Iraqi security forces and Sadrist fighters in Baghdad in 2007 and in Basra during the spring and early summer of 2008.

Abd al-Aziz is aided by his two sons, Muhsin (1974–) and Ammar (1972–), who both head various offices and departments within the SIIC. Ammar is the secretary-general of the al-Mihrab Martyr Foundation, an SIIC-affiliate organization that has built mosques, Islamic centers, and schools throughout southern Iraq and Shia areas of Baghdad, the Iraqi capital; he is also the second-in-command of the SIIC.

The SIIC publicly recognizes Grand Ayatollah Sayyid Ali al-Sistani, Iraq's senior resident Shia religious authority, as its official religious guide and scholar, although the degree to which it actually follows his religious edicts is unclear because SIIC and Sistani have their own networks of mosques, which reinstituted Friday sermons after the fall of Hussein. SIIC and Badr fighters have notably ignored Sistani's calls for intercommunal harmony and a cessation of sectarian/intercommunal killings by both Sunnis and Shias. Hakim and other SIIC leaders have also publicly denied that they seek to establish a religious state in Iraq, as this was the original goal of the SIIC. The party has insisted on a prominent role for Islamic morals, sharia, and institutions, particularly Shia ones, in the present and future Iraqi state.

Christopher Paul Anzalone

See also: Badr Organization; Supreme Iraqi Islamic Council

Further Reading

Dagher, Sam. "Rising Player with a Vision for Shiite Iraq." *Christian Science Monitor*, November 20, 2007.

Jabar, Faleh A. *The Shi'ite Movement in Iraq.* London: Saqi Books, 2003.

Samii, A. William. "Shia Political Alternatives in Postwar Iraq." *Middle East Policy* 10 (May 2003): 93–101.

Visser, Reidar. *Shi'a Separatism in Iraq: Internet Reverie or Real Constitutional Challenge?* Oslo: Norwegian Institute of International Affairs, 2005.

Halliburton

A multinational corporation based in Houston, Texas, that provides specialty products and services to the oil and gas industries and also constructs oil fields, refineries, pipelines, and chemical plants through its main subsidiary KBR (Kellogg, Brown, and Root). Although Halliburton conducts operations in more than 120 countries, controversy regarding Halliburton Energy Services has focused on U.S. government contracts awarded to the company following the 2003 Iraq War and allegations of conflict of interest involving Vice President Richard (Dick) Cheney, who was a former Halliburton chief executive officer (CEO).

In 1919 during the midst of the oil boom in Texas and Oklahoma, Mr. and Mrs. Erle P. Halliburton began cementing oil wells in Burkburnett, Texas. That same year the Halliburtons established their business in Dallas, Texas. They then moved the business to Ardmore, Oklahoma. In 1924 the Halliburton Oil Well Cementing Company was incorporated. A significant expansion of the company occurred in 1962 with the acquisition of Brown and Root, a construction and engineering firm that became a wholly owned subsidiary of Halliburton. Brown and Root had been established in 1919 by brothers George and Herman Brown along with their brother-in-law Dan Root. Employing political patronage with influential figures such as Lyndon B. Johnson, Brown and Root grew from fulfilling small road-paving projects to garnering military contracts constructing military bases and naval warships. Brown and Root was part of a consortium responsible for providing approximately 85 percent of the infrastructure required by the U.S. military during the Vietnam War.

The relationship between Halliburton and the U.S. military establishment was enhanced in 1992 when the Pentagon, under the direction of Secretary of Defense Dick Cheney, offered the company a contract for the bulk of support services for U.S. military operations abroad. Three years later Cheney was elected chairman and CEO of Halliburton. One of his first initiatives at Halliburton was the acquisition of rival Dresser Industries for $7.7 billion.

Halliburton, however, also inherited the legal liabilities of Dresser for asbestos poisoning claims. The asbestos settlement caused Halliburton's stock price to plummet 80 percent in 1999. Nevertheless, during Cheney's five-year tenure at Halliburton (1995–2000), government contracts awarded to the company rose to $1.5 billion. This contrasts with just $100 million in government contracts from 1990 to 1995.

Upon assuming the vice presidency in the George W. Bush administration in 2001, Cheney declared that he would be severing all ties with the company. He continued, however, to earn deferred compensation worth approximately $150,000 annually along with stock options worth more than $18 million. Cheney assured critics that he would donate proceeds from the stock options to charity.

Even if Cheney did not personally profit, Halliburton secured several lucrative government contracts to rebuild Iraq and support the U.S. military presence in that nation following the U.S.-led invasion of Iraq in March 2003. It is estimated that Halliburton's Iraq contracts are worth as much as $18 billion. The company also received contracts worth several hundred million dollars for support work in Afghanistan after the beginning of Operation ENDURING FREEDOM in late 2001. Although the company enjoys relatively low profit margins from its military contracts, Halliburton stock hit a record high in January 2006.

These profits have been subject to charges of corruption. For example, in 2003 a division of Halliburton overcharged the government by some $61 million for buying and transporting fuel from Kuwait into Iraq. Halliburton insisted that the high costs were the fault of a Kuwaiti subcontractor. Halliburton also received criticism for a $7 billion no-bid contract to rebuild Iraqi oil fields. This endeavor was largely a failure, as Iraq's oil production grew only slowly, and international access to Iraqi oil supplies has been limited. An effort to construct a pipeline under the Tigris River at Fatah was a dismal failure and was undertaken against the advice of experts who cautioned that the area was geologically unstable and could not support such a project. Halliburton spent $75.7 million dollars on the failed project, including approximately $100,000 per day as its crews were idle because of broken drill bits and other damaged equipment. Nevertheless, the U.S. government issued Halliburton another contract, for $66 million, to complete the pipeline. Once completed, the project will have cost 110 percent more than the original estimate.

Defenders of Halliburton insist that few companies have the resources and capital necessary to carry out the large-scale assignments given to Halliburton. Company executives also point out that if Halliburton were not providing support operations, far more troops would be needed in Iraq. The controversies surrounding Halliburton's role in the Iraq War continue to raise questions as to the rationale for the initial March 2003 invasion of Iraq, the mismanagement of the postwar stability and reconstruction efforts there, and the company's close relationship to the George W. Bush administration, whose wars in Afghanistan and Iraq have allowed the company to garner handsome profits.

Ron Briley

See also: Bush, George Walker; Cheney, Richard Bruce; Iraqi Freedom, Operation

Further Reading

Briody, Dan. The *Halliburton Agenda: The Politics of Oil and Money*. Hoboken, NJ: Wiley, 2004.

Purdum, Todd S., and the Staff of *The New York Times. A Time of Our Choosing:* *America's War in Iraq.* New York: Times Books/Henry Holt, 2003.

High Mobility Multipurpose Wheeled Vehicle

Multipurpose wheeled vehicle used by the U.S. armed forces. The High Mobility Multipurpose Wheeled Vehicle (HMMWV, popularly called the Humvee) has been in service since 1983. A commercial, civilian version was successfully marketed as the Hummer. The Humvee first saw service in Operation Just Cause in Panama in December 1989. It has seen extensive service in Iraq and Afghanistan since the 1991 Persian Gulf War.

Since the invention of the internal combustion engine, the world's militaries have developed and used a wide variety of wheeled and tracked vehicles to transport personnel and cargo and to serve as platforms for weapons and other uses. During World War II the most common wheeled utility vehicle was the Jeep. Developed for the U.S. Army, the Jeep had various official designations and was a small, quarter-ton truck with four-wheel drive for off-road capability. It served through the 1970s with many changes over time. The Jeep's limited capacity and high center of gravity, which resulted in numerous rollovers, led the Army to develop other wheeled vehicles, such as the six-wheel-drive 1.5-ton M-561 Gamma Goat and the M-715, a 1.25-ton truck. The Army also procured commercial trucks like the 0.75-ton Dodge, designated the M-880. In 1975 and 1976 the Army tested the commercial CJ-5 Jeep, the Dodge Ram Charger, Chevrolet Blazer, and Ford Bronco. Funding cuts in the post–Vietnam War era and the need for a platform for the TOW (tube-launched, optically tracked, wire-guided) missile led the Army

Members of the U.S. Air Force 170th Security Police Squadron patrol an air base flight line in an M998 High Mobility Multipurpose Wheeled Vehicle (Humvee) mounting an M-60 machine gun, during Operation DESERT STORM. (U.S. Department of Defense)

to consider other options, such as the Cadillac Gage Scout, various dune buggies, and the Combat Support Vehicle (CSV) dedicated to the TOW mission. The plan was to produce 3,800 CSVs, but Congress scrapped that program in 1977, deeming that vehicle too limited.

In 1980 Congress approved the development of the Humvee with the objective of producing 50,000 1.25-ton four-wheel-drive vehicles to replace the multiplicity of vehicles, many worn out by years of use, in the Army inventory. This was a break-through, as up to this time the Army had opted for vehicles of varying sizes and carrying capacities. In 1981 three contractors were asked to bid on the Humvee: Chrysler Defense, Teledyne Continental, and AM General, whose parent company, American Motors, had purchased Kaiser-Jeep in 1969. All three produced prototypes for testing,

which was done at Aberdeen Proving Ground, Maryland, and Yuma, Arizona, in 1982. The AM General model, nicknamed the Hummer as a play on the military designation and thought to be catchier than Humvee, won.

The first production contract in 1983 was for 55,000 vehicles to be produced over 5 years, a number later raised to 70,000 vehicles. The Army received 39,000, the Marines 11,000, and the remainder went to the Air Force and Navy. By 1995 over 100,000 Humvees had been produced. Production would double by 2005 for both U.S. and foreign sales. American Motors began marketing the Hummer commercially in 1983, and the brand is still marketed by General Motors.

Designated the M-998, the Humvee four-wheel-drive vehicle weighs 5,200 pounds; measures 15 feet long, 7.08 feet wide, and

6 feet high (reducible to under 5 feet); and is powered by a 150-horsepower, 378-cubic-inch, V-8 diesel engine. Its ground clearance of more than 16 inches and four-wheel drive make the Humvee an effective off-road carrier. Its 25-gallon fuel tank allows for a range of 350 miles at speeds up to 65 miles per hour. It can ford water up to 2.5 feet deep and double that with a deep-water-fording kit. It can climb a 60 percent incline and traverse a 40 percent incline fully loaded. Its very wide stance and low center of gravity make it difficult to turn over.

The Humvee replaced several military vehicles and became a platform for many tasks. In addition to the Humvee's basic configuration as a truck with more than a ton of carrying capacity, there are variants that function as an ambulance, a TOW-missile platform, a machine-gun or grenade-launcher platform, a prime mover for towing a 105-millimeter (mm) howitzer, and a shelter carrier. Some variants are equipped with a winch on the front, which provides additional capabilities, especially self-recovery. The Humvee can be delivered to the battlefield by helicopter. The weight of the vehicle can be reduced by using versions without roofs or with canvas roofs and sides. As the Humvee has matured over time, it has been reconfigured and manufactured in what the military calls M-A1 and M-A2 versions.

Not designed to be an armored combat vehicle, the Humvee in its original configuration posed serious problems in the conflicts in Iraq and Afghanistan. The military had already been exploring how to armor Humvees in light of experience in the peacekeeping mission in the Balkans in the 1990s. The canvas roofs and sides of some models offered no protection from small-arms fire, and the metal versions were little help against roadside mines. The solutions were not simple, but there have been several programs to alleviate this serious hazard in the M-1114 and M-1151 up-armored variants.

The up-armored vehicle is now in service in combat areas, and armor kits were made available for installation in the theater of operations. The basic upgrade in armament is a 2,000-pound kit that added steel plating and ballistic-resistant windows. The steel plating under the vehicle was designed to absorb an 8-pound explosive. The kit for in-theater installation weighs about 750 pounds. As the Humvee mission expanded, changes were made in engine power, transmission, suspension, and engine cooling. Some changes can be made in theater, but many have to be done at depot level in the United States as Humvees are modified for deployment or repaired after combat damage. The operational tempo in combat also produces vehicle wear seven times that found in peacetime. This fact, the loss of 250 Humvees in combat, and the aging of the inventory stress the ability of the military to maintain readiness and prepare for future challenges. The cost of updating the inventory as it rotates through the depot system is $52,000 per vehicle.

Daniel E. Spector

See also: U.S. Army, Iraq War

Further Reading

Cordesman, Anthony H., and Abraham R. Wagner. *The Lessons of Modern War*, Vol. 4, *The Gulf War*. Boulder, CO: Westview, 1996.

Green, Michael, and Greg Stewart. *HUMVEE at War*. St. Paul, MN: Zenith, 2005.

Scales, Robert H. *Certain Victory: The U.S. Army in the Gulf War*. Washington, DC: Brassey's, 1994.

Thompson, Loren B., Lawrence J. Korb, and Caroline P. Wadhams. *Army Equipment after Iraq*. Arlington, VA: Lexington Institute, Center for American Progress, 2006.

Zaloga, Steven J. *HMMWV, Humvee, 1980–2005: U.S. Army Tactical Vehicle.* Oxford, UK: Osprey, 2006.

Hormuz, Strait of

Narrow body of water that connects the Persian Gulf to the Gulf of Oman and the Indian Ocean. The Strait of Hormuz is bounded in the north by Iran and on its south by the United Arab Emirates (UAE) and the Sultanate of Oman. The waters of the Strait of Hormuz are predominately within the claimed territorial waters of these three nations because the United Nations Convention on the Law of the Sea (UNCLOS) defines territorial waters as 12 nautical miles from shore. At its narrowest point, the strait is 21 nautical miles wide, but there are islands throughout its length, most of which belong to Iran. The strait is designated as an international shipping lane. As such, ships are allowed to transit it under the rules of "innocent" or "transit" passage, which permit maritime traffic in key straits that separate international bodies of water.

Because of its location, the Strait of Hormuz is considered a strategic choke point. About 20 percent of world oil shipments transit the strait on any given day aboard commercial tankers. The key nation in this regard is Iran, whose largest port and naval base, Bandar Abbas, is located at the northernmost tip of the strait.

Iran has fortified several islands—the Tunb Islands and Abu Musa—that dominate the strait. Abu Musa, in particular, has long been a source of conflict between Iran and the UAE, especially since Iran's occupation of it in the early 1970s.

The Strait of Hormuz has always been a significant factor in modern wars. During World War II, it was the key conduit for American Lend-Lease aid through Iraq and Iran to the Soviet Union. Since then the strait has been the chief avenue for U.S. seaborne trade into the Gulf region and oil out of it. The strait became even more an issue after the 1979 Islamic Revolution in Iran, which deposed pro-U.S. Mohammad Reza Shah Pahlavi. After that the United States began to station warships in the Persian Gulf to protect U.S. interests in the region.

Near the end of the Iran-Iraq War (1980–1988), Iran attempted to close the strait by mining it to deprive Iraq and other Gulf states of their oil revenues. The United States responded by reflagging oil tankers and forcibly reopening the strait in Operation ERNEST WILL.

Not long after, the United States used the strait as the main conduit for sea-supplied military matériel in support of Operations DESERT SHIELD (1990) and DESERT STORM (the Persian Gulf War, 1991). Thereafter the United States maintained a strong naval presence in the region, including at least one, and often several, aircraft carrier battle groups.

Most recently, the strait was critical to the maritime power projection of Operation IRAQI FREEDOM, the 2003 Anglo-American–led invasion of Iraq. Without access to the Strait of Hormuz, the United States and other Western powers would be severely limited in influencing events in the Middle East. U.S. policy makers in particular continue to keep a wary eye on the Strait of Hormuz, especially given Iran's nuclear ambitions and the often harsh rhetoric coming from its rightist leaders.

John T. Kuehn

See also: IRAQI FREEDOM, Operation

Further Reading

Bowden, Mark. *Guests of the Ayatollah: The First Battle in America's War with Militant Islam.* New York: Atlantic Monthly, 2007.

Marolda, Edward, and Robert Schneller. *Shield and Sword: The United States Navy and the Persian Gulf War.* Annapolis, MD: U.S. Naval Institute Press, 2001.

Husaybah, Battle of

Battle near the Iraqi town of Husaybah, close to the Syrian border, on April 17, 2004, which involved U.S. marines from the I Marine Expeditionary Force. The 14-hour battle occurred concurrently with the First Battle of Fallujah (April 4–May 1, 2004), an operation by the United States to capture the city of Fallujah, also known as Operation VIGILANT RESOLVE. From Husaybah, the insurgents had been attempting to launch an offensive against U.S. forces to divert resources from the attack against Fallujah. The insurgent force numbered about 300 and was operating from positions in the vicinity of the former Baath Party headquarters in Husaybah. U.S. forces numbered 150.

On April 17 the insurgents drew the Americans from their base on the outskirts of Husaybah with a roadside bombing and then with a mortar assault. When the marines retaliated, they encountered an ambush during which they were hit with small-arms and machine-gun fire. The marines then called in reinforcements. The resulting street fighting lasted the entire day and late into the night, with the marines having to advance block by block to clear buildings of insurgents. During the night, Bell AH-1 Cobra helicopter gunships also attacked insurgent positions in the city. The American forces defeated the insurgents after fierce fighting. Five marines were killed and nine wounded in the fight. The insurgents suffered an estimated 150 killed in action, an unknown number of wounded, and 20 captured. The insurgent losses

represented more than 50 percent of their original strength.

Richard B. Verrone

See also: Fallujah

Further Reading

Murray, Williamson, and Robert H. Scales Jr. *The Iraq War: A Military History.* Cambridge, MA: Belknap, 2005.

Ricks, Thomas E. *Fiasco: The American Military Adventure in Iraq.* New York: Penguin, 2006.

West, Bing. *No True Glory: A Frontline Account of the Battle for Fallujah.* New York: Bantam, 2006.

Hussein, Qusay

Iraqi government and military official and son of Iraqi dictator Saddam Hussein. At the time of the U.S.-led invasion of Iraq in March 2003, Qusay Hussein was considered the second most powerful man in Iraq and the likely successor to his father. Qusay Hussein was born in Tikrit, Iraq, on May 17, 1966, the second son of Saddam Hussein and Sajida Talfah. As Arab custom dictates, Saddam Hussein's elder son, Uday, was the most prominent and was raised as his father's successor. Although out of the limelight, Qusay Hussein remained loyal to his father to the point of even imitating his dress and trademark mustache.

While Uday Hussein proved to be mentally unstable and a flamboyant sexual sadist whose antics embarrassed the ruling family, Qusay was much more reserved. Complying with his father's wishes, in 1987 he married the daughter of Mahir Abd al-Rashid, an influential military commander. The marriage produced four children. Although possessing numerous mistresses, Qusay Hussein portrayed himself as a devoted family man.

Qusay's loyalty and patience eventually bore dividends. When Uday's behavior became more erratic in the late 1980s, Saddam Hussein began to turn more to his second son. For example, Qusay was granted broad authority in crushing the Shiite Muslim and Marsh Arabs' uprisings following Iraq's defeat in the 1991 Persian Gulf War. He responded ruthlessly, using torture and executing entire families believed to be disloyal to the regime.

As Uday's position declined, Qusay began to emerge as the likely successor to Saddam Hussein. For his role in crushing the 1991 rebellions, Saddam entrusted Qusay with command of the Special Security Organization (SSO), including Internal Security and the Presidential Guard. In his role as security head, Qusay Hussein oversaw Iraqi's chemical, biological, and nuclear programs. He was also responsible for the repression of opponents of his father's regime. It is believed that Qusay, with his father's approval, had a hand in the attempted assassination of Uday on December 12, 1996.

Clearly Saddam Hussein's favorite, Qusay was named "caretaker" in the event of Saddam's illness or death and given command of the elite Republican Guard. Possessing no formal military training, Qusay Hussein refused to accept advice from more experienced commanders. None dared to question his orders for fear of the consequences, however. The dismal performance of the Republican Guard in failing to slow the American-led invasion in 1991 is often blamed on the lack of military experience of Qusay and his advisers.

Following the terror attacks of September 11, 2001, foreign pressure on Iraq began to increase, and the United States began preparing for a second invasion of Iraq, this time to topple the Hussein regime. Saddam Hussein and his sons temporarily rallied in the face of the overwhelming military force gathering to confront them. On March 18, 2003, U.S. president George W. Bush called on Saddam Hussein and his sons to leave the country, a demand that was rebuffed.

Following the invasion on March 20, 2003, Qusay Hussein went into hiding. On July 22, 2003, Qusay; his 14-year-old son, Mustapha; Uday; and their bodyguard were cornered in Mosul. During the course of a four-hour firefight, all were killed. Following identification, the bodies were buried in Awja.

Robert W. Malick

See also: Hussein, Saddam; Hussein, Uday

Further Reading

Balaghi, Shiva. *Saddam Hussein: A Biography.* Westport, CT: Greenwood, 2006.

Bengio, Ofra. "How Does Saddam Hold On?" *Foreign Affairs* (July/August 2000): 90–103.

Bennett, Brian, and Michael Weisskopf. "The Sum of Two Evils." *Time*, June 2, 2003, 34.

Thomas, Evan, and Christopher Dickey. "Saddam's Sons." *Newsweek*, October 21, 2002, 34.

Woods, Kevin, James Lacy, and Williamson Murray. "Saddam's Delusions." *Foreign Affairs* (May/June 2006): 2–16.

Hussein, Saddam

Iraqi politician, leading figure in the Baath Party, and president of Iraq (1979–2003). Born on April 28, 1937, in the village of Awja, near Tikrit, to a family of sheepherders, Saddam Hussein attended a secular

Saddam Hussein, who ruled Iraq as national president and Revolutionary Command Council chairperson from July 1979 until he was driven from power by a U.S.-led coalition during the Iraq War, in April 2003. (Reuters/Ina/Hulton Archive/Getty Images)

school in Baghdad and in 1957 joined the Baath Party, a socialist and Arab nationalist party. Iraqi Baathists supported General Abd al-Karim Qasim's ouster of the Iraqi monarchy in 1958 but were not favored by President Qasim.

Wounded in an unsuccessful attempt to assassinate Qasim in 1959, Hussein subsequently fled the country but returned after the 1963 Baathist coup and began his rise in the party. He was imprisoned in 1964. Escaping in 1966, Hussein continued to ascend through the party's ranks, becoming second in authority when the party took full and uncontested control of Iraq in 1968 under the leadership of General Ahmad Hassan al-Bakr, a relative of Hussein's. The elderly Bakr gradually relinquished power

to him so that Hussein eventually controlled most of the government.

Hussein became president when Bakr resigned, allegedly because of illness, in July 1979. A week after taking power, Saddam led a meeting of Baath leaders during which the names of his potential challengers were read aloud. They were then escorted from the room and shot. Because Iraq was rent by ethnic and religious divisions, Hussein ruled through a tight web of relatives and associates from Tikrit, backed by the Sunni Muslim minority. He promoted economic development through Iraqi oil production, which accounted for 10 percent of known world reserves. Hussein's modernization was along Western lines, with expanded roles for women and a secular legal system based in part on sharia and Ottoman law. He also promoted the idea of Iraqi nationalism and emphasized Iraq's ancient past, glorifying such figures as kings Hammurabi and Nebuchadnezzar.

Before assuming the presidency, Hussein had courted both the West and the Soviet Union, resulting in arms deals with the Soviets and close relations with the Soviet Union and France. He was also instrumental in convincing the Mohammad Reza Shah Pahlavi of Iran to curb his support of Iraqi Kurds. Hussein's efforts to take advantage of the superpowers' Cold War rivalry, including rapprochement with Iran, fell apart with the overthrow of the shah in the 1979 Iranian Revolution. The shah's successor, Ayatollah Khomeini, a radical, fundamentalist Muslim, bitterly opposed Hussein because of his Sunni background and secularism.

After a period of repeated border skirmishes, Iraq declared war on Iran in September 1980. Hussein's ostensible dispute concerned a contested border, but he also feared Iran's fundamentalism and its support for the Iraqi Shia Muslim majority. Initial success gave way to Iraqi defeats in the face of human-wave attacks and, ultimately, a stalemate. By 1982 Hussein was ready to end the war, but Iranian leaders desired that the fighting continue. In 1988 the United Nations (UN) finally brokered a cease-fire, but not before the war had devastated both nations. The war left Iraq heavily in debt, and Hussein requested relief from his major creditors, including the United States, Kuwait, and Saudi Arabia. He also sought to maintain high oil prices. His efforts were in vain; creditors refused to write off their debts, and Kuwait maintained a high oil output, forcing other oil-producing nations to follow suit.

Hussein responded by declaring Kuwait a "rogue province" of Iraq. He was also enraged by Kuwaiti slant drilling into Iraqi oil fields. Hussein's demands became more strident, and after securing what he believed to be U.S. acquiescence, he ordered Iraqi forces to attack and occupy Kuwait on August 2, 1990. Hussein miscalculated the U.S. reaction. President George H. W. Bush assembled an international military coalition, built up forces in Saudi Arabia (Operation DESERT SHIELD), and then commenced a relentless bombing campaign against Iraq in January 1991. The ground war of February 24–28, 1991, resulted in a crushing defeat of Iraqi forces. Although Hussein withdrew from Kuwait, coalition forces did not seek his overthrow, and he remained in power, ruling a nation devastated by two recent wars.

Hussein retained control of Iraq for another decade, during which he brutally suppressed Kurdish and Shia revolts, relinquished limited autonomy to the Kurds, acquiesced to the destruction of stockpiles of chemical weapons, and pursued a dilatory response to UN efforts to monitor his weapons programs. Convinced—wrongly as it turned out—that Hussein had been building and stockpiling weapons of mass destruction, President George W. Bush asked for and received authorization from Congress to wage war against Iraq. U.S. and coalition forces invaded Iraq in March 2003. Coalition forces took Baghdad on April 10, 2003, and captured Hussein on December 14, 2003, to be brought to trial on charges of war crimes and crimes against humanity.

On November 5, 2006, the Iraqi Special Tribunal found Hussein guilty in the 1982 deaths of 148 Shiite Muslims, whose murders he had ordered. That same day he was sentenced to hang. Earlier, on August 21, 2006, a second trial had begun on charges that Hussein had committed genocide and other atrocities by ordering the systematic extermination of northern Iraqi Kurds during 1987 and 1988, resulting in as many as 180,000 deaths. Before the second trial moved into high gear, however, Hussein filed an appeal, which was rejected by the Iraqi Court on December 26, 2006. Four days later, on December 30, 2006, the Muslim holiday of Eid al-Adha, Hussein was executed by hanging in Baghdad. Before his death, Hussein told U.S. Federal Bureau of Investigation interrogators that he had misled the world to give the impression that Iraq had weapons of mass destruction in order to make Iraq appear stronger in the face of its enemy Iran.

Daniel E. Spector

See also: Bush, George Walker; Hussein, Qusay; Hussein, Uday; Kurds; Shia Uprising

Further Reading

Bengio, Ofra. *Saddam's Word: Political Discourse in Iraq.* New York: Oxford University Press, 1998.

Karsh, Efraim. *Saddam Hussein: A Political Biography.* New York: Grove/Atlantic, 2002.

Miller, Judith, and Laurie Mylroie. *Saddam Hussein and the Crisis in the Gulf.* New York: Times Books, 1990.

Wingate, Brian. *Saddam Hussein: The Rise and Fall of a Dictator.* New York: Rosen, 2004.

Hussein, Uday

Iraqi government official, commander of the Fedayeen Saddam, and eldest son of Iraqi president and dictator Saddam Hussein. Uday Hussein was born in Baghdad on June 18, 1964, and was initially groomed to succeed his father as dictator of Iraq. Uday's mental instability, cruelty, and alcoholism, however, resulted in his being passed over for his younger brother, Qusay

Hussein. Uday's fall from favor began in 1988. During a dinner party that year, he murdered his father's favorite bodyguard and food taster, Kamil Hanna Jajjo. Jajjo had supposedly introduced Saddam to his most recent mistress, which Uday viewed as insulting to his own mother. Originally sentenced to death, Uday was instead imprisoned and tortured. Upon his release, he was exiled to Switzerland as an assistant to the Iraqi ambassador. After six months, however, Swiss authorities quietly expelled Hussein after he threatened to kill a Swiss citizen in a restaurant.

Upon his return to Iraq, Uday attempted to rebuild his power base but was unable to control his sadistic and volatile nature. As head of the Iraqi Olympic Committee, he ordered the torture of athletes whom he believed were not performing to the best of their ability. In one instance, a missed soccer goal resulted in the offending athlete being dragged though gravel and then submerged in raw sewage. Uday also began to dominate the state-owned media, controlling state radio and the youth magazine *Babel*. As minister of youth affairs, Uday headed the paramilitary organization Fedayeen Saddam.

In 1994 Saddam granted Uday control of Iraq's oil-smuggling operations, which were in violation of sanctions by the United Nations (UN) that had been imposed following the 1991 Persian Gulf War. Supervising up to 150,000 barrels of smuggled oil a day provided a vast income. With this revenue, Uday lived a life of ostentatious luxury. He purchased hundreds of foreign sports cars, storing them in underground garages throughout Baghdad. At his numerous palaces, staffs were maintained around the clock, including a personal shopper and two trainers for his pet lions. At the palaces, Uday set up torture chambers, and he reportedly ordered the kidnapping, rape, and torture of scores of Iraqi women, including married women, even brides. Brides were sometimes taken from their wedding celebrations if Uday favored them sexually.

On December 12, 1996, a botched assassination attempt riddled Uday's sports car and two escort vehicles with bullets as they sped through the upper-class Baghdad neighborhood of Mansur. Although hit eight times in the arm, leg, and stomach, Uday survived the attack. Official blame for the attack centered on Iran, although some sources claim Qusay had a hand in the assassination attempt with the approval of his father.

Following the terror attacks on the United States of September 11, 2001, foreign pressure on Iraq began to mount. President Hussein and his sons rallied in the face of the overwhelming military force gathering to confront them, however. On March 18, 2003, on the eve of the Iraq War, U.S. president George W. Bush demanded that Saddam Hussein and his sons leave the country immediately or face an invasion. After they refused this ultimatum, coalition forces invaded Iraq on March 20. Uday went into hiding following the invasion, but on July 22, 2003, he and his brother, Qusay, were cornered by Special Operations Task Force 20 and elements of the U.S. Army's 101st Airborne Division in Mosul, Iraq. After a four-hour firefight, Uday, Qusay, Qusay's 14-year-old son, and a bodyguard were shot dead. Saddam Hussein, meanwhile, was apprehended by American forces on December 13, 2003, and was executed for war crimes on December 30, 2006.

Robert W. Malick

See also: Bush, George Walker; Hussein, Qusay; Hussein, Saddam

Further Reading

Cockburn, Andrew, and Patrick Cockburn. *Out of the Ashes: The Resurrection of Saddam Hussein.* New York: HarperCollins, 2000.

Marr, Phebe. *The Modern History of Iraq.* 2nd ed. Boulder, CO: Westview, 2003.

I

Intelligence

This entry is intended to describe the intelligence issues faced by the U.S. and coalition forces in Iraq, not the problems surrounding the misjudgments around Iraqi weapons of mass destruction (WMD). In some ways, however, Iraqi WMD continued to plague the coalition even after the invasion: major intelligence resources continued to be assigned to the largely abortive search for WMD for a significant time. Therefore, these intelligence assets were not available for more critical intelligence targets during a period when they might have been the most useful.

A more important weakness of the U.S. intelligence support of operations in Iraq after the invasion was that it simply was not prepared for the insurgency environment that developed. In fairness, at least significant precipitants for the insurgency were a series of disastrous decisions by the Coalition Provisional Authority (CPA). Such decisions can change an operational environment sufficiently that intelligence analysts can face a completely different picture as a result of "friendly" actions. Most critically, however, other than a largely discounted Central Intelligence Agency (CIA) report on the probability of an insurgency developing, operational-level intelligence units simply did not plan for or predict a widespread insurgency such as became reality. Although speaking for the operational side rather than intelligence, the commanding general of the U.S. V Corps probably summed up the working

assumptions best when he stated, "The enemy we're fighting is different from the one we'd war gamed against."

In fairness, however, after the initial problems in providing adequate intelligence support to the coalition operations, the United States and other countries involved developed much better systems and procedures. Over time, these initiatives began to pay major dividends in terms of operational success. Fusion centers were established at the major headquarters, bringing together virtually all intelligence agencies from the United States and several other coalition members. These fusion centers (of various names) provided analysis on topics not normally associated with military operations, such as insurgent and terrorist group financing, larger political and cultural issues, and regional impacts of coalition operations.

Other intelligence procedures and techniques at both the operational and tactical levels were developed or refined somewhat "on the fly." Network analysis was used at all levels of intelligence and proved critical in understanding the plethora of insurgent groups. As a result, analysts developed much better skills at targeting the truly critical nodes of the insurgents, such as leaders, bomb makers, and media specialists. Although very much outside of formal doctrine, many U.S. units established company intelligence support teams to provide the tactical commanders better and quicker intelligence on their tactical areas of operation. New intelligence communications architectures were built to pass critical intelligence more quickly from strategic to tactical levels and vice versa. Finally, of course, unmanned aerial vehicles (UAVs) truly came into their own during this war as a crucial surveillance and collection asset.

Despite these major improvements, some difficulties remained for the intelligence system throughout the war. A technical problem was that the vastly expanded use of UAVs and other technical means of collecting intelligence resulted in tightness of the available electronic bandwidth. Coalition forces began a proliferation of headquarters of various types within the theater, almost all of which established their own intelligence cells, creating both overlapping reporting and high demand for personnel to fill positions in these cells. Finally, intelligence sharing—long a problem with multinational operations—remained subject to many roadblocks, particularly between the U.S. and Iraqi intelligence systems.

Lawrence Cline

See also: Central Intelligence Agency; Coalition Provisional Authority; Weapons of Mass Destruction

Further Reading

Burton, Brian, and John Nagl. "Learning as We Go: The US Army Adapts to Counterinsurgency in Iraq, July 2004–December 2006." *Small Wars and Insurgencies* 19, no. 3 (2008): 303–27.

Grau, Lester W. "Guerrillas, Terrorists, and Intelligence Analysts." *Military Review* (July–August 2004): 42–49.

Larson, Eric V. et al. *Assessing Irregular Warfare: A Framework for Intelligence Analysis.* Santa Monica, CA: RAND Arroyo Center, 2008.

Perry, Walter L., and John Gordon IV. *Analytical Support to Intelligence in Counterinsurgencies.* Santa Monica, CA: RAND Corporation, 2008.

Teamey, Kyle, and Jonathan Sweet "Organizing Intelligence for Counterinsurgency." *Military Review* (September–October 2006): 24–29.

Interceptor Body Armor

A form of body armor employed by U.S. military forces, first introduced in 1998. It has been used extensively in Operations Enduring Freedom and Iraqi Freedom. Manufactured by Point Blank Body Armor, Inc., Interceptor body armor replaced the Personnel Armor System for Ground Troops (PASGT) and is considerably more effective in protecting troops than traditional bulletproof outerwear. Interceptor body armor is considered a personnel protection "system," the individual parts of which work together to provide superior protection from bullets, shrapnel, and other projectiles.

The system is comprised of an outer tactical vest (OTV) and two small-arms protective inserts (SAPI). The outer vest and the inserts are made of finely woven Kevlar KM2 fibers, which are both heat and bullet resistant. The armor was tested to be able to withstand and stop a 9-millimeter (mm) 124-grain full metal jacket bullet (FMJ) traveling at a velocity of 1,400 feet per second. The system will stop a variety of slower-moving bullets and shrapnel fragments, and it features removable inserts for shoulder, neck, throat, and groin protection. The two SAPIs that may be added to the front or back of the outer vest significantly increase the system's protective capacity. Made of boron carbide ceramic, the inserts can stop a 7.62-mm NATO rifle round with a muzzle velocity of 2,750 feet per second.

Interceptor body armor also features numerous configurations that mimic existing backpacks and carrying systems, so soldiers can tailor their body armor for specific tasks or missions. The body armor system is available in several exterior patterns, including coyote brown, traditional woodland camouflage, three-color desert camouflage, and the newer universal camouflage pattern. When worn with the two inserts, the total weight of the armor system is 16.4 pounds (the outer vest weighs 8.4 pounds, while the two inserts weigh 4 pounds each). This is markedly less than the Interceptor's predecessor, the PSAGT, which weighed in at a hefty 25.1 pounds. Nearly 10 pounds lighter, Interceptor body armor also allows soldiers considerably more freedom to maneuver. More recently, SAPIs designed for side protection have also been introduced. Heavier than the standard inserts, they weigh in at 7.1 pounds each. A complete armor system costs $1,585.

During the Iraq War, many infantry soldiers complained that Interceptor body armor was too cumbersome and too stout for the generally lightly armed Iraqi insurgents they were battling. Some argued that they were unable to pursue the enemy with the full armor system and the many supplies and arms they had to carry. On the other hand, U.S. troops who principally rode in vehicles praised the system for its ability to protect against improvised explosive devices (IEDs) and ambushes.

Interceptor body armor has not been without its problems and detractors, however. In May 2005 the U.S. Marine Corps ordered the recall of more than 5,000 OTVs because they allegedly were unable to stop a 9-mm bullet, which was the requirement upon manufacture. The problems soon received press attention, and in November 2005 the Marines recalled an additional 10,342 OTVs because ballistics tests had proven their inadequacy against 9-mm bullets. The problems with the armor system led a

sizable number of American troops to purchase their own civilian body armor, a development that deeply troubled the Pentagon. Furthermore, many soldiers and marines refused to wear the additional side inserts because of their added weight, making them more vulnerable to injury or death. One Marine Corps study has suggested that 43 percent of marines killed by torso wounds may have been saved had Interceptor body armor been more effective.

The problems with Interceptor armor received high-profile media coverage, and the U.S. Congress launched several investigations into its manufacturing and deployment. In May 2006 the U.S. Army announced that it would be sponsoring a competition for a new body-armor system that would replace the Interceptor body armor. In the meantime, numerous improvements and additions have been made to the existing body armor, including the use of an entirely new and improved outer tactical vest. In September 2006 the Marine Corps announced that its personnel would begin receiving modular tactical vests in lieu of the Interceptor OTV, made by Protective Products International. The controversies surrounding Interceptor body armor proved to be a public-relations fiasco for the Pentagon, raising claims that the Department of Defense was not adequately protecting U.S. soldiers.

Paul G. Pierpaoli Jr.

See also: U.S. Army, Iraq War

Further Reading

Savage, Robert C. Woosnam. *Brassey's Book of Body Armor.* Dulles, VA: Potomac Books, 2002.

Solis, William M. *Defense Logistics: Army and Marine Corps Individual Body Armor System Issues.* Washington, DC: U.S. Government Printing Office, 2007.

Iraq, Air Force

The Iraqi Air Force, initially created under the direction and guidance of the British Mandate government in 1931, grew steadily through six decades by importing technology and hardware from multiple sources, most notably Great Britain, France, and the Soviet Union. Its expansion was largely driven by the aftermath of unsuccessful attacks on Israel, which often led to the destruction of significant numbers of Iraqi warplanes. In 1991 it was virtually destroyed by the combined air forces of the international coalition formed to evict Iraqi occupation units from Kuwait (Operation DESERT STORM). Just prior to the 1991 Persian Gulf War, in the hope of preserving the airplanes for future use, much of the pre-1991 Iraqi air fleet was flown to Iran. The government of Iran seized control of the warplanes, however, further degrading Iraq's aerial defense capability. In the years after the Persian Gulf War, Iraq's remaining warplanes slowly degenerated due to poor maintenance, a lack of trained aircraft technicians, and a shortage of vital repair parts. During the 2003 Anglo-American–led invasion of Iraq (Operation IRAQI FREEDOM), coalition forces reported virtually no aerial activity by the Iraqi military.

In 1931 the air arm of the Iraqi Army was created, primarily using obsolete British equipment. Throughout the next four decades, the growing Iraqi Air Force continued to use equipment considered obsolete by Western standards, but of sufficient quality to become one of the most powerful Arab air forces in the Middle East. Regionally, only the Israeli and Egyptian air forces were of superior size and quality. When Iraq became an independent nation in 1947, it continued to pursue surplus equipment from Great Britain, France, and the Soviet Union. By using cast-off warplanes, the fledgling Iraqi government kept the purchase and maintenance costs of its air force manageable.

In 1948 the Iraqi Air Force saw its first significant action outside of the national borders. When the state of Israel proclaimed its independence on May 14, 1948, it was immediately invaded by the armies of Egypt, Iraq, Lebanon, Syria, and Transjordan. Because Israel had no warplanes at the start of the Israeli-Arab War (1948–1949), Iraqi attack aircraft held complete air superiority and could attack Israeli ground forces with impunity. They proved largely ineffective, however, and over the course of the war the nascent Israeli Air Force proved equal to the task of driving back the Iraqi warplanes. In June 1967 Israel launched preemptive strikes against Egypt, Jordan, and Syria, fearing that an attack from the Arab nations was imminent. This prompted the Six-Day War. After the initial assaults, the Israeli Air Force turned its attention to Iraq, launching massive raids against Iraqi airfields and destroying much of the Iraqi Air Force on the ground. The few warplanes that survived the attacks remained grounded at airfields in eastern Iraq, presumably outside the range of Israeli raids. In the October 1973 Yom Kippur (Ramadan) War, elements of the Iraqi Air Force joined the conflict in support of the Syrian Army and performed well enough against the Israeli Air Force that Iraq exited the war with its aerial fleet largely intact.

Throughout the 1970s and 1980s, Iraq used France and the Soviet Union as its primary warplane suppliers. Over 100 French Mirage F1 jets replaced the obsolete fleet of British Hawker Hunters. These were supplemented by approximately 100 French-built

Gazelle, Super-Frelon, and Alouette helicopters. The most advanced Soviet fighter in the Iraqi arsenal was the MiG-29 Fulcrum; 24 joined a fleet of more than 200 MiG-21 Fishbed aircraft in 1987. Air transport capacity was primarily supplied by the Il-76 Candid transport and aerial tanker. During the Iran-Iraq War (1980–1988), the Iraqi Air Force served primarily in support of Iraqi ground forces. Iraq was able to maintain local air superiority over the primary battle zone of the war but could not withstand the numerically superior Iranian Army. Soon the Iraqi Air Force began to deploy chemical weapons in a desperate attempt to hold off massive Iranian offensives.

After only two years of peace the Iraqi Air Force was again committed to combat. On August 2, 1990, Iraqi president Saddam Hussein ordered an invasion of Kuwait in the form of an overwhelming combined-arms assault on the small Persian Gulf nation. The world reaction was outrage, as American and Saudi Arabian military units scrambled into position to prevent further aggression. The United Nations (UN) imposed economic sanctions and threatened the use of force to drive Iraq from Kuwait. When Hussein refused to withdraw his troops, a U.S.-led multinational invasion of Kuwait and Iraq ensued (Operation DESERT STORM). The invasion began on January 17, 1991, and lasted several weeks, involving massive air strikes against Iraqi command and control centers, airfields, and antiair defenses.

Despite the fact that Iraq owned the sixth-largest air fleet in the world, including as many as 750 warplanes in 1990 and 1991, the Iraqi Air Force offered minimal resistance to the coalition's establishment of complete air superiority. During the entire aerial campaign, Iraqi fighters did not shoot down a single coalition aircraft and rarely attempted to intercept coalition warplanes. Coalition forces downed 42 Iraqi aircraft, including 9 Mirage F1s and 5 MiG-29s, and reported that Iraqi pilots were poorly trained and ineffective in aerial combat. Rather than face annihilation, approximately 130 Iraqi combat pilots flew to Iran, where they were interned by the Iranian government for the duration of the war. When the conflict ended, the pilots were released, but the aircraft were integrated into the Iranian military. According to American estimates, more than 200 Iraqi aircraft were destroyed on the ground during DESERT STORM. By the end of the war the air force contained only 50 Mirage F1s, 15 MiG-29s, and fewer than 100 older aircraft models.

In the period after the Persian Gulf War, coalition forces established a pair of no-fly zones over Iraq, prohibiting Iraqi warplanes from overflying all but the central third of the nation. Coalition aircraft frequently bombed targets in Iraq to enforce compliance with the terms of the 1991 cease-fire. From 1991 until 2003, the Iraqi Air Force rapidly deteriorated due to massive shortages of spare aircraft parts and trained mechanics. As of 2002 Iraq owned only 5 serviceable MiG-29 fighters and fewer than 40 serviceable Mirage F1s, supplemented by fewer than 100 older warplanes. By the beginning of the Anglo-American–led coalition invasion of Iraq in March 2003 (Operation IRAQI FREEDOM), the Iraqi Air Force had virtually ceased to exist.

Coalition forces routinely found derelict aircraft as they captured Iraqi airfields. Some advanced Iraqi warplanes were found literally buried in the desert in an attempt to preserve them from enemy air strikes. After Iraqi president Saddam Hussein was deposed in April 2003, coalition forces began to slowly rebuild the Iraqi military as a key component of the establishment of a democratic Iraqi government. The resurgent air force now serves primarily in a transport capacity, and it has been outfitted with American-built C-130 Hercules transport planes and UH-1 helicopters. Iraq has not been able to import new aircraft since the 1991 Persian Gulf War, and thus its few remaining aircraft have become increasingly obsolete.

In August 2009 the Iraqi Defense Ministry revealed that Iraq owned 19 MiG-21 and MiG-23 fighter jets that were in storage in Serbia. Saddam Hussein had sent the aircraft to Serbia for repairs in the late 1980s during the Iran-Iraq War. The aircraft could not be returned to Iraq because of the subsequent international sanctions. Upon learning of the existence of the aircraft in 2009, the Iraqi government arranged with the Serbs to refurbish and return the aircraft on a priority basis.

The United States has agreed to provide Iraq with propeller-driven Hawker Beechcraft T-6A aircraft that would be used to train Iraqi jet pilots to fly the Lockheed Martin F-16 Fighting Falcon. In October 2012, Iraq signed a contract to purchase 18 F-16 fighter aircraft.

Paul Joseph Springer

See also: IRAQI FREEDOM, Operation

Further Reading

Butler, Richard. *The Greatest Threat: Iraq, Weapons of Mass Destruction and the Growing Crisis in Global Security*. New York: PublicAffairs, 2000.

Herzog, Chaim. *The Arab-Israeli Wars: War and Peace in the Middle East from the War of Independence to Lebanon*. Westminster, MD: Random House, 1984.

Hiro, Dilip. *The Longest War: The Iran-Iraq Military Conflict*. London: Routledge, 1991.

Murray, Williamson, and Robert H. Scales Jr. *The Iraq War: A Military History*. Cambridge, MA: Belknap, 2005.

Rubin, Barry, and Thomas A. Keaney, eds. *Armed Forces in the Middle East: Politics and Strategy*. Portland, OR: Frank Cass, 2002.

Iraq, Army

The Iraqi Army has historically been one of the most technologically advanced and aggressive military forces in the modern Middle East. Since the end of World War II Iraq has joined three wars against Israel, launched invasions of Iran and Kuwait, and been attacked by two multinational forces under American leadership. The Iraqi Army has also frequently engaged in internal strife, fighting to put down repeated Kurdish and Shiite revolts against the government. In addition, the Iraqi Army has played a fundamental role in the Iraqi government, having participated in a series of coups d'état against the existing government beginning in the late 1950s. After the most recent invasion and occupation of Iraq, which began in 2003 with Operation IRAQI FREEDOM, the Iraqi Army was declared dissolved by the Coalition Provisional Authority (CPA), the interim occupation government. The CPA then began to rebuild the Iraqi military from the ground up, including its complete retraining.

The military history of Iraq stretches back several thousand years. The region of Mesopotamia, situated astride the Tigris and Euphrates rivers, is often considered the "cradle of civilization." The ancient Sumerian, Akkadian, and Babylonian empires each dominated the region. By the ninth century CE, Baghdad was an economic and cultural center for the entire Muslim world. In 1638 the region was assimilated into the Ottoman Empire through military conquest. Iraq remained a part of Ottoman Turkey until World War I, when it was invaded and

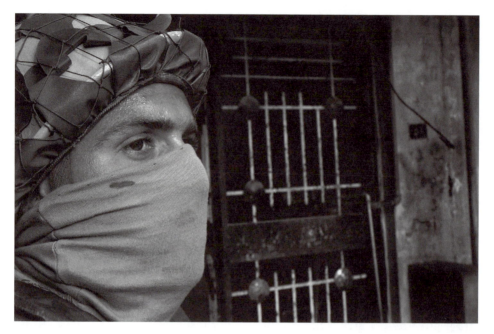

A member of the Iraqi Civil Defense Corp watches an apartment complex while team members search rooms during a raid on March 29, 2004, in Baghdad. (U.S. Department of Defense)

occupied by a British expeditionary force that landed at Basra and gradually moved northward. The British troops were assisted by Iraqi Arabs, emboldened by promises of independence at the end of the war. When World War I ended the Ottoman Empire was dissolved, but the modern state of Iraq was largely controlled by the British and remained a British Mandate until 1947.

In the interwar period a series of rebellions against British rule erupted in Iraq. The first began in May 1920, when Iraqi nationalists, angered at the creation of the British Mandate, led a general Arab insurrection against the newly constituted government. In addition to feeling frustrated by their failure to obtain independence, the rebels also resented the actual composition of the mandate government. It consisted almost entirely of foreign bureaucrats, particularly British colonial officials transplanted from India. By February 1921

British military forces had successfully quelled the rebellion, only to see a Kurdish revolt begin the following year. The Kurdish attempt to form an independent Kurdish state was primarily stymied through the use of airpower, against which the Kurds had no defense. Iraqi Army units under British control assisted in the suppression of the Kurdish revolt. In the 1930s two more major uprisings occurred. In August 1933 Assyrian Christians rebelled against the government, provoking a harsh retaliation by the Iraqi Army that left 600 dead. A religious-based revolt occurred again in 1935, when Shiite Muslims attempted to overthrow the reigning government and were brutally suppressed by British and Iraqi troops.

In 1941, with World War II raging in Europe, Iraqi politician Rashid Ali al-Gaylani and his military colleagues known as the Golden Square perceived an opportunity to overthrow British control. After they seized power, Ali proclaimed an independent Iraq. The Allied powers feared that he would align his government with the Axis nations of Germany and Italy because Germany had been directing propaganda efforts in neighboring Syria and Iraq. British residents and officials took refuge in the British legation, and to rescue them, the British sent in forces that quickly defeated the Iraqi Army and reestablished the mandate government. Three separate Kurdish revolts broke out in the 1940s, each led by Mullah Mustafa Barzani. All were quickly suppressed by the Iraqi Army, bolstered by British air power.

On May 14, 1948, Jews in Palestine led by David Ben-Gurion proclaimed the State of Israel. The announcement provoked an immediate invasion by Egypt, Iraq, Lebanon, Syria, and Transjordan; thus began the Israeli-Arab War of 1948–1949. Iraqi forces operated in conjunction with Syrian and Transjordanian troops and were occasionally aided by members of the Palestinian Arab Liberation Army. The Arab forces did not have a technological advantage as had been claimed, and the Arab coalition was incapable of overrunning the new nation. The Iraqi expeditionary force made small initial gains but could not withstand the eventual Israeli counterattack. The Iraqi Army in 1948 included more than 20,000 troops, of which 5,000 were initially committed to the war effort. The Iraqi troops were supported by an armored battalion and 100 warplanes. After initial rapid advances on the central front, Iraqi general Nur ad-Din Mahmud ceded the operational initiative and shifted to a defensive stance. The Iraqi troop contingent grew to over 20,000 men during the war, including thousands of poorly trained recruits who volunteered for service in Palestine. Despite maintaining numerical superiority for the entire war, Iraqi troops

made no progress in Israel after June 1948. By mid-1949 Iraqi troops had withdrawn from Israel, although the formal state of war remained through 2006.

In 1956 the Suez crisis threatened to expand into a larger regional conflict. While Egyptian and Israeli units sparred for control of the Sinai Peninsula, Iraqi Army troops crossed into Jordan to prevent an Israeli attack there. Shortly after Iraqi troops returned home, Brigadier General Abd al-Karim al-Qasim led the Iraqi military in a coup against King Faisal II's government. Faisal had been installed as monarch in 1947, with British support. During the seizure of power, the king and Prime Minister Nuri al-Said were both killed. Qasim then consolidated his power and put down repeated counterrevolutions, including an attempted coup by Sunni officers of the army and another Kurdish revolt. In 1961 Britain relinquished control of Kuwait, which was immediately claimed by the Iraqi government. In response, Britain deployed troops to Kuwait to defend it from a potential Iraqi invasion. The longest and most successful Kurdish revolt against Iraqi rule commenced in 1961. Mustafa Barzani led yet another uprising in the hope of gaining autonomy for the Kurdish people.

The Iraqi Army proved incapable of quelling the rebellion, however, even when assisted by the Iraqi Air Force. By 1963 Syrian military forces moved into Iraq to assist in ending the rebellion, hoping to prevent an expansion of the uprising. With the exception of a one-year cease-fire that ended in April 1965, the conflict continued until 1970, when the Iraqi government finally admitted defeat and granted Kurdish autonomy without full independence.

In 1967 the June Six-Day War erupted between Israel and an Arab coalition. Israeli intelligence, detecting a massive Arab military buildup on its borders, compelled Israel to launch a series of preemptive strikes to prevent or delay the invasion. The majority of the Egyptian Air Force was destroyed in the first raids, and a similar raid against Iraqi airfields achieved modest success, destroying some aircraft and driving the rest to airfields in eastern Iraq, beyond the reach of Israeli attack aircraft. Although Iraq did not formally participate in the 1967 war, Iraqi troops again moved into defensive positions in Jordan, helping to deter a major Israeli advance across the Jordan River.

On October 6, 1973, Arab armies surprised Israel with a massive invasion on three fronts, sparking the Yom Kippur (Ramadan) War. Although the Iraqi Army did not participate in the first days of the conflict, within a week Iraqi armored units were fighting the Israelis on the Golan Heights. Over 60,000 Iraqi troops were deployed in the war, supplemented by 700 tanks. The decision to attack Israel proved to be a debacle for the Iraqi Army, however. On October 13, an Israeli ambush destroyed 80 Iraqi tanks in a single day without the loss of any Israeli tanks. Iraqi military performance improved little throughout the war. The Iraqi military coordinated poorly with its Arab allies and was repeatedly mauled by the aggressive tactics of Israeli commanders. Although Iraq itself was never threatened with invasion, the Iraqi Army at the conclusion of the war showed the effects of devastating battlefield losses. During the spring of 1974 Barzani led another Kurdish revolt, this time supported by Mohammad Reza Shah Pahlavi of Iran. This rebellion was brutally put down by the Iraqi Army, forcing Pahlavi to withdraw his support. For the remainder of the decade, Iraq attempted to rebuild its army, relying primarily upon the Soviet Union for the supply of heavy weapons.

After five years of border disputes with Iran, Iraqi president Saddam Hussein ordered an invasion of Iran, beginning on September 22, 1980. At the time of the invasion the Iraqi Army had grown to almost 200,000 troops, supplemented by 4,500 tanks, mostly of Soviet design. By gradually increasing tank imports while maintaining older designs in service, the Iraqi armored divisions fielded a very mixed force of vehicles, ranging from the T-55, designed in 1947, to the T-80 model of 1976. Initially the army managed to advance into Iranian territory. However, the advance was soon halted by stronger-than-expected Iranian resistance. Eight years of bloody stalemate ensued, costing almost 1 million total casualties. In an effort to end the stalemate, Hussein ordered the use of chemical weapons on Iranian troops and the Iranian civilian population. The use of chemical weapons alarmed the entire region, particularly because the Iraqi government had a well-established nuclear weapons program in place and was actively seeking atomic weapons. On June 7, 1981, Israel launched an air raid to destroy Iraq's Osiraq nuclear reactor, destroying the bulk of the nuclear program in a single strike.

After eight years of combat, Iran and Iraq agreed to an armistice returning to the status quo antebellum. In 1988 Iraq possessed the largest army in the Middle East, capable of fielding 1 million troops from a population of only 17 million. In addition, imports of Soviet hardware made the Iraqi Army the most advanced in the region. Iraqi armored divisions relied on the Soviet T-80 main battle tank. The army contained 70 divisions of veteran troops, with a large number of artillery pieces. The Soviet Union also provided Iraq with tactical and strategic missiles capable of delivering biological and chemical weapons to Israel.

The Iraqi military did not remain idle for long after the Iran-Iraq War. Following two years of rebuilding, Iraq again looked to expand its territory along the Persian Gulf coast. After renewing claims that Kuwait was a renegade province of Iraq, the Iraqi government accused Kuwait of stealing oil reserves through illegal slant-drilling techniques and manipulating the price of oil. When Kuwait refused a series of Iraqi demands, Hussein ordered the invasion of Kuwait, beginning on August 2, 1990. The invasion quickly overwhelmed the small Kuwaiti military. The United States immediately deployed forces to Saudi Arabia to prevent further Iraqi aggression, and within four months, 500,000 American troops defended Saudi Arabia, bolstered by detachments from dozens of nations (Operation DESERT SHIELD). Included in the defensive forces were units from many of Iraq's Arabic neighbors. When Hussein ignored United Nations (UN) resolutions demanding the evacuation of Kuwait, the coalition forces launched a series of air strikes against targets in Iraq and Kuwait beginning in January 2001. Eventually, during Operation DESERT STORM, a massive ground assault forced Iraqi units to retreat from Kuwait.

Although Hussein threatened that coalition forces would face "the mother of all battles" if they dared to invade Iraq, the coalition ground attack quickly overwhelmed Iraqi units entrenched in prepared positions. The Iraqi military had no defense against coalition air supremacy, and thousands of destroyed Iraqi tanks and armored vehicles littered the retreat route. The vaunted Republican Guard divisions, elite units of the Iraqi Army, were eviscerated by coalition aircraft and tanks. Although the exact number of Iraqi soldiers killed remains unknown, estimates put the number at between 11,000 and 15,000, with a further 300,000 wounded in the fighting.

Even after Iraqi forces were driven from Kuwaiti soil, Iraq remained under tight economic sanctions in the decade after the Persian Gulf War. Because Hussein refused to account for the entire Iraqi biological and chemical weapons arsenal, UN weapons inspectors roamed the nation. Restrictions on imports into Iraq prevented Hussein from rebuilding the devastated Iraqi Army, and even vehicles that survived the coalition onslaught could not be maintained for want of spare parts.

On March 20, 2003, the United States led a thin coalition in a new invasion of Iraq (Operation IRAQI FREEDOM). Ostensibly, the invasion was triggered by Iraqi refusals to comply with UN weapons inspections. However, the new coalition did not include any of Iraq's Middle Eastern neighbors. Regardless of the much smaller size of the invading forces, the 2003 invasion conquered Iraq in only three weeks, deposing Hussein in April. Weapons inspectors did not find the expected stockpiles of chemical and biological weapons, although some small caches of illegal weapons were discovered in the aftermath of the fighting. At the time of the invasion, the Iraqi Army was a mere shadow of its 1990 size, with less than 400,000 poorly trained troops using obsolete equipment. Estimates for total Iraqi casualties in the 2003 war vary greatly, but U.S. general Tommy Franks reported in April 2003 that approximately 30,000 Iraqi soldiers died during the invasion.

After conquering Iraq, the Anglo-American–led forces established a provisional government. One its earliest directives, proposed by Paul Bremer, head of the Coalition Provisional Authority (CPA), and announced on May 23, 2003, dissolved the Iraqi military, a move that in retrospect proved to be a disaster because occupying and pacifying the nation without the army proved impossible, especially considering that American forces in theater were only a fraction of what would have been needed. Rather, the provisional government planned to completely rebuild and retrain the Iraqi Army. This decision created a massive power vacuum in Iraqi society, and contributed to the high unemployment, lawlessness, and insurgency that have characterized occupied Iraq. The Iraqi Army continues to operate Soviet-built tanks, but the vast majority of Iraq's top-quality armored vehicles were destroyed in 1991 and 2003, ensuring that most remaining Iraqi tanks are of long-obsolete designs, such as the T-62 and T-55. From the 70 divisions of 1988, the Iraqi Army was down to only 10 divisions by 2006. One division is currently mechanized; the remainder is composed of motorized infantry units. Many analysts fear that the Iraqi Army would be incapable of defending the nation from a determined assault from one of its stronger neighbors. As of this writing, coalition forces remain in occupation of Iraq, attempting to rebuild the Iraqi Army into an effective force capable of maintaining internal and external security. These efforts have been hindered by a continuing insurrection bolstered by foreign fighters attempting to defeat the occupation and destroy the newly formed Iraqi Army. The army has proven unwilling or unable to halt the insurrection and protect the civilian population, and the Iraqi government has likewise been unable to effectively mobilize its military and security forces to stanch the insurgency.

Paul Joseph Springer

See also: Hussein, Saddam; IRAQI FREEDOM, Operation

Further Reading

Butler, Richard. *The Greatest Threat: Iraq, Weapons of Mass Destruction and the Growing Crisis in Global Security*. New York: PublicAffairs, 2000.

Finnie, David H. *Shifting Lines in the Sand: Kuwait's Elusive Frontier with Iraq*. Cambridge, MA: Harvard University Press, 1992.

Herzog, Chaim. *The Arab-Israeli Wars: War and Peace in the Middle East from the War of Independence to Lebanon*. Westminster, MD: Random House, 1984.

Hiro, Dilip. *The Longest War: The Iran-Iraq Military Conflict*. London: Routledge, 1991.

Murray, Williamson, and Robert H. Scales Jr. *The Iraq War: A Military History*. Cambridge, MA: Belknap, 2005.

Rubin, Barry, and Thomas A. Keaney, eds. *Armed Forces in the Middle East: Politics and Strategy*. Portland, OR: Frank Cass, 2002.

Iraq, History of, 1990 to Present

From 1990 until the U.S.-led coalition invasion of Iraq on March 20, 2003, which overthrew the government of President Saddam Hussein, Iraq was in perpetual crisis, and many of its citizens suffered from severe economic and military hardships. To make matters worse, Iraqi government policies during that period only exacerbated the chaos that defined the nation between 1990 and 2003. After Hussein was overthrown, Iraq was convulsed by violence due to sectarian strife and a potent Iraqi insurgency, and occupation forces have had mixed success in dealing with the unrest. Reconstruction has proceeded slowly, and, with no longstanding tradition of a freely elected democratic government, the new Iraqi government has proven to be not very adept at managing the nation's affairs. During much of the time period, Iraq was ruled by Saddam Hussein, who was president of Iraq from July 16, 1979, until April 9,

2003. On April 9, 2003, coalition forces captured Baghdad and established the Coalition Provisional Authority (CPA) to govern Iraq, which was later formed into the Iraqi Interim Government. The permanent government was elected in 2005. Large numbers of coalition forces—most of them American—remained in the country as part of an effort to quell the violence and help the government gain control of the country.

Following the conclusion of the eight-year Iran-Iraq War in 1988, Iraq faced economic disaster. The nation's foreign debt was estimated to be between $100 billion and $120 billion, with recovery costs estimated at more than $450 billion. Iraq's estimated 100-billion-barrel oil reserve, however, continued to be a viable asset. Nevertheless, Iraq's economy was incapable of absorbing most of the nearly 500,000 soldiers who were still in active service in the Iraqi military. Hussein had hoped that neighboring Saudi Arabia or Kuwait would write off Iraq's war debts or even offer funds for reconstruction. When this did not occur, he became angry and accused Kuwait of deliberately keeping oil prices low by overproducing in an effort to further injure the Iraqi economy. He also accused the Kuwaitis of illegally slant-drilling oil from the Rumaila Oil Field, located in southeastern Iraq.

On August 2, 1990, Iraqi troops invaded Kuwait and quickly occupied it. Immediately following the invasion, Kuwaiti officials and much of the international community condemned the action and demanded the withdrawal of Iraqi troops. The United Nations (UN) also denounced the act and immediately passed UN Resolution 661, which imposed wide-ranging sanctions on Iraq. These sanctions provided for a trade embargo that excluded only medical supplies, food, and other essential items.

The embargo further depressed the Iraq economy. The UN also authorized a naval blockade of Iraq. The United States, meanwhile, was deeply concerned about the occupation of Kuwait, a potential Iraqi incursion into Saudi Arabia, and a potential disruption to world oil supplies; what is more, it worried over Iraqi programs that had called for the production of weapons of mass destruction (WMD). U.S. officials feared that these developments would upset the balance of power in the region and might imperil Israel.

The United States and Great Britain soon spearheaded a military coalition of 34 countries, including many Arab nations, to face down the Iraqi aggression. When diplomatic negotiations yielded no progress, coalition forces began a massive aerial campaign against Iraq on January 17, 1991. Nearly a month of aerial attacks against Iraq destroyed much of the entire infrastructure of Iraq and killed an estimated 12,000–15,000 Iraqi soldiers and civilians. The aerial bombardment was followed by a quick ground assault in February 1991 in which coalition forces advanced into Kuwait and southern Iraq. Kuwait was liberated and Iraq resoundingly defeated in just 100 hours of ground combat. Some 60,000 Iraqi troops surrendered without a fight. On February 27, 1991, U.S. president George H. W. Bush ordered coalition forces to stand down. Estimates of Iraqi deaths during Operation DESERT STORM, including civilian casualties, range from approximately 24,000 to 40,000 soldiers and civilians. Meanwhile, Iraq's military had been badly mauled, the economy was in tatters, and the nation's infrastructure was badly damaged.

Despite the destruction caused by the Persian Gulf War, Hussein's government survived. Bush called for the Iraqi people to force Hussein to step aside, and uprisings occurred among various groups, including

Iraqi Army troops returning from their defeat. These began in March 1991 and soon engulfed much of the country. Shiite Muslims in southern Iraq and Kurds in northern Iraq, two religious sects that had been violently persecuted throughout Hussein's presidency, also rebelled against the Iraqi government. The refusal of the coalition governments to support the insurgents, however, allowed the government to suppress the rebellions with brutal force. Unfortunately for the opponents of Hussein, the Iraqi government was allowed under the terms of the agreements ending the war to employ helicopters, which it used with devastating effectiveness against the insurgents. Many Kurds fled north to Turkey to avoid the violent suppression that followed, and Shiite Muslims and Kurds continued to face persecution throughout the rest of Hussein's presidency.

The brutal campaigns against the Shiites and Kurds—especially those against the Kurds in the north—received wide-ranging media coverage and garnered much sympathy for the Kurdish population. Partly because of such coverage, a no-fly zone, an area over which the Iraqi Air Force had to relinquish its control, was established in northern Iraq, followed by a similar zone in southern Iraq.

Following the successful suppression of the uprisings, the Iraqi government set out to strengthen its hold on power. Hussein favored his most loyal supporters, Arab Sunnis from the area of his hometown of Tikrit. With the economy in shambles, many Iraqi people had begun seeking old institutions, such as Arab tribes, for support. At the same time, Hussein shrewdly sought backing from tribal leaders within Iraq. The government thus established an Assembly of Tribes, and Hussein made a public apology for past land reforms that had hurt tribal leaders. Tribalism and favoritism soon led to violence and ruthless competition among the various groups, however. In 1994, in order to quell such unrest, the government responded by implementing harsh new laws designed to limit the power of tribal groups. However, because of selective enforcement of such laws, there was little reduction in violence.

At the same time UN sanctions devastated the Iraqi economy. Also, government policies supported large military and internal security forces at the expense of other sectors. The sanctions had declared that 30 percent of Iraqi oil exports had to be set aside for war reparations, but the Iraqi economy had grown to depend on its oil exports at the expense of other industries, especially agriculture. Thus, when money from the oil trade was diminished, many Iraqis suffered from malnourishment and grinding poverty. The effects of the sanctions, combined with the large debts incurred during the war with Iran, brought on hyperinflation, which nearly wiped out the Iraqi middle class. The value of the Iraqi currency, the dinar, plummeted, and food prices rose rapidly after the war. Cancer rates also increased, reportedly as a result of the 300–800 tons of depleted uranium used in Iraq during the war.

Medical supplies were scarce in Iraq as a result of the sanctions, and the government hoarded them. Mortality rates in children under the age of five increased steeply. The Iraqi government implemented food rationing, but that did little to improve the situation. Illiteracy rates in Iraq also rose because many roads and schools had been damaged or destroyed. To add to the problem, the government withdrew much of its support for teachers and other salaried professionals. Power shortages caused widespread problems in homes and industries throughout Iraq, and many modern manufacturing facilities were forced to shut down.

In 1991 the Iraqi government rejected UN proposals to trade its oil for food and other humanitarian supplies. On May 20, 1996, however, a Memorandum of Understanding was signed between the United Nations and the Iraqi government. The memorandum stated that the Iraqi government could sell oil to purchase food and other humanitarian supplies. The first shipments of food arrived in Iraq in March 1997. Unfortunately, the program suffered from rampant corruption, and did little to improve the lot of average Iraqis, who continued to suffer from extreme poverty. By the late 1990s the People's Republic of China and Russia were calling for a significant easing of UN sanctions. Such calls went unheeded, however, as the United States and other Western powers refused to grant any leniency to the Iraqi regime. By 2000 as many as 16 million Iraqis depended on some form of government assistance for survival.

Following the Persian Gulf War the United States and its allies continued to limit Hussein's power through numerous punitive military operations. These operations, mostly air and missile strikes, damaged infrastructure and put even more of a strain on the Iraqi economy. On October 8, 1994, Operation VIGILANT WARRIOR began as a response to the deployment of Iraqi troops toward the Kuwaiti border. After some 170 aircraft and 6,500 military personnel were deployed to southern Iraq, Hussein recalled his troops and the crisis passed. On September 3, 1996, Operation DESERT STRIKE was launched in response to the movement of 40,000 Iraqi troops into northern Iraq, which threatened the Kurdish population. More than two years later, on December 16, 1998, the United States and Great Britain began Operation DESERT FOX, a four-day

bombing campaign against select Iraqi targets. It was in response to the Iraqi government's refusal to comply with UN Security Council (UNSC) resolutions that called for the dismantling of certain weapons and the government's interference with UN weapons inspectors, whose goal was to ensure that the Iraqi government was complying with UN resolutions. The stated goal of DESERT FOX was to destroy any hidden weapons of mass destruction and the Iraqi government's ability to produce and deploy them. The bombing targeted research and development installations.

On February 16, 2001, the United States and Great Britain launched a bombing campaign to damage Iraq's air defense network. Throughout the interwar period, bombing efforts meant to force Iraq's compliance with UN mandates caused much destruction while doing little to weaken Hussein's hold on power.

In response to such attacks, the Iraqi government, which had essentially been controlled by the decidedly secular Baath Party, began using Islam as way to rally its citizens. The struggle against the United States was depicted as a jihad, or holy war, against the Western world. In 1994 the government encouraged the building of mosques as part of a new "faith campaign." Large murals portraying Hussein in prayer were exhibited, and government money was set aside to construct the largest mosque in the world. Hussein and his government also encouraged loyalty to the regime, and Hussein was depicted as a hero in his conflict against the United States.

In northern Iraq the Kurds were now separated from the rest of the country, and self-rule was largely implemented. Kurdish political parties allowed cable television from outside Iraq to be broadcast into their region. The UN and international aid groups with access to the north were able to distribute aid to the region. On the eve of the March 2003 invasion of Iraq, the Kurdish economy was performing much better than the rest of the country. Many Kurdish villages had been resettled, medical facilities were restored, and the infant mortality rate had improved dramatically.

Following the terror attacks on the United States of September 11, 2001, the George W. Bush administration took a more assertive stance with Iraq. Bush and his closest advisers believed that Iraq posed a threat to the United States and its allies, including Israel. Many of Bush's advisers mistakenly believed that Iraq possessed weapons of mass destruction and suggested an attack against Iraq, which would at once remove Hussein from power, secure the alleged WMD, and serve as a warning to other rogue states. Beyond that, they hoped that a democratic Iraq might be a force for change in the entire region.

Bush hoped to secure approval from the UN before proceeding with an attack. On September 12, 2002, Bush addressed the UN Security Council and attempted to make his case for an invasion of Iraq. Much of the international community was critical of such a move, however. Other world leaders did not believe that Iraq posed a threat or had links to such terrorist organizations as al-Qaeda, which the Bush administration alleged. On November 8, 2002, the UN Security Council passed Resolution 1441, which offered Iraq a final chance to comply with its disarmament agreements. The resolution required that the Iraqi government destroy all chemical, biological, and nuclear weapons as well as the means to deliver them, and to provide complete documentation of such.

On February 5, 2003, U.S. secretary of state Colin Powell addressed the UN General Assembly and presented evidence, some of which was later proven to be false, that Iraqi officials were impeding the work of the weapons inspectors, continuing to develop weapons of mass destruction, and directly supporting al-Qaeda, which had carried out the September 11 attacks. Following the presentation, the United States and Great Britain, among others, proposed a UN resolution calling for the use of force against Iraq. Other countries, such as Canada, France, Germany, and Russia, urged continued diplomacy. Although the American effort failed, the United States decided to pursue an invasion without UN authorization.

On March 20, 2003, a U.S.-led coalition invaded Iraq with the objectives of disarming Iraq, ending Hussein's reign as president, and freeing the Iraqi people. Coalition forces were able to advance quickly through Iraq. On April 9 they captured Baghdad and officially toppled the Iraqi government, forcing Hussein to go into hiding.

On May 1, 2003, Bush declared that major combat operations in Iraq were over and that the postinvasion reconstruction phase had begun. However, the postinvasion period would prove very difficult for coalition forces. With the absence of government authority and social order, the country soon experienced widespread civil disorder, with many people looting palaces, museums, and even armories that the Iraqi government had once controlled. To complicate things, the coalition did not have enough troops on the ground to prevent such disorder and keep an insurgency at bay.

In an attempt to bring order in Iraq, the United States established the Coalition Provisional Authority to govern Iraq, and put it in place on April 20, 2003. While many of Hussein's palaces were looted, their physical structures remained intact. It was from these palaces that the CPA governed Iraq.

On May 11, 2003, President Bush selected diplomat Lewis Paul Bremer III to head the CPA. On June 3, 2003, as part of the first act of the CPA, Bremer ordered the de-Baathification of Iraq. Senior officials within the Baath Party were removed from their positions and banned from future employment in the public sector. In all, about 30,000 party members became instantly unemployed. The next day Bremer dissolved Iraq's 500,000-member army. This left Iraq without a military or police force to stop the widespread looting. It also ensured a huge number of disgruntled, unemployed dissidents who viewed the CPA with great enmity. Violence against the occupation armies steadily increased. Notwithstanding the apparent early successes of the coalition forces, individuals opposed to the coalition presence in Iraq engaged in acts of violence, such as the use of ambush tactics, improvised explosive devices, and suicide bombings against coalition forces. Despite a quick military victory, coalition forces faced a long battle with Iraqi insurgents in their attempt to bring peace to Iraq.

Sectarian strife was also increasing, and by mid-2004 some analysts claimed that Iraq was perched on the edge of a full-blown civil war. The Arab Sunni leadership capitalized on Sunni fear of Shiite dominance of a new government. Sunnis extremists routinely employed bombing and suicide bombing attacks against Shiite civilians. Also, Shiite members of the new Iraqi Army used extralegal means to execute Sunni civilians. Shiites organized death squads, which killed many Iraqi civilians.

In the face of such violence, on June 28, 2004, governing authority was transferred to the Iraqi Interim Government, which was led by Prime Minister Iyad Allawi. The generally pro-Western Allawi launched a campaign to weaken the rebel forces of Muqtada al-Sadr, who had spoken out against the CPA. On September 1, 2004, Allawi pulled out of peace negotiations with Sadr. Eventually, however, Sadr agreed to a cease-fire and took part in the legislative elections, which were held on January 30, 2005.

As part of the January 2005 elections, the Iraqi people chose representatives for the 275-member Iraqi National Assembly. With 58.4 percent voter turnout, a total of 8.4 million people cast their ballots. At least every third candidate on the candidate lists was female. There were nine separate attacks in Iraq on election day that killed 44 people, although these numbers were less than most experts had expected.

Two parties supported largely by Shiite Muslims won a majority of the seats, and 85 of the 275 members were women. Many Sunni Arabs, who had largely supported Hussein and held power in the previous government, boycotted the elections, leading some observers to challenge the legitimacy of the elections. The assembly was immediately charged with writing a constitution for Iraq and approved the Iraqi Transitional Government on April 28, 2005. The transitional government gained authority on May 3, 2005. The Iraqi constitution was approved on October 15, 2005, and described Iraq as a democratic, federal, representative republic.

On December 15, 2005, a second general election was held to elect a permanent Iraqi Council of Representatives. Following approval from the members of the National Assembly, a permanent government of Iraq was formed on May 16, 2006. Turnout for this election was high, at 79.4 percent, and the level of violence was lower than during the previous election. The United Iraqi Alliance, a coalition of Arab Shiite parties, won the most votes with 41.2 percent.

Ibrahim al-Jafari was nominated for the post of prime minister, but he was passed over after growing criticism by Nuri al-Maliki, a member of the Islamic Dawa Party, a conservative Shiite group. As prime minister, Maliki successfully negotiated a peace treaty with Sadr's rebel forces in August 2007.

Meanwhile, on December 13, 2003, U.S. forces captured Saddam Hussein in Dawr, a small town north of Baghdad and near Tikrit, his birthplace. An Iraqi Special Tribunal charged Hussein with crimes committed against the inhabitants of the town of Dujail in 1982. Dujail had been the site of an unsuccessful assassination attempt against Hussein. The former Iraqi president was charged with the murder of 148 people, with having ordered the torture of women and children, and with illegally arresting 399 others. On November 5, 2006, he was found guilty and sentenced to death by hanging. On December 30, Hussein was executed by Iraqi authorities.

In January 2007 President Bush presented his plan for "a new way forward" in Iraq. This was a new U.S. military strategy whose stated goal was to reduce the sectarian violence in Iraq and help the Iraqi people provide security and stability for themselves.

Five additional U.S. Army brigades were deployed to Iraq between January and May 2007, totaling about 40,000 troops. Operations to secure Baghdad began immediately. The U.S. troop surge, as many commentators called the plan, continued into 2009.

The interpretations of the results of the surge were mixed. Many U.S. media outlets, including CNN, reported that violence had dropped anywhere from 40 to 80 percent in Iraq following the surge. ABC ran many reports on its nightly news show that highlighted the progress in Iraq. *New York Times* writer David Brooks argued that even President Bush's harshest critics would have to concede that he finally got one right. Barack Obama, who was elected president of the United States in November 2008 and was once a harsh critic of the surge, later asserted that the new military strategy had led to an improved security situation in Iraq, although he was quick to point out that the war should not have been launched in the first place.

Critics have argued that while violence may have fallen in Iraq following the surge, such evidence did not indicate that the surge was truly successful. A 2008 study of satellite imagery suggested that Shiite ethnic cleansing of Sunni neighborhoods had been largely responsible for the decrease in violence in Sunni areas. Some independent journalists argued that violence was down because the Shiites had won the battles of Baghdad in 2006 and 2007 and had controlled nearly three-fourths of the capital city. Others praised Maliki's government, not the U.S. government, for its efforts to stop the violence. Still others attributed it to deals struck by the occupying troops with the Sunnis to turn against al-Qaeda and other extremists.

Public opinion in Iraq seemed to suggest that Iraqis did not believe that the surge had led to any reduction in violence. A multi–news agency poll conducted in March 2008 showed that only 4 percent of Iraqis gave the U.S. surge any credit for any reduction in violence following the surge. Instead, many Iraqi people gave Iraqi institutions credit for the lowering of violence. Despite the reduction in violence, 50 percent of Iraqis still view security as the nation's main concern. In 2007 the Iraqi population was 29.267 million.

On December 4, 2008, the U.S. and Iraqi governments concluded the Status of Forces Agreement, which stipulated that U.S. troops would depart from all Iraqi cities by

June 30, 2009, and would leave Iraq entirely by December 31, 2011. U.S. forces were no longer allowed to hold Iraqi citizens without charges for more than 24 hours. Also, immunity from prosecution in Iraqi courts was taken away from U.S. contractors. Maliki, however, was faced by detractors who called for the immediate removal of foreign troops from Iraq. They believed the agreement only prolonged an illegal occupation. Iraq's grand ayatollah, Sayyid Ali Husayn al-Sistani, led many of these protests and contended that Maliki was ceding too much control to the Americans. Such dissent forced the government to promise to hold a referendum on the agreement no later than June 20, 2009. If Iraqi citizens vote down the agreement, the Iraqi government would inform the U.S. that its troops would have to leave by June 2010, and the U.S. would be forced to accept the referendum. The referendum was not held by the June 2009 deadline and was put off until sometime in 2010.

Despite the effect of two wars and a continued insurgency against coalition forces in the country, the Iraqi economy has improved largely due to an influx of money pouring in from abroad. Wages rose over 100 percent between 2003 and 2008, and taxes were cut by 15–45 percent, allowing many Iraqi citizens to increase their spending power. However, despite such successes, Iraq faced many economic problems as well. Unemployment remained high; the Iraq government estimated that unemployment was between 60 and 70 percent in 2008. At the same time, the Iraqi foreign debt rose as high as $125 billion. Internal fragmentation and acts of sectarian violence continued to pose a large problem in Iraq, and U.S. and Iraqi forces have been unable to completely stop the violence.

Gregory W. Morgan

See also: Allawi, Iyad; Baghdad; Bush, George Walker; Hussein, Saddam; IRAQI FREEDOM, Operation; Iraq, Sanctions on; Maliki, Nuri Muhammed Kamil Hasan al-

Further Reading

Abdullah, Thabit. *A Short History of Iraq*. London: Pearson, 2003.

Allawi, Ali A. *The Occupation of Iraq: Winning the War, Losing the Peace*. New Haven, CT: Yale University Press, 2007.

Inati, Shams Constantine. *Iraq: Its History, People, and Politics*. Amherst, MA: Humanity Books, 2003.

Marr, Phebe. *The Modern History of Iraq*. 2nd ed. Boulder, CO: Westview, 2003.

Tripp, Charles. *A History of Iraq*. Cambridge: Cambridge University Press, 2007.

Iraq, Sanctions on

The international community imposed sanctions on Iraq beginning on August 6, 1990, four days after the Iraqi invasion of Kuwait. Various sanctions remained in place until May 22, 2003, at which time the Saddam Hussein government had been overthrown by the Anglo-American–led invasion of Iraq in March 2003. This was one of the longest and hardest sanction regimes ever imposed by the international community and the United Nations (UN) on one of its member states.

On August 2, 1990, Iraq's armed forces occupied Kuwait. Four days later UN Security Council Resolution 661 imposed comprehensive trade sanctions on Iraq. The sanctions prohibited the importation of any Iraqi commodities or products into all UN member states as well as the sale or supply of any products to Iraq. The resolution excluded the sale of medical supplies to Iraq as well as foodstuffs for humanitarian purposes.

Although the Persian Gulf War officially ended on February 28, 1991, the Security Council continued to employ sanctions against Iraq. Security Council Resolution 687 of April 3, 1991, instructed the government of Iraq to destroy, remove, and render harmless all its weapons of mass destruction (WMD) and medium-range missiles. The UN also decided to send to Iraq a team of international inspectors to supervise the implementation of the resolution. Continuing economic sanctions were supposed to maintain international pressure on Iraq to cooperate with the inspectors.

Because the 1991 war caused major damage to Iraq's infrastructure, including power plants, oil refineries, pumping stations, and water treatment facilities, the sanctions crippled Iraqi efforts to revive the economy and created a humanitarian crisis. In response to the plight of Iraqi civilians, UN secretary-general Javier Pérez de Cuéllar submitted a report to the Security Council on March 20, 1991, describing in detail the humanitarian crisis existing in Iraq after the war. In its conclusions, the report recommended that the international community work rapidly to reconstruct Iraq to improve the humanitarian situation there.

As a means of improving the humanitarian situation in Iraq, the Security Council passed Resolutions 706 and 712 in August and September of 1991, respectively. These resolutions allowed for the limited sale of Iraqi crude oil for the strict purpose of purchasing basic humanitarian goods for the Iraqi population. The government of Iraq rejected the offer, however, and demanded that all sanctions be immediately abolished.

The sanctions inflicted much more damage on Iraqi society during the 1990s. United Nations Children's Fund (UNICEF) surveys revealed that in the southern and central regions of Iraq, home to approximately 85 percent of the country's population, the mortality rate of children under the age of five had nearly tripled, from 56 deaths per 1,000 live births between 1984 and 1989 to 131 deaths per 1,000 live births between 1994 and 1999. Infant mortality (defined as children in their first year) increased from 47 per 1,000 live births to 108 per 1,000 live births within the same time frame.

The harsh conditions in Iraq soon caused a rift among the Security Council's permanent members. The United States and the United Kingdom advocated continuing the sanctions until the Iraqi government fulfilled all its obligations in compliance with Security Council Resolution 687. Their stance, however, was challenged by China, France, and Russia, which claimed that the sanctions only enhanced the suffering of the Iraqi people without influencing the Iraqi government to comply with Resolution 687.

On April 14, 1995, the UN Security Council suggested in Resolution 986 that the Iraqi government accept international supervision of the sale of Iraq's crude oil in return for humanitarian aid and basic needs such as food, medicine, and other essential civilian supplies. This diplomatic initiative finally bore fruit in May 1996 when the UN and Iraq signed a Memorandum of Understanding (MOU). Iraq began exporting crude oil under UN supervision in December 1996.

The MOU began the Oil for Food Program, which operated until the invasion of Iraq by American- and British-led forces on March 20, 2003. The program was officially terminated on November 21, 2003, when authority was handed to the Coalition Provisional Authority (CPA), the entity that assumed the governance of Iraq headed by an American. On May 22, 2003, the Security Council abolished all sanctions against Iraq.

When the Oil for Food Program began, Iraq was permitted to sell $2 billion of oil every six months. Two-thirds of the profits were channeled to humanitarian needs. In 1999 the Security Council decided to abolish the ceiling.

Under the program, the government of Iraq sold oil worth $64.2 billion. Of that amount, $38.7 billion was spent on humanitarian aid. Another $18 billion was given as compensation for lawsuits stemming from the occupation of Kuwait by Iraq. Finally, $1.2 billion was used to fund the program itself.

A total of $31 billion in humanitarian aid and equipment was transferred to Iraq under the program. Additional supplies and equipment totaling $8.2 billion were planned to be delivered to Iraq when the war broke out in March 2003. The program also helped to minimize the damage wrought by severe droughts in Iraq between 1999 and 2001.

During its seven years of operation, the program had a positive impact on civilian nutrition and health. It raised the average daily caloric intake for every Iraqi from 1,200 calories to 2,200 calories per day. The spread of contagious diseases such as cholera was also contained. The sewage system improved slowly during the 1990s, as did the delivery of medicine, particularly after the Oil for Food Program was launched.

While the Oil for Food Program succeeded in improving humanitarian conditions in Iraq, the diet quality was still poor. This caused malnutrition because of deficiencies in vitamins and minerals, which led to the spread of anemia, diarrhea, and respiratory infections, especially among young children. Furthermore, the program was criticized for restricting aid to food rather than also allowing the repair of infrastructure and the generation of employment. Because the aid was distributed through the government of Iraq, it actually helped the government maintain its hold over the people.

The full deficiencies of the aid plan became known after the occupation of Iraq began in 2003. In 2004 following complaints from U.S. senators and congressional representatives regarding irregularities in the UN-managed Oil for Food Program, the UN created an independent inquiry committee (IIC) led by American banker Paul A. Volcker. The IIC completed its work at the end of 2005. The committee report pointed to mismanagement by the UN, corruption and bribery by top UN officials, and manipulation of the aid scheme by the government of Iraq, which received $1.8 billion in illegal aid. Also, IIC experts estimated that the government of Iraq was able to illicitly smuggle approximately $11 billion of oil outside Iraq, thereby circumventing the Oil for Food Program.

Chen Kertcher

See also: Bush, George Walker; IRAQI FREEDOM, Operation; Weapons of Mass Destruction

Further Reading

Arnove, Anthony. *Iraq under Siege: The Deadly Impact of Sanctions and War.* London: Pluto, 2000.

Lopez, George A., and David Cortright. "Containing Iraq: the Sanctions Worked." *Foreign Affairs* 83, no. 4 (2004): 90–103.

Malone, David M. *The International Struggle over Iraq: Politics in the UN Security Council, 1980–2005.* Oxford: Oxford University Press, 2006.

IRAQI FREEDOM, Operation

Those who take the long view of history may be inclined to blame British prime minister David Lloyd George as much as U.S. president George W. Bush for the current situation in Iraq. British and French actions after World War I to fill the Middle Eastern

Iraqi and U.S. forces in An Najaf during Operation IRAQI FREEDOM, August 2004. Imam Ali Mosque is pictured. (U.S. Department of Defense)

void left by the collapse of the Ottoman Empire created modern Iraq and other Arab nations without regard for traditional ethnic and religious boundaries. Conditions in the European-created, artificial country of Iraq (especially the long-held animosity between the country's three major ethnic and religious populations of Kurds, Sunni, and Shia) made it a perfect breeding ground for such strong-arm dictators as Saddam Hussein to seize and hold power over a divided population, while incubating simmering ethnic and religious rivalries.

Iraq, compared with Afghanistan, the other major theater of combat operations for President Bush's Global War on Terror, played out with mixed success in two very different campaigns: a stunning conventional assault that rapidly destroyed the Iraqi army, captured Baghdad, ousted Saddam Hussein, and paved the way for a U.S.-led occupation of the country, and a smoldering insurgency conducted by al-Qaeda fighters and both Sunni and Shia faction Iraqi militia groups that began shortly after Hussein's defeat.

Although the two Iraq campaigns bear a superficial similarity to what transpired in Afghanistan (large-scale conventional combat operations to defeat the enemy's main forces followed by an insurgency), the Iraq War and occupation have shown striking differences in scope, intensity, and even in the justification U.S. leaders gave for invading the country. While Operation ENDURING FREEDOM was launched to strike directly at those presumed responsible for masterminding the September 11, 2001, terror attacks and the Afghan Taliban regime that harbored them, no such justification can be claimed for the Bush administration's decision to launch the March 2003 invasion of Iraq. Despite Iraqi president Saddam Hussein's track record of general support for terrorist organizations hostile to the United States and the West, no direct link to al-Qaeda has ever been proven. And while U.S. strategy regarding Afghanistan might be classified as *reactive*, the decision of America's leaders to invade Iraq can only be termed *proactive*, a surprising and controversial preemptive action.

In the wake of the 1990 and 1991 Persian Gulf War, Hussein used chemical weapons on Iraq's Kurdish minority. Subsequently, Hussein was often vilified for using chemical weapons on "his own people," but he did not consider the Kurds to be his people; his loyalty lay only with his Baathist Party cronies and his own tribe. What is perhaps surprising about his use of chemical weapons is that he did not use them more extensively. Iraqi officials were recalcitrant to inspections by the United Nations (UN) and failed, by late 2002, to produce an adequate accounting of the disposition of the weapons of mass destruction the country was known to possess (and use) in 1991. Further, the Iraqis failed to provide a full and open disclosure of the status of its suspected nuclear weapons program. If Iraq had added nuclear weapons to its 1991 chemical arsenal, as was charged by Iraqi émigrés (such as Khidhir Hamza, self-proclaimed "Saddam's Bombmaker," who toured U.S. college campuses in the autumn of 2002 trumpeting his "insider" knowledge of Iraq's alleged nuclear program), it would be foolish to ignore the threat such weapons posed. By failing to cooperate promptly, fully, and openly with UN weapons inspectors, Hussein had almost literally signed his own death warrant.

Opting for a preemptive strategy instead of risking a potential repeat of the September 11 terror attacks—with the added specter of chemical, biological, or nuclear weapons—Bush and his advisers (principally Vice President Dick Cheney and Deputy Secretary of Defense Paul Wolfowitz, described as "a major architect of Bush's Iraq policy ... and its most passionate and compelling advocate") decided to act, unilaterally if necessary. Armed chiefly with what would later be exposed as an egregiously inaccurate Central Intelligence Agency (CIA) report about Iraq's possession of nuclear and other weapons of mass destruction, Bush obtained a legal justification for invading Iraq when the Senate approved the Joint Resolution Authorization for Use of Military Force against Iraq Resolution of 2002 in October 2002. In February 2003 Secretary of State Colin Powell addressed the UN Security Council with information based largely on the same flawed CIA report, but action was blocked by France, Germany, and Russia. Although the three powers bolstered their opposition with claims that military action against Iraq would threaten "international security," their true motives were suspect to some who supported military action (France and Germany, for example, already had made billions of dollars by illegally circumventing the UN Oil for Food Program with Iraq). Regardless of their motives, all three countries had a vested interest in maintaining the status quo in Iraq and little motivation to participate in an American-led preemptive strike. Although Britain joined Bush's "coalition of the willing" (from 2003, 75 countries contributed troops, matériel, or services to the U.S.-led effort), the absence of France and Germany left his administration open to strong criticism for stubbornly proceeding without broad-based European support.

Bush's proactive rather than reactive strategy was heavily criticized by administration opponents as a sea-change departure from that of past U.S. presidents and slammed for its unilateralism. Yet, as historian John Lewis Gaddis points out in *Surprise, Security and the American Experience*, it was not without historical precedent. He cites the preemptive, unilateral actions of presidents John Adams, James K. Polk, William McKinley, Woodrow Wilson, and even Franklin D. Roosevelt. Yet, with U.S. ground forces already stretched thin by Operation Eɴᴅᴜʀɪɴɢ Fʀᴇᴇᴅᴏᴍ, mounting a major, preemptive invasion of Iraq was considered by many—particularly U.S. military leaders—as risky. Military drawdowns during Clinton's presidency, for example, had reduced U.S. Army active duty strength from 780,000 to about 480,000.

Even in the years before the 2003 Iraq invasion, Army Chief of Staff general Eric Shinseki had clashed with Secretary of Defense Donald Rumsfeld over Department of Defense proposals to reduce army end strength even further. Rumsfeld had taken office in 2001 firmly convinced that technology could replace large numbers of ground combat forces, and he doggedly clung to that conviction. Moreover, Rumsfeld, who had previously served as president Gerald Ford's secretary of defense between 1975 and 1977, often acted as if he were unaware of how profoundly the 1986 Goldwater-Nichols Act had affected U.S. military culture by eliminating much of the petty, interservice bickering that he had earlier witnessed. Shinseki further provoked Rumsfeld's ire when he told the Senate Armed Services Committee on the eve of the Iraq invasion that an occupation of that country would require "several hundred thousand" troops, an estimate that, in hindsight, seemed prescient indeed, but which was sharply criticized in 2003 by Rumsfeld and Paul Wolfowitz as "wildly off the mark." On March 20, 2003, U.S. and British forces (plus smaller contingents from Australia and Poland) invaded Iraq in Operation Iʀᴀǫɪ Fʀᴇᴇᴅᴏᴍ. The 297,000-strong force faced an Iraqi army numbering approximately 375,000, plus an unknown number of poorly trained citizens' militias. U.S. combat strength was about half of that deployed during the 1990 and 1991 Persian Gulf War. With U.S. Central Command general Tommy Franks in overall command, the U.S. ground forces prosecuting the invasion were led by U.S. V Corps commander Lieutenant General William Scott Wallace.

Preceded by a shock-and-awe air campaign reminiscent of the one that blasted Hussein's forces and Iraqi infrastructure in the Persian Gulf War, ground forces (including U.S. Marines and British combat units) executed another "desert blitzkrieg" that quickly smashed the Iraqi army. Despite the failure of the Turkish government at the last minute to allow the United States to mount a major invasion of northern Iraq from its soil, two ground prongs struck north from Kuwait, while Special Forces and airborne forces worked with the Kurds in the north in a limited second front. The ground advance north was rapid. Baghdad fell on April 10, and Hussein went into hiding. (He was captured in December 2003, brought to trial, found guilty, and executed on December 30, 2006.)

President Bush declared the "mission accomplished" and the end of major combat operations while aboard the U.S. aircraft carrier *Abraham Lincoln* on May 1, 2003. Subsequent events during the postinvasion occupation of Iraq would prove Bush's dramatic statement to be wildly premature: although only 139 U.S. personnel and 33 British soldiers died during the invasion, more than 4,000 Americans were to die thereafter in the insurgency that accompanied the occupation. Bush administration decisions to include the dismissal of Baathist Party officials (essentially, Iraq's only trained administrators), and the disbanding of the Iraqi Army (that, at one stroke, dumped nearly 400,000 trained soldiers and potential insurgent recruits into the Iraqi general population) contributed to the insurgency.

Jerry D. Morelock

See also: Bush, George Walker; Franks, Tommy Ray; Hussein, Saddam; IRAQI FREEDOM, Operation, Air Campaign; IRAQI FREEDOM, Operation, Coalition Ground Forces; IRAQI FREEDOM, Operation, Coalition Naval Forces; IRAQI FREEDOM, Operation, Ground Campaign; Rumsfeld, Donald Henry; U.S. Air Force, Iraq War; U.S. Army, Iraq War; U.S. Navy, Iraq War

Further Reading

Atkinson, Rick. *In the Company of Soldiers: A Chronicle of Combat.* New York: Henry Holt, 2005.

Cavaleri, David. *Easier Said Than Done: Making the Transition between Combat Operations and Stability Operations.* Fort Leavenworth, KS: Combat Studies Institute Press, 2005.

DiMarco, Louis A. *Traditions, Changes and Challenges: Military Operations and the Middle Eastern City.* Fort Leavenworth, KS: Combat Studies Institute Press, 2004.

Franks, Tommy, with Malcolm McConnell. *American Soldier.* New York: Regan Books, 2004.

Gaddis, John Lewis. *Surprise, Security and the American Experience.* Cambridge, MA: Harvard University Press, 2005.

Gordon, Michael R., and General Bernard E. Trainor. *Cobra II: The Inside Story of the Invasion and Occupation of Iraq.* New York: Pantheon Books, 2006.

Murray, Williamson, and Robert H. Scales Jr. *The Iraq War: A Military History.* Cambridge, MA: Belknap, 2005.

Ricks, Thomas E. *Fiasco: The American Military Adventure in Iraq.* New York: Penguin, 2006.

Sanchez, Ricardo S., and Donald T. Phillips. *Wiser in Battle: A Soldier's Story.* New York: Harper, 2008.

Woodward, Bob. *Bush at War.* New York: Simon and Schuster, 2002.

Woodward, Bob. *Plan of Attack.* New York: Simon and Schuster, 2004.

Woodward, Bob. *State of Denial: Bush at War, Part III.* New York: Simon and Schuster, 2006.

Zinmeister, Karl. *Boots on the Ground: A Month with the 82d Airborne Division in the Battle for Iraq.* New York: St. Martin's, 2004.

Zinmeister, Karl. *Dawn over Baghdad: How the U.S. Military Is Using Bullets and Ballots to Remake Iraq.* New York: Encounter Books, 2004.

IRAQI FREEDOM, Operation, Air Campaign

The air campaign was an important part of the U.S.-led invasion of Iraq (Operation IRAQI FREEDOM) and contributed enormously to its rapid success. For IRAQI FREEDOM, the U.S.-led coalition assembled a formidable array of air power. The United States contributed 64,246 air personnel, including reserve and National Guard, and 1,663 aircraft. The latter included 293 fighters, 51 bombers, 182 tankers, and 337 aircraft of other types operated by the U.S. Air Force; 232 fighters, 52 tankers, and 124 aircraft of other types operated by the U.S. Navy; 130 fighters, 22 tankers, and 220 aircraft of other types operated by the U.S. Marine Corps; and 20 aircraft operated by the U.S. Army.

Aircraft participating in the operation included almost all models in the U.S. inventory: the North American/Rockwell/Boeing B-1B Lancer, Northrop Grumman B-2 Spirit, and Boeing B-52H Stratofortress bombers; Fairchild Republic A-10A Thunderbolt II and Lockheed AC-130 Spectre combat support aircraft; Boeing F-15 Eagle, Lockheed Martin F-16 Fighting Falcon, McDonnell

Douglas (now Boeing) F/A-18 Hornet, and Lockheed F-117 Nighthawk fighters; Lockheed KC-130 Hercules transports; and McDonnell Douglas KC-10 Extender and Boeing KC-135 Stratotanker tankers.

The Royal Air Force contributed some 8,000 personnel and 113 aircraft, including 66 fighters, 12 tankers, and 35 aircraft of other types. The Royal Australian Air Force contributed 22 aircraft, including 14 fighters, and 250 airmen. Canada contributed 3 transport aircraft. The Iraqi side at the beginning of the hostilities had 20,000 air force personnel, 325 combat aircraft, and 210 surface-to-air missiles.

The air campaign was designed as an integral part of a joint military operation, serving as a force multiplier to supplement the firepower of a relatively light land component. The allied air campaign was able to take advantage of Operations NORTHERN WATCH and SOUTHERN WATCH, which the U.S. Air Force and Royal Air Force had been conducting since 1991, effectively transforming the United Nations–sanctioned policing of no-fly zones over northern and southern Iraq into a de facto sustained air campaign to conduct reconnaissance and suppress Iraqi air defenses. Thus, the coalition was able to prepare for battle well before the start of Operation IRAQI FREEDOM.

The air campaign of Operation IRAQI FREEDOM began early in the morning of March 20, 2003, with an unsuccessful air strike near Baghdad, involving two F-117A stealth fighter-bombers, aimed at killing top Iraqi leaders, including President Saddam Hussein. The strike was followed by massive cruise-missile attacks on key Iraqi command and control centers in and around Baghdad. By March 23–25, the air assault developed into the strategic phase of a so-called shock-and-awe campaign aimed to prevent the use of weapons of mass destruction by the Iraqis and to disorganize the enemy, forcing its rapid defeat.

Afterward, the coalition air campaign changed its focus to aiding ground forces moving into Iraq from Kuwait; at this point, more than half of the new targets were not preplanned targets of opportunity. The Iraqis returned fire with sporadic and highly ineffective antiaircraft fire and random launches of surface-to-air missiles. They also managed to launch seven Ababil-100 tactical ballistic missiles, five of which were destroyed by U.S. Patriot batteries; two others missed their targets.

The growing flexibility of allied targeting reflected the proliferation of precision-guided munitions (PGM, smart bombs) in the coalition air force, which allowed more options in strike capabilities, redirecting of aircraft, performing close air support, and striking targets of opportunity. The air campaign also demonstrated the impressive global-reach capabilities of allied air power. Indeed, bombers were flying in from bases as far away as Missouri, Diego Garcia in the Indian Ocean, and Great Britain. Others were operating from aircraft carriers in the Persian Gulf and the Mediterranean, and from bases across the Middle East. The allies enjoyed uncontested air supremacy, as the remnants of the Iraqi air defense system were unable to operate effectively, and the enemy was unable to master a single sortie during the war. The coalition also benefited from the use of unmanned aerial vehicles (UAVs) as sensors and decoys to confuse the Iraqis.

The arrival of a major sandstorm on March 25 and 26 canceled about 65 percent of all sorties. Nevertheless, the coalition was able to adjust its reconnaissance and surveillance missions to harsh weather using the Joint Surveillance and Target Reader System (JSTARS) aircraft and long-range UAVs, which provided high-flying bombers with necessary information and data.

With the resumption of the ground march toward Baghdad, the allied air campaign shifted its focus to providing ground support, particularly targeting Iraqi Republican Guard units and militia formations, which were defending road approaches to the Iraqi capital. Finally, the air and ground assault on Baghdad merged into one coordinated effort.

Coalition air power was able to destroy or significantly degrade the Republican Guard formations and to open a new dimension in the urban warfare, providing constant surveillance, reconnaissance, intelligence, and fire support to allied ground forces. Coalition air power was also instrumental in the opening of the second front in northern Iraq. Major air operations in Iraq effectively ended with one final unsuccessful attempt on April 7 to eliminate Hussein when a B-1 bomber attacked a palace in Baghdad where the dictator was allegedly staying.

The aerial campaign during the Iraq War again demonstrated that there is no substitute for air dominance in modern warfare, a lesson that was gleaned from the 1990 to 1991 Persian Gulf War. Additionally, the technological superiority and application of air power in joint warfare operation allowed the coalition to enjoy unprecedented efficiency in reconnaissance, surveillance, and flexible, real-time targeting, while combining centralized control with decentralized execution of air operations. This also provided the coalition air force with almost instant capability to evaluate its performance as ground forces rapidly advanced into Iraq.

At the same time, however, the operation also witnessed an insufficiency in allied intelligence, particularly in regard to "decapitation" air strikes. Some observers have noted that the planners of the operation displayed overconfidence that a massive initial air assault on limited command and control targets would lead to the quick collapse of the regime. The campaign also revealed a shortage of aerial tankers, as the prosecution of combat missions deep inside Iraq put serious pressure on the allied tanker fleet.

Overall, coalition air forces conducted 41,404 sorties in the skies over Iraq. The U.S. Air Force contributed 24,196 sorties of those sorties; the U.S. Navy conducted 8,945 sorties; the U.S. Marine Corps contributed 4,948 sorties; the U.S. Army contributed 269 sorties; the Royal Air Force conducted 2,481 sorties; and the Royal Australian Air Force flew 565 sorties. Of 29,199 munitions used, 68 percent were precision-guided. The coalition lost just seven aircraft to enemy fire (six helicopters and one combat/ support aircraft A-10A, and two pilots). One Royal Air Force fighter was lost due to friendly fire.

Peter J. Rainow

See also: Iraqi Freedom, Operation; Iraqi Freedom, Operation, Coalition Ground Forces; Iraqi Freedom, Operation, Ground Campaign

Further Reading

Boyne, Walter J. *Operation Iraqi Freedom: What Went Right, What Went Wrong and Why.* New York: Forge Books, 2003.

Keegan, John. *The Iraq War: The Military Offensive, from Victory in 21 Days to the Insurgent Aftermath.* New York: Vintage, 2005.

Murray, Williamson, and Robert H. Scales Jr. *The Iraq War: A Military History.* Cambridge, MA: Belknap, 2005.

Iraqi Freedom, Operation, Casualties of

Casualties as a result of combat operations in Iraq during Operation Iraqi Freedom, which began on March 19, 2003, and continued through the end of 2011, were a constant source of controversy, particularly in the United States. The quick and decisive victory won by the United States in the 1991 Persian Gulf War, which saw few American casualties, and the low initial American casualty count for the Afghanistan War, Operation Eɴᴅᴜʀɪɴɢ Fʀᴇᴇᴅᴏᴍ, had conditioned U.S. citizens and politicians to expect a speedy and relatively easy victory in Iraq. Although the initial combat phase (March 19–April 30, 2003) produced few U.S. and coalition combat deaths, the subsequent insurgency led to several thousand more, with the toll continuing to climb. Many responded to the mounting Iʀᴀϙɪ Fʀᴇᴇᴅᴏᴍ casualty numbers with incredulity and calls for a full or total withdrawal of American troops from Iraq. Other nations with large troop deployments in Iraq—particularly Great Britain—experienced similar developments.

The U.S. Department of Defense provides a continuously running tally of American casualties. Its figures include numbers of American personnel killed in action (KIA) and wounded in action (WIA) in both official Operation Iʀᴀϙɪ Fʀᴇᴇᴅᴏᴍ combat operations (March 19, 2003–April, 30, 2003) and postcombat operations (May 1, 2003–2011). In the first phase of the war, 139 American military personnel were killed, and 545 were wounded. Total U.S. military deaths from both phases of Iʀᴀϙɪ Fʀᴇᴇᴅᴏᴍ were 4,487 through the end of 2011, while the total number of American military personnel wounded in action during the same period is some 31,500. Of those wounded, a majority returned to active duty within 72 hours, classified as wounded in action, returned to duty (WIA RTD). Each fatality milestone has occasioned an outcry of opposition to the war, and when the casualty count topped 4,000 in the spring of 2008 and

coincided with a particularly heated presidential primary campaign, these numbers became a source of even greater political controversy. In addition to the U.S. casualties a total of 318 coalition troops had been killed, including 179 Britons and 139 others. Also, the Iraq War has claimed the lives of 139 journalists. A total of 1,264 contractors have also been killed.

Although the Department of Defense makes information on U.S. casualties publicly available, precise figures documenting Iraqi casualties, both military and civilian, are more difficult to access, and nearly all figures come with caveats. Iraqi sources have reported that government agencies are not permitted to report the numbers of bodies buried daily. Credible sources indicate roughly 9,200 Iraqi combatant fatalities during the first phase of Operation Iʀᴀϙɪ Fʀᴇᴇᴅᴏᴍ; estimates range from a low of 7,600 to a high of 10,800. According to the Iraq Coalition Casualty Count, an estimated 8,298 members of the Iraqi Security Forces (ISF) have been killed in combat, fighting Iraqi insurgents. The Iraq Coalition Casualty Count is one of the most thorough databases compiling this information, although the group does not provide numbers of wounded ISF personnel and its information is not considered reliable by European, Arab, or American academics. Current and credible estimates of the number of insurgents killed are among the hardest statistics to obtain, because membership in those groups is both fluid and clandestine. According to calculations made in September 2007, the number of insurgents killed after the fall of Baghdad in April 2003 was 19,492; casualties continue to accumulate, although a reliably sourced updated estimate has not been released.

The number of Iraqi civilians killed during Iʀᴀϙɪ Fʀᴇᴇᴅᴏᴍ has been widely disputed. The Lancet study of 2006, so-called for its publication in the British medical journal of that name, was carried out by Iraqi and American physicians and researchers from al-Mustansiriyya University and Johns Hopkins University through a cluster-survey of households where respondents had to show death certificates. It estimated a total of 426,369 to 793,663 Iraqi deaths to that date.

A third study, by experts from the Federal Ministry of Health in Baghdad, the Kurdistan Ministry of Planning, the Kurdistan Ministry of Health, the Central Organization for Statistics and Information Technology in Baghdad, and the World Health Organization carried out the Iraq Family Health Survey Study (IFHS) Group (known as the WHO study in the media). The IFHS study estimated 151,000 Iraqi deaths from March 2003 to June 2006. The study actually presented a range of deaths from 104,000 to 223,000 for those years.

Other sources have estimated Iraqi civilian casualties from the war and sectarian violence from 600,000 to more than 1,000,000. The independent British-based Opinion Research Bureau estimated 1,220,580 Iraqis deaths by September 2007. Other than deliberate underreporting, some sources pointed to the suppression of statistics by the Iraqi government in the belief that to do so would compromise efforts to quell violence.

Although there is disagreement on the actual number of civilian deaths in Iraq, there is general agreement that the numbers have been very high. Generally speaking, those who supported the war have denied the higher civilian casualty counts, while those who opposed the war held them to be valid.

The Iraq Coalition Casualty Count serves as a thorough clearinghouse for information on all coalition fatalities. During the period of official Iraqi Freedom combat (March 19–May 1, 2003), 33 soldiers from the United Kingdom were killed; no other coalition nation suffered any fatalities during this phase of operations. Coalition Casualty Count cites the following fatality numbers for other coalition nations: Australia, 2; Azerbaijan, 1; Bulgaria, 13; Czech Republic, 1; Denmark, 7; El Salvador, 5; Estonia, 2; Fiji, 1; Georgia, 5; Hungary, 1; Italy, 33; Kazakhstan, 1; Latvia, 3; Netherlands, 2; Poland, 22; Romania, 3; Slovakia, 4; South Korea, 1; Spain, 11; Thailand, 2; Ukraine, 18; United Kingdom, 176. The group does not provide WIA casualty figures.

A high suicide rate among U.S. military and veterans has become a special matter of concern. Although no clear answers for this have emerged, it has been attributed to extended tours, too little time off between tours, the nature of the conflict, circumstances at home, and other factors.

Periodic lulls in violence and the achievement of certain strategic objectives have resulted in temporary decreases in the rates of injury and death, but the nature of the guerrilla-style, low-intensity conflict that has characterized the Iraq insurgency and the continuing sectarian conflicts mean that casualties on all sides will likely continue to accumulate.

Rebecca Adelman and Sherifa Zuhur

See also: Iraqi Freedom, Operation

Further Reading

Baker, James A., III, and Lee Hamilton. *The Iraq Study Group: The Way Froward, a New Approach.* New York: Vintage, 2006.

Burnham, Gilbert, Riyadh Lafta, Shannon Doocy et al. "Mortality after the 2003 Invasion of Iraq: A Cross-Sectional Cluster Sample Survey." *Lancet* 368, no. 5945 (October 21, 2006): 1421–29.

Capdevila, Luc, and Danièle Voldman. *War Dead: Western Society and Casualties of War.* Translated by Richard Veasey. Edinburgh, UK: Edinburgh University Press, 2006.

"Documented Civilian Deaths from Violence." Iraq Body Count, http://www.iraqbodycount.org/database.

Fischer, Hanna. "Iraqi Civilian Casualties Estimates." Washington, DC: Congressional Research Service, January 12, 2009.

Iraq Family Health Survey Study Group. "Violence-Related Mortality in Iraq from 2002 to 2006." *New England Journal of Medicine* (January 31, 2008): 484–92.

Mueller, John. "The Iraq Syndrome." *Foreign Affairs* 84 (2005): 44–54.

"Operation Iraqi Freedom (OIF) U.S. Casualty Status." U.S. Department of Defense, http://www.defenselink.mil/news/casualty.pdf.

Roberts, Les, Riyadh Lafta, Richard Garfield et al. "Mortality before and after the 2003 Invasion of Iraq: Cluster Sample Survey." *Lancet* 364, no. 9448 (October 29, 2004): 1857–64.

Wood, Trish. *What Was Asked of Us: An Oral History of the Iraq War by the Soldiers Who Fought It.* New York: Little, Brown, 2006.

IRAQI FREEDOM, Operation, Coalition Ground Forces

During Operation IRAQI FREEDOM, the 2003 invasion of Iraq, U.S. forces led a small coalition of allied states to overthrow the regime of Saddam Hussein. The coalition was officially designated as Combined and Joint Task Force 7 (CJTF-7), with "combined" meaning more than one nation and "joint" meaning more than one military service.

In an effort to avoid past problems in coalition warfare that included political interference and a lack of unity in the chain of command and in light of limited potential contributions to the invading force, the United States developed an invasion plan that emphasized U.S. forces and those of the nation's close ally the United Kingdom. When the government of Turkey refused to grant the United States permission to launch a second front from its territory, the invasion plan was revised to call for the major ground assault to occur from Kuwait, supported by airborne assaults and action by special operations forces in the north.

The coalition consisted of 248,000 U.S. personnel along with 45,000 British; 2,000 Australian; 1,300 Spanish; and 200 Polish troops. The majority of the Australian and Polish troops were special operations forces. The main British ground unit was the 1st Armoured Division. Prior to the invasion, the U.S. Army provided command and control gear to some of the British units to facilitate interoperability (the U.S. Army had to provide similar equipment to U.S. Marine Corps units). The equipment allowed the allied forces to communicate and exchange information through satellite systems and to employ tactical Internet capabilities. Nonetheless, national liaison officers had to be stationed among the units to coordinate air support and ground fire.

Coalition units were under the overall operational command of U.S. Army lieutenant general David McKiernan, who was appointed as the head of Coalition Forces Land Component Command. McKiernan was second-in-command to the overall operation commander, U.S. general Tommy Franks. The senior British military officer was Air Chief Marshal Brian Burridge.

Prior to the onset of hostilities, coalition special operations forces crossed into Iraqi territory to gather intelligence and identify targets. On March 20 the invasion began.

The majority of non-U.S. coalition forces were placed under the operational umbrella of the U.S. I Marine Expeditionary Force (I MEF). The southern area of Iraq was the main target of the British-led forces, which included most of the Australian and Polish troops. British and Polish commandos and U.S. marines attacked and captured the port city of Umm Qasr, including the majority of the area's oil wells, and gradually took control of the Faw peninsula. The British then secured Basra and worked to open the port to coalition shipping and humanitarian supplies. The British then moved northward and linked with U.S. forces at Amarah. The Spanish troops did not take part in offensive combat operations and instead provided engineering and support for the coalition from Kuwait. In the north, Polish and U.S. special operations units, along with the U.S. 173rd Airborne Brigade, collaborated with anti-Hussein Kurdish militias to create a second front in Operation NORTHERN DELAY. The coalition forces were able to capture the strategic city of Kirkuk in April 2003.

The coalition's main offensive was a two-pronged advance on Baghdad conducted mainly by U.S. forces. The western advance was led by the U.S. V Corps, in turn led by the 3rd Infantry Division, while the eastern attack was undertaken by the I MEF as the British forces continued operations in the south. The 3rd Infantry Division reached the Iraqi capital on April 4 and had control by April 10. On May 2, U.S. president George W. Bush announced an end to major combat operations. However, an insurgency arose with former Hussein loyalists and foreign fighters fighting against coalition forces.

Additional countries meanwhile contributed troops to the coalition war effort. In September 2003 Iraq was divided into zones of occupation. The British took charge of the multinational forces in the four southern provinces, designated the South Zone. Coalition forces in the South Central Zone, consisting of four provinces and parts of two others, came under Polish command. Poland maintained elements of either an armored or mechanized division as its core contribution, rotating units such as the 12th Mechanized Division or the 11th Lubusz Armored Cavalry Division through multiple tours in Iraq beginning in May 2003. Poland's peak contribution to the coalition was 2,500 troops, but the country withdrew its forces in October 2008.

A number of other countries also had significant deployments of more than 1,000 troops. In 2004 South Korea dispatched 3,600 troops, mainly medical, construction, and engineering units, but all forces were withdrawn in December 2008. The South Korean units were formed into the Zaytun Division (*zaytun* is Arabic for "olive"). Italy deployed 3,200 soldiers in 2003; however, these troops were withdrawn in November 2006. Georgia contributed 2,000 troops but withdrew the bulk of its forces during the brief Soviet-Georgian War of August 2008. Ukraine deployed the 5th, 6th, and 7th Mechanized brigades in succession, beginning in 2003, with a top commitment of about 1,800 troops. Ukraine withdrew its troops in December 2005. Australia deployed about 1,400 ground troops, including units from the Royal Australian Regiment, the 2nd Cavalry Regiment, and the Light Horse Regiment (Queensland Mounted Infantry). The Netherlands provided approximately 1,350 troops in July 2003 and withdrew its forces two years later. Spain contributed 1,300 troops in 2003 but withdrew the forces in 2004.

By 2008, 40 countries had deployed forces at some point to support CJTF-7, which was renamed the Multi-National Force–Iraq (MNF-Iraq) on May 15, 2004. However, the cost in both economic terms and loss of life led to growing antiwar sentiment in coalition states, leading many to draw down or completely withdraw their forces. As of the end of 2008, there were approximately 6,100 non-U.S. coalition troops in Iraq, the bulk of which (4,100) were British. By then, 314 non-U.S. coalition soldiers had been killed in Iraq. As of August 2009, all non-U.S. coalition forces had withdrawn from Iraq.

In addition to the larger contingents, the following countries contributed at least 100 soldiers (mostly support, medical, or engineering units): Albania, Azerbaijan, Bulgaria, the Czech Republic, Denmark, the Dominican Republic, El Salvador, Honduras, Hungary, Japan, Latvia, Lithuania, Mongolia, Norway, Nicaragua, Portugal, Romania, Slovakia, and Thailand.

The following countries contributed fewer than 100 troops: Armenia, Bosnia-Herzegovina, Estonia, Iceland, Kazakhstan, Macedonia, Moldova, New Zealand, the Philippines, Singapore, and Tonga. Several of these deployments were symbolic; for instance, Iceland deployed only 2 soldiers. In addition, Fiji deployed 150 troops in support of the United Nations (UN) mission in Iraq.

Tom Lansford

See also: Iraqi Freedom, Operation

Further Reading

Cockburn, Patrick. *The Occupation: War and Resistance in Iraq.* New York: Verso, 2007.

Keegan, John. *The Iraq War: The Military Offensive, from Victory in 21 Days to the Insurgent Aftermath.* New York: Vintage, 2005.

Murray, Williamson, and Robert H. Scales Jr. *The Iraq War: A Military History.* Cambridge, MA: Belknap, 2005.

Iraqi Freedom, Operation, Coalition Naval Forces

Naval forces from the United States and other nations played an important role in Operation Iraqi Freedom. Military operations opened on March 20, 2003, with the firing of 40 Tomahawk cruise missiles by British and American warships and air strikes by both U.S. Air Force and U.S. Navy fixed-wing aircraft; meanwhile, U.S. Navy Grumman EA-6 Prowlers jammed Iraqi radar systems. This was followed by the seizure of two offshore gas and oil platforms by Navy SEALs.

When coalition ground forces invaded Iraq, carrier aircraft provided close air support and struck targets in support of the bombing campaigns. The five U.S. Navy carrier battle groups operating in the Persian Gulf, the Indian Ocean, and the eastern Mediterranean Sea flew more than 7,000 sorties during the first three weeks of operations. Marines landed from two amphibious ready groups and joined army troops in the invasion of Iraq. The campaign was swift, and only a week after the Iraqi capital at Baghdad fell on April 10, 2003, Vice Admiral Timothy Keating, commander of the 140 U.S. warships in the region, suggested the return home or redeployment elsewhere of naval units. By April 30, at the end of operations, 35 coalition ships had fired 1,900 Tomahawks, one-third of them from submarines.

There were no significant naval surface engagements because Iraqi leader Saddam Hussein did not possess naval forces capable of posing a credible threat to coalition naval operations. After British and American marines captured the Iraqi port of Umm Qasr 30 miles south of Basra on March 30, four U.S. and six British minesweepers (operating with the mother ship RFA *Sir*

Belvedere) began clearing the narrow Khor Abd Allah waterway that linked the port to the Persian Gulf. Working with unmanned underwater vehicles (UUVs) and with more than 20 trained dolphins of the navy's Marine Mammals System (MMS), a Navy Very Shallow Water (VSW) detachment consisting of Navy SEALs, Marine Force Reconnaissance divers, and Explosive Ordnance Disposal divers opened the waterway so that supplies could be funneled through the city to troops advancing inland.

President George W. Bush consistently referred to the Iraq War as "the central front in the War on Terror," contributing to the difficulty in distinguishing between naval forces involved in operations in Operation IRAQI FREEDOM, Operation ENDURING FREEDOM–Afghanistan (OEF-A), and Operation ENDURING FREEDOM–Horn of Africa (OEF-HOA). Warships of Great Britain's Royal Navy joined U.S. Navy forces in OIF, and the two navies often shifted forces between bilateral operations in the Persian Gulf and multinational operations farther afield. The invasion phase of the war was declared over on April 30, 2003, after which time the line between operations was further blurred with the establishment of Combined Task Force 150 (CTF-150) to support OIF, OEF-A, and OEF-HOA by monitoring shipping and countering piracy in the northern Persian Gulf.

Australia, Canada, Denmark, France, Germany, Italy, the Netherlands, New Zealand, Pakistan, Turkey, the United Kingdom, and the United States assigned warships to CTF-150 at varying times. CTF-150 usually contains about 15 ships, the command of which rotates among the participating navies in four- to six-month intervals. Commanders have included Spanish rear admiral Juan Moreno, British commodore Tony Rix, French vice admiral Jacques

Mazars, Dutch commodore Hank Ort, Pakistani rear admiral Shahid Iqbal, German rear admiral Heinrich Lange, and British commodore Bruce Williams.

In 2003, Combined Task Force 158 (CTF-158) was formed by U.S., British, Australian, and Iraqi naval forces to operate jointly with units of the Iraqi armed forces to train Iraqi naval personnel, protect Iraqi assets such as the Khawr al Amayah and Al Basrah oil terminals (KAAOT and ABOT, respectively) located on platforms off the coast of the Faw (Fao) peninsula in southern Iraq, operate jointly with Kuwaiti naval patrol boats, and patrol international waters in a cone-shaped area extending into the Persian Gulf beyond the territorial waters of Iraq. Its commanders have included British commodore Duncan Potts and U.S. rear admiral Kendall Card.

James C. Bradford

See also: IRAQI FREEDOM, Operation; IRAQI FREEDOM, Operation, Air Campaign; IRAQI FREEDOM, Operation, Ground Campaign

Further Reading

Boyne, Walter J. *Operation Iraqi Freedom: What Went Right, What Went Wrong and Why.* New York: Forge Books, 2003.

Holmes, Tony. *US Navy Hornet Units in Operation Iraqi Freedom.* 2 vols. Oxford: Osprey, 2004–2005.

Lambeth, Benjamin S. *American Carrier Air Power at the Dawn of a New Century.* Santa Monica, CA: RAND Corporation, 2005.

Miller, Richard F. *A Carrier at War: On Board the USS Kitty Hawk in the Iraq War.* Washington, DC: Potomac Books, 2003.

IRAQI FREEDOM, Operation, Ground Campaign

For some time the United States and its coalition partners had been building up their forces in Kuwait. More than 300,000 personnel were deployed in the theater under U.S. Army Central Command (CENTCOM) commander General Tommy Franks. Actual coalition combat strength on the ground to implement COBRA II, the ground invasion of Iraq, numbered some 125,000 U.S. troops; 45,000 British troops; 2,000 Australian troops; and 200 Polish troops. Other nations supplied support or occupation troops. Unlike the 1990–1991 Persian Gulf War, there was no broad-based coalition helping to bear the cost of the war. Although Kuwait and Qatar supported the United States, Saudi Arabia refused the use of its bases for air strikes against Iraq. The United States also experienced a major setback when the Turkish Parliament, despite pledges of up to $30 billion in financial assistance, refused to allow the United States to use its territory to open up a northern front, a key component of the U.S. military plan. Three dozen ships laden with equipment for the 30,000-strong U.S. 4th Infantry Division lay off Turkish ports. Only after the war began were they redirected through the Suez Canal and around the Arabian Peninsula to Kuwait. The Turkish government's decision meant that the 4th Infantry Division would have to be part of the follow-on force and that Iraq could concentrate its military efforts to the south.

Although some air strikes were launched on the night of March 19 (one—the Dora Farms Strike—was an unsuccessful effort to kill Saddam Hussein and his sons, but most strikes were directed against Iraqi air defense and missile systems threatening coalition forces in Kuwait as well as leaflet drops with capitulation instructions), the Iraq War began at 5:34 a.m. Baghdad time on March 20, 2003 (9:34 p.m., March 19 EST). Initially known as Operation IRAQI LIBERATION, it was later renamed Operation IRAQI FREEDOM (the British code name was Operation TELIC, while the Australian forces knew it as Operation FALCONER). The war commenced just hours after the expiration of U.S. president George W. Bush's 48-hour ultimatum to Saddam Hussein to step aside.

Baghdad was repeatedly hit with cruise missile attacks and air strikes by B-1, B-2, and B-52 bombers against key headquarters and command and control targets. This shock-and-awe campaign did not appear to be on the massive scale that CENTCOM had suggested. Part of this was the use of 70 percent smart bombs (guided) and 30 percent dumb aerial munitions (unguided), as opposed to only 10 percent smart weapons during the 1990–1991 Persian Gulf War. Also, a good many of the air strikes occurred away from the capital.

As the air attacks unfolded, the ground war also began. The coalition advance from Kuwait was along two main axes northwest toward Baghdad by U.S. Army and marine units, and one supporting thrust due north toward Basra. British forces on the far right under 1st Armoured Division commander Major General Robin Brims were assigned the task of securing the Shatt al-Arab waterway and important Shiite city of Basra, Iraq's second largest. At the same time, Lieutenant General James Conway's I Marine Expeditionary Force in the center and Lieutenant General William Scott Wallace's U.S. Army's V Corps to the west would drive on the Iraqi capital of Baghdad, 300 miles to the north. Major General Buford Blount's 3rd ID, with the 7th Armored Cavalry Regiment leading, made the most rapid progress, largely because it moved through more sparsely populated areas.

In the center part of the front, the I Marine Expeditionary Force, carrying out the longest march in its storied history, skirted to the west of the Euphrates River, through the cities of Nasiriyah and on to Najaf and

Karbala. Key factors in the allied success were coalition air power (Iraqi aircraft and helicopters never got off the ground), including Apache helicopter gunships and the highly resilient tank-busting A-10 Thunderbolt, the rapidity of the advance, and the ability of coalition troops to fight at night.

The marines were successful in seizing by coup de main the oil fields north of Basra, some 60 percent of the nation's total, including key refineries. Having secured the Shatt al-Arab, and wishing to spare civilians, the British were hopeful of an internal uprising and did not move into Basra itself. They were not actually encamped in the city until the night of April 2. In the meantime they imposed a loose blockade and carried out a series of raids into Basra to destroy symbols of the regime in an effort to demoralize the defenders and to convince them that coalition forces could move at will. At the same time, British forces distributed food and water to convince the inhabitants that they came as liberators rather than conquerors.

U.S. Special Forces secured airfields in western Iraq, and 1,000 members of the 173rd Airborne Brigade dropped into Kurdish-held territory in northern Iraq on the night of March 26. Working in conjunction with lightly armed Kurdish forces, the brigade opened a northern front and secured the key oil production center of Mosul. U.S. Special Forces also directed air strikes against the Islamic Ansar al-Islam camp in far northeastern Iraq, on the Iranian border.

A number of Iraqi divisions moved into position to block the coalition drive north. These troops largely evaporated, however, with many of their personnel simply deserting. Meanwhile, so-called Saddam Fedayeen, or "technicals"—irregulars often wearing civilian clothes—carried out attacks using civilian vehicles with mounted machine guns

and rocket-propelled grenades on supply convoys along the lines of communication from Kuwait north, which came to be dubbed Ambush Alley. Indeed, on March 23, the 507th Maintenance Company, part of a convoy moving north near the Euphrates, took a wrong turn, was ambushed, and in an ensuing firefight lost nine killed, five wounded, and six captured.

On March 26, U.S. 7th Cavalry regiment and 3rd Infantry Division elements defeated an Iraqi force near Najaf in the largest battle of the war thus far, killing some 450 Iraqis. On March 28, with U.S. forces some 100 miles south of Baghdad, there was an operational pause because of a fierce sandstorm extending over March 25 and 26 and the need for some army units to resupply.

The Iraqi leadership, meanwhile, repositioned its six Republican Guard divisions around Baghdad for a defense of the capital. As some of these divisions moved to take up new positions south of the city, they came under heavy air attack and lost much of their equipment. The coalition advance quickened again during April 1 and 2, following the serious degrading of the Baghdad and Medina divisions.

On April 3, U.S. forces reached the outskirts of Baghdad and over the next two days secured Saddam International Airport, some 12 miles from the city center. The speed of their advance allowed U.S. forces to take the airport with minimal damage to its facilities, and it soon became a staging area. By that date, too, the Iraqi people sensed the shift of momentum and an imminent coalition victory. Advancing U.S. troops reported friendly receptions from civilians and increasing surrenders of Iraqi troops, including a reported 2,500 Republican Guards north of Kut on April 4.

By April 5, the 3rd Infantry Division was closing on Baghdad from the southwest, the marines from the southeast, and the 101st Airborne Division was preparing to move in from the north. Baghdad was in effect under a loose blockade, with civilians allowed to depart. On that day also, the 3rd Infantry Division's 2nd Brigade, commanded by Colonel David Perkins, pushed through downtown Baghdad in a three-hour-long operation, called a "Thunder Run," inflicting an estimated 1,000 Iraqi casualties. This proved a powerful psychological blow to the Iraqi regime, which had claimed U.S. forces were nowhere near the city and that it still controlled the international airport. It also led to an exodus of many Baath Party officials and Iraqi military personnel.

This process was repeated on April 6 and 7. In a fierce firefight on April 6, U.S. forces killed an estimated 2,000–3,000 Iraqi soldiers for 1 killed of their own. Three battalions of the 3rd Infantry Division remained in the city on April 7. The next day marine elements moved into southeastern Baghdad. With the 101st Airborne closing on the city from the northwest and the 3rd Infantry Division from the southeast, the ring around the capital was closed. On April 9, resistance collapsed in Baghdad as Iraqi civilians assisted by U.S. Marines toppled a large statue of Saddam Hussein. There was still fighting in parts of the city as diehard Baath loyalists sniped at U.S. troops, but Iraqi government central command and control had collapsed by April 10.

Elsewhere on April 10, following the collapse of resistance in Baghdad, a small number of Kurdish fighters, U.S. Special Forces, and the 173rd Airborne Brigade liberated Kirkuk. The next day, Mosul, Iraq's third largest city, fell when the Iraqi V Corps commander surrendered some 30,000 men. Apart from some sporadic shooting in Baghdad and massive looting there and in other cities, the one remaining center of resistance was Hussein's ancestral home of Tikrit.

On April 12, the 101st Airborne relieved the marines and 3rd Infantry Division in Baghdad, allowing them to deploy northwest to Tikrit. Meanwhile, the 173rd Airborne Brigade took control of the northern oil fields from the Kurds in order to prevent any possibility of Turkish intervention. The battle for Tikrit failed to materialize. Hussein's stronghold collapsed, and on April 14 allied forces entered the city. That same day the Pentagon announced that major military operations in Iraq were at an end; all that remained was mopping up. Through the end of April, the coalition suffered 139 U.S. and 31 British dead. The coalition reported that 9,200 Iraqi military personnel had also been slain, along with 7,299 civilians, the latter figure believed by many critics of the war to be far too low.

On May 1, 2003, President Bush visited the U.S. aircraft carrier *Abraham Lincoln* off San Diego, the carrier having just returned from a deployment to the Persian Gulf. There the president delivered his "Mission Accomplished" speech, broadcast live to the American public. Bush's characterization that the war was won proved premature. The administration had given insufficient thought to the postwar occupation of Iraq, and long-simmering tensions between Sunni, Shiite, and Kurds erupted into sectarian violence. A series of ill-considered policy decisions, including disbanding the Iraqi Army, abetted the poor security situation, as angry Sunnis, supported by volunteers from other Arab states, took up arms and launched suicide attacks against Iraqi civilians and the U.S. occupiers. Unguarded ammunition dumps provided plentiful supplies for the improvised explosive devices (IEDs) that claimed growing numbers of allied troops.

Spencer C. Tucker

See also: Baghdad, Battle for; Bush, George Walker; Franks, Tommy Ray; IRAQI FREEDOM, Operation; IRAQI FREEDOM, Operation, Coalition Ground Forces; Republican Guard; Rumsfeld, Donald Henry

Further Reading

Atkinson, Rick. *In the Company of Soldiers: A Chronicle of Combat*. New York: Henry Holt, 2005.

Franks, Tommy, with Malcolm McConnell. *American Soldier*. New York: Regan Books, 2004.

Murray, Williamson, and Robert H. Scales Jr. *The Iraq War: A Military History*. Cambridge, MA: Belknap, 2005.

Purdum, Todd S., and the Staff of the *New York Times*. *A Time of Our Choosing: America's War in Iraq*. New York: Times Books/Henry Holt, 2003.

West, Bing, and Ray L. Smith. *The March Up: Taking Baghdad with the 1st Marine Division*. New York: Bantam, 2003.

IRAQI FREEDOM, Operation, Planning for

On September 15, 2001, U.S. president George W. Bush and his national security team met to discuss how to respond to the September 11 terrorist attacks on the United States. Secretary of Defense Donald Rumsfeld and his aides offered three targets for retaliation: al-Qaeda, Afghanistan's Taliban regime, and Iraq. In November Pentagon planners began to ponder formally how to attack Iraq. From the outset Rumsfeld and his circle of civilian planners argued with senior military officers over whether to attack Iraq and how many ground troops to employ. As pressure built for a U.S. invasion, based on the premise that Iraq possessed weapons of mass destruction (WMD), the U.S. Central Command (CENTCOM), commanded by General Tommy Franks, assumed responsibility for planning and executing the invasion of Iraq. For a variety of reasons, particularly civilian pressure from Rumsfeld and his aides, a perceived urgency that imposed undue haste, an overburdened staff that also had to address Afghanistan, and Franks's command style that squashed dissent, war planners focused on the relatively easy task of defeating the Iraqi military. They gave little thought to what would come afterward.

During the years following the 1990–1991 Persian Gulf War, military planners had prepared a plan for a second war against Iraq. Dubbed Operation DESERT CROSSING, it envisioned a large invasion force of about 350,000 men, with some variants involving a force of upwards of 500,000 men. The Rumsfeld circle argued that this was far too many ground forces. They pointed to the tremendous improvement in the U.S. military's ability to deliver precision-guided weapons as well as technical advances in reconnaissance systems and command and control networks and asserted that the military was now more mobile and more lethal than during the Persian Gulf War. Proponents of a smaller invasion force argued that these changes, coupled with the deterioration of the Iraqi military that had begun during the Persian Gulf War, implied that a second war against Iraq would not be a difficult undertaking. The Rumsfeld circle also wanted the flexibility to launch the ground invasion without a long, prewar buildup of forces.

The demand for a lean force that could attack without a long logistical buildup constrained military planners. CENTCOM created a list of things that it wanted to be able to affect or influence, including the Iraqi leadership, internal security, its WMD, and the Republican Guard. They then matched this list against such U.S. military capabilities as Special Operations Forces, air power, and conventional ground forces.

Meanwhile, a group of military planners, notably Secretary of State (and retired four-star general) Colin Powell, warned the Bush administration that the Iraqi Army was the glue holding Iraq together. If the United States dissolved that bond by destroying the army, it would inherit the responsibility for occupying and governing Iraq for a very long time. However, this minority viewpoint had little influence on the development of war plans.

During his 2002 State of the Union address President Bush identified Iraq, Iran, and North Korea as hostile nations, part of an "axis of evil." He asserted that the United States would not stand idle while these nations threatened American interests with WMD. In June 2002 Bush spoke at the U.S. Military Academy, West Point, and formally announced the adoption of a strategy of preemption, known as the Bush Doctrine. These two speeches provided the intellectual rationale for the March 2003 invasion of Iraq.

In August 2002 the Bush administration drafted a secret document titled "Iraq: Goals, Objectives and Strategy." It was an ambitious statement that sought to eliminate the Iraqi WMD threat once and for all, end the Iraqi threat to its neighbors, liberate the Iraqi people from Saddam Hussein's tyranny, and end Iraqi support for international terrorism. The intention was that a stable democracy would be planted in Iraq that would grow and spread throughout the Middle East. In addition, the stupendous show of U.S. force would overawe potential future adversaries.

In its final form, the war plan called for army Special Operations helicopters and air force aircraft to begin operations on the evening of March 19 against Iraqi observation posts along the Saudi and Jordanian borders. Then, coalition special operations units would infiltrate western Iraq to eliminate missile sites that threatened Israel. Two days later, at 9:00 p.m. on March 21, Tomahawk cruise missiles, Lockheed F-117 Nighthawk stealth fighters, and Northrop Grumman B-2 Spirit stealth bombers would strike targets in and around Baghdad. The next morning, COBRA II, the ground invasion, would begin. The army's V Corps, built around the tank-heavy 3rd Infantry Division, along with the 101st Airborne Division, would conduct the main thrust toward Baghdad. Simultaneously, the 1st Marine Division would seize the Rumaila oil field, drive north across the Euphrates River, and protect the V Corps' flank. The converging army and marine units would then form a cordon around Baghdad to prevent senior Iraqi leaders or WMD from escaping. British forces would seize the largely Shiite city of Basra in southeastern Iraq.

Plans had also called for an attack south from Turkey, mounted by the 4th Infantry Division. Last-minute Turkish obstinacy, despite financial incentives offered by the United States, blocked this part of the plan, forcing the 4th Infantry Division to become a follow-on force and allowing the Iraqis to concentrate their forces to the south. The northern front consisted of the 173rd Airborne Brigade working with lightly armed Kurdish forces to secure the key oil production center of Mosul. In total, the invading ground force was to number about 145,000 men, which was enough to provide a breakthrough force but insufficient to pacify conquered territory.

Planners thought that the ground invasion coming so soon after the air strike would surprise Iraqi military leaders. Air attacks began ahead of schedule, however, when intelligence reports indicated a meeting of Hussein and his senior leaders. The intelligence proved wrong.

COBRA II began on March 21 (local time), 2003. Conventional operations proceeded relatively smoothly, reaching an apparent high-water mark on April 9, when a live television broadcast showed U.S. troops helping a jubilant Iraqi crowd topple a giant statue of Saddam Hussein in downtown Baghdad. Thereafter, the failure to plan adequately for the subsequent occupation led to an insurgency that has persisted for years.

James Arnold

See also: Bush, George Walker; Desert Crossing, OPLAN; Franks, Tommy Ray

Further Reading

Cordesman, Anthony H. *The Iraq War: Strategy, Tactics, and Military Lessons.* Westport, CT: Praeger, 2003.

Gordon, Michael R., and General Bernard E. Trainor. *Cobra II: The Inside Story of the Invasion and Occupation of Iraq.* New York: Pantheon Books, 2006.

Record, Jeffrey. *Wanting War: Why the Bush Administration Invaded Iraq.* Dulles, VA: Potomac Books, 2009.

Ricks, Thomas E. *Fiasco: The American Military Adventure in Iraq.* New York: Penguin, 2006.

Iraqi Insurgency

A violent resistance by segments of the Iraqi population against the foreign occupation powers deployed in Iraq and the new Iraqi government set up after the fall of the Baathist state. The term "insurgency" is employed in U.S. governmental circles and by coalition forces but is not used in the Arab media, except in discussions with U.S. spokespersons. The term was not initially employed by the U.S. government, but its appearance in 2004 led to a major emphasis on insurgency theory and new approaches to counterinsurgency.

The Iraqi insurgency commenced soon after the official end of hostilities that followed the overthrow of Iraqi president Saddam Hussein in the spring of 2003. Until the U.S. military gained control of Iraq and President George W. Bush declared "mission accomplished" on May 1, 2003, Operation Iraqi Freedom was essentially a war between the Iraqi government and military and the coalition powers that overthrew it. Since then, Iraqi Freedom has morphed into a battle between coalition and allied Iraqi forces and a wide array of insurgent groups, now characterized as an insurgency war.

A number of factors led to the insurgency, but the chief cause was the power vacuum created by the sudden collapse of the highly centralized Iraqi government and by the failure of the U.S. armed forces to properly fill that void in a timely manner with a power structure acceptable to those governed. Many Iraqis did not welcome a change in government, or feared the opposition elements who assumed power. Coalition forces have sometimes argued that the lack of electricity, fuel, potable water, and basic social services created daily personal grievances among many Iraqis, but far more resentment was engendered by attacks, arrests, and detentions, and later, by Iraqi-on-Iraqi campaigns that led those who could afford or were able to flee Iraq to do so. The Iraqi people expected the occupying American forces to provide for their security, but the latter either had insufficient numbers to do so effectively or were not assigned to protect Iraqis, their property, or their state institutions.

The U.S.-led invasion of Iraq and subsequent fall of the country's dictator, Saddam Hussein, made conditions ripe for power struggles to emerge among various sectarian and political groups. Even though Iraqis had a history of intermarriage and mixed communities, many had been suppressed and mistreated by Hussein's government and had scores to settle.

The U.S. government hoped that the period immediately following the overthrow of Hussein would see the installation of a broadly based Iraqi government led by those who had opposed Saddam. However, the Iraqi people viewed many of the new leaders as pursuing their own narrow interests or those of their parties.

Also, the initial U.S. governmental appointees in the Interim Authority were intent on wiping out all vestiges of the previous government and institutions through de-Baathification. This led many Sunni Iraqis to conclude that they had absolutely nothing to gain and could possibly force the occupying troops to leave Iraq if they took up arms and established control in those areas of the country where they were a majority. Initially, the coalition refused to accept both the severity of this fighting and its toll on Iraqis, but a virtual civil war began to engulf Iraq in 2006.

A telling feature of the Iraqi insurgency has been its decentralized nature. It is conducted by a large number of disparate groups, many of which are ideologically different, although temporary alliances are not uncommon. For example, there were at least 40 different Sunni Muslim insurgent factions, although the coalition primarily focused on the threat presented by al-Qaeda in Iraq. Others were local nationalists, made up of former Iraqi security service members and soldiers of the old Iraqi armed forces, some of whom aligned with new Islamist groups. Their goal, broadly speaking, was to drive the United States and its allies from Iraq and regain the power that they once had enjoyed, or at least, sufficient power to force the central Shia-dominated Iraqi government to grant them autonomy in certain areas. This

segment of the resistance was motivated by a mixture of nationalism, opposition to occupation, loss of status and income, fear of future discrimination, and the lure of financial incentives provided by various groups. These predominantly Sunni groups had valid reasons to fear that the new security services dominated by Shia and Kurds would oppress them. Some of these insurgents were believed to be trained and equipped soldiers with previous combat experience and knowledge of the local terrain.

A second element within the Sunni Iraqi community consisted of Jihadist Salafiyya (or Salafis) whose ultimate goal was the establishment of an Islamic state in Iraq while excluding the Shia and/or non-Islamists from power altogether. The U.S. government identified this group as consisting primarily of foreign volunteer fighters, who indeed traveled to Iraq from Saudi Arabia, Jordan, Syria, Egypt, and Libya. Actually, there were far fewer of these foreign volunteers than was claimed, and a far larger number of Salafist or Jihadi Salafists were Iraqis who adopted this role in desperation, or who had become Salafist in the Saddam Hussein era. These groups targeted coalition forces as well as Iraqi military, police, government, and civilians in suicide attacks. Among these groups was al-Qaeda in Iraq, which was originally the Tawhid wal-Jihad group headed by now-deceased Abu Musab al-Zarqawi.

Although al-Qaeda leaders in Afghanistan warned the Iraqi group, which had sworn allegiance to them, that attacking Iraqi Shia was a dubious policy, they went on doing so. The leaders of al-Qaeda in Iraq considered the Shia to be renegades (and apostates) and held them accountable for collaborating with the occupying forces.

In 2008 the coalition began to claim that many insurgents were not ideologically committed (perhaps because efforts to convince Iraqis that they were un-Islamic were failing). They asserted that many fighters were motivated by the need for a source of income because of the economic collapse of Iraq and the general state of lawlessness. This claim appears to have been true in some limited areas where kidnapping rings operated just after the initial defeat of Hussein's government. It is the type of claim that can be made in civil wars generally, but is demonstrably untrue, for most of the insurgent statements claim religious convictions.

The insurgents have employed a wide array of tactics against their targets. Some rely on sabotage of electric stations, oil pipelines and facilities, and coalition reconstruction projects. Others use small-arms gunfire against coalition forces and attempt assassinations of public officials and private citizens. Firing rockets and mortar shells at fixed coalition positions has also been an insurgent tactic. The use of improvised roadside bombs and improvised explosive devices (IEDs) has proven especially lethal to coalition troops. Suicide bombers, car bombs, and truck bombs have also been used to great effect by the insurgents.

Insurgents have deployed ambushes that involve the simultaneous use of mines, grenades, and rocket-propelled grenades. Insurgents also engage in the kidnapping of local citizens and foreigners to exchange them for ransom, or simply to execute them. Initially, insurgent violence was primarily directed at coalition forces. As the occupation has persisted, however, attacks by various insurgency groups have begun shifting toward the Iraqi police and security forces as well as opposing militias representing the various warring sects. Attacks on Iraqi civilians, especially those associated with the government or

seeking employment with the police force, also escalated after 2004.

The United States accused Syria and Iran of aiding various insurgency groups in the funding and planning of their activities. There was evidence that some former Baathists, including the acknowledged leader of the resistance, Ibrahim al-Duri, were in Syria. Both Syria and Iran oppose the establishment of a pro-American democracy in Iraq, and fear that their influence in the region would be jeopardized by the long-term stationing of U.S. troops in Iraq.

The United States has employed several strategies to squelch the insurgency in Iraq. The initial phase of counterinsurgency efforts in late 2003 and early 2004 consisted mainly of occupation forces engaging in indiscriminate and sometimes culturally insensitive tactics that alienated many Iraqis, such as mass arrests, night searches, heavy-handed interrogations, and blanket incarcerations. Such actions enraged and embittered formerly friendly or neutral Iraqis. The United States then responded to insurgents by engaging in a variety of counterinsurgency measures, including Operation DESERT THRUST, Operation PHANTOM FURY in Fallujah, Operation TOGETHER FORWARD, and Operation PHANTOM THRUST, just to name a few. These full-scale assaults on insurgency bases have had only a temporary and limited effect, however.

The most notable counterinsurgency effort was mounted during 2007. The so-called troop surge accounted for an increase in U.S. troop size by about 30,000 additional soldiers. The move has been hailed a success by U.S. officials for bringing down the levels of violence in Iraq. Critics, however, contend that the levels of violence have gone down only in some areas of the country, and only through methods that have cordoned off and imposed barriers around neighborhoods that have been cleansed on a sectarian basis. In spring 2009 there was, for example, an upsurge of bombings targeting both Shia and Sunni areas in Baghdad. While most insurgent activity involved only Sunnis, other groups have also been involved. Thus, there was also armed resistance by members of Muqtada al-Sadr's Mahdi Army when Iraqi government forces engaged them. They had not been a part of the insurgency but rather sought to enhance their power within the body politic.

Another reason for a drop in the violence was the fact that the U.S. military struck a bargain with various Sunni groups, some of them Jihadist Salafists. This permitted coalition forces to concentrate on fighting al-Qaeda in Iraq in these areas. However, these so-called Awakening Councils were subject to numerous attacks and have been clashing with the government. Since their support rested on financial incentives, their continued compliance is unclear. It remains uncertain if the reduction in the Iraq insurgency will survive the withdrawal of U.S. troops from Iraq.

Kristian P. Alexander and Sherifa Zuhur

See also: al-Qaeda in Iraq; Anbar Awakening; Bush, George Walker; Counterinsurgency; Iraqi Freedom, Operation; Mahdi Army; Sadr, Muqtada al-

Further Reading

Chehab, Zaki. *Iraq Ablaze: Inside the Insurgency.* New York: I. B. Tauris, 2006.

Cordesman, Anthony. *Iraqi Security Forces: A Strategy for Success.* Westport, CT: Praeger Security International, 2005.

Hafez, Mohammed. *Suicide Bombers in Iraq: The Strategy and Ideology of Martyrdom.* Washington, DC: United States Institute of Peace Press, 2007.

Hashim, Ammed S. *Insurgency and Counterinsurgency in Iraq.* Ithaca, NY: Cornell University Press, 2006.

Pelletiere, Stephen. *Losing Iraq: Insurgency and Politics.* Westport, CT: Praeger Security International, 2007.

Iraqi Police Forces

After the U.S. invasion of March 2003, many Iraqi police officers simply took off their uniforms and went home. The Coalition Provisional Authority (CPA) quickly viewed the deteriorating security situation with considerable alarm, and it issued requests for Iraqi police to return to service. Some police did return, but initially they were unarmed and clearly reluctant to engage in street patrols. As the reconstitution of the police proceeded, two police forces were established: the Iraqi National Police (INP) and the Iraqi Police Service.

The Iraqi National Police, renamed the Federal Police in August 2009, has approximately 42,000 members. It has been much more focused on counterinsurgency than regular policing. As a result, it has tended to be more a paramilitary force than "cops on the beat." Reinforcing its paramilitary ethos, the INP has been organized in military-style units of four divisions and 17 brigades. The INP is under control of the ministry of the interior. As with the ministry of the interior itself, the INP is overwhelmingly Shia. This situation almost certainly has led to some distrust of the INP by the Iraqi Sunni population.

After the CPA finally began to re-establish Iraqi security forces, training for the Iraqi police was placed under the defense department, which almost certainly impacted the types of training and the effectiveness of training the police received. The coalition

Iraqi police investigate at the scene of a roadside attack on an Iraqi police patrol on January 20, 2006, in Baghdad, Iraq. The attack injured three police and two civilians. Security forces went on high alert in Baghdad and four other large provinces in the country to try to prevent terror attacks ahead of Friday's announcement of preliminary election results, police and military said. (AP Photo/Hadi Mizban)

has trained over 31,000 members of the INP, with around 6,000 INP members receiving paramilitary training from the Italian Carabinieri under a NATO training mission. It should be noted that the various Iraqi police forces were among the first Iraqi security services to be reconstituted and to receive external training, with training programs starting as early as December 2003.

The Iraq Police Service (IPS) is responsible for law enforcement at the local and provincial levels, and consists of about 230,000 members. The actual number of "effectives" is difficult to judge, with reports of "ghost" police and padding of local commanders' rosters. The IPS has been marked by significant corruption and almost certainly has been infiltrated by various militia members and criminals. The IPS

also has suffered from poor training, equipment, and investigative capabilities.

There are three police academies for officers and six regional training centers for new recruits. In theory, well over half the police have been trained by the U.S. Civilian Police Assistance Transition Team (CPATT), but the level of attrition of trained Iraqis has been significant, reportedly with only 40–70 percent remaining in the police. Members who have been trained by the CPATT have been hired directly by provincial authorities, with the increased prospect of these members being political and/or ethnic hires.

The coalition activated local police transition training teams in 2006, comprised of a mix of military and civilian police advisers who work with local Iraqi police stations. Given the lack of available coalition personnel, only about 30 percent of Iraqi police stations had coalition advisers, therefore limiting both the actual advising efforts and the ability to monitor the activities of the local police.

Lawrence Cline

See also: Coalition Provisional Authority

Further Reading

Baker, James A. III, and Lee H. Hamilton. *The Iraq Study Group Report*. Washington, DC: United States Institute of Peace, 2006.

Deflem, Mathieu, and Suzanne Sutphin. "Policing Post-War Iraq: Insurgency, Civilian Police, and the Reconstruction of Society." *Sociological Focus* 39, no. 4 (November 2006), 265–83.

Perito, Robert M. *Special Report: The Iraq Federal Police: U.S. Police Building Under Fire*. Washington, DC: United States Institute of Peace, October 2011.

Iraq Liberation Act

Legislation passed by the United States Congress to establish a program to support a transition to democracy in Iraq. The act was sponsored by Representative Benjamin A. Gilman (R-N.Y.) and passed by Congress on October 7, 1998. President William Jefferson Clinton signed the act into law on October 31, 1998.

The Iraq Liberation Act of 1998 (ILA) encapsulated sentiment on the part of Congress that the United States should support efforts to remove Iraqi dictator Saddam Hussein from power and replace his regime with a democratic government. Enactment of the ILA coincided with growing tensions and frustrations within the international community in 1997 and 1998 over Iraq's continued failure to comply with United Nations (UN) resolutions mandating United Nations Special Commission (UNSCOM)

inspections of suspected Iraqi nuclear, biological, and chemical weapons sites. Residual concerns and mistrust stemming from the 1991 Persian Gulf War and the Iraqi suppression of Kurdish and Shiite opposition factions within the country also contributed to the rising tensions.

The ILA evolved from two prior pieces of legislation, the Emergency Supplemental Appropriations Act for Fiscal Year 1998, and the Omnibus Consolidated and Emergency Supplemental Appropriations Act for Fiscal Year 1999. Both acts provided monetary assistance to identified democratic opposition groups in Iraq. Pursuant to the Fiscal Year 1998 act, the U.S. Department of State also submitted a report to Congress detailing plans to establish a program of assistance for Iraqi democratic opposition groups. In spite of doubts over democratic opposition capabilities, the ILA provided additional assistance and, more importantly, encapsulated Congress's wishes for Iraq's future.

The ILA first delineated the historical chronology of Iraqi actions from its invasion of Iran on September 22, 1980, to Iraqi obstruction of UNSCOM inspection efforts in 1998 and the U.S. response of financial assistance to democratic opposition groups. The descriptive chronology provided a supportive framework for the third section, and core, of the ILA: the articulation of Congress's sentiment that U.S. policy toward Iraq should entail the removal of President Saddam Hussein's regime and support of democratic tendencies within the country. To that end, the ILA authorized the president to grant broadcasting, military, and humanitarian assistance to certain Iraqi democratic opposition groups. Seed money in the amount of $2 million for Fiscal Year 1999 was provided for television and radio broadcasting. Military assistance included up to $97 million in defense material and services from the Department of Defense, as well as military education and training for these groups. However, a separate but significant section made it clear that beyond providing materials, services, and training, the ILA should not be considered as authorizing direct U.S. military force to effectuate regime change in Iraq. Finally, the ILA authorized humanitarian assistance for individuals living in areas of Iraq controlled by democratic opposition groups. A particular emphasis was placed on providing humanitarian assistance to refugees fleeing from areas controlled by the Hussein regime.

A restrictive clause in the ILA prohibited the provision of such assistance to any group actively cooperating with Hussein's regime at the time when such assistance was to be provided, but Congress proceeded further in a separate section to clearly set out criteria to determine which opposition groups were eligible to receive assistance under the ILA. A number of religious and secular opposition groups had emerged in Iraq, and Congress wished to ensure assistance was provided to appropriate groups in accordance with congressional intent. Thus, Congress restricted presidential authorization of assistance to only those organizations composed of a diverse array of Iraqi individuals or groups opposed to Hussein's regime, with a corresponding commitment to democratic values, human rights, peace within the region, Iraq's territorial integrity, and the cultivation of cooperation among all democratic opposition groups. The ILA further urged the president to make an appeal to the United Nations to establish a war crimes tribunal for Iraq. Finally, the ILA contemplated additional U.S. support and assistance for democratic Iraqi parties when Hussein lost power in Iraq.

President Clinton signed the ILA into law the same day Iraq ceased all cooperation with UNSCOM. Six weeks later, beginning on December 16, 1998, the United States and Great Britain responded by launching Operation DESERT FOX, an air-strike campaign to degrade Iraqi command centers, airfields, and missile installations. The ILA and DESERT FOX served as further steps in the evolving U.S. policy toward Iraq. It took only a short step from there to reach a revised policy of active and direct regime change in Iraq after the terrorist attacks of September 11, 2001.

Mark F. Leep

See also: Hussein, Saddam

Further Reading

Condron, Sean M. "Justification for Unilateral Action in Response to the Iraqi Threat: A Critical Analysis of Operation Desert Fox." *Military Law Review* 161 (1999): 115–80.

Katzman, Kenneth. *Iraq: U.S. Regime Change Efforts and Post-Saddam Governance*. Washington, DC: Congressional Research Office, March 2006.

Paulus, Andreas. "The War against Iraq and the Future of International Law: Hegemony or Pluralism?" *Michigan Journal of International Law* 25 (2004): 691–733.

Iraq Sanctions Act of 1990

On November 5, 1990, the United States enacted the Iraq Sanctions Act of 1990 (Public Law 101-513; H.R. 5114) in response to the invasion and occupation of Kuwait by Iraq that began on August 2, 1990. Among other things, the act imposed on the government of Iraq sweeping economic sanctions and a trade embargo on most imports and exports.

In the Iraq Sanctions Act, the U.S. Congress supported the actions taken by the president in response to the invasion of Kuwait, called for the immediate and unconditional withdrawal of Iraqi forces from that country, supported the efforts of the United Nations Security Council (UNSC) to end the violation of international law and threat to peace, supported the imposition and enforcement of multinational sanctions against Iraq, called upon allies and other countries to support the UNSC resolutions to help bring about the end of the Iraqi occupation of Kuwait, and condemned the Iraqi violations of Kuwaiti human rights associated with the occupation, including mass arrests, torture, summary executions, rapes, pillaging, and mass extrajudicial killings.

The Iraq Sanctions Act also continued the trade embargo and economic sanctions that were imposed upon Iraq and Kuwait following Iraq's invasion of Kuwait on August 2, 1990 (as they were enumerated in Executive Orders 12722 and 12723 [August 2, 1990] and 12724 and 12725 [August 9, 1990]). Consistent with UNSC Resolution 666, foodstuffs or payment for foodstuffs for humanitarian assistance were exempt from the embargo.

The sanctions applied to Iraq included the following goods and services: foreign military sales; commercial arms sales; exports of certain goods and technology; nuclear equipment, materials, and technology; assistance from international financial institutions; assistance through the Import-Export Bank; assistance through the commodity credit corporation; and all forms of foreign assistance other than emergency humanitarian assistance.

Under the Iraq Sanctions Act, the United States denied funds from the Foreign Assistance Act of 1961 and Arms Export Control Act to any country that did not comply with UNSC sanctions against Iraq, unless those funds promoted the interest of the United States, assisted needy people in Iraq, or helped foreign nationals who were fleeing Iraq and Kuwait. In addition, the Iraq Sanctions Act authorized penalties of $25,000 to $1 million on individuals or corporations who deliberately evaded Executive Orders 12722, 12723, 12724, and 12725.

The Iraq Sanctions Act stated that Iraq violated the charter of the United Nations and other international treaties. It described Iraq's abysmal human rights record and referenced Iraq's history of summary executions, mass political killings, disappearances, widespread use of torture, arbitrary arrests, prolonged detention, deportation, and denial of nearly all civil and human rights. In addition, it highlighted Iraq's repression of the Kurdish people, cited its use of chemical weapons, and named it a state sponsor of terrorism. Congress sought multilateral cooperation to deny potentially dangerous technology transfers to Iraq and to encourage the country to improve its human rights record.

Under the act, the president retained the right to waive the sanctions if there were fundamental changes to Iraqi policies and actions, or if there were fundamental changes in Iraqi leadership and policies. The president was also required to consult fully with, and report periodically to, Congress, to transmit new regulations before they went into effect, and to advise Congress of his intentions at least 15 days before terminating the embargo.

The sanctions were originally viewed as a nonviolent, diplomatic mechanism to apply pressure to the regime in Iraq. The sanctions achieved some, but not all, of the intended policy goals, but they also negatively affected the civilian population of Iraq. Over the next decade, members of the international community questioned the legitimacy and purpose of the sanctions, given the widespread human suffering in Iraq. According to some, the sanctions were the most damaging part of the Persian Gulf War.

As part of the Iraq Sanctions Act, the United States also supported the UN sanctions on Iraq. Indeed, the U.S. and UN sanctions resulted in a near-total embargo on Iraq, but they did not succeed in creating fundamental change in Iraq's policies, removing Saddam Hussein from power, or ending Iraq's weapons of mass destruction (WMD) programs.

The main criticism of the sanctions is that they had little impact on regime behavior, yet the civilian population suffered immensely. Under the sanctions, Iraq could not export oil (its primary source of wealth), and its imports were dramatically reduced. Food and medicine were permissible imports, but fertilizer, pesticide, livestock, seeds, dual-use chemicals (including many medicines and vaccines), agricultural machinery, books, journals, and parts for electrical and water purification systems were banned. As a result, there was widespread malnutrition and disease in Iraq. Infant mortality rates increased dramatically to the highest levels in over 40 years. Estimated numbers of deaths related to the sanctions are disputed, but the UN estimates that over 1 million Iraqis died because of the sanctions. Children were disproportionately affected.

The devastating humanitarian suffering led the United Nations to create the Oil for Food Program (UNSC Resolution 986), which allowed Iraq to sell limited quantities of oil in order to meet the population's humanitarian needs. The program was established in April 1995, but oil was not exported until December 1996, and the first shipment of food did not arrive in Iraq until March 1997. The Oil for Food Program eased, but did not eliminate, the human suffering in Iraq, a good bit of which, however, was the direct result of President Saddam Hussein's policies.

The U.S.-imposed sanctions continued until the 2003 U.S.-led invasion of Iraq. On May 7, 2003, after the Hussein regime had been toppled, President George W. Bush suspended the Iraq Sanctions Act of 1990. On May 22, 2003, the United Nations passed UNSC Resolution 1483, which lifted its sanctions on Iraq.

Alison Lawlor

See also: Hussein, Saddam

Further Reading

Haass, Richard N., ed. *Economic Sanctions and American Diplomacy.* Washington, DC: Council on Foreign Relations, 1998.

Katzman, Kenneth. *Iraq: Oil for Food Program, International Sanctions, and Illicit Trade.* Washington, DC: Congressional Research Services, Library of Congress, April 16, 2003.

Tripp, Charles. *A History of Iraq.* Cambridge: Cambridge University Press, 2007.

Iraq Study Group

A bipartisan commission empowered by the U.S. Congress on March 15, 2006, to examine and analyze the situation in Iraq following the March 2003 invasion of that country and to recommend courses of action to curb the insurgency and end sectarian strife there. The Iraq Study Group was chaired by former secretary of state James Baker III and former U.S. representative Lee Hamilton. Also known as the Baker-Hamilton Commission, the group consisted of five Democrats and five Republicans, and was aided in its work by the United

Iraq Study Group co-chairmen James A. Baker III, left, and Lee Hamilton take part in a news conference on Capitol Hill in Washington, D.C., on December 6, 2006, to present the Iraq Study Group's report on the situation in Iraq. (AP Photo/Dennis Cook)

States Institute of Peace. In addition to Baker, the other Republicans on the commission included Edwin Meese III (former U.S. attorney general); Lawrence Eagleburger (former secretary of state); Sandra Day O'Connor (former U.S. Supreme Court justice); and Alan K. Simpson (former U.S. senator from Wyoming). The Democrats, in addition to Hamilton, included Leon Panetta (former chief of staff to President Bill Clinton); Charles Robb (former U.S. senator from Virginia); Vernon Jordan (informal adviser to Bill Clinton); and William J. Perry (former secretary of defense). The group's final report was issued on December 6, 2006. During its deliberations, however, it maintained contact with the George W. Bush administration, and in particular with National Security Advisor Stephen Hadley.

Creation of the Baker-Hamilton Commission was prompted by the steadily increasing violence in Iraq, which had continued to result in casualties and deaths to U.S. soldiers and Iraqi military personnel as well as civilians. By early 2006 the situation on the ground was growing ever more dire, and it was clear that U.S. public support for the war was eroding at an alarming rate. Although much congressional disapproval toward the war came from the Democratic ranks, an increasing number of Republicans were also questioning the conflict and the Bush administration's handling of it. With critical midterm congressional elections in the offing, many in Congress believed the time had come to reassess the situation in Iraq and assert congressional authority over the conduct of the war there. In public, the Bush White House voiced its approval of the commission, welcoming its bipartisanship, and appeared reassured that the group was being co-chaired by James Baker. At the same time, the White House stated that it would not be beholden to the commission's recommendations if these were deemed antithetical to American interests. Privately, however, there was considerably more consternation about the Iraq Study Group, and on several occasions White House officials allegedly clashed with commission members over their recommendations. In mid-November, about three weeks before the commission's report was released, President Bush and key members of his national security team met with the group so that it could question them about specific details and give them a preview of the report to come. Just prior to that, the commission had also met with British prime minister Tony Blair, the Bush administration's primary ally in the war in Iraq.

Several U.S. news magazines and other media outlets reported that there was considerable contention among the members of the Baker-Hamilton Commission. Some of these conflicts centered on different philosophies toward national security policy and the implementation of Middle East policy, while others involved the Bush administration's opposition to key recommendations. Among the recommendations was the group's position that the United States should engage in discussions with Iran and Syria to stem the external influences on the Iraqi insurgency. The White House was adamantly opposed to this idea, and squabbling among the commission's members on this point nearly led to a deadlocked conclusion. Nevertheless, consensus was reached, and the commission's report was issued on December 6, 2006. It offered 79 specific recommendations. The timing was crucial,

as the Republicans had just lost control of Congress in the November elections, and Secretary of Defense Donald Rumsfeld, a chief architect of the Iraq War, had been recently forced to resign. The White House stated, for the first time, that new approaches to the war were needed, but it also let it be known that it would not implement all of the commission's recommendations.

The report stated clearly that the situation in Iraq was grave and deteriorating rapidly. It also criticized the Pentagon for having underreported the sectarian violence in Iraq and underreporting the number of Iraqi casualties. It went on to suggest that the Iraqi government must quickly ramp up the number of Iraqi soldiers and accelerate their training. During this time, the United States should increase significantly its troop presence in Iraq to enable the Iraqis to take over their own affairs. Once that was accomplished, U.S. troops should be withdrawn rapidly from the country. The report was careful not to suggest a timetable for these developments, however, which the Bush administration had been on record as strongly opposing. The report also called for the United States to engage in a dialogue with the Syrians, Iranians, and other regional groups that might lead to their assistance in curbing the Iraqi insurgency. The commission hoped to see gradual, phased U.S. troop withdrawals beginning in 2007 and a complete withdrawal by the end of 2008. Overall, the commission's report was well received, both in the United States and abroad.

In the end the Bush administration did not follow many of the report's prescriptions. In early 2007 the White House announced its surge strategy, which saw the insertion of as many as 30,000 additional U.S. troops in Iraq.

Paul G. Pierpaoli Jr.

See also: Bush, George Walker; IRAQI FREEDOM, Operation; Rumsfeld, Donald Henry

Further Reading

Baker, James A., III, and Lee Hamilton. *The Iraq Study Group: The Way Forward, a New Approach.* New York: Vintage, 2006.

Stiglitz, Joseph E., and Linda J. Bilmes. *The Three Trillion Dollar War: The True Cost of the Iraq Conflict.* New York: Norton, 2008.

Islamic Dawa Party

Iraqi Shia political party founded in 1958 by junior Islamic clerics (*ulama*), merchants, and religious intellectuals in the Shiite holy city of Najaf. The party sought to achieve a staged implementation of an Islamic governing system based on Islamic law. The party's name in Arabic, Hizb al-Dawa al-Islamiyyah, translates roughly as the "Islamic Call Party." The Arabic word *dawa* in this context refers to "call" or "invitation" in the religious missionary sense. The party's founding council included several Shiite clerics who would rise to prominence in later decades, including Muhammad Mahdi al-Hakim and Muhammad Baqir al-Hakim, sons of Grand Ayatollah Muhsin al-Hakim, the preeminent Shiite religious scholar in Iraq from 1955 until his death in 1970.

Baqir al-Hakim founded the Supreme Council for Islamic Revolution in Iraq (recently renamed the Supreme Islamic Iraqi Council) in 1982 while in exile in Tehran, Iran, with the support of Grand Ayatollah Ruhollah Khomeini and the Iranian revolutionary government. The Dawa Party's unofficial religious guide was Ayatollah Muhammad Baqir al-Sadr (1935–1980), an activist Iraqi cleric, a noted Islamic thinker and author, and a student of Muhsin al-Hakim. Subsequently, many Dawa Party members were arrested, imprisoned, and killed by Iraqi Baathists, and hundreds of others went into self-imposed exile in Iran, the Persian Gulf states, and Europe. Some returned to Iraq in 2003 following the overthrow of Iraqi dictator Saddam Hussein and his Baath Party in the spring of 2003.

Baqir al-Sadr was a prolific writer who penned numerous books on subjects ranging from Islamic economics and philosophy to the establishment of an Islamic state and is probably best known for an early two-volume work on Islamic economics. His ideas influenced the formation of the Islamic state in Iran, and he was known as the "Khomeini of Iraq." He also wrote several textbooks on Islamic jurisprudence and Qur'anic hermeneutics, which remain classics in modern Shiite thought and are still used in Shiite and even Sunni seminaries today. His theory of *wilayat alummah* (governance or authority of the people) and proposals for a four-stage implementation of an Islamic system of governance were the basis of the Dawa Party's founding political platform.

In the first stage of this process, Islamic principles and ideas would be spread by Dawa members to build party membership and create a viable political constituency. In the second stage, once it had laid this groundwork, the party would enter the political realm and seek to build up its power and influence. The third stage would witness the party removing the ruling secular elite from power. In the final stage, triumphant Dawa members would establish an Islamic system of government in which clerics would play a substantial role but would not govern day-to-day affairs.

Baqir al-Sadr broke formal ties with the party in 1961 at the insistence of his teacher,

Grand Ayatollah Hakim, because affiliation with the party would have compromised Sadr's scholarly status; clerics were to remain at least somewhat separate from political parties. However, he reportedly maintained ties to the party and continued to serve as a *marja*, or spiritual leader, to Dawa members. Sadr was executed because of his political activism in April 1980, along with his sister Amina bint Haydar al-Sadr (also known as Bint al-Huda), on the direct orders of Saddam Hussein.

The Dawa Party expanded its membership between 1958 and 1963, taking advantage of a series of military coups beginning with the overthrow of the Hashemite monarchy in 1958 by Abd al-Karim Qasim. During his tenure of office, the Dawa Party competed with secular Iraqi political parties, such as the Iraqi Communist Party, that were gaining ground among Iraqi youths, including many Shia. The growing number of Iraqi Shiite activists came under increasing pressure during the 1960s, and the detachment of the senior Shiite *ulama* from politics convinced these activists that an alternative to the religious elite was needed to achieve their political goals. The party recruited in Najaf, at Baghdad University, and in the Thawra slum of Baghdad, later known as Saddam City (and now Sadr City).

The Baath Party's seizure of power in July 1968 marked a new chapter in the relationship between the Dawa Party and the central Iraqi government. In April 1969 Grand Ayatollah Hakim refused to issue a fatwa (juridical opinion) in support of Iraqi president and Baath Party chief Ahmad Hassan al-Bakr in his dispute with Mohammad Reza Shah Pahlavi of Iran over control of the Shatt al-Arab waterway. Angered, Bakr cracked down on Shiite political, social, and religious institutions. In response, Hakim issued a fatwa prohibiting Muslims from joining the Baath Party. Hakim's death in 1970 led to a split within the Iraqi Shia, with political activists looking to Baqir al-Sadr and political quietists following Ayatollah Abu al-Qasim al-Khoi, another student of Hakim's.

Baath suppression of the Dawa Party continued in the 1970s. Hundreds of party members were arrested, imprisoned, tortured, and even executed. Despite increasing government pressure, Baqir al-Sadr continued to call for activism against the ruling Baath regime. In 1977 the government banned religious processions commemorating Ashura, a 10-day period of mourning that commemorates the martyrdom of the third Shiite imam, Hussein bin Ali, and his companions at Karbala in October 680 during the Islamic month of Muharram. Hundreds of Shia were arrested for ignoring the ban. Shortly before the arrest of Baqir al-Sadr and his sister Amina, a decree was issued by new Iraqi president Saddam Hussein that sentenced all members of the Dawa Party to death for treason. Following Baqir al-Sadr's execution, hundreds of Dawa members fled abroad to escape Baathist suppression. During their two decades in exile, party members participated in the Committee for Collection Action and the Iraqi National Congress, two major Iraqi exile political coalitions.

The exiled Dawa Party leadership and many members returned to Iraq following the U.S.- and British-led invasion during the spring of 2003. Along with the Supreme Islamic Iraqi Council, the Dawa Party was a key ally of the American, British, and coalition forces and it held seats on the Iraqi Governing Council, an advisory body set up following the collapse of the Baath Party government. Dawa Party secretary-general Ibrahim al-Jafari served as the interim prime minister from April 2005 to May 2006.

After losing the political backing of the U.S. government and, more importantly, key Iraqi Shia leaders including Grand Ayatollah Ali al-Sistani, Jafari was replaced as prime minister and Dawa secretary-general by Nuri (Jawad) al-Maliki, also a Dawa adherent, in May 2006.

Christopher Paul Anzalone

See also: Maliki, Nuri Muhammed Kamil Hasan al-; Supreme Iraqi Islamic Council

Further Reading

Aziz, T. M. "The Role of Muhammad Baqir al-Sadr in Shii Political Activism in Iraq from 1958 to 1980." *International Journal of Middle East Studies* 25 (May 1993): 207–22.

Baram, Amatzia. "Two Roads to Revolutionary Shi'i Fundamentalism in Iraq: Hizb al-Da'wa Islamiyya and the Supreme Council of the Islamic Revolution of Iraq." In *Accounting for Fundamentalisms*, edited by Martin E. Marty and R. Schott Appleby, 531–88. Chicago: University of Chicago Press, 1994.

Jabar, Faleh A. *The Shi'ite Movement in Iraq.* London: Saqi Books, 2003.

Mallat, Chibli. *The Renewal of Islamic Law: Muhammad Baqer as-Sadr, Najaf, and the Shi'i International.* Cambridge: Cambridge University Press, 2004.

Nakash, Yitzhak. *Reaching for Power: The Shi'a in the Modern Arab World.* Princeton, NJ: Princeton University Press, 2006.

al-Ruhaimi, Abdul-Halim. "The Da'wa Islamic Party: Origins, Actors and Ideology." In *Ayatollahs, Sufis and Ideologues: State, Religion, and Social Movements in Iraq*, edited by Faleh A. Jabar, 149–55. London: Saqi Books, 2002.

Shanahan, Rodger. "Shi'a Political Development in Iraq: The Case of the Islamic Da'wa Party." *Third World Quarterly* 25 (2004): 943–54.

Islamic Radicalism

This term is used to describe radical movements, organizations, and parties that, regardless of doctrinal and political differences, promote and legitimize their political objectives by invoking Islam. A radical is an individual who espouses extreme views and seeks major, if not revolutionary, change in government and society and often favors illegal means, including violence, to promote such change.

Islamic radicals, also known as Islamic fundamentalists, espouse a literal interpretation of Islam and Sharia (Islamic law) and favor the establishment of an Islamic state based on that law. They share these goals with Islamists, who are sometimes incorrectly deemed radicals, since not all support revolutionary means for Islamization. Some claim that Islamic radicals eschew Western ideas and values, including secularism, democracy, and religious tolerance and pluralism. However, this is untrue of many who value Western ideas but not existing morals in Western society. To certain extreme Islamic radicals, governments and laws that are based on anything but their interpretation of Islam are considered heretical. These radicals feel bound to impose their values on others, and even, if possible, to overthrow heretical governments.

Al-Qaeda, the Taliban, the Armed Islamic Group of Algeria, the Salafist Group for Preaching and Combat of Algeria, Laskar Jihad, and Egyptian Islamic Jihad are some of the better-known radical Islamic groups. Others, such as the Muslim Brotherhood in Egypt have forsworn violence and imposing change on others, and are thus less radical. Hezbollah and Hamas have employed violence against Israelis.

Some Islamic radical groups are Shia, and some are Sunni. Iran, one of the few countries with a majority Shia population, is an example of a radical Islamic state, but radical Shia movements also exist in Iraq, Yemen, and the Gulf states.

The origins of Islamic radicalism are threefold. First, although the Islamic world was once a great and powerful civilization, beginning in the 11th century with the Crusades, followed by Ottoman rule and then European colonial rule after World War I, it has been in decline, eclipsed, and in its own view, dominated and exploited by the West. This view is also shared by Bernard Lewis and other such Western thinkers as Samuel Huntington, but many Muslims argue that the reason for the domination and exploitation is their own fault—that Muslims abandoned jihad in its fighting form and must now return to it. Second, other movements, like nationalism and socialism, failed to bring about a better political solution, and Muslims sought out Islamist or radical Islamic groups as an alternative. Third, many Muslims have come to regard the West, and particularly the United States, with contempt for its alleged social, moral, and economic decadence. They also see that while preaching democracy, the Western powers have supported the very authoritarian governments that oppress them.

To Islamic radicals, the Islamic world has lost its way because it has forsaken Islamic values, amalgamated Western and Islamic law, and transposed foreign cultures onto its own peoples. Accordingly, the solution for the revival of Islamic civilization is a return to an allegedly authentic or purified Islamic way of life. Islamic radicalism is thus, in many ways, an explicit rejection of the current ills of Muslim society. Certain, but not all, Islamic radicals thus seek to overthrow the regimes and rulers they regard as un-Islamic, and some of these are supported by the West and the United States, such as those in Saudi Arabia, Egypt, Jordan, and Kuwait. Islamic radicals were responsible for the overthrow in 1979 of the pro-American Mohammad Reza Shah Pahlavi Iran and the assassination two years later of President Anwar Sadat of Egypt. They have also been responsible for myriad terror attacks against Western interests, including the September 11, 2001, attacks in the United States that killed some 3,000 people.

Islamic radicals played a significant role in the Iraqi insurgency. While many insurgents fought to expel the coalition and regain control of their country, others were motivated by radical ideology. Comprised largely of foreign mujahideen, al-Qaeda Iraq embraced the same extremist views espoused by Osama bin Laden. They sought to keep Iraq in a state of chaos in order to kill as many Americans as possible and eventually to establish an Islamist government in Baghdad. Their radical ideas and extreme violence cost them support among the Iraqi people and made possible the Anbar Awakening.

Stefan Brooks

See also: al-Qaeda in Iraq; Anbar Awakening

Further Reading

Choueri, Youssef. *Islamic Fundamentalism.* New York: Continuum, 2002.

Esposito, John. *What Everyone Needs to Know about Islam.* New York: Oxford University Press, 2002.

Esposito, John. *Unholy War: Terror in the Name of Islam.* New York: Oxford University Press, 2003.

Lewis, Bernard. *What Went Wrong? The Clash between Islam and Modernity in the Middle East.* New York: Oxford University Press, 2002.

Lewis, Bernard. *The Crisis of Islam: Holy War and Unholy Terror.* New York: Random House, 2003.

Milton-Edwards, Beverly. *Islamic Fundamentalism since 1945.* New York: Routledge, 2002.

Sidahmed, Abdel Salam. *Islamic Fundamentalism.* Boulder, CO: Westview, 1996.

Tibi, Bassam. *The Challenge of Fundamentalism: Political Islam and the New World Disorder.* Berkeley: University of California Press, 1998.

J

Jafari, Ibrahim al-

Iraqi politician and prime minister of Iraq in the transitional government from 2005 to 2006 before being ousted under intense pressure from the U.S. government. Jafari is a former member of the Party of Islamic Call (Hizb al-Da'wa al-Islamiyya) but was reportedly expelled in June 2008 for his vocal public criticisms of his successor and fellow Dawa official, Nuri al-Maliki, and for forming a rival faction within the party. Ibrahim al-Jafari, an Arab Shia, is a *sayyid* (descendant of the Prophet Muhammad) and was born on March 25, 1947, in the southern Iraqi shrine city of Karbala to the prominent al-Ishayker family.

Jafari received his university education in medicine at the University of Mosul and is a medical doctor. He subsequently joined the Dawa Party, an Iraqi Shia political party founded in 1958. Some reports say that he joined in 1966; others claim 1968. The party sought to achieve the staged implementation of an Islamic governing system and received guidance from one of its founding members, Ayatollah Muhammad Baqir al-Sadr, who was tortured and executed by the Iraqi Baath Party in April 1980. Jafari, along with many other Dawa Party members, left Iraq following the execution of Sadr. In 1989 Jafari took up residence in London after living in Iran for a time and became one of the party's chief spokespeople in Great Britain. The party was a key member of the coalition of opposition parties active against the Iraqi government during the 1980s and 1990s.

Jafari and the Dawa Party leadership were publicly opposed to the U.S.- and British-led invasion and subsequent occupation of Iraq in 2003, but they returned en masse to the country shortly after Saddam Hussein's regime collapsed in April of that year. Jafari was one of those selected to serve on the Iraqi Governing Council, an interim governing body formed by the U.S.-dominated Coalition Provisional Authority (CPA), that exercised limited political control over Iraq from 2003 until the transfer of power from the CPA to the Iraqi government in June 2004. Following the transfer of power, Jafari served as one of the two vice presidents in the interim government until the January 2005 elections.

The United Iraqi Alliance (UIA), a loose coalition of mainly Shia Arab political parties of which the Dawa Party is a member, dominated the January 2005 elections, and it became clear that a member of one of the UIA's two largest parties, Dawa or the Supreme Islamic Iraqi Council (SIIC), would most likely become prime minister. On April 7, 2005, Jafari formally became Iraq's first post-Hussein prime minister after his chief rival for the post, the Iraqi exile Ahmad Chalabi, who had fallen from the good graces of the United States and many of his Iraqi colleagues because of his duplicity and corruption, withdrew his name from consideration. Jafari is a strong supporter of the idea that Islamic law should

Ibrahim al-Jafari, head of al-Dawa Party in Iraq and member of the parliament, at a press conference after the meeting with Syrian vice president Farouk in Damascus, Syria, on December 13, 2006, after Syria and Iraq restored diplomatic relations the previous month. The U.S. administration was under pressures to reach out to Syria to help bring about stability and security in Iraq. (AP Photo/Bassem Tellawi)

play a key role in Iraq's legal code but is opposed to the formation of an Iranian-style governmental system in Iraq and does not support the formation of a clerically run Islamic state.

Jafari enjoyed widespread support and popularity initially, with some 2004 polls indicating that his popularity among Iraqis was second only to Grand Ayatollah Ali al-Husayni al-Sistani, Iraq's senior resident Shia religious scholar, and the militant Iraqi Shia nationalist Muqtada al-Sadr. Despite this popularity, Jafari's tenure as Iraq's first postinterim government prime minister (April 7, 2005–May 20, 2006) was marked with a noticeable increase in politically motivated sectarian tensions. The SIIC, unlike the Dawa Party, has a large paramilitary wing (the 10,000-man Badr Organization, also commonly called the Badr Corps). During

Jafari's premiership, the SIIC leader, Abd al-Aziz al-Hakim, gained control over several key ministries, including the Ministry of the Interior, which controls the Iraqi police and internal security forces. The ministry, police, and internal security forces, including elite commando units, were staffed with Badr Corps officers and paramilitaries who were more loyal to Hakim than to Iraq as a nation-state. Hakim used these units against political and communal rivals, both Shia, namely the Sadr Movement led by Muqtada al-Sadr, and Sunni insurgents and civilians.

Jafari's inability or unwillingness, or both, to address such issues lost him the support of U.S. president George W. Bush, who began to pressure Iraq's chief political leaders to choose a replacement. The UIA again dominated the December 2005 parliamentary elections, winning the right to select the next prime minister. Jafari narrowly defeated, by one vote, Adil Abd al-Mahdi, a senior SIIC official. This victory was largely due to the support of members of parliament loyal to Muqtada al-Sadr, who vocally opposed U.S. pressure on the Iraqi parliament and political elite to replace Jafari. President Bush bluntly remarked in early 2006 that his administration, which designed and launched the invasion and occupation of Iraq, "doesn't want, doesn't support, doesn't accept" the continuation of Jafari's premiership. Although Jafari initially refused to bow to U.S. pressure and domestic pressure from Sunni and Kurdish political rivals as well as pressure from Iraqi secular parties, he finally succumbed to pressure from Grand Ayatollah al-Sistani and the *marjaiyya*, the informal council of Iraq's senior resident Shia scholars sitting in the southern shrine city of Najaf, and stepped down. Jafari was replaced as Iraqi prime minister by a fellow Dawa Party official, Nuri al-Maliki, who also took over from Jafari as the party's secretary-general in May 2007.

In late May 2008 Jafari announced the formation of a new political party, the National Reform Party, which led to his public expulsion from the Dawa Party.

Christopher Paul Anzalone

See also: Bush, George Walker

Further Reading

Ghosh, Bobby. "The Doctor of Politics." *Time*, February 22, 2005.

Seattle Times News Services. "Al-Maliki Aims to Smooth Ties with Iran." *Seattle Times*, June 8, 2008.

Wong, Edward. "Shiites Say U.S. Is Pressuring Iraqi Leader to Step Aside." *New York Times*, March 28, 2006.

Jihad

The term "jihad" (*jehad*) is often translated as "holy war." It means "striving" or "to exert the utmost effort" and refers both to a religious duty to spread and defend Islam by waging war (lesser jihad) and an inward spiritual struggle to attain perfect faith (greater jihad). The distinction between lesser and greater is not accepted by all Muslims in all circumstances. Many distinguish between jihad as an individual versus a collective duty, as when Muslims face attack or cannot practice their faith (individual duty) or when led by an appropriate Muslim authority (collective duty). In general, mainstream modern Islam emphasizes the greater jihad, the struggle to be a good Muslim, while recognizing the lesser jihad, the struggle through war, as a historical necessity.

Within the spectrum of Islamic belief, definitions of jihad have also rested on historical circumstances. Nineteenth-century Indian reformer Sayyid Ahmad Khan argued for a more limited interpretation of jihad whereby believers could perform acts of piety or charity in place of armed struggle and that it was incumbent only if Muslims could not practice their faith. But others held that Khan's ideas were innovative and thus false. The reform movement of Muhammad ibn abd al-Wahhab in 18th-century Arabia, in contrast, reasserted the incumbency of jihad as armed struggle for all believers. As the Qur'an contains verses that promote mercy and urge peacemaking but also verses (referred to as the Sword Verses) that more ardently require jihad of believers, there is a scriptural basis for both sides of this argument.

Interpretations of the Qur'anic statements about the nature of jihad began when the early Muslims at Medina created an Islamic state in 622 CE but faced the armed warriors of Mecca. The initial mention of jihad in the Qur'an (22:39) deals with defensive warfare only, and the statement "those who stay at home" could be taken as a condemnation of those who abstained from an early key battle of the Muslims against the Meccan forces. Many Muslim scholars believed that the admonition to pursue an aggressive jihad "with their wealth and their persons" (Qur'an 4:95) overrode verses revealed earlier on. Fighting and warfare (*qital*) are, however, differentiated from jihad, which is always accompanied by the phrase "*ala sabil Allah*" ("on the path of God"), similar to the way that just war is differentiated from other forms of conflict in the Christian tradition.

Some scholars differentiate the fulfilling of jihad by the heart, the tongue, or the sword as a means of preserving the Muslim community, but such teachings have by and large been contradicted by the revival of activist jihad, first in response to European 19th-century colonialism and then again in the 20th century.

Mainstream Islam considers foreign military intervention; foreign occupation; economic oppression; non-Islamic cultural realignment; colonialism; and the oppression of a domestic government, either secular or Islamic, of an Islamic people or country to be a sufficient reason, if not a Qur'anic mandate, to participate in a defensive jihad. The more militant and fundamental end of the Islamic spectrum asserts that a social, economic, and military defensive jihad is justifiable and necessary. A widespread discussion of jihad is ongoing in the Muslim world today in response to the rise of militancy, however, and there is a concerted effort to separate the concepts of jihad and martyrdom when they are the rallying call of irresponsible extremists.

Notable defensive jihads in the more recent history of Islam include the resistance of the Afghan (1979) and Chechnyan (ongoing) mujahideen against their respective Soviet and Russian occupations, and the struggle of Algerians to gain independence from France in the Algerian War (1954–1962). Some Islamic religious scholars, such as Abdullah Yusuf Azzam, a former professor of bin Laden, have argued for jihad against the West. Numerous clerics and scholars have held, along with the views of their communities, that the Palestinian struggle against Israel is a defensive jihad because of the infringements on life and liberty, the use of collective punishment, and the seizure by Israel of *waqf* (endowment) lands.

Essentially, the early Muslim community adopted offensive jihad because no defensive action would have protected it against the allied tribal forces determined to exterminate it. In such a jihad, the Peoples of the Book (*dhimma*), meaning other monotheistic traditions like Judaism and Christianity, must be treated differently than enemies who are unbelievers (*kuffar*). The Peoples of the Book must submit to Islamic rule, however, including the paying of poll and land taxes. Rules of engagement, truces, and treatment of prisoners and non-Muslims were all specified in medieval texts concerned with *siyar*, or Islamic international law.

Classical Islamic law and tradition assert that a jihad that is a collective duty (simplified in Western texts as an offensive jihad) can be declared only by the caliph, the successor to the prophet Muhammad and the lawful temporal and spiritual authority for the entire Islamic community. On the other hand, no authority other than conscience or the awareness of an oppression targeting Islam or Islamic peoples is necessary to participate in an individually incumbent jihad.

When the Mongols attacked Baghdad in 1258, the caliphate, long since a divided patchwork of sultanates and emirates, ceased to exist. It was the only political structure recognized by the classical interpretation of Islamic doctrine as being capable of leading a (offensive) jihad. That did not prevent the Ottoman sultans from declaring themselves caliphs and calling for jihad, but the Muslim world did not recognize them as such. Other jihads were declared in the early modern period, for instance by the Mahdiyya of the Sudan, the Wahhabi in Arabia, and the Sanusiyya in present-day Libya.

Leaders of such movements, like contemporary jihadists, have sometimes proclaimed jihads by issuing a fatwa, or statement. Although a fatwa is supposed to be a legal response issued by a qualified jurist, self-proclaimed leaders and clerics sometimes say that the traditional *ulema*, or mullahs, crushed by modern state governments, have failed in their duty and therefore claim the right to speak in their stead.

Although many Muslims recognize their respective governments and political leaders as worthy of defining and declaring defensive jihads, many others perceive their governments as illegitimate Islamic states or their leaders as illegitimate Islamic leaders. Turkey, Egypt, and Pakistan, for example, are quasi-democratic states that grant secular political parties and politicians the same rights as Islamic political parties and politicians. Islamic militant groups in all three countries see these governments and their leaders as heretical and illegitimate under Sharia (Islamic law). In a similar vein, some Muslims, most notably the Takfiri (apostates), declare jihad against Muslim governments perceived as oppressive, anti-Islamic, or corrupt (that is, being "non-Muslim," in their eyes). Additionally, many of the Islamic theocratic monarchies, such as Saudi Arabia, are deemed illegitimate by fundamentalist Muslims. This perception is due in part to the willingness of some of these monarchies and democracies to cooperate and form alliances with non-Islamic nations or with nations that wage economic, cultural, or military war against Islam and Muslims. Some of these monarchies and democracies also limit the power of the clerics within their countries.

Various Islamic movements, most notably al-Qaeda, have stepped into the void created by the disappearance of the caliphate and the resultant fractured Islamic political and religious world. Al-Qaeda in Iraq has exploited the chaos following the U.S.-led invasion of 2003. These movements have interpreted Islam as they wish and declared jihad as they desire, although often with the assistance and support of some clerics as well as leaders with a degree of religious knowledge. Because early Muslims killed in jihad were considered martyrs, there is an extensive tradition that exalts martyrdom. The possibility of martyrdom appeals to modern jihadists, particularly younger or more desperate followers. Defensive jihad, inclusive of martyrdom, is deemed appropriate in order to end Israel's occupation of the perceived Islamic territories of the West Bank, East Jerusalem, and Gaza Strip, if not all of Palestine.

A martyr secures a place in paradise and may intercede for other Muslims. Antiterrorist campaigns in the Muslim world have argued, against the weight of literature and popular belief, that modern jihadists are not martyrs if they set out to martyr themselves, because suicide is forbidden in Islam. Noncombatant Muslims who perish in a jihad are also considered martyrs. Jihadists thus excuse the deaths of innocents caught in their crossfire with targets or authorities. They explain the deaths of non-Muslim civilians as being deserved for their failure to submit to Islam or for their open oppression of Islam or Islamic peoples. In the case of Israeli civilians, the fact that all provide military service to their country means that they are not really considered civilians by the jihadists.

The term "jihad" is incorporated into the organizational names of numerous militant groups, including the Egyptian Islamic Jihad, the Egyptian and former Iraqi Tawhid wal-Jihad, and the Palestinian Islamic Jihad.

The struggle in contemporary Islam to redefine jihad and detach its meaning from adventurism, martyrdom, and attacks on Muslim governments as well as Westerners is one of the most significant challenges at this time in history.

Richard M. Edwards and Sherifa Zuhur

See also: al-Qaeda in Iraq; Suicide Bombings

Further Reading

Bostrom, Andrew G., ed. *The Legacy of Jihad: Islamic Holy War and the Fate of Non-Muslims*. Amherst, NY: Prometheus, 2005.

Delong-Bas, Natana. *Wahhabi Islam: From Revival and Reform to Global Jihad*. Oxford: Oxford University Press, 2004.

Esposito, John. *Unholy War: Terror in the Name of Islam*. New York: Oxford University Press, 2003.

Fregosi, Paul. *Jihad in the West: Muslim Conquests from the 7th to the 21st Centuries*. Amherst, NY: Prometheus, 1998.

Kepel, Gilles. *Jihad: The Trail of Political Islam*. Cambridge, MA: Belknap, 2003.

K

Karbala, First Battle of

Karbala is located in central Iraq some 60 miles southwest of Baghdad and is regarded as one of the holiest cities in Shia Islam. Three notable battles have occurred there: one in October 680 CE among Islamic factions, one during Operation IRAQI FREEDOM in 2003, and one between Iraqi factions in 2007. The March 31 to April 6, 2003, battle occurred during the Iraq War when U.S. forces attempted to evict Iraqi forces from Karbala. Units involved in the fight included those from the U.S. 3rd Infantry Division, the 1st Armored Division, and the 101st Airborne Division; Iraqi forces consisted of members of the Fedayeen Saddam and Syrian mercenaries.

During the initial phase of the 2003 invasion of Iraq, advance units of the U.S. 3rd Infantry Division, having pushed their way through Republican Guard forces southeast of Karbala, arrived in the area on March 31. While some troops kept a watchful eye on the Iraqis in Karbala, the main body bypassed the city and attacked Baghdad through the Karbala Gap. This meant that U.S. forces would have to clear the Iraqis out of Karbala later.

This task fell principally to the 101st Airborne Division, supported by the 2nd Battalion, 70th Armored Regiment, 1st Armored Division. On April 2, 2003, a U.S. Army Sikorsky UH-60 Black Hawk helicopter was shot down near Karbala, killing seven soldiers and wounding four others. This event appeared to indicate a significant enemy presence in the city.

The 101st Airborne Division decided to insert three battalions via helicopter at three landing zones (LZs) on the outskirts of the city, designated LZ Sparrow, LZ Finch, and LZ Robin. M-1 Abrams tanks and M-2 Bradley fighting vehicles of the 2nd Battalion, 70th Armored Regiment, were to support these forces.

On the morning of April 5, 23 UH-60 Black Hawks escorted 5 CH-47 Boeing Chinook helicopters ferrying three battalions of the 502nd Infantry Regiment to their LZs. The 3rd Battalion landed at LZ Sparrow and met heavy but uncoordinated resistance. The 2nd Battalion landed to the south at LZ Robin and found numerous arms caches hidden in schools as well as a suspected terrorist training camp. As night fell, the battalion had cleared 13 of its 30 assigned sectors.

The 1st Battalion landed at LZ Finch in the southeast, where it captured a large store of weapons. As the infantry moved forward, it was constantly supported by helicopters and artillery. While the soldiers went house to house, armored vehicles from the 2nd Battalion, 70th Armored Regiment, arrived and engaged the enemy.

The following morning, April 6, the Americans continued operations until 5:00 p.m., when all sectors were secured. Symbolic of the victory, members of the 2nd Battalion, 70th Armored Regiment, tore down a large statue of Iraqi dictator Saddam Hussein in the middle of the city. Reported casualties were as many as 260 for the Iraqis; the Americans suffered 8 killed. One UH-60 helicopter was also lost. One U.S.

M1 Abrams tank was disabled but not destroyed.

William P. Head

See also: Iraqi Freedom, Operation; Karbala, Second Battle of

Further Reading

Atkinson, Rick. *In the Company of Soldiers: A Chronicle of Combat.* New York: Henry Holt, 2005.

NBC Enterprises. *Operation Iraqi Freedom: The Insider Story.* Kansas City, MO: Andrews McMeel, 2003.

Karbala, Second Battle of

Karbala is located in central Iraq some 60 miles southwest of Baghdad and is one of the holiest cities in Shia Islam. There have been three notable battles there: one in October 680 CE among Islamic factions, one during Operation Iraqi Freedom in 2003, and one between Iraqi factions in 2007. The Second Battle of Karbala (August 27–29, 2007) began as thousands of Shia pilgrims gathered in the city for the annual festival of Nisf Sha'ban (Laylat al-Barat). The fighting occurred between members of the Mahdi Army, who were charged with providing security for the pilgrims, and Iraqi Security Forces (police), most of whom belonged to the Badr Brigades.

By August 27, 2007, a large security force was present in the city because pilgrims had been killed during previous pilgrimages. Early that evening, small-arms fire broke out between the Mahdi Army and local police. The number of forces on each side has not been determined.

The Mahdi Army is a militia force loyal to Iraqi leader Muqtada al-Sadr. Senior members of Iraq's Interior Ministry soon accused the Mahdi Army of attacking government forces in Karbala who were guarding two shrines under the control of the Supreme Islamic Iraqi Council.

On August 28 the Iraqi government deployed more troops to the city. On August 29 Prime Minister Nuri al-Maliki imposed a curfew that directed pilgrims to end their devotions early. Although he claimed that the situation was then under control, sporadic shooting continued. Only after additional Iraqi security forces had arrived and most of the pilgrims had departed did the violence end. Casualties in this factional struggle were estimated at 30–40 killed and more than 100 wounded. It is believed that 10 Iraqi policemen died in the confrontation.

In the aftermath of this fighting, the head of the Mahdi Army in Karbala, Ali Sharia, was arrested and tried for inciting the violence at Karbala. In August 2008 he was convicted and sentenced to death.

William P. Head

See also: Mahdi Army; Maliki, Nuri Muhammed Kamil Hasan al-; Sadr, Muqtada al-

Further Reading

Craig, Charles. "Iraq Militias Fighting for Supremacy." *Time*, August 29, 2007, http://www.time.com/time/world/article/0,8599,1657449,00.html.

"Iraqi PM Orders Curfew in Karbala." BBC News, August 29, 2007, http://news.bbc.co.uk/2/hi/middle_east/6968236.stm.

"Toll Rises in Karbala Fighting." Al Jazeera, August 28, 2007, http://english.aljazeera.net/news/middleeast/2007/08/2008525141014347965.html.

Kerry, John

Vietnam War veteran, U.S. senator (1985–2013), 2004 Democratic presidential candidate, and Secretary of State since 2013,

John Forbes Kerry was born in Aurora, Colorado, on December 11, 1943, the son of a World War II Army Air Corps test pilot, foreign service officer, and attorney. His mother, a nurse, was a member of the distinguished and wealthy Forbes family of Boston. As a child Kerry lived abroad for a time and also attended an exclusive college preparatory school in New Hampshire.

Kerry attended Yale University, graduating in 1966. That same year he joined the U.S. Navy, serving on a destroyer off the coast of Vietnam. During 1968 and 1969 he volunteered to command a swift (navy patrol) boat; he was stationed first at Cam Ranh Bay and then on the island of Phu Quoc. He received three Purple Heart medals for combat wounds, returned to the United States in the spring of 1969, and left the service on March 1, 1970.

Upon his return Kerry, who was proud of his service in the war, nevertheless dedicated much energy to opposing the war and speaking out on policies that he believed had failed the U.S. mission in Vietnam. Some of his actions were not without controversy. His antiwar activity included membership in several antiwar organizations, writings against the war, testimony to the U.S. Senate Foreign Relations Committee, the publicizing of alleged war crimes committed by American and Vietnamese soldiers, and participation in numerous demonstrations, including a famous one in which he and nearly 1,000 fellow Vietnam veterans threw down their service medals on the steps of the U.S. Capitol before television cameras.

In 1972 Kerry decided to run for a U.S. House of Representatives seat, representing northeastern Massachusetts as a Democrat. He lost the race and decided to attend law school at Boston College, from which he earned a degree in 1976. He then became a full-time prosecutor in Middlesex County.

He left that post in 1979 to establish his own law firm, which was a modest success. In 1982 he successfully ran for the post of lieutenant governor in Massachusetts and served under Governor Michael Dukakis. Two years later Kerry ran for a U.S. Senate seat and won. He served in the Senate from January 1985 until he became Secretary of State in 2013.

In the Senate, Kerry earned a reputation for his earnestness, deep grasp of national issues, and ability to reach across the aisle when necessary to effect bipartisan legislative compromises. He is considered a moderate to left-leaning Democrat. In 2000 he was on Vice President Al Gore's short list of potential running mates for the autumn 2000 presidential election.

Kerry decided to run for president in 2004 and soon established himself as one of the front-runners in an unusually crowded slate of Democratic hopefuls. After winning the January 2004 Iowa Caucus, Kerry went on to win a string of state primaries, and by the early spring he was the presumptive Democratic presidential nominee. After choosing North Carolina senator John Edwards as his vice presidential running mate, Kerry was formally nominated at the Democratic National Convention that summer and began a hard-fought campaign to unseat the incumbent George W. Bush.

Kerry's main platform in the election was his opposition to the war in Iraq and Bush's handling of the Global War on Terror after the September 11, 2001, terror attacks. Kerry also scoffed at Bush's economic policies, which had caused huge budget deficits and an uneven economy, and had skewed income toward those who already possessed the vast majority of wealth in the country. Kerry also made vague promises of health care reform. Without a doubt, however, the Iraq War was the most important subject of debate in 2004. In this, Kerry's past voting record did not serve him particularly well, as he strongly backed the October 2002 joint congressional resolution authorizing the use of force against Iraq. After the March 2003 invasion of Iraq and the subsequent revelation that Iraq did not have weapons of mass destruction (WMDs), Kerry turned sharply against the war and became an outspoken critic of the Bush administration.

Not surprisingly, the Bush campaign jumped on Kerry's position vis-à-vis the Iraq War, particularly Kerry's ill-considered comment that he "first voted for it before he voted against it," opening himself up to charges of flip-flopping on the war. Over the course of the late summer and into the autumn, seeds of doubt were planted in the electorate's mind as to Kerry's competence, decisiveness, and ability to handle national security issues. Indeed, Kerry was portrayed as a weak and effete Massachusetts liberal who was out of step with American voters. The Kerry campaign was sometimes slow and tepid in its reactions to these attacks, which only compounded the damage. A series of searing television ads by the Swift Boat Veterans for Truth group also hobbled Kerry's campaign. Among other things, the group accused Kerry of dishonorable conduct during and after his Vietnam War service and charged that he had lied or greatly exaggerated his role in the war.

Kerry went on to lose the 2004 election by a close margin (Bush won 31 states to Kerry's 19 plus the District of Columbia but bested him by less than 3 percent of the popular vote and 35 electoral college votes). Remaining in the U.S. Senate, Kerry continued to criticize the Bush administration's policies, especially those toward the Iraq War.

Paul G. Pierpaoli Jr.

See also: Bush, George Walker; Weapons of Mass Destruction

Further Reading

Kerry, John. *A Call to Service: My Vision for a Better America.* New York: Viking, 2003.

Kranish, Michael, Brian C. Mooney, and Nina J. Easton. *John F. Kerry: The Complete Biography.* New York: PublicAffairs, 2004.

Kirkuk

The oldest site of continuous human occupation in Iraq, Kirkuk is located approximately 142 miles north of Baghdad and rests along the Hasa River, atop the remains of the 11th century BCE Assyrian capital city of Arrapha, in Iraqi Kurdistan. Kirkuk is a city of some 710,000 people. Its predominant population of Iraqi Kurds and Turkomen, along with the city's position as a hub of the Iraqi petroleum industry, has made Kirkuk a critically strategic center during all of Iraq's political turmoil since World War I. The city played a significant political and geostrategic role during the run-up to the 2003 Iraq War.

In its early incarnation, Kirkuk was a bloody battleground for at least three empires—the Assyrian, the Babylonian, and the Median—for whom the city on the banks of the Hasa was a strategic stronghold. Under the Babylonians the city was called Kurkura, while under the Greeks it was known as Karkha D-Bet Slokh, which translates as "citadel of the house of Selucid." By the seventh century CE, following the Arab invasion of the Sassanid Empire, Muslim Arabs were calling the city Kirkheni, or "citadel."

With the discovery of oil in 1927 at Bab Gurgur, near Kirkuk, the city became the center of petroleum production in northern Iraq. The oil rush led to the Iraqi annexation of the former Ottoman Mosul wilayah, of which Kirkuk was a part. From 1963 onward the Iraqi Arabs attempted to transform the ethnic makeup of the entire region to take power away from the Kurds and ensure that Iraqi Arabs stayed in control of the oil fields. In 1975 the Iraqi Baath Party, under Ahmad Hassan al-Bakr, began to "Arabize" the Kirkuk area by imposing restrictions on Kurds and Turkomen who lived there, while trying to replace them with Arabs from central or southern Iraq. As many as 1,400 Kurdish villages were razed, and more than half a million Kurds were forcibly relocated. The Arabization process intensified following the failed Kirkuk/Kurdish uprising after the Persian Gulf War in 1991, and between 1991 and 2003 an estimated 120,000 Kurds and Turkomen were forcibly relocated out of Kirkuk.

In the lead-up to the Iraq War (2003), Kirkuk, along with Mosul, proved to be a sticking point that prevented the United States from being able to launch a prong of its assault into Iraq from bases in Turkey. The Turkish Parliament wanted guarantees that Kurdish fighters would not be allowed to capture Kirkuk or Mosul. Because the United States would not, or could not, make such a promise, Turkey refused to grant the Americans and their allies permission to launch attacks from Turkish soil. The Turks also saw this move as a means of squelching the Iraqi Kurds' nationalism, since many of the Kurds view Kirkuk as the "Kurdish Jerusalem."

On April 11, 2003, after days of heated battles, the U.S.-led coalition forces and Kurdish Peshmerga fighters secured Kirkuk from Saddam Hussein's Baath Party loyalists. Victims of the Kirkuk's Arabization attempted to return once the area was free of the Baath Party, yet the new postwar Iraqi government has done little to resolve this crisis, leaving most returning Kurds in a refugee limbo.

Keith Murphy

See also: Iraqi Freedom, Operation; Kurds

Further Reading

Astarjian, Henry D. *The Struggle for Kirkuk: The Rise of Hussein, Oil, and the Death of Tolerance in Iraq*. Westport, CT: Praeger Security International, 2007.

Polk, William R. *Understanding Iraq: The Whole Sweep of Iraqi History, from Genghis Khan's Mongols to the Ottoman Turks to the British Mandate to the American Occupation*. New York: Harper Perennial, 2006.

Kurdistan Democratic Party

Kurdish political party operating in Kurdish-dominated northern Iraq. The Kurdistan Democratic Party (KDP) was founded in Baghdad in 1946. Mustafa Barzani, tribal chief, fervent Kurdish nationalist, and Naqshbandi sheikh, was its elected president in exile. The KDP, which generally embraces a social democratic ideology and has consistently fought for a Kurdish state, finds its support base in northern Kurdistan (i.e., Irbil, about 50 miles east of Mosul). Most members belong to the Naqshbandi Sufi order and speak the Kurmanji dialect. There are also KDPs in Iran, Syria, and Armenia as well as a KDP-Bakur in Turkey. This entry describes only the KDP operating in and around Iraq.

In 1958 Barzani returned to Iraq from exile in the Soviet Union, claiming that he could unify all Kurdish groups under his control. His return coincided with the overthrow of the Iraqi monarchy that same year. When Iraqi prime minister Abd al-Karim Qasim began forcibly deporting Kurds from Kirkuk, Barzani responded in 1961 by leading a rebellion against the Iraqi regime that lasted on and off until 1975. The Baathists controlling Iraq committed the full strength of their army and air force to destroy the Kurds and drive them into the Zagros and Taurus mountains.

Barzani, along with thousands of Kurds, fled to neighboring Iran, for Iran provided the KDP with weapons, supplies, and sanctuary. Barzani and the KDP would thus become a permanent enemy of successive Iraqi governments. In 1979 on the death of Mustafa Barzani, his son, Masud Barzani, became the leader of the KDP. He is currently the president of the Kurdistan Regional Government (KRG).

In the late 1980s Iraqi dictator Saddam Hussein tried to eradicate the Kurds during the Anfal Campaign. As many as 4,000 Kurdish villages were destroyed, and more than 100,000 Kurds were killed. A number of members of the Barzani family, tribe, and associated relatives were among those murdered. This campaign caused the Kurds to change their strategy prior to Operation DESERT STORM, which included union with competing political groups.

The KDP, the Patriotic Union of Kurdistan (PUK), and other Kurdish groups now formed the Iraqi Kurdistan Front (IKF) to combine forces to fight Hussein. Once DESERT STORM began in January 1991, 50 percent of the Kurdish soldiers in the Iraqi Army deserted, and some fought in conjunction with coalition troops. After Iraq's defeat in the Persian Gulf War, Kurds from all walks of life joined the IKF. Barzani and Jalal Talabani, leader of the PUK, jointly directed IKF attacks, using Peshmerga (Kurdish fighters). They seized Kirkuk and 75 percent of Kurdistan, and added many Iraqi army deserters to their ranks, thereby obtaining large numbers of heavy weapons. However, immediately after the Persian Gulf War

cease-fire, the Iraqi Republican Guards destroyed many Kurdish irregular units, and by March 1991 nearly 1.5 million Kurds had become refugees.

On April 5, 1991, the United Nations (UN) passed Resolution 688, which codified the no-fly zones in northern and southern Iraq and provided for the airdropping of food and medicine to the Kurds. At the same time, the United States and several of its allies implemented Operation PROVIDE COMFORT, a major humanitarian mission to help the embattled Kurds. On April 10, 1991, the United States established the northern no-fly zone at the 36th parallel. On April 18, 1991, the UN created a Kurdish-controlled enclave in northern Iraq. However, because there was no political support for a long-term occupation of the region, the UN withdrew all forces on July 5, 1991.

The KDP and PUK now established control in the UN-mandated Kurdish zone. In May 1992 the Kurds founded the KRG, which is composed of, among other groups, the KDP, the PUK, and the Iraqi Communist Party. The Kurds held elections and established a joint legislative assembly with a cabinet. However, the KDP and PUK each tried to seize control of the autonomous region. Amnesty International later reported that in 1994 and 1995 both groups committed scores of killings during their battle for power.

In August 1996, 2,000 Iranian Revolutionary Guard Corps (IRGC) soldiers entered Iraq and attacked the KDP on behalf of the PUK. Barzani turned to Hussein for help. Soon a force of as many as 60,000 Iraqi Republican Guards entered the autonomous Kurdish region and drove the PUK from Irbil. The KDP then pushed the remnants of the PUK to the Iranian border. Hussein and the KDP now controlled all of northern Iraq.

On February 5, 1999, U.S. president Bill Clinton issued Presidential Decision Directive 99-13, which authorized the KDP and the PUK to receive U.S. military assistance through the Iraq Liberation Act (Public Law 105-338). During the 2003 invasion of Iraq, the PUK and KDP cooperated with the Anglo-American–led coalition and sent soldiers into the fight. They also removed Ansar al-Islam from the Kurdish region.

Most recently, the Kurdistan Brigades, led by Dilshad Kalari (Dilshad Garmyani), have publicly called for jihad against the KDP and PUK. The Kurdistan Brigades considers both Masud and PUK leader Talabani apostate politicians. Among other things, the Kurdistan Brigades decries the cooperation between the Peshmerga and the Nuri al-Maliki administration in Baghdad and has criticized the loss of control over certain areas in Kurdistan.

Many Iraqi Kurds have fully assimilated into Iraq and do not support Kurdish separatism. The Kurdish region has few resources with which to develop a viable economy, which is one reason why Kurdish nationalists want control of the Kirkuk oil fields. Since 2003 the KDP and PUK have once again united to form the Democratic Patriotic Alliance of Kurdistan in an attempt to realize a Kurdish state. The parties hotly contested the 2005 Iraqi elections, but continued infighting among them has led some to believe that a truly unified and effective Kurdish popular front may be very difficult to achieve.

Donald Redmond Dunne

See also: Hussein, Saddam; Kirkuk

Further Reading

Batatu, Hanna. *The Old Social Classes and the Revolutionary Movement of Iraq: A Study of Iraq's Old Landed and Commercial Classes and of Its Communists, Ba'athists, and Free Officers.* Princeton, NJ: Princeton University Press, 1978.

Bengio, Ofra. *Saddam's Word: Political Discourse in Iraq.* New York: Oxford University Press, 1998.

Marcus, Aliza. *Blood and Belief: The PKK and the Kurdish Fight for Independence.* New York: New York University Press, 2007.

Natali, Denise. *International Aid, Regional Politics, and the Kurdish Issue in Iraq after the Gulf War.* Abu Dhabi: Emirates Center for Strategic Studies and Research, 1999.

O'Leary, Brendan, John McGarry, and Khaled Smith. *The Future of Kurdistan in Iraq.* Philadelphia: University of Pennsylvania Press, 2005.

Stansfield, Gareth R. V. *Iraqi Kurdistan: Political Development and Emergent Democracy.* New York: Routledge, 2003.

Kurds

People of Indo-European origin who inhabit the upcountry and mountainous areas chiefly in Iran, Iraq, Syria, and Turkey. Their primary area of concentration in southern Turkey, and northern parts of Iran and Iraq, is known as Kurdistan, although this is not an autonomous region. There are also small enclaves of Kurds in southwestern Armenia, Azerbaijan, and Lebanon. The total Kurdish population worldwide is estimated to number between 30 million and 35 million people, making the Kurds one of the biggest ethnic groups in the world who do not enjoy their own autonomous homeland. The Kurds, whose language is of Indo-European background, are not Arabs. However, numerous Kurds have intermarried with Arabs and have played an important role in Arab and Muslim history. Salah al-Din al-Ayyubi (Saladin, one of the

Kurdish children bunch together to have their photograph taken at a refugee camp near Turkey's border with Iraq. The camp is one of several that have been established by Kurds who left their homes in northern Iraq to escape Iraqi government forces. Troops from the United States and other countries aided the Kurds in these camps as part of Operation Provide Comfort, a movement to help displaced Kurds in the aftermath of Operations Desert Shield and Desert Storm. (U.S. Department of Defense)

greatest of Muslim leaders) was of Kurdish origin. There have also been numerous Kurdish dynasties, such as the Ziyarids, the Jastanids, and the Kakuyids.

The great majority of Kurds are Sunni Muslims, and their language is related to Persian (which is spoken chiefly in Iran, Afghanistan, and Tajikistan). There are numerous dialects of Kurdish divided into two primary dialect groups: Sorani and Kumanji. Just as they have their own language, the Kurds maintain their own unique culture and traditions.

Until the first few decades of the 20th century, most Kurds lived a pastoral, nomadic existence and divided themselves into tribes. For centuries, they led a somewhat isolated lifestyle that clung to tradition and was well ordered by tribal hierarchy and customs. The mountain Kurds' principal avocation was goat- and sheepherding, which was migratory in nature. In this sense, they were not unlike the Bedouins to the south. However, when the Ottoman Empire broke apart as a result of World War I, the Kurds found themselves circumscribed within newly created states, none of which was interested in allowing them to continue their centuries-old lifestyle and customs.

As new nations such as Iraq and Turkey (where the bulk of Kurds live) organized themselves into nationalistic nation states, the Kurds came under great pressure to abandon their tribal ways and assimilate into the majority culture. They were also greatly limited in their migratory patterns, which served only to further marginalize them.

Soon after World War I, Kurds began to call for their own nation, Kurdistan. They expected support in this endeavor from the United States. But as an Associated Power in World War I, rather than an Entente Power, the United States had not declared war on the Ottoman Empire and therefore after the war had no voice in its dismemberment and the subsequent League of Nations Mandates. Beyond that, however, the American public had little interest in such a course of action.

While the British gave some lip service to the establishment of a Kurdish state, the Turks effectively quashed the idea, with Iraq and Iran agreeing that they would recognize no Kurdish state encompassing any part of their territory. The Kurds were now subjected to discrimination and oppression in general. This situation was particularly bad in Turkey. The Turkish government refused to recognize the Kurds as a distinct ethnic group (a state of affairs that continues today), forced them to abandon their language, banned their traditional garb, and lured them into urban areas to curtail their pastoral life. This, of course, only brought more discrimination and resulted in high unemployment and poverty rates for urbanized Kurds.

In Turkey the Kurds have periodically risen up in rebellions that have been promptly crushed by the Turkish government. However, an underground Kurdish guerrilla group, formed out of the Kurdish Workers' Party (PKK) in the 1980s, continues to pursue the dream of an independent Kurdish state and has engaged Turkish, Iranian, and Syrian troops in an ongoing military struggle. In the late 1940s and again in the late 1970s, Kurds attempted to form their own autonomous region in Iran. These efforts were both put down by the Iranians.

For decades Kurds have been subjected to brutal oppression by the Iraqi government. From 1960 to 1975, Iraqi Kurds under the leadership of Mustafa Barzani waged a guerrilla-style war with Iraqi regular forces. This brought significant casualties to the Iraqis and forced them in 1970 to enter into talks with the rebelling Kurds. That same year, the Iraqi government offered a peace deal to the Kurds that would have brought them their own autonomous region (but not sovereignty) by 1974. Meanwhile, Barzani continued his campaign, and the peace offer never took hold. In 1975 the Iraqis began moving thousands of people into northern Iraq in an attempt to Arabize the region while simultaneously exiling close to 200,000 Kurds.

The Iran-Iraq War (1980–1988) brought great misery and many fatalities to Iraqi Kurds. Saddam Hussein's government was brutal in its treatment of the minority, and in 1988 Hussein launched his so-called Anfal ("spoils of war") Campaign. Over a period of several months, Iraqi forces killed perhaps as many as 100,000 Kurds and destroyed some 2,000 villages, often employing chemical weapons. In 1991, in the immediate aftermath of the Persian Gulf War, Iraqi Kurds rebelled again, and they were again crushed.

The Kurdish region of northern Iraq, comprising three provinces, is roughly divided in two by two competing political parties—the Kurdistan Democratic Party, headed by Massoud Barzani, and the Patriotic Union of Kurdistan, led by Jalal Talabani. Although there is much political infighting between the two groups, their goals and programs are remarkably similar, and they have been able to work together effectively, especially in post-Hussein Iraq. Indeed, the Kurdish fighting groups known as the Peshmerga have fought for decades in Iraq, Iran, and Turkey. Some have fought alongside U.S. troops in a joint effort to defeat Kurdish Islamic extremist groups, such as Ansar al-Islam.

After the 2003 Anglo-American invasion of Iraq and Hussein's overthrow, Kurds took control of Kirkuk and most of Mosul. Ironically, while the United States and its allies have been unable to build a stable, democratic regime in central and southern Iraq, the Kurds in the north have been more successful in creating a stable environment in their sphere of influence. The Kurds are strongly pro-democratic, and somewhat more pro-American than other Iraqis. Northern Iraq has experienced some attacks and bombings, and Mosul and Kirkuk remain key problem areas as of 2009, but other areas of historic Iraqi Kurdistan have been less dangerous for coalition forces.

The major Kurdish political parties decry Islamic extremism and do not support a theocratic government, although many smaller Kurdish groups do. There is still a great deal of support for the creation of a separate Kurdish nation among Kurds. Such a move, however, would be vociferously opposed by the Turks and Iranians. There is as yet no resolution over the status of Kirkuk, where Arabs and Turkomen dispute Kurdish claims. However, if this issue and some other matters can be resolved, and the Kurds exercise autonomy over their region, they will have a nation in everything but name.

Paul G. Pierpaoli Jr.

See also: Hussein, Saddam; Kirkuk; Kurdistan Democratic Party

Further Reading

Bulloch, John, and Harvey Morris. *No Friends but the Mountains: The Tragic History of the Kurds*. New York: Oxford University Press, 1993.

Ciment, James. *The Kurds: State and Minority in Turkey, Iraq, and Iran*. New York: Facts on File, 1996.

Izady, Mehrdad R. *The Kurds: A Concise Handbook*. Washington, DC: Crane Russak, Taylor and Francis, 1992.

Lawrence, Quil. *Invisible Nation: How the Kurds' Quest for Statehood Is Shaping Iraq and the Middle East*. New York: Walker, 2008.

McDowall, David. *A Modern History of the Kurds*. New York: I. B. Tauris, 2000.

Kurds, Massacres of

The Kurdish people are spread across a number of countries in the Middle East, including Turkey, Iraq, Syria, and Iran. Kurds have campaigned for their own homeland for many years and have suffered persecution throughout their history. During recent times the Kurds have been subjected to repeated repressions and massacres.

Following an uprising led by Mustafa Barzani from 1961 to 1963, the Kurds were given some representation in the Iraqi government. However, following the outbreak of the Iran-Iraq War in September 1980, the Kurdish leadership tended to side with Iran, and as a result Iraqi dictator Saddam Hussein began a program of systematic persecution against the Kurds. Iraqi attacks increased dramatically from 1986 on. The lead figure directing these attacks was Ali Hasan al-Majid, a cousin of President Hussein. The use of chemical weapons during the attacks on the Kurds would earn Majid the sobriquet "Chemical Ali."

During the campaign as a whole, the Iraqi army deployed more than 200,000 troops against the Kurds. The campaign, launched by Majid himself, was split into seven phases between February and September 1988. This campaign against the Kurds became known as the Anfal Campaign, meaning "the spoils of war." In each phase,

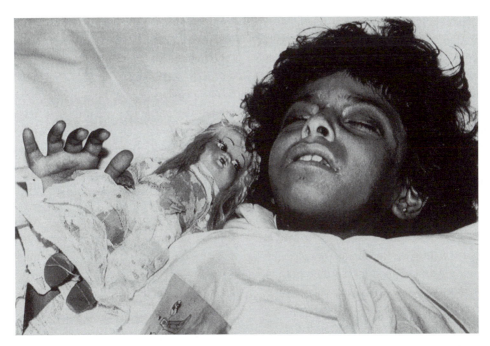

Six-year-old Mahnaz Mohan, from Halabjeh, 150 miles north of Baghdad, was one of six people receiving medical treatment in Vienna, Austria, on March 29, 1988, after suffering from mustard gas poisoning in the March 16–17 Iraqi gas attack. More than 30 other victims were taken to other hospitals. Iran claims that 5,000 people were killed and more were wounded during Saddam Hussein's chemical attack in the Kurdish north. (AP Photo/Bernard J. Holzner)

an area of Kurdish-dominated territory was sealed off and then attacked. Tactics against the Kurds included the employment of aircraft to bomb the Kurdish villages, as well as ground forces to secure Kurdish settlements and detain and interrogate all males between the ages of 15 and 70. It was then official Iraqi policy either to execute these men immediately or transport them, along with their families, to the Topzawa Camp just outside the northern Iraqi town of Kirkuk. Here the men of proscribed age were segregated and summarily shot; the bodies were then bulldozed into shallow burial pits.

This deliberate plan of genocide grew as the campaign progressed. In the first stage (February 23–March 19, 1988), there was no official policy calling for the killing of all adult males; however, by the last phase (August 25–September 6, 1988) Majid did promulgate such a policy. Within Kirkuk, there was mass deportation of Kurdish families. The Baath Party then built large-scale housing projects and encouraged poor Arabs from the south of Iraq to settle in them. This policy of "Arabization" allowed Baghdad to better control the oil-rich area around Kirkuk.

Perhaps the most infamous incident during the Anfal operation was the chemical attack that took place against the Kurdish town of Halabja. Although there were a total of 40 separate chemical attacks in the entire six-month campaign against the Kurds, the one against Halabja was by far the most significant. Halabja, located 150 miles northeast of Baghdad, had an estimated population of 80,000 people. Eight Iraqi Air Force aircraft struck the town on the evening of March 16, 1988, and the attacks continued throughout the night. Chemical agents employed in the attack included mustard gas and nerve agents such as sarin and tabun. During this one attack, more than 5,000 civilians were killed and many thousands of others were injured.

Initially, Baghdad claimed that the attack had been intended to strike Iranian troops, but between 1992 and 1994 the organization Human Rights Watch effectively proved Iraqi culpability in the Halabja massacre. In total, the Anfal Campaign claimed perhaps as many as 50,000 civilian lives and destroyed some 2,000 villages, 1,750 schools, and 2,500 mosques.

Following the outbreak of the 1991 Persian Gulf War, the Kurds in Iraq rose up against the Hussein regime, and under the protection of an allied air umbrella were able to establish their own governments in so-called safe havens established by the United Nations (UN). In 2003 the Kurdish leadership supported the American-led invasion of Iraq and has now established effective control over Kirkuk and the surrounding areas. Thus far, it has prevented any further atrocities against the Kurdish people in Iraq.

Yet Iraq is not the only place where the Kurds have recently suffered. Within Turkey, Turkish security forces have leveled more than 3,000 Kurdish villages and displaced some 378,000 Kurds since 1982. In Iran, during the revolutionary period from 1979 to 1982, Islamic Revolutionary Guards campaigned against the Kurds, killing some 10,000 civilians. And attacks on Kurdish settlements continue. The most recent incidents occurred on July 9, 2005, following the murder of a Kurdish activist. In Syria, too, there have been incidents. On March 12, 2004, 180 Kurdish civilians were killed or injured in clashes with Syrian forces in Qamishli, a Kurdish city in the northeastern part of the country.

Former Iraqi dictator Saddam Hussein and Ali Hasan al-Majid were both tried and convicted by the Iraqi Special Tribunal of crimes against humanity for their role in the Anfal Campaign.

Ralph Martin Baker

See also: Hussein, Saddam

Further Reading

Lawrence, Quil. *Invisible Nation: How the Kurds' Quest for Statehood Is Shaping Iraq and the Middle East.* New York: Walker, 2008.

McDowall, David. *The Kurds: A Nation Denied.* Austin, TX: Harry Ransom Humanities Research Center, 1992.

Potter, Lawrence G., and Gary G. Sick, eds. *Iran, Iraq, and the Legacies of War.* New York: Palgrave Macmillan, 2004.

Rudd, Gordon W. *Humanitarian Intervention: Assisting the Iraqi Kurds in Operation Provide Comfort, 1991.* Washington, DC: Department of the Army, 2004.

Yildiz, Kerim, and Tom Blass. *The Kurds in Iraq: The Past, Present and Future.* London: Pluto, 2004.

L

Libby, I. Lewis

Attorney, author, leader in the neoconservative movement, and the central figure in the Valerie Plame Wilson incident. I. "Scooter" Lewis Libby was born in New Haven, Connecticut, on August 22, 1950. Lewis has never divulged publicly his actual first name, using only the initial "I." He grew up in an affluent family and graduated from the exclusive Philips Academy (Andover, Massachusetts) in 1968. He enrolled at Yale University, from which he graduated magna cum laude in 1972, and then earned a law degree from Columbia University School of Law in 1975. While an undergraduate at Yale, Libby was greatly impressed and influenced by a young political science professor there, Paul Wolfowitz, who would later become deputy secretary of defense in the George W. Bush administration. Libby began a lifelong friendship and mentorship with Wolfowitz and also began to write a novel during his Yale days, which was ultimately published as *The Apprentice* in 1996. Despite his connection with Wolfowitz, as a young man Libby had Democratic leanings, and he worked in Massachusetts governor Michael Dukakis's gubernatorial campaign.

From 1975 to 1981 Libby practiced law with a prestigious law firm, becoming a junior partner in 1976. With the advent of the Republican Ronald Reagan administration, Wolfowitz invited Libby to join him on the State Department's influential policy planning staff, an opportunity that Libby believed he could not refuse. He remained in the State Department until 1985, at which time he left government service to take up the practice of law. In 1989 he again entered government service, this time with the Department of Defense working for Wolfowitz as deputy under-secretary for strategy and resources. In 1992 Libby became deputy undersecretary for defense policy, a post he held until 1993, at which time he went back to private law practice. During his stints in government, Libby had become allied with both established and up-and-coming neoconservatives, including Secretary of Defense Donald Rumsfeld and future national security adviser and secretary of state Condoleezza Rice. In the late 1990s Libby was active in the Project for the New American Century, a favored group of neoconservatives.

In 2001 Libby joined the George W. Bush administration, serving as an adviser to the president and, more importantly, as chief of staff for Vice President Richard B. Cheney. Libby's role in the West Wing was a large one, and he had considerable access to policy-making decisions. He was a staunch defender of Cheney, and the two men were reportedly very close both professionally and personally. From 2001 to 2003 Libby also played a significant role on the Defense Policy Board Advisory Committee, which was chaired by the vaunted neoconservative Richard Perle. Libby was reportedly much involved in the formulation of U.S.-Israeli policies and had a direct role in the promulgation of the so-called Road Map to Peace in late 2002 and early 2003. Libby, unlike some of his fellow neoconservatives, kept a very low profile while in office; he rarely granted interviews and preferred to work behind the scenes, where he was especially adept.

Libby's greatest role in the Bush administration came in the Valerie Plame Wilson incident, a multiyear saga that embroiled the White House in a Central Intelligence Agency (CIA) leak case that was allegedly undertaken in retribution for Ambassador Joseph Wilson's unflattering comments made about the Iraq War in July 2003. Valerie Plame, who at the time was a covert CIA operations officer, was Wilson's wife. It was alleged that Libby had a direct role in revealing the identity of Plame during interviews he granted with Judith Miller, a reporter for the *New York Times*, in July 2003. They took place in the immediate aftermath of an op-ed piece that Wilson wrote for that same newspaper in which he questioned the legitimacy of the Bush administration's claims concerning Iraqi attempts to buy enriched uranium from Niger, claims that had been strongly disputed by Plame and some of her colleagues. Wilson also questioned other justifications for the March 2003 invasion of Iraq. Knowingly revealing the identity of an undercover intelligence officer is a federal offense.

When questioned by Federal Bureau of Investigation (FBI) agents and testifying before a federal grand jury, Libby claimed that he had learned of Plame's identity from a television reporter and had "forgotten" that Vice President Cheney had previously told him about Plame's identity. In September and October 2005 Libby's story began to fall apart. It was soon revealed to the special counsel investigating the case that Libby had had numerous conversations about Plame, including ones with Miller

in which he divulged her identity. Other contradicting testimony led investigators to believe that Libby had not, in fact, learned the identity of Plame from a television reporter. As a result, on October 28, 2005, Libby was indicted on five felony counts: obstruction of justice, making false statements to FBI officers (two counts), and perjury in his grand jury testimony (two counts). He immediately resigned from the White House staff. On March 6, 2007, Libby was convicted of four of the five counts against him. Libby's lawyers filed appeals and indicated that they would seek a retrial, although they decided against the latter.

On June 5, 2007, Libby was sentenced to 30 months in prison and a $250,000 fine. He was also disbarred and will not be able to practice law in the future. On July 2 President Bush commuted Libby's sentence, terming it "excessive." While the commutation saved Libby from a prison term, the $250,000 fine remains, as do the felony convictions themselves. Only if Libby were to be issued a full pardon would his record be wiped clean. From January 6, 2006, to March 7, 2007, Libby served as a senior adviser to the Hudson Institute. He is not now actively engaged in work and may be writing his memoirs. Many believed that Libby's conviction was at least in part politically motivated and that he was a scapegoat for higher-ranking members of the Bush White House. Indeed, Cheney never testified at any of the legal proceedings, and it is still unclear who actually initiated the leak.

Paul G. Pierpaoli Jr.

See also: Bush, George Walker; Central Intelligence Agency; Cheney, Richard Bruce; Weapons of Mass Destruction; Wilson, Joseph Carter, IV; Wilson, Valerie Plame; Wolfowitz, Paul Dundes

Further Reading

Plame Wilson, Valerie. *Fair Game: My Life as a Spy, My Betrayal by the White House.* New York: Simon and Schuster, 2007.

Wilson, Joseph. *The Politics of Truth: Inside the Lies That Led to War and Betrayed My Wife's CIA Identity.* New York: Carroll and Graf, 2004.

Woodward, Bob. *State of Denial: Bush at War, Part III.* New York: Simon and Schuster, 2006.

Lynch, Jessica

U.S. Army soldier who was taken prisoner early in Operation IRAQI FREEDOM and who, upon being rescued, became a national celebrity and a controversial symbol of the Iraq War. Born in Palestine, West Virginia, on April 26, 1983, Jessica Lynch joined the army largely because she was interested in traveling. On the eve of the war she was deployed to Iraq as part of the 507th Maintenance Company. On March 23, 2003, after an element of her supply convoy became separated from other vehicles and became disoriented, she was injured in a Humvee accident during an ambush and taken captive by the Iraqis. The attack took place in the city of Nasiriyah.

After the engagement ended Private First Class Lynch lost consciousness. She later awoke in an Iraqi military hospital. There, and subsequently at Saddam Hussein General Hospital, Iraqi doctors and nurses treated Lynch for the severe injuries she had sustained. She remained hospitalized until April 1, 2003, when an American Special Forces team raided the hospital and freed her, carrying her out on a stretcher and delivering her to military authorities for medical treatment. Footage of the rescue operation was released to the media, and Lynch quickly became a symbol of

Former U.S. Army private Jessica Lynch testifies before the House Oversight and Government Reform hearing on Capitol Hill, April 24, 2007. (AP Photo/Susan Walsh)

American fortitude and resolve in the early days of IRAQI FREEDOM.

Although much of the media portrayed Lynch as a hero, the details of her ordeal remain unclear. Some reports, for example, suggested that during the ambush she had fired her weapon in an effort to fend off the attackers; others maintained that the firing mechanism of her assault rifle was inoperable because it was jammed with sand. The nature of her captivity also became a source of speculation. While there is a great deal of evidence that the Iraqi medical staff treated her professionally and in accordance with the provisions dictated for prisoners of war, questions persist about the possibility that she was interrogated and abused. Additionally, many critics are skeptical of whether the operation to reclaim her was as dangerous as it appeared to be, and there are conflicting reports about whether the soldiers encountered any resistance as they entered the hospital. Some have suggested that the George W. Bush administration and the media embellished the story to increase public support for the war and turn her rescue into compelling headlines.

Beyond the disagreement about the details of her captivity, Lynch's story reignited much larger debates about gender, race, and the military. For opponents of the combat exclusion that bars women from frontline duty, Lynch's courage indicated the fitness of women for combat situations. Conversely, for those who support the ban on women in combat, her apparent helplessness proved the rightness of their claims. Other observers wondered why Lynch was the only captive whose cause became famous, particularly because there were two other female casualties of the Nasiriyah ambush, Private First Class Lori Piestewa and Specialist Shoshana Johnson. Piestewa died of injuries sustained during the skirmish, while Johnson was held captive for 22 days. Despite being the first Native American woman to die in combat and the first female African American prisoner of war, respectively, neither woman received as much media attention as did Lynch, and some have claimed that this disparity was a result of race and that mainstream America was more interested in the suffering of a white woman than that of her nonwhite peers.

Whatever the reasons, Lynch became an instant celebrity. Multiple television networks developed her story into full-length programs. In an effort to capitalize on her iconic status, some media outlets may have exaggerated certain aspects of the story, and Lynch later contested the accuracy of an NBC-TV dramatization in particular. Seeking to make her own voice heard, Lynch told her story to Pulitzer Prize–winning journalist Rick Bragg, who developed it into the popular book *I Am a Soldier, Too: The Jessica Lynch Story* (2003). Throughout the text, which covers everything from Lynch's idyllic childhood to her postwar return to her home in Palestine, West Virginia, Lynch resists being labeled a hero and instead tries to provide an accurate account of her life and her time in Iraq. Now a decorated veteran, Lynch returned to civilian life, earned a college degree, and is now teaching. She became a mother for the first time in January 2007.

Rebecca Adelman

See also: Iraqi Freedom, Operation

Further Reading

Bragg, Rick. *I Am a Soldier, Too: The Jessica Lynch Story.* New York: Vintage, 2003.

Conroy, Thomas. "The Packaging of Jessica Lynch." In *Constructing America's War Culture: Iraq, Media, and Images*, edited by Thomas Conroy and Jarice Hanson, 61–84. Lanham, MD: Lexington Books, 2008.

Holland, Shannon L. "The Dangers of Playing Dress-Up: Popular Representations of Jessica Lynch and the Controversy Regarding Women in Combat." *Quarterly Journal of Speech* 92 (2006): 27–50.

Takacs, Stacy. "Jessica Lynch and the Regeneration of American Identity and Power Post-9/11." *Feminist Media Studies* 5 (2005): 297–310.

M

M-1A1 and M-1A2 Abrams Main Battle Tanks

The M-1A1 (and its successor the M-1A2) Abrams is the most powerful U.S. tank and one of the top main battle tanks (MBTs) in the world. Designed to replace the M60 (which entered service in 1960), the M1 began as a project by the Federal Republic of Germany (FRG, West Germany) and the United States for an MBT able to engage and defeat the vast number of tanks that the Soviet Union and its satellites might field in an invasion of Central Europe. Designated the MBT-70, the new tank was centered on the Shillelagh gun/missile launcher and a 1,500-horsepower engine, neither of which, however, worked out as planned.

Collapse of the MBT-70 project and cancellation of the follow-on XM803 program led to a brand new program, begun from the ground up, in 1972. That same year the U.S. Army came up with a concept of what it wanted in the new MBT, and two companies—Chrysler Defense and the Detroit Diesel division of General Motors—built prototypes of what was then designated the XM1 MBT. Both were tested in early 1976, and that November the army declared Chrysler the winner. Following manufacture of a number of test vehicles, the first production model M1 tank came off the assembly line in February 1980. The new tank was named for General Creighton Abrams, armor tank battalion commander in World War II, commander of allied forces in Vietnam, and then army chief of staff.

The M1 was a revolutionary design and a sharp departure from previous U.S. tanks, with their rounded surfaces and relatively high profile. The M1 was more angular, with flat-plate composite Chobham-type armor and armor boxes that can be opened and the armor changed according to the threat. It was also considerably lower (8 feet) than the M60 (10 feet 9 inches).

From the start the army's intention was to arm the M1 with the 105-millimeter (mm) gun. As a result of a program aimed at securing a common main armament for U.S., British, and West German tanks, the army made the decision, after initial M1 production had begun, to arm the M1 with a German-designed Rheinmetall 120-mm smoothbore gun. But that gun was still under development when the tank was ready, so the army decided to continue with the 105-mm M68 gun utilized in the M60. The 120-mm M256 gun, essentially the German-designed gun with a U.S. breech, was available in 1984, and the first M-1A1 with this new armament came off the production line in August 1985. The M-1A1HA introduced a new steel-encased depleted uranium armor, which is virtually impenetrable but also dramatically increased the tank's weight to nearly 146,000 pounds. A total of 3,273 M1s were produced for the U.S. Army.

The M-1A1 (production began in 1985) mounts the 120-mm main gun, and the next modification was the introduction of almost-impenetrable steel-encased depleted-uranium armor, designated HA (heavy armor). Prior to the 1991 Persian Gulf War, upgrades were carried out in Saudi Arabia on all in-theater

M-1A1 tanks to bring them to M-1A1HA status.

A total of 4,796 M1As were produced for the U.S. Army. The U.S. Marine Corps received 221, along with 403 M1s transferred from the army, to replace its more than 700 M60A1s. Kuwait also purchased 218 Abrams tanks, and Saudi Arabia bought 315. Egypt also arranged to produce 551 of them under a coproduction arrangement in which they were built in Egypt by the Halwan Tank Plant. In 2006 and 2007 the Australian Army took delivery of 59 M-1A1s. In July 2008 Iraq issued a formal request to purchase 140 upgraded M-1A1Ms from the United States.

In the Persian Gulf War, the M-1A1 Abrams and British Challenger proved their great superiority over their Soviet counterparts, especially in night fighting. Of some 600 M-1A1 Abrams that saw combat, only 18 were disabled by enemy action. None were penetrated by an enemy round, but 3 were struck by depleted uranium shells fired from other M1s, although none of these were permanently disabled, and there were no crew fatalities. This reflected the survivability features built into the tank, including armored bulkheads to deflect blasts outward. Conversely, the M-1A1's 120-mm gun proved lethal to Iraqi MBTs. The M-1A1 could engage Iraqi armor at some 3,000 yards, twice the Iraqi effective range, and its superior fire-control system could deliver a first-round hit while on the move. The depleted uranium penetrators could almost guarantee a kill.

The M-1A2 was first produced in 1986. Most changes are internal. These include a thermal viewer for the tank commander, a new land navigation system, and the Inter-Vehicular Information System (IVIS). The latter is a datalink compatible with other advanced armored fighting vehicles (AFVs) and helicopters. Although only 77 M-1A2s were delivered new, more than 500 M-1A1s were upgraded to M-1A2s. The M-1A2 weighs some 139,000 pounds, mounts a 120-mm main gun and three machine guns: two M-240 7.62-mm (.30-caliber), one for the loader and the other mounted coaxially to the right of the main gun, and one M-2 12–7-mm (.50-caliber) mounted on the tank commander's cupola. A six-barrel smoke grenade launcher is located on each side of the turret, and the tank can also lay a smoke-screen by an engine-operated system.

During the Iraq War, no Abrams tanks were disabled by enemy action during the initial battles in March and April 2003. During the occupation that followed, some 80 Abrams were knocked out of action as of March 2005. Five crew members have been killed inside their tanks when the vehicles were hit by large improvised explosive devices (IEDs) using explosively formed penetrators (EFPs). Ten crew members also died after being hit while riding partially exposed in open hatches.

Production of the M-1A2 was completed in 1996 but can be renewed if necessary. The M-1A2 is also in service in Kuwait and Saudi Arabia.

Spencer C. Tucker

See also: Iraqi Freedom, Operation

Further Reading

Foss, Christopher F., ed. *The Encyclopedia of Tanks and Armored Fighting Vehicles.* San Diego: Thunder Bay, 2002.

Tucker, Spencer C. *Tanks: An Illustrated History of Their Impact.* Santa Barbara, CA: ABC-CLIO, 2004.

Mahdi Army

Paramilitary wing of the Iraqi political movement Tayyar al-Sadr (the Sadr Movement) led by Iraqi junior Shiite cleric

Muqtada al-Sadr. Muqtada al-Sadr is the son of Ayatollah Muhammad Sadiq al-Sadr, a prominent and outspoken critic of the Iraqi Baath Party and of President Saddam Hussein's regime during the 1990s. The elder Sadr was assassinated along with two of his other sons, Mustafa and Muammal, on February 18, 1999. Sadiq al-Sadr was a cousin of both Grand Ayatollah Muhammad Baqir al-Sadr, a prominent Iraqi Shiite activist cleric in the 1960s and 1970s, and Musa al-Sadr, the prominent cleric who oversaw the political mobilization of Lebanese Shia from the late 1950s until his disappearance on a trip to Libya in 1978.

Sadiq al-Sadr received his religious education in the seminary of Najaf and studied with his cousin, Baqir al-Sadr, and Iranian Grand Ayatollah Ruhollah Khomeini, who lived in exile in Najaf from 1965 to 1978. Sadiq al-Sadr's popularity among Iraqi Shia began to grow beginning in the mid-1980s, and by the end of that decade, despite debates among clerical circles about his qualifications for the rank, he had come to be recognized by many as an elevated religious leader known as a *marja' al-taqlid*, meaning a source of authority whom a follower might emulate.

Sadr was a rising star in the 1990s because of his vocal criticism of the Baathists and his belief in an active seminary, a dangerous position in Iraq. He challenged the silent seminary, which was represented by the politically quietist Grand Ayatollah Ali al-Husayn al-Sistani and the other members of the *marjaiyya*, the council of Iraq's resident grand ayatollahs that sits in Najaf. Sadr took advantage of government crackdowns on the traditional Shiite seminaries in southern Iraqi cities, such as Najaf, Karbala, and Kufa, following the suppression of the 1991 Shiite and Kurdish rebellions in Iraq.

While senior clerics such as Sistani came under increasing government scrutiny and were basically placed under house arrest, Hussein's regime initially tolerated Sadr because he was seen as a potential counterweight to Sistani. A divided Iraqi Shiite community was more advantageous to the ruling Baathists than a unified one. However, by the mid-1990s Sadr had begun to take more confrontational positions vis-à-vis the government, issuing a fatwa (juridical opinion) forbidding his followers from joining the Baath Party, holding Friday prayers in defiance of a government ban, and calling for the implementation of a clerically governed Islamic state in Iraq.

Sadr was also critical of Sistani and the marjaiyya for remaining politically disengaged in the face of government suppression. An Iraqi native and Arab, Sadr presented himself as the native alternative for Iraqi Shiites to follow in opposition to the Iranian-born Sistani and the other members of the marjaiyya, all of whom were foreign born. Sadr's speeches and sermons drew tens of thousands of people, and his representatives successfully took over thousands of mosques, local religious centers, and Husseiniyyas (buildings used to commemorate the lives and martyrdom of the Shiite imams, such as the third imam Hussein).

After the assassination of Sadr in February 1999, control of his grassroots movement in Iraq was assumed by his son Muqtada al-Sadr, a low-ranking seminary student, although most of his followers took as their marja' al-taqlid Ayatollah Kadhim Hairi, one of Sadiq al-Sadr's best students. Hairi, however, resided in Qum, where he remains today, and thus was not well placed to assume control of Sadiq al-Sadr's movement in Iraq. For a time Muqtada al-Sadr recognized Hairi as the spiritual guide of the Sadr Movement; however, the two had a falling out in late 2003 after Hairi declined to return to Iraq.

In early April 2003 following the March U.S.- and British-led invasion of Iraq, Muqtada al-Sadr's representatives and clerical allies reopened mosques and religious centers in Sadrist strongholds in places such as the southern city of Kufa and the sprawling Shiite district known as Sadr City in eastern Baghdad. These mosques and centers form the social support base for the Sadr Movement and remain as key elements of Sadr's influence and authority. Sadr City and large swaths of southern Iraq are Sadrist strongholds, giving the movement significant popular support among the Iraqi Shiite population, which makes up an estimated 60–65 percent of Iraq's 28 million people. Despite its continued prominence, the Sadr Movement began to splinter in 2005. Ayatollah Muhammad Yaqubi and Mahmoud Sarkhi al-Hassani, two former students of Sadiq al-Sadr, broke away from the movement and formed their own sociopolitical groups. Yaqubi created the Fadhila (Islamic Virtue) Party, and Hassani formed a smaller movement popular among more messianic Iraqi Shiites who await the return of the Twelfth Shia Imam, Muhammad al-Mahdi.

The Mahdi Army was formed soon after the collapse of the Iraqi government in the spring of 2003, and by the spring of 2004 its membership had swelled to an estimated 6,000–10,000 fighters, of whom a core group of 500–1,000 were highly trained. Muqtada al-Sadr has been blamed for ordering the murder of Hujjat al-Islam Abd al-Majid al-Khoi, a midlevel cleric and son of the late prominent Iraq-based grand ayatollah Abu al-Qasim al-Khoi, who was a U.S. ally; the younger Khoi was stabbed to death in a crowd in Najaf on April 10, 2003. Sadr has repeatedly

denied that he was involved in the murder. Later that month Mahdi Army fighters surrounded the Najaf homes of Sistani and other members of the marjaiyya, demanding that they leave Iraq. The Mahdi Army was forced to stand down when several thousand Shiite Arab tribes-men loyal to the marjaiyya came to Najaf to protect the grand ayatollahs. Sadr has maintained a tenuous relationship with the grand ayatollahs and has publicly recognized their authority, although he may simply be paying them lip service.

Sadr ordered the Mahdi Army into the streets in April 2004 after the Coalition Provisional Authority (CPA), the U.S.-dominated governing body headed by L. Paul Bremer that ran Iraq from 2003 to June 28, 2005, closed the offices of the main Sadrist newspaper, al-Hawza, and pressured an Iraqi court to indict Sadr and several of his aides for the murder of Khoi. Fighting between the Mahdi Army and coalition forces continued until early June, when a tenuous cease-fire was negotiated.

Heavy fighting between the two sides began again on August 3, 2005, when U.S. and Iraqi forces tried to arrest Sadr. The fighting lasted until August 25, when Sistani, who had recently returned to Iraq after undergoing medical treatment in Great Britain, brokered a cease-fire. During the height of the fighting, Sadr and several hundred of his supporters took over Najaf's Shrine of Imam Ali, a revered Shiite holy site where the first imam is buried. The old city of Najaf was heavily damaged in the fighting. After meeting with Sistani on August 25, Sadr and his armed supporters left the shrine compound and turned over its keys to Sistani's representatives.

Following the December 2005 national elections, the Sadr Movement gained control of four ministries and reportedly infiltrated branches of the security services with

Mahdi Army militiamen, who were accused of carrying out attacks on Sadr's rivals and Sunni Arabs. Despite such allegations, Sadr remained the most popular Iraqi Shiite leader with Sunni Iraqis, many of whom respected and admired his resistance to continued U.S. and British occupation. His crossover popularity, however, was shattered following the February 22, 2006, bombing of the revered Shiite Askari shrine in Samarra. Mahdi Army militiamen and other rogue elements, some of them former members of his movement, ignored instructions from Sadr not to carry out random revenge attacks and instead attacked Sunni mosques and murdered Sunni religious leaders and random passersby in retaliation.

The ensuing descent of Iraq into a virtual civil war has made it more difficult to determine which elements are truly a part of the Sadr Movement and the Mahdi Army, whose membership reportedly has swelled to some 60,000 according to the Iraq Study Group report. Many groups that are carrying out sectarian killings are thought to be led by former Mahdi Army commanders who were expelled from the movement or even individuals who have never been Mahdi Army members but use its name to carry out extortion and kidnappings for ransom. The real Mahdi Army and the Sadr Movement, although initially supportive of Iraqi prime minister Nuri al-Maliki, began to face government-led attacks in April 2008 when Iraqi forces and U.S. aircraft attacked Mahdi Army positions in the southern port city of Basra. These assaults were reportedly spearheaded by Iraqi Army and police units dominated by the Supreme Islamic Iraqi Council, headed by Sadr's chief Shiite rival, Abd al-Aziz al-Hakim. The attacks are believed to have been an attempt to damage the Sadrists' political chances in provincial elections set for 2009.

The Mahdi Army and the Supreme Council's paramilitary wing, the Badr Organization (also known as the Badr Corps) have engaged in running gun battles since 2005, with a large-scale battle between the two occurring in Karbala in January 2008 during Ashura religious processions. Despite these attacks, in early May 2008 Sadr announced the six-month renewal of a 2007 cease-fire agreement between the Sadr Movement and the Iraqi government. He ordered his supporters not to engage in violence and instead requested that they focus on grassroots nonviolent political protests against the continued occupation of Iraq.

Christopher Paul Anzalone

See also: Hakim, Abd al-Aziz al-; Iraqi Insurgency; Shia Islam

Further Reading

Cockburn, Patrick. *Muqtada: Muqtada al-Sadr, the Shia Revival, and the Struggle for Iraq.* New York: Scribner, 2008.

Cole, Juan. "The United States and Shi'ite Religious Factions in Post-Ba'athist Iraq." *Middle East Journal* 57 (2003): 543–66.

Jabar, Faleh A. *The Shi'ite Movement in Iraq.* London: Saqi Books, 2003.

Nakash, Yitzhak. *Reaching for Power: The Shi'a in the Modern Arab World.* Princeton, NJ: Princeton University Press, 2006.

Visser, Reidar. *The Sadrists of Basra and the Far South of Iraq: The Most Unpredictable Political Force in the Gulf's Oil-Belt Region?* Oslo: Norwegian Institute of International Affairs, 2008.

Mahmudiyah Incident

Four soldiers from the 101st Airborne Division raped a 14-year-old Iraqi girl and killed her family on March 12, 2006. The four soldiers left their post manning a checkpoint in order to commit the murders. After killing the family and the girl, Abir Qasim Hamza al-Janabi, they set her body on fire. This fire spread to the rest of the house and alerted neighbors. Initially suspected as an insurgent attack, Private First Class Justin Watt came forward to voice suspicions about the role of American soldiers in the attack. Then the investigation shifted to the 101st Airborne Division soldiers. In response to the killings, there were several attacks by insurgent groups in Iraq that claimed their actions were in retaliation for the rape and killing of Abir.

After the investigation and trial, two of the soldiers involved, Specialists James Barker and Paul Cortez, received 90 and 100 years in prison respectively. Private Jesse Spielman received a sentence of 110 years for his role in the rape and killings. Private First Class Steven Green, the ringleader of the attack, was out of the army when arrested for the crimes. He faced a civilian trial and received a sentence of life in prison without parole.

The attack in Mahmudiyah was one of several events that showcased the problems associated with long-term conflicts. Similar to the problems at Abu Ghraib prison, Mahmudiyah was an example of what can happen when leadership does not exercise proper oversight or instill proper discipline in subordinates.

Gates Brown

See also: Abu Ghraib

Further Reading

Frederick, Jim. *Black Hearts: One Platoon's Descent into Madness in Iraq's Triangle of Death*. New York: Harmony Books, 2010.

Von Zielbauer, Paul. "G.I. Gets 100 Years for Rape and Killing in Iraq." *New York Times*, August 5, 2007. http://www.nytimes.com/2007/08/05/us/05abuse.html.

Majid al Tikriti, Ali Hassan al-

High-ranking Iraqi government official, minister of defense (1993–1995), cousin of Baath Party leader and Iraqi dictator Saddam Hussein, and known as Chemical Ali because of his role in the use of chemical weapons to suppress ethnic uprisings by the Kurds and Shiites. Ali Hassan al-Majid al Tikriti was born sometime in 1941 in Tikrit to a relatively modest family.

Majid, along with many others from Tikrit, joined the Baath Party in 1958 and enlisted in the Iraqi Army that same year. He was arrested during the 1963 coup when Colonel Abd al-Salam Arif seized power and moved against the Baathists. After the Baath Party seized power in 1968, Majid rose steadily within the party ranks, along with his cousin Saddam Hussein and many other men from Tikrit, a number of them interrelated. This cadre formed the base of Hussein's power, as all were family members or members of the same tribe, people whom he could trust. By 1978 Majid headed the Regional Secretariat Office of the Baath Party. That same year, after graduating from the National Defense Academy, he was appointed to the Military Bureau.

When Hussein became president of Iraq in 1979, replacing Ahmad al-Hassan Bakr, Majid's star continued to rise. In 1982 he became a member of the Regional Command. After an assassination attempt on Hussein in 1983, Majid was charged with punishing those connected—even tangentially—with the attempt. Between 1984 and 1987 he was the director-general of internal security, making him a key part of Hussein's security apparatus that ensured the survival and continuation of the regime.

In 1987 Hussein appointed Majid governor of the northern bureau, which included

Kurdistan in northern Iraq. By 1987, with the pressures of the Iran-Iraq War (1980–1988) weighing heavily upon Baghdad, the security situation in northern Iraq was seen as very precarious, with a growing Kurdish resistance movement distracting the government from the war effort against Iran. To bring an end to the Kurdish insurgency, Majid ordered civilian Kurds to be attacked using chemical weapons, including mustard gas and sarin. One attack on Halabja resulted in more than 5,000 deaths, leading to the sobriquet of Chemical Ali. Following the Halabja massacre, Majid oversaw an Arabization campaign in Anfal that involved the forced transfer of Kurdish populations and the continued use of chemical weapons to break the Kurdish resistance.

In 1989 Majid became minister of local administration, a position designed to oversee the repopulation with Arabs of the areas that he had depopulated in Kurdistan in his last posting. After the invasion of Kuwait in August 1990 Majid was made governor of Kuwait, in which position he oversaw the organized Iraqi looting and sacking of the nation and the elimination of opposition to Iraqi rule.

With the 1991 Persian Gulf War and the Shiite rebellion centered in Basra against the regime, Hussein placed Majid in charge of the southern forces to put down the insurgency, which he did with brute force. In 1991 Majid became a member of the Revolutionary Command Council. He served as minister of the interior from 1991 until 1993, and from 1993 to 1995 he headed the Ministry of Defense. These appointments to key security posts clearly illustrated Hussein's trust in Majid, but the constant shifts in assignments also revealed Hussein's paranoid nature. No official served in any key military or security post for long, lest he come to pose a threat to the regime. Rotation in office was a key element of Hussein's modus operandi, even if the rotation occurred among a limited elite.

In 1995 Majid was removed from office for allegedly having traded with Iran, but in 1998 he reemerged to govern the southern portion of Iraq, where government power was limited because of the no-fly zone established by the allies after the Persian Gulf War. Shortly before the Iraq War began in March 2003, Hussein divided the nation into four administrative areas, with Majid having charge of the southern portion. During the American-led invasion, Majid was reportedly killed in an air raid on Basra, but this proved false. Indeed, he was arrested on August 17, 2003, and handed over to Iraqi authorities to be put on trial on charges of crimes against humanity and genocide arising from his campaign against the Kurds. During the trial Majid was unapologetic, arguing that his actions had been approved by the legitimate Iraqi government and that he was simply carrying out orders. On June 24, 2007, an Iraqi court found Majid guilty. The court gave him five death sentences. A series of judicial and political hurdles delayed the sentence from being carried out until January 25, 2010, when Majid was executed by hanging.

Michael K. Beauchamp

See also: Baath Party; Hussein, Saddam; Kurds, Massacres of

Further Reading

Aburish, Said K. *Saddam Hussein: The Politics of Revenge*. New York: Bloomsbury, 2000.

Cleveland, William L. *A History of the Modern Middle East*. 3rd ed. Boulder, CO: Westview, 2004.

Khalil, Samir al-. *Republic of Fear: The Politics of Modern Iraq*. Berkeley: University of California Press, 1989.

Maliki, Nuri Muhammed Kamil Hasan al-

Iraqi political leader and prime minister since May 20, 2006. For many years, Nuri Muhammed Kamil Hasan al-Maliki was a leader of the Islamic Dawa Party, an Islamist organization that was ruthlessly suppressed by former Iraqi president Saddam Hussein. He remains the secretary-general of the party. Until 2006 Maliki was known by the pseudonym "Jawad," which he adopted while in exile in Syria.

Maliki was born in Abi Gharq, Iraq, near Karbala, on June 20, 1950. He received a bachelor's degree at the Usul al-Din College

Iraqi prime minister Nuri al-Maliki attends a meeting with Iranian president Mahmoud Ahmadinejad, unseen, in Tehran on August 8, 2007. Al-Maliki went to Iran for talks expected to focus on bilateral relations and overcoming "terrorism challenges" in his war-torn nation. (AP Photo/Hasan Sarbakhshian)

in Baghdad and a master's degree in Arabic literature at Salahaddin University in Sulamaniyah. It was during his college years that he became politically active and joined the Islamic Dawa Party in 1968, steadily rising in the organization's hierarchy. Maliki represents the jihadist faction within the party.

When Iraqi president Saddam Hussein cracked down on the Dawa Party in the 1970s, its members were sentenced to death, even in absentia. Maliki was forced to flee Iraq in October 1979. Fleeing through Jordan, he first traveled to Syria and remained there until 1982, when he moved to Iran. He resided for a year in Ahwaz and then moved to Tehran. In September 1989 he returned to Damascus. He remained in Syria until the fall of Saddam's government in April 2003.

While in Syria Maliki supervised the Dawa Party's publication, *Al-Mawqif*, and became the head of the organization in Damascus and in Lebanon, participating in the Iraqi opposition coalition known as the Joint Action Committee in 1990. He toured the Middle East and Europe to solicit support for the Iraqi opposition movement and convened an important conference representing the various Iraqi opposition groups held in Beirut in 1991.

On his return to Iraq in 2003, Maliki served in various positions in the new Iraqi interim government; he was named to the National Council, headed the security committee of the transitional Iraqi National Assembly, and was then elected to the new National Assembly, where he served on the National Sovereignty Committee. He also became the chief spokesperson and negotiator for the alliance of the various Shia parties and groups known as the United Islamic Alliance during the drafting of the new Iraqi constitution.

When Ibrahim al-Jafari, Iraq's first prime minister, was unable to obtain support from the United States and certain Iraqi groups, Maliki was nominated as prime minister. He took office on May 20, 2006; he also served as the acting minister of the interior until June 2006.

Maliki has been described by Iraq experts as a pragmatic individual who represents the Arab-Iraqi-centered orientation of the Dawa Party and is not overly influenced by Iran. However, it has been difficult for Iraqi officials to steer clear of pressure from the United States and to deal with sectarian and party loyalties in the context of intersectarian fighting, which has further delayed reestablishing stability in Iraq. U.S. senator Carl Levin (D-Mich.), chairman of the Senate Armed Services Committee, attacked the Maliki government in August 2007 for being "too beholden to religious and sectarian leaders." At the same time, Senator Hillary Clinton (D-N.Y.) charged that Maliki was too "divisive" a figure. Yet, his political skills have been demonstrated, certainly prior to his assuming the office of prime minister, in his generally good working relationships with various opposition parties. These relationships were strained later, in part because of the tension between Washington's and Baghdad's differing goals and priorities.

Under the Maliki government, the U.S. military has forged new alliances with Sunni tribal elements to defeat al-Qaeda in Iraq and other Sunni insurgency groups and has urged measures to reverse de-Baathification, causing concerns among Iraqi Shiites. A point of controversy has been legislation regarding the sharing of oil revenues, resisted by Sunni and Kurdish leaders. A major Maliki triumph, however, was passage of the Status of Forces Agreement of December 2008.

On these issues, Maliki has been responsive to Iraqi concerns and has consistently called for a definite time frame for a U.S.

troop withdrawal, despite various American warnings that setting a withdrawal date is unwise. The United States has reportedly monitored all of Maliki's and other Iraqi government leaders' communications, perhaps because of these differences.

Maliki has also had to deal with inter-Shiite tensions, such as when the Fadhila Party withdrew its representatives from the Shiite coalition in 2007 and when he responded to pressures to counter the power of the Mahdi Army of Muqtada al-Sadr and the Badr Organization/militia. Indeed, he moved against the latter two in 2008. In November 2008, tension with the Kurds expressed itself in directives made to the Peshmerga forces.

Sherifa Zuhur

See also: Islamic Dawa Party

Further Reading

Raghvan, Sudarsan. "Maliki's Impact Blunted by Own Party's Fears: Hussein-Era Secrecy Persists, Analysts Say." *Washington Post*, August 3, 2007, A-1.

Shanahan, Rodger. "The Islamic Da'wa Party: Past Development and Future Prospects." *Middle East Review of International Affairs* 8, no. 2 (June 2004): 112–25.

Woodward, Bob. *The War Within: A Secret White House History, 2006–2008.* New York: Simon and Schuster, 2008.

Zuhur, Sherifa. *Iran, Iraq and the United States: The New Triangle's Impact on Sectarianism and the Nuclear Threat.* Carlisle Barracks, PA: Strategic Studies Institute, 2006.

Marsh Arabs

Indigenous people, known as the Madan (Ma'dan), who have traditionally inhabited the marshlands in southern Iraq (hence "Marsh Arabs"). The Marsh Arabs have a unique seminomadic 5,000-year-old water-borne culture, derived from the ancient Sumerians and Babylonians. They live in the marshy lowlands of southern Iraq in the disputed border area near the Iranian border (historically known as Persia), an area also known as the Tigris-Euphrates alluvial salt marsh and Hawizeh. They are ethnically Arab and are Shiite Muslim, the majority religious group in Iraq. Although the marshes provided a refuge from persecution by the Sunni Muslim Ottoman Turks, the Persians, and the British, the wetlands did not insulate the Marsh Arabs from the Iran-Iraq War (1980–1988), Iraqi president Saddam Hussein's wrath following his defeat in the 1991 Persian Gulf War, or the 10 years of United Nations (UN) economic sanctions that followed.

At the beginning of the Iran-Iraq War, there were between 250,000 and 500,000 Marsh Arabs inhabiting approximately 7,700 square miles of wetlands. That conflict saw great pressure on the Marsh Arabs, and their numbers plummeted. The subsequent Persian Gulf War removed Hussein's forces from Kuwait, but U.S. president George H. W. Bush also encouraged an internal revolt against Hussein. The Marsh Arabs joined the resultant short-lived Shiite uprising in southern Iraq. It lasted for just a month, in March 1991. Hussein brutally crushed the rebellion.

Also, starting in the 1950s, British engineers working for the Iraqi government planned and began carrying out a project to build embanked canals that would concentrate the water of the Tigris and Euphrates Rivers and reclaim the water of the marshes, so as not to waste it. The project, which began in 1953, was reenergized during the Iran-Iraq War. The problems with the project are both ecological and social, since the Iraqi government was essentially forcing the

Madan from their homelands, apparently for political purposes. The destruction of the wetlands' rich biodiversity drastically reduced the Marsh Arabs' primary food sources (rice, barley, wheat, pearl millet, fish, sheep, and cattle) as well as the reeds used to create their boats and homes. By 1993 about two-thirds of the rivers waters had been diverted from the marshes into the constructed Third Waterway. The Marsh Arabs' sources of income were sharply curtailed, and the desertification decimated the Marsh Arabs' commercial fisheries.

Between 1991 and 2000 or so, many Marsh Arabs were killed and many others fled to Iran or to other Shiite areas within Iraq, leaving approximately 40,000 of the original Marsh Arab population in their ancestral region. By 2001, the United Nations Environment Program (UNEP) estimated that Hussein's efforts had reduced the marshes to no more than 386 square miles. Hussein and his supporters asserted that the diversion was not intended to destroy the Madan people and culture. Rather, they argued that the draining of the marshes was intended to make rich oil reserves more accessible and to create new agricultural opportunities for an impoverished region.

The American- and British-led March 2003 invasion of Iraq that ousted Hussein and overthrew Iraq's Sunni-led Baathist government (Operation IRAQI FREEDOM) was followed by a planned restoration of the marshes. This was aided initially by the ending of a four-year drought in 2003 and the destruction of Hussein's diversion dams by the Marsh Arabs. By 2007 the marshes had been restored to approximately 50 percent of their area prior to the wars. The restoration of Madan culture and the resettlement of the region by the indigenous population has been slow and fitful, however, hindered by the continuing conflict in Iraq, growing tensions with Iran, and the vastly reduced number of Marsh Arabs.

Richard M. Edwards

See also: Hussein, Saddam; IRAQI FREEDOM, Operation

Further Reading

Brown, Sarah Graham. *Sanctioning Saddam: The Politics of Intervention in Iraq.* London: I. B. Tauris, 1999.

Coughlin, Con. *Saddam: His Rise and Fall.* New York: Harper Perennial, 2005.

Hiro, Dilip. *The Longest War: The Iran-Iraq Military Conflict.* London: Routledge, 1991.

Ochsenschlager, Edward L. *Iraq's Marsh Arabs in the Garden of Eden.* Philadelphia: University of Pennsylvania Museum Publication, 2004.

Thesiger, Wilfred. *The Marsh Arabs.* 2nd rev. ed. London: HarperCollins, 1985.

Martyrdom

The act of dying for principles or a particular cause, usually religious. The term is derived from the Greek *martys*, meaning "witness," and was first used in a religious context in reference to the apostles of Jesus Christ, who were "witnesses" of the life and deeds of Jesus, although the idea of death and suffering for religious beliefs appears earlier in Egyptian, Hindu, and Mesopotamian faiths.

Martyrdom acquired its current usage in the Western, Christian world in the early Christian period, when Christians were being persecuted by authorities of the Roman Empire. Those killed for upholding their beliefs were called martyrs, their acceptance of death being considered a testimony of their faith. Some Christian martyrs sought out and welcomed martyrdom as a means of emulating Jesus's willingness to be sacrificed on the cross. Judaism does not connect martyrdom to the idea of witnessing faith but rather refers to it as sanctification of the name of God, or *kiddush ha-Shem*. In both Christianity and Judaism, martyrdom refers to a case in which the believer accepts death rather than denies or changes his or her religious beliefs.

In Islam, martyrdom (*shuhada*) or becoming a martyr for the faith (*istishhad*) is connected to the concept of declaring or witnessing Islam and to struggle for the sake of Islam (*jihad*). The most important Qur'anic verse usually connected with martyrdom is 4:69: "Whosoever obeys Allah, and the Messenger—they are with those whom God has blessed, Prophets, just men, martyrs [shuhada], the righteous; the best of company are they!" According to Islam, martyrs are not questioned after death by the two angels Munkar and Nakir, bypass purgatory, and do not require the intercession of the Prophet to proceed to paradise, as they are free of sin. Martyrs can serve as intercessors for others and are buried in the clothes they die in and not washed after death.

In the early period of Islam, martyrdom referred to those Muslims killed in battle against the armies of Mecca, for example at the Battle of Uhud, and to 11 of the Shia imams. Today, the term also refers to suicide attackers who believe they are defending the cause of Islam. A true martyr (*shahid*) is, according to doctrine, one who does not seek his own death deliberately but accepts it and is granted religious legitimacy and assured a place in heaven. However, suicide committed for personal reasons is prohibited by Islamic law and may be punished by an endless repetition of the same form of death in hell.

Present-day Islamic terrorist organizations alluded to the concept of martyrdom when they began using suicide attacks as a tactic. This was not a new phenomenon but both a revival of an ancient tradition dating back to the early wars of Islam and an adaptation of the discourse of radical Islamic leaders who believed that martyrdom was inevitable for those struggling in the Islamic cause.

Suicide attacks provide two significant advantages over standard attacks. First, if successful, they are tactically and logistically easier to execute because no escape route or retreat is needed, and they are therefore more efficient. Second, they provide a shock to the enemy that goes beyond the actual casualty figure, as they suggest great vulnerability and further probable use of this tactic. Third, they provide a martyr symbol that makes recruiting new members for the organization an easier task by strengthening the ideology behind a group's agenda. The fact that the martyr is willing to commit suicide is used by the group as "testimony" and "evidence" of the worthiness of its cause.

Terrorist suicide attacks in contemporary times began outside the Middle East, in Sri Lanka by Tamil separatists. Much used there, it has no connection with Islamic ideology and demonstrated only the resolve of the attackers. Claims of martyrdom, however, were made for those killed in demonstrations against the Iranian government prior to the Islamic Revolution. Suicide attacks were not used in that revolution, however. Suicide attacks that involved claims of martyrdom did occur in Syria in the late 1970s and early 1980s in battles between Islamic groups and the Syrian government in Damascus, Hama, and Homs.

The term "martyr" was used in the Lebanese civil war by both Christians and Muslims. The connection between martyrdom and suicide attacks came with the Islamic resistance, which responded to the Israeli invasion and occupation of Lebanon in 1982. These actions were undertaken by only a few, but some of the large attacks launched in 1983, as by Islamic Jihad against the U.S. Marine barracks and French forces, were truck bombings involving suicide.

Much of the present-day discussion of martyrdom comes out of the War on Terror. This depends on one's point of view. Thus Americans note suicide bomber attacks in Iraq, while some Iraqis style such events as martyrdom operations and part of the resistance against the occupation.

A long-standing discussion of martyrdom in acts of resistance also arose among Palestinians opposing Israeli occupation of what they perceive to be their homeland. Those killed in all stages of the resistance to Israel—but particularly those active in political movements—have been referred to by most Palestinians as martyrs. Suicide attacks began to be employed in the Palestinian-Israeli struggle in 1994 and were at the time very controversial among Palestinians. Were these necessary acts of desperation or a bona fide tactic in a war of the weak? That question led to discussions among religious leaders that only expanded after the September 11, 2001, al-Qaeda terrorist attacks on the United States. Although these later were largely condemned by Muslim leaders, Palestinian suicide attacks were not because of the conditions of the Israeli occupation and collective punishment and other tactics employed by the Israeli government. Sheikh Qaradawi, a popular Egyptian preacher who now lives in Qatar, has pronounced those who engage in such attacks in Palestine to be reacting under defensive jihad, justified by the Qur'an.

Some prominent Muslim religious leaders have given their public support for various types of martyrdom. Iranian leader Ayatollah Ruhollah Khomeini approved self-sacrifice by Iranian troops and citizens during the war against Iraq (1980–1988), when these forces, which included civilian volunteers, were forced to advance in human wave assaults against Iraqi defensive fire, in what would have to be classified as suicidal attacks. Other organizations that adopted the suicide/martyr method for attacks include al-Qaeda, Abu Sayyaf, and a Bedouin group called Tawhid wa-l Jihad by the Egyptian security services, as well as the non-Islamist al-Aqsa Martyrs Brigades. Even al-Qaeda leaders such as Sayf al-Adl indicate that they have sought to rein in the desire for suicide attacks by younger and less self-controlled members for, if such fervor were uncontrolled, there would be few operatives to run the movement.

Controversial aspects of the present-day link between jihad and martyrdom include the deaths of innocent civilian victims who are not the primary targets of such attacks. Extremist groups employing suicide attacks excuse these victims away as simply additional martyrs. There is also the issue of motivation—whether the suicide bombers are impelled to act by the wrong intent (*niyah*)—because if so, then they are not true martyrs. According to the companion of the Prophet and early caliph Umar, those waging jihad should not set out deliberately to die and become martyrs in an egotistical aim to be known as a hero. There is also a financial aspect to this, as those who engage in jihad (including those who are martyred) are enjoined not to leave their families without support or in debt. In contemporary times, would-be suicide martyrs sometimes ignore or reinterpret these rules, or organizations promise to provide for their widows and families.

All of this has led to a serious effort to deradicalize by uncoupling the concepts of jihad and martyrdom within Muslim communities and by Muslim governments. While not uniform in approach and content, these attempts generally stress moderation and peaceful efforts rather than violence to change society. This task is extremely difficult where foreign occupation and military campaigns are ongoing, as in Pakistan and Afghanistan, but also in Saudi Arabia, where alliances with the United States are blamed for violence against Muslims.

Elliot Paul Chodoff and Sherifa Zuhur

See also: al-Qaeda in Iraq; Jihad; Suicide Bombings

Further Reading

Ayoub, Mahmoud M. *Redemptive Suffering in Islam: A Study of the Devotional Aspects of "Ashura" in Twelver Shi'ism*. The Hague: Brill, 1978.

Gambetta, Diego, ed. *Making Sense of Suicide Missions*. Oxford: Oxford University Press, 2005.

Oliver, Anne Marie, and Paul Steinberg. *The Road to Martyrs' Square: A Journey into the World of the Suicide Bomber*. Oxford: Oxford University Press, 2005.

Shay, Shaul. *The Shahids: Islam and Suicide Attacks*. New Brunswick, NJ, and London: Transaction Publishers, 2004.

Smith, Jane I., and Yvonne Haddad. *The Islamic Understanding of Death and Resurrection*. Albany: State University of New York Press, 1981.

McCain, John Sidney, III

U.S. Navy pilot, prisoner of war (POW) during the Vietnam War (1967–1973), U.S. Representative (1983–1987), U.S. Senator (1987–present), advocate of normalized U.S. relations with Vietnam, and Republican

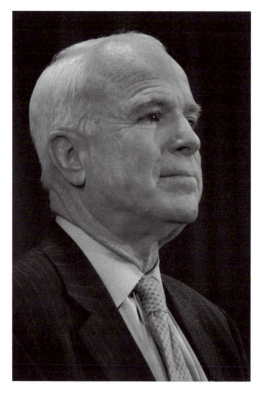

Sen. John McCain (R-Ariz.) ran for the Republican Party's presidential nomination in 2000. Although McCain was unsuccessful, his campaign raised important ethical questions about politics. McCain won his party's nomination in 2008 but lost the national election to Democrat Barack Obama. (Shutterstock)

presidential nominee in 2008. Born on August 29, 1936, in the Panama Canal Zone, John Sidney McCain III came from a line of navy admirals. His father, Admiral John S. McCain Jr., was commander in chief, Pacific Command (CINCPAC) from 1968 to 1972; his grandfather John S. McCain Sr. was a four-star admiral who served in both World War I and World War II.

McCain was a rebel who graduated fifth from the bottom of his class at the U.S. Naval Academy, Annapolis, in 1958. He became a naval aviator and his devil-may-care attitude and leadership skills made him a highly effective pilot. On October 26, 1967, Lieutenant Commander McCain was piloting a Douglas A4 Skyhawk when he was shot down and he crashed in Western Lake in the middle of Hanoi in the Democratic Republic of Vietnam (North Vietnam). The Vietnamese made the site and plane into a military memorial, which McCain visited on his return to Hanoi in 1992.

With two broken arms, a broken leg, a broken shoulder, and a deep wound in his foot, McCain was probably the most seriously injured pilot to enter the Hoa Lo Prison (also known as the Hanoi Hilton). "The crown prince," as the Vietnamese guards called him because of his father's high position, was a tough and highly respected POW who, despite his serious condition and being subjected to torture by his captors, refused the opportunity to be sent home in June 1968.

Released at the end of the war on March 14, 1973, McCain retired from the Navy to enter politics. In 1980 he divorced his first wife and married Cindy Lou Hensley, the daughter of a wealthy beer distributor. For a time he worked in the family business, but he seemed destined for political office. In 1982 he was elected to the House of Representatives from Arizona's 1st District, and in 1986 he was elected a U.S. Senator from Arizona as a Republican, taking office in January 1987.

McCain had a generally distinguished record in the Senate, and on several occasions he was on the short list to be a vice-presidential candidate. In Congress, he naturally gravitated toward foreign, military, and national security matters. The only blight on his record was his involvement, in the mid-1980s, in a scandal involving Charles Keating and the Lincoln Savings and Loan Association, which had bilked depositors and investors out of millions of dollars. Although McCain had been involved with Keating without knowing of his nefarious dealings, he nonetheless admitted that he had used poor judgment in accepting contributions and other perks from him.

McCain made several trips to Vietnam after he reached Congress. The first visit was in 1985; the second one came in 1992, as part of his work on the Senate Select Committee on POW/MIA Affairs. McCain met with some of his former captors in 1992 during what was an emotion-filled visit. McCain, along with other committee members, concluded in 1993 that there were no known POWs or soldiers missing in action (MIA) still residing in Vietnam. He came under attack from some who strongly believed that Americans were indeed still being held by the Vietnamese. After his second visit, McCain became a strong supporter of normalized relations with Vietnam and an end to economic sanctions, which was realized beginning in 1995.

In 2000 McCain ran in the Republican presidential primary, ultimately losing to George W. Bush in a fairly close contest. McCain's allure was that he was not an ideologue and was not afraid to go against his own party. McCain generally backed the Bush administration's War on Terror after the September 11, 2001, terror attacks, but he parted company with Bush on several issues, including the use of torture against enemy combatants, tax cuts for the wealthy, gun legislation, and climate change.

McCain backed the Iraq War from the beginning, but by 2004 he had begun to question the prosecution of that conflict; he openly challenged Secretary of Defense Donald Rumsfeld to put more ground troops into the theater to deal with the mounting Iraqi insurgency. He traveled to Iraq numerous times to see for himself the situation on the ground, and what he saw did not impress him. In August 2006, McCain publicly charged the Bush administration with having constantly underestimated the Iraqi insurgency and took military commanders in Iraq to task for having provided unrealistic assessments of the ground situation. McCain repeatedly urged the Bush administration to prosecute the Iraq war with more zeal and greater commitment, and so it is no surprise that he strongly backed the troop surge strategy implemented in 2007.

In 2008 McCain sought and gained the Republican presidential nomination. From the start, however, he was hobbled by his relatively close association with President Bush, who by then was wildly unpopular; his stance toward the Iraq War; and a failing U.S. economy. His campaign began strongly but fell victim to repeated verbal and strategic gaffes. He shifted from one issue to another while his opponent, Senator Barack Obama, successfully portrayed McCain as Bush redux. McCain's charge that Obama's call for withdrawing U.S. troops from Iraq as quickly as possible was tantamount to defeat fell on deaf ears. McCain touted his role in the successful troop surge, but Obama stuck with his position that the Iraq War had been a mistake in the first place. McCain's choice of Sarah Palin as a running mate, the governor of Alaska who had little national recognition, may not have helped his candidacy. In the end, McCain lost by a large margin in both the popular and electoral vote, but he opted to remain in the Senate as one of its most senior—and seasoned—members.

Paul G. Pierpaoli Jr.

See also: Bush, George Walker; Obama, Barack Hussein, II; Surge, U.S. Troop Deployment, Iraq War

Further Reading

Howes, Craig. *Voices of the Vietnam POWs: Witnesses to Their Fight.* New York: Oxford University Press, 1993.

McCain, John, with Mark Salter. *Faith of My Fathers.* New York: Random House, 1999.

McCain, John, with Mark Salter. *Worth the Fighting For: A Memoir.* New York: Random House, 2002.

McKiernan, David Deglan

U.S. Army officer, commander of the Coalition Force Land Component Command (Middle East) between 2002 and 2004, and commander of the International Security Assistance Force–Afghanistan (ISAF) led by the North Atlantic Treaty Organization (NATO) during 2008 and 2009. As such, David Deglan McKiernan was the top military official in Afghanistan for all international military forces and commander of all U.S. armed forces in Afghanistan. McKiernan was born on December 11, 1950. He attended the College of William and Mary, where he was a member of the Reserve Officers' Training Corps (ROTC). Upon his graduation in 1972, he entered active service in the army as an armor officer. He later earned a master's degree in public administration from Shippensburg University and graduated from the U.S. Army Command and General Staff College and the Army War College. As an advancing career officer, McKiernan spent his years as a junior officer in the United States, South Korea, and Germany and held several staff positions in Germany and at the U.S. Army Training and Doctrine Command (TRADOC).

During Operation DESERT STORM in 1991, McKiernan ran the army's VII Corps mobile command post in Saudi Arabia as the assistant G-3 (operations). He was the G-3 for the 1st Cavalry Division, later becoming the division's 1st Brigade commander from 1993 to 1995. McKiernan was promoted to brigadier general in October 1996 when serving as the deputy chief of staff in the Allied Command Europe Rapid Reaction Corps, which was stationed in Germany and deployed in Sarajevo, Bosnia. After becoming the assistant division commander of the 1st Infantry Division in Germany, he served as the deputy chief of staff for operations for the U.S. Army Europe during military operations in Bosnia, Albania, and Kosovo in 1998 and 1999. Promoted to major general, he commanded the 1st Cavalry Division. McKiernan became a lieutenant general shortly after becoming the army's deputy chief of staff for plans and operations in October 2001.

As the United States prepared for an invasion of Iraq in 2002, McKiernan assumed command of the U.S. Third Army and U.S. Army Forces Central Command, known by the acronym ARCENT. He assisted with the plans for the initial Iraq invasion in March 2003, which embroiled him in a conflict between Secretary of Defense Donald Rumsfeld and other top army commanders about the appropriate number of troops to deploy. McKiernan was among those army officers who advocated that more troops be sent to the region. In interviews, McKiernan claimed that he had sufficient troops to accomplish his mission for the invasion. As the Coalition Forces Land Component Command (CFLCC) commander from 2002 to 2004, McKiernan directed all U.S. and coalition ground forces during the initial phases of the war. As such, he was also involved in the controversies surrounding the lack of clear postconflict plans and the slow recognition of the Iraqi insurgency. In October 2004 McKiernan served as the deputy commander and chief of staff at the U.S. Army Forces Command. Promoted to full general in December 2005, McKiernan became the commanding general of U.S. Army Europe and Seventh Army.

In June 2008 McKiernan assumed command of ISAF and called for additional troops to help contain the Taliban insurgency and prevent the resurgence of the al-Qaeda terrorists who had previously used Afghanistan as their base of operations. In February 2009 President Barack Obama authorized an additional force of 17,000 soldiers to deploy to Afghanistan, which would raise U.S. force levels to 50,000. Many of those troops were deployed to southern Afghanistan, where the fighting was fiercest. McKiernan believed that further resources, including the deployment of more civilians, had to be dedicated to Afghan police training, eliminating corruption, and combating the drug trade.

In May 2009 after only 11 months on the job, in a surprise announcement, Secretary of Defense Robert Gates said that he was replacing McKiernan with Lieutenant General Stanley A. McChrystal, a former commander of the Joint Special Operations Command. Gates said that McKiernan had done nothing wrong but that "new leadership and fresh eyes" were needed in a war that Washington admitted was not being won. It was the first replacement of a field commander during combat operations since the dismissal of General Douglas MacArthur during the Korean War. Factors behind the dismissal of McKiernan were that he and Central Command (CENTCOM) commander General David Petraeus had not developed a close relationship and that leadership believed greater emphasis should be placed on counterinsurgency initiatives. Although McKiernan had an unblemished record, his expertise lay in conventional rather than insurgent warfare.

Lisa Marie Mundey

See also: IRAQI FREEDOM, Operation

Further Reading

Bumiller, Elisabeth, and Thom Shanker. "Pentagon Ousts Top Commander in Afghan War." *New York Times*, May 12, 2009.

Fontenot, Gregory et al. *On Point: The United States Army in Iraqi Freedom.* Annapolis, MD: Naval Institute Press, 2005.

Metz, Steven. *Iraq and the Evolution of American Strategy.* Washington, DC: Potomac Books, 2008.

Ricks, Thomas E. *Fiasco: The American Military Adventure in Iraq.* New York: Penguin, 2006.

Woodward, Bob. *Plan of Attack.* New York: Simon and Schuster, 2004.

Military Strategic Tactical Relay Satellite Communications System

Joint service satellite communications system that provides secure, jam-resistant, worldwide communications to meet essential wartime needs for high-priority military users. The multisatellite constellation links command authorities with combat operations centers, ships, submarines, aircraft, and ground stations.

The operational Military Strategic Tactical Relay (MILSTAR) satellite communications system constellation consists of five satellites placed in geosynchronous orbits around the earth. Each satellite weighs approximately 10,000 pounds and has a design life of 10 years. Each MILSTAR satellite serves as a space-based "switchboard" by directing traffic from terminal to terminal anywhere on the earth. The need for ground-controlled switching is thus significantly reduced because MILSTAR satellites actually process the communications signal and can link with each other through crosslinks. MILSTAR terminals provide encrypted voice, data, teletype, or facsimile communications and interoperable communications among the users of U.S. Army, Navy, and Air Force MILSTAR terminals. Geographically dispersed mobile and fixed control stations provide survivable and enduring operational command and control for the MILSTAR constellation.

The first MILSTAR satellite was launched on February 7, 1994, by a Titan IV expendable launch vehicle. The second was launched on November 5, 1995. The third launch, on April 30, 1999, placed the satellite into an unusable orbit. The fourth, fifth, and sixth satellites have a greatly increased capacity because of an additional medium data rate payload and were launched on February 27, 2001; January 15, 2002; and April 8, 2003.

The MILSTAR system is composed of three segments: space (the satellites), terminal (the users), and mission control. The Air Force Space Command's Space and Missile Systems Center (SMC), Los Angeles Air Force Base, California, developed the space and mission control segments. The Electronics Systems Center, Hans-com Air Force Base, Massachusetts, developed the air force portion of the terminal segment. The 4th Space Operations Squadron, Schriever Air Force Base, Colorado, is the front-line organization providing real-time satellite platform control and communications payload management.

During Operation ALLIED FORCE, the North Atlantic Treaty Organization (NATO) bombing campaign against Yugoslavia, two first-generation MILSTAR satellites provided low data rate, extremely high frequency (EHF) communications support. Because of their onboard processing and crosslink capabilities, they served as a global space network without the need for ground relay stations. The U.S. Navy especially used MILSTAR's capabilities to link command authorities, ground stations, aircraft, and ships for the majority of its communications needs during this operation, including the transmission of air tasking orders and other tactical requirements. Unfortunately, a launch failure on April 9, 1999, left a damaged MILSTAR satellite in a useless orbit and limited MILSTAR support.

MILSTAR and Defense Satellite Communications System (DSCS) satellites continued to anchor the U.S. military's satellite communications network after the September 11, 2001, terrorist attacks. In October 2001 anti-Taliban forces of the Northern Alliance, supported by U.S. Special Operations Forces (SOF), launched Operation ENDURING FREEDOM (OEF) to oust the Taliban, which had supported Islamic terrorists and protected al-Qaeda training camps in Afghanistan. Because of the primitive nature of the in-theater communications system and the mountainous terrain of Afghanistan, satellite communications were the most viable means by which commanders, operations centers, strike aircraft, SOF ground controllers, and Northern Alliance forces could communicate among each other.

The successful launch of a second MILSTAR Block II satellite on January 5, 2002, allowed the four-satellite constellation to operate as a fully cross-linked network. The deployment of large numbers of EHF terminals provided badly needed capability for rising satellite communications (SATCOM) capability to support requirements, especially for precision-guided munitions strikes and mobile user communications. Unfortunately, Unmanned Aerial Vehicles (UAVs) could not link to either MILSTAR or DSCS satellites. As a result, military planners had to turn to civil and commercial satellite providers to supplement MILSAR and DSCS satellites for satellite communications.

Because of the limitations encountered in the first year of OEF combat operations, the Joint Staff appointed a team of experts to examine the OEF experience and propose options for increasing SATCOM capability for a possible conflict with Iraq. In the spring of 2003, war fighters had access to newer DSCS and MIL-STAR satellites in orbit. As a result, when coalition forces invaded Iraq in March 2003, the MILSTAR constellation handled secure communications, UAV surveillance video feeds, and reach-back intelligence routed from the United States to the Iraq theater. MIL-STAR, acting as a spaced-based switchboard, served to enhance network-centric warfare by providing mobile forces with essential video, facsimile, and data messages. Additionally, the Combined Air Operations Center stayed informed of evolving combat conditions and provided airborne strike aircraft with up-to-date target coordinates. The U.S. Navy used MILSTAR to send current targeting coordinates to ships in the Persian Gulf region, which, in turn, updated Tomahawk attacks.

Robert B. Kane

See also: Iraqi Freedom, Operation

Further Reading

Levis, Alexander H., John C. Bedford, and Sandra Davis, eds. *The Limitless Sky: Air Force Science and Technology Contributions to the Nation*. Washington, DC: Air Force History and Museums Program, 2004.

Spires, David N. *Beyond Horizons: A Half Century of Air Force Space Leadership*. 2nd ed. Maxwell Air Force Base, AL: Air Force Space Command and Air University Press, 2007.

Mine Resistant Ambush Protected Vehicles

The mine resistant ambush protected (MRAP) vehicle is an armored truck developed by the U.S. military Operation Iraqi Freedom in Iraq and Operation Enduring Freedom in Afghanistan to protect troops from improvised explosive devices (IEDs). IEDs are field-expedient explosives developed by insurgents or guerrillas from whatever material is available. (A better name might be homemade bombs.) They can be simple artillery rounds rigged to a detonator that is set off remotely or by physical contact with vehicles or people, preferably enemies of those setting the mines. They can also be very sophisticated devices, with explosives designed to pierce armored vehicles. IEDs have been the cause of almost half the fatalities suffered by U.S. forces in Iraq, while about half the fatalities in Afghanistan have been from IEDs.

While IEDs can sometimes be effective against the Abrams tank and the Bradley Fighting Vehicle, they are very highly effective against unarmored transport vehicles. These include the High Mobility Multipurpose Wheeled Vehicle (Humvee), the modern equivalent of the World War II–era Jeep, and the 2.5- and 5-ton trucks and tanker trucks used to move personnel, ammunition, provisions, and fuel over the extensive roadways of Afghanistan and Iraq. These vehicles were not designed as armored combat vehicles; rather, they were specially designed and reinforced versions of commercial transports for military logistics purposes.

The threat from IEDs led to a program to armor Humvees and other transport vehicles, a program that continues. The basic problem of refitting such vehicles is how to cope with the added weight of the armor without making major modifications to engine power, transmissions, engine cooling, and suspension systems. This has to be balanced with the differences between up-armoring vehicles in the theater of war versus the extended choices of doing so at depots in the United States.

A parallel approach to retrofitting existing vehicles has been the development and fielding of MRAPs to provide better protection for vehicles and crews. MRAPs are wheeled vehicles with a "V" shaped hull and armored plating designed to deflect the impact of IEDs. They were used in small numbers in Iraq and Afghanistan in 2003 for route clearance and explosive ordnance disposal (EOD). The protection they provided led to the U.S. Department of Defense decision in 2007 to make deployment of MRAPs a high priority.

The resulting program involves three categories of MRAPs based on size and mission. Category I MRAPs are 7–15 tons, carrying a crew of two plus four passengers, mainly for urban transportation. Category II vehicles weigh between 15 and 25 tons, carry a crew of two and eight passengers, and are designed for road escort, ambulance, and EOD missions. Category III vehicles weigh 25 tons or more, carry a crew of two plus four passengers, and are designed for EOD missions that require more equipment than can be carried in Category II vehicles. The dimensions and missions have already changed, and will likely be further refined as testing and fielding proceeds.

Several companies, both domestic and foreign, have had various types of vehicles under development or in production, and as the U.S. military began to invest in armored vehicles, many companies competed for the new market, potentially worth several billion dollars. The vehicles are called Cougar, Buffalo, Maxx-Pro, Caiman, and Alpha. The Defense Department continues to prefer referencing the vehicles as Category I, II, and III MRAPs, but the commercial names have also remained, leading to some confusion, as the Cougar and Caiman come in both 4X4 and 6X6 versions. Domestic production companies have included Force Protection Industries, BAE Systems of North America, Navistar subsidiary International Military and Government LLC, Armor Holdings LLC, Oshkosh Truck, General Dynamics, Textron, and Protected Vehicles. Companies in Canada, Germany, Israel, and South Africa have also been involved because they have also been developing new, armored wheeled vehicles.

The designs of the vehicles vary. Some have a one-piece hull and chassis. Others have the hull bolted to the chassis. Some have the "V" shaped armor covering the entire vehicle, while others have that protection only for the crew and passengers. There are variations in mobility both on and off the road, engine size, and dimensions. All have been through extensive tests at Aberdeen Proving Ground and elsewhere, and are being evaluated by in-field performance in Iraq and Afghanistan.

By the end of 2007 the Defense Department had placed orders for 7,774 MRAPs and projected a total requirement of 23,000 if troop levels remained steady in Iraq. By April 2008 there were about 5,000 MRAPs in Iraq, with projections of having about 6,000 by December 2008. Costs through fiscal year 2009 were estimated at $25 billion. Costs are based on the actual cost of the various vehicles, which vary widely even within category, and mode of shipment. The military prefers air transport to bring the vehicles into the war zone, but doing so costs $135,000 for each vehicle, compared with just $18,000 by ship.

Although several vehicle models are in Iraq and Afghanistan, there are three that represent the categories well. Their characteristics demonstrate the flux in the scope of the Defense Department categories in a very short time. For Category I, the Navistar MaxxPro, a model that dominates that category with $3.5 billion in orders, has an 8.7-liter six-cylinder diesel engine that produces 330 horsepower. It is 21 feet long, 8.5 feet wide, and 10 feet high. It weighs 40,000 pounds, has a ground clearance of 11 inches, and carries a 2-man crew and up to 10 passengers. The cost is $549,000.

For Category II, the Force Protection Cougar 6X6 has a 7.2 liter diesel engine that produces 330 horsepower. It is 23 feet long, 8.5 feet wide, and 8.8 feet high. Weighing in at 39,000 pounds, it has a 15-inch ground clearance. It carries a crew of two and eight passengers. Unit cost is $649,000.

The Force Protection Buffalo represents Category III. Its 12-liter six-cylinder diesel engine produces 400 horsepower. It is 27 feet long, 8.25 feet wide, and 13 feet high. The weight is 45,320 pounds, ground clearance is 16 inches, and it has a crew of two plus four passengers. The $855,000 cost includes a remote-controlled external arm to help with EOD. Its large size allows more EOD equipment.

The armored Humvee has a 6.5-liter diesel V-8 engine producing 190 horsepower. It is 16 feet long, 7.5 feet wide, and 6.25 feet high. It weighs 12,000 pounds and has a ground clearance of 16.8 inches. Carrying four people, its unit cost is $150,000.

It is impossible to determine what the U.S. military, both army and marines, will eventually choose for transport vehicles, both wheeled and tracked, armored or not. It is clear that the decisions will be based not only on testing in the United States but also on performance of the many versions of transport vehicles. They will be expected to perform in the varied terrain presented by Iraq and Afghanistan, which ranges from desert to densely populated urban areas and from sea level to mountain ranges higher than any in the continental United States, with climates of intense heat to below-zero temperatures and widely different challenges posed by rain, snow, drought, and blinding sandstorms. Ground clearance will be a critical factor for off-road travel. Size will be important not only for maneuverability in crowed urban areas but for transport to the field of battle, especially by air. The height of the vehicles will be important as bigger targets are more vulnerable to attack from armor-piercing rounds from rocket-propelled grenades (RPGs) and other weapons. If applied with thought, the lessons learned from actual combat in Iraq and Afghanistan should lead to a U.S. military equipped with the best possible range of transport vehicles for future challenges.

Daniel E. Spector

See also: IRAQI FREEDOM, Operation

Further Reading

Dixon, Chris. "Blast Proof Wheels for the Mean Streets of War Zones." *New York Times*, February 24, 2008.

Feickert, Andrew. *Mine-Resistant, Ambush-Protected (MRAP) Vehicles: Background and Issues for Congress.* Washington, DC: Congressional Research Service, Library of Congress, 2007.

Schwartz, General Norton A. *Statement before the Senate Homeland Security and Government Affairs Committee.* Washington, DC: U.S. Government Printing Office, September 27, 2007.

Mines and Mine Warfare, Land

Land mines are stationary explosive weapons planted in the path of an enemy to hinder movement or to deny access to certain territory. Mines may be considered both offensive and defensive weapons. Mines are generally concealed and rigged so that they will be initiated by the presence of either enemy troops or vehicles, save in instances when they are exploded by remote control. Land mines produce casualties by direct explosive force, fragmentation, shaped-charge effect, or the release of harassing agents or lethal gas. Land mines include improvised explosive devices (known today as IEDs), which were employed extensively by insurgents during the Iraq War.

There are two main types of land mines: antitank (AT) and antipersonnel (AP). Antitank mines are large and heavy. They are triggered when vehicles such as tanks drive over or near them. These mines contain sufficient explosives to destroy or damage the vehicle that runs over them. They also frequently kill people in or near the vehicle. Antitank mines are laid in locations where enemy vehicles are expected to travel: on roads, bridges, and tracks.

Antipersonnel mines are triggered much more easily and are designed to kill or wound people. They may be laid anywhere and can be triggered by stepping on them, pulling on a wire, or simply shaking them. Antipersonnel mines may also be rigged as booby traps to explode when an object placed over them is removed. Generally speaking, AP mines contain small amounts of explosives. They are therefore smaller and lighter than antitank mines. They may be as small as a pack of cigarettes. Antipersonnel mines come in all shapes and colors and are made from a variety of materials.

Mines are normally laid in groups to form minefields. There are several types of these fields. Defensively, the hasty protective minefield provides local, close-in security protection for small units. This minefield employs no standard pattern in laying the mines. An example of a hasty protective minefield would be placing mines to cover a likely avenue of approach by an enemy force. A second type is the point minefield. It is utilized primarily to reinforce other obstacles, such as road craters, abatis, or wire obstacles not associated with hasty protective minefields. A third type is the tactical minefield. Its primary use is to arrest, delay, and disrupt an enemy attack. The field may be employed to strengthen defensive positions and protect their flanks. A fourth type is the interdiction minefield. It is utilized to trap or harass an enemy deep in his own territory, assembly areas, or defensive positions. Artillery- or air-delivered scatterable mines are ideal for this type of minefield.

Modern land mines may be said to date from the Russo-Japanese War (1904–1905), but World War I witnessed continuous use of land mines to protect trench lines. Land mines continued to play an important role during World War II. Two important developments took place in land-mine warfare during that conflict: the appearance of the antitank mine; and the introduction of antipersonnel mines employed against infantry and to protect antitank mines from detection and removal.

Many current antitank mines are derived from those of World War II. For example, the TMM1, produced in the former Yugoslavia, and the PT Mi-Ba, produced by the Czech Republic and Slovakia, are descendants of the German antitank Tellermine 43 and 42. The American designs are the M-15 and M-21 series; the Russians produce a similar mine, the TM-46, the Italians the M-80, and the Chinese the Type 72. These are canister-shaped mines that are buried using tilt rod fusing and pressure fusing. They range from 10 to 30 inches in diameter and 3 to 7 inches in height. They contain between 7 and 15 pounds of high explosives. Another popular design is the square AT mine, such as the American M-19, Italian VS-HCT2, or Belgian PRB-ATK M3. The square mine is approximately 10 inches square and 4–5 inches high with 5–25 pounds of explosives. Many of these are magnetic-influence mines with pressure as a backup fusing system.

Antipersonnel mine models introduced during World War II are still in service with only minor modifications. Examples are the Russian antipersonnel mine POMZ (and the later model POMZ-2M, a stake mine consisting of a wooden stake with a cast-iron fragmentation body). The Russian PDM-6 APM is basically the wooden-cased mine used during the Russo-Finnish War of 1939–1940. Its successors, the PDM-7, PDM-7ts, and PDM-57, are employed worldwide. There are also bouncing mines similar to the U.S. M16 series or the Russian OMZ (fragmentation obstacle APM or "Bouncing Betty")—canister mines topped with a pressure fuse. Such mines stand five to seven inches tall (including the fuse) and are three to four inches in diameter, with approximately one pound of explosive. The improvised version of these APMs consists of an artillery shell or a mortar bomb buried nose down in the ground. It is similar to IEDs used in both the Vietnam and Iraq wars.

After World War II the trend in land mines has been toward miniaturization and substitution of plastic parts for metal ones. For example, the American M14 series, first used in Vietnam, and the Russian APM PFM-1 and PFM-1S, first used during the Israeli-Syrian conflict of October 1973 and

massively by Soviet troops in Afghanistan, are small air-delivered plastic weapons with a low metallic signature. Other common APMs with low metallic content are the Type-72 series (People's Republic of China), encountered throughout Southeast Asia; and the PMN (Russia) present in Asia (Afghanistan, China, Iraq, Vietnam) and in southern Africa, where it is known as the "Black Widow." These are all small canister-type mines 2.5–4 inches in diameter and 1.5–4.5 inches in height. They all use pressure fusing. They carry one to four ounces of explosive.

The Korean War (1950–1953) saw widespread use of mines, particularly in the intense, largely static warfare of the second half of the war following the entry of the PRC in the fighting. The demilitarized zone across Korea remains one of the most heavily mined areas in the world. The Vietnam War of the 1960s and 1970s saw an increase in the use of APMs offensively as part of ambushes, with the American M18 Claymore as well as its copies in the Soviet MON 50 and Chinese Type 66. These mines are generally command-detonated. All are of curved rectangular shape. The Claymore was about 1 inch thick, 3.5 inches tall, and 8–12 inches long, filled with 1.5 pounds of explosive with a layer of metal balls (similar to 00-Buck shotgun pellets) faced toward the target area. These mines are never buried but are positioned on bipod legs that allow aiming. These mines were employed in Vietnam offensively but were also defensively employed around fire bases (U.S. and allied forces) and sanctuaries (for communist forces).

The United Nations (UN) estimates that 24,000 people are killed and at least 10,000 are maimed each year as a result of active and inactive minefields. A high percentage of these casualties are children. The present method for clearing mines involves painstaking detection and careful destruction of the devices. In 2004 the UN listed 35 countries with minefields of more than 1,000 mines. Egypt leads the list with 23 million mines planted, followed by Iran with 16 million; Angola with 15 million; and Afghanistan, the PRC, and Iraq with an estimated 10 million each. It can take one person 80 days to clear 2.5 acres.

Those who clear the mines, known as deminers, are at great risk of becoming victims themselves. More than 80 deminers died in mine-clearing operations in Kuwait following the 1991 Gulf War. French deminers still clear mines and unexploded artillery shells from World War I and as far back as the Franco-Prussian War (1870–1871). It is estimated that worldwide up to 85 million antipersonnel mines await clearance. In 2004 the UN estimated the cost of laying a single mine at less than $10 but its removal at $1,800.

In 1991 nongovernmental organizations and individuals began discussions regarding a ban on antipersonnel land mines. In October 1992 the International Campaign to Ban Landmines (ICBL) was formed by founding organizations Handicap International, Human Rights Watch, Medico International, Mines Advisory Group, Physicians for Human Rights, and Vietnam Veterans of America Foundation. The ICBL called for an international ban on the production, stockpiling, transfer, and use of antipersonnel land mines, and for increased international resources for mine clearance and mine victim assistance programs.

An international treaty often referred to as the Ottawa Mine Ban Treaty was negotiated in 1997. It is formally named The Convention on the Prohibition of the Use, Stockpiling, Production and Transfer of AntiPersonnel Mines and On Their Destruction. Among the first governments ratifying the treaty were Belgium, Canada, France, Germany, and the United Kingdom. The treaty went into effect in March 1999. In recognition of its achievements, the campaign was awarded the Nobel Peace Prize in 1997. Signa-tories to the treaty include all Western Hemisphere nations except the United States and Cuba, all NATO states except the United States and Turkey, all of the European Union except Finland, 42 African countries, and 17 nations in the Asia-Pacific region, including Japan. Important military powers not ratifying the treaty include the United States, Russia, China, India, Pakistan, and North and South Korea.

The treaty binds states to destroy their stockpiled antipersonnel mines within 4 years and those already in the ground must be removed within 10 years. In addition to comprehensively banning antipersonnel mines, the treaty requires signatories to perform mine clearance and urges mine victim assistance programs. Despite the treaty, mines continued to be laid in such nations as Angola, Cambodia, Senegal, and Sudan.

Herbert F. Merrick

See also: Iraqi Freedom, Operation

Further Reading

Crol, Mike. *History of Landmines.* London: Pen and Sword Books, 1998.

Davies, Paul. *War of the Mines: Cambodia, Landmines and the Impoverishment of a Nation.* London: Pluto, 1994.

Heyman, C. *Trends in Land Mine Warfare: A Jane's Special Report.* London: Jane's Information Group, 1995.

Matthew, Richard, Bryan McDonald, and Ken Rutherford, eds. *Landmines and Human Security: International Politics and War's Hidden Legacy.* New York: State University of New York (SUNY) Press, 2004.

McGrath, Rae. *Landmines: A Resource Book.* Milwaukee: University of Michigan Press, 2000.

Missile Systems, Iraqi

Among weapons in the Iraqi missile arsenal, one system stood out: the Soviet-designed Scud B missile and its variants. Scud missiles were very much in the news during the 1991 Persian Gulf War. The Scud B carries a 1,000-pound warhead and has a range of 175 miles. Modified Iraqi models developed during the war against Iran (1980–1988), like the al-Hussein and al-Abbas missile, could strike up to 375 and 575 miles, respectively. The most modern of the Scud variants was the al-Hijarah, with a range of 466 miles. To obtain this longer range, Iraqi scientists had to reduce the missile's payload. The modified Scuds lacked a sophisticated guidance system, and an al-Abbas missile fired to maximum range could hit anywhere within about a 3-mile radius. The Iraqi leadership apparently chose not to use the al-Hussein and al-Abbas missiles during Operation DESERT STORM.

Before DESERT STORM began, U.S. intelligence had identified 64 fixed Scud missile sites in western Iraq, all aimed at Israel. Twenty-eight of those sites were complete, with the balance nearing completion. The fixed sites were easy targets to attack with the precision weapons systems available to the U.S. military at the time. Iraq also had an unknown number of mobile Scud launchers placed on Soviet-made tractors or locally manufactured tractors and trailers. Intelligence estimates held that Iraq possessed 48 such mobile launchers, but this was not certain.

Because of their potential to deliver chemical weapons and indiscriminately

An Iraqi FROG artillery rocket system captured during Operation DESERT STORM in February 1991. (U.S. Department of Defense)

strike both civilian and military targets, the Scuds received the most attention of any Iraqi weapons during the Persian Gulf War. The threat posed by Iraq's surface-to-surface ballistic missiles greatly worried coalition military and political leaders. If Iraqi missiles were used to attack Israel, it seemed likely that Israel would retaliate and that this would cause the allied coalition, which included a number of Arab nations, to break apart.

During the Persian Gulf War, Iraq fired 91 Scuds. About half of them were directed at Saudi Arabia and 3 at Bahrain; the balance struck Israel. Although the missile strikes against Israel caused some public panic and caused 4 people to die from heart attacks, the missiles directly killed only 2 people while wounding another 200 Israelis.

The political impact of the missile attacks against Israel was nonetheless considerable. As expected, the Israeli public and some political leaders demanded retaliation. In response, the George H. W. Bush administration rushed Patriot antimissile missiles to Israel. Their presence helped calm the Israeli public and end the likelihood that Israel would enter the war.

Simultaneously, the United States devoted enormous effort to locating and destroying mobile Scud launchers. This proved to be the most difficult problem of the war. The Scud crew loaded and prepared the launcher in a hidden position, and then drove the vehicle to a separate launch site that the crew had already surveyed. Set up and launch occurred quickly. Essentially, the mobile launchers could fire from almost anywhere inside Iraq.

From January 18 to February 6, 1991, the Iraqis fired 29 Scuds from their western desert. Thereafter, the effect of the intense coalition anti-Scud efforts reduced the rate of fire. Iraqi launch teams had to fire blindly, making the already inaccurate Scud even less likely to hit its target. For three weeks following February 6, Iraq launched only 11 missiles, 2 of which fell harmlessly in the desert.

Iraq protected its forward troops in Kuwait from coalition air attack with a mixture of missiles and guns. The missile systems included short-range SA-9s and SA-13s as well as shoulder-fired SA-14s and SA-16s. Behind the front lines, the older SA-2 and SA-3 formed the backbone of the Iraqi air defense system. The SA-2 has a range of 31 miles. The SA-3, which has a range of 14 miles, was specifically designed to destroy aircraft flying at low and medium altitudes. The Iraqis positioned SA-6s in fixed sites to defend airfields, command and control centers, and important logistical centers. They composed the centerpiece of the Baghdad air defense system. A few SA-8s also were used to defend other strategically important areas.

At the time of the Persian Gulf War, most of the ships in the Iraqi Navy were obsolete. However, Iraq did possess 13 missile boats armed with the French-built Exocet but principally with the Soviet-designed Styx antiship missile. The Exocet had a range of more than 100 miles and warhead of 75 pounds. The larger Styx had a range of 16–45 miles and carried a far larger 1,100-pound warhead. The Persian Gulf War showed that coalition warships, with their overwhelming numerical and technological superiority, had little to fear from Iraqi naval missiles, however.

The Iraqi Air Force presented a potentially more serious threat to coalition forces. During the Persian Gulf War, the Iraqi Air Force possessed a small number of sophisticated missiles for attacks against land or sea targets. Iraq had purchased most of these missiles from France. In addition, Iraqi development programs had produced the

Faw family of air-to-surface cruise missiles derived from the Soviet Styx. The threat posed by Iraqi air-launched missiles was demonstrated well prior to the Persian Gulf War. On March 17, 1987, the Iraqis mistakenly hit the U.S. Navy frigate *Stark* (FFG-31), which was operating in the Persian Gulf, with 2 air-launched AM-39 Exocet antiship missiles. The attack badly damaged the frigate and killed 37 crewmen. Nevertheless, during the Persian Gulf War the Iraqis achieved no hits with air-launched missiles.

Iraq also possessed about 50 land-based antiship missiles called Silkworms, derived from the Chinese design. The Silk-worms had a range of about 70 miles. On February 25, 1991, the Iraqis fired two Silkworms at the U.S. battleship *Missouri*. A U.S. Navy radar warning system detected 1 incoming missile. The British destroyer *Gloucester* then destroyed this Silkworm. The second Silkworm fell harmlessly into the Persian Gulf. A coalition air strike then destroyed the Iraqi missile site.

The Iraqi missile arsenal also included the Soviet-designed FROG-7 (Free Rocket Over Ground). The Frog-7 was able to deliver chemical and possibly nuclear weapons. The FROG-7 could propel a 990-pound chemical warhead about 37 miles from a mobile launcher. Because it was obsolete by 1991, its major threat was as a potential terror weapon. The Iraqi leadership apparently chose not to utilize this weapon during the Persian Gulf War.

The number of missiles Iraq retained after the Persian Gulf War was unclear. However, Iraq did still possess significant stocks of modern air-to-air missiles. Consequently, the Iraqi air defense system was considered to be among the world's most formidable. The Iraqi air defense arsenal included a heavy surface-to-air arsenal with an estimated 130 to 180 SA-2s, 100 to 125 SA-3 launchers, 100 to 125 SA-6s, 20 to 35 SA-8s, 30 to 45 SA-9s, some SA-13s, and about 30 Roland VII and 5 Crotale surface-to-air missiles. Republican Guard air defense units used the proven SA-6 mobile surface-to-air missile to protect high-value strategic targets. The Iraqi command also positioned SA-7 and SA-10 antiaircraft missiles near key buildings to provide a last line of defense. In addition, Iraqi ground units carried an estimated 2,000 man-portable SA-7s and SA-14 antiaircraft missiles along with a handful of SA-16s.

Under the allied aerial onslaught beginning during the Persian Gulf War, the Iraqis learned to rapidly move their missile and radar units to avoid allied retaliation. In addition, the Iraqis skillfully employed decoys. However, overall the Iraqi air defense system was completely overshadowed by the sophisticated, state-of-the-art, allied aerial attacks. During tens of thousands of allied aerial sorties over Iraqi territory between 1991 and 2003, the Iraqis never managed to shoot down an allied manned aircraft. This trend continued through the 2003 Iraq War. The Iraqis were unable to effectively engage high-altitude coalition aircraft. Although they tried to defend major strategic targets including the command posts of senior Iraqi leaders, they failed.

The Iraqi missile arsenal on the eve of the Iraq War (Operation IRAQI FREEDOM) included French-designed Matra 530, Matra 550, and Matra Super 530 air-to-air missiles. The only major improvement the Iraqi Air Force made between the Persian Gulf War and the Iraq War was the installation of French-designed Matra Magic 2 air-to-air missiles on the Dassault Mirage F-1, a French-built fighter/attack aircraft. This missile gave the Mirages a useful "dogfight" missile. However, the Iraqi Air Force never flew during IRAQI FREEDOM.

Iraq also retained a variety of air-to-surface missiles, such as the AM-39 Exocet and some surface-to-surface, long-range missiles including the Al-Samoud 2 and Ababil-100 missiles and an estimated 12–25 surviving Scuds dating from the early 1990s. However, these missiles lacked the range, accuracy, and destructive capacity to be a serious threat to allied aircraft.

On March 20, 2003, Iraq launched its first theater ballistic missile against Kuwait. Subsequently, Iraq fired such additional theater ballistic missiles as the Ababil-100 and such cruise missiles as the CSS-C-3 Seersucker. A typical Iraqi missile operation occurred on March 20 and 21, when the Iraqis fired seven missiles at Kuwait, four of which were intercepted by Patriot batteries and three of which were allowed to strike unpopulated areas.

James Arnold

See also: Iraq, Air Force; IRAQI FREEDOM, Operation, Air Campaign; U.S. Air Force, Iraq War

Further Reading

Cordesman, Anthony H. *The Iraq War: Strategy, Tactics, and Military Lessons.* Westport, CT: Praeger, 2003.

Dunnigan, James F., and Austin Bay. *From Shield to Storm: High-Tech Weapons, Military Strategy, and Coalition Warfare in the Persian Gulf.* New York: William Morrow, 1992.

Jane's Armour and Artillery, 1990–1991. London: Jane's Information Group, 1990.

Jane's Armour and Artillery, 2001–2002. London: Jane's Information Group, 2001.

Spencer, Jack. *Ballistic Missile Threat Handbook.* Washington, DC: Heritage Foundation, 2002.

Missiles, Cruise

One of the most effective long-range weapons of modern warfare, cruise missiles essentially are unmanned aircraft that cruise at various altitudes until they dive or crash into their targets. Cruise missiles have also figured prominently in warfare in the Middle Eastern wars. Conceptually, all cruise missiles trace their roots to the German World War II V-1 buzz bomb. The only real differences between today's cruise missiles and the V-1 are the improved propulsion and guidance systems, increased range, far better accuracy, and a much more powerful warhead. The V-1's pulse jet engine and simple gyro-timing guidance system have given way to highly efficient turbofans and a variety of guidance systems tailored to the missile's specific mission or target. With those improvements has come a significant increase in price ($5,000 for a V-1 and $500,000 for a modern U.S. Tomahawk) as well as in capabilities. Today's cruise missiles can fly a terrain-hugging deceptive flight route to a target 1,000 miles distant and have a 70 percent probability of a direct hit (99 percent chance of hitting within 30 feet).

The United States and the Soviet Union both exploited the German V-1 in trying to develop their own cruise missiles after World War II. By 1950 both countries had working prototypes of turbojet-powered flying bombs under development. The best known of the American cruise missile models were the U.S. Navy's Regulus and the U.S. Air Force's Hound Dog. Like the V-1, these missiles were seen as area attack weapons, but the American missiles carried nuclear instead of conventional warheads. The Regulus had a range of 600 miles and was designed to be launched from submarines, while the similarly ranged Hound Dog was air-launched from Boeing B-47 Stratojet and Boeing B-52 Stratofortress bombers. Neither American missile was particularly accurate, and both left service by the mid-1960s.

With more accurate and more powerful submarine-launched ballistic missiles entering service, the major Western naval powers dropped their cruise missile programs. Moreover, their possession of aircraft carriers obviated the need for their surface ships to have a long-range strike capability. However, the carrier-shy Soviet Union lacked the resources and experience to build aircraft carriers and therefore pursued a different path, developing in 1958 the SS-N-1, a cruise missile intended to attack ships. It was followed two years later by the SS-N-2. These missiles differed from their American counterparts primarily in having a radar-based terminal guidance system that took them into the targeted ship. France was the only country to see any value in developing its own antiship missiles, but the program enjoyed only a low priority.

All this changed with Egypt's sinking of the Israeli destroyer *Eilat* in 1967 with an SS-N-2 Styx ship-to-ship missile. Suddenly all navies saw antiship cruise missiles (ASCMs) as the poor man's naval strike weapon. They also recognized the value of such weapons in situations where increasingly expensive aircraft carriers were not available. That led the United States and other powers to initiate accelerated cruise missile programs. ASCMs, such as the French Exocet and the American Harpoon and Tomahawk, were the first to enter service, but their relative light weight and expense, compared to that of an aircraft carrier and its air wing, led some to examine their use in the land-attack role. Meanwhile,

the Soviets developed their own family of long-range ASCMs: the SS-N-3, SS-N-12, SS-N-19, and SS-N-22.

The Yom Kippur (Ramadan) War in October 1973 saw the first naval engagements fought entirely between ASCM-equipped patrol boats. Having been stung by these weapons in the 1967 Six-Day War, Israel had developed its own ASCM, the Gabriel missile, and installed it on a new class of small patrol boats and corvettes. More importantly, Israel had developed tactics and electronic countermeasures to defeat the Soviet-built ASCMs supplied to Egypt and Syria. The October 7, 1973, Battle of Latakia saw six Israeli patrol boats sink five Syrian naval units. During October 12–13, the Israelis sank three more Egyptian missile patrol boats in the Battle of Baltim. Superior electronic countermeasures and tactics enabled the Israelis to win those battles without suffering any losses or damage. The Syrian fleet and Egypt's Mediterranean-based fleets remained in port for the rest of the war. Unfortunately for Israel, it had not deployed missile patrol boats to its Red Sea port, Eilat, and Egypt's Red Sea blockade remained unbroken.

By the early 1980s advances in micro-miniaturization, avionics, and navigation systems brought land-attack cruises back into vogue for both conventional and nuclear missions. The U.S. Land-Attack Tomahawk cruise missile initially was equipped with a Terrain Contour Matching guidance system, which enabled it to navigate over land by matching its onboard radar's picture of the terrain below against a computer-developed map of its flight route to the target. By the late 1990s, this system was replaced by a module that guided the missile by using the Global Positioning System (GPS), making the missile accurate to within three to six feet. Finally, a Digital Scene Matching

Area (DSMA) correlation feature was added to ensure that the missile would select the right target as it entered the target area by matching a digital image of the target scene (radar, optical, or infrared, or a combination of them) against an onboard image database. DSMA is particularly useful against mobile targets.

By the end of the Cold War, treaties and other considerations had driven all of the nuclear cruise missiles out of service. Conventional cruise missiles were now so accurate that Western political and military leaders had come to see them as politically safe precision weapons that could be employed in an infinite variety of situations.

ASCMs figured prominently in the 1982 Falklands War, with Argentine naval air force units sinking two British warships and damaging four others with their French-supplied AM-39 Exocet missiles. Iraq employed the same weapon in larger numbers against Iranian shipping during the Iran-Iraq War (1980–1988). Although the missiles failed to sink any tankers or merchant ships, they damaged more than 200, driving up insurance rates and forcing the United States to escort tankers through the Persian Gulf during the war's final year. More ominously, on March 17, 1987, the Iraqis hit the U.S. Navy frigate *Stark* (FFG-31) with two Exocets, killing 37 crew members and injuring 21 (the total casualties represented more than a third of the crew). The crew saved the ship, but it took more than 18 months to repair the damage and return it to service.

The 1991 Persian Gulf War saw the first major employment of land-attack cruise missiles. The anti-Iraq coalition opened Operation DESERT STORM by launching 122 of the U.S. Navy's Tomahawk land-attack missiles (TLAMs) against key Iraqi air defense posts, radar systems, and communications facilities. The TLAMs were employed almost entirely against targets considered too dangerous or risky for attack by aircraft. Typically, they preceded an air strike, taking out a key facility that was critical to the Iraqis' local or area air defense. The United States fired nearly 300 TLAMs during the war at a total cost of approximately $360 million.

The TLAMs then became the weapon of choice for U.S. retaliation against terrorist attacks, used to strike al-Qaeda and related camps in Afghanistan and the Sudan in the late 1990s. More than 250 were fired during Operation IRAQI FREEDOM in 2003, and America's 2001 invasion of Afghanistan was also preceded by a series of TLAM strikes against Taliban-related targets.

Cruise missiles are a relatively inexpensive, expendable alternative to expensive aircraft and ballistic missiles. Unlike bomber aircraft, they do not put crew members in harm's way. For nations not concerned with accuracy, cruise missiles remain a cheap solution to their long-range strike problem. However, for militaries seeking precision, for both antiship and land-attack missions, cruise missiles have become the complex weapons of choice for retaliatory strikes and the initial military operations conducted during a war. The newest have incorporated stealth technologies to make them more difficult to detect and engage. Others rely on supersonic dash speeds to defeat air defenses. In any case, cruise missiles are used to take out key enemy command centers, air defense sites, and airfields before manned aircraft are committed to the fight. In peacetime, cruise missiles are used for situations where a rapid and precise attack is required and the political-military leadership doesn't want to risk pilot losses.

China, France, India, Israel, Russia, Taiwan, and the United States produce ASCMs, but only two countries—the United

States and Russia—manufacture land-attack cruise missiles. China, India, and Pakistan are developing indigenous cruise missiles that are expected to enter operational service. Undoubtedly, the 21st century will see a proliferation of cruise missiles. In combination with unmanned aerial vehicles, they will become an increasingly prominent element of modern warfare.

Carl Schuster

See also: IRAQI FREEDOM, Operation; IRAQI FREEDOM, Operation, Air Campaign; U.S. Air Force, Iraq War

Further Reading

Finlan, Alastair. *The Gulf War, 1991.* Oxford: Osprey, 2004.

Frieden, David R. *Principles of Naval Weapons Systems.* Annapolis, MD: Naval Institute Press, 1985.

Herzog, Chaim. *The Arab-Israeli Wars: War and Peace in the Middle East from the War of Independence to Lebanon.* Westminster, MD: Random House, 1984.

Hewson, Robert. *Jane's Air-Launched Weapons, 2001.* London: Jane's Information Group, 2002.

Hooten, Ted. *Jane's Naval Weapons Systems, 2001–2002.* London: Jane's Information Group, 2002.

Knight, Michael, ed. *Operation Iraqi Freedom and the New Iraq.* Washington, DC: Washington Institute for Near East Policy, 2004.

Tripp, Robert. *Lessons Learned from Operation Enduring Freedom.* Santa Monica, CA: RAND Corporation, 2004.

Mosul

Iraq's third largest city, Mosul is located on the west bank of the Tigris River, some 250 miles north of Baghdad. Mosul's 2008 population was estimated at about 1.8 million; only Baghdad and Basra are larger. The city was the site of the Battle of Mosul (November 8–16, 2004). Muslin, a finely woven cotton fabric, was once produced in the city in great quantities, and it may have been named for Mawsil, the French version of the town's Arabic name.

This predominantly Kurdish city is the hub of both Iraq's oil and domestic electricity production and was the scene of ongoing Arabization efforts by Iraqi president Saddam Hussein's Baath Party. Mosul's Kurdish majority proved to be the stumbling block in the U.S. and Turkish negotiations prior to the March 2003 invasion of Iraq. The Battle of Mosul in 2004 was one of the last steps in the Anglo-American–led fight for control of Iraq during Operation IRAQI FREEDOM.

Mosul is built on a site rich in Assyrian history. The city is located where, in 850 BCE, King Assurnasirpal II of Assyria chose to build Nineveh where the city of Nimrud had been located. Later, in 700 BCE, Sennacherib, king of Assyria, made Nineveh the capital of Assyria. After changing hands a number of times over the next few hundred years, the city remained a critical trade center because of its position on key trade routes. Mosul would remain a critical part of the trade route until the opening of the Suez Canal in 1869. The discovery of oil and the construction of the Qyurrah refinery in the 1920s led to Mosul's return to strategic and economic importance.

In 1958 Abd al-Karim Qasim, as a part of his plan to integrate non-Arab ethnic groups into Iraqi cities, began encouraging Kurds to relocate to Mosul. Hussein and his Baath Party undertook an aggressive plan to Arabize Mosul, however, and many of those Kurds who had survived the Arabization returned to traditionally Kurdish regions either by choice or by force. After the overthrow of Hussein in March 2003, some Iraqi Kurds called for

Mosul to be included in the Kurdish regional government. These displays of Kurdish nationalism have angered Sunni Arabs and certainly soured U.S.-Turkish relations.

In 2003 the United States had planned to launch an arm of its invasion into Iraq from bases in Turkey, with the goal of quickly securing the oil fields at Mosul. Because of questions about the disposition of the Kurds, however, the Turks refused to allow the Americans to stage any part of the invasion from Turkish soil. Therefore, instead of being secured in the initial hours of the war, Mosul was not taken until April 11, 2003, two days after the fall of Baghdad, when Kurdish fighters assumed control after Hussein's forces abandoned the town. After days of looting and fighting between Kurds and Arabs, the Kurds relinquished control of the city to U.S. troops.

Mosul was also the scene of the shoot-out between Hussein's sons Uday and Qusay and coalition troops on July 22, 2003, in which both men were killed. In November 2004 after insurgents conducted coordinated attacks on Iraqi police installations, the Mosul police fled the city. This precipitated the Battle of Mosul, in which U.S. and Iraqi forces together with Kurdish fighters retook the city on November 16.

Since the Battle of Mosul, the city has been plagued by violence and disorder. In December 2004 a suicide bomber killed scores of people, including 14 U.S. soldiers and 4 Halliburton employees.

In 2005 an Iraqi government official was assassinated in the city. Ethnic and sectarian violence in Mosul increased sharply between 2005 and 2007, and the city's buildings and infrastructure have been in increasingly poor repair. In January 2008 another suicide bombing leveled an apartment building in Mosul, killing 36 people; the following day, the city's police chief was assassinated. The continuing unrest has coincided with a large exodus of middle-class and professionals from the city, only complicating the situation in Mosul. In May 2008 the Iraqi army, with U.S. support, launched a major campaign to bring law and order back to Mosul. A 2009 investigation concluded that more than 2,500 Kurds had been killed in the city since 2003.

Keith Murphy

See also: Hussein, Qusay; Hussein, Uday; IRAQI FREEDOM, Operation; Kurds

Further Reading

Ricks, Thomas E. *Fiasco: The American Military Adventure in Iraq.* New York: Penguin, 2006.

Tucker, Mike. *Among Warriors in Iraq: True Grit, Special Ops, and Raiding in Mosul and Fallujah.* Guilford, CT: Lyons, 2005.

Mosul, Battle of

Pitched battle fought in the city of Mosul, located in northern Iraq some 250 miles northwest of Baghdad, during November 8 through 16, 2004. The battle involved the United States Army 1st Battalion, 24th Infantry Regiment, Iraqi Security Forces (Iraqi police, Iraqi Army, Iraqi National Guard, and Iraqi Border Patrol), and Kurdish Peshmerga fighting Iraqi insurgents (former Baath Party members, fundamentalist factions with ties to the al-Qaeda in Iraq organization, and fighters from other "extremist" groups). The Battle of Mosul was brought on as much by political expediency as it was by the need to protect civilians from harassment by the insurgents. It ended in a clear-cut victory for coalition forces.

The Battle of Mosul occurred simultaneously with another furious battle between coalition forces and insurgents in Fallujah. The

Second Battle of Fallujah (November 7–23, 2004) drew insurgents and foreign fighters in droves. The coalition responded to the insurgent attacks with overwhelming force, which included recalling Lieutenant General David Petraeus and the 101st Airborne Division to Fallujah. The 101st had been maintaining a peaceful occupation of the primarily Sunni Mosul for the preceding year. Coalition troops took little time to rout the insurgency, and the surviving insurgents fled Fallujah. A number of them then went to Mosul.

The 25th Infantry Division was deployed to Mosul in mid-October 2004 to replace the 101st Airborne. This was approximately the same time that displaced insurgents began arriving from Fallujah. The insurgents announced their arrival with an enormous wave of kidnappings and beheadings that left more than 200 of Mosul's residents dead in the streets for resisting the insurgents.

On November 8, 2004, Iraqi insurgents began to carry out coordinated attacks within Mosul. It was on this day also that the 1st Battalion, 24th Infantry Regiment reported the first major engagement of what would become the Battle of Mosul, near the Yarmuk traffic circle in the western part of the city. Soldiers of the regiment were pinned down by coordinated mortar fire from the north and were being pounded from the other three directions by rocket-propelled grenades (RPG) and machine gun fire in a daylong firefight.

The insurgents also used this opening day of the battle to overrun two Iraqi police stations. The insurgents then cleaned out the station armories, taking weapons and flak jackets, and killed a dozen Iraqi policemen. The western media reported that the majority of the policemen had deserted their posts after reporting attacks by "hundreds" of insurgents against their stations.

However, when the Americans retook the stations, they estimated that only 20–30 insurgents had taken each station.

On November 9 insurgents successfully attacked a Forward Operating Base in Mosul, killing two American army officers. By November 10 Iraqi insurgents were openly taking to the streets in defiance of coalition forces, and by November 11 they had taken another Iraqi police station and destroyed two others. The time had come for a coalition counteroffensive.

Members of the U.S. 24th Infantry Regiment were sent out in an effort to crush the insurgents between two companies. The blow was aimed, again, at the strategically critical Yarmuk traffic circle. The 24th encountered fierce resistance as it pushed from house to house in close-quarter urban fighting. Yet with air support, the 24th was able to regain control of four of the five bridges over the Tigris River.

In the meantime, the insurgents sacked nine more police stations, destroying eight and occupying the ninth. On November 12, additional insurgent reinforcements arrived and, despite U.S. Air Force bombing, by November 13 insurgent forces held as much as 70 percent of Mosul. The insurgents became so secure in their military superiority that they began seeking out members of the Iraqi Security Forces to behead.

Coalition reinforcements began to arrive by November 13, including a battalion of the U.S. 25th Infantry Regiment, a group of Kurdish Peshmerga fighters, and elements of the Iraqi Special Forces and National Guard. On November 16 U.S. forces retook the fifth insurgent-held bridge over the Tigris and began to sweep through all of Mosul except for the western sector. The Americans met little resistance, but the insurgents burned many of the police stations they had occupied. By November 16, the major fighting was over. The western sector of Mosul, however, would remain in insurgent hands until another coalition surge involving an influx of 12,000 troops arrived in December and January 2005. This was timed to secure Mosul for Iraq's first democratic elections in January.

The coalition official casualty report for the Battle of Mosul was 4 U.S. soldiers killed, 9 Peshmerga fighters killed, and 116 Iraqi Security Forces killed (as many as 5,000 are believed to have deserted). Total losses for insurgents are unknown, although 71 were confirmed killed. Also, 5 civilians were reported killed, as were 2 contractors (1 British and 1 Turkish). Precise casualty figures, including the number of wounded, remain unknown, and some estimates claim much higher death tolls for both the civilians and insurgents.

The importance of the battle could be measured by the fact that, although there were mass desertions of Iraqi police and security forces targeted by insurgents, a sense of esprit de corps and pride among Iraqi forces developed, which had been sorely lacking before the event. In turn, the police and the security forces became better equipped to handle the insurgency, and the Iraqi citizenry gained trust in them, which led to the citizenry providing more information to coalition forces regarding insurgent activity. The terrorist tactics employed by the insurgents in the battle backfired. However, Mosul remained one of the most violent places in Iraq as of the spring of 2009.

Keith Murphy

See also: Fallujah, Second Battle of; Mosul

Further Reading

Allawi, Ali A. *The Occupation of Iraq: Winning the War, Losing the Peace.* New Haven, CT: Yale University Press, 2007.

Tucker, Mike. *Among Warriors in Iraq: True Grit, Special Ops, and Raiding in Mosul and Fallujah.* Guilford, CT: Lyons, 2005.

Mullen, Michael Glenn

U.S. Navy admiral and chairman of the Joint Chiefs of Staff since 2007, Michael Glenn Mullen was born in Los Angeles, California, on October 4, 1946. After graduation from the U.S. Naval Academy at Annapolis, he was commissioned in the navy in 1968. He first served in the waters off Vietnam in a variety of surface warfare positions. Additional deployments and exercises took him to the Caribbean and the Mediterranean. In 1973 Mullen assumed command of his first ship, the gasoline tanker *Noxubee*.

Mullen next reported to the U.S. Naval Academy, where he served as a company tactical officer and later as executive assistant to the commandant of midshipmen. He then returned to sea duty, gaining further experience aboard the guided missile cruisers *Fox* and *Sterett*. These ships featured increasingly advanced naval weapons systems with vastly improved capabilities that transformed naval operations during the 1980s. Mullen gained operational experience in the Western Pacific, Indian Ocean, and Red Sea.

In 1985 Mullen graduated from the Naval Postgraduate School in Monterrey, California with a master's degree in operations research. He then assumed command of the guided missile destroyer *Goldsborough*. Deploying to the Persian Gulf, he participated in the maritime escort of Kuwaiti oil tankers during the Iran-Iraq War (1980–1988).

Following command of the *Goldsborough*, Mullen served as director of the division officer course at the Navy Surface

Warfare Officer School and, following promotion to captain on September 1, 1989, became a staff officer in the office of the secretary of defense for the director, Operational Test and Evaluation Force. He then assumed command of the Ticonderoga-class cruiser *Yorktown*, conducting a broad range of missions, from support of the United Nations (UN) embargo of Haiti to counter-drug operations and joint and multinational exercises in the North Atlantic. Mullen was then assigned to the Bureau of Naval Personnel, where he served as the director, Surface Officer Distribution and later as director, Surface Warfare Plans, Programs and Requirements Division. Still later, following his promotion to rear admiral on April 1, 1996, he became the bureau's deputy director, affording him invaluable experience in manpower and resource management.

Later in 1996 Mullen was named commander of Cruiser-Destroyer Group 2, where he was in command of the ships, submarines, and aircraft of the *George Washington* Battle Group. The battle group deployed to the Mediterranean, where it participated in peacekeeping operations. The following year, it served as the cornerstone of the U.S. military presence in the Persian Gulf, compelling Iraq to comply with UN disarmament inspections, as well as enforcing the no-fly zone over southern Iraq. Following promotion to rear admiral on October 1, 1998, Mullen was chosen to serve as the director, Surface Warfare Division, Office of the Chief of Naval Operations. Responsible for the direction of acquisition plans and programs for the navy surface force, Mullen gained vital understanding of resource management, planning, programming, and budgeting.

On November 1, 2000, Mullen was promoted to vice admiral and was named the combined commander, U.S. Second Fleet and North Atlantic Treaty Organization (NATO) Striking Fleet Atlantic. Mullen soon found himself back in Washington, D.C., however, assuming responsibility for the direction and management of all navy acquisition programs as the deputy chief of Naval Operations for Resources, Requirements and Assessments. He guided the navy's resource decisions during critical reevaluations in the aftermath of the September 11, 2001, terror attacks, directing such key programs as the Next Generation Destroyer, Littoral Combat Ship, and Theater Ballistic Missile Defense. After two years as the navy resource director, Mullen was promoted to full admiral on August 28, 2003, and named the 32nd vice chief of naval operations. He had served as vice chief for just over a year when he was reassigned as the commander of the NATO Allied Joint Force Command Naples and simultaneously commander of U.S. Naval Forces Europe. Mullen immediately established clear priorities for these separate but closely connected commands, but as quickly as they were on course, Mullen was recalled to Washington.

On July 22, 2005, Mullen became the 28th chief of naval operations. He assumed command of a service facing issues of relevance, an apparent loss of operational significance, and the profound cost of continuing war in the Middle East. In response, Mullen committed the navy to easing the strain on the nation's land forces by assigning naval personnel to serve in an unusually broad range of supporting roles. Faced with a tight fiscal environment, Mullen ensured that the navy's budget priorities were clearly aligned with the realities of the strategic environment. In regard to the navy crisis of mission, Mullen immediately directed that a new maritime strategy be developed to guide the efforts of the nation's maritime services. After nearly two years of study and collaboration, "Co-operative Strategy for 21st Century Sea-power" was released. It was the nation's first maritime strategy document developed collaboratively and signed by all three of the nation's maritime services, the navy, marines, and coast guard.

On October 1, 2007, Admiral Mullen was appointed the 17th chairman of the Joint Chiefs of Staff. He assumed the post amid the most divisive and politically charged environment since the Vietnam War era. Almost immediately, he demonstrated a pragmatic, long-term view of U.S. military requirements by voicing concern over the broader effects of continuing U.S. military commitments in Afghanistan and Iraq, and campaigned for a broad, strategic reassessment.

Mullen explained that a rebalancing of global strategic risks was needed and that a comprehensive, sustainable long-term Middle East security strategy was a vital priority. He also asserted the requirement for a more balanced, flexible, and ready force. Describing a future characterized by persistent conflict and irregular warfare, but simultaneously uncertain and unpredictable, Mullen argued that U.S. forces must not only possess the ability to conduct counter-insurgency operations but also remain unmatched in their ability to fight a conventional war. Mullen helped secure legislation passed by Congress to increase military strength by 100,000 personnel. He also instituted efforts to ease the tempo of operational deployments and began a measured troop redeployment from Iraq.

Kenneth Szmed Jr.

See also: Iraqi Freedom, Operation

Further Reading

Baer, George W. *One Hundred Years of Sea Power: The U.S. Navy, 1890–1990.* Stanford, CA: Stanford University Press, 1994.

Love, Robert W. *History of the U.S. Navy, 1775–1991.* Mechanicsburg, PA: Stackpole Books, 1992.

Polmar, Norman. *The Naval Institute Guide to the Ships and Aircraft of the U.S. Fleet.* 18th ed. Annapolis, MD: Naval Institute Press, 2005.

Multinational Force, Iraq

U.S.-led military command of coalition forces in Iraq, established on May 15, 2004 and disbanded December 31, 2009. The Multi-National Force–Iraq (MNF-I) was created ostensibly to combat the growing Iraqi insurgency, which began in earnest in late 2003 and early 2004; it replaced Combined Joint Task Force 7, which had been in operation from June 2003 to May 2004.

Commanders of the MNF-I have included lieutenant generals Ricardo Sanchez (May–June 2004), George W. Casey (June 2004–January 2007), David Petraeus (January 2007–September 2008), and Raymond Odierno (September 2008–January 1, 2010). The MNF-I was tasked with bringing the growing Iraqi insurgency to an end but was largely unsuccessful in that effort until the George W. Bush administration placed General Petraeus in command and implemented a troop surge that placed as many as 30,000 additional U.S. troops on the ground in Iraq. The strategy seemed to have worked, for violence had fallen off markedly beginning by late 2007; Petraeus was given much of the credit for this development. At the same time, the so-called Anbar Awakening groups in Iraq also helped to curb sectarian and insurgent violence. The current MNF-I commander, General Odierno, while acknowledging that the surge has provided strengthened security forces, credits a change in counterinsurgency strategy more than the surge itself in reducing the level of violence. Referring to it as an "Anaconda strategy," Odierno has explained the strategy as a comprehensive approach that has shown success in, among other areas, cutting off insurgents from their support within the Iraqi population.

Since its inception, the MNF-I has overwhelmingly comprised U.S. troops; the second-largest deployment is from Great Britain. The size of the MNF-I has been fluid, but on average it has contained around 150,000 combat-ready personnel, the vast majority of whom have been American. The troop surge brought the total closer to 180,000, but that number has dwindled as troop withdrawals began in 2008. Working with the MNF-I, but not falling under its direct command, are the United Nations (UN) Assistance Mission–Iraq, which provides humanitarian aid and observation, and the North Atlantic Treaty Organization (NATO) Training Mission–Iraq, whose goal is to train Iraqi security, police, and military personnel. The major component parts of the MNF-I are Multi-National Security Transition Command; Gulf Region Division, U.S. Corps of Engineers; Joint Base Balad; Multi-National Corps–Iraq; Multi-National Division–Baghdad; Multi-National Division–North; Multi-National Force–West; Multi-National Division Center; Multi-National Division–Southeast.

In addition to battling the Iraqi insurgency and other indigenous violence, other goals of the MNF-I include support and aid to the Iraqi government, reconstruction efforts, specialized training of Iraqi military personnel, intelligence-gathering, and border patrols. When the MNF-I is withdrawn in its entirety, it is expected that Iraq will have been pacified; will have a stable, representative democratic government; and will be able to protect itself from internal pressures and foreign intrusions. The December 2008 Status of Forces Agreement between the U.S. and Iraqi governments stipulates that all U.S. troops be withdrawn by December 31, 2011. Under the terms of this arrangement, U.S. troops vacated Iraqi cities by July 31, 2009. The Iraqis concluded similar agreements with other coalition forces that still maintained a presence in Iraq.

Numerous nations supplied troops to the MNF-I, many of which were withdrawn by the end of December 2008. The participating members, along with the size of their deployments included: United States (145,000 troops as of December 2008), Great Britain (4,000 as of December 2008), Romania (500 as of December 2008), Australia (350 as of December 2008), El Salvador (300 as of December 2008), and Estonia (40 as of December 2008).

Those nations that participated but were withdrawn by December 31, 2008, included (figures in parentheses represent peak deployments): South Korea (3,600), Italy (3,200), Poland (2,500), Georgia (2,000), Ukraine (1,650), Netherlands (1,345), Spain (1,300), Japan (600), Denmark (545), Bulgaria (458), Thailand (423), Honduras (368), Dominican Republic (302), Czech Republic (300), Hungary (300), Azerbaijan (250), Albania (240), Nicaragua (230), Mongolia (180), Singapore (175), Norway (150), Latvia (136), Portugal (128), Lithuania (120), Slovakia (110), Bosnia-Herzegovina (85), Macedonia (77), New Zealand (61), Tonga (55), Philippines (51), Armenia (46), Kazakhstan (29), Moldova (24), and Iceland (2).

To entice potential coalition partners to join the MNF-I effort, the U.S. government offered a plethora of financial aid and other incentives. Because the invasion of Iraq had not been sanctioned by the UN, the United States found it more difficult to convince other nations to become involved in the postwar stabilization effort in Iraq. Some nations, and previously close allies, however, refused to take part in the mission, despite U.S. promises of financial and other rewards. The United States reportedly offered Turkey up to $8.5 billion in loans if the country sent peacekeeping troops to Iraq; Turkey, which had forbade the use of its bases during the March 2003 invasion of Iraq, demurred. France and Germany refused any participation in Iraq. Some countries, such as Great Britain and Australia, were offered lucrative private-contractor business that would help fuel their economies. The Bush administration, however, refused to acknowledge that there were any quid pro quo arrangements in the assembling of international forces in Iraq.

Paul G. Pierpaoli Jr.

See also: Iraqi Insurgency; Odierno, Raymond; Petraeus, David Howell

Further Reading

Cockburn, Patrick. *The Occupation: War and Resistance in Iraq.* New York: Verso, 2007.

Keegan, John. *The Iraq War: The Military Offensive, from Victory in 21 Days to the Insurgent Aftermath.* New York: Vintage, 2005.

Myers, Richard Bowman

A U.S. Air Force general and chairman of the Joint Chiefs of Staff (JCS) from 2001 to 2005, Richard Bowman Myers was born in Kansas City, Missouri, on March 1, 1942.

He graduated from Kansas State University in 1965 and entered the air force through the Reserve Officers' Training Corps (ROTC) program. He served as a fighter pilot during the Vietnam War, accumulating 600 combat flying hours. In 1977 he earned a master's degree in business administration from Auburn University.

Myers was promoted to brigadier general in April 1990 and was assigned as director of Fighter, Command and Control and Weapons Programs in the Office of the Assistant Secretary of the Air Force for Acquisition in Washington, DC. In September 1992 he was promoted to major general, and in November 1993 he was promoted to lieutenant general. From July 1996 to July 1997 he was the assistant to the chairman of the JCS. He then commanded the Pacific Air Forces at Hickham Air Force Base, Hawaii, during July 1997 to July 1998. He was promoted to full general in September 1997.

From August 1998 to February 2000 Myers headed the North American Aerospace Defense Command and U.S. Space Command. He also commanded the Air Force Space Command and was the Department of Defense manager of the space transportation system contingency support at Peterson Air Force Base, Colorado.

Myers was vice chairman of the JCS from March 2000 to September 2001. As vice chairman, he served as chairman of the Joint Requirements Oversight Council, as vice chairman of the Defense Acquisition Board, and as a member of the National Security Council (NSC) Deputies Committee and the Nuclear Weapons Council. In addition, Myers acted for the JCS chairman in most aspects of the planning, programming, and budgeting system, including participation in the Defense Resources Board.

In August 2001 President George W. Bush nominated Myers as chairman of the JCS. Myers thus had held his new position for only a few weeks—and had not yet been confirmed by the U.S. Senate—when the terrorist attacks of September 11, 2001, took place. After the second plane hit the World Trade Center during the attacks, Myers called the Pentagon's command center and ordered the military's alert status to defense condition (DEFCON) 3, the highest state of military readiness since the October 1973 Yom Kippur (Ramadan) War. Myers was confirmed to the chairman's position by the Senate and was sworn in on October 1, 2001.

Myers closely analyzed the status of both Afghanistan and Iraq prior to U.S. military involvement in those two countries in Operation ENDURING FREEDOM beginning in 2001 and Operation IRAQI FREEDOM beginning in 2003, respectively. While much of the blame for the debacle of the war in Iraq fell on Secretary of Defense Donald Rumsfeld, Myers has also been sharply criticized. Many argue that, among others things, he underestimated the potential likelihood of a postinvasion insurgency and failed to provide enough troops to secure the country from the very beginning.

Myers retired on September 30, 2005. Two months later he was awarded the Presidential Medal of Freedom. The following year he was named Foundation Professor of Military History at Kansas State University. Myers has also served on several boards, including those of Northrop Grumman and United Technologies Corporation. He holds the Colin L. Powell Chair for National Security, Leadership, Character and Ethics at the National Defense University, and in 2009 he published his memoirs, *Eyes on the Horizon*.

Charlene T. Overturf

Air Force general Richard Myers was chairman of the Joint Chiefs of Staff between 2001 and 2005. He has been criticized for underestimating the number of ground troops required in the invasion of Iraq in 2003 and ignoring the possibility of an Iraqi insurgency. (U.S. Department of Defense)

See also: Bush, George Walker; IRAQI FREEDOM, Operation

Further Reading

Fawn, Rick, and Raymond A. Hinnebusch, eds. *The Iraq War: Causes and Consequence*. Boulder, CO: Lynne Rienner, 2006.

Lifton, Robert Jay, Richard Falk, and Irene Gendzier. *Crimes of War: Iraq*. New York: Nation Books, 2006.

Myers, Richard B., and Malcom McConnell. *Eyes on the Horizon: Serving on the Front Lines of National Security*. Riverside, NJ: Threshold Editions, 2009.

Woodward, Bob. *State of Denial: Bush at War, Part III*. New York: Simon and Schuster, 2006.

N

Najaf, First Battle of

Iraq War battle between U.S. forces and the Islamist Mahdi Army militia, controlled by Muqtada al-Sadr, during August 5–27, 2004. The Iraqi city of Najaf is located about 100 miles south of Baghdad and had a prewar population estimated at 585,000 people. Najaf is one of the holy cities of Shia Islam and a major center for Shia religious pilgrimages, education, and political power.

In March 1991, following the Persian Gulf War, the residents of Najaf rebelled against the regime of Iraqi dictator Saddam Hussein as part of a larger Shiite uprising against the government. Hussein's forces suppressed the uprising in the city with great brutality. Early in the Iraq War (Operation IRAQI FREEDOM), following two days of heavy fighting, Najaf was assaulted and then captured on April 1, 2003, by units of the U.S. 101st Airborne (Air Assault) Division, commanded by Major General David Petraeus.

Following the overthrow of Hussein's regime later that same month, Najaf witnessed the gradual emergence of the powerful cleric Muqtada al-Sadr, whose Mahdi Army militia was based in the city, as were the Badr Brigades. In April and May 2004 Sadr's militia led an uprising in Najaf that largely usurped control of the city from U.S. forces. Sadr's militia also took on U.S. and coalition military forces across the Shia-controlled areas of southern Iraq. On May 27 Sadr reached a deal with the Americans by which both sides agreed to withdraw

their forces from Najaf. The Mahdi militia soon began rebuilding their forces in the city, however.

On July 31, 2004, the 11th Marine Expeditionary Unit, commanded by Colonel Anthony Haslam, took up positions around Najaf, relieving the army's Task Force Dragon. The marines first clashed with the Mahdi militia on August 2, when a marine patrol approached a house believed to be occupied by Sadr. Major fighting erupted on August 5 when the Mahdi militia attacked an Iraqi government police station and the marines responded in force. On August 9 three additional battalions of troops from the 1st Cavalry Division were sent from Baghdad to Najaf to reinforce the marines. Combat took the form of street fighting, with the Mahdi militia employing rocket-propelled grenades, mortars, and automatic rifles against U.S. Abrams tanks, Bradley Fighting Vehicles, attack helicopters, and infantry. A number of Abrams tanks and Bradley Fighting Vehicles were knocked out or heavily damaged by rocket-propelled grenades, and one U.S. helicopter was shot down.

After a few days, the scene of the fighting had approached the Imam Ali Mosque and a huge adjacent cemetery known as the Wadi of Peace. Because the mosque and cemetery represent some of the holiest sites in Shiite Islam, concerns were expressed throughout the Arab world for their safety, but the heavy fighting continued.

The turning point in the battle came on August 26, when two F-16s dropped four

2,000-pound Joint Direct Attack Munition (JDAM) bombs on hotels near the Imam Ali Mosque, then occupied by the Mahdi militia. The air strike prompted Sadr to negotiate a truce the next day. The Mahdi militia agreed to turn in its weapons and leave Najaf. In return, U.S. forces also left Najaf, and security was turned over to the Iraqi police. The Imam Ali Mosque did not suffer any significant damage during the Battle of Najaf.

Casualty figures remain in dispute. The Americans claim that several hundred members of the Madhi Army were killed in the fight, but militia spokesmen claim the toll was fewer than 30 dead. Eight U.S. service personnel were killed and 30 more were wounded. The Battle of Najaf showcased not only the rise to prominence of such radical extremists as Sadr but also the general elevation of tensions between Shia, Sunnis, and Kurds in Iraq. By the end of 2004 U.S. and coalition forces found themselves locked in a deadly struggle with all the signs of a civil war, despite protestations to the contrary by both U.S. president George W. Bush and British prime minister Tony Blair. Indeed, the situation in Iraq continued to deteriorate until the summer of 2008, when some signs indicated that the Iraq insurgency violence had subsided a bit, a development the British and Americans said was the result of the troop surge, implemented in 2007.

Paul William Doerr

See also: IRAQI FREEDOM, Operation; Mahdi Army; Sadr, Muqtada al-

Further Reading

Bremer, L. Paul, with Malcolm McConnell. *My Year in Iraq: The Struggle to Build a Future of Hope*. New York: Simon and Schuster, 2006.

Ricks, Thomas E. *Fiasco: The American Military Adventure in Iraq*. New York: Penguin, 2006.

Woodward, Bob. *State of Denial: Bush at War, Part III*. New York: Simon and Schuster, 2006.

Najaf, Second Battle of

Fierce battle between the Iraqi army and police, heavily aided by U.S. and British military units and air power, and hundreds of well-armed followers of Ahmad al-Hassan al-Basri. The battle occurred on January 28, 2007, in Zarqa, a town located 10 miles from the southern Iraqi Shia shrine city of Najaf. Details about Basri, his messianic religious movement known as the Soldiers of Heaven (Jund al-Samaa), and the battle itself are hotly debated.

According to some accounts, based on interviews with captured members of the group, Basri was the deputy to Dhia Abd al-Zahra Khadhim al-Krimawi (who died in 2007), a shadowy Iraqi Shia leader who claimed to be Imam Mahdi, the 12th in a line of religious and political leaders who Shias believe will return at a time decided by God to usher in a period of absolute justice that will precede the Day of Judgment. The fate of Basri remains unknown, with some sources in the Shia religious establishment in southern Iraq claiming that he survived the battle and is living in seclusion, possibly in the southern shrine city of Karbala.

Following the suppression of the group, the Iraqi government and military spokespeople claimed that Basri, Krimawi, and their followers were really Sunnis and not Shias, although evidence of this is sketchy at best. The Iranian government, al-Qaeda, and remnants of the Iraqi Baath Party have all been accused of supporting the group. Initial Iraqi government reports claimed that foreign Sunnis from countries as far as Pakistan and Afghanistan were killed or captured fighting against Iraqi security forces. These reports were challenged, however, when dead and captured Jund fighters were identified as Iraqis instead of foreigners.

Anonymous sources in the Hawza Ilmiyya, the Shia seminary system in Najaf, have stated that Basri was a former student who left because of disagreements over religious theology with the seminary's religious scholars. Shia clerics loyal to Mahmoud Sarkhi al-Hassani, who heads another Shia messianic party in southern Iraq, denied that Basri and Krimawi were associated with their group. Hassani is a former student of Grand Ayatollah Sayyid Muhammad Sadiq al-Sadr, the father of Muqtada al-Sadr, and claims to be the representative of Imam Mahdi. His group broke with the larger Sadr Movement (Tayyar al-Sadr) over theological and political disputes, including a disagreement about who should assume command of the movement, Muqtada or Hassani. The latter has a relatively small but devoted following in southern Iraq. According to other sources, Basri was also a former student of the late Sadiq al-Sadr, a popular Shia religious opposition leader who was assassinated with two of his sons in 1999, probably by Baath Party operatives. These sources claim that the two had a falling out when the Iraqi Baathists attempted to split Sadiq al-Sadr's increasingly powerful sociopolitical network by sponsoring a rival splinter group, the Mehwadiya led by Basri.

Fighting began on January 28, 2007, when Iraqi police and a battalion of soldiers from the Iraqi 8th Army Division attempted to carry out a morning raid on an alleged safe house used by the Jund. They were acting on information that the group planned to assassinate Grand Ayatollah Sayyid Ali Husayn al-Sistani, Iraq's senior resident Shia religious authority, and other grand ayatollahs and senior religious leaders in Najaf. The assassinations allegedly were to be carried out during Ashura, the Shia period of mourning in commemoration for the martyrdom of Imam Hussein bin Ali and dozens of his companions and family members at Karbala in 680 by soldiers sent by the Umayyad caliph Yazid I. The Jund were reportedly acting on the orders of Basri to prepare for the return of Imam Mahdi and the establishment of a religious state governed with absolute justice, as foretold in Shia religious sources and traditions. Reportedly, group members planned to hide their weapons and use the sheer number of people, millions of Iraqis and foreign Shia, who flood into the southern Iraqi shrine cities of Najaf, Karbala, and Kufa during Ashura, to their advantage, hiding in the crowds to get close to the grand ayatollahs' residences.

The Iraqi soldiers and police were soon overwhelmed by hundreds of armed Jund fighters and became pinned down by heavy gunfire, forcing them to call for U.S. and British air support, which came in the form of air strikes by Lockheed Martin F-16 Fighting Falcons and Hughes/McDonnell Douglas AH-64 Apache helicopter gunships along with a small contingent of British fighter jets. The aircraft dropped 500-pound bombs on Jund positions, including significant numbers of fighters in a grove of trees in Zarqa. In the early afternoon, the U.S. 25th Infantry Division and other units were sent from bases near Baghdad to aid the besieged Iraqi units.

During the 15 hours of fighting, one U.S. Apache helicopter was shot down, killing its 2 crew members, and 25 Iraqi soldiers and police were also killed. Iraqi government and U.S. military estimates place the number of Jund casualties at somewhere between 250 and 400, although the number was probably closer to 250–263, among them Krimawi. More than 450 Jund fighters were captured alive and later tried by Iraqi courts. Millions of dollars and a large cache of weapons, including antiaircraft guns, rockets, and automatic rifles, were seized from the Jund's well-equipped compound.

In September 2007 an Iraqi court sentenced 10 Jund leaders to death and 384 fighters to prison terms ranging from 15 years to life. It freed 54. Despite the trial and the apparent decimation of the Jund, the group is but one of several messianic Mahdist Shia groups active in post-Hussein Iraq. The largest is the party led by Mahmoud al-Hassani, who claims the rank of grand ayatollah despite the fact that his religious scholarly credentials do not support his claims and he is not recognized as such by Iraq's Shia religious establishment, the *marjaiyya*. Hassani's popularity is reportedly growing in southern Iraq as a greater number of the country's Shias become disenchanted with the marjaiyya traditionalists and the ruling Shia political parties such as the Islamic Dawa Party, the Sadr Movement, and the Supreme Islamic Iraqi Council.

Christopher Paul Anzalone

See also: Najaf, First Battle of; Shia Islam

Further Reading

Cave, Damien. "Mystery Arises over Identity of Militia Chief in Najaf Fight." *New York Times*, February 1, 2007.

Cave, Damien. "250 Are Killed in Major Iraq Battle." *New York Times*, January 29, 2007.

Cockburn, Patrick. "US 'Victory' against Cult Leader Was 'Massacre.'" *Independent*, January 31, 2007.

Colvin, Ross. "US Military Still Probing Iraqi Cult Battle." *Reuters*, February 2, 2007.

Hardy, Roger. "Confusion Surrounds Najaf Battle." *BBC News*, January 31, 2007.

Jamail, Dahr, and Ali al-Fadhily. "Pilgrims Massacred in the 'Battle' of Najaf." *Asia Times*, February 2, 2007.

Santora, Marc. "Fierce Militia Fighters Catch Iraqi Army by Surprise." *International Herald Tribune*, January 30, 2007.

Visser, Reidar. *The Sadrists of Basra and the Far South of Iraq: The Most Unpredictable Political Force in the Gulf's Oil-Belt Region?* Oslo: Norwegian Institute of International Affairs, 2008.

Nasiriyah, Battle of

The Shiite-dominated town of Nasiriyah occupies an important location in southern Iraq. Situated some 225 miles southeast of the capital of Baghdad, Nasiriyah is the fourth most populous city of Iraq after Baghdad, Basra, and Mosul. In 2003 Nasiriyah had a population of some 560,000 people. It is also an important transportation hub, with key bridges spanning the Euphrates River on either side of the city. Located close to Tallil Airfield and the headquarters of the Iraqi Army III Corps of three divisions, Nasiriyah was thus a key objective in the first phases of the Iraq War. During the 1991 Persian Gulf War, Nasiriyah had been the most northerly point in Iraq for U.S. forces, with the 82nd Airborne having reached the city's outskirts.

In 2003 the task of taking Nasiriyah and the bridges over the Euphrates fell to U.S. Marine Corps Task Force Tarawa (TF Tarawa), commanded by Brigadier General Richard Natonski. TF Tarawa was the code

A U.S. marine assisting displaced Iraqi civilians caught in a firefight north of An Nasiriyah, Iraq, on March 26, 2003. (U.S. Department of Defense)

name for the 2nd Marine Expeditionary Brigade, centered on the 2nd Marine Regiment, Marine Aircraft Group 29, Company A of the 8th Tank Battalion (with M-1 Abrams tanks), and Combat Service Support Battalion 22. TF Tarawa was the vanguard of the I Marine Expeditionary Force (I MEF), commanded by Lieutenant General James Conway, that was centered on the 1st Marine Division led by Major General James Mattis.

TF Tarawa's assignments were to first secure Jalibah Air Base and then secure the bridges across the Euphrates and the Saddam Canal. Taking and holding these crossing points were essential for enabling the 1st Marine Division to continue its drive northward on Highway 7 toward Kut. With this accomplished, TF Tarawa was to keep open the supply corridor that would enable the 1st Marine Division to continue north and engage and defeat the Republican

Guard divisions defending the southern approaches to Baghdad.

In its drive north into Iraq from Kuwait, TF Tawara was obliged to move through the desert to get to Jalibah Air Base because the supply vehicles of the U.S. Army's 3rd Infantry Division, which had movement priority, occupied the roads. Meanwhile, the 3rd Infantry Division also advanced toward Baghdad, taking a crossing over the Euphrates west of Nasiriyah. As the 3rd Infantry Division defeated Iraqi forces in and around Tallil Airfield and bypassed Nasiriyah to the west, TF Tarawa moved on that city.

TF Tarawa departed Jalibah Air Base for Nasiriyah early on March 23, but taking the city did not go according to plan. Natonski had planned for the 1st Battalion, 2nd Marine Regiment, to move through the eastern part of Nasiriyah and seize one of the northern bridges, after which another battalion was to secure the city, thereby allowing the three regimental combat teams of the I MEF to continue the drive north on Route 7.

The marines had anticipated fighting at Nasiriyah but not the level of resistance encountered. One thing did go according to plan: much of the Iraqi 11th Division simply deserted. What the marines had also expected did not occur, however: an uprising by the population of Nasiriyah against the regime. The inhabitants had done so in 1991, and many had been massacred by the Saddam Hussein regime. The survivors had learned their lesson. Indeed, they now prepared to defend the city. The composition of those fighting is still disputed, with some of the fighters certainly being members of the Fedayeen Saddam who began arriving in the city on March 22 in private vehicles and commandeered buses. Although poorly trained, they were fanatical fighters and willing to die in a jihad. Under the command of ruthless Iraqi general Al Hassan al-Majid, a relative of Hussein who had charge of the south, the defenders of Nasiriyah prepared to do battle with the marines.

Fighting began as soon as the leading marine element, the 1st Battalion, 2nd Marine Regiment, supported by some armor, arrived at the city outskirts. The marines quickly destroyed nine stationary T-72 tanks—a number of them bereft of engines—that had been dug in to defend a railroad bridge south of the river.

At about 7:30 a.m., marines of A Company were startled to make contact with an American military truck belonging to the army's 507th Maintenance Company. The men in it informed the marines that their 18 trucks had been part of a 3rd Infantry Division supply column. The 507th Maintenance Company, which included female soldiers Jessica Lynch and Lori Piestewa, had taken a wrong turn on Route 7 and proceeded into Nasiriyah, where it had been ambushed. In the ensuing fighting, 11 American soldiers had been killed and 6 others, including Lynch and Piestewa, were taken prisoner. Piestewa died of her wounds shortly after capture, while the remaining 5 prisoners, including Lynch, were later rescued. Piestewa was a member of the Hopi tribe and is thus believed to have been the first Native American woman killed in combat in a foreign war. On learning of the plight of the 507th Maintenance Company, the marines immediately headed north and rescued a dozen wounded members of that unit.

Unfortunately for the marines, the appearance of the 507th Maintenance Company trucks had alerted the defenders of Nasiriyah to the imminent arrival of other American forces. The ensuing firefight and the desperate effort of the members of the maintenance company to escape also served to give the defenders a false sense of their ability to stop the Americans.

After a pause to refuel, the marines then drove to the Euphrates. The Iraqis had not blown the bridge, but a major firefight soon erupted. One company took a wrong approach to another bridge over the Saddam Canal, and a number of its vehicles became bogged down in soft sand. The marines resumed their advance to the canal down the city's main road, which they soon dubbed "Ambush Alley."

Supported by tank fire, the marines succeeded in getting across the canal, but one of their amphibious assault vehicles (AAV) took a hit from a rocket-propelled grenade (RPG) on the bridge. Four marines were wounded, and the AAV barely made it across the span. Worse, a Fairchild-Republic A-10 Warthog aircraft, supporting the marines, attacked marines on the north side of the bridge, mistaking them for Iraqis and killing six. Two other marine vehicles sent south of the river back down Ambush Alley as part of a convoy to remove wounded were struck and destroyed by RPG and small-arms fire that killed most of those inside. Heavy fighting for the bridgehead raged during the night, with the marines supported by Bell AH-1S Cobra attack helicopters. By the morning of March 24 the marines had control of both bridges and had suppressed some of the resistance along Ambush Alley. Determined to press on as quickly as possible in order to threaten Kut and thereby present the Iraqis with two threats to Baghdad, Conway, Mattis, and Natonski decided to push the 1st Marnie Regiment up Ambush Alley through Nasiriyah and up Highway 7. At the same time, the 5th and 7th Marine regiments were able to secure the bridge outside the urban area and reach Highway 1.

The 5th and 7th Marine regiments had a relatively easy time of it, but it was a different story for the members of the 1st Marine Regiment, pushing up Highway 8 on the evening of March 24. They came under heavy small-arms fire including RPGs and mortar fire. Sustaining relatively few casualties, however, the lst Marine Regiment passed through the city on the night of March 24–25 and was soon on its way to Kut.

TF Tarawa now was faced with the difficult task of clearing Nasiriyah in order to protect the marine supply line north to Routes 1 and 7. These efforts were severely impacted by the arrival of a *shamal*. This fierce sandstorm lasted several days and not only reduced air support available to the marines but also made the efforts to clear out snipers and fighters more difficult, complicating fighting conditions. Artillery proved to be the only all-weather continuous fire support asset for TF Tarawa. On March 26 high-explosive (HE) rounds with concrete-piercing fuses were fired against a

hospital that was serving as a paramilitary strong point and that was then seized by the marines. A concentrated artillery fire mission against an estimated 2,000 fedayeen at a railroad station in the southern part of the city reported to be preparing to launch a counterattack not only ended that threat but also killed some 200 of the fedayeen.

A number of marine vehicles were lost to RPGs, but the situation was eased by a cordon around the city that cut off resupply to the Iraqi fighters. With the end of the shamal and the arrival of unmanned aerial vehicles over Nasiriyah, more accurate targeting information was soon available. Marine aircraft also took part. Also, some residents began to come forward to identify Iraqi sniper nests and command centers, and Special Forces units also assisted in the targeting.

Intelligence provided by friendly Iraqis also enabled a team of marines, navy SEALs, and army Rangers to rescue Private Lynch and the other Americans who had been captured earlier. The fighting was largely over by March 29, but it was not until early April that Nasiriyah was completely secure. The fighting for the city had claimed 18 marines killed and more than 150 wounded.

Spencer C. Tucker

See also: Fedayeen; IRAQI FREEDOM, Operation

Further Reading

Cordesman, Anthony H. *The Iraq War: Strategy, Tactics, and Military Lessons.* Westport, CT: Praeger, 2003.

Keegan, John. *The Iraq War: The Military Offensive, from Victory in 21 Days to the Insurgent Aftermath.* New York: Vintage, 2005.

Livingston, Gary. *An Nasiriyah: The Fight for the Bridges.* North Topsail Island, NC: Caisson, 2004.

Lowry, Richard S. *Marines in the Garden of Eden: The True Story of Seven Bloody Days in Iraq.* New York: Berkley, 2006.

Murray, Williamson, and Robert H. Scales Jr. *The Iraq War: A Military History.* Cambridge, MA: Belknap, 2005.

Pritchard, Tim. *Ambush Alley: The Most Extraordinary Battle of the Iraq War.* New York: Ballatine, 2007.

National Intelligence Council

The center for midterm and long-term intelligence planning within the U.S. intelligence community. The National Intelligence Council (NIC) officially began operating in 1979. Its origins date back to 1947, when the U.S. government reorganized the nation's intelligence services via the National Security Act and created the Central Intelligence Agency (CIA). The director of central intelligence (DCI) had the responsibility of ensuring that all intelligence data was properly evaluated and shared among appropriate U.S. government organizations. Toward that end, Congress gave the DCI a permanent staff. However, intelligence estimates continued to be flawed. Consequently, acting in his capacity as DCI, in 1950 General Walter Bedell Smith created the Board of National Estimates. It was charged with preparing and disseminating assessments of both international trends and foreign threats to American interests. The Board of National Estimates operated as a council composed of experts in the various fields of intelligence and oversaw the production of National Intelligence Estimates.

In 1973 DCI William J. Colby reformed the way in which the board produced the National Intelligence Estimates. Colby was persuaded that the board had become too insular and out of touch. He thus eliminated the Board of National Estimates, replacing its council of experts with regional and functional specialists called national intelligence officers. These officers had the responsibility of drafting the National Intelligence Estimates. The CIA's Directorate of Intelligence and the analytical branches of the national intelligence community provided the national intelligence officers with staff and research support. In 1979 the national intelligence officers became the National Intelligence Council (NIC), with the mission of reporting directly to the DCI.

The NIC's mission is to serve as the intelligence community's center for midterm and long-term strategic thinking. The NIC's overall mission is to manage the intelligence community's estimative process, incorporating the best available expertise from inside and outside the government. It speaks authoritatively on substantive issues for the entire intelligence community. The NIC is charged with five formal functions: supporting the director of national intelligence in his role as head of the intelligence community, acting as a focal point for receiving and responding to queries from policy makers, broadening the intelligence community's perspective by reaching outside of the intelligence community to engage experts in academia and the private sector, assisting the intelligence community in responding to the changing requirements from policy makers, and leading the intelligence community in the production of National Intelligence Estimates and related products.

The NIC's National Intelligence Estimates are considered the most authoritative written judgments concerning national security issues. They contain comprehensive judgments regarding the likely course of future events of the entire intelligence community, an entity that after 2004 consists of the CIA; the Defense Intelligence Agency; the National Security Agency; the National

Geo-spatial Intelligence Agency; the National Reconnaissance Office; the State Department's Bureau of Intelligence and Research; Air Force, Army, Coast Guard, Marine Corps and Navy Intelligence; the Federal Bureau of Investigation (FBI); the Department of Homeland Security; the Department of Energy; and the Treasury Department. The NIC's stated goal is "to provide policymakers with the best, unvarnished, and unbiased information—regardless of whether analytic judgments conform to U.S. policy."

The formal structure of the NIC has a chairman, a vice chairman, a counselor, and a director of strategic plans and outreach. There are seven national intelligence officers assigned to geographic regions: Africa, East Asia, Europe, the Near East, Russia and Eurasia, South Asia, and the Western Hemisphere. Six national intelligence officers deal with specific areas of concern: economics and global issues, military issues, science and technology, transnational threats, warnings, and weapons of mass destruction (WMD) and proliferation. By the terms of the Intelligence Reform and Terrorism Prevention Act of 2004, the NIC reports directly to the director of national intelligence (DNI) and represents the coordinated views of the entire intelligence community.

Throughout its history, the NIC's process of creating National Intelligence Estimates has been fraught with uncertainty and subject to controversy. By definition, estimates are speculative. Estimates were performed when analysts often did not know something with precision or confidence. Effective estimates rely upon sound data—a problematic foundation given the active efforts of other nations to conceal their plans—and careful analysis. Because the estimates are used by the executive branch to craft policy and by

political parties to evaluate presidential choices, the analysts who craft the National Intelligence Estimates have frequently been subject to political pressures.

In the aftermath of the September 11, 2001, terrorist attacks followed by the U.S. invasion of Afghanistan and the U.S. invasion of Iraq, two NIC publications represented the council's efforts to provide U.S. policy makers with an assessment of how the world would evolve and to identify opportunities and negative developments that might require policy actions. "Mapping the Global Future 2020" sought to depict what the world would look like in 2020. "Global Trends 2025: A World Transformed" sought to provide a fresh examination of how global trends would unfold. The NIC, like other organizations within the intelligence community, came under scrutiny for its perceived failings in providing actionable information that may have prevented the September 11 attacks. But in fairness, the failings pervaded the entire intelligence apparatus as well as the FBI. The NIC again came under scrutiny after it became apparent that prewar intelligence concerning Iraq's WMD was either faulty or misrepresented. No WMD were found after the 2003 invasion of Iraq, even after a 16-month search.

James Arnold

See also: Central Intelligence Agency; Intelligence; Weapons of Mass Destruction

Further Reading

Ford, Harold P. *Estimative Intelligence: The Purpose and Problems of National Intelligence Estimating*. Washington, DC: Defense Intelligence College, 1993.

Steury, Donald P., ed. *Sherman Kent and the Board of National Estimates: Collected Essays*. Washington, DC: History Staff, Center for the Study of Intelligence, Central Intelligence Agency, 1994.

Theoharis, Athan, ed. *The Central Intelligence Agency: Security under Scrutiny*. Westport, CT: Greenwood, 2006.

National Security Agency

U.S. intelligence-gathering agency. Headquartered at Fort Meade, Maryland, the National Security Agency (NSA) is the component of the U.S. intelligence community that specializes in activities related to cryptography and signals intelligence (SIGINT). Established on November 4, 1952, by President Harry S. Truman in the wake of a series of intelligence failures regarding the Korean War, the NSA has served as the U.S. government's primary technical intelligence–collection organization since that time.

The United States was renowned for its success in the realm of SIGINT (the gathering and analysis of intercepted voice communications intelligence, or COMINT) and electromagnetic radiation (electronic intelligence, or ELINT) during World War II. Yet Americans entered the early years of the Cold War with a disorganized SIGINT apparatus loosely coordinated among the independent and oftentimes redundant cryptologic agencies of the U.S. Army, the U.S. Navy, and the U.S. Air Force. In line with the centralizing theme of the 1947 National Security Act, Secretary of Defense Louis A. Johnson established the Armed Forces Security Agency (AFSA) in 1949 to streamline SIGINT collection. Plagued by the weaknesses of limited jurisdiction and ill-defined authority, however, deficiencies in AFSA's relationship with the service agencies were made readily apparent prior to and during the outbreak of the Korean War in June 1950.

At the urging of President Truman, Secretary of State Dean Acheson appointed New York attorney George Abbott Brownell to head a probe investigating AFSA's failings. The resultant "Brownell Committee Report" advocated replacing AFSA with a centralized national agency capable of unifying all U.S. SIGINT efforts. Fully agreeing with this recommendation, within months President Truman had dissolved AFSA and quietly signed into law the NSA.

Throughout the 1950s and early 1960s the NSA established itself as a key intelligence player in virtually all major Cold War political and military conflicts. In 1953 the NSA began overflights of Soviet airspace using converted B-47 Stratojets equipped with various receivers capable of intercepting Soviet air defense radar signals. By intentionally triggering the activation of the Soviet air defense radar system, the B-47s could pinpoint and map the locations of Soviet systems on the ground, providing crucial information for U.S. pilots. By the late 1950s the Stratojets had been replaced by the high-flying U-2 reconnaissance jet, and over-flights to collect Soviet SIGINT data continued, focusing on radar emissions and telemetry information related to intercontinental ballistic missile (ICBM) launches. The overflight program ended suddenly amid an international crisis. On May 1, 1960, U-2 pilot Francis Gary Powers was shot down over the central Soviet city of Sverdlovsk. Initially disavowing any knowledge of the overflight program, the Eisenhower administration, when faced with irrefutable evidence presented by Soviet premier Nikita Khrushchev, was forced to concede that it had ordered the flights.

Although direct flights over Soviet airspace were terminated in the wake of the Powers controversy, the NSA maintained a robust collection effort utilizing ground, air, sea, and space-based antennas and sensors to monitor the transmissions of the Eastern bloc as well as nonaligned and allied nations. In an often contentious relationship with the U.S. Navy, NSA listening posts were established on both adapted warships such as USS *Liberty* and on smaller dedicated collection platforms such as USS *Pueblo* to loiter in international waters collecting transmissions, while NSA-directed submarines tapped into undersea communication cables. Ground stations concentrating on intercepting shortwave and very high frequency (VHF) emissions were established in strategically important locations around the globe, including Ellesmere Island in the upper reaches of the Arctic Circle, Ayios Nikolaos in Cyprus, Field Station Berlin in West Berlin, and Misawa Air Force Base in Japan. After the undisclosed launch of the first SIGINT satellite in June 1960, the NSA also began to establish an array of ground-based relay centers in remote locations on the periphery of the Soviet Union.

By the late 1970s the NSA was enjoying great success in decoding the encrypted Soviet messages that had previously eluded the U.S. intelligence community. As the NSA's mission grew, its budget increased exponentially. Exact budgetary figures from the Cold War period continue to be withheld as classified information as is the current budget, but during that time the NSA established itself as the largest U.S. intelligence agency in terms of both manpower and financial resources.

The proliferation of consumer-oriented electronic communication devices that began in the 1980s proved a boon to the NSA. With the advent of fax machines, cell phones, personal computers, and handheld computers, the NSA has greatly increased its ability to monitor transmissions of all kinds and from all around the world. Because of this, the NSA has been central in U.S. antiterrorism efforts. It is believed that

the NSA has the capability of intercepting and monitoring transmissions of most of the planet's electronic devices. This ability has come in handy since the Global War on Terror began in 2001, but it has also caused much consternation among those who fear further encroachments on privacy and civil liberties. In December 2005 the NSA came under great scrutiny when the *New York Times* published a story about the George W. Bush administration's order to tap telephone conversations of select Americans placing calls out of the country. The operation was carried out largely by the NSA and without the requisite court warrants. There have also been concerns that the NSA, working with Internet service providers, may be monitoring customers' Internet communications even between Americans, a situation with serious implications regarding U.S. civil liberties.

In early March 2003 an NSA memo revealed that the agency had been spying on UN delegates in order to learn their views and bargaining positions on the upcoming Iraq War vote. The operation included tapping the phones of delegates and staff members. The spying revelation does not appear to have affected the UN vote, which did not authorize invading Iraq.

Robert Berschinski

See also: Bush, George Walker; Central Intelligence Agency

Further Reading

Bamford, James. *Body of Secrets: Anatomy of the Ultra Secret National Security Agency.* New York: Anchor, 2002.

Bamford, James. *The Puzzle Palace: A Report on America's Most Secret Agency.* New York: Penguin, 1983.

Bright, Mark et al. "Revealed: U.S. Dirty Tricks to Win Vote on Iraq War." *Guardian/Observer*, March 1, 2003, http://www

.guardian.co.uk/world/2003/mar/02/usa
.iraq.

Johnson, Chalmers. *The Sorrows of Empire: Militarism, Secrecy, and the End of the Republic.* New York: Metropolitan Books, 2004.

National Security Council

U.S. agency utilized by the president of the United States and his chief military and political advisers to analyze and determine foreign (sometimes domestic) and military policy that will best protect the national security of the United States. The National Security Council (NSC) was established in 1947 under the auspices of the National Security Act of that year, which established the NSC as the central organization for coordinating foreign policy that would bring together all key national security policy makers. The act called for a small NSC staff and an executive secretary who would supervise the council's workings, resulting in a membership that was much smaller than today's NSC staff.

With the end of World War II, the United States became a global superpower. As the competition between the United States and the Soviet Union intensified into the Cold War, it was clear that a more centralized structure was necessary in order to discuss national security decisions. The resulting NSC has steadily grown in power since it was first convened by President Harry S. Truman, and today it is comparable to that of a cabinet-level agency.

The NSC is composed of the president (chair), vice president, secretary of state, secretary of the treasury, secretary of defense, and the national security adviser (assistant to the president for national security affairs). Serving as the military adviser

to the NSC is the chairman of the Joint Chiefs of Staff (JCS). The director of national intelligence (a position established only in 2005) serves as the NSC's intelligence adviser. Other regular but nonpermanent attendees include the chief of staff to the president, the counsel to the president, the assistant to the president for economic policy, the U.S. attorney general, and the director of the Office of Management and Budget. Other officials and representatives are invited to attend meetings as required.

Since the NSC was established it has continued to change and evolve with each presidential administration. Different events and situations have called for different processes and policies emanating from the NSC. Today the national security adviser is much more than an executive secretary who controls the flow of information. Instead, the national security adviser is a powerful adviser to the president. This has been accompanied by an exponential growth in the NSC staff. The NSC has also lost much of its earlier formality, and weekly meetings have not been common since the 1950s. More informal episodic meetings are the norm.

Despite the significant changes in the structure and operations of the NSC throughout the decades, its fundamental mission has not changed. The NSC continues to be used as a forum for discussion and debate before the president makes a final decision on matters relating to foreign, military, or national security policy. Since 1986 each president has been required to submit a National Security Strategy (NSS) annually. The NSS is a document that outlines the current threats to the national security of the United States and how the presidential administration plans to deal with these. Each administration chooses how best to use the NSC to create the NSS, but the process usually involves different committees, each drafting an NSS.

Since the 1991 Persian Gulf War the NSC has been deeply involved in conflicts in the Middle East. President George H. W. Bush used the NSC to good effect before and during the Persian Gulf War (Operation DESERT STORM). Brent Scowcroft, a former U.S. Air Force general, was perhaps one of the most effective NSC advisers in history, serving the George H. W. Bush administration from 1989 to 1993. Scowcroft's tenure was marked by unusually cordial relations with Secretary of State James A. Baker III, and the NSC dealt successfully with the end of the Cold War, the collapse of the Soviet Union, rocky relations with the People's Republic of China (PRC), the unification of Germany, and the invasion of Panama as well as DESERT STORM and its aftermath.

When President William J. Clinton took office in 1993, he greatly expanded NSC membership. Clinton used the NSC mainly to focus on using American power to create a safer world through humanitarian intervention, free trade, and the spread of democracy. His administration did, however, engage in military operations, with input from the NSC, including the bombardment of Iraq to punish it for failing to abide by United Nations (UN) sanctions, the bombing of suspected terrorist sites in Afghanistan and Sudan in retaliation for the U.S. embassy bombings in Kenya and Tanzania, and the North Atlantic Treaty Organization (NATO) bombing campaign against Serbia in 1999, designed to end the Kosovo War.

After President George W. Bush came into office in 2001, the terror attacks of September 11, 2001, greatly impacted the sessions of the NSC, which was headed by Condoleezza Rice until January 2005 and Stephen Hadley from January 2005 to January 2009. The president's 2002 NSS argued that while deterrence was a workable solution for the Cold War, such a policy could not effectively combat terrorism. This marked the implementation of the Bush Doctrine, which was shaped by Rice and other neoconservatives in the White House and argued for the use of preemptory force to foil terrorist acts before they could be perpetrated. This thinking led to the March 2003 invasion of Iraq. Rice went on to become secretary of state in Bush's second term, although she since seemed to moderate her position on the use of force. The Department of Home-land Security, created in 2002, also interacts with great frequency and on many issues with the NSC.

Following the election of President Barack Obama, in January 2009 retired U.S. Marine Corps general James L. Jones became national security adviser.

Arthur M. Holst

See also: Bush, George Walker; Central Intelligence Agency; Intelligence

Further Reading

Doyle, Richard B. "The U.S. National Security Strategy: Policy, Process, Problems." *Public Administration Review* 67 (2007): 624–629.

Newmann, William W. "Reorganizing for National Security and Homeland Security." *Public Administration Review* 62 (2002): 126–137.

Zegart, Amy B. *Flawed by Design: The Evolution of the CIA, JCS, and NSC*. Stanford, CA: Stanford University Press, 1999.

Negroponte, John Dimitri

U.S. diplomat and the first director of national intelligence (2005–2007). John Dimitri Negroponte was born in London, England, on July 21, 1939. His father,

John Negroponte, national intelligence director between 2005 and 2007, shown testifying before the Senate Armed Services Committee on February 28, 2006. Negroponte introduced much needed reforms in the U.S. intelligence community. (AP/Wide World Photos)

Dimitri, was a Greek shipping tycoon. Negroponte attended elite schools in the United States, including Phillips Exeter Academy and Yale University, from which he earned an undergraduate degree in 1960. Attending Harvard University Law School for only a brief time, he joined the Foreign Service in 1960 and stayed with the State Department until 1997. During his long career, Negroponte served in eight overseas posts, including in Asia, Latin America, and Europe. He also held a series of increasingly important positions with the State Department in Washington, DC. In 1981 he was appointed to his first ambassadorship, to Honduras, a post he held until 1985. He subsequently served as ambassador to Mexico (1989–1993) and the Philippines (1993–1996). From 1987 to 1989 Negroponte was

deputy assistant to the director of national security affairs in the Ronald Reagan administration.

Negroponte retired from the Foreign Service in 1997 and joined the publishing firm of McGraw-Hill as a senior executive. In 2001 President George W. Bush tapped him to become the U.S. ambassador to the United Nations (UN), a post he held until 2004. Negroponte worked at the UN to secure support for U.S. policies in the aftermath of the September 11, 2001, terror attacks and vowed not to bend to international pressure in the ensuing Global War on Terror. This stance did not always make him popular among his UN colleagues. In the run-up to the 2003 Iraq invasion, Negroponte was the Bush administration's reliable point man in dealing with the sometimes intransigent UN.

In April 2004 Negroponte was named ambassador to Iraq. He assumed his duties on June 30, when Anglo-American occupation forces turned sovereignty of Iraq over to the provisional government. Negroponte, who replaced L. Paul Bremer, was immediately faced with a rapidly expanding insurgency and the problems of stabilizing and rebuilding a war-torn nation.

A year later, in February 2005, President Bush named Negroponte as the first director of national intelligence, a new cabinet-level position. Negroponte was charged with coordinating the work of all of the nation's intelligence-gathering services. As such, he was largely responsible for establishing the budgetary requirements of the new intelligence apparatus, which approached $40 billion by 2006. Negroponte's appointment was lauded by many who saw in him the required steadiness of a diplomat combined with the ability to organize and lead. Having worked under both Democratic and Republican administrations, he was seen as a relatively bipartisan public servant who could be counted on to do the right thing in the face of considerable political pressures.

Negroponte wasted no time in instituting needed reforms in the intelligence community and reorganizing the intelligence-gathering apparatus to make it far more efficient and less vulnerable to leaks and political infighting. Indeed, his policies earned high praise from both executive-branch and congressional officials. In January 2007 Negroponte left his post to become deputy secretary of state, a position that he had long coveted and that he held until January 2009.

Paul G. Pierpaoli Jr.

See also: Bremer, L. Paul, III; Bush, George Walker; Intelligence

Further Reading

Draper, Robert. *Dead Certain: The Presidency of George W. Bush*. New York: Free Press, 2008.

U.S. Senate, Committee on Foreign Relations. *The Nomination of Hon. John D. Negroponte to be U.S. Ambassador to Iraq, April 27, 2004*. Washington, DC: U.S. Government Printing Office, 2004.

Neoconservatism

A form of conservative political thought and also a political movement that had its genesis in the 1964 presidential campaign of Republican candidate Barry Goldwater. Neoconservatism is most prevalent among rightist Republicans and has steadily gained followers over the years. It was said to be the prevailing mind-set in the foreign policy of President George W. Bush and many of his senior officials, including Vice President Richard (Dick) Cheney, Secretary of State Condoleezza Rice, Secretary of Defense Donald Rumsfeld, and Deputy Secretary of Defense Paul Wolfowitz. Irving Kristol, William Kristol, Charles Krauthammer, Richard Perle, Robert Kagan, and William Bennett are also identified as prominent neoconservatives (neocons). The term "neoconservative" can be controversial, however, because it is said to be pejorative or a code word used by those espousing anti-Semitic and/or anti-Israeli views. Many neoconservatives are either Jewish or strong supporters of Israel.

Neoconservatism rose to maturity in the 1970s as a reaction to the policies of détente pursued by presidents Richard Nixon, Gerald Ford, and Jimmy Carter in dealing with the Soviet Union. Some disenchanted liberals and conservatives favored confronting the

Soviet Union rather than tolerating or seeking to accommodate its allegedly aggressive policies. The foreign policy of the Ronald Reagan administration largely embraced neoconservative principles, the first administration to do so. Reagan placed renewed emphasis on military force and deterrence and promoting democracy by supporting what he called "freedom fighters" battling communist regimes or insurgencies. Reagan's staunch anticommunism and controversial 1983 speech denouncing the Soviet Union as "an evil empire" and blaming it for the arms race was vintage neoconservative thought, even if the term itself was not yet in vogue. In the same speech, Reagan characterized the Cold War as a struggle between "right and wrong, good and evil," just as George W. Bush labeled Iraq, Iran, and North Korea an "axis of evil" and the Global War on Terror as a war of moral righteousness against the forces of evil and tyranny. Part of neoconservative rhetoric—if not philosophy—tends to view the world in stark contrasts of black and white, leaving few gray areas that might yield to diplomacy rather than force.

One of the earliest neoconservative statements by George W. Bush came in a speech he delivered at the U.S. Military Academy, West Point, on June 1, 2002. In this speech, formalized in a document three months later titled "The National Security Strategy of the United States of America," Bush indicated that the Cold War–era doctrines of deterrence and containment were now less relevant because the new threats posed by al-Qaeda and other nonstate terrorist groups required new thinking. According to Bush, deterrence could not succeed against terrorist groups because, unlike governments, they do not have a nation or citizens to defend. Containment could not work with dictators, he claimed, who could deliver weapons of mass destruction (WMD) or secretly provide them to their terrorist allies.

Thus, Bush built the case for preemptive action to defend the United States. No longer would the United States wait for threats to materialize fully before taking action. Indeed, a central premise of the so-called Bush Doctrine and neoconservative thought is that the United States must take advantage of its military superiority and neutralize threats before they are capable of threatening American interests, even if this means acting unilaterally without the support of the international community. President Bush justified the invasion and overthrow of Iraqi dictator Saddam Hussein's regime in March 2003 by arguing that Hussein posed a growing threat to both American security and the stability of the Middle East. Therefore, Bush undertook military action before Hussein had rearmed with WMD.

Another important neoconservative theme is the so-called democratic peace theory: that the United States should promote democracy and freedom around the world because, as Democratic president Woodrow Wilson believed, democracies do not wage war with each other. This line of reasoning holds that it is dictatorships that are responsible for causing wars and threatening peace.

Critics of the Bush Doctrine and neoconservatism in general object to its alleged aggressiveness and militarism and its de-emphasis on diplomacy and international law to promote peace. Instead, critics find the ever-present willingness to use force as a threat to peace and stability, which can lead to wars such as the one in Iraq, predicated on faulty intelligence that was never questioned by civilian leaders until it was too late.

In more recent years, neoconservatism has lost some of its former luster. The apparent lack of WMD in Iraq, which had been a primary motivation for the March 2003 invasion of Iraq, led many to question the use of preemptive force in the absence of reliable intelligence. The Iraq insurgency, which has been raging since 2004, also gave pause to those who had previously believed that invading Iraq was a prudent course of action. Finally, the November 2006 mid-term elections sent a powerful signal to the Bush administration and neoconservatives. The electorate apparently had not bought the precepts of the neocons, and this likely was a major factor in the Republicans losing control of both houses of Congress in the November 2006 congressional elections. Rumsfeld was forced out within days of the election, and others of like mind also left the administration. Vice President Cheney, perhaps the most militant of the neocons, kept an exceedingly low profile after the 2006 elections and was rarely in the public eye until after he left office in January 2009.

Stefan Brooks

See also: Bush, George Walker; Bush Doctrine; Cheney, Richard Bruce; Perle, Richard; Rice, Condoleezza; Rumsfeld, Donald Henry; Wolfowitz, Paul Dundes

Further Reading

Bennett, William J. *Why We Fight: Moral Clarity and the War on Terrorism.* New York: Regnery, 2003.

Chernus, Ira. *Monsters to Destroy: The Neoconservative War on Terror and Sin.* Boulder, CO: Paradigm, 2006.

Dolan, Chris J. *In War We Trust: The Bush Doctrine and the Pursuit of Just War.* Burlington, VT: Ashgate, 2005.

Kaplan, Lawrence, and William Kristol. *The War over Iraq: Saddam's Tyranny and America's Mission.* San Francisco: Encounter Books, 2003.

Murray, Douglas. *Neoconservatism: Why We Need It.* New York: Encounter Books, 2006.

Night-Vision Imaging Systems

Night-vision technology utilizes image intensification and infrared thermal imaging to provide soldiers the ability to engage in their mission in the darkness of night and at other times of restricted light and reduced visibility.

At present engineers and scientists of the United States Army Research, Development and Engineering Command (RDECOM) at the Night Vision and Electronic Sensors Directorate (NVSED) are developing the military's night-vision devices (NVDs) in their directive to "own the night." NVDs intensify existing light, capturing ambient light from the moon, stars, and human-made sources. NVDs are sensitive to a broad segment of the spectrum of light, and therefore they intensify lights that are both visible and invisible to the human eye.

Light, a form of electromagnetic radiation, consists of extremely fast oscillations creating frequencies that define in which part of the spectrum individual types of light are found. The spectrum from the highest to lowest frequencies is defined as X-rays, ultraviolet, visible light (violet to red), infrared, and radio waves. NVDs collect light from the visible and infrared sections of the spectrum to form images.

Light enters the NVD through a lens and strikes a high-powered photo cathode located within a vacuum tube that emits free electrons when struck by light. These electrons then strike a phosphor screen, where the image is focused. A soldier

U.S. marines employ night-vision scopes to help them see in low-light situations while clearing and assessing objectives during training at Camp Lejeune, North Carolina, on September 14, 2009. (U.S. Department of Defense)

views this picture through an eyepiece that also magnifies it. Engineers designed the screen to display the image in green because the human eye can differentiate more shades of green than any other color produced by phosphor when chemically activated. In this way NVDs enable soldiers to accomplish their objectives without activating their own light source, which could compromise mission stealth and expose troop positions and maneuvers.

Night-vision imaging systems had their genesis during World War II when the United States, Great Britain, and Germany experimented with development of the technology. Improving the German cascade image tube became the goal of night-vision engineers during the 1950s. About this time, the U.S. Army Corps of Engineers produced an infrared sniper scope, but the equipment required to use the scope proved

too bulky and required infrared searchlights that gave away troop positions to anyone who also had an infrared detecting scope. Additionally, the Radio Corporation of America (RCA) developed a near-infrared two-stage cascade image tube that used a multialkali photocathode to intensify ambient light. However, this technology had its limitations: the output was inverted and provided minimal gain in imaging. RCA solved this problem by adding a third stage, which corrected the inversion and increased the image gain but also made the tube too large for military use.

NVSED continued its development of NVDs and in the 1960s manufactured the first personal devices for troops as part of the First Generation Image Intensifier Program. The primary first-generation NVD was a small starlight scope that could be mounted as a rifle sight or used as a handheld viewer. The Vietnam War marked the first war in which U.S. troops used NVDs when the U.S. Army issued soldiers the small starlight scope in 1964. These first-generation image intensifiers lasted about 2,000 operating hours and could amplify light only 1,000 times.

The second generation of image intensifiers came into production during the late 1960s and early 1970s. Engineers were able to compact more electron gains into a smaller tubes. Second-generation NVDs increased operating time from 2,500 to 4,000 hours. Equally important, these additions enhanced the amplification ability of these devices 20,000 times.

The development of linear scanning imagers in the 1970s offered a high-quality image by using multiple-element detector arrays and allowed for the creation of Forward Looking Infrared (FLIR) systems. FLIR provides an advantage over image intensification because it layers infrared scans to provide the final image. This enables FLIR to work in total darkness and produce images despite fog, smoke, dust storms, and other masking agents that would obscure image-intensification NVDs.

FLIR systems saw first combat use in Kuwait and Iraq in 1991 during Operation DESERT STORM and proved invaluable to American soldiers. Night-vision imaging systems using image intensification and FLIR were fitted on M-1A1 and M-1A2 Abrams and M-60 Patton tanks, helicopters, airplanes, and tube-launched optically tracked wire-guided (TOW I and TOW II) antitank missile systems. Additionally, ground troops received individual NVDs and outfitted Bradley infantry fighting vehicles (IFVs) with night-vision capabilities to aid in safely transporting infantrymen and firing TOW missiles to knock out Iraqi tanks. Targeting systems utilizing

FLIR technology aided troops in hitting Iraqi armored vehicles and other targets through intense smoke, dust, fog, and haze.

Lockheed F117A Nighthawks, known as stealth fighters, also utilized night-vision imaging systems in their support of ground troops. The AH-64 Apache helicopter was created as an all-weather day-night military attack helicopter in large part because of the Target Acquisition and Designation System, Pilot Night Vision System (TADS/PNVS), which combines night-vision sensors and the targeting unit to enhance the ability of the pilot and the copilot/gunner to accurately engage enemy contacts. However, Operation DESERT STORM also revealed flaws in the individual systems and led to the integration of image intensification and FLIR technologies.

The third generation of image intensifiers combined light amplification technology with FLIR. These intensifiers multiply the light-gathering power up to 30,000–50,000 times. Additionally, these NVDs boost the tube life expectancy up to 10,000 hours, greatly improving their cost-effectiveness.

The third-generation NVDs were developed in time for use in Operation ENDURING FREEDOM (2001–) in Afghanistan and Operation IRAQI FREEDOM (2003–2011). These imaging systems, along with first- and second-generation NVDs, fulfilled the same role in Afghanistan and Iraq as they had in Kuwait a decade earlier. Third-generation devices provided upgrades to the troops' helmet units with the development of the AN/PVS-14 Monocular Night-Vision Device (MNVD), a lighter-weight and enhanced viewing piece. The AN/PVS-10 Night-Vision Sniper Night Sight connected to the M24 sniper rifle system for both day and night optical improvements. The night channel incorporates a third-generation image intensifier that aided snipers in both Iraq and Afghanistan after its implementation in 2002.

Fairchild Republic A10 Thunderbolt IIs, known as Warthogs, were workhorses for the U.S. Air Force in Kuwait and received NVDs shortly after Operation DESERT STORM to increase their support ability. The U.S. Army added second-generation FLIRs to the Abrams tanks' System Enhancement Package (SEP) tanks, Bradley A3 IFVs, LRAS3 Scout Humvees, and Stryker reconnaissance vehicle systems to increase their combat effectiveness prior to the wars in Afghanistan and Iraq. These enhancements not only increased the weapons capabilities of these vehicles but also improved survivability of troops.

By 2008 scientists had developed a new technology that could replace image-intensifier tubes in NVDs. The suggested alteration would replace image intensifiers with liquid crystal (LC) materials. Despite the combination of infrared sensors, FLIR, and image intensification in third-generation NVDs, these night-vision imaging systems are still affected by visible light, which can obscure images. Placing LC materials that are spectrally tunable with a semiconductor can produce an NVD that is unaffected by visible light and allows users the ability to see through other objects. Proponents claim that LC technology should revolutionize night-vision imaging systems because of its high sensitivity, spatial resolution, and contrast. Additionally, LC affords the possibility of much cheaper NVDs by cutting the expensive optics and high-voltage components.

Adam P. Wilson

See also: IRAQI FREEDOM, Operation; M-1A1 and M-1A2 Abrams Main Battle Tanks

Further Reading

Erwin, Sandra I. " 'Owning the Night' Means Fusing Sensors: Night-Vision Goggles Designed for Next-Generation Information-Centric Force." *National Defense* 87, no. 588 (November 2002): 32–35.

Youst, Gregory. *Desert Storm's Night Vision and Electro-Optical Equipment Suitability Survey.* Fort Belvoir, VA: Night Vision and Electro-Optics Directorate, 1992.

No-Fly Zones

Restrictions imposed on the flight of Iraqi military aircraft following the 1991 Persian Gulf War (Operation DESERT STORM). As part of the March 3, 1991, cease-fire agreement ending the war, coalition forces insisted on a no-fly zone in the northern part of Iraq. Extending north from 36° north latitude, it was designed to protect the Kurds from Iraqi government aircraft. In discussions with the Iraqis over the cease-fire agreement, coalition military commander General H. Norman Schwarzkopf allowed the Iraqis to continue to fly armed helicopters. Not until April 10 did the United States order Iraq to cease all military action in the northern zone.

No prohibition was imposed on the flight of military aviation in the southern part of the country. During the Persian Gulf War the Shiites in the south had answered the call of the George H. W. Bush administration to rebel, and after the war they were abandoned by the United States. Iraqi dictator Saddam Hussein ordered a bloody repression in which as many as 50,000 Shiites died. Not until a year and a half later, on August 2, 1992, did the Bush administration proclaim a no-fly zone in the south that covered Iraqi territory south of the 32nd Parallel. On September 3, 1993, the William J. Clinton administration extended the southern no-fly zone north to reach to the 33rd Parallel and the suburbs of Baghdad. The northern and southern no-fly zones were designed to protect civilians in these areas from air attack and to demonstrate to the Iraqi people that their government would not have full sovereignty over these regions until Hussein was driven from power. In effect the no-fly zones led to a continuation of warfare, albeit at a low level, between the United States and Britain on the one hand and Iraq on the other extending from Operation DESERT STORM to the March 2003 invasion of Iraq in Operation IRAQI FREEDOM.

Initially American, British, and French pilots conducted the no-fly patrols, but the French withdrew from participation in 1996. Most patrols were fairly routine, but on December 29, 1992, a U.S. plane shot down an Iraqi MiG-25 when it entered the southern no-fly zone. To circumvent the southern no-fly ban, the Iraqi government used its ground forces to begin a program of draining the Euphrates River marshes inhabited by the rebellious Shiite Marsh Arabs.

The air patrols and air strikes against ground targets were controversial. The United States and Britain alone among United Nations (UN) Security Council members justified the no-fly zones as being in accordance with UN Security Council Resolution 688. This resolution of April 5, 1991, condemned the repression of the civilian population in many parts of Iraq but made no mention of no-fly zones. Other Security Council members, most notably the People's Republic of China (PRC) and Russia, sharply criticized the British and U.S. air actions.

In the last weeks of the Bush administration, Iraqi air defenses fired on British and U.S. aircraft patrolling the no-fly zones. In response, on January 13, 1993, the Bush administration ordered air attacks against Iraqi air defense sites. More than 100 sorties were flown against Iraqi radar and missile air defense sites near Nasiriyah, Samawah, Najaf, and Amarah. Then, in response to Hussein's noncompliance with UN inspectors searching for weapons of mass destruction (WMD), on January 17, 1993, the Americans attacked the Zafraniyah nuclear weapons program factory on the outskirts of Baghdad. Fearful of the possible loss of pilots in the downing of aircraft, the Bush administration decided to carry out this attack with 42 Tomahawk cruise missiles alone.

President Clinton continued the retaliatory air strikes of his predecessor. These met increasing opposition from the governments of France, Russia, and Turkey. Tragedy struck in the northern no-fly zone in April 1994 when two U.S. F-15Cs mistakenly shot down two U.S. Army helicopters carrying allied officers to meet with Kurdish officials in northern Iraq.

The undeclared air war continued. Iraqi forces used their radar sites to target British and U.S. aircraft and occasionally to fire missiles at them. Under the rules of engagement, pilots were authorized to attack the ground targets in the event of a radar lock-on, which would be preparatory to a missile launch. In December 1998 in Operation DESERT FOX, U.S. and British aircraft carried out an extensive bombing campaign to destroy suspected Iraqi WMD programs. By 1999 the United States maintained at considerable expense some 200 aircraft, 19 naval ships, and 22,000 American military personnel to enforce the no-fly zones.

The no-fly zones and the low-level warfare that ensued there reflected, at least as far as the United States and Great Britain were concerned, the lack of a satisfactory end to DESERT STORM in 1991. At the time, Bush administration officials assumed that Hussein would soon be driven from power, but that proved incorrect. At least the northern no-fly zone provided de facto autonomy for a large portion of the Kurdish population. The no-fly zones ceased to exist with the beginning of the Iraq War (Operation IRAQI FREEDOM) on March 19, 2003.

Spencer C. Tucker

See also: IRAQI FREEDOM, Operation; Kurds

Further Reading

Byman, Daniel, and Matthew C. Waxman. *Confronting Iraq: U.S. Policy and the Use of Force since the Gulf War.* Santa Monica, CA: RAND Corporation, 2002.

Gordon, Michael R., and Bernard E. Trainor. *The Generals' War: The Inside Story of the Conflict in the Gulf.* New York: Little, Brown, 1995.

U.S. Congress, House of Representatives, Committee on Armed Services. *United States Policy toward Iraq.* Hearing, 106th Congress, 1st Session. Washington, DC: U.S. Government Printing Office, 1999.

Nuclear Weapons, Iraq's Potential for Building

From 1968 to 1991 Iraq sought to obtain uranium and create an industrial base for uranium enrichment and nuclear weapons production. Operation DESERT STORM and the resulting United Nations (UN) sanctions assured the destruction of Iraq's nuclear infrastructure in 1991. From 1991 to 2003 Iraq attempted to preserve the scientific talent needed to restart its nuclear program. American suspicions, based on faulty intelligence, that Iraq was secretly reconstituting its nuclear program and Iraqi dictator Saddam Hussein's recalcitrance in cooperating with UN inspectors greatly influenced the George W. Bush administration's decision to invade Iraq in March 2003.

From 1968 to 1990 the Iraqis sought and received foreign assistance for nuclear weapons programs. In the late 1970s the French built a light water reactor at the Al Tuwaitha Nuclear Center, located some 11 miles southeast of Baghdad. This type of reactor was known as Osiris; the French named it Osiraq, for the reactor and Iraq. The Iraqis called it the *Tammuz I* for the month in the Babylonian calendar when the Baath party took power in Iraq in 1968. In June 1981, during Operation OPERA, Israeli aircraft largely destroyed Osiraq; it was entirely destroyed in the Persian Gulf War in 1991.

Thereafter the United States claimed that Iraq pursued clandestine uranium enrichment. With German assistance, by 1990 Iraq was operating industrial-scale electromagnetic isotope separation facilities and had built prototype centrifuges. Iraq constructed a facility able to make 1,000–4,000 centrifuges annually (1,500 centrifuges can enrich sufficient uranium for one nuclear weapon a year). Iraq also began designing a first-generation nuclear weapon and a ballistic missile delivery vehicle. In 1992 some experts estimated that Iraq was six months to three years from completing a nuclear bomb. However, the Persian Gulf War crippled Iraq's nuclear infrastructure, and it never recovered.

In April 1991 UN Security Council Resolution 687 required Iraq to abstain from the acquisition, research, development, and manufacture of nuclear weapons. To ensure compliance, the UN Special Commission (UNSCOM) conducted inspections in Iraq from 1991 to 1998. UNSCOM discovered and destroyed many Iraqi nuclear-related capabilities and facilities, despite determined Iraqi efforts to frustrate the inspectors. It was alleged that Hussein hoped to conceal key elements of his nuclear program and preserve its scientific potential until UN sanctions on Iraq were lifted. However, Hussein might also have been trying to demonstrate his sovereign rights, since it seemed to many in Iraq that the United States and some European nations were pressuring the International Atomic Energy Agency (IAEA) process. In 1995 General Hussein Kamil al-Majid, Hussein's son-in-law, defected from Iraq along with his brother. Majid subsequently revealed that he personally had ordered the destruction of all stockpiles of weapons of mass destruction (WMD) in Iraq. He also divulged extensive information on Iraqi weapons programs and facilities, which greatly assisted UNSCOM. Majid and his brother and their wives, Hussein's daughters, were then tricked into returning to Iraq, where the two men were killed three days after they arrived.

In 1998 Hussein ended cooperation with UNSCOM and the IAEA. Britain and the United States launched a punitive air strike, and Iraq responded by renouncing compliance with all UN resolutions. From then on, many in the American intelligence community believed that Iraq had begun to reconstitute its nuclear program. To support this view, intelligence assessments cited Iraq's efforts to obtain equipment necessary for uranium enrichment, to enhance its cadre of weapons personnel, and to acquire yellow-cake uranium from Africa.

In 2001 U.S. intelligence learned that Iraq was trying to obtain high-strength, high-specification aluminum tubes. The Central Intelligence Agency (CIA) believed that Iraq would use these tubes for uranium-enrichment centrifuges. The Department of Energy, however, claimed that the tubes were unsuitable for centrifuge production and were probably intended for conventional 81-millimeter (mm) rocket production. Investigations conducted after the

2003 overthrow of Hussein showed that the latter assessment was correct.

U.S. intelligence also detected Iraqi efforts to obtain carbon filament winding machines, flow-forming machinery, magnets, and other "dual use" machine tools. Such machinery could support both nuclear research and nonnuclear programs. The Central Intelligence Agency (CIA) assumed the former, but postwar investigations revealed that the machinery actually supported conventional military programs.

U.S. intelligence discovered Hussein's direct personal interest in the Iraqi Atomic Energy Commission (IAEC) after 1999, when he provided IAEC scientists with increased security and funding. The CIA believed that this development indicated his intent to restart nuclear work immediately. In fact, Hussein did not order IAEC scientists to conduct nuclear work. Rather, he wanted to sustain their morale, keep Iraq's scientific base intact, and have them conduct nonnuclear research.

British and U.S. intelligence also learned that Iraqi officials had visited Niger in 1999, and they assumed that Iraq had sought to purchase yellow-cake uranium for a reconstituted nuclear program. Whether the Iraqis actually obtained an agreement was uncertain, and in 2002 the CIA sent Ambassador Joseph C. Wilson to Niger to investigate. He reported that Niger's government denied any deal with Iraq and that a forged document had been the evidence. The CIA leadership in Washington did not believe this denial, and did not change its assessment that Iraq had sought to purchase uranium from Africa. Indeed, this assessment was a major part of President Bush's justification for war. Yet the postinvasion investigations revealed that Iraq indeed did not seek any foreign uranium after 1991.

The final National Intelligence Estimate, published in October 2002, noted Iraq's efforts to acquire aluminum tubes. The estimate concluded that Iraq could make a nuclear weapon within a year if foreign states provided fissile material, but otherwise would not be able to make a weapon "until the last half of the decade." In order to justify U.S. military action against Iraq, President George W. Bush and Secretary of State Colin Powell issued public warnings that Iraq could soon make nuclear weapons. Following the U.S.-led invasion, former UNSCOM inspector Charles Duelfer led the Iraq Survey Group, a 1,400-member team that comprehensively studied Iraq's weapons programs. Duelfer determined that prewar warnings about Iraq's weapons were based on incorrect intelligence. In fact, Iraq had made no concerted effort to restart its nuclear program after 1991, and never intended to do so while UN sanctions were in force.

James D. Perry

See also: Blix, Hans; Central Intelligence Agency; UN Special Commission; Weapons of Mass Destruction

Further Reading

Brockwell, The Lord Butler of. *The Review of Intelligence on Weapons of Mass Destruction*. London: Stationery Office, 2004.

Duelfer, Charles. *Comprehensive Report of the Special Advisor to the DCI on Iraq's WMD*. Washington, DC: U.S. Government Printing Office, 2004.

U.S. Senate, Select Committee on Intelligence. *Report on the U.S. Intelligence Community's Prewar Intelligence Assessments on Iraq*. Washington, DC: U.S. Government Printing Office, July 9, 2004.

Obama, Barack Hussein, II

Attorney, Democratic Party politician, U.S. senator from Illinois (2005–2008), and president of the United States (2009–). Barack Hussein Obama II was born on August 4, 1961, in Honolulu, Hawaii, the son of a white American woman and an African from Kenya. Obama's parents separated when he was just two years old, and they divorced in 1964. Obama's father returned to Kenya and had limited contact with his son after that time; Obama saw his father, who died in a car crash in 1982, only once after he left for Kenya. Obama's maternal grandparents were a major force in his life and in many ways served as his surrogate parents.

Obama's mother subsequently married a man from Indonesia, and Obama moved to Jakarta, Indonesia, where he attended several schools until he returned to live with his grandparents in Hawaii in 1971. In 1979 Obama entered Occidental College before transferring to Columbia University, from which he graduated in 1983. From 1985 to 1988 he worked as a community organizer on the South Side of Chicago; his experiences there led to his adoption of Chicago as his home city.

In 1988 Obama entered Harvard Law School, where his keen intellect and engaging personality earned him the presidency of the *Harvard Law Review;* he was the first African American ever to hold the position. In 1991 he secured his law degree and returned to Chicago; the following year he led a successful voter-registration drive in Illinois that registered as many as 150,000 previously unregistered African American voters. In 1992 Obama joined the faculty of the University of Chicago School of Law, serving in various teaching capacities until 2004. From 1993 to 2004 Obama was also a member of a small Chicago law firm that specialized in civil rights issues and local economic development. In 1997 Obama became an Illinois state senator, a post he held until 2004. As a state senator, Obama garnered much praise for his grasp of important issues and his ability to sponsor and guide bipartisan-backed legislation through the senate.

In 2004 Obama, a gifted orator, made a run for the U.S. Senate, winning by the largest landslide in Illinois electoral history. He campaigned on a platform that was sharply critical of the Iraq War and that promised to reorder the United States' social and economic priorities. He also vowed to help unite Americans and heal racial, social, and economic divisions.

In July 2004 Obama delivered the keynote address at the Democratic National Convention, as a result of which he became a national phenomenon. His electrifying speech caught the attention of many and helped pave the way for his run for the White House in 2008. Obama was sworn in as a U.S. senator in January 2005. He worked closely with Republican senator Richard Lugar, chairman of the Senate Committee on Foreign Relations; the two visited nuclear missile launch sites in Russia in an effort to ensure the safety of the armaments. Obama also continued his criticism of the Iraq War, arguing that it had been an unnecessary operation badly managed by the George W. Bush administration.

In February 2007 Obama announced his intention to run for the U.S. presidency on the Democratic ticket in 2008. At the time many dismissed his intentions, pointing to his relative inexperience and the likely candidacies of such heavy-hitters as Senators Hillary Clinton, Joseph Biden, Christopher Dodd, and John Edwards, among others. But Obama ran an impressively earnest and well-executed primary campaign, and by the mid-winter of 2008 his many rivals had all dropped out of the race, except for Senator Clinton. Meanwhile the Obama campaign's brilliant use of the Internet to raise money and get out his message began to tell, and in early June 2008 Obama became the presumptive Democratic nominee when Clinton conceded the race. From then on Obama, who eschewed public funding of his campaign, continued to raise massive sums of money and garnered an impressive list of endorsements from both Democrats and Republicans, including former secretary of state and Republican Party stalwart Colin L. Powell. By the early fall, Obama had raised more money by far than any other presidential candidate in history.

In the general election Obama faced off against Republican senator John S. McCain, a war hero and prisoner of war during the Vietnam War, and the son and grandson of U.S. Navy admirals. Until September the tenor of the race focused chiefly on Obama's insistence that U.S. troops be withdrawn from Iraq as expeditiously as possible, his calls for energy independence, his desire to implement universal and affordable health care for all, and his hope to lessen the power of Washington lobbyists and special interests. In an attempt to bolster his foreign

Democrat Barack Obama became president of the United States in 2009. The first African American to hold that position, he promised a new era of engaging foreign governments and of multinationalism in U.S. foreign policy. (U.S. Department of Defense)

policy bona fides, he traveled to the Middle East and several European nations in July 2008 amidst much fanfare. The McCain camp sought to portray Obama as too inexperienced and naive to be president, and McCain argued that the troop surge in Iraq, begun in early 2007, had made a quantifiable difference in the course of the conflict. He suggested that Obama's plan for a specific timetable for the withdrawal of U.S. troops from Iraq represented a "cut and run" mentality that would play into the hands of the insurgents. Obama's suggested timetable ended up being embraced by the Iraqi government and became the basis for the U.S.-Iraq Status of Forces Agreement, finalized in late 2008.

Obama continued to argue that the Iraq War had been unnecessary from the start, based on flimsy intelligence and poor judgment on the part of the Bush administration. He also asserted that the conflict had caused the United States to dilute its efforts in the Afghanistan War, resulting in the increasingly deadly Taliban insurgency there. Obama promised to redouble U.S. efforts in Afghanistan and to dispatch significantly more troops there.

In August 2008 Obama named Senator Joseph Biden, from Delaware, to be his vice presidential running mate. Biden added his years of governmental experience to the ticket, and the choice was generally hailed as a wise move. Just a few days later, McCain revealed his choice for a running mate: Governor Sarah Palin of Alaska, a 44-year-old with no experience in national politics. She had been governor for only 20 months and before that had been the mayor of a small town in Alaska. The choice proved controversial, although it energized election coverage of the McCain campaign that, until then, had largely been dominated by Obama. Meanwhile, Obama continued to run a highly disciplined campaign, which portrayed McCain as another version of George W. Bush, who by the autumn of 2008 had the lowest approval ratings in modern presidential history. McCain's not infrequent gaffes—uneven debate performances and unfocused messages—began to work against him, while Obama's tactics and campaign strategy aided his own campaign.

In September the focus of the campaign shifted dramatically as the U.S. economy plunged into a downward spiral. By midmonth, the Iraq War had taken a distant second place to the struggling economy. Each day brought more bad news: the financial system was paralyzed by a series of spectacular bank and investment house

failures; the stock market gyrated wildly but in a persistently downward trajectory; unemployment rose dramatically; and the housing market was in full-fledged crisis. Obama made the most of the situation, asserting that a vote for McCain would be a vote for more economic chaos. By Election Day, Obama enjoyed a comfortable lead over McCain, and he went on to win the presidency, garnering 52.9 percent of the popular vote and 365 electoral votes.

Obama's transition to power went smoothly, although Republicans, in the now well-established pattern of U.S. partisan politics, consistently challenged both his appointees and statements. His nomination of former rival Senator Hillary Clinton for secretary of state proved an adroit move, and she won easy confirmation in the Senate. Choosing stability over change, Obama chose to keep Robert M. Gates, a holdover from the Bush administration, in the key post of secretary of defense.

Obama's early efforts to solve the financial crisis through massive government bailouts to the financial and auto industries generated some opposition but nothing like the opposition to his health care plan, which passed in March 2010 amid much acrimony among the Republicans, who rejected it en masse. Obama's public approval ratings began to sag late in 2009 and continued to fall into 2010. Internationally, Obama's taking over the reins of the U.S. government was generally well received, particularly his apparent willingness to reach out to European and other allies, "reset" deteriorating relations with Russia, and undertake new diplomatic initiatives and approaches to the Muslim world. In December 2009 after much study and internal debate, the Obama administration announced a troop surge in Afghanistan. The surge would deploy as many as 30,000 additional troops to deal with the worsening Taliban insurgency and would occur over a 6-month period, from January to June 2010. Obama, however, stipulated that troop withdrawals from Afghanistan would begin 18 months after the surge ended in June 2010. Obama's strategy met some opposition. Many Democrats disagreed with the surge, and many Republicans found a mandated timetable for troop withdrawals ill-advised.

On May 2, 2011, U.S. Special Operations Forces killed al-Qaeda leader Osama bin Laden at his hideout in Abbottabad, Pakistan. In December 2011, President Obama withdrew remaining forces from Iraq and ended Operation Iraqi Freedom. These two foreign policy successes helped him win re-election in December 2012. While Iraq continues to recover from decades of dictatorship and war, U.S. concern in the region has turned to Iran and Syria.

Paul G. Pierpaoli Jr.

See also: Clinton, Hillary Rodham; Gates, Robert Michael; McCain, John Sidney, III

Further Reading

Life Magazine. *The American Journey of Barack Obama*. Boston: Little, Brown, 2008.

Obama, Barack. *The Audacity of Hope: Thoughts on Reclaiming the American Dream*. New York: Three Rivers, 2007.

Obama, Barack. *Dreams from My Father: A Story of Race and Inheritance*. New York: Three Rivers, 2004.

Obama for America. *Change We Can Believe In: Barack Obama's Plan to Renew America's Promise*. New York: Three Rivers, 2008.

Odierno, Raymond

U.S. Army general appointed commander of Multinational Forces-Iraq (MNF-I) on September 16, 2008. Born in Rockaway, New Jersey, on September 8, 1954, Raymond Odierno graduated from the U.S. Military Academy, West Point, in 1976 and was commissioned in the field artillery. During his career he earned a master's degree in nuclear effects engineering from North Carolina State University and another in national security and strategy from the Naval War College.

Odierno's initial tours of duty took him to the Federal Republic of Germany, where he served as platoon leader and survey officer of the 1st Battalion, 41st Field Artillery, 56th Field Artillery Brigade, as well as aide-de-camp to the brigade's commanding general. Following completion of the Field Artillery Officer Advanced Course at Fort Sill, Oklahoma, Odierno was assigned to the XVIII Airborne Corps Artillery at Fort Bragg, North Carolina, where he commanded a battery and served as S3 in the 1st Battalion, 73rd Field Artillery. Additionally, upon completion of his master's degree in nuclear effects engineering, he served as arms control officer for the Office of the Secretary of Defense. During operations Desert Shield and Desert Storm, Odierno was the executive officer of the 2nd Battalion, 3rd Field Artillery, and then held the same position in the Division Artillery of the 3rd Armored Division.

Following Desert Storm, Odierno went on to command 2nd Battalion, 8th Field Artillery, 7th Infantry Division, from 1992 to 1994. After attending the Army War College and being promoted to colonel, he commanded the Division Artillery, 1st Cavalry Division, from 1995 to 1997. Following an assignment at the Army War College in Carlisle Barracks, Pennsylvania, he served as chief of staff, V Corps, U.S. Army Europe, and assistant division commander (support) of the 1st Armored Division, during which time he acted as deputy commanding general of Task Force Hawk, Albania. Upon promotion to brigadier general in July 1999, he became director of Force Management in the Office of the Deputy Chief of Staff for Operations and Plans in the Pentagon.

From October 2001 to June 2004 Odierno commanded the 4th Infantry Division (Mechanized) at Fort Hood, Texas. Promoted to major general in November 2002, he deployed with his division to participate in Operation IRAQI FREEDOM from March 2003 to April 2004. Originally the division planned to enter Iraq from the north through Turkey; however, the Turkish government refused permission to move the unit through its territory, and the division deployed into Iraq through Kuwait. Subsequently the 4th Infantry Division acted as a follow-on force and conducted operations in the Sunni Triangle north of Baghdad.

In December 2003 Odierno's troops captured deposed Iraqi dictator Saddam Hussein. Despite this success, Odierno's area of responsibility, which centered on Tikrit and Mosul, experienced ever-increasing insurgent violence. Subsequently some critics characterized as overly heavy-handed Odierno's attempts to suppress the growing insurgency through confrontational armed measures, thereby driving some Iraqis into the insurgent fold. He has since argued that these measures were justified, as similar tactics had been successfully employed to suppress radical insurgents, notably al-Qaeda in Iraq, in 2007.

Upon his return to the United States in August 2004, Odierno served briefly as special assistant to the vice chief of staff of the army. From October 2004 until May 2006 he was the assistant to the chairman of the Joint Chiefs of Staff, serving as military adviser to Secretary of State Condoleezza Rice. He was promoted to lieutenant general in January 2005.

In May 2006 Odierno took command of III Corps at Fort Hood, Texas, assuming command of Multinational Corps-Iraq (MNC-I) on December 14, 2006, the second-most senior command position in Operation IRAQI FREEDOM responsible for implementing the campaign plan of the MNF-I commanding general. Shortly thereafter General David Petraeus assumed command of MNF-I and implemented a thorough revision of strategy that emphasized counterinsurgency operations in conjunction with his rewriting of army doctrine on counterinsurgency.

In February 2007 Odierno launched Operation ENFORCING THE LAW, also known as the Baghdad Security Plan. U.S. and Iraqi troops were dispersed throughout Baghdad and maintained a continual presence to establish security for its inhabitants through a system of joint security stations. His subsequent operations aimed to deny al-Qaeda in Iraq its operational sanctuaries throughout the various provinces and to deny it an opportunity to regroup. The so-called Awakening Councils in Anbar Province aided these efforts.

Following rotation back to Fort Hood in February 2008, Odierno was selected to succeed Petraeus as commanding general of MNF-I. He assumed that position on September 16, 2008, with promotion to full general.

Karl Lee Rubis

See also: IRAQI FREEDOM, Operation; Multinational Force, Iraq

Further Reading

Kagan, Frederick W., and Kimberly Kagan. "The Patton of Counterinsurgency." *Weekly Standard* 13 (2008): 27–33.

Ricks, Thomas E. *Fiasco: The American Military Adventure in Iraq*. New York: Penguin, 2006.

Woodward, Bob. *The War Within: A Secret White House History, 2006–2008*. New York: Simon and Schuster, 2008.

Oil

A strategic nonrenewable energy resource at the center of debates regarding the U.S. role in international politics and economics, particularly in the Middle East. Oil from the Middle East has long been an essential security priority of the United States and other industrialized nations, and a major source of energy for the world economy. Strategic concerns about access to petroleum reserves played a role in regional Middle East conflicts after World War II, including the Suez Crisis (1956), the Six-Day War (1967), the Yom Kippur (Ramadan) War (1973), the Iranian Revolution (1979–1980), the Iran-Iraq War (1980–1988), the Persian Gulf War (1991), and the Iraq War (2003–).

In Paris at the end of 1968, the director of the U.S. State Department Office of Fuels and Energy informed delegates of the Oil Committee of the Organization of Economic Cooperation and Development that American oil production would soon reach capacity. Since then growing oil demand has caused U.S. economic and military dependence on foreign petroleum production to be an important part of national and international political and economic debates.

The Persian Gulf basin is the source of approximately two-thirds of all known global petroleum reserves. Of the major oil producers, Saudi Arabia has the largest proven reserve, with 264 billion barrels. Iraq has the third largest reserve of conventional oil in the world, with a total of 115 billion barrels; Kuwait has the fifth position at 97 billion barrels. Oil production in the Middle East played a central role in the 1991 Persian Gulf War, the Global War on Terror that began in 2001, and the Iraq War that began in 2003. The geopolitical importance of oil is clear in the international dialogue regarding these conflicts.

After a decade of relative energy stability and steady oil prices, Kuwait increased its oil production in 1988, causing a decrease in world oil prices. This had a negative effect on the Iraqi economy, which relied heavily on income from oil exports. Iraq was also significantly in debt to Saudi Arabia and Kuwait, which meant that its ability to repay the loans was undermined by falling oil prices. Iraqi president Saddam Hussein used the situation as a principal justification for his invasion of Kuwait in August 1990, arguing that the Kuwaiti production increases were tantamount to economic warfare against Iraq.

The Iraqi invasion of Kuwait placed a large proportion of Middle Eastern oil supplies under Iraqi control. The invasion also placed the Iraqi army adjacent to the vastly productive Hama oil fields of Saudi Arabia, a source of further international anxiety. Despite some domestic and international protest under the banner "No blood for oil," U.S. president George H. W. Bush invoked the (Jimmy) Carter Doctrine (which had identified the uninterrupted flow of Persian Gulf oil as a vital interest of the United States since 1980) and announced Operation DESERT SHIELD to protect Saudi Arabia from a potential Iraqi attack. As DESERT SHIELD grew, oil supplies to the West remained largely uninterrupted, but speculation in the commodities market and angst over the potential of more Iraqi aggression pushed world oil prices sharply higher. This in turn stoked fears of inflation and other economic difficulties usually associated with the 1970s.

After bringing together an international coalition through the United Nations (UN), the United States justified its support of Saudi Arabia and Kuwait based on the violation of the latter's territorial integrity and the former's geopolitical importance as a key supplier of oil. In early January 1991 the U.S. Congress authorized the use of military force to free Kuwait, and the coalition began Operation DESERT STORM on January 17. On January 23 media sources reported the dumping of more than 400 million gallons of crude oil in the Persian Gulf as a purposeful Iraqi tactic to prevent the landing of coalition naval forces in Kuwait. The Iraqi government claimed that the spill, the largest in history at that time, resulted from the coalition bombing campaign, which was untrue.

While retreating from Kuwait in February, the Iraqi army set many Kuwaiti oil fields on fire, causing a significant short-term oil shortage in the world market and a major spike in oil prices. The shortage was quickly remedied by increased production within the Organization of Petroleum Exporting Countries (OPEC) and the utilization of U.S. and International Energy Agency strategic petroleum reserves. Despite these measures, the instability of the global oil supply caused the international price of oil to rise to a record of $40.42 per barrel in late winter of 1991. Following the war, Iraq received heavy economic sanctions but was later permitted by the United Nations to import certain products under the Oil for Food Program.

Despite the fact that Iraqi oil output had been severely limited, world oil supplies became plentiful by the mid-1990s, and by 1999 an oil glut caused prices to drop to as low as $22 per barrel. In the United States

gasoline was selling in most places for less than 95 cents per gallon.

After the terrorist attacks of September 11, 2001, the fact that 15 of the 19 Islamist terrorists who hijacked the airliners used to carry out the attacks were Saudis initiated a close examination of the political and economic relationship between the United States and Saudi Arabia, the country's largest supplier of foreign oil.

The resultant War on Terror also sharply increased U.S. military involvement in the Middle East. The United States invaded Afghanistan in October 2001 (Operation ENDURING FREEDOM) with a considerable amount of world support. In March 2003 the United States, the United Kingdom, and a small international coalition extended the war by invading Iraq (Operation IRAQI FREEDOM) with the stated goal of ending the international threat posed by the regime of Saddam Hussein, which allegedly sponsored international terrorism and possessed weapons of mass destruction (WMDs). The coalition forces quickly defeated the Iraqi army, but they were unable to establish a stable government, and no WMDs were found.

The inability to achieve political stability had a profoundly negative effect on Iraqi oil production. In 2003 Iraqi production ceased, causing a loss of 2 million barrels a day. This affected the global oil market and sent prices higher. In 2006 Iraq's oil production was still down 600,000 barrels per day from prewar production levels. By the end of 2007, however, production had reached prewar levels.

The Iraqi production lapse had a profound impact on the international oil market. The lack of excess production capacity, refinery shortages, and individual production problems in the OPEC nations only exacerbated the effects of the Iraqi shortage on the global economy. The United States also decided not to tap oil from its strategic petroleum reserve. Because of continuing growth in world demand in a time of relative oil scarcity and instability, petroleum prices increased dramatically, reaching $80–$90 per barrel at the beginning of 2007 and $140 per barrel by mid-2008. From that high, however, oil prices dropped substantially by the end of 2008 and early 2009.

The Iraq War effort has faced domestic and international criticism from both popular and official sources. Many of the protests against the war have centered around the themes of U.S. dependency on foreign oil, control of oil production, and rising oil prices. Among other nations, the war enhanced tensions among the United States, Iran, and Venezuela, also major international oil producers.

As early as 2003 international commentators alleged that the Bush administration had used military force in Iraq because the country had the potential to destabilize the international oil market. In 2003 the White House and the Department of Defense denied that oil was part of the motivation for the Iraq War. However, in the summer of 2005 President George W. Bush argued that U.S. troops needed to continue fighting in Iraq to prevent the country's oil fields from coming under the control of terrorist extremists. The Energy Task Force, headed by Vice President Richard Cheney, also noted the fundamental importance of the region, especially considering U.S. dependence on oil imports. By 2008, thanks to the situation in Iraq, disruptions due to unrest in Nigeria, and growing demand in such nations as China and India, oil prices had reached historic highs, hitting more than $140 per barrel. In the United States the surging fuel prices spiked inflation to its highest level in 17 years and, along with depreciating home prices, a major slump in

homes sales, and the subprime mortgage crisis, threatened to tilt the economy into a full-blown recession. By the summer of 2008 gasoline prices were averaging more than $4 per gallon, drying up demand for large vehicles such as sport utility vehicles and light trucks, and hammering the domestic car industry. Skyrocketing gas prices hit all sectors of the economy and reined in consumer spending as a whole. Since 2008 gasoline prices have fluctuated but have generally remained high. This problem has led the Obama administration to make energy autonomy a major policy focus.

Christopher Dietrich

See also: Bush, George Walker; Iraqi Freedom, Operation; Organization of Petroleum Exporting Countries

Further Reading

Bush, George, and Brent Scowcroft. *A World Transformed.* New York: Knopf, 1998.

Klare, Michael T. *Blood and Oil: The Dangers and Consequences of America's Growing Dependency on Imported Petroleum.* New York: Owl Books, 2005.

Roberts, Paul. *The End of Oil: On the Edge of a Perilous New World.* Boston: Houghton Mifflin, 2004.

Yergin, Daniel. *The Prize: The Epic Quest for Oil, Money, and Power.* New York: Simon and Schuster, 1993.

Organization of Petroleum Exporting Countries

Oil cartel founded on September 14, 1960, during the Baghdad Conference to give oil-exporting countries leverage in negotiations with foreign oil companies that, at the time, controlled production and dictated prices as well as the share of profits going to producing nations. In the late 1960s and early 1970s the Arab member nations of the

Organization of Petroleum Exporting Countries (OPEC) enacted embargoes against supporters of Israel during the 1967 Six-Day War and the 1973 Yom Kippur (Ramadan) War in an effort to influence Middle East policy. Since the 1980s OPEC has acted largely apolitically, seeking to stabilize oil production and prices to maximize members' profits while guaranteeing a reliable oil supply to the world economy.

As early as 1945 oil-producing nations recognized that a unified stance on pricing and output would improve their effectiveness in bargaining with the major oil companies. In 1959 the U.S. government established a mandatory quota on all imported oil to the United States in an attempt to give preferential treatment to oil producers in Canada and Mexico. In so doing, the world's largest oil consumer effectively imposed a partial boycott on Middle Eastern oil. The net result was depressed prices for Persian Gulf crude. To make matters worse, the oil companies enacted a series of unilateral price cuts in 1959 and 1960 that caused oil prices to fall even lower.

The severe impact that these policies had on Middle Eastern oil provided the impetus for the world's five largest oil exporters—Saudi Arabia, Iran, Iraq, Kuwait, and Venezuela—to band together with the express purpose of reversing these price cuts. During its first two decades of operations OPEC expanded its membership to include Qatar, Indonesia, Libya, United Arab Emirates (UAE), Algeria, Nigeria, Ecuador, and Gabon. During its first decade of operations OPEC enjoyed little success. Prices continued to float lower well into 1971. In 1958 oil sold for $10.85 per barrel (in 1990 dollars). In 1971 it sold for just $7.46 per barrel. The cartel doggedly negotiated with oil companies but had little success in eroding the oil companies' power to set prices. Beginning in 1973, however, OPEC finally succeeded in wresting pricing power from the oil companies, which were increasingly vulnerable to political decisions made in the oil-producing states that housed their operations. On October 16, 1973, in reaction to the Yom Kippur (Ramadan) War, OPEC cut production, which ultimately quadrupled the price of oil and began a series of price hikes that effectively ended the companies' control over all but the technical side of oil production.

As Arab nations' production made up an increasing share of the world oil market, they began to use their power politically, applying oil embargoes against Britain and France during the 1956 Suez Crisis and against the United States, Britain, and West Germany during the 1967 Six-Day War. These embargoes failed, however, in large part because of U.S. willingness to make up the oil shortfalls of its allies. Also, because oil is a worldwide commodity, limited embargoes have little effect, as nations targeted by an embargo usually find other ways to purchase petroleum.

Arab oil producers' attempts to use the oil weapon to influence the Arab-Israeli conflict enjoyed great success in October 1973 during the Yom Kippur (Ramadan) War, precipitated by Egypt and Syria's surprise attack on Israel. On October 17, one day after OPEC initiated production cuts that spiked sharp price increases, the Organization of Arab Petroleum Exporting Countries (OAPEC) decreased overall oil production and initiated a five-month oil embargo against the United States and the Netherlands to protest their support for Israel. The oil price shock, together with worldwide production cuts and the embargo, caused severe economic disruptions in much of the world. The impact on the United States was particularly severe. The nation's economy, which was already groaning under inflation, relatively high unemployment, low growth, and budget deficits, tilted into a serious recession. Government efforts to cap prices and control supplies only worsened the situation, as shortages and even limited rationing of gasoline became widespread. From 1973 to 1974, the price of oil catapulted from about $8 per barrel to more than $27 (1990 dollars). The American economy remained in a virtual recession into the mid-1980s.

The Soviet Union, an oil exporter, had little to lose from the Arab states' use of oil as a weapon. As such, it encouraged the oil embargo because it weakened the West economically and resulted in increased oil revenues for itself. At the same time the Soviets took advantage of decreased Arab production and higher prices, significantly increasing its oil exports to the United States during the embargo, a fact that neither nation publicized at the time.

The oil embargo caught Americans largely unprepared. As a result, the U.S. government instituted gasoline rationing that resulted in long lines at gasoline stations and national anxiety over energy supplies. In response to the price increases and embargo, the United States sought to establish a cartel of oil-consuming nations to confront OPEC directly, but the major importers' diverse oil needs and political positions on the Arab-Israeli conflict stymied this plan. In 1975 the U.S. Congress did pass legislation to establish a Strategic Petroleum Reserve (SPR) to protect against future supply disruptions. Since then the government has stored millions of barrels of oil in massive underground salt caverns along the Gulf Coast. The SPR may exist more for psychological reasons than anything else, however. The reserve would run out quickly in the event of a partial or complete oil-supply shutdown, and there is not enough oil in the caverns to affect the worldwide price of oil.

Although the Arab states ended the oil embargo soon after hostilities ceased and without securing the desired Israeli withdrawal from territories occupied in 1967, this unprecedented attempt transformed the position of oil-producing states, gave OPEC major clout, and fueled Arab nationalism. Since 1973 both the United States and the Soviet Union have devoted increasing attention to the Middle East as a strategic battleground. The Arab world, meanwhile, endeavored to exercise political influence independent of the superpowers.

OPEC's achievement of higher oil prices in 1973 and 1974 ultimately damaged the oil producers' economies by the late 1970s, when the resulting worldwide recession produced inflation and falling demand for oil. Two major crises in the Middle East during 1979 and 1980 resulted in yet another oil price spike. As a result of the 1979 Iranian Revolution, which saw the ousting of Mohammad Reza Shah Pahlavi, the imposition of an anti-Western Islamic fundamentalist government in his stead, and the taking of American embassy personnel by radical Iranian students, oil prices shot up from $24.46 per barrel (1990 dollars) to $49.52 by mid-1980. The effects on the world's economy were stunning. In the United States inflation peaked at more than 13 percent, while interest rates approached 20 percent. The 1979–1980 oil shock was not part of OPEC's strategy, although the organization did benefit handsomely from it in the immediate term. Clearly the markets were reacting to great regional instability in the Middle East, which began with the Iranian Revolution and was exacerbated by the start of the Iran-Iraq War (1980–1988).

Since the 1980s OPEC has pursued a policy of relatively prudent price control, ensuring substantial profits without adversely affecting the world economy. Beginning in the mid-1980s the price of oil dropped and continued to fall until the Iraqi invasion of Kuwait in August 1990 precipitated more jolting price hikes. After mid-1991, however, when an international coalition reversed the Iraqi invasion and soundly defeated Iraqi dictator Saddam Hussein's army, oil prices fell again. They would continue to drift downward, reaching new inflation-adjusted lows by the late 1990s. Following 2002, however, OPEC again began to reap record revenues as war and unrest in the Middle East and simple greed drove oil prices to record highs. This situation was reversed at the end of 2008 with the onset of the world economic crisis, when oil plunged to $38 a barrel, more than $100 less than it had been trading six months before.

Today OPEC has 12 member states; Ecuador and Gabon left OPEC prior to the 1990s. Angola joined in 2007. Iraq remains a member, although its oil production has not been part of any OPEC quota agreements since March 1998. Having become a net importer of oil and unable to meet its production quota, Indonesia resigned at the end of 2008.

Elun A. Gabriel

See also: Iraq, History of, 1990 to Present

Further Reading

Ahrari, Mohammed E. *OPEC: The Failing Giant*. Lexington: University Press of Kentucky, 1986.

Al-Sowayegh, Abdulaziz. *Arab Petro-Politics*. New York: St. Martin's, 1984.

Klinghoffer, Arthur Jay. *The Soviet Union and International Oil Politics*. New York: Columbia University Press, 1977.

Rustow, Dankwart A. *Oil and Turmoil: America Faces OPEC and the Middle East*. New York: Norton, 1982.

Skeet, Ian. *OPEC: Twenty-Five Years of Prices and Politics*. Cambridge: Cambridge University Press, 1988.

P

Pace, Peter

U.S. Marine Corps general and chairman of the Joint Chiefs of Staff from 2005 to 2007. Peter Pace was born on November 5, 1945, in Brooklyn, New York, to Italian American parents, and raised in Teaneck, New Jersey. He graduated from Teaneck High School in 1963. Pace secured an appointment to the U.S. Naval Academy at Annapolis and graduated in 1967, taking a commission in the Marine Corps. Following officer basic training at Quantico, Virginia, Pace was assigned in the summer of 1968 as a rifle platoon leader in Vietnam. He returned to the United States in March 1969 and subsequently held a series of posts both in the United States and abroad, advancing steadily through the ranks.

Pace received a master's of business administration from George Washington University in 1972 and completed advanced training at the Marine Corps Command and Staff College in Quantico, Virginia, in 1980. In 1986 he graduated from the National War College in Washington, D.C. Pace was promoted to brigadier general on April 6, 1992; major general on June 21, 1994; lieutenant general on August 5, 1996; and full general on September 8, 2000.

Pace served as president of the Marine Corps University from 1992 until 1994. In 1996, following his promotion to lieutenant general, he was assigned as director of operations, Joint Staff, in Washington, D.C. From 1997 to 2000 he served as commander, U.S. Marine Corps Forces, Atlantic/Europe/ South. In 2000 he assumed the position of commander in chief, U.S. Southern Command, before returning to Washington in 2001 to serve as vice chairman of the Joint Chiefs of Staff. He became chairman of the Joint Chiefs of Staff, the highest-ranking U.S. military post, on September 30, 2005. He was the first marine officer to hold either the vice chairman or the chairman positions.

As vice chairman and then chairman of the Joint Chiefs of Staff, Pace was a key player in the planning and implementation of the War on Terror and the March 2003 invasion of Iraq. A loyal soldier to the end, he publicly supported the White House and his direct superiors, especially Secretary of Defense Donald H. Rumsfeld, as the invasion of Iraq was being formulated. Certainly, Rumsfeld relied heavily on Pace's support during the war planning. As the Iraq War lost public support because of the growing Iraqi insurgency, Pace saw his direct superior, chairman of the Joint Chiefs of Staff General Richard B. Myers, come under increased pressure to step aside. Upon the end of Myers's term in office, Pace became the 16th chairman of the Joint Chiefs of Staff on September 30, 2005.

In private Pace had questioned the planning, strategy, and implementation of many aspects of the Iraq War, although publicly he always loyally supported his superiors. Pace's position on the war was that U.S. troops were not in Iraq simply to eradicate insurgents and run up body counts. Rather, he was unwavering in his position that the military's job in Iraq was to provide a stable

General Peter Pace, chairman of the Joint Chiefs of Staff between 2005 and 2007, was the first U.S. Marine Corps officer to hold that position. (U.S. Department of Defense)

environment within which Iraqis could rebuild their infrastructure and society while humanitarian and development aid could flow into the war-torn nation. Remembering the consequences of the fixation with enemy body counts during the Vietnam War, Pace urged his superiors not to ask for or give these out, but rather to emphasize humanitarian successes and positive developments achieved by the new government in Iraq. His advice was mostly ignored.

Pace's public position against gays in the military and the fact that the American public saw the Iraq War in an increasingly negative light were key factors in the decision of newly appointed secretary of defense Robert Gates not to recommend Pace for a second term as chairman of the Joint Chiefs of Staff. Gates sought thereby to avoid a long, drawn-out confirmation hearing in Congress, now controlled by Democrats. Pace also had largely lost the confidence of many senior military leaders because of his failure to stand up to Rumsfeld's ideas about how wars should be fought. Gates asked Pace to step down, which he did on October 1, 2007, after serving only two years as chairman. Pace was succeeded by Admiral Michael G. Mullen, chief of naval operations.

Randy Jack Taylor

See also: Gates, Robert Michael; IRAQI FREEDOM, Operation; Mullen, Michael Glenn

Further Reading

Cloud, David S. "A Marine on Message." *New York Times*, April 23, 2005.

Keegan, John. *The Iraq War: The Military Offensive, from Victory in 21 Days to the Insurgent Aftermath*. New York: Vintage, 2005.

Woodward, Bob. *State of Denial: Bush at War, Part III*. New York: Simon and Schuster, 2006.

Perle, Richard

Highly influential lobbyist, political adviser and pundit, and vocal leader of the neoconservative movement. Richard Perle was born in New York City on September 16, 1941, but moved to southern California with his family as a youth. He graduated from the University of Southern California in 1964, studied in Copenhagen and at the London School of Economics, and earned a master's degree in political science from Princeton University in 1967. Perle entered the public arena in 1969, when he took a job on Senator Henry M. "Scoop" Jackson's staff. As a Senate staffer from 1969 to 1980, Perle gained considerable political insight and expertise and soon became known as an expert on arms control and national security issues.

Despite his considerable reputation, Perle preferred to work behind the scenes and was not a well-know figure outside the halls of Congress. By the late 1970s he had become an anti-Soviet hard-liner and derided the Jimmy Carter administration's attempts to engage in arms control agreements with the Kremlin, which Perle believed were detrimental to U.S. defense and global security. During this time he also forged lucrative contacts with the private sector, which caused some to question his motives.

In 1981 the incoming Ronald Reagan administration named Perle assistant secretary of defense for international security policy, a post he held until 1987. Perle was predictably a champion of Reagan's get-tough approach with the Soviets and endorsed efforts to fight communism in Central America and the arming of the mujahideen in Afghanistan, who were waging an anti-Soviet insurgency. His tenure in office was not without controversy, however. In 1983 he was accused of conflict of interest after recommending that the Pentagon purchase an Israeli-made weapons system. The company that made the system had recently paid Perle a $50,000 consulting fee. Perle pointed out that the payment was for work done prior to his joining the Reagan administration, but his detractors used the incident to tarnish his image.

When not employed in the public sector, Perle busied himself with lucrative consulting jobs, served as an informal political adviser, wrote several books, composed myriad essays and op-ed pieces for foreign and domestic newspapers and magazines, and often appeared on television as a political commentator. He has subscribed to numerous conservative and neoconservative causes and think tanks, including the Jewish Institute for National Jewish Affairs, the Center for Security Policy, the Hudson

Institute, and the American Enterprise Institute for Near East Policy, among others. He was one of the signatories to the Project for the New American Century's open letter to President Bill Clinton in 1998 that advocated the overthrow of Iraqi dictator Saddam Hussein. Perle cultivated close ties to fellow neoconservative Paul Wolfowitz, deputy secretary of defense from 2001 to 2005 and a key architect of the Iraq War, as well as Secretary of State Donald Rumsfeld.

Between 2001 and 2003 Perle was well placed to advocate for his neoconservative outlook as chairman of the Defense Policy Board Advisory Committee, which was charged with advising the Pentagon on matters of defense and national security issues. As such, he was an early and vocal proponent of war with Iraq, and within days of the September 11, 2001, terror attacks was on record as having linked Hussein to al-Qaeda, ties that have never been proven. Perle was also on record as having proposed to invade Iraq with as few as 40,000 ground troops and was dismissive of U.S. Army chief of staff General Eric Shinseki's call for more than 600,000 troops to attack Iraq. Perle envisioned a scenario in Iraq similar to that which had unfolded in Afghanistan during Operation ENDURING FREEDOM, which had left most of the ground fighting to indigenous forces.

After leaving the chairmanship of the Defense Policy Board Advisory Committee in 2003, Perle continued writing and consulting. He has served as the chief executive officer of Hollinger International (a newspaper holding corporation) and is the director of the *Jerusalem Post*, a subsidiary of Hollinger. Because of his close ties to Israel (especially the rightist Likud Party, for which he has served as an adviser), Perle's advocacy of the Iraq War had been linked —rightly or wrongly—to his coziness with

Israeli leaders. Indeed, in the 1990s he wrote a position paper for Likud that included the overthrow of Hussein as a tenet of Israeli policy. Perle has vigorously denied any connection between his war stance and past dealings with Israel, and in recent years he has downplayed his role in the run-up to the Iraq War, claiming that his influence had been greatly exaggerated. Perle has also attacked the efficacy of the United Nations (UN), arguing that it is essentially an ineffective organization that is incapable of policing the world in any meaningful way.

After the Iraqi insurgency began in earnest in 2004, Perle made a concerted attempt to distance himself from some of the George W. Bush administration's policies in Iraq. While Perle has yet to call his Iraq War advocacy a mistake, he has expressed regret about the way in which the war was waged and blamed "dysfunction" in the Bush administration for the failings of U.S. occupation and pacification policies. David Brooks, a conservative columnist, wrote in the *New York Times* in 2004 that Perle had "no noteworthy meetings with either Bush or [Vice President Dick] Cheney" since 2001 and intimated that Perle's influence over official policy was entirely overblown.

In 2004 Perle and other Hollinger executives were accused of fiduciary manipulation after they allegedly funneled company funds from stockholders' accounts into compensation packages for top company executives. Perle's compensation, at some $5.4 million, was questioned, but as of this writing, no judgments against Perle have been made in this case. Perle continues to write and consult.

Paul G. Pizerpaoli Jr.

See also: Bush, George Walker; Cheney, Richard Bruce; Neoconservatism

Further Reading

Frum, David, and Richard Perle. *An End to Evil: How to Win the War on Terror.* New York: Random House, 2003.

Ricks, Thomas E. *Fiasco: The American Military Adventure in Iraq.* New York: Penguin, 2006.

Petraeus, David Howell

U.S. Army officer, commander of the Multi-National Force–Iraq (2007–2008), commander the U.S. Central Command (CENTCOM) (2008–2011), and director of the Central Intelligence Agency (CIA) (2011–2012). Born on November 7, 1952, David Howell Petraeus grew up and graduated from high school in Cornwall, New York. Petraeus graduated 10th in his class from the United States Military Academy, West Point, in 1974. Commissioned a second lieutenant of infantry, he graduated from Ranger School and served as a platoon leader in the 1st Battalion, 509th Airborne Infantry, in Italy. As a first lieutenant he served as assistant battalion operations officer, and as captain he served as company commander, battalion operations officer, and then commanding general's aide-de-camp, all in the 24th Infantry Division (Mechanized).

From 1982 to 1995 Petraeus served in a progression of command and staff assignments, with alternating assignments for both professional military and civilian academic education. He graduated from the Army Command and General Staff College in 1983 after which he attended Princeton University's Woodrow Wilson School of Public Affairs, where he earned a master's degree in public administration in 1985 and a doctorate in international relations in 1987. His doctoral dissertation dealt with the U.S. Army in Vietnam and the lessons learned there.

Petraeus returned to West Point as an assistant professor of international relations and then was a military fellow at Georgetown University's School of Foreign Service. In 1995 he was assigned as the chief operations officer of the United Nations (UN) mission during Operation UPHOLD DEMOCRACY in Haiti.

Petraeus's commanded assignments included the 3rd Battalion, 187th Infantry Regiment, 101st Airborne Division, during 1991–1993 and the 1st Brigade, 82nd Airborne Division, from 1995 to 1997. He was promoted to brigadier general in 1999.

Petraeus's first combat assignment, now at the rank of major general, came as commander of the 101st Airborne Division (Air Assault) in Operation IRAQI FREEDOM in March 2003. The division engaged in the Battle of Karbala and the Battle of Najar as well as the feint at Hilla. Petraeus later oversaw the administration and rebuilding of Mosul and Niveveh provinces. Subsequently, Petraeus commanded the Multinational Security Transition Command–Iraq and North Atlantic Treaty Organization (NATO) Training Mission–Iraq between June 2004 and September 2005. Petraeus's next assignment was as commanding general of Fort Leavenworth, Kansas, and the U.S. Army Combined Arms Center, where he exercised direct responsibility for the doctrinal changes to prepare the army for its continued efforts in Afghanistan and Iraq. He also co-authored *Field Manual 3-24, Counterinsurgency.*

On January 5, 2007, Petraeus, now a lieutenant general, was selected by President George W. Bush and later unanimously confirmed by the U.S. Senate to command the Multi-National Force–Iraq. Petraeus took formal command on February 10, 2007, replacing Lieutenant General George Casey. The

U.S. Army general David Petraeus commanded the Multi-National Force–Iraq in 2007 and 2008. He then assumed command of the U.S. Central Command (CENTCOM). (U.S. Army)

Petraeus appointment was the keystone in Bush's troop surge strategy in Iraq designed to bring an end to the mounting violence there and to bring about peace in Iraq. Many welcomed the change in command but also remained skeptical that Petraeus could reverse the violence in Iraq.

In April 2007 Petraeus was tasked with reporting to Congress the progress of the Bush administration's surge strategy, begun that January, and met stiff and sometimes combative resistance. To his credit, however, Petraeus deftly handled the pressure and stated confidently that the strategy, given time, would show positive results. At the same time, he firmly argued against setting a timetable for the withdrawal of ground troops from Iraq. In July he submitted to Congress his first progress report, which was positive and upbeat. It met with derision, however, because it did not appear that Iraq was any more secure than it had been in January. His September 2007 report cited progress on the military and security fronts but admitted that the political climate in Iraq remained troubled. The September report drew sharp criticism from some Democrats and the antiwar lobby, compelling a bipartisan group of congressional representatives and senators to sponsor resolutions—which eventually passed—that condemned the recent attacks on Petraeus. Petraeus was promoted to four-star rank in December 2007.

By early 2008, defying high odds and most critics of the war, the surge strategy appeared to be paying off, as violence had fallen off markedly in the last quarter of 2007. Talk of troop drawdowns, however, were still subject to interpretation, as the possible numbers being cited would account mainly for the surge, meaning that troop strength in Iraq would remain unchanged from January 2007, even after troop reductions.

By the spring of 2008, however, Petraeus could point to a significant reduction in sectarian and insurgency-based violence in Iraq. In addition, the Iraqis themselves seemed increasingly willing and able to take over security and police tasks. As a result, U.S. and coalition troop withdrawals accelerated throughout 2008, and violence in Iraq hit four-year lows. Petraeus was largely hailed in the United States for his efforts at undermining the Iraqi insurgency, and because of this President Bush tapped him to command CENTCOM. Petraeus took command on October 1, 2008; General Raymond Odierno succeeded him as commander of the Multi-National Force–Iraq.

During congressional hearings, Petraeus was careful to point out that talk of victory in Iraq was still premature; instead, he viewed the situation with a great deal of realism, suggesting that an Iraq that is "at peace with itself, at peace with its neighbors, and has a government that is representative of—and responsive to—its citizens" might be considered a victory. As the head of CENT-COM, Petraeus became responsible for U.S. military operations in 20 nations from Egypt to Pakistan as well as the ongoing conflicts in Afghanistan and Iraq.

On June 24, 2010, the same day that he removed General Stanley A. McChrystal as commander of U.S. and NATO forces in Afghanistan, President Barack Obama tapped Petraeus as McChrystal's successor, thereby sending a signal that there was no change in U.S. Afghanistan policy. Then, on April 28, 2011, Obama nominated Petraeus to become the new director of the CIA. On June 30, he was confirmed by the Senate in a 94–0 vote. Petraeus was sworn in on September 6. On November 8, 2012, Petraeus, who had been married for 37 years, submitted his letter of resignation with the admission that he had engaged in an extramarital affair.

Marcel A. Derosier

See also: Counterinsurgency; Iraqi Freedom, Operation; Odierno, Raymond

Further Reading

Atkinson, Rick. *In the Company of Soldiers: A Chronicle of Combat.* New York: Henry Holt, 2005.

Day, Thomas L. *Along the Tigris: The 101st Airborne Division in Operation Iraqi Freedom: February 2003–March 2004.* Atglen, PA: Schiffer, 2007.

Fontenot, Gregory et al. *On Point: The United States Army in Iraqi Freedom.* Annapolis, MD: Naval Institute Press, 2005.

Phantom Strike, Operation

A Multi-National Force–Iraqi Army offensive launched on August 13, 2007. The force included 28,000 troops, many of whom were present as a result of the George W. Bush administration's troop surge, which had begun earlier in the year. Following on the heels of recent coalition offensive operations, which began in June 2007, including FARDH AL-QANOON (Baghdad Security Plan) and PHANTOM THUNDER (a nationwide counteroffensive), Operation PHANTOM STRIKE was designed to root out remaining al-Qaeda in Iraq terrorists and Iranian-backed extremist elements (including the Mahdi Army) and to reduce sectarian violence, with the goals of restoring law and order for the Iraqi people. PHANTOM STRIKE was led by U.S. Army lieutenant general Ray Odierno, then commander of the Multi-National Corps–Iraq. It was a joint mission conducted with the Iraqi Security Force. Opposing them were Abu Omar al-Baghdadi and Abu Ayyub al-Masri, leaders of al-Qaeda in Iraq. PHANTOM STRIKE was begun one month before General David Petraeus, commander of all coalition forces in Iraq, was to report to the U.S. Congress on progress in Iraq.

During the operation, coalition and Iraqi security forces went into previously unsecured regions and attempted to eliminate terrorist groups from safe havens in the capital city of Baghdad and the provinces of northern Babil, eastern Anbar, Salahuddin, and Diyala. Considerable emphasis was placed on destroying the terror cells in Baghdad, Diyala, and central and northern Iraq. Largely an intelligence-driven operation, PHANTOM STRIKE had coalition forces move into previous no-go zones and establish local security forces and intelligence networks designed to pinpoint the exact makeup and location of Sunni and Shia extremist groups while also rooting out al-Qaeda operatives in outlying regions of Baghdad and the more violent provinces. Both the Baghdad Security Plan and PHANTOM THUNDER shaped the culminating operations for PHANTOM STRIKE.

Coalition and Iraqi security forces launched dozens of raids in and around Baghdad. These included units of varying sizes and composition. Among those American and Iraqi units participating in the total operation were troops of the 3rd Stryker Brigade Combat Team, the 2nd Infantry Division, the 3rd Brigade Combat Team, the 1st Cavalry Division, the 25th Combat Aviation Brigade, and the 1st and 4th Iraqi Army divisions. Strike forces went into action by land and air. In some of the attacks, it was a matter of getting in and out quickly. In others, the forces remained for an extended period in order to keep the insurgents on the defensive and thus turn former "safe" insurgent areas into places too risky for them to return. Commanders of the surge forces were told only to take territory they could hold. As part of General Petraeus's new counterinsurgency strategy, PHANTOM STRIKE resulted in coalition forces moving out of their bases and into neighborhoods all across Baghdad and other major urban centers in the country in order to establish a security area based on the doctrine of clear, control, and retain (CCR).

PHANTOM STRIKE marked the last military offensive of PHANTOM THUNDER and lasted until January 2008. From June 16 to August 19, 2007, alone, some 1,196 insurgents were killed and 6,702 captured. The precise number of killed or captured during the entire effort is uncertain. Eleven U.S. military personnel died during the operation; the number of Iraqi government casualties is unknown. The operation was termed a success in that insurgent groups were ejected from their strongholds in northern Babil, eastern Anbar, and Diyala provinces and the southern outskirts of Baghdad. Furthermore, the raids conducted during Phantom Strike gathered valuable information on al-Qaeda and Iranian-backed terror cells countrywide.

Charles Francis Howlett

See also: Baghdad; Phantom Thunder, Operation

Further Reading

Filkins, Dexter. *The Forever War.* New York: Knopf, 2008.

Roggio, Bill. "Coalition, Iraqi Forces Launch Operation Phantom Strike." *Long War Journal*, August 13, 2007, http://longwarjournal.org/archives.

West, Bing. *The Strongest Tribe: War, Politics, and the Endgame in Iraq.* New York: Random House, 2008.

Phantom Thunder, Operation

A corps-size operation carried out by coalition forces in Iraq (American and Iraq Security Forces) that commenced on June 16, 2007, under the command of General David Petraeus (Multi-National Force–Iraq, overall headquarters) and Lieutenant General Raymond Odierno (Multi-National Corps–Iraq, major troop force). Operation Phantom Thunder was part of the U.S. troop surge strategy implemented in January 2007 and was designed to root out extremist groups, including al-Qaeda, from Iraq. Phantom Thunder was comprised of several subordinate operations, including Operations Arrowhead Ripper in Diyala Province, Marne Torch and Commando Eagle in Babil Province, Fardh Al-Qanoon in Baghdad, Alljah in Anbar Province, and special forces attacks against the Mahdi Army in southern Iraq. In preparation for this campaign against the so-called Baghdad Belt, an additional five American brigades were deployed to Iraq between January and June 2007.

As the buildup began, Operation Law And Order began on February 14, 2007, in an effort to resecure Baghdad, with estimates running as high as almost 70 percent of the city under insurgent control. It became part of Operation Phantom Thunder when American and Iraqi forces moved to clear Sunni insurgents, al-Qaeda fighters, and Shiite militiamen from Baghdad's northern and southern flanks. The United States wanted to take quick advantage of the arrival of 30,000 additional troops, so the offensive was begun as soon as possible. During Law And Order, 311 insurgents were killed.

Operation Marne Torch began on June 16 in Arab Jabour and Salman Pak, major transit points for insurgent forces in and out of Baghdad. By August 14 some 2,500 allied troops had killed 88 insurgents, captured more than 60 suspected terrorists, destroyed 51 boats, and destroyed 51 weapons caches.

On June 18 Operation Arrowhead Ripper commenced when multinational troops assaulted al-Qaeda forces in the city of Baquba in Diyala Province with nighttime air strikes. As the ground forces moved in, intense street fighting engulfed the center of the city near the main market. By August 19, U.S. and Iraqi forces had killed 227 insurgents.

Multinational forces began Operation Commando Eagle on June 21 in the Mahmudiyyah region southwest of Baghdad. The area was known as the Triangle of Death because three U.S. soldiers had been kidnapped and killed there in mid-May 2007. Employing Humvee-based attacks supported by helicopter gunships, the operation resulted in roughly 100 insurgents killed and more than 50 captured.

Operations Fardh Al-Quanoon and Alljah were also conducted by multinational forces, this time west of Baghdad. The primary targets were Fallujah (Alljah), Karma, and Thar Thar. Allied planners developed a concept of attack similar to the one that took Ramadi in 2003. On June 17 a raid near Karma killed a known Libyan al-Qaeda fighter and six of his aides. Four days later, six al-Qaeda leaders were killed and five were captured near Karma. By the end of July ground commanders reported that Karma and Thar Thar had been secured.

Throughout the summer U.S. air strikes also proved effective against insurgents in Fallujah. However, on June 22 insurgents retaliated with two suicide bombing attacks on off-duty police officers that left four dead. On June 29 U.S. forces killed Abu Abd al-Rahman al-Masri, a senior Egyptian al-Qaeda leader east of Fallujah. They also captured and killed many others in the ensuing weeks. Fallujah proved hard to secure, and while officials declared it secure in late August, periodic incidents continued to occur well into 2008.

The final part of Phantom Thunder was the action against the Mahdi Army. In June, Iraqi Special Forces, the core of the joint Iraqi-American operation, killed and captured dozens of troops belonging to the Mahdi Army.

Several lesser operations were also conducted against retreating insurgent forces in which an additional 234 were killed by August 14, when the operation officially came to an end, and Operation Phantom Strike began. Operation Arrowhead Ripper continued for another five days until street fighting in Baquba ended. This action blended into Operation Phantom Strike.

Official reports of the action stated that coalition and Iraqi security forces had pushed into areas previously not under their control and had killed or expelled insurgent forces from northern Babil, eastern Anbar, and Diyala provinces as well as from the southern outskirts of Baghdad. During the operation, Iraqi and coalition forces conducted intelligence raids against al-Qaeda in Iraq and the Iranian-backed cells nationwide.

Iraqi and coalition forces conducted 142 battalion-level joint operations, detaining 6,702 insurgents; killing 1,196; and wounding 419. Of this number, 382 were high-value targets. They captured 1,113 weapons caches and neutralized more than 2,000 improvised explosive devices (IEDs) and vehicle-borne IEDs. Of the approximately 28,000 U.S. and Iraqi military personnel who took part in Phantom Thunder, 140 American soldiers died; the number of wounded has not been determined. Of the Iraqi security forces who fought with the Americans, 220 died; the number of wounded is not known. An additional 20 Iraqis died fighting in U.S.-allied militia units.

William P. Head

See also: Arrowhead Ripper, Operation; Phantom Strike, Operation

Further Reading

"Operation Phantom Thunder." Institute for the Study of War Military Analysis and Education for Civilian Leaders, http://www.understandingwar.org/operation/operation-phantom-thunder.

Roggio, Bill. "Operation Phantom Thunder: The Battle of Iraq." *Long War Journal*, June 21, 2007, http://www.longwarjournal.org/archives/2007/06/operation_phantom_fu.php.

Private Security Firms

Legally established for-profit enterprises contracted by government agencies to provide the contracting agency with armed security or to engage in security assistance aid—advisers, training, equipment and weapons procurement, and so on—to foreign military forces. Although broadly falling into the category of "government contractors," private security firms performing protective functions—providing armed guards whose duties may involve the use of deadly force—are set apart from the vast majority of government contractors, who provide only logistical, communications, administrative, and other service support. Indeed, the use of deadly force by some U.S.-contracted private security firms in Afghanistan and Iraq in recent years has generated significant controversy.

The use of private contractors by governments to provide military support dates back to at least the 18th century, when armies hired civilian drivers and teams to move artillery cannon around the battlefield. During the American Civil War (1861–1865), civilian teamsters were hired to drive army supply wagons, and "sutlers" (businessmen selling to soldiers food, drink, and other items not available in the military supply system) contracted with the army for the privilege of accompanying units in the field. During the Vietnam War, U.S. military forces hired commercial firms such as Pacific Architects and Engineers (PA&E) to provide construction and other services that were beyond the military's capability to accomplish. Widespread contracting of services previously performed by military personnel (such as dining hall workers) began in earnest in the U.S. armed forces during the Jimmy Carter administration and has increased since the military drawdown that began with the end of the Cold War (1991). Government contractors were employed during Operations Desert Shield and Desert Storm (1990–1991), and private security firms providing military assistance (advising, training, etc.) have been used extensively in support of several Balkan nations since the collapse of

Yugoslavia. Since 2001, the Department of Defense has employed private security firms to provide military training assistance and advisers to the Afghan and Iraqi military and security forces.

However, the Defense Department is only one U.S. government agency employing civilian contractors in general, and private security firms providing armed guards in particular are most often contracted by non–Defense Department agencies, such as the State Department. Private armed security guards contracted by the State Department normally work for the Regional Security Officer (a career U.S. Foreign Service Officer) who is responsible for the security of a U.S. mission in a foreign country. Well-established American firms such as Halliburton, Blackwater, DynCorp, Kroll, Triple Canopy, Custer Battles, Military Professional Resources, Inc. (MPRI) have all competed and won U.S. government contracts from various government agencies and for a wide range of services in Iraq and Afghanistan (although most are in Iraq). In Iraq, Blackwater Worldwide Security Consulting provided security guards and helicopters for the now-defunct Coalition Provisional Authority. Similarly, British firms such as ArmorGroup, Global Risk Strategies, and Aegis have also won contracts to operate in these areas. Many private security firms recruit not only retired military and police personnel from their home country, but also people with similar skills from all over the world. Many of these companies are also currently recruiting Iraqis or joining with upstart security companies in Iraq.

In Afghanistan, the United States employs some 29,000 private contractor employees who provide a variety of services, but only about 1,000 of those likely are security contractors. The largest companies in Afghanistan are either U.S.- or British-based, and include DynCorp, USPI, ArmorGroup, Saladin, and Global Risk Strategies.

Critics of the use of private security firms claim they have eroded national sovereignty by diminishing the nation's monopoly on the use of force and point to alleged instances of abuse of local nationals by private security firm personnel. Proponents of private security firms counter that the firms perform vital functions that would otherwise be difficult to accomplish given scarce personnel resources.

The lack of clarity surrounding the legal status of contractors also poses concerns about their employees' accountability. Unlike military personnel, private security personnel working for the U.S. government are not subject to the Uniform Code of Military Justice (UCMJ)—indeed, they are security guards, not soldiers, and most do not even work for the Defense Department—and those who are not nationals of the hiring nation often are not subject to that nation's laws. In Iraq, for example, until the U.S.-Iraq security agreement signed in January 2009 stated that civilian contractors may face criminal charges in Iraqi courts, private security contractors were immune from legal prosecution under Coalition Provisional Authority Order 17, which effectively barred the Iraqi government from prosecuting contractor crimes in its own courts. There also have been several reported incidences in which armed guard security contractors working for the U.S. State Department have killed Iraqi civilians through the apparent use of excessive force. Such overly aggressive behavior is counterproductive as it undermines U.S. efforts at nation-building by alienating the Iraqi population in general. Indeed, the prevailing attitude among most U.S. military personnel toward private security guard contractors is overwhelmingly negative—a reaction that cannot simply be explained away by envy over the fact that private security firm employees may earn up to four times what uniformed military personnel are paid. U.S. military personnel tend to believe that those carrying weapons and authorized to exercise deadly force in the name of the United States should be limited to: uniformed military personnel subject to the UCMJ; sworn and commissioned law enforcement officers; and designated and trained operations officers of official government intelligence agencies.

Yet, despite the problems posed by the increasing use of private security firms, there is no indication that their influence is likely to decrease. In addition, there has been no public commitment by the Barack Obama administration to change current U.S. policy regarding the use of private security firms.

Kristian P. Alexander, Jerry D. Morelock, and David T. Zabecki

See also: Blackwater; Halliburton

Further Reading

Avant, Deborah D. *The Market for Force: The Consequences of Privatizing Security.* Cambridge: Cambridge University Press, 2005.

Caparini, Marina, ed. *Private Military and Security Companies: Ethics, Policies and Civil-Military Relations.* New York: Taylor and Francis, 2008.

Chesterman, Simon, and Chia Lehnardt, eds. *From Mercenaries to Markets: The Rise and Regulation of Private Military Companies.* New York: Oxford University Press, 2007.

Engbrecht, Shawn. *America's Covert Warriors: Inside the World of Private Military Contractors.* Dulles, VA: Potomac Books, 2010.

Mandel, Robert. *Armies without States: The Privatization of Security.* Boulder, CO: Lynne Rienner, 2002.

Scahill, Jeremy. *Blackwater: The Rise of the World's Most Powerful Mercenary Army.* Saddle Brook, NJ: Avalon, 2007.

Singer, Peter W. *Corporate Warriors: The Rise of the Privatized Military Industry.* Ithaca, NY: Cornell University Press, 2003.

Putin, Vladimir Vladimirovich

Prime minister of the Russian Federation (1999–2000 and 2008–present), acting president (December 1999–March 2000), and second president of the Russian Federation (2000–2008). Vladimir Vladimirovich Putin

Vladimir Putin became president of the Russian Federation in 2000 upon the resignation of Boris Yeltsin and held that office until 2008. He is currently prime minister. (President of Russia)

was born on October 7, 1952, in the city of Leningrad (present-day St. Petersburg). He graduated with a law degree from Leningrad State University in 1975 and then joined the foreign intelligence directorate of the Komitet Gosudarstvennoi Bezopasnosti (KGB), with which he served until 1990. For obvious reasons, little information has been made public regarding the details of Putin's KGB career other than that he spent some time during the Cold War in the German Democratic Republic (East Germany). However, since he became president, speculation about his intelligence career has flourished, with claims that he was involved in economic espionage in Western Europe; others allege that he was little more than a low-level domestic spy. Although international sources have raised concerns over Putin's background as an officer of one of history's most brutal internal police organizations, his KGB career has done little to detract from his growing popularity among Russians since his rise to power.

Returning to St. Petersburg after retiring from the KGB with the rank of colonel in 1990, Putin began his political career in the early 1990s under the tutelage of Anatoly Sobchak, who was then the mayor of St. Petersburg. Because Sobchak was known as a liberal democrat, Putin's role in his administration provides some of the few clues to his political orientation, which at the time of his later appointment to the federal government was not at all evident. Putin became deputy mayor of St. Petersburg in 1994 and proved himself a capable administrator. With just two years of political experience, he was brought to the Kremlin in 1996 to serve on President Boris Yeltsin's presidential staff. In 1998, Yeltsin appointed him to head the KGB's main successor organization, the Federal Security Service (FSB), where Putin managed all of Russia's intelligence agencies and ministries; on August 9, 1999,

Yeltsin appointed Putin prime minister and indicated publicly that he favored him as his presidential successor.

As Yeltsin's fifth prime minister in less than two years, Putin quickly accomplished the improbable task of gaining the confidence of a wary Russian public that had grown tired and frustrated with government corruption and a flagging economy. He was swift and firm in his response to an Islamic insurgency in Dagestan that was threatening to erupt into war with Chechnya by the time of his confirmation as premier. This earned him a reputation among Russians as a pragmatist for his tough-minded conduct of a government invasion of Dagestan in the wake of a string of terrorist bombings that struck large apartment complexes in Moscow in September 1999.

Although Yeltsin's surprise resignation from the Russian presidency on New Year's Eve 1999 came as a shock to many, his appointment of Putin as acting president was not a surprise. Drawing speculation that a deal had been struck between the two, Putin, in his first official move as acting president, signed a decree granting Yeltsin, among other perks, full immunity from criminal prosecution as well as a lifetime pension.

While Putin did not win the March 2000 presidential elections by as large a margin as analysts had predicted, he nevertheless easily defeated his closest challenger, Communist Party leader Gennady Zyuganov, by some 20 percentage points. The vote demonstrated what experts and pollsters described as a profound shift in Russian public opinion, which for the first time in a decade rallied around one candidate—a newcomer to politics—who had amassed a significant support base from formerly split constituencies and disparate parties. Putin was inaugurated in May 2000 in the first democratic

transfer of power in Russia's 1,100-year history.

Putin moved quickly to solidify his power base, and he acted aggressively to curb corruption in government and in Russia's large industries. His detractors claimed that he sometimes subverted democratic ideals in doing so. His administration also struggled to jump-start Russia's troubled economy, a task that was made considerably easier after 2001, when the soaring price of oil brought an economic windfall to the world's second largest oil producer.

Putin's relations with Western leaders, particularly with President George W. Bush, began on a cordial and cooperative note. He voiced full support for the War on Terror after the September 11, 2001, terror attacks, and supported Operation Enduring Freedom in Afghanistan. Those relations suffered dramatically after the 2003 Iraq War, however, which Putin refused to endorse without a full United Nations (UN) authorization. He has also been angered over the expansion of the North Atlantic Treaty Organization (NATO) and is vehemently opposed to a U.S.-built missile defense system that would be deployed in Central and Eastern Europe. In December 2007 Putin pulled Russia out of the 1990 Treaty on Conventional Armed Forces in Europe (CFE), a move that was likely a show of Russian disdain for the missile defense plans. By that point, many in the West had begun to talk about a renewed Cold War. Russia has also refused to ratify tougher sanctions against Iran and began to move closer to the People's Republic of China in an attempt to check U.S. hegemony. Meanwhile, Putin's government was compelled to fight against a guerrilla insurgency in Chechnya from 2000 to 2004.

Putin came under fire by many in the West and in his own country for what were perceived as harsh crackdowns on the media and critics of his government. Nevertheless, Putin was reelected in March 2004 with over 70 percent of the vote. The result was never truly in doubt, as few sought to oppose him and those that did were unable to pierce the media blockade imposed on his critics. European and American election observers criticized both the media coverage and polling irregularities. In response, Putin said, "In many so-called developed democracies there are also many problems with their own democratic and voting procedures," a not so veiled reference to U.S. president George W. Bush's controversial victory over Vice President Al Gore in 2000. By the time he reluctantly gave up the presidency on May 7, 2008, the Russian economy was faring very well, and the Russian government was already making plans to augment its military capabilities. Putin's handpicked successor, Dmitry Medvedev, easily won the May 2008 election, although most believe that Putin, who is now prime minister, continues to hold the majority of power in the Kremlin. He is also head of the powerful United Russia Party, which currently exercises sweeping power within the Russian political arena.

Paul G. Pierpaoli Jr.

See also: Bush, George Walker; Iraqi Freedom, Operation

Further Reading

Kampfner, John. *Inside Yeltsin's Russia: Corruption, Conflict, Capitalism.* London: Cassell, 1994.

Politkovskaya, Anna. *Putin's Russia: Life in a Failing Democracy.* New York: Holt, 2007.

Sakwa, Richard. *Putin: Russia's Choice.* 2nd ed. London: Routledge, 2007.

R

Ramadi, First Battle of

Military engagement between U.S. forces and Iraqi insurgents (mainly Sunnis) on April 6–10, 2004, in Ramadi in central Iraq. Ramadi is the capital of Anbar Province, with a population of some 450,000, and lies along the Euphrates River 70 miles west of Baghdad along a main highway that continues eastward to the Iraqi capital and to the west across the Syrian desert to Jordan. Most of the city's inhabitants are Sunni Muslims. The battle was precipitated when Sunni forces in Ramadi rose in rebellion against U.S. forces garrisoned there.

Situated in the western part of the so-called Sunni Triangle, Ramadi's population had long been a center of support for the government of deposed dictator Saddam Hussein, and as such became a focal point for anticoalition forces after the March 2003 invasion of Iraq. In the days immediately after the fall of Baghdad in April 2003, the *muqawama* (resistance), including those who supported the former regime as well as Sunni Iraqis opposed to the invasion and Iraqi and foreign jihadists, began to fight coalition forces. The insurgents routinely ambushed lightly armored coalition vehicles and attacked convoys with small-arms and rockets, set off bombs in public places and near police stations, and planted improvised explosive devices (IEDs), which they detonated by remote control to destroy or disable coalition vehicles. While U.S. forces sought to maintain a low-profile presence in the city and engaged in efforts to win the support of the city's population through constructive projects, they found that many of the Sunnis held them in contempt.

U.S. troops were blamed when a bomb-making group accidentally set off a charge in a local mosque and when another explosive device exploded in the city's marketplace. By September 2003 the U.S. camp at Ramadi was coming under nightly mortar and artillery fire, with 19 soldiers killed and more than 100 wounded. The Americans sought to turn the town over to Iraqi officials, but insurgents also targeted these alleged collaborators. The resistance also became increasingly brazen; there were even large, noisy pro-Saddam public demonstrations in the city's streets.

Thus, 13 months after the invasion, Ramadi had become one of the most perilous places in all of Iraq. When members of the Iraqi Governing Council agreed on a new constitution in March 2004 and drafted plans for elections the following January, an upsurge in violence occurred in Anbar Province. The most dramatic incident in this escalation occurred in Fallujah, which was another epicenter of the insurgency located just 30 miles east of Ramadi. There a mob lynched four civilian contractors who had been dragged from an ambushed convoy, desecrated their burned bodies, and hanged the corpses on a bridge over the Euphrates on March 31, 2004. As coalition forces moved to pacify Fallujah, insurgents in Ramadi confronted U.S. marines at a level of intensity not seen since the early days of the Iraq War.

The worst of the Battle of Ramadi, from the American perspective, occurred on April 6, the first day of pitched battle. On that day, the 2nd Battalion, 4th Marine Regiment, 1st Marine Division, which was charged with maintaining order in the city, received intelligence that insurgents intended to seize a government building. Marine patrols entered the city to carry out a sweep in support of loyalist Iraqis to prevent the takeover and to disperse antigovernment elements. On their way, they fell into well-laid ambushes set up by scores of fighters who were thought to be former members of the Special Republican Guards. Thus, the marines of Golf Company, who were carrying out the foot patrols, came under sniper fire, ran into insurgent ambushes, and spent much of the day pinned down and taking casualties. As other units moved to relieve the beleaguered marines, they, too, were ambushed. Several platoons engaged in firefights before they could extricate themselves with the help of other marines as well as members of the U.S. Army's 1st Brigade, 1st Infantry Division, which committed M1 Abrams tanks and Bradley fighting vehicles to the fight.

The deadliest of the attacks that day took place in the city's marketplace, where a group of perhaps 50 anticoalition fighters set up a .50-caliber machine gun on a rooftop and took positions atop other buildings or in nearby shops and behind trees with AK-47s, rocket-propelled grenade launchers, and other small arms. There they waylaid a group of some 20 marines from Echo Company as they entered the marketplace in 3 Humvees followed by 2 trucks. The hard-pressed marines were unable to call in helicopter air support, which was then committed elsewhere, and the heavy machine-gun fire ripped apart the lead vehicle with all but one of its occupants trapped inside.

By the time reinforcements arrived and the marines were able to move forward again, they found that many of their Iraqi opponents had fled. Ten marines were killed and many others were wounded in this action.

Heavy fighting occurred in Ramadi over the next few days. On April 7 the marines returned in force to take the fight to the enemy and complete their original mission. They came under similar ambushes and sustained additional casualties, but no combat deaths, in a series of firefights, which occurred throughout the city all that day. The marines also inflicted heavy losses on the insurgents. Ultimately, the marines conducted street-by-street and house-by-house raids that led to the capture and interrogation of dozens of suspects and the seizure of arms caches. Altogether before the battle ended on April 10, the marines suffered 16 killed in action and 25 wounded. Insurgent losses remain unclear, as many of those killed and wounded were removed before U.S. forces regained the upper hand; however, most estimates put insurgent casualties at around 250 killed and hundreds more wounded.

The insurgency swung into high gear with the fighting in Ramadi and elsewhere in March and April 2004. Heretofore coalition leaders continued to hope that they would win the battle for the "hearts and minds" of Iraqi civilians. Now many wondered whether this was possible. Others questioned whether there were sufficient numbers of "boots on the ground" to quell a growing resistance that was developing new and more lethal tactics. Rather than the desultory, hit-and-run efforts mounted by the insurgents in the past, the marines at Ramadi encountered well-coordinated attacks, with their opponents proving themselves adept at ambushes, laying down suppression fire, and making effective use of cover and concealment. Although the marines had won this battle, they and other forces in Iraq still faced a stiff resistance in many other towns and districts of Iraq that would not easily be extinguished.

George L. Simpson Jr.

See also: Iraqi Freedom, Operation; Ramadi, Second Battle of

Further Reading

Fitzgerald, Paula M. "Marines Recall Ramadi Battle." *Marine Corps News*, April 19, 2004.

Negus, Steve. "The Insurgency Intensifies." *Middle East Report* (Fall 2004): 22–27.

Swanson, David, with Joseph L. Galloway. "Battle at Ramadi." *Philadelphia Inquirer*, August 15, 2004, A-4.

Ramadi, Second Battle of

Military engagement in which U.S. Army and Marine forces, along with elements of the Iraqi Army, fought for control of Ramadi, the capital of Anbar Province in western Iraq. After U.S.-led forces took Fallujah for the first time during November and December 2004, Ramadi became the center of the growing insurgency in Iraq. In this city of some 400,000 people, about 80 miles west of Baghdad, insurgent leaders created the Islamic State of Iraq, a coalition of Islamist fighting groups that included al-Qa'ida fi Bilad al-Rafhidayn (al-Qaeda in the Land of the Two Rivers, meaning Iraq). At the time marine leaders believed that if Ramadi remained in insurgent hands, all of Anbar Province would be insecure.

In June 2006, with the situation worsening, the U.S. command dispatched the 1st Brigade Combat Team of the 1st U.S. Armored Division to the Ramadi area to initiate plans to attack the insurgents. Many

feared another full-scale Fallujah-style assault that might kill dozens of noncombatants and level the city. However, U.S. commanders were determined to proceed with caution and they carefully planned their operation, which involved some 5,500 U.S. soldiers and marines along with 2,000 Iraqi Army troops.

By June 10 the U.S. and Iraqi troops had cordoned off the city, and a growing number of air strikes were mounted on specific targets. Using loudspeakers, U.S. forces warned residents to evacuate before the impending attack. The main goal of the operation was to sever insurgent supply and reinforcement lines into Ramadi. The Americans also planned to set up locations outside Ramadi where noninsurgent Iraqis from the city could find safe haven.

On June 18 operations began in earnest when two U.S. mechanized columns and an Iraqi Army unit of some 2,000 men entered the city's suburbs from the south and cut off two access routes into the city. Concurrently, marine units captured and held the western portion of the city center, controlling the river and its two main bridges. While armored forces controlled the city's eastern exits, marine units established outposts east of Ramadi along the main road between Baghdad and Syria.

With these key points secured, several hundred coalition forces, supported by Lockheed AC-130 gunships, moved into eastern Ramadi. The gunships killed several insurgents as coalition troops established an outpost in Ramadi's Mulab neighborhood to allow U.S. and Iraqi troops to better patrol this problem area. There they discovered numerous weapons caches and improvised explosive device (IED) components in many homes.

While this part of the operation met with some success, the Americans soon found themselves in intense street fighting throughout the city. Insurgents would mount widely scattered points simultaneously and then vanish. On July 24 the jihadist forces launched a major attack and, while they suffered heavy casualties, they continued to press toward their main objective, the Ramadi Government Center, in which dozens of marines were barricaded.

To meet the threat, U.S. troops demolished several smaller surrounding structures, with the plan to turn the area into a park later. Still, all the coalition troops who ventured into the city faced IEDs, suicide attacks, and patrol ambushes. Sniper fire was a near constant.

In early July U.S. troops captured the Ramadi General Hospital, which had been used as an insurgent barracks. Coalition wounded who had been taken to the hospital were found beheaded, and nearly every room on every floor of the seven-story building was rigged with explosive devices.

On August 21 the insurgents killed and defiled the body of Sunni Sheikh Abu Ali Jassim, who had encouraged many of his tribesmen to join the Iraqi police in their efforts to root out the insurgents. In response, on September 9, 2006, with funding and organizational efforts coming from the coalition, 50 sheikhs from 20 tribes from across Anbar Province formally organized an anti-insurgent council, named Anbar Awakening. Some of its members had been fighters with al-Qaeda in Iraq. However, as the council gained strength, its tribal members began attacking al-Qaeda fighters in the suburbs of Ramadi. By October representatives from many tribes in northern and western Ramadi had joined the Awakening.

In mid-September 2006 new marine units relieved those holding western Ramadi. Throughout the next three months, truck bombs as well as suicide and sniper attacks continued as part of the daily routine for the occupying forces. U.S. Navy SEAL Michael A. Monsoor was posthumously awarded the Medal of Honor for having thrown himself on a grenade that threatened the lives of the other members of his team on September 29, 2006.

One of the more tragic events in the battle occurred in mid-November when, during a firefight, an air attack in central Ramadi inadvertently killed more than 30 civilians, many of them women and children. The Battle of Ramadi also marked the first time insurgents employed chlorine bombs. On October 21, 2006, they detonated a car bomb of two 100-pound chlorine tanks, injuring three Iraqi policemen and a civilian.

The battle formally ended on November 15. It had claimed the lives of 75 American soldiers and marines and more than 200 were wounded. U.S. officials estimated insurgent dead at 750. The number of Iraqi Army deaths was not known. Coalition forces claimed to have secured 70 percent of the city by the end of November.

On December 1, 2006, with insurgents still entrenched in parts of Ramadi, the United States launched Operation Squeeze Play. Supported by Anbar Awakening tribal fighters, by January 14, 2007, coalition forces had secured a much larger portion of the city and killed or captured roughly 200 additional insurgents.

By the spring of 2007 U.S. officials believed that they had finally gained control over all of Ramadi. On June 30, 2007, a group of 64 insurgents attempted to infiltrate the city but were wiped out by U.S. marines, who had been alerted by Iraqi police.

William P. Head

See also: al-Qaeda in Iraq; Ramadi, First Battle of

Further Reading

Barnes, Julian E. "In Ramadi, the Battle Is Ever Changing." *Los Angeles Times*, August 6, 2006, A5.

Campbell, Donovan. *Joker One: A Marine Platoon; Story of Courage, Sacrifice, and Brotherhood.* New York: Random House, 2008.

Regime Change

A phrase that first appeared in American vocabulary in the early 2000s, in the aftermath of the September 11, 2001, terror attacks. Generally the term refers to action taken by external actors to replace another state's government. In its contemporary American usage, "regime change" refers specifically to former president George W. Bush's policy goal of removing Iraqi dictator Saddam Hussein from power. The stated belief that Iraq had weapons of mass destruction (WMD) was the chief reason advanced by the Bush administration for the U.S.-led invasion of Iraq in March 2003 (Operation IRAQI FREEDOM). As a side issue, the poor human rights record and repression of Hussein's dictatorship were given as additional reasons for advocating a democratic Iraq. Neoconservatives believed that a democratic Iraq would help to transform the Middle East. When no WMD were found in Iraq, regime change became the Bush administration's chief justification for the war.

Although the descriptor "regime change" is relatively new, the ideas behind it are not. Indeed, the United States has been involved in a number of military and diplomatic conflicts with similar goals. The United States has explicitly stated a policy of encouraging regime change in Iran for some years, although not by military means. Combined action by the United States and Britain indeed brought regime change to Iran in 1953, and covert U.S. actions fostered regime change in Latin America, specifically in Chile and Nicaragua. Operation ENDURING FREEDOM, the U.S.-led effort to topple the Taliban government in Afghanistan in late 2001, was clearly an effort to effect regime change there.

The origins of the U.S. aspiration for regime change in Iraq lie in the 1991 Persian Gulf War, in which the United States, under the leadership of President George H. W. Bush and within a broad international coalition, went to war with Iraq, then led by Saddam Hussein, to expel the Iraqis from Kuwait. In November 1998 President Bill Clinton signed the Iraq Liberation Act, which refers specifically to the regime of Saddam Hussein and the importance of ousting it.

In President George W. Bush's estimation, in the post–September 11 environment, the goal of regime change, along with the presumed threat of WMD and the assumption that Hussein had ties to terrorist networks, necessitated military action. In his State of the Union Address on January 29, 2002, Bush identified Iraq as part of a global "axis of evil," which also included Iran and North Korea. This speech presaged his new foreign/military policy strategy of preemption, known as the Bush Doctrine, and was a break with past policy toward Iraq, which emphasized sanctions, containment, and localized bombing operations. Colin Powell, then secretary of state, made the case for an invasion of Iraq before the United Nations (UN) Security Council in February 2003, based partly on faulty intelligence. He later regretted his actions.

Operation IRAQI FREEDOM, which began in March 2003, has had various outcomes. To date, no WMD have been found, and the

Central Intelligence Agency (CIA) has established that there were no clear links between Hussein's government and al-Qaeda operatives from Afghanistan, in contrast with the Bush administration's claims that such links existed. President Bush and other administration officials also confused many Americans when they subsequently portrayed al-Qaeda in Iraq as being essentially the same as al-Qaeda in Afghanistan.

The goal of regime change was realized, although the Iraqi government still remains unstable and insurgents continue to clash with coalition and Iraqi troops. After the collapse of his government, Hussein was captured on December 13, 2004; tried before an Iraqi court; and executed by Iraqi authorities on December 30, 2006. In the meantime, the Iraqi government and military have been restructured. Democratic elections were held in January 2005, and a new constitution was adopted on October 15. Furthermore, U.S. troops trained Iraqi military and police personnel so that they can take charge of their nation's defense.

Although there was widespread recognition of the dictatorial nature of Hussein's regime, which held many political prisoners and was guilty of major human rights abuses against the Kurds and Shia Iraqis, significant portions of the international community remained unconvinced that regime change in Iraq was a goal worth pursuing. This was especially true given the skepticism over Iraqi WMD or ties to al-Qaeda, as evidenced by the failure of the UN Security Council to support military action against Iraq when permanent members France and Russia exercised their veto power. Regime change by an international power without an additional casus belli is considered illegal under international law. Thus other American actions in this regard, such as the CIA's participation in the 1953 coup in Iran, had been

covert, and underlying reasons, such as securing access to oil, were not discussed widely. Furthermore, many scholars, activists, and world leaders expressed concern that regime change was simply American imperialism by another name.

Regime change as foreign policy remained controversial within the United States as well. Although there was widespread popular dislike and fear of Hussein and his regime, only a slim majority of the country supported taking military action to remove him from power. Furthermore, as fighting persisted well beyond Bush's declaration of the end of major combat operations in May 2003, the war became increasingly unpopular, and a counterdiscourse of domestic regime change emerged. Democratic candidate John Kerry, in his failed 2004 presidential bid, called for regime change in the United States.

With Hussein removed from power, the Bush administration backed off the language of regime change and switched its emphasis to the rhetoric of spreading freedom and democracy in the Middle East. Popular support for the war continues to wane, however, and many critics wonder whether the removal of a dictatorial government justifies the continuing loss of American lives in Iraq. Although Hussein was eventually found guilty of war crimes and executed in December 2006, the debate over the wisdom of regime change in Iraq has continued, especially in the political realm. In the 2008 presidential race, the rhetoric of regime change was downplayed, especially among the Republicans, but the Democrats continued to assert that the invasion of Iraq should not have taken place.

Rebecca Adelman

See also: Bush, George Walker; Bush Doctrine; Central Intelligence Agency; Hussein, Saddam; Iraqi Freedom, Operation; Neoconservatism

Further Reading

Bolton, M. Kent. *U.S. Foreign Policy and International Politics: George W. Bush, 9/11, and the Global Terrorist Hydra.* Upper Saddle River, NJ: Pearson/Prentice Hall, 2005.

Dodge, Toby. *Iraq's Future: The Aftermath of Regime Change.* Adelphi Paper #372. New York: Routledge for the International Institute for Strategic Studies, 2005.

Republican Guard

Iraqi army formation created in 1978 that served as the elite force of Iraqi dictator Saddam Hussein's army. The Republican Guard was permanently disbanded after the 2003 Iraq War (Operation IRAQI FREEDOM). Throughout its existence, the Republican Guard was one of the mainstays of Hussein's regime and received the best equipment, training, and personnel. When first constituted, the Republican Guard was a palace guard of one brigade. At the outbreak of the Iran-Iraq War in 1980, the Guard was expanded to take on the role of an elite offensive force, and by 1988 it numbered seven divisions and had been redesignated as the Republican Guard Forces Command (RGFC). The total strength of this force was estimated at 50,000 men and 400 tanks in seven divisions. There were an additional 10,000 troops in the Special Republican Guard, which was composed of the most loyal troops, usually stationed close to Baghdad.

The names of the seven divisions reflected either past military victories or past monarchs, such as the 6th Nebuchadnezzar Division named after the 6th-century BCE king of Babylon. Republican Guard divisions were organized similarly to those of the regular army, apart from the fact that the tank battalions had more tanks. However, soldiers in the Republican Guard were volunteers rather than conscripts and received subsidized housing and new cars as incentives. These incentives were to help ensure the loyalty of the Guard to Hussein and his regime. Many members of the Republican Guard were either from the Tikrit area or from other bases of support for the regime. In terms of equipment, much of the armored forces of the Guard were equipped with Soviet-produced T-72 tanks, and training in their use was more thorough than in the regular army.

The Republican Guard was not under the control of the defense ministry, but rather served as Iraq's special security apparatus. By 1990 the RGFC was officially under the command of Saddam Hussein's son Qusay, although it is possible that he directed only the Special Republican Guard, which guarded the palaces and important headquarters of the regime.

The Republican Guard was the main strike force in the Iraqi invasion of Kuwait in August 1990. In response to the deployment of coalition forces in operations DESERT SHIELD and DESERT STORM, the majority of the Republican Guard was held in reserve. For the U.S.-led coalition against Iraq, destruction of the Republican Guard was a high priority. This was largely achieved by the 1st and 3rd U.S. Armored divisions. Following the end of the Persian Gulf War on February 28, 1991, Hussein rebuilt the Republican Guard, although, as with the rest of the Iraqi army, it was not to pre-1990 standards.

In 1995 an attempted military coup against Hussein led a battalion of the Guard from the al-Dulaymi tribe to rebel as well. They were subsequently defeated by two loyal brigades, and the clans of the al-Dulaymi tribe were severely punished. In July 1995 the Republican Guard was purged of all officers whom Hussein suspected of disloyalty. In 2002 there were reports that the Guard was being trained in urban warfare and guerrilla tactics. The U.S. military claimed that former Guardsmen constituted many of the insurgent forces in Iraq that fought the coalition and new Iraqi government after 2003; however these assertions have never been proven.

Before the March 2003 Anglo-American-led invasion of Iraq (Operation IRAQI FREEDOM), the Republican Guard was dug in along the Tigris River close to Baghdad. The Republican Guard was then thought to number between 55,000 and 60,000 troops; some estimates placed the number as high as 75,000–80,000 (including some 7,000–12,000 Special Republican Guards). The force had at its disposal between 350 and 450 Soviet-made T-62 and T-72 tanks and various other armored and unarmored mechanized vehicles. When some of these units advanced to meet the U.S. drive on the capital, they were largely destroyed by U.S. air strikes. Those that escaped the aerial bombardment were annihilated during the Battle for Baghdad, which took place April 3–12, 2003; particularly hard hit during that engagement was the Special Republican Guard. Following the end of official hostilities in May 2003, coalition forces broke up any remaining Republican Guard formations. Some of its personnel, however, were subsequently recruited into internal security formations because of their comparatively high level of training.

Ralph Martin Baker

See also: Baghdad; Hussein, Saddam; IRAQI FREEDOM, Operation

Further Reading

Carhart, Tom. *Iron Soldiers: How America's 1st Armored Division Crushed Iraq's Elite Republican Guard*. New York: Pocket Books, 1994.

Ripley, Tom. *Desert Storm Land Power: The Coalition and Iraqi Armies*. London: Osprey, 1991.

Xenos, Nicolas. *Republican Guard: Leo Strauss, Foreign Policy, and the American Regime*. Oxford: Routledge, 2006.

Rice, Condoleezza

U.S. national security adviser (2001–2005) and secretary of state (2005–2009). Condoleezza Rice was born on November 14, 1954, in Birmingham, Alabama, to a prominent African American family. She graduated in 1973 from the University of Denver at age 19, then earned a master's degree from Notre Dame University in 1975. After working in the State Department during the Jimmy Carter administration, Rice returned to the University of Denver and received a doctorate in international studies in 1981. She joined the faculty at Stanford University as a professor of political science and fellow at the Hoover Institute.

In 1989 Rice joined the administration of George H. W. Bush, where she worked closely with Secretary of State James Baker. She was the director of Soviet and East European affairs on the National Security Council (NSC) and a special assistant to the president on national security affairs. She impressed the elder Bush, who subsequently recommended her to George W. Bush when the Texas governor began to prepare for his 2000 presidential campaign. From 1993 to 2000 Rice was the provost of Stanford University.

Rice served as a foreign policy adviser to George W. Bush in the 2000 presidential campaign, and on assuming the presidency Bush appointed her in January 2001 as the nation's first female and second African American national security adviser. Following the September 11, 2001, terrorist attacks on the

United States, Rice emerged as a central figure in crafting the U.S. military and diplomatic response and in advocating war with Iraq. She played a central role in the successful implementation of Operation Enduring Freedom in Afghanistan in late 2001.

In 2002 Rice helped to develop the U.S. national security strategy commonly referred to as the Bush Doctrine, which emphasized the use of preemptive military strikes to prevent the use of weapons of mass destruction (WMD) and acts of terrorism, although many associate this policy more with Vice President Dick Cheney, Paul Wolfowitz, and other individuals, such as Douglas Feith. She was also instrumental in the administration's hard-line policy toward the Iraqi regime of Saddam Hussein, including the effort to isolate Iraq and formulate an international coalition against it. Rice was one of the main proponents of the 2003 U.S.-led invasion of Iraq, Operation Iraqi Freedom.

During the 2004 presidential campaign, Rice became the first national security adviser to openly campaign on behalf of a candidate. She faced criticism by Democrats for her hard-line security policies and for her advocacy against affirmative action policies. After the election, upon the resignation of Colin Powell, Rice was appointed secretary of state.

Once in office in 2005, Rice worked to repair relations with such U.S. allies as France and Germany, the governments of which opposed the U.S.-led invasion of Iraq. She also endeavored to increase international support for the continuing U.S. efforts in Iraq. Rice's closeness with Bush provided her with greater access, and therefore more influence, than Powell had enjoyed. Following Rumsfeld's replacement as secretary of defense, Rice's influence may have increased.

In 2005 Rice led the U.S. effort to develop a multilateral approach toward Iran in light of

U.S. secretary of state Condoleezza Rice addresses the media following a meeting at the U.S. Embassy in Baghdad, Iraq, April 2006. Rice was secretary of state in the George W. Bush administration between 2005 and 2009. (U.S. Department of Defense)

that country's refusal to suspend its nuclear program. In June 2006 the permanent members of the United Nations (UN) developed a plan to offer incentives in exchange for the cessation of Iran's nuclear program. Rice supported European Union (EU) high commissioner for foreign policy Javier Solana's efforts to negotiate with Iran after Tehran refused to meet an August 2006 deadline to suspend its nuclear enrichment.

Rice has been a staunch supporter of Israel. She endeavored to gain support for the Road Map to Peace, which endorsed the creation of a Palestinian state in exchange for democratic reforms and the renunciation of terrorism by the Palestinians. Rice supported the 2006 Israeli unilateral withdrawal from the Gaza Strip. When Israel began bombarding Lebanon in July 2006, following the kidnapping of Israeli soldiers by members of

Hezbollah in the border town of Ghajar, Rice supported the Israeli action. She enraged the Lebanese by initially opposing a cease-fire in the hopes that Hezbollah would be destroyed. It was only after weeks of destruction that she supported a UN-brokered cease-fire based on UN Security Council Resolution 1701. In her last year of office, Rice was unsuccessful in moving forward the Palestinian-Israeli peace process of Israeli soldiers. She took a hard-line stance against the Russian incursion into South Ossetia and invasion of Georgia in the summer of 2008.

Rice left office with the end of the Bush administration in January 2009. She is currently the Thomas and Barbara Stephenson Senior Fellow on Public Policy at the Hoover Institution and professor of political science at Stanford University. She also serves on a number of boards, including the board of trustees of the Kennedy Center for the Performing Arts.

Tom Lansford

See also: Bush, George Walker; Bush Doctrine; Cheney, Richard Bruce; Feith, Douglas; Iraqi Freedom, Operation; Rumsfeld, Donald Henry; Wolfowitz, Paul Dundes

Further Reading

Felix, Antonia. *Condi: The Condoleezza Rice Story*. New York: Newmarket, 2002.

Lusane, Clarence. *Colin Powell and Condoleezza Rice: Foreign Policy, Race, and the New American Century*. Westport, CT: Praeger, 2006.

Morris, Dick, and Eillen McGann. *Condi vs. Hillary: The Next Great Presidential Race*. New York: Regan Books, 2005.

Rocket-Propelled Grenades

A short-range, shoulder-fired, infantry anti-tank and antimatériel weapon. Rocket-propelled grenades (RPGs) have also been used from time to time against aircraft, especially helicopters. RPG has been popularly translated as "rocket-propelled grenade," but the acronym actually stands for *ruchnoy protivotankovy granatomyot*, Russian for "handheld antitank grenade launcher." In the 1950s the production of RPGs was taken over by the Bazalt State Research and Production Enterprise, which continues to produce the Russian-made RPG today. The RPG fires a fin-stabilized, oversized explosive charge to penetrate armored vehicles. RPG warheads, ranging from 70 millimeter (mm) to 85 mm in diameter, come in thermobaric (fuel-air explosive), fragmentation, HEAT (high-explosive anti-tank), and high-explosive configurations. The most successful and commonly used RPG version today is the RPG-7 and its variants. It has been in service since 1961, when it replaced the earlier RPG-2 that had been introduced in 1949.

The RPG is a single-shot weapon, requiring reloading after each firing. In its regular military deployment, the RPG is used by a two-man team, with the gunner carrying the weapon and two additional rounds of ammunition. The assistant gunner carries an additional three rounds of ammunition, and is also trained to fire the weapon if the gunner is incapacitated. A well-trained RPG team can fire four to six rounds per minute.

The weapon comprises a reusable smooth-bore 40-mm tube that fires a front-loaded projectile. The tube is 37.4 inches long and weighs 17.4 pounds, unloaded. With the grenade loaded, it weighs 22 pounds. The weapon is controlled by two pistol-grip handles with an unusual configuration, which has the trigger mechanism located in the forward handle, with the rear grip used for additional stability. The projectile itself is made up of two parts, the warhead with a sustainer motor and the booster charge. These parts must be screwed together before loading and firing.

The RPG is recoilless, with the recoil of the rocket exiting through the breech exhaust opening. The projectile is rocket-propelled and is fired from the launcher tube by a small strip-powder charge at a velocity of about 380 feet per second. After traveling about 36 feet, a sustainer rocket ignites and increases the projectile's velocity to a maximum 960 feet per second. As the projectile leaves the launch tube, a set of stabilizing fins opens in the tail section of the projectile.

Firing the new PG-7VR tandem-charge ammunition, the RPG-7 can penetrate nearly 2 feet of steel with explosive reactive armor, 5 feet of reinforced concrete, 6.5 feet of brickwork, or 12 feet of log or sand. The RPG round can put a 2-inch hole in walls, but does not knock down the entire wall. It is highly effective in urban warfare against troops inside buildings. In this manner, it was used to great effect against American forces during the Vietnam War at the Battle of Hue in 1968.

The RPG-7 has two standard sights, a primary 2.5 power optical telescopic sight, and a permanently attached iron sight as a backup. In addition, night-vision sights may be attached in place of the optical sight. Two factors make accurate firing difficult, particularly at longer ranges, even in ideal weather conditions. First, the gunner must estimate range with a high degree of precision. This is facilitated to some degree by the optical sight, but remains a crucial factor in achieving a hit. Second, the weight of the war-head at the forward end of the projectile makes it difficult to hold the weapon steady for any length of time. This means that the gunner must line up his sights and fire quickly. Without practice, a gunner can hit a vehicle-sized target most of the time at ranges of 150–300 feet. With training, the RPG has an effective range of 1,000 feet against moving targets and about 1,600 feet against stationary targets.

Firing the RPG into a crosswind is difficult, as is the case with all unguided projectiles. In a crosswind of seven miles per hour (mph), a first round hit at 600 feet may be expected about 50 percent of the time. Insurgents have often compensated for poor accuracy by firing large numbers of RPGs at a single target. This technique was employed against the Soviets in Afghanistan in the 1980s, during the Afghanistan-Soviet War, and against the Israelis by Hezbollah in Lebanon in the summer of 2006.

The short effective range of the RPG forces the shooter to get close to the target, either by advancing or allowing the target to approach until within effective range. Rapid firing is critical, and the launcher is carried loaded to speed the firing procedure. When fired, the RPG emits a telltale puff of exhaust smoke. This factor, combined with the short range, necessitates evasive action by the gunner immediately after firing, unless the action is meant to be a suicide mission.

The RPG can be fired from the standing, crouching, or prone positions. Relatively low "back-blast" from the rocket's exhaust also allows the use of the RPG from enclosed spaces, such as rooms in fortified positions, making the RPG particularly useful in the covered, short-range combat environment of urban operations. This feature has been used to considerable advantage in Northern Ireland, Lebanon, Gaza, and Iraq since 2003.

Originally designed as an antitank weapon, the RPG was copied from the World War II–era German Panzerfaust. Improvements in armor technology, particularly the incorporation of gapped and reactive armor in main battle tanks in the 1970s and 1980s, reduced the effectiveness of RPGs as antitank weapons. However, an advanced grenade, the PG-7BR, featuring a tandem two-stage warhead designed to defeat reactive armor, was introduced in 1988.

Nonetheless, with the development of precision antitank guided missiles, such as the Russian AT-3 Sagger, deployed in 1963, and the American BGM-71 tube-launched, optically tracked, wire-guided missile, deployed in 1971, use of RPGs against tanks declined considerably, and they were adapted thereafter mainly for use against personnel, fixed positions, and light vehicles. In addition, the fact that the RPG round self-detonates after a range of about 3,000 feet allows it to be used as a form of light artillery, spraying the target area with fragmentation.

In Mogadishu, Somalia, in 1993, RPGs shot down two American UH-60 Black Hawk helicopters. This triggered an extensive battle between U.S. forces and local militiamen, resulting in the deaths of 17 Americans. That in turn ultimately led to the withdrawal of American forces from Somalia in March 1994. Specially modified RPGs were also used by the mujahideen against Soviet helicopters in Afghanistan during the 1980s, to great effect.

In its antipersonnel role, the RPG fires two different grenades. One, a thermobaric, air-fuel explosive round, TBG-7VR, has the blast equivalent of an artillery projectile or a 120-mm mortar shell. The second, a fragmentation round, OG-7V, is particularly effective against troop emplacements. In addition, the HEAT round sprays lethal metal fragments as far as 500 feet from the point of impact.

The RPG, while originally Russian and still produced in that country, is also produced in more than a dozen other countries and is in use in some 40 countries worldwide. In addition to regular armed forces, RPGs can be found in the arsenals of almost every nonstate military organization in the world, including terrorist groups. RPGs are easy to use and maintain, are relatively inexpensive to manufacture, and, like the AK-47 assault rifle, are readily available on the black market at low cost. These factors, coupled with low training requirements and ease of use, have made it a chosen weapon of insurgents, terrorist groups, and other nonstate militias around the world. The RPG has been used extensively in Vietnam, Afghanistan (both during the Afghanistan-Soviet War and in the ongoing Operation Enduring Freedom since 2001), Chechnya, the Middle East, and Africa. The Provisional Irish Republican Army (PIRA) also used it against British troops in Northern Ireland during the 1970s.

In Iraq during Operation Iraqi Freedom, RPGs were the favored weapon of various insurgent forces. While they are not capable of penetrating the M-1 Abrams tank, they have been successfully used against light-armored vehicles and U.S. and coalition infantry forces. Nevertheless, a perfectly aimed RPG-7 can disable tanks, which can cause problems of a different sort. In August 2006 and again in January 2008, an RPG-29, the most potent RPG to date, did partially penetrate the FV4034 Challenger 2 tank, which is the United Kingdom's main battle tank.

Additional versions, the RPG-26 and RPG-27, are single-shot, disposable antitank rocket launchers, similar to the American M-72 light antitank weapon entered into service in 1989. Firing a variant of the tandem two-stage warhead developed for the RPG-7, these are for use only against armored vehicles.

Elliot Paul Chodoff

See also: Iraqi Freedom, Operation

Further Reading

Brassey's Infantry Weapons of the World. New York: Crane Russak, 1979.

Jane's Infantry Weapons, 2008–2009. Coulsdon, Surrey, UK: Jane's Information Group, 2008.

U.S. Army. *Soviet RPG-7 Antitank Grenade Launcher*. Bulletin No. 3. Fort Monroe, VA: United States Army Training and Doctrine Command, 1976.

Rumsfeld, Donald Henry

Congressman, government official, ambassador, and U.S. secretary of defense (1975–1977, 2001–2006). Born in Chicago, Illinois, on July 9, 1932, Donald Rumsfeld graduated from Princeton University in 1954. He was commissioned in the navy through the Naval Reserve Officers' Training Corps (NROTC) and served from 1954 until 1957 as a pilot and flight instructor. Rumsfeld remained in the reserves, retiring as a navy captain in 1989.

Rumsfeld began his long association with Washington as an administrative assistant to Representative David S. Dennison Jr. of Ohio (1957–1959) then joined the staff of Representative Robert Griffen of Michigan. From 1960 through 1962 he worked for an investment-banking firm. In 1962 Rumsfeld was elected to the U.S. House of Representatives as a Republican from Illinois and served until 1969, when he resigned to accept appointment as director of the Office of Economic Opportunity and assistant to President Richard M. Nixon (1969–1970). He was then counselor to the president and director of the Economic Stabilization Program (1971–1973). During 1973 and 1974 he was U.S. ambassador to the North Atlantic Treaty Organization (NATO) and thus avoided any involvement with the Watergate scandal.

Donald Rumsfeld was U.S. secretary of defense between 1975 and 1977, and again from 2001 to 2006. The confrontational Rumsfeld was one of the strongest proponents of a U.S. invasion of Iraq but has been roundly criticized for his failure to provide adequate ground forces for the invasion and to recognize the potential for insurgency operations. (U.S. Department of Defense)

When Nixon resigned and was succeeded by Gerald Ford, Rumsfeld returned to Washington in August 1974 to serve as chair of the new president's transition team. He was then Ford's chief of staff. From 1975 until 1977 Rumsfeld served as secretary of defense. At age 43, he was the youngest person to hold that position. During Rumsfeld's 14 months in office, he oversaw the transformation of the military to an all-volunteer force, as well as post–Vietnam War reforms. He also actively campaigned for additional defense appropriations and to develop weapons systems, such as the B-1 bomber, the Trident missile system, and the MX missile. Ford honored Rumsfeld for his government service in 1977 with the Presidential Medal of Freedom, the nation's highest civilian award.

Rumsfeld left government service when President James (Jimmy) E. Carter took office in January 1977. Following a brief period as a university lecturer, Rumsfeld entered private business. He was chief executive officer, then chairman, of G. D. Searle, the pharmaceutical company, from 1977 to 1985. From 1990 until 1993 Rumsfeld served as chairman and chief executive officer of General Instrument Corporation. From 1997 until 2001, Rumsfeld was chairman of Gilead Sciences, Inc. Concurrent with his work in the private sector, Rumsfeld served on numerous federal boards. He also served in the Ronald Reagan administration as special presidential envoy to the Middle East during 1983 and 1984.

In January 2001 newly elected president George W. Bush appointed Rumsfeld to be secretary of defense for a second time. Rumsfeld then became the oldest individual to hold the post. Bush charged him with transforming the military from its Cold War emphasis on major conventional warfare into a lighter, more efficient force capable of rapid deployment around the world. Rumsfeld worked to develop network-centric warfare, an approach to military operations that relies on technological innovation and integration of weapons and information systems to produce more firepower with fewer personnel. In addition, Rumsfeld initiated the restructuring of the U.S. military presence throughout the world and the closure and consolidation of bases. Rumsfeld also refocused the strategic forces of the United States by emphasizing missile defense and space systems following the 2002 U.S. withdrawal from the Anti-Ballistic Missile Treaty. He made certain of the loyalty of top officers by personally reviewing all higher promotion decisions at

the three-star level and above. He angered a number of congressional representatives when he canceled such weapons programs as the Comanche helicopter and Crusader self-propelled artillery system.

Rumsfeld's reform efforts and his restructuring of the military were overshadowed by his role in the post–September 11, 2001, Global War on Terror. As secretary of defense and a proponent of neoconservatism, Rumsfeld oversaw the military operation that overthrew the Taliban regime in Afghanistan (Operation ENDURING FREEDOM), although the failure to capture Osama bin Laden tarnished the otherwise successful military campaign.

Rumsfeld was one of the foremost proponents of military action against Iraq, teaming up with President Bush and Vice President Richard Cheney to overcome opposition from within the cabinet by Secretary of State Colin Powell. Indeed, Rumsfeld was a major architect of the Bush Doctrine, which called for preemptive military action against potential adversaries. Rumsfeld then directed the 2003 invasion of Iraq (Operation IRAQI FREEDOM). In the campaign, Rumsfeld employed a strategy that relied on firepower and smaller numbers of "boots on the ground."

While the overthrow of the Iraqi regime of Saddam Hussein was highly successful, the subsequent occupation of Iraq did not go well. Within the Pentagon, there were complaints of Rumsfeld running roughshod over those who disagreed with him. Certainly he was much criticized for his outspoken, combative management style, as when he pointedly referred to the French and German governments, which had opposed the war, as "Old Europe." But there was good reason to criticize his military decisions and specifically his overly optimistic assessment of the situation that would follow the overthrow of Hussein. Disbanding the Iraqi Army to rebuild it from scratch came to be seen in retrospect as a major blunder. Rumsfeld had also ignored previous recommendations that 400,000 U.S. troops would be required for any occupation of Iraq. The actual number of troops involved was only about one-third that number. As a consequence, Iraqi arms depots, oil-production facilities, and even the national museum were looted in the immediate aftermath of the invasion.

Occupation troops were unable to halt a growing insurgency. As U.S. casualties escalated and Iraq descended into sectarian violence, calls for Rumsfeld's ouster came from Republicans as well as Democrats, and even a number of prominent retired generals. Just prior to the 2006 midterm elections, an editorial in all the *Military Times* newspapers demanded his removal.

Rumsfeld resigned on November 8, 2006. This came a week after President Bush had expressed confidence in his defense secretary and said that he would remain until the end of his term, but it was also one day after the midterm elections, in which the Republican Party lost its majorities in both the House of Representatives and the Senate. The election was widely seen as a referendum on the Iraq War and, by extension, Rumsfeld's leadership of it. President Bush named former Central Intelligence Agency (CIA) director Robert Gates to succeed Rumsfeld. His book *Knowns and Unknowns: A Memoir* was published in 2011.

Tom Lansford and Spencer C. Tucker

See also: Bush, George Walker; Bush Doctrine; Central Intelligence Agency; Gates, Robert Michael

Further Reading

Graham, Bradley. *By His Own Rules: The Ambitions, Successes, and Ultimate Failures of Donald Rumsfeld*. New York: PublicAffairs, 2009.

Scarborough, Rowan. *Rumsfeld's War: The Untold Story of America's Anti-Terrorist Commander*. Washington, DC: Regnery, 2004.

Woodward, Bob. *Bush at War*. New York: Simon and Schuster, 2002.

Woodward, Bob. *Plan of Attack*. New York: Simon and Schuster, 2004.

Woodward, Bob. *State of Denial: Bush at War, Part III*. New York: Simon and Schuster, 2006.

S

Sadr, Muqtada al-

Influential religious figure in the Iraqi Shia community, leader of the Sadriyun that included the Mahdi Army militias, and considered by many to be the most populist of Iraqi Shiite leaders. The fourth son of the famous Iraqi cleric Muhammad Sadiq al-Sadr, Muqtada al-Sadr was born on August 12, 1973, in Baghdad. Sadr became a political leader with an enhanced following as a consequence of his nationalist stance against the coalition presence in Iraq, beginning in 2003. In Shia Islam in Iraq, believers follow a living cleric, but since Sadr had not attained the rank of his illustrious father in scholarly training or publications, he did not inherit the loyalty of many in his father's network of mosques who preferred a more senior cleric. Yet Sadr acquired a loyal following of his own and, during a period of political truce with the Iraqi government, sought to enhance his standing by continuing his own religious training. Like his father and Iraq's highest Shiite religious authority, Grand Ayatollah Sayyid Ali Husayn al-Sistani, Sadr drew support from a network of mosques but also from extensive charitable and social services provided to impoverished Shia communities in various areas of Baghdad. He also has followers in many other cities and areas of southern and central Iraq. Sadr became especially popular in the large slum areas in Baghdad, including the Thawra area, which became known as Sadr City from the strength of his followers there.

The elder Sadr was a revered member of the Iraqi Shiite clergy who was assassinated, along with his two elder sons, in 1999. It is widely believed that the assassination was ordered by Iraqi leader Saddam Hussein. Muqtada al-Sadr is also related to the late highly respected leader Imam Musa al-Sadr, who created a popular movement among the Shia of Lebanon.

Muqtada al-Sadr spoke out fiercely against the actions of the U.S.-led coalition in Iraq despite his opposition, and that of his followers, to Saddam Hussein's dictatorial government. Sadr's opposition to the coalition presence was based on both political and religious considerations. After the U.S. Coalition Provisional Authority (CPA) closed Sadr's newspaper *al-Hawza* on March 28, 2004, and there had been numerous attacks against him in the American-funded Iraqi press, Sadr mobilized his militia, known as the Mahdi Army. This was to protest what he perceived as the CPA's attempt to eliminate his organization prior to the transfer of authority to Iraqi officials, scheduled for June 30, 2004. The subsequent protests turned violent when a key Sadr aide was arrested on April 3, 2004. The situation was further enflamed two days later when CPA administrator L. Paul Bremer issued a warrant for Sadr's arrest and essentially declared him an outlaw. Sadr's Mahdi Army subsequently seized control of several cities in southern Iraq, provoking the worst crisis for the U.S.-led occupation since the spring of 2003, especially as the Mahdi Army held the loyalty

of the most fiercely anti-Baathist groups in the country.

During the ensuing week of violence, Sadr sought refuge in the Imam Ali Mosque in Najaf, the holiest shrine in Shia Islam. Sadr's popularity soared during this period because he appeared to be the only Iraqi leader willing to actively resist the occupation. All others, even Ayatollah Sistani, appeared to be passively silent or even acquiescent to the Western authorities. Sadr declared a cease-fire on April 10, 2004, ostensibly to observe a three-day religious holiday, but momentum had also shifted as the CPA retook certain key bases in southern cities. In subsequent negotiations, the CPA called for Sadr to surrender but refrained from overt attempts to arrest him.

In late August 2004, following more than three weeks of renewed fighting between Mahdi Army fighters and U.S. forces, Sadr's forces withdrew from the Imam Ali Mosque. Sadr issued a statement urging his fighters to lay down their arms in line with an agreement he had reached with Ayatollah Sistani. On August 27, 2004, members of the Mahdi Army began surrendering their arms to Iraqi police. But Iraqi prime minister Iyad Allawi renewed the violence when he refused to honor the tenuous truce; fighting ensued, especially in Sadr City. Sadr, in an attempt to distance himself from the acrimony, was thereafter careful not to involve himself directly in Iraqi politics.

In October 2006 the Mahdi Army seized control of Amarah in southern Iraq. A pitched battle ensued between Iraqi security forces and the militiamen. Sadr implored the Mahdi soldiers to lay down their arms, and some have speculated that he had not authorized the Amarah offensive and had lost control over Mahdi Army groups in that area. Sadr's plea was largely ignored. In February 2007 the U.S. media reported

Muqtada, the son of the late Ayatollah Muhammad Sadiq al-Sadr, who was assassinated with his two sons on February 19, 1999, by Saddam Hussein, sits in his offices in the holy Shiite city of Najaf, 112 miles south of Baghdad, on July 3, 2003. Muqtada said during an interview with the Action Francaise Press (AFP) that he condemned the attacks on coalition forces and advocated peace through Islamic means. (AFP/Getty Images)

that Sadr had fled to Iran in anticipation of the security crackdown attendant with the U.S. troop-surge strategy. Sadr, however, had merely gone into seclusion in Iraq, and during his two-month hiatus he sharply condemned the U.S.-led occupation and called for Iraqi security forces not to cooperate with occupation forces. In 2008 Sadr called for a truce and implored the Mahdi Army to lay down its arms, in response to myriad negotiations with Iranian and Iraqi leaders following several months of brutal fighting between the Mahdi Army and Iraqi government forces. Sadr continued to condemn the U.S. government and coalition forces' occupation in Iraq, as that was the primary concern of his followers. In late 2008 he called for attacks against U.S. troops in Iraq in retaliation for the Israeli incursion into the Gaza Strip seeking to defeat the radical Palestinian group Hamas. However, this was largely a rhetorical gesture, as his followers continued to observe the truce in place.

Paul G. Pierpaoli Jr. and Sherifa Zuhur

See also: Coalition Provisional Authority; Mahdi Army; Sadr City, Battle of; Sistani, Sayyid Ali Husayn al-

Further Reading

Cockburn, Patrick. *Muqtada: Muqtada al-Sadr, the Shia Revival, and the Struggle for Iraq*. New York: Scribner, 2008.

Diamond, Larry. *Squandered Victory: The American Occupation and the Bungled Effort to Bring Democracy to Iraq*. New York: Times Book, 2005.

Nasr, Vali. *The Shia Revival: How Conflicts within Islam Will Shape the Future*. New York: Norton, 2006.

Sadr City, Battle of

A battle during the Iraq War that occurred from March 26 until May 11, 2008. In the Battle of Sadr City, coalition forces principally fought elements of the Mahdi Army. Sadr City is one of nine administrative districts of Baghdad, built in 1959 to ease a housing shortage in the capital city. It is home to more than 1 million Shia Muslims, many of them poor. Part of the district had been known as Thawra and was termed Saddam City by the Americans in 2003. American forces in the coalition then began

to call the area Sadr City from the strength there of Muqtada al-Sadr's followers, known as the Sadriyun. The coalition forces in Iraq had long sought permission from Iraqi prime minister Nuri al-Maliki to subdue the Jaysh al-Mahdi (JAM) militias, which they called the Mahdi Army. The Sadriyun, or Sadrists, possessed militias just as did the Dawa Party and the Supreme Council of the Islamic Revolution in Iran (SCIRI). However, these militias also clashed with them, and therefore the coalition had to some degree been influenced by the competition of the various Shia political forces. The Americans claimed that certain elements from the Jaysh al-Mahdi were obtaining arms from Iran, although their competitors, such as the Badr Brigades, were more clearly linked with Iranian support, or at least had been in the past. Maliki was reluctant to approve coalition operations against fellow Shiites, particularly as he might not have been elected had it not been for his good relations with Muqtada al-Sadr and his followers. Also, the largest Shia party in the country had been even closer to Iran than the Sadriyun, who were seen as an Iraqi-based party. Another concern was the vulnerability of the poor civilian population of Sadr City. However, under pressure from Washington, when 12 rockets were launched from the Sadr City area into the Green Zone on March 25, 2008, Maliki approved a joint Iraqi-American response.

Forces of the Iraqi Army 11th Division entered Sadr City on March 26, supported by the U.S. Army 3rd Brigade Combat Team, 4th Infantry Division, commanded by Colonel John Hort. As the Iraqis moved in, American combat engineers began construction of a concrete barrier across the southern one-third of Sadr City in order to push insurgent forces back beyond rocket range of the coalition-controlled Green Zone. An American Stryker brigade and other supporting coalition units, including troops from the 2nd Stryker Cavalry Regiment, succeeded over the course of a month in building a three-mile-long wall across the southern third of the neighborhood. The concrete "Gold Wall" was constructed from sections 12 feet high by 5 feet wide, placed individually by crane. The Gold Wall and the construction of barriers has been highly criticized by Iraqis and others who believe that defense of perimeters or erection of "sanitized zones" is untenable in the long run.

The fighting in Sadr City was some of the heaviest in the Iraq War. Significantly, for the first time, an unmanned aerial vehicle (UAV), or drone, was placed under the direct control of a battlefield commander. Utilizing helicopters and armed and unarmed UAVs, and leveraging the persistent surveillance ability of the surveillance drones—which could follow a target on the ground for hours—American forces were able to strike insurgent targets deep within Sadr City. Precision attacks directed or conducted by UAVs killed numerous insurgent mortar and rocket teams.

The heaviest fighting took place on April 28 as militia forces, emboldened by the lack of American air support during a heavy sandstorm, attacked along the heavily contested area of al-Quds Street, known to allied forces as Route Gold. Dozens of militia fighters were killed in ensuing firefights. Mahdi Army forces marshaled heavy firepower to oppose the construction of the concrete wall. Although they employed .50-caliber sniper rifles and RPG-29 rockets, and detonated more than 120 Iranian-made mines with explosively forged projectiles against coalition forces, the militias nevertheless failed to prevent construction of the wall.

Of the some 2,000 American troops in the battle, 6 were killed. Some 5,000 men of the Iraqi Army took part in the battle; their casualty figures were not reported. The Mahdi militia numbered perhaps between 2,000 and 4,000 members; they are believed to have suffered some 700–1,000 casualties.

The forces of the Supreme Islamic Council of Iraq (Majlis al-'A'la al-Islami al-'Iraqu, or SIIC), formerly known as the SCIRI, are heavily represented in the new Iraqi Army; consequently the action was understood as one of intrasectarian and political warfare. Muqtada al-Sadr took refuge in Iran but called for his fighters to adhere to a truce, or this campaign could have led to a much wider popular rebellion against the new Iraqi government. Unfortunately, violence continued in Baghdad with numerous large-scale suicide bombings there and in other cities in the spring of 2009. These, however, were primarily Sunni attacks on Shia or Iraqi and coalition forces, or against the Awakening Shaykhs.

The Battle of Sadr City was seen as a significant victory for coalition forces; however, it came at the expense of Prime Minister Maliki's impartiality and credibility to some degree, making him appear to be a creature of the coalition. Sadrist forces and Maliki reached a cease-fire agreement on May 11, 2008, bringing an end to the major fighting in Sadr City.

Shawn Fisher and Sherifa Zuhur

See also: Mahdi Army; Maliki, Nuri Muhammed Kamil Hasan al-; Sadr, Muqtada al-; Supreme Iraqi Islamic Council

Further Reading

Gordon, Michael R., and Stephen Farrell. "Iraqi Troops Take Charge of Sadr City in Swift Push." *New York Times*, May 21, 2008.

Gordon, Michael R., and Alissa J. Rubin. "Operation in Sadr City Is an Iraqi Success, So Far." *New York Times*, May 22, 2008.

Paley, Amit R. "U.S. Role Deepens in Sadr City." *Washington Post*, April 21, 2008.

Salafism

Term describing branches of reformist Islam as well as a widespread contemporary purist movement, an attempt to return to traditional Islamic roots and practices. Salafism (*salafiyya* in Arabic) is derived from the Arabic *salaf* and means "(righteous) predecessors" or "(righteous) ancestors" in reference to the first three generations of Muslims. Some adherents seek a return to the spirit of that period.

Modernist reformers in the late 19th and early 20th centuries have been considered Salafists. The name also applies to fervently observant or activist Sunni Muslims who follow the teachings of Muhammad abd al-Wahhab from the 18th century and other scholars. These latter are sometimes called the neo-Salafis.

A key concept undergirding Salafism is that the first several generations of Muslims were intent on following the Sunnah, or tradition of the Prophet, and were sincere in their efforts to live according to Islamic teaching. One common thread in the different branches of Salafism is that Islam must be cleansed of illicit innovations, known as *bid'ah*. The modernist school argued that tradition had rendered various principles rigid and imitative, and that a return to previous creative principles would be of benefit. This school implicitly supported some innovations.

Both the modernist and purist strands of Salafism have impacted such organizations as the Muslim Brotherhood. The purist trend of Salafism has informed the worldviews of such organizations as al-Qaeda in Mesopotamia or al-Qaeda in Afghanistan and Pakistan. However, most Muslims who abide by the precepts of Salafism and who may be found in many countries are neither violent nor radical.

The terms "Salafiyya" and "Salafism" date back hundreds of years and were applied to movements like the Ikhwan al-Safa that arose in previous centuries. The term "salaf" appears in a number of early *hadith*, or sayings of the Prophet and his companions, as well as other writings, such as the *tafsirs* of al-Tabari and Ibn Kathir. The title was applied in the late 19th century to various Muslim thinkers, including Jamal ad-Din al-Afghani and his disciple Muhammad Abduh, mainly in response to British colonialism in the Middle East.

Jamal ad-Din al-Afghani was born and raised in eastern Iran and was probably Shiite by doctrinal association. Nevertheless, in his effort to see the revival of Islam as a counter to British colonial policy, he strove to hide his doctrinal sympathies, focusing instead on building a philosophical opposition movement to oppose British occupation of Muslim lands. He traveled extensively and typically portrayed himself in ways that were not consistent with his background and training. In each instance when his benefactors, whether in Great Britain, Egypt, or Istanbul, became suspicious of him and his motives, Afghani would depart to another area of the world to continue his self-appointed mission to throw off the British yoke. Wherever he went he continued to preach the revival of the Islamic community, or *ummah*, as based on the lives of the Prophet and his early companions.

In his desire to defeat British colonialism, Afghani was willing to engage in a wide range of political and insurgency-type activities, ranging from simple fund-raising to endorsing assassination attempts against those Middle Eastern rulers he considered to be British puppets. He spoke openly of killing the leader of Persia, Nasir ad-Din Shah, and one of his disciples eventually carried out the deed in 1896. Although supportive of the Ottoman Empire as the current seat of the Islamic caliphate, Afghani spent his last years in Istanbul virtually as a political prisoner of the empire's sultan, and he died of cancer in 1897.

Afghani's influence almost vanished after his death, but later he became a folk hero to the revived Islamic movement in the Middle East. The principles of Salafism would be pushed eloquently by one of his main disciples, Muhammad Abduh. Abduh collaborated with Afghani on a number of publishing projects and helped to popularize Salafist ideas through what became known as "the Islamic League." He was savvy politically and was able to secure the position as Grand Mufti of Egypt in 1899, a post he held until his death.

In some ways Abduh's influence was greater than Afghani's because Abduh was seen by many as more moderate and mainstream, even though his ideas were essentially no different than his mentor's. His writings were more readily accepted and included a *tafsir* of the Qur'an along with other works defending the unity of Allah from Christian influences stemming from British colonial policy.

Abduh's ideas would have a tremendous impact on the thinking of Hassan al-Banna and the founding of the Muslim Brotherhood in Egypt in 1928. The focus of the brotherhood as well as other revivalist Muslim societies was initially based on personal piety and raising money through the imposition of *zakat*, or the charitable tax. Soon these activities turned to political activism, and the brotherhood surged to the forefront of political thought in the struggle against British colonial occupation of the country. Although Banna was assassinated in 1949, the ideas of the brotherhood spread throughout the Middle East and into the rest of the Islamic world, especially through the work of such apologists as Sayyid Qutb and Yusuf al-Qaradawi, and have in large measure become the foundation of the Islamic revival movement.

The principles of Salafism revolve around several key issues that involve the literal interpretation of the Qur'an and adopting certain aspects of the lifestyle of the Prophet and his companions. Shunning Western dress and grooming became important outward displays of this movement, although for political reasons, this was not always consistently done. Coupled with this was a revival of interest in the writings of the Hanbalite jurist Ibn Taymiyyah, who discussed the conflict inherent between the *salaf* and the *khalaf*, or the authentic believers of the Prophet with those who are merely substitutes of the real thing.

This led to sporadic conflict in the Muslim world between the members of the Salafist movement and the governments of the region. Efforts by Arabic governments to suppress Salafism culminated in the judicial execution of Sayyid Qutb by the Egyptian government of Gamal Abdel Nasser in 1966 and the government of Hafiz al-Asad's 1982 destruction of the town of Hama, in which close to 30,000 people died. Hama had become the base of the movement in Syria. These attempts to destroy the movement were only temporary, however. Rebounding from these setbacks, the brotherhood continued its political activities throughout the Islamic world, spreading even into Europe and the United States.

Another important aspect of the Salafist movement is the call to revive *ijtihad* and the rejection in general of the concept of *taqlid*. Taqlid, often incorrectly called blind following, stresses the need for a Muslim to simply follow the rulings of a particular *madhhab*, or school of law, without doing the necessary research himself or herself. This is a convenient approach because it does not require an inordinate amount of time and energy to be expended on learning the fundamentals of Islam, particularly those considered well established a few hundred years after the death of the Prophet Muhammad. Taking a ruling on faith, a Muslim can practice his or her religion on the basis of these early rulings by those much more learned than he or she.

The weakness of taqlid, however, is obvious, as for one to be a truly devoted follower it is best to learn the foundational material for oneself. This requires long hours of study and sometimes even formal training to become well versed in the early writings of Islam. This approach reopened the door to ijtihad, the revival of personal interpretation of Qur'anic texts as well as other early writings. For many centuries the learned within Islam had considered ijtihad closed because of the solidification and codification of Islamic practice through the *madhhabs*. Salafism called for the return of ijtihad to allow the typical believer to make up his or her mind for himself or herself, and this led to a massive revival in interest in the classical and medieval works of Islam. Translations of the hadith and Sunnah writings flourished, and the works of medieval scholars such as Qadi Iyad, Ibn Taymiyyah, and Ibn Qayyim were resurrected. Even the writings of some early Sufi scholars such as Imam Ghazzali became popular, even though the Salafist movement by and large considers Sufism a heretical interpretation of Islam.

The return of ijtihad meant that many devout Muslims began to question some aspects of the juristic rulings from later scholars of the madhhabs, while still retaining interest in the rulings of the founders of those schools. This revival of personal interpretation had significant influence on bringing back the earliest teachings regarding *zakat*, the proper forms of prayer, and the need to engage in jihad. Zakat became the means for the Salafists to influence local politics through provision of welfare and family support, while jihad became more than an inward struggle, returning to the Prophet's own conception that jihad was a form of warfare to make Islam supreme. This revival not only spawned such groups as the Muslim Brotherhood, but also led to a whole series of other lesser groups generally striving for the same goals, that is, the imposition of Islamic Sharia in the Muslim world and a return to evangelistic operations to spread Islam throughout the non-Muslim world. The Salafist movement's teachings can be found in virtually every Islamic revival today, largely because those teachings were built upon the earliest ideas and writings of the Prophet and his companions.

Russell G. Rodgers

See also: Sunni Islam

Further Reading

Abduh, Muhammad. *Risalat al-Tauhid.* [The Theology of Unit]. Translated by Ishaq Musa'ad and Kenneth Craig. Kuala Lumpur, Malaysia: Islamic Book Trust, 2004.

Al-Hashimi, Muhammad Ali. *The Ideal Muslim Society: As Defined in the Qur'an and Sunnah.* Riyadh, Saudi Arabia: International Islamic Publishing House, 2007.

Al-Qaradawi, Yusuf. *The Eye of the Beholder: The Muslim Brotherhood over the Past 70 Years.* Cairo: Al-Falah Foundation, 2003.

Keddie, Nikki. *An Islamic Response to Imperialism: Political and Religious Writings of Sayyid Jamal ad-Din "al-Afghani."* Translated by Nikki Keddie and Hamid Algar. Berkeley: University of California Press, 1968.

Philips, Abu Ameenah Bilal. *The Evolution of Fiqh: Islamic Law and the Madh-habs.* Kuala Lumpur, Malaysia: A. S. Noordeen, 2005.

Sanchez, Ricardo S.

U.S. Army officer best known for his command of coalition forces in Iraq from June 2003 to June 2004 (Operation Iraqi Freedom). Born on May 17, 1951, in Rio Grande City, Texas, Ricardo S. Sanchez began his military career in the Reserve Officers' Training Corps (ROTC) program at the University of Texas at Austin and Texas A&I University (now Texas A&M–Kingsville). A 1973 graduate of the latter institution, Sanchez was commissioned in the U.S. Army as a second lieutenant that same year. He served in both infantry and armor units early in his career. He was a platoon leader, an executive officer, an assistant logistics officer, and an operations officer. Sanchez's military education included both the Command and General Staff College and the U.S. Army War College. He also earned a master's degree in operations research and systems analysis engineering from the Naval Postgraduate School.

As a lieutenant colonel, Sanchez served in Operation Desert Storm in 1991 as commander of the 2nd Battalion, 69th Armor, 197th Infantry Brigade. His performance in the Persian Gulf War contributed to his early promotion to colonel in September 1994. Between July 1994 and June 1996 he commanded the 2nd Brigade of the 1st Infantry Division (Mechanized) at Fort Riley, Kansas.

Lieutenant General Ricardo Sanchez, the commander of U.S. forces in Iraq. Sanchez held the top military position in Iraq throughout one of the most critical periods of the war. During his tenure as commander in Iraq, the killing of Saddam Hussein's sons Uday and Qusay and the capture of Saddam Hussein were his major accomplishments. (AP Photo)

Sanchez then served as an investigator in the Office of the U.S. Army Inspector General Agency and in various roles at U.S. Southern Command. After promotion to brigadier general in November 1998, Sanchez served as assistant division commander (support) of the 1st Infantry Division during 1999 and 2000. From July 2000 to June 2001 he was deputy chief of staff for operations, U.S. Army Europe and Seventh Army, Germany. Between July 2001 and June 2003 he commanded the 1st Armored Division, being promoted to major general in July 2002. Promoted to lieutenant general in

August 2003, from July 2003 to June 2004 he was the commanding general of V Corps, U.S. Army Europe and Seventh Army, Germany, including duty as commanding general, Combined Joint Task Force 7, Operation Iraqi Freedom.

With the rapid withdrawal of U.S. Central Command (CENTCOM) and its Combined Forces Land Component Command (CFLCC), Sanchez by default became the commander of Coalition Ground Forces in Iraq, the top military position in Iraq. This critical period after the end of major hostilities saw the emergence of the Iraqi insurgency, the deaths of Uday and Qusay Hussein, and the capture of deposed Iraqi president Saddam Hussein. The major challenges facing Sanchez were the reestablishment of essential services and basic security, and ending the counterinsurgency. According to multiple sources, communications between Sanchez and L. Paul Bremer, head of the Coalition Provisional Authority (CPA), were strained and often nonexistent. This poor communication and lack of unified leadership is often cited as one of the contributors to the turmoil that followed the end of major conflict in Iraq. Compounding Sanchez's problems during this period was the fact that he was essentially a corps commander with little more than a corps staff yet was responsible for commanding an entire theater. With the vacuum created by the rapid withdrawal of the CFLCC, Sanchez was left with a staff that was nowhere near large enough for his responsible span of control or trained and experienced at the higher level of theater operations.

Despite progress in certain areas, this period of Iraqi Freedom was marked by a burgeoning insurgency, widespread lawlessness, and the challenge of detaining thousands of prisoners. The most glaring controversy during Sanchez's tenure was the prisoner abuse at Abu Ghraib prison. In September 2003 Sanchez approved in writing 29 interrogation methods authorized for use with Iraqi detainees. At the direction of CENTCOM, 10 of those methods were later repealed after having been deemed unacceptably aggressive. However, the actual methods employed at Abu Ghraib went beyond even what Sanchez had authorized, as evidenced by the graphic photographs that were ultimately seen on worldwide media. On January 16, 2004, Sanchez issued a press release announcing the investigation of "detainee abuse at a Coalition Forces detention facility."

Sanchez left his post in June 2004. Ultimately several low-ranking military members were court-martialed over the abuse scandal, and Sanchez believed that he was denied his fourth star and was forced into retirement on November 1, 2006, because of it.

In 2008 Sanchez published his autobiography, *Wiser in Battle: A Soldier's Story*, a sweeping indictment of the handling of the Iraq War by Defense Secretary Donald Rumsefeld and the George W. Bush administration. Sanchez now lives in Texas.

Benjamin D. Forest

See also: Abu Ghraib; Iraqi Freedom, Operation; Iraqi Insurgency

Further Reading

Gordon, Michael R., and General Bernard E. Trainor. *Cobra II: The Inside Story of the Invasion and Occupation of Iraq*. New York: Pantheon Books, 2006.

Ricks, Thomas E. *Fiasco: The American Military Adventure in Iraq*. New York: Penguin, 2006.

Sanchez, Ricardo S., and Donald T. Phillips. *Wiser in Battle: A Soldier's Story*. New York: Harper, 2008.

Woodward, Bob. *State of Denial: Bush at War, Part III*. New York: Simon and Schuster, 2006.

SEAL Teams

The U.S. Navy SEALs (Sea, Air, and Land) are part of the U.S. Navy Special Warfare Command, which in turn is a unit of the U.S. Special Operations Command (SOCOM). SOCOM was formed in 1987 to better coordinate military special operations, including the U.S. Army Delta Force, the U.S. Army Special Forces, and U.S. Air Force and U.S. Marine Corps special operations elements. U.S. Navy SEALs have played important roles in Operations DESERT STORM, ENDURING FREEDOM, and IRAQI FREEDOM.

With nearly 2,500 members, SEALs have a distinguished tradition to draw upon. Tracing their heritage to the World War II navy frogmen who cleared underwater obstacles on Japanese-held islands in the Pacific prior to amphibious landings, SEAL Teams were officially formed by order of President John F. Kennedy on January 1, 1962. From the Vietnam War in the 1960s to the invasion of Grenada in 1983 and the 1989 invasion of Panama, SEALs played an important role in American covert and special operations missions.

While SEALs operate in small units from two to eight members, the organizational structure of the SEAL Teams is larger. There are eight SEAL Teams (four on the West Coast and four on the East Coast). Each team is subdivided into six platoons, with supporting units that make up a Naval Special Warfare Squadron.

SEALs have become a lead element in executing the Global War on Terror. From 2002 to the end of 2008 SEALS were undermanned by about 12 percent, but a mandate to remedy the shortfall has resulted in a slow expansion in their numbers. Since augmentation efforts began in 2005, the rate of completion for the Basic Underwater Demolition/SEAL Course has risen from 26 percent to about 32 percent. Training, at a cost of around $350,000 per individual, takes on average 30 months before a SEAL candidate is ready to deploy to a team.

The international response to the Iraqi invasion of Kuwait in August 1990 led to Operation DESERT SHIELD and then to Operation DESERT STORM. Beginning in August 1990 SEAL Teams 1, 3, and 5 were in country and served in various missions. Prior to combat they operated on the Kuwait-Iraq border, gathering intelligence on Iraqi dispositions and helping to train Kuwaiti and Saudi sailors. SEAL Teams were the first U.S. combat forces to face Iraqi forces. When the war began in January 1991, SEALs performed maritime missions such as inspecting ships and capturing oil platforms. This included the first nonaerial combat of the war when SEALs assaulted Iraqis firing from a platform on U.S. helicopters. This SEAL operation killed 5 Iraqis and captured 23 others with no American casualties. Other tasks performed included combat search-and-rescue missions (including securing an American pilot who had ejected into the sea off Kuwait) and conducting beach reconnaissance to determine potential landing areas in Kuwait. Additionally, SEALs performed mine-clearing operations. During a 16-day period in January 1991 SEALs destroyed or rendered harmless 25 maritime mines. This activity went undetected by the Iraqis.

One SEAL mission during DESERT STORM was diversionary in nature and was designed to convince the Iraqi leadership that an amphibious assault was in the offing, fixing Iraqi coast defense units in place when the ground offensive began. SEALs planted explosive charges in Iraqi-held Kuwaiti beaches. These were later detonated remotely, part of a major deception operation involving more than 17,000 U.S. marines on landing ships off the coast.

The wars in Afghanistan and Iraq found the SEALs operating inland. During these conflicts they have performed various missions including covert combat action, escorting VIPs in Iraq and Afghanistan, the rescue of American and allied prisoners of war (including the April 2003 rescue of U.S. Army private Jessica Lynch in Nasiriyah, Iraq), search and rescue of downed pilots, and the capture or apprehension of high-value targets. Some examples in Afghanistan include the search for al-Qaeda organization leader Osama bin Laden and Taliban Mullah Khairulla Kahirkhawa in February 2002 and stability operations performed with indigenous forces. In January 2002 Seal Team 3 searched for weapons being smuggled into Afghanistan. In the Iraq War, SEAL operations have included safeguarding offshore oil platforms and dams (the latter included the April 2003 capture of Dam 57 in conjunction with Polish Special Operations forces before Saddam Hussein loyalists could destroy it) and reconnaissance and intelligence gathering.

Operations in conjunction with both conventional forces and special operations units of the other armed services have expanded the SEAL missions as well. A major strength of the SEAL Teams continues to be their great flexibility, which gives them tremendous force-multiplying capability. They tie up more enemy troops defending against their real or perceived threats than their actual numbers would seem to dictate.

The conflicts in Afghanistan and Iraq have taken a toll on the SEAL Teams. Between October 2001 and November 2008 SEAL deaths were estimated to exceed 25, a fairly large number for this small organization. By April 2010 that number had risen to

30. Decorations include a posthumous Medal of Honor to Master-at-Arms Second Class Michael A. Monsoor, a 25-year-old member of SEAL Team 3 who fell onto a grenade on September 26, 2006, in Ramadi, Iraq, to save the lives of his teammates. Another posthumous Medal of Honor was awarded to Lieutenant Michael P. Murphy for heroic actions in Afghanistan on June 27 and 28, 2005.

Scott R. DiMarco

See also: IRAQI FREEDOM, Operation

Further Reading

Couch, Dick. *Down Range: Navy SEALs in the War on Terrorism.* New York: Three Rivers, 2006.

Dockery, Kevin. *Navy SEALs: A Complete History from World War II to the Present.* New York: Berkley Books, 2004.

Fuentes, Gidget. "The Search for SEALs: Changes to Special-Warfare Recruiting, Training, Practices Shows Promise to Growing Unit." *Navy Times* (April 26, 2007): 18.

Luttrell, Marcus, with Patrick Robinson. *Lone Survivor: The Eyewitness Account of Operation Redwing and the Lost Heroes of SEAL-10.* Boston: Little, Brown, 2007.

Roth, Margaret. "Recent Conflicts Mark Turning Point for SEALS, Other Special Ops Forces." *Seapower* (February 2005): 14–16.

Sharia

Sharia is Islamic law, which Muslims regard as divine and a guide to an Islamic lifestyle. Islamic law is not monolithic; many differences in its principles and positions have occurred, and it is continually evolving. Sharia guides the believer's relationship with God (theology) as well as human relationships (ethics). Moreover, there are traces of tribal or customary law (*urf*) within the criminal principles of jurisprudence and penalties of Sharia. Especially since the terrorist attacks on the United States of September 11, 2001, but also earlier, some non-Muslims have attacked Muslims seeking to live under Sharia and have described Sharia in pejorative terms.

The term "Sharia" (Shari'ah) means the "straight path" or "the way." In the Qur'an (surah 1), which is part of daily prayers, Muslims ask to be guided on the straight path (*sirat al-mustaqim*) and not the path of those who have gone astray. Sharia provides that guidance. Reference to Sharia is found in the Qur'an in surah 45:18, where the Prophet is told that Allah (God) has "set Thee on the Way of our religion; so follow it, and follow not the desires of those who know not."

Sharia developed gradually over a considerable period and is based on the roots of jurisprudence (*usul al-fiqh*) as interpreted by Muslim scholars. The actual literature on Sharia deals with either the roots of Islamic jurisprudence, which differ slightly in each of the formal schools of Islamic law, or with *furu' al-fiqh*, the branches of Islamic law. The works on *usul al-fiqh* discuss the Qur'an as well as the *hadith*, the collections of the sayings and deeds of the Prophet Muhammad and in some cases those of his Companions or wives. The hadith are intended to illustrate the Sunnah, or tradition of the Prophet.

Islamic legal experts and scholars use the hadith, the Qur'an, and other legal principles of Sharia in order to determine the correctness of any action. The works that explain the *usul al-fiqh* acknowledge differences between scholars and discuss methodology. The *furu'* literature, on the other hand, concerns the ritual of Islam (*ibadat*) and social relations (*mu'amalat*). The first branch considers ritual purity, prayer, *zakat* (almsgiving), pilgrimage,

fasting, and jihad, whereas the second might consider divorce; marriage; inheritance; the rules of buying, selling, lending, bequests, deposits, crimes, torts, *dhiyya* (compensatory payment to the family of the dead, or to the injured), or *talion* (retaliatory injury for injury); judicial procedure; contracts; rules about slaves; land ownership; the slaughter of animals for licit (*halal*) food; oaths; and many other topics, as virtually all aspects of life should be governed by Islamic law. Each action considered under the *furu'* is graded into one of five categories—neutral, reprehensible, forbidden, allowed, or recommended in Islam—and there may be further refinements of these gradations. In this literature, there are both expansive works with many subdivisions called *mahsus* and concise works called *mukhtasars*.

In Islam, the ultimate source of law is Allah. The Prophet Muhammad arbitrated disputes in Medina during his lifetime. After his death, lawmaking was carried out by secular rulers but also increasingly by scholars trained to be jurists. The Shia Muslims considered all the executive legislative functions of the ruler to be rightfully those of the Hidden Imam, so their scholars, *fuqaha* (those who make *fiqh*), were responsible for them.

During their lifetimes, the first four caliphs (*khulafa*) were considered the *rashidun* (rightly guided). They had an input into lawmaking as well as the arbitration of disputes. However, as the Muslim empire expanded, the need arose for a more formalized methodology to deal with the myriad of cases.

The first step to this formalization was the compilation and recension of the Qur'an. Next came the systematization of the hadith literature in the period between 800 and 960 CE. Some of these individual hadiths were considered sound, or *sahih*, while others were considered weak (available only from single sources or possibly incorrect). The collections considered to be sound or most accurate included those by Muhammad ibn Ismail ibn Ibrahim ibn al-Mughirah al-Bukhari, Abu al-Husayn Muslim ibn al-Hajjaj Qushayri al-Nishapuri (simply referred to as Muslim), Abu Issa Muhammad ibn Issa al-Tirmidhi, Abu Abdullah ibn Yazid ibn Majah al-Rabiah al-Qazwini (Ibn Majah), Abu Dawud Sulayman ibn Ashath al-Azadi al-Sijistani, Abu Abdullah Malik ibn Anas ibn Malik ibn Amr al-Asbahi (Ibn Malik), and Ahmad ibn Shuayb ibn Ali ibn Sinan Abu Abd al-Rahman al-Nasai. The most widely used today are those by Muslim and Bukhari.

The earliest collection of hadith was the *Muwatta* of Ibn Malik. He interviewed numerous individuals whose early family relatives knew the Prophet and heard key sayings from him. Ibn Malik was also the founder of the Maliki *madhhab* (school of law). Bukhari then developed a list of more than 600,000 oral traditions, but he only accepted 7,000 as sufficiently authentic to be followed. This systematic approach to the collection of hadith literature was soon followed by the development of the *madhahib* (sing., *madhhab*), or schools of law.

The early *madhahib* were quite numerous, being developed by those who were disciples of scholars of the Qur'an and hadith. In addition to these sources of law, the jurists exercised opinion (*ra'y*) and used analogy (*qiyas*) and also consensus (*ijma'*), which could refer to scholarly agreement, or what scholars believed the consensus of the Muslim community at Medina to have been.

Another method was known as *ijtihad*, a form of creative inference and interpretation in making legal judgments. This process, coupled with practical application, led to a series of digests of legal rulings. From 800 to 1300 CE, these schools of law developed, matured, and consolidated until five Sunni schools had emerged as well as several Shiite schools. Today four Sunni and three Shiite legal traditions exist as well as the Ibadi tradition. The major Sunni *madhahib* differ in methodology and rulings, but they agree on the basic commonalities of Muslim practice, such as the need for prayer or *zakat*. The basic process that each school follows was generally the same, starting with the Qur'an and then working through hadith literature, followed by the consensus opinions of the Prophet's Companions and then their individual opinions. Failing this, solutions to problems could be derived through *ijtihad* at least until the 10th century or with reference to other principles such as *istislah* (consideration of the common good). Certain Sunni *madhahib* had put more emphasis on aspects of law other than the use of *ijtihad;* however, the tradition continued on in the Jafari *madhhab* followed by the Twelver Shiite Muslims.

The Hanafi *madhhab* was based on the teachings and writings of Abu Hanifa (703–767). He had the opportunity during his lifetime to meet some of those who actually saw and heard the Prophet speak and was thus able to ascertain some hadith from them. The *Kitab al-Athar* of Ibn Hanafi, compiled around 750, serves as a key digest of hadith collections for this *madhhab*, while a number of other digests of legal rulings have come forth from its early days. Another important early writing of this school was the *Siyar* of Shaybani, written around 800 and called the "law of nations," while another was *al-Hidayah* (*The Guidance*) of Marghinani, which was penned around 1190. The Hanafi *madhhab* was the official school of the Ottoman Empire, so it is followed by the Sunni Muslims of Iraq and

Syria and is one of the two schools followed in Egypt.

The Maliki *madhhab* was established by Malik Ibn Anas (717–801), sometimes called Imam Dar al-Hijra, or the Imam of the House of the Migration. A later Maliki work of Qadi Iyad ibn Musa al-Yahsubi called *al-Shifa*, written around 1140, was an important collection of material on the life of the Prophet and its impact on the life of the Muslim. Maliki law prevails in North Africa and is characterized as being moderate; however, Maliki jurists, like others, are often influenced by the Salafist movement.

The Shafii *madhhab* was founded by Muhammad bin Idris al-Shafi (769–820). Shafi was born in Gaza and belonged to the legal school of Medina, but developed his own legal school. The *Risala al-Fiqh of al-Shafi*, written around 800, is extremely important in that Shafi created a conservative methodology different from the Hanafiyya use of private judgment and also distinct from the Traditionists of the Maliki and Hanbali schools. Shafi's method is rigorous hierarchy of the use of Qur'an, hadith, *ijma'*, and then *qiyas* (analogy). His other great work of jurisprudence was *Kitab al-Umm*. Another important source text is the *Umdat al-Salik wa Uddat al-Nasik (Reliance of the Traveller and the Tools of the Worshipper)* by Ahmad ibn Naqib al-Misri, which was written around 1050 and contains the rulings and concepts of Imam Nawawi regarding Islamic public and foreign policy. Among many great Shafi scholars were Imam Ghazali and Abu al-Hasan Ashari. The Shafi legal school is found in Kurdistan, India, Sri Lanka, Ethiopia, Somalia, the Hijaz, Palestine, and throughout Southeast Asia and in some Egyptian and Chechen communities.

The Hanbali *madhhab* was developed by the disciples of Ahmad ibn Hanbal al-Shaybani (778–855). This school is considered by some scholars today to be more restrictive or purist than others. Hanbal's method of instruction revolved around a collection of 30,000 hadiths called the *Musnad*, and it was said that he knew 100,000 traditions by heart. Solutions to legal problems were sought first in the Qur'an and then in this collection, followed by recourse to the other sources of *fiqh* (*usul al-fiqh*) specified by Hanbal. Hanbal adamantly refused to allow his students to record his decisions. Hanbali law is not codified, and our knowledge of his own fatawa (response) comes from his disciples, including the two greatest hadith collectors Bukhari and Imam Muslim. Two of Hanbal's other followers were the distinguished jurists Ibn Taymiyyah (1263–1328) and his disciple Ibn Qayyim (1292–1350). Some of Ibn Taymiyyah's writings and ideas—for instance, some parts of his questions about the rightful authority of the Mongol rulers—have been instrumental in much of the Salafist revival movement of the 19th and 20th centuries. The best collection of early Hanbali juristic decisions is found in Khiraqi's *al-Mukhtasar*, compiled around 940. Ibn Hamid, Ibn al-Jawzi, Shams al-Din ibn Muflih, Sharaf al-Din al-Hajjawi, Muhammad al-Saffarini, and Muhammad ibn Abd al-Wahhab are among the many Hanbali jurists. The Hanbali *madhhab* was followed in Jerusalem, Greater Syria, and Saudi Arabia.

Applying Sharia principles in the modern world is complex. Sharia is considered immutable, but in fact scholars created jurisprudence (*fiqh*) in response to the questions that arose. Although every aspect or action in life is to be considered on the basis of Sharia, investigation into questions of jurisprudence and responses by Muslim jurists is deeply shaped by precedent and the way that the question (fatwa) is formulated.

In the 19th century the Ottomans partially codified their use of Hanafi law, to some degree in response to the thinking that Sharia ought to be more systemized as was Western law. Important arguments were made during this century by Egyptian jurist Muhammad Abduh about the use of *ijtihad*, disregarding the strict traditions of the *madhahib* and instead using a kind of patchwork approach called *talfiq*, whereby a jurist could borrow from different legal schools.

As modern states subsumed or limited the activities of the traditional *ulama* (scholars), civil laws began to adjudicate individual activities, particularly in commercial, civil, and penal law. In certain countries, scholars only retained power over family law, sometimes called personal status law, and Islamic education.

This shift in legal authority has been contested by some in the Muslim world. The development of civil legal systems has certainly complicated the application of Sharia, as have developing civil legal systems that incorporate aspects of Sharia. This has led to advocacy by some to Islamize civil codes partially based on Sharia or to oppose further changes in them in the form of many proposed legal reforms. Still other groups have sought to establish an Islamic government based upon Sharia. This occurred in Iran, where the laws of the Pahlavi era were completely reworked.

Currently many Muslim countries still include aspects of Sharia in family courts, maintain dual legal systems, or still incorporate Sharia in other areas of law. The use of Sharia impacts all areas of law in Iran, Sudan, Saudi Arabia, and parts of Malaysia and also in the criminal codes of Libya, Pakistan (now partially reformed), and parts of Nigeria. In the case of Kelantan in Malaysia, there is an effort to eventually impose Sharia on all aspects of life, as the Sharia law courts in that country have been gradually assuming many of the functions of the state-supported civil courts.

In Iraq there is today a dual legal system administering family law. Many elements of family law under Sharia have been classified as statutory discrimination against women by the Convention on the Elimination of All Forms of Discrimination against Women (CEDAW), adopted by the General Assembly of the United Nations (UN). These also impact civil laws that were partially based on Ottoman law and included exemptions for those who carried out murder in the name of family honor and for rapists who married their victims. Supporters of Sharia have argued that incorrect interpretations of Sharia might have prevailed but that Western-style reforms will destroy the morals of their societies.

Much criticism has come from the West and the UN against penal codes that utilize the severe *hadd* punishments, as in Iran, Libya, and Saudi Arabia; in the revised penal code adopted in Pakistan; and in areas controlled by the Taliban. These included capital punishment, amputations of hands or feet, and lashings. Some Muslim leaders, such as Tariq Ramadan in Switzerland, have called for a moratorium on such penalties on the grounds that true Sharia is not actually being applied today and requires revision and discussion, but other Muslim authorities oppose his idea of a moratorium.

The major reason for considering Sharia in a study of modern U.S. wars in the Middle East is the disagreements about its role either in violent extremism or in political opposition to regimes backed by or in conflict with the United States, such as the Taliban in Afghanistan. Images of corporal punishment being meted out in public by the Taliban in Pakistan prior to reconquest of the Swat Valley evoked widespread criticism in the United States of the Pakistani government's decision to conclude a truce there with the Taliban.

Russell G. Rodgers and Sherifa Zuhur

See also: Shia Islam; Sunni Islam

Further Reading

Al-Hashimi, Muhammad Ali. *The Ideal Muslim Society: As Defined in the Qur'an and Sunnah*. Riyadh, Saudi Arabia: International Islamic Publishing House, 2007.

Doi, 'Abdur Rahman. *Shari'ah: The Islamic Law*. London: Taha Publishers, 1997.

Dutton, Yasin. *The Origins of Islamic Law: The Qur'an, the Muwatta, and Madinan 'Amal*. London: RoutledgeCurzon, 2002.

Gibb, H. A. R. *Mohammedanism*. London: Oxford University Press, 1970.

Hughes, Thomas Patrick. *Dictionary of Islam*. Reprint ed. Chicago: Kazi Publications, 1994.

Philips, Abu Ameenah Bilal. *The Evolution of Fiqh: Islamic Law and the Madh-habs*. Kuala Lumpur, Malaysia: A. S. Noordeen, 2005.

Shia Islam

The smaller of the two predominant branches of Islam, the larger being Sunni Islam. The name "Shia" derives from the Arabic term "Shiat Ali" (Party of Ali), whereas the name "Sunni" derives from the term "Ahl al-Sunnah wa al-Jama'ah" (People of the Prophet's Practice and Unified Community). Adherents to Shia Islam account for 12–15 percent of all Muslims worldwide. The Sunni sects, or schools, of Islam account for approximately 85 percent.

Shia Islam grew out of political struggles against the Umayyad caliphs. As a result of its political and theological evolution, it came to incorporate the descendents of several different trends: activists, moderates, and extremists. In addition, Shiite leadership is divided into different positions and differs in the degree of approved activism by clerics. The Ithna Ashariyya, called Twelvers by Westerners and Jafariyya by adherents for their school of Islamic law, were historically moderates; the Ismailiyya (Seveners) were labeled extremists, or *ghulat*, by their enemies; and the Zaydiyya (Fivers) were activists (in their support of Zayd in his jihad against the caliph). The three groups are named according to the prominent figures in the chain of religious leaders (*a'imah*, or imams) whom each recognizes as constituting the proper line of religious authority passed down to them from the Prophet Muhammad.

Shiism is the dominant branch of Islam in Iran (90 percent of the population), Iraq, Lebanon, Bahrain, and Azerbaijan. Shiism also has adherents in Syria, Yemen, East Africa, India, Pakistan, Afghanistan, Tajikistan, Turkey, Qatar, Kuwait, the United Arab Emirates, the Eastern Province of Saudi Arabia, and many areas outside the Middle East, such as the United States, Canada, South Asia, the United Kingdom, Europe, Australia, and East Africa. In the United States, Dearborn, Michigan, has a large Shiite population.

The Shiat Ali (Party of Ali) were those who preferred the succession of Ali ibn Abu Talib as *khalifa* (caliph) when the Prophet Muhammad died. Ali ibn Abu Talib was the son-in-law of Muhammad by marriage to Muhammad's only surviving daughter, Fatima. Some suggest that in the mixture of southern and northern Arab Muslim tribes, it was the southerners, Aws and Khazraj of Medina, who most strongly supported hereditary rights in leadership rather than a leader chosen on a different basis.

Ali accepted Abu Bakr as caliph, or political leader of the Muslims, even though Ali's supporters preferred Ali, and he also accepted the caliph Umar. The caliphate was then offered to him, but he was told he would have to follow the precedents of Abu Bakr and Umar, and Ali refused to do this. His supporters agitated again when Uthman became the third caliph. Uthman was so disliked for nepotism and the enrichment of his Umayyad relatives that a revolt occurred in which he was killed. Ali's followers recognized him as the fourth caliph in 656 CE. However, the Umayyads claimed the caliphate for Muawiya, and this led to two civil wars in Islam and Ali's assassination in 661. Following Ali's death, his son Hasan was forced to abdicate, and his other son Husayn fought the Umayyads and was killed at Karbala. These events are commemorated in Shiism and given a deeply symbolic meaning.

While all Muslims revere the Prophet and his family (known as Ahl al-Bayt, or People of the House), Sunni Muslims recognize a large number of the Prophet's early companions at Medina as transmitters of *hadith*, the short texts relating Muhammad's words, actions, or preferences. In contrast, the Shia do not recognize the authority of certain Companions and teach the traditions (hadith) transmitted by others or the Ahl al-Bayt from the Prophet, his daughter Fatima, and Ali on to Ali's sons Hasan and Husayn and also the succession of imams who followed them. More importantly, because Ali had rejected the injunction to follow the precedents of the first two caliphs rather than the *sunnah* (traditions or practices) of the Prophet, the foundational logic for Shiism to develop its own *fiqh*, or legal school, was set.

In the Umayyad period, the followers of Ali began to develop their own attitudes and worldview in contrast to other Muslims.

The Battle of Karbala in October 680 between the supporters and relatives of Muhammad's grandson Husayn ibn Ali and forces of Yazid I, the Umayyad caliph, reinforced the Shia belief in *walaya*, or devotion to the Prophet's family, and also provided a reason for rebellion. A movement called the *tawabbun* (penitents) rose up to fight the Umayyads a year after the Battle of Karbala because they had not defended Husayn then, and 3,000 of them were killed.

Shiites believe that Ali was the first imam, thereby inheriting the *nass*, or spiritual legitimacy, of the Prophet. The imam is the sole legitimate religious successor of the Prophet, and each imam designates his own successor. In Shia Islam, each imam is held to have special knowledge of the inner truth of the Qur'an, Muhammad's *sunnah*, and Islam. This institution is called the imamate in English (*a'imah*). The *a'imah*, or chain of imams, are believed to be infallible, sinless, and personally guided by Allah (God) and are also believed to possess the divine authority over Islam and humanity granted to Ali by the Prophet Muhammad.

Shiites and Sunnis have the same beliefs about Allah, who has omnipotence over all beings and is also perceived as Merciful and Beneficent, closer to a person than his or her own jugular vein and one who cares deeply about his creation. In both branches of Islam there is also a dynamic between faith and the acceptance of divine will along with the responsibility of the human believer. Indeed, apart from the differences in the Shia view of leadership, the two sects are similar in many aspects. They diverge, however, in their legal systems.

The Shia recognize all the same religious duties as the Sunnis, which are described in the study of Islam in the West as the Five Pillars with two additional duties. However, the Ismailiyya sect and its subsects also stress the inner truths, or esoteric knowledge of Islamic principles. Therefore, to their spiritual elite simply reading the Qur'an is inadequate; one must understand its hidden meaning.

The Shia stress the unicity or oneness (*tawhid*) of Allah, a strict monotheism, and the avoidance of any trace of polytheism. They support social justice (*'adalah*), which means equity within society, and aid to the oppressed and the needy. As with Sunni Muslims, the Shia adhere to the principle of the *hisba*, or commanding the good and forbidding the reprehensible. This refers to all that is licit or recommended in Islamic law as opposed to sins that are forbidden. Entrance into Paradise is based on doing more good than evil or upon martyrdom. All Muslims, Shia as well as Sunni, respect the prophets, including Abraham, Moses, Jesus, and Muhammad, whom they believe revealed to humans the true religion of Allah.

The concept of the *a'imah* (imamate)— that specific leaders are appointed by Allah and then designated by other imams (*nass*)— grew in strength thanks to the sixth imam, Jafar al-Sadiq. His followers developed the Twelver legal and theological tradition. The last of these 12 imams, Muhammad al-Mahdi, did not make himself known at the death of the 11th imam, al-Hasan al-Askari; however, texts revealed his presence. Mahdi is believed to be hiding on Earth, neither alive nor dead but in a state of occultation, and will return at the Day of Judgment and the Resurrection (*qiyamah*) when Allah will decide the fate of all humanity, Muslim and non-Muslim alike.

The Twelvers believe that Mahdi, born in 689, was the son of Hasan. The Shia believe that Mahdi was in hiding from the caliph and that between the years 874 and 941 he communicated by letters with his people.

During this period, called the Lesser Occultation, the community recognized four regents for Mahdi. In his last letter, he wrote that he would no longer communicate with humanity. Thus the period from 941 to the present is known as the Greater Occultation.

In Islam, every human is held accountable for his or her deeds. The deeds of each individual are judged by Allah and weighed on a scale. If the good outweighs the evil, then the individual gains entrance into Paradise. If the evil outweighs the good, the individual spends eternity in Hell. The Shia, like the Sunni, also believe that the prophets, imams, and martyrs can intercede with Allah for a soul on the Day of Judgment and may seek this intercession (*shafa'a*) if possible through prayer, religious rituals, or appeals to the Fourteen Infallibles: the Prophet Muhammad, his daughter Fatima, the Twelve Imams, or martyrs. They also seek redemption through the ritual of repentance performed on the Day of Ashura, the commemoration of Imam Husayn's death.

Shiism's Twelvers, the largest Shia group, proclaim the necessity of obligatory religious duties or acts of outward worship. The first is the *shahada*, or testimony that there is no God but God and that Muhammad is his prophet and Ali his imam. The next is prayer (*salat*), recited five or more times a day. The third is fasting (*sawm*) during the daylight hours for all of the month of Ramadan, the ninth month of the Islamic calendar. The fourth religious practice is the pilgrimage (*hajj*), a journey to the holy city of Mecca that should be made at least once during a person's life if he or she is physically and financially able to undertake it. The fifth religious practice is the paying of *zakat*, a voluntary tax that is used to support the poor, to spread Islam, or sometimes for other purposes such as aid to travelers and the funding of jihad. The assessment of *zakat* should be 2.5 percent of one's income and assets in any given year. (All Muslims also give gifts of money during and at the end of Ramadan and the Id al-Adha, but these are in addition to *zakat*.) Another form of tithing, the *khums*, is a 20 percent tax on all annual profits from any source levied on all adult males and is used to support the mosque and the clerics. Jihad is also a commanded duty in Shiism and refers to the struggle of the faithful to please Allah as well as to defend Islam by waging war against those who attack Muslims. The idea of the *walaya* is important in Shiism (but also in Sufi Islam), as is the *tabarra*. These mean a special reverence for all members, past and descended, of the Ahl al-Bayt; the guardianship of the imamate; and the disassociation from all enemies of the Ahl al-Bayt.

In addition to the Shia groups mentioned previously, there are others. The Shaykhiyya of Basra and Bahrain are a subsect of the Twelver Shia, influenced by Akhbari thought. The Druze (who call themselves *muwahiddun*, or unitarians) are an offshoot of the Ismailiyya sect, and the Alawites found in Syria and Turkey are a distinct subsect of Shiism. Sunni Muslims and some Shia, however, consider the Alawi sect extreme because of some of its syncretic practices. Nonetheless, it was declared a licit school of Islam in a fatwa issued by Imam Musa al-Sadr in order to legitimate the rule of President Hafiz al-Asad, an Alawi, in Syria. Although all branches of Islam believe in a divine savior, the Mahdi (the Guided One) who will come at the Day of Judgment, the Twelfth branch of Shiism holds that the Twelfth Imam, or Hidden Imam since he is in occultation, is the Mahdi and call him the Imam Mahdi.

Mahmoud Ahmadinejad, president of Iran, and his cabinet have pledged to work to make the conditions right for the return of the Imam Mahdi, a return that Shia Muslims believe will lead Islam to world domination. In Iran, many believe that the Imam Mahdi will reappear from a well at the mosque in Jamkaran just outside of the holy city of Qum, Iran. The site is frequently visited by Shiite pilgrims who drop messages into the well hoping that the Hidden Imam will hear them and grant their requests. Along with the Imam Mahdi's return at the Day of Judgment, there are various beliefs about other millenarian events and wars that will occur before this period.

Since the disappearance of the Twelfth Imam, the Shia *ulama* (clerics) have served as his deputies, interpreting the law and leading the Shiite faithful under the authority of the Hidden Imam. In Twelver Shiism it is believed that four persons acted as the deputies or special vice-regents (*wakala al-khassa*) of the Hidden Imam during the Lesser Occultation. These persons were called the *bab* (gate) or *na'ib* (deputy) for the imam. From 941 there have been no overt claims of a *bab* except for Sayyid Ali Muhammad (known as The Bab), who established Babism in the 19th century, and the Shaykhi Shia, who put forth the idea of the perfect Shia who lives in each age. Generally in this period, the idea is that there is a *wakala al-'amma*, or a general vice-regency, that has been delegated to the Shia clerics. When Iran's Ayatollah Ruhollah Khomeini and his government established the system of rule of the cleric (*vilayat-e faqih*) in Iran, there were disputes about whether he was to be considered the *na'ib* al-Imam, or deputy of the Hidden Imam. The idea of rule of the cleric, developed from the increasingly activist opinions of one branch of Shiism—the Usulis (*usuliyya*)—opposed the Akhbaris, a different intellectual tradition. This notion that clerics should rule, therefore becoming a part of the political system, is still controversial even among many Usulis.

Khomeini's official title became Supreme Faqih (Jurist), and he governed the Council of Guardians as its supreme religio-political authority. There had been several clerics more senior to Khomeini who were, however, marginalized or even assassinated after the Islamic Revolution. Khomeini's successor, Ali Husayni Khamenei, was not the most senior of the clerics who might potentially have followed Khomeini in power. Khamenei was granted the title of ayatollah to ensure his authority. Some described him as a political appointee.

Ismaili Shiites, also known as Ismailiyya, or the Seveners, are followers of the living Agha Khan and constitute the second-largest branch of Shia Islam. Ismailis believe that the imamate is a position that continues unbroken since the caliphate of Ali, although the living imams since the Seventh Imam serve as regents awaiting the return of the Hidden Imam. Ismailis acknowledge only six of the Twelve Imams and assert that the real Seventh Imam was Ismail Ibn Jafar. Other Muslims assert that Ismail's son Muhammad was the Seventh Imam and that he is presently occulted awaiting the end of time to reveal himself as the last imam. The Ismaili movement spread through missionary activity as a secret organization beginning in the later ninth century. It split in a factional dispute about leadership in 899. Ismaili Shia are found primarily in South Asia, Syria, Saudi Arabia, Yemen, China, Tajiki-stan, Afghanistan, and East Africa but have also, in recent years, immigrated to Europe and North America.

Ismailis mandate the same religious practices as the Twelvers, but their emphasis is on esoteric teachings and thus on an inner or deeper interpretation of each that can make them distinct. As with the Twelvers, the Ismailis evince love and devotion (*walayah*) for Allah, the prophets, the Ahl al-Bayt, the imam, and the Ismaili *da'i* (preacher) and also believe in personal purity and cleanliness (*taharah*). As with all other Muslims, they must also practice prayer and *zakat*, or almsgiving. In addition, they fast during Ramadan, carry out the *hajj*, and believe in jihad.

Zaydis, also known as Zaydiyya or the Fivers, are theologically and in the view of Islamic law closer to a Sunni school of the law. There are Zaydi communities in India, Pakistan, and Yemen. Zaydis derive their name from Zayd ibn Ali ibn Abi Talib, the son of Husayn ibn Ali ibn Abi Talib (626–ca. 680), the grandson of the Prophet Muhammad. Most Zaydis regard Husayn as the third rightful imam. After Ali, Hasan, and Husayn, the followers of Zayd had asserted that the succession of the imamate would be determined after engaging in armed rebellion against the Umayyad caliphs. Zayd's followers did not want a Hidden Imam, but a living one who would rule instead of the Umayyads, and so the Zaydiyya are considered activists. Although Zayd's rebellion against the corrupt Umayyad caliph Hisham ibn Abd al-Malik (691–743) in 740 was unsuccessful, his followers thereafter recognized Zayd as the fourth Zaydi imam.

Zaydism does not support the infallibility of the imams and asserts that no imam after Husayn received any divine guidance. Zaydis reject the Hidden Imam and the idea that the imamate must be passed from father to son, although they do believe that the living imam must be a descendant of Ali, and some of their own leaders passed on their leadership to their sons. Zaydi Islamic law (*fiqh*) is most like the Sunni Hanafi school.

While there was never a concept of Sunni Islam as a sect as it is described today, the non-Alid Muslims (those who did not insist on Ali gaining political leadership) accepted the institution of the caliphate even though the caliph was not a spiritual descendant of the Prophet. Still, the caliph received an oath of allegiance from his people and had to be pious and promote and protect Islam. Alids (supporters of Ali), later called the Shia, accepted their temporal rulers but did not regard them as being spiritually legitimate in the manner of the imams. For purposes of survival, they could deny their Shia beliefs if need be in the practice known as *taqqiya* (dis-simulation). There are major legal and philosophical differences in Shia Islam, such as the theme of the oppressed Muslims who act out their penitence for their inability to defend Husayn at Karbala, the imamate, the concept of the Occultation and the Return, and the concept of *marjaiyya*, the idea that a believer should follow a particular cleric as a guide. Minor differences pertain to aspects of daily prayer and the commencement of holidays, which often begin on one day in Iran and, typically, a day earlier in Saudi Arabia and other Sunni centers.

Shiite Islamic education is centered in Najaf and Karbala in Iraq and in Qum and Mashhad in Iran, with other religious authorities in Tehran and additional centers of learning elsewhere. Shia clerics from Lebanon typically studied in Iraq or in Iran. One of the most influential Shia theorists in Iran following the Islamic Revolution was probably Abd al-Karim Sorush, who is famous for his idea of the expansion and contraction of Islamic law (*qabz va baste shari'at*). The most senior cleric in Iraq today is the Shia Grand Ayatollah Sistani. The clerical establishment in Iraq is referred to as the *hawzah*, and its duty is to train the future clerics of Shiism, provide judgments, and officiate over pilgrimages and those who wish to be buried at the holy sites. Other important cities of Shia learning are Qum, Mashhad, and Tehran, all in Iran.

In Iran the great leaders of Tehran, Ayatollah Sayyid Muhammad Tabatabai (1841–1920) and Sayyid Abd Allah Bahbahani (d. 1871), were part of the revolutionary organization of the constitutional movement early in the 20th century, but other clerics opposed that movement. Shiite authorities also resisted British colonialism and encroachments on their power by Reza Shah Pahlavi in Iran.

The last great single *marja' al-mutlaq* (the absolute source of emulation), Ayatollah Burujerdi, died in 1961. Debate then began between different reformist leaders and the degree of activism in which clerics should engage. In the 1960s a more radical, or activist, Shiism began to develop. Informal gatherings and new publications began to spread new radical Shiite thought. Ayatollah Khomeini's resistance to Mohammad Reza Shah Pahlavi was significant, but so too was the work of Dr. Ali Shariati (1933–1977).

Educated in Mashhad and Paris, Shariati challenged the quietism of many religious scholars, writing essays and giving lectures to galvanize a new activism in Shiism that combined with existentialism and Third Worldist views. Another major influence on radical Shiism in this period was Murtaza Mutahari (1920–1979).

Sunnis and Shiites have different approaches to jurisprudence, or the making of Islamic law, and therefore also in the issuance of fatawa to broader religious questions of Muslims. The different Sunni schools of law use as sources (*usul al-fiqh*) the Qur'an, the hadith, analogy (*qiyas*), and *ijma*, or the consensus of the community at Medina or of the jurists. In earlier periods, these legal schools also used *ray* (opinion of the jurist) or *ijtihad*, a particular technique of intellectual problem solving. In the 10th century the Sunni jurists decided to stop using *ijtihad* so as to avoid the introduction of too many innovations into Sharia (Islamic law). However, the Shia legal school of the Twelvers retained this principle. Consequently, Shia cleric-jurists who train in this technique and qualify receive the title of *mujtahid*, or one who can enact *ijtihad*.

Ijtihad has come to mean more than a principle of Islamic jurisprudence. As contemporary activist Shiism was developing, Ali Shariati began to apply *ijtihad* to Muslim life, including a vibrant definition of monotheism and the application of Muslim principles.

There are various ranks of clerics in Shia Islam in addition to the *mujtahid*, such as the elevated designations of ayatollah and grand ayatollah that other clerics should agree on. In addition, the Shia may follow his or her own preferred *marja' al-taqlid* (source of emulation). Above all of these clerics, there may be one agreed-upon *marja' al-mutlaq*, or source of emulation of the age.

These are not the only differences between Sunni and Shia Islam. Shia constituted minorities in such countries as Lebanon and Saudi Arabia, where they were an underclass socially and economically. In the modern period, leaders such as Ali Shariati and Imam Musa Sadr in Lebanon supported populism and addressed the discrimination against and suffering of the Shiite masses.

While at times some Sunni groups have expressed both discrimination and hatred toward Shia Muslims, there have also been efforts at ecumenism and more cooperation between the sects. Al-Azhar University in Egypt teaches about the Jafariyya (Twelver) *madhhab*, or legal school of Islam, in spite of the government of Egypt having outlawed Shiism. It should also be noted that Shia and Sunni Muslims had coexisted peacefully and have frequently intermarried in Iraq. Shia Muslims were often members of the Communist Party or the Baath Party, and just like the Iranian clerics responding to the inroads made by secular ideologies in that country, the clerics in Iraq began an Islamic movement in part to encourage youths to reengage with Islamic education. When this movement developed from a clerical organization into an activist one, Iraqi president Saddam Hussein ruthlessly suppressed it. Sadly, the end of Hussein's rule brought Shia-Sunni sectarian conflict to Iraq, fueled in part by Sunni Islamists and nationalists who viewed the new Shia-dominated majority as conspirators with the Americans and who call the Shia apostates or renegades.

Richard M. Edwards and Sherifa Zuhur

See also: Sunni Islam

Further Reading

Ajami, Fouad. *The Vanished Imam: Musa al-Sadr and the Shia of Lebanon*. Ithaca, NY: Cornell University Press, 1986.

Daftari, Farhad. *The Isma'ilis: Their History and Doctrines*. Cambridge: Cambridge University Press, 1990.

Fuller, Graham E., and Rend Rahim Francke. *The Arab Shi'a: The Forgotten Muslims*. Hampshire, UK: Palgrave Macmillan, 2001.

Gregorian, Vartan. *Islam: A Mosaic, Not a Monolith*. Baltimore: Brookings Institute Press, 2004.

Halm, Heinz. *Shi'a Islam: From Religion to Revolution*. Princeton, NJ: Markus Wiener, 1997.

Momen, Moojan. *An Introduction to Shi'i Islam: The History and Doctrines of Twelver Shi'ism*. New Haven, CT: Yale University Press, 1987.

Nasr, Seyyed Hossein. *Islam: Religion, History, and Civilization*. New York: HarperCollins, 2003.

Sobhani, Ayatollah Jafar, and Reza Shah Kazemi. *Doctrines of Shi'i Islam: A Compendium of Imami Beliefs and Practices*. London: I. B. Tauris, 2001.

Shia Uprising

Shia opposition groups in Iraq long predated the U.S. invasion, with their focus, of course, against Saddam Hussein. The most prominent groups were the Dawa Party and the Supreme Council for the Islamic Revolution in Iraq (SCIRI), which after the U.S. occupation renamed itself the Islamic Supreme Council of Iraq. The armed wing of SCIRI was the Badr Corps, which fought alongside the Iranians during the Iran-Iraq War (1980–1988). The Dawa Party did not have a formal militia. Following the Iran-Iraq War, most SCIRI and Badr Corps members remained in Iran. In fact, after they return to Iraq in 2003, some members spoke better Farsi than Arabic. After Operation DESERT STORM, the Dawa Party was deeply involved in the brief ill-fated Shia uprising against the Iraqi regime in the south, but SCIRI was in many ways somewhat sidelined. Both SCIRI and the Dawa Party generally were cooperative with the U.S. occupation forces, but a major player quickly emerged after the U.S. invasion: Muqtada al-Sadr and his Jaish al Mahdi.

Muqtada al-Sadr, born in 1974, comes from a highly distinguished family of Shia religious scholars. In particular, his father, Ayatollah Muhammed Sadiq al-Sadr, was revered by most Iraqi Shia. Sadiq was actively pushed Shia political goals. He was murdered in February 1999, almost certainly by the Iraqi government. Another relative (and Muqtada's father-in-law), Ayatollah Muhammed Baqir al-Sadr, was key in mobilizing Shia political activism against the previous Iraqi regime and founded the al Dawa party. As a result of his activism, he was executed by the Saddam regime in April 1980.

One aspect of al-Sadr's background might be important. As noted, his family has provided a number of Ayatollahs and senior religious figures for the Iraqi Shia. al-Sadr, on the other hand, has much weaker religious credentials. Even after his father's death, and before 2003, al-Sadr appeared to receive little support from his father's former supporters. In fact, there were reports that many of the Shia referred to him as an "ignorant child."

A "godfather" for al-Sadr was Ayatollah Kadhim al Haeri, a senior cleric from Karbala who had been in exile in Iran since 1973. In April 2003 al Haeri formally appointed al-Sadr as his deputy and official representative in Iraq. At the same time Haeri stated that all "Baathists"—which many Sunni with some justification viewed as being broadly directed at all Sunni—should be killed. During the same period the major Shia ceremony of Arbain in Karbala was marked by millions of Shia pilgrims, with almost universal calls for a Shia government for Iraq.

al-Sadr's influence quickly began to grow. In the chaos following the U.S. invasion, many younger Shia imams collected armed followers and began seizing large swathes of Shia areas of Baghdad, particularly in Saddam City—which was renamed Sadr City after Sadiq al-Sadr—and much of Southern Iraq. These seizures also included Sunni mosques that had been built in predominantly Shia areas. Probably largely because of the Sadr "brand," these largely unorganized armed groups began coalescing around Muqtada.

Major armed confrontations between co-alition forces and Sadrists began as early as March 2004, with a coalition arrest warrant for al-Sadr issued in April 2004. al-Sadr condemned the Interim Governing Council, appointed in July 2003, as "lackeys of the occupation" and tried to establish a parallel government. During the same period he established the Jaish as Mahdi (JAM), or Army of the Mahdi, as his formal armed militia. Its primary stated goals were to pro-tect Shia interests and to oppose U.S. occu-pation. For a brief period, al-Sadr received some support not only from Shia, but also Iraqi Sunnis, as a result of what they viewed as his nationalist struggle. As JAM increas-ingly began to conduct anti-Sunni opera-tions, this early support collapsed among the Sunnis.

Since much of the Shia establishment more or less cooperated with the U.S. occu-pation forces, Muqtada's followers began to oppose both the U.S. forces and much of the Iraqi "collaboration." Many of the early armed actions in particular were directed both against the U.S. and the Shia structure. There were low-level clashes between JAM and members of the Supreme Council for the Islamic Revolution in Iraq. Although there were some ideological differences between the groups, most of these battles appeared to be primarily over political power and turf. Despite these street battles, al-Sadr was invited to join the United Iraqi Alliance by SCIRI and Dawa parties in a joint slate to contest the 2005 elections.

In general al-Sadr's support base and JAM membership has come from the poor, lesser educated, and younger part of Iraqi Shia. The actual strength of JAM at its peak was more a matter of guesswork than a solid estimate, but it usually has been assessed to be in the 25,000–40,000 range of active members. Elements of JAM have

operated under a number of different titles, including Promised Day Brigades, Hezbollah Brigades in Iraq, and Islamic Resistance in Iraq.

During much of JAM's existence, al-Sadr remained in Iran for "religious studies," with only occasional short visits to Iraq. In large part, this almost certainly was a matter of maintaining a safe haven but also likely involved his desire to burnish his religious credentials and status. He finally returned to Iraq for a more extended stay in Janu-ary 2011. During his lengthy absences, how-ever, a steady stream of decrees, orders, and manifestos ascribed to him flowed into Iraq for his followers.

In some ways following the Lebanese Hezbollah model, JAM has focused not only on security, but also on the provision of social services. The social and political wing of the Sadrist movement usually is known as the Office of the Martyr Sadr. It has provided food and other supplies to the poor and especially to families of "martyrs." Also, since a number of Sadrists have positions in local governments, they have formed a network that has helped their supporters find jobs.

Although frequently in opposition to the Iraqi political establishment, al-Sadr and JAM also have been players in the political system. In January 2005 elections the Sad-rists won 23 out of 275 seats in parliament, doing particularly well in Baghdad, Basra, and Maysan. They also entered the govern-ment, including holding the ministries of health, transportation, and agriculture. How-ever, by 2007 relations with the other Shia parties had soured so badly that the Sadrists pulled out of the government.

al-Sadr consistently has had difficulties in controlling all elements of JAM. Although some of his protestations as to his inability to stop specific operations may be two-faced,

JAM has always been a loosely structured group. Many of the actual militiamen were formed in what were called special groups. These normally were the ones most likely to engage coalition forces. al-Sadr's actual control of these groups was somewhat variable. Clearly he had a chain of command that incorporated some of the special groups, while others apparently obeyed his orders as it suited them. It also became increasingly difficult with some of them to determine if they were engaged in operations to further a broader ideological goal or if they simply were street thugs engaged in criminality for profit.

Iran clearly played a role in the operations of JAM. Publicly available reports and evidence linked Iran to some of the weapons used by JAM, particularly materials used for more advanced improvised explosive devices (IEDs). The Iranian Quds Force—an arm of the Iranian Revolutionary Guard Corps—also provided training to elements of JAM. There also has been speculation that some of the special groups owed more allegiance to Iran than they did to al-Sadr. Having said this, however, JAM certainly was a predominantly local movement, though it did receive significant external support from Iran. JAM also has received training assistance from Lebanese Hezbollah, likely at the behest of the Iranians.

As already noted, JAM has engaged in widespread violence, which has been along three primary axes: anti–U.S. occupation, anti-Sunni, and to a lesser extent anti–other Shia groups and the Iraqi government. al-Sadr's anticoalition and pronationalist attacks generally were concentrated in Baghdad, Basra, and surrounding areas. For much of the U.S. occupation, JAM was the principal threat to coalition forces, in Baghdad in particular. JAM rocket and mortar attacks against the International (Green)

Zone became a rather routine occurrence, along with ambushes and IEDs against coalition forces in Shia areas.

Anti-Sunni operations became pronounced from 2006. The key symbol for the shift toward Sunni-Shia civil war in Iraq was the February 22, 2006, bombing of the Shia Askari Shrine in Samarra. In response, Shia militias—along with the Shia-dominated Ministry of Interior forces—killed about 1,300 Sunnis. JAM was particularly prominent in this anti-Sunni campaign.

Along with various Sunni groups, JAM was active in ethnic cleansing operations, particularly in Baghdad. Which side actually started ethnic cleansing remains a subject of debate, but it is fair to say that both Sunni and Shia militias took to this with a vengeance. These actions seemed to reach their peak in 2006 and 2007, when JAM tried to evict all Sunnis from predominantly Shia areas, particularly Sadr City. Along with driving out Sunni families, they also focused on mixed-confessional couples. Cross-sectarian marriage has been a fairly common situation in Iraq, particularly in urban areas such as Baghdad. The choice given such couples was to divorce or to be killed, usually after torture.

The peak of JAM's anti-Iraqi government armed activities came in 2008, with an Iraqi-led offensive in Basra. By 2008 the British—who putatively were in charge of security in Basra Province—had abandoned all pretense of actually securing the city. As a result, three Shia groups vied for control: the government-supporting ISCI, JAM, and the Fadhila Party. The Fadhila Party, together with its associated militia, became a major player in the Basra area. It was led by Muhammed al Yaqubi, who although a student of al-Sadr's father, rejected the authority of the younger al-Sadr. Although geographically limited, the Fadhila Party gained importance because it maintained political control of Basra and of the Oil Facilities Protection Force in the oil facilities around Basra.

As a result of the lack of governmental control of Basra, Prime Minister Maliki launched what was dubbed Operation KNIGHT'S CHARGE on 25 March 2008. This major military operation began with minimal coordination with coalition forces, and initially met with severe resistance and minimal success in restoring security. Also, some Iraqi troops either deserted or refused to fight. Coalition elements, particularly air assets and intelligence support, quickly were brought in to assist the Iraqis. A cease-fire was arranged with JAM and Fadhila, but after a short period, the government resumed its offensive. By late May armed JAM power in Basra and surrounding areas had largely been negated.

After the battle for Basra and associated operations around Sadr City in Baghdad, al-Sadr reached a cease-fire with the government in May 2008. After this cease-fire, al-Sadr announced that he was splitting JAM into two components. The first, and largest, was to be a political and social wing. The second was what he called special companies that were to consist of the core fighting element. The special companies should not be confused with the special groups, although it is likely that he wanted to incorporate many of the special groups into the new "elite" force. al-Sadr also announced that he was shifting JAM into a "cultural and social institution," with less emphasis on armed operations. In response, a splinter group, the League of the Righteous, formed to continue attacks. By 2011, however, the League appeared to be reconciled with al-Sadr.

Although the withdrawal of U.S. forces from Iraq removed much of the raison d'être of JAM and the overall Sadrist movement, JAM remains an independent political and security identity. Although continuing its

involvement in Iraqi politics—as of 2011, the Sadrists had 41 of 325 seats in the Iraqi parliament—the Sadrist trend and JAM retained a somewhat adversarial relationship with the government. At the very least, with al-Sadr's continued popularity with a significant segment of the Shia population, he likely will be able to circumscribe the freedom of action of any Iraqi government.

Lawrence Cline

See also: Badr Organization; Islamic Dawa Party; Sadr, Muqtada al-

Further Reading

Cordesman, Anthony H., and Jose Ramos. *Sadr and the Mahdi Army: Evolution, Capabilities, and a New Direction.* Washington, DC: Center for Strategic and International Studies, August 4, 2008.

International Crisis Group. *Middle East Report Number 55: Iraq's Muqtada al-Sadr: Spoiler or Stabiliser?* July 11, 2006.

Johnson, David E., M. Wade Markel, and Brian Shannon. *The 2008 Battle of Sadr City.* Santa Monica, CA: RAND Corporation, 2011.

Katzman, Kenneth. "Iran's Activities and Influence in Iraq." *CRS Report for Congress.* January 24, 2008.

Rahimi, Babak. "The Future of Moqtada al-Sadr's New Jaysh al-Mahdi." *CTC Sentinel* 2, no. 1 (January 2009).

Schwarz, Anthony J. "Iraq's Militias: The True Threat to Coalition Success in Iraq." *Parameters* (Spring 2007): 55–71.

Shinseki, Eric Ken

U.S. Army general and chief of staff of the army (1999–2003). Born in Lihue on the island of Kauai, Hawaii, on November 28, 1942, Eric Shinseki graduated from the United States Military Academy, West

U.S. Army general Eric Shinseki was chief of staff of the U.S. Army between 1999 and 2003. He became secretary of veterans' affairs in 2009. Shinseki sharply disagreed with Defense Secretary Donald Rumsfeld on the number of troops that would be required during an invasion of Iraq. (U.S. Department of Defense)

Point, in 1965 and was commissioned a second lieutenant. His military education included the Armor Officer Advanced Course from 1968 to 1969, the United States Army Command and General Staff College in 1979, and the National War College in 1986. Shinseki also earned a master's degree in English literature from Duke University in 1976.

Shinseki served two combat tours in Vietnam with the 9th and 25th Infantry divisions. He was wounded during each of those tours, the second time by a land mine that took off most of his right foot. After recovering, he had to fight the military personnel system to stay in the army with his handicap.

Shinseki's subsequent command and staff assignments included more than 10 years in Europe, with assignments in command and staff at Schweinfurt, Kitzingen, Würzburg, and Stuttgart in the Federal Republic of Germany. Promoted to brigadier general (July 1991), Shinseki served in Verona, Italy, as deputy chief of staff of Allied Land Forces Southern Europe, a component of Allied Command Europe, and later as the assistant division commander for maneuver of the 3rd Infantry Division in Würzberg. Promoted to major general in June 1994, he commanded the 1st Cavalry Division at Fort Hood, Texas. Promoted to lieutenant general (August 1996), Shinseki became U.S. Army deputy chief of staff for operations and plans. Promoted to full general in August 1997, he commanded United States Army Europe and Seventh Army. In that capacity, he was directly responsible for the peace-keeping and stabilization operations, led by the North Atlantic Treaty Organization (NATO), in Croatia and Bosnia.

From June 22, 1999, to June 11, 2003, General Shinseki was the U.S. Army's chief of staff. He was both the first four-star Asian American general in U.S. history and the first Asian American to head one of the armed services. As chief of staff he initiated the controversial Army Transformation Campaign, by which the army was to be transformed into a lighter, more mobile force to address contemporary emerging strategic challenges. These included anti-terror operations such as the invasion of Afghanistan (Operation ENDURING FREEDOM) in 2001 and the more conventional campaign against Iraq (Operation IRAQI FREEDOM) in 2003. Shinseki launched his Army Transformation Campaign well before Donald Rumsfeld became secretary of defense and announced his own strategic vision of smaller and more flexible forces. Nonetheless, Shinseki found himself constantly at loggerheads with the brusque and imperious defense secretary. In 2001 Shinseki resisted Rumsfeld's call for additional reductions in army strength. Some insiders suggest that Shinseki's opposition to Rumsfeld's overzealous force reductions bordered on insubordination. Others considered Shinseki to be one of the few senior military leaders willing to challenge Rumsfeld's farfetched and unfounded notions about fighting modern wars, which almost all proved failures.

In February 2003, just one month prior to the launching of Operation IRAQI FREEDOM, Shinseki testified before the Senate Armed Service Committee that "something on the order of several hundred thousand soldiers" would be needed for the pacification and occupation of Iraq. Shinseki's estimate was based on his own experience with such operations in the Balkans, but his troop estimate for Iraq was immediately dismissed by Rumsfeld and others because it directly contradicted their theories about high-technology military operations on the cheap. If Shinseki's recommendations had been followed, there can be no doubt that the Iraq War would have played out much differently.

In what was considered by many to be an unbelievably shabby and small-minded bureaucratic maneuver, Rumsfeld undercut Shinseki's authority by selecting his successor more than a year before Shinseki was due to step down as chief of staff. Shinseki retired from active duty in August 2003. Despite his disagreements with Rumsfeld and the Pentagon's planning for Iraq, Shinseki has kept silent on the issue, choosing not to engage in any public discussions or castigations concerning the defense secretary or the ongoing war in Iraq. Nevertheless, the apparent success of the Bush administration's troop surge—accompanied by a revitalized counterinsurgency strategy—seems to have vindicated Shinseki's view that more troops were required in Iraq. When Barack Obama became president in 2009, he selected Shinseki as his administration's secretary of veterans affairs. Shinseki's appointment was greeted enthusiastically by both members of the military and veterans' groups.

Michael Doidge

See also: Bush, George Walker; IRAQI FREEDOM, Operation; Obama, Barack Hussein, II; Rumsfeld, Donald Henry

Further Reading

Bell, William. *Commanding Generals and Chiefs of Staff, 1775–2005: Portraits and Biographical Sketches of the United States Army's Senior Officer.* Washington, DC: Center of Military History, 2005.

Fontenot, Gregory et al. *On Point: The United States Army in Iraqi Freedom.* Annapolis, MD: Naval Institute Press, 2005.

Sistani, Sayyid Ali Husayn al-

Islamic cleric and the most imposing traditional religious authority in Iraq, a prolific author (38 books), and a key presence in post-2003 Iraq. Grand Ayatollah Sayyid Ali Husayn al-Sistani was born in Mashhad, Iran, on August 4, 1930, into a *sayyid* family that traced its lineage to the Prophet Muhammad. The family has produced scholars since the 17th century. Sistani began his religious training in Mashhad and then moved to Qum, Iran, to study Islamic jurisprudence and theory when the supreme and only *marja'-e mutlaq* (source of emulation) of his time, Muhammad Husayn Burujerdi, taught there.

Sistani moved to Najaf, Iraq, in 1951. There he attended lectures by grand ayatollahs Abu al-Qassim Khoi and Sheikh

Hussayn Hilli. Upon his return to Mashhad, Sistani received the certificate of *ijtihad* by both Khoi and Hilli. Ijtihad is a source of law in Jafari jurisprudence involving independent deductive and creative reasoning attainable only after sufficient study and with acknowledgment by certain clerics.

Sistani later returned to Najaf to teach, remaining a quietist during the Islamic revival and rise of activist parties, such as the Islamic Dawa Party, and surviving when other Shiite clerics were persecuted by the Baathist government. Sistani served as the prayer imam in Khoi's own mosque from 1987 to 1993 and announced his status as a *marja' al-taqlid* (religious source of emulation) after Khoi's death. This led to challenges to his authority by clerics in Qum, but Sistani shrugged them off thanks largely to responses of his *wakil* (agent) and son-in-law Javad Shahrastani. Sistani's mosque was closed in 1994, and he was placed under house arrest. Sistani rarely traveled except for pilgrimages, but he went to London in 2004 to be treated for a heart condition.

Grand Ayatollah Sistani and his wakils, including Shahrastani, built and continue to maintain a vast network of adherents and centers of learning and charity. This includes a main office in Qum, which manages his mosques, scholarly libraries, charities, schools, hospitals, seminaries, the publishing of Islamic legal codes, and the distribution of preachers' and students' salaries. The main office also manages the transfers to other agents of his international network, which consists of mosques, charitable organizations, Internet sites, and seminaries, all of which operate on a multimillion-dollar budget. Sistani's activities in Najaf further the *hawzah* (scholarly establishment) there, shaping the future role of clerics, supporting pilgrims and other religious traffic to Iraq's holy cities, and managing educational, Internet, and publishing outlets.

Beyond his religious reach, since 2003 Sistani has significantly impacted the political life of Iraqis, facilitating the integration of clerical influence in the country with government agencies, for the dominant political parties are Islamist and extremely powerful within the various ministries. He has helped move the Iraqi polity more toward an Islamic democratic system than the secular, liberal democracy envisioned by American administrators.

From the beginning of the Iraqi occupation, the Americans realized that Sistani was an important contact point for them in postinvasion Iraq, but they did not fully understand his beliefs or stances vis-à-vis Islamic life and government, Iraqi sovereignty, Iran's role in the country, or Shiism. He refused to meet with them, as he did not support a lengthy occupation of Iraq and did not wish to be compromised. Communications were thus carried on through intermediaries.

With his thick Iranian accent and image as a cleric steeped in the Iranian tradition, Sistani has garnered ire from those who oppose Islamic clerics, the Shia, and Iran in general. He could have initially more forcefully opposed the American occupation, but he instead urged Iraqi cooperation to build stability and independence. However, on June 26, 2003, Sistani's office called for an immediate general election instead of the formation by the Coalition Provisional Authority (CPA) of a transitional government. He then opposed the CPA-supported plan for caucuses that would precede an election. His followers staged protests throughout Iraq and ultimately defeated the plan. Sistani, however, was sustaining his legacy as a quietist scholar who had to preserve clerical independence from politicians and the media. At the same time, he had to oppose undue Western interference in Iraqi affairs.

Sistani nevertheless encouraged all Iraqis to participate in the 2005 elections as their Islamic duty. The result was the emergence of a democratically elected coalition of Shiite parties with an Islamist agenda. One may conclude that Sistani's interpretation of the role of the cleric (*ulama*) differs from that of the late Ayatollah Ruhollah Khomeini's in that Sistani does not argue for *vilayat al-faqih* (rule of the cleric) and opposes authoritarianism. Instead, he holds that the cleric's role in Muslim society is a holistic defense of Islam.

Sistani has decried the civil and sectarian violence that has raged in Iraq since 2005, calling for restraint in revenge attacks against Sunni Iraqis, although his ability to moderate these conflicts, or inter-Shiite conflict, in central and southern Iraq is limited. He opposed the Iraqi government's 2008 attacks on the Mahdi Army, the militia controlled by cleric Muqtada al-Sadr, because of the need for Iraqi unity.

Sherifa Zuhur

See also: Coalition Provisional Authority; Islamic Dawa Party; Mahdi Army; Sadr, Muqtada al-; Shia Islam

Further Reading

Khalaji, Mehdi. *The Last Marja: Sistani and the End of Traditional Religious Authority in Shiism.* Policy Focus #59. Washington, DC: Washington Institute for Middle Eastern Affairs, September 2006.

Nasr, Vali. *The Shia Revival: How Conflicts within Islam Will Shape the Future.* New York: Norton, 2006.

Rahimi, Babak. *Ayatollah Sistani and the Democratization of Post-Ba'thist Iraq.* Special Report No. 187. Washington, DC: U.S. Institute of Peace, June 2007.

Visser, Rieder. *Sistani, the United States and Politics in Iraq: From Quietism to Machiavellianism?* No. 700. Oslo: Norwegian Institute of International Affairs, 2006.

Special Air Service, United Kingdom

Established in the summer of 1941 in Egypt, the Special Air Service (SAS) is the special forces regiment within the British Army. The regiment saw extensive action during the Persian Gulf War (1990–1991) as well as the wars in Afghanistan (2001–present) and the conflict in Iraq (2003–2009).

The SAS consists of four squadrons: A, B, D, and G, as well as a number of smaller specialty units, such as operations Research, Demolitions, Parachute Section, Boat Section, and Army Air Corps Section. The SAS insignia is the winged sword, and its unit motto is "Who Dares Wins."

The SAS has its roots in the Long-Range Desert Group, a group of commandos who fought against Italian forces in North Africa during World War II. Lieutenant Colonel David Stirling, the regiment's founder, began his army career with the Scots Guards in 1939, and thereafter transferred to No. 8 Commando unit in the Middle East. Convinced that small, self-sufficient units of 4 or 5 men each could be more effective than groups of 200, Stirling established the SAS in July 1941. The regiment began with approximately 60 men and a few trucks. By the end of World War II, the force numbered more than 1,000 men.

After the war, the remnants of the SAS (known as the Artists Rifles) were reorganized. Between 1950 and 1966 the SAS carried out combat operations against communist guerrillas in Malaya and against Indonesian forces and rebel guerrillas in Borneo.

Additionally, SAS D-Squadron conducted operations in Jebel Akhdar, Oman, during 1958 and 1959, and in Aden between 1964 and 1967. Between 1970 and 1977 the SAS returned to Oman to fight guerrillas there who were attempting to overthrow the government. From the late 1960s SAS elements also spent 25 years in Northern Ireland, supporting the British army and the Royal Ulster Constabulary (RUC) in their fight against the Provisional Irish Republican Army (PIRA).

In April 1980, back on home soil and under the glare of the world's media, the SAS took a mere 46 minutes to rescue 26 hostages from the Iranian embassy in London, during Operation NIMROD. In May 1982 the SAS carried out operations in the Falkland Islands against Argentine forces during the Falklands War.

In 1990, after the Iraqi invasion of Kuwait and formation of a military coalition spearheaded by the United States to drive out the Iraqis, some 700 men of the SAS (almost the entire regiment) were deployed to Iraq. General Sir Peter de la Billiére, the joint British commander-in-chief in the Persian Gulf, convinced U.S. general H. Norman Schwarzkopf, overall commander of coalition ground forces, to allow the SAS to operate in Iraqi territory. Dividing into separate fighting columns, with 30 SAS men assigned to each, A and D squadrons drove almost 250 miles behind enemy lines.

The SAS operations generally took place under cover of darkness and included missions to interrupt Iraqi communications. Tactics included blowing up underground fiber-optic cables, placing booby traps, and destroying communication towers. In addition to the disruption of Iraqi communication networks, the SAS destroyed Scud missile launch sites through a series of coordinated attacks.

However, not all SAS missions in Iraq proved successful. Two missions were aborted, and an SAS team known as Bravo Two Zero found itself in considerable difficulty behind Iraqi lines. After being discovered by Iraqi forces and splitting into two groups, the team battled harsh weather conditions and hypothermia. Four men were lost in this mission.

After seeing further action in the Balkans and Sierra Leone between 1994 and 2000, SAS units deployed to Afghanistan in 2001 in the ongoing fight against the Taliban and al-Qaeda (Operation ENDURING FREEDOM). Tasked with training the anti-Taliban Northern Alliance, the SAS instructed men in standard British Army assault tactics. The SAS also conducted surveillance and ground assaults on al-Qaeda training camps. Allegedly, during one of these missions in the cave complexes at Tora Bora in late 2001, the SAS believed that it had located the hiding place of al-Qaeda leader Osama bin Laden. However, for political reasons, the SAS operatives withdrew until U.S. forces could arrive, and the chance to capture bin Laden was lost. In addition to their regular assignments, the SAS has undertaken humanitarian assignments in Afghanistan, including locating suitable sites for food aid drops.

In 2003 the SAS returned to Iraq to support the Anglo-American–led military coalition that toppled the Saddam Hussein regime. The SAS deployed units for several operations behind Iraqi lines before the main ground campaign began in March. SAS teams helped to pinpoint the whereabouts of Hussein, who was apprehended in December 2003, and to monitor oil fields. Select SAS units remain in Iraq, although the nature of their work remains, necessarily, guarded.

Kirsty Anne Montgomery

See also: Hussein, Saddam; IRAQI FREEDOM, Operation

Further Reading

Carew, Tom. *Jihad! The Secret War in Afghanistan.* Edinburgh and London: Mainstream Publishing, 2000.

Kemp, Anthony. *The SAS: The Savage Wars of Peace, 1947 to the Present.* London: John Murray, 1994.

McCrery, Nigel. *The Complete History of the SAS: The Full Story of the World's Most Feared Special Forces.* London: Carlton Books, 2003.

Ryan, Mike. *Secret Operations of the SAS.* Barnsley, South Yorkshire: Pen and Sword Books, 2003.

Special Republican Guards

An elite military unit created in 1992 by Iraqi president Saddam Hussein to protect his regime and himself from revolt or assassination by other Iraqi military units. The Special Republican Guards (SRG) was composed of men from clans and towns that were particularly loyal to Hussein (such as Tikrit). They were better paid and received more benefits than members of the regular army or the Republican Guards, and had the best military equipment at their disposal. After the fall of Hussein's government in April 2003, the SRG was believed to have been responsible for much of the violence of the Iraqi insurgency that followed.

During the 1991 Persian Gulf War most of Hussein's elite Republican Guard units were decimated. Although those who survived remained loyal to Hussein and helped keep him in power, he apparently feared that some might turn on him. For that reason, in 1992 (some sources say 1995) Hussein created the SRG. From the very beginning the SRG was intended to protect the regime from internal foes more than from external threat. To ensure loyalty, SRG members were recruited from Hussein's clan and those closely allied to it. The members were also required to be from Tikrit, Bayji, Sharqat, or other smaller towns in the region in which Hussein was born. Recruits were almost always Sunni Muslims, rather than Kurds or Shiites. By insisting on these membership criteria, Hussein was able to better ensure that the SRG would be loyal to him and his family, through ties of family, regional origin, and shared religion. In addition to better pay than their military compatriots, members of the SRG received enlistment bonuses and subsidized housing, which were not offered to other units.

The SRG was the only armed force allowed to garrison Baghdad. Regular army troops were never stationed in the city, and Republican Guard divisions were stationed in the city's outer defenses. The SRG was not under the authority of the Defense Ministry but rather the State Special Security Apparatus, which was tightly controlled by Hussein himself. Indeed, the commander of the SRG was Qusay Hussein, the dictator's son.

The SRG was originally composed of one brigade, but later was expanded to five brigades with a total of 14 battalions of 1,300–1,500 men each. Four of the brigades were mechanized infantry, equipped with the best weapons available in Iraq. A fifth brigade was armored, equipped with T-72 main battle tanks. Antiaircraft weapons were also available, including handheld weapons and antiaircraft artillery. Because the SRG's purpose was to protect the regime, it had to be able to resist assaults by regular military units. At its peak, the SRG numbered about 26,000 men. By March 2003, however, its strength had declined to some 12,000 troops.

The SRG's duties included protecting Hussein's various presidential palaces and residences, along with his farms and other real estate holdings. It also guarded key installations in Baghdad. The 1st Brigade in particular was charged with presidential security. Various units drove and maintained the limousines used by Hussein, and they provided security for motorcades and members of the government and their families. One gruesome task assigned to the 1st Brigade was the apprehension and execution of military officers and government leaders accused of disloyalty to the regime. Other units are believed to have been charged with guarding sites that might have contained weapons of mass destruction (WMD).

In 1998 a dispute between the Iraqi government and the United Nations (UN) arose when weapons inspectors wanted to examine SRG facilities believed to contain WMD. Although the situation was resolved without violence, the episode convinced some intelligence experts that Hussein continued to work on forbidden weapons and used his most loyal units to keep prying eyes away.

During the March 2003 Anglo-American–led invasion of Iraq, many American military leaders believed that the SRG would be their most dangerous opponent. While the Republican Guard was largely destroyed outside of Baghdad, the SRG was first encountered in the fighting for Baghdad International Airport on April 4. In a three-hour engagement with troops of the U.S. 3rd Infantry Division, the SRG was soundly defeated. Three tanks were destroyed, and an estimated 250 SRG members were killed; American losses were 1 dead and 8 wounded. Following this battle, the SRG largely melted into the population. Fears that SRG members might fight house-to-house for Baghdad proved unfounded. On May 23, 2003, the provisional Iraqi government ordered the SRG dissolved.

SRG members are believed to have launched the insurgency against coalition forces in the Sunni triangle around Tikrit during the summer of 2003. Ironically, the Sons of Iraq and Anbar Awakening home guard militias that have been funded, trained, and equipped by the Americans beginning in 2007 contain cadres composed of former SRG members.

Tim J. Watts

See also: Baghdad, Battle for; Hussein, Qusay; Hussein, Saddam; Republican Guard

Further Reading

Carlisle, Rodney P. *Iraq War.* New York: Facts on File, 2005.

Keegan, John. *The Iraq War: The Military Offensive, from Victory in 21 Days to the Insurgent Aftermath.* New York: Vintage, 2005.

Woods, Kevin M., and Michael R. Pease. *The Iraqi Perspectives Report: Saddam's Senior Leadership on Operation Iraqi Freedom from the Official U.S. Joint Forces Command Report.* Annapolis, MD: Naval Institute Press, 2006.

STEEL CURTAIN, Operation

A major anti-insurgent operation mounted by U.S. marines and Iraqi forces during November 5 through 22, 2005, as part of the broader al-Sayyad operation that aimed to control the resistance in the Euphrates River Valley, deal with Anbar Province, and also establish control by the Iraqi Army in the Al Qaim region. Operation STEEL CURTAIN (also known as Al Hajip Elfulathi) was significant in that it was the first military operation to include significant numbers of Iraqi Army personnel recruited and trained by the coalition government for

Iraq. For the first time, Iraqi soldiers took the lead in some of the house-to-house searches and extensively patrolled in insurgent areas. The U.S. command considered the operation to be a success, although it was costly in terms of civilian casualties and the creation of strong tensions.

After the fall of President Saddam Hussein's regime in April 2003, many U.S. leaders considered the war in Iraq to be over. This proved not to be the case when a major insurgency broke out that summer and intensified over the succeeding months. Some of the resistance came from Islamist groups, others did not, but all wanted American troops out of Iraq. The resistance was particularly active in Anbar Province in western Iraq, adjoining the Syrian border, but was not restricted to this area. The Anbar region is dominated by tribes, and the Sunni tribes expected nothing but violence and a diminution of their role in Iraq under a government dominated by Shia groups. This area had also long been used by smugglers. Consisting mostly of rough desert terrain, the province held many routes for men, arms, and supplies to flow from Syria to desert camps and urban locations inside Iraq. Major urban centers included Husaybah, Karabilah, and Ubaydi. Ubaydi in particular was considered a key location for insurgents and was heavily fortified. Indeed the earlier Operation MATADOR in May 2005 had been an attempt to secure Ubaydi. Although coalition forces took the city, they failed to garrison it, and insurgents quickly resumed control over the city.

Most observers believed that coalition success in Iraq would depend upon whether or not a viable Iraqi military could be established. When Hussein was forced from power, the United States took what many now consider to be the unwise course of completely disbanding the Iraqi military as part of the attempt to rid the country of Baathist influences. This decision left a power vacuum that coalition forces could not fill, and it forced the building of a new Iraqi army from scratch. The process was slow and difficult, and Operation STEEL CURTAIN appeared to be an opportunity to speed along the process.

In June 2005 U.S. forces launched Operation SPEAR, an effort to oust insurgents from Anbar Province. In that operation, only 100 Iraqi soldiers participated. By November 2005, however, the number of Iraqi soldiers nationwide had increased dramatically. Special efforts had also been made to recruit and station new units in and around Anbar. Two Iraqi division headquarters were formed, along with four brigade headquarters. Ten infantry battalions were recruited and deployed to Anbar. A total of 15,000 Iraqi soldiers were stationed in the province by November 2005, with 1,000 deployed to help the American troops in Operation STEEL CURTAIN.

The most hopeful sign for the coalition was that some of the new troops were locally recruited. A number were assigned to specially trained Scout Platoons, also known as Desert Protectors. Comparisons were made between the Scout Platoons and Native Americans recruited by the U.S. Cavalry during the 19th-century Native American wars in the American West. Like the Native American units, the Scout Platoons were familiar with the territory in which STEEL CURTAIN took place. They served as a liaison between American units and local tribal leaders, and the Scouts also provided information about which individuals belonged in the area and which individuals might be foreign fighters. American military leaders also viewed the increased number of recruits as a sign that the local population was increasingly unhappy with the foreign fighters, especially members of al-Qaeda.

In July 2005 coalition forces launched Operation HUNTER, which was intended to sweep through the Euphrates River Valley. Coalition planners recognized that in the western provinces most of the insurgents in 2005 were al-Qaeda operatives. The goal of Operation HUNTER had been to force the insurgents out of the region and cut off the supply lines that funneled fresh resources and men into Iraq and permitted operatives to escape to camps in Syria and beyond. Unlike earlier anti-insurgent campaigns, Operation HUNTER was also expected to establish a permanent Iraqi army presence in the area.

American operational forces for STEEL CURTAIN included marines from the 3rd Battalion, 6th Marine Regiment, and the 2nd Battalion, 1st Marine Regiment. Both were part of the 2nd Marine Division. The marines were reinforced with supporting units and specialists, including forward air controllers, to total approximately 2,500 men.

STEEL CURTAIN began on November 5 with an assault on Husaybah. It took coalition forces four days to clear the city. Many of the insurgents that were forced from Husaybah fled to Karabilah. Another four days were needed to secure Karabilah. The final phase of the operation was to secure Ubaydi. Fighting in this center of al-Qaeda operations was difficult and more protracted, involving house-to-house combat. After seven days, coalition commanders declared the city secure.

From the Iraqi perspective, the operation resulted in hundreds of civilian casualties and destroyed much of Husaybah, including government buildings, schools, and two mosques. Citizens were also very angry and upset because they were not allowed to reclaim their dead.

Operation STEEL CURTAIN officially ended on November 22. Iraqi soldiers were praised for their participation in the operation, especially their work inside the cities. Unlike earlier operations, the coalition forces established forward operating bases in the region as they cleared out the al-Qaeda insurgents. The goal was to establish an ongoing presence that would prevent the return of al-Qaeda.

Coalition losses were relatively light. Ten marines were killed and 30 others were wounded. Losses among the Iraqi troops are unknown. Coalition spokesmen claimed that 139 insurgents were killed and another 256 captured.

Coalition commanders were pleased that five al-Qaeda leaders were killed in the air strikes on Husaybah. Although planners had hoped to capture or kill Jordanian-born al-Qaeda associate Abu Musab al-Zarqawi, he was not among the casualties. He was later killed in an American air strike in June 2006.

Coalition leaders considered the operation a success and held that the new Iraqi Army could now aid in operations against insurgents. Only three weeks after the conclusion of STEEL CURTAIN, the Iraqi provisional government held the first democratic election in years on December 15. A permanent legislative body was elected. Although many in the Al Qaim region and Anbar region refused to vote, the reduction in the harassment and intimidation of voters was considered an important goal of Operation STEEL CURTAIN and similar military operations.

Tim J. Watts

See also: al-Qaeda in Iraq

Further Reading

Benhoff, David A., and Anthony C. Zinni. *Among the People: U.S. Marines in Iraq.* Quantico, VA: Marine Corps University, 2008.

Navarro, Eric. *God Willing: My Wild Ride with the New Iraqi Army.* Washington, DC: Potomac Books, 2008.

West, Bing. *The Strongest Tribe: War, Politics, and the Endgame in Iraq.* New York: Random House, 2008.

Stryker Brigades

Rapidly deployable, multioperational, highly mobile infantry brigade combat teams. As part of broader Defense Department reform and realignment efforts, the U.S. Army spent much of the 1990s planning a new force structure for the early 21st century. The transformed army would boast new equipment to take advantage of what some saw as a revolution in military affairs. Its units would be more flexible, deployable, and sustainable than those of the Cold War, but every bit as lethal. The Stryker Brigades emerged as a deliberate intermediate step between the Cold War army and this new, objective force.

On October 12, 1999, General Eric K. Shinseki, the U.S. Army's newly appointed chief of staff, delivered the traditional keynote speech to the annual meeting of the Association of the United States Army. In that speech, General Shinseki announced his intent to begin implementing the long-studied reforms. He established many specific goals, including reducing the army's logistics requirements, shrinking the size of support forces, and replacing existing armored vehicles with smaller, lighter counterparts. Army units would adopt a standard modular structure capable of rapid deployment. Most significantly, Shinseki called

for the creation of a prototype unit within the next year.

That unit would use readily available equipment to begin moving toward the eventual objective force. It would both validate that future force's design theory and begin providing the army with experience in new operating concepts. By design, the brigade would form both an intermediate step between the existing light and heavy combat brigades and an interim force between the existing and future units. It would be able to deploy almost as quickly as lighter infantry units, but have combat power approaching that of heavier armored units. By using a standard vehicle chassis, state-of-the-art electronics, and a number of other innovations, the new formation would require fewer personnel and supplies.

The 3rd Brigade of the 2nd Infantry Division was selected as the first of seven brigades to adopt the new design. After evaluating 35 U.S. and foreign vehicles, the army settled on a Canadian Light Armored Vehicle as the new unit's mount. In February 2002 this vehicle, modified for the army's needs into several different variations, was officially named to honor two infantrymen with the same last name who had been awarded the Medal of Honor. The Stryker, with eight wheels, became the symbol of the new units, subsequently designated as Stryker Brigade Combat Teams.

The prototype unit technically existed within a year of Shinseki's speech. But it required substantially more time to acquire hundreds of new types of equipment and reconsider the way army brigades traditionally fought. At 19 tons, the basic Stryker infantry carrier provided a medium-weight platform that could be adopted to meet nearly all of the brigade's vehicle needs. The Stryker family included a mortar carrier, a mobile gun system, and reconnaissance, command, fire support, engineering, ambulance, and anti-tank variations. The vehicles and the troops they carried shared information through a sophisticated electronic network. Through experiments, tests, and training the Stryker Brigades learned how to make the most of their new capabilities.

After September 11, 2001, many viewed the new type of brigade as a critical component of the War on Terror. Its new equipment, organization, and techniques theoretically allowed the Stryker Brigade to shoot, move, and communicate with unprecedented ease and coordination. That theory was soon to be tested in combat.

On December 3, 2003, with the beginning of the Iraq War, the first Stryker Brigade crossed the Kuwaiti border bound for the Iraqi city of Mosul. Rapidly changing conditions forced a change in plans while it moved north, and the unit drove into the city of Samarra instead. The brigade's ability to alter plans on the march without pause proved to be but one of its chief assets.

In the course of its initial deployment, the first Stryker Brigade met and exceeded the army's expectations. The medium-weight force proved ideal for a number of missions. With its modern information systems and modular structure, the brigade's subordinate units could be rapidly reconfigured as need arose. Special training and equipment provided for its individual soldiers increased the effectiveness of even the smallest units. The Stryker vehicle itself also offered unexpected advantages in Iraq. While it proved as fast and easy to support as had been hoped, its silence in comparison to tracked vehicles provided a valuable advantage in urban settings. Following the success of the 3rd Brigade, 2nd Infantry Division, additional units completed their conversions into Stryker Brigades and deployed to Iraq.

This did not stop criticism of the Stryker vehicle and the units that used it, however. Many observers, familiar with tactics designed for heavier armored vehicles, have criticized the Stryker's comparative lack of armor and use of wheels rather than tracks. Others have complained about the vehicle's high center of gravity, a deliberate choice to protect its passengers from roadside mines.

Despite such criticisms, the performance of the Stryker Brigades in combat has fulfilled General Shinseki's intent. The new units proved more flexible, deployable, and sustainable than previous designs without sacrificing lethality. Also, techniques and equipment developed for the new brigades quickly found their way into other units. Along the way, the Stryker Brigades and their signature vehicle became an icon of American forces in Iraq since 2003.

Jeffery A. Charlston

See also: IRAQI FREEDOM, Operation, Ground Campaign

Further Reading

Gonzales, Daniel. *Network-Centric Operations Case Study: The Stryker Brigade Combat Team.* Santa Monica, CA: RAND Corporation, 2005.

Peltz, Eric. *Speed and Power: Toward and Expeditionary Army.* Santa Monica, CA: RAND Corporation, 2003.

Reardon, Mark, and Jeffery Charlston. *From Transformation to Combat: The First Stryker Brigade at War.* Washington, DC: Center of Military History, 2007.

Suicide Bombings

Bombings in which an explosive is delivered and detonated by a person or persons who expect to die in the explosion along with

Smoke and flames fill the air after a suicide bomber set off an explosion that killed 33 people and injured another 50 in Tal Afar, Iraq, on October 11, 2005. (U.S. Department of Defense)

the intended target or targets. In recent years the number of suicide bombings or attacks has risen exponentially, and not just in the Middle East. The United States was struck by four hijacked aircraft piloted by Islamic fanatics associated with the al-Qaeda terrorist organization on September 11, 2001, resulting in the deaths of almost 3,000 people. Certainly, this was the worst—and most dramatic—example of a suicide operation. Other shocking attacks took place in Bali, Jakarta, Madrid, London, the Sinai Peninsula, and Amman, in addition to those in Iraq, Afghanistan, and Pakistan.

Suicide bombers employ several different techniques. Japanese pilots in World War II were known for crashing their airplanes straight into targets, causing tremendous devastation. These were known as kamikaze ("divine wind"), the name given to a typhoon that destroyed a Mongol invasion fleet off Japan in the 13th century. Kamikazes exacted a heavy toll on Allied warships at the end of World War II, especially off Okinawa. The Tamil Tigers of Sri Lanka utilized suicide bombings during their long struggle against the central government between 1983 and 2009. Other attackers have employed bombs secured in cars or trucks.

Individual suicide bombers often strap explosives and shrapnel to their bodies and wear vests or belts specially designed for the purpose. They then drive or walk to their targets. Because military targets are heavily defended, typical targets include crowded shopping areas, restaurants, or buses. Suicide bombers may also approach softer targets directly linked to the military or police, such as a line of recruits in the street, as has occurred during the Iraq War. Detonating the explosives kills and injures people in the vicinity and can also destroy notable property, such as religious shrines. One technique is to send two or more suicide bombers against a single target; after the first blast, the second bomber works his way into the crowd of responders and then detonates his explosives.

An explosion in an enclosed area is more destructive than one in the open, and suicide bombers pick their targets accordingly. Forensic investigators at the site of a suicide bombing can usually identify the bomber and the general type of device he or she used. A suicide vest decapitates the bomber; a belt cuts the bomber in two.

The explosive devices themselves are easily constructed. They might include an explosive charge, a battery, a cable, a light switch detonator, and a custom-made belt or vest to hold the explosives. Scrap metal might be employed to act as shrapnel, which in the blast would kill or maim those nearby. Explosives may also be carried in a briefcase or other bag. The bomber sets off the explosive by flipping a switch or pressing a button, sometimes remotely as in the case of a car or truck bombing.

Muslim extremists in the latest wave of violence might leave a written or video *shahada*, which is partially a statement of their intent and partially a will and settlement of any debts. Suicide bombings have been used in the Middle East since the late 1970s. The Islamic resistance employed them in Syria against the Baathist government, although many more conventional attacks also occurred. During the Lebanese civil war, car bombings evolved in some cases into suicide attacks; and in 1981 the Islamic Dawa Party bombed the Iraqi embassy in Beirut.

In response to the Israeli invasion of Lebanon in 1982, the Islamic Resistance, a loosely organized group, formed, and some of its elements planned bombing attacks. In November 1982 an Islamic Resistance suicide bomber destroyed a building in Tyre, Lebanon, and killed 76 Israelis. The Organization of Islamic Jihad and other militant Islamist groups including Hezbollah, as well as numerous Christians, carried out another 50 suicide attacks between 1982 and 1999, when the Israelis withdrew from Lebanon. A massive suicide bombing of their barracks in October 1983 forced American and French troops from Lebanon.

The belief that such attacks bring martyrdom has encouraged suicide bombings in countries all over the world, including Afghanistan, Chechnya, Croatia, Tajikistan, Pakistan, Yemen, Panama, Argentina, and Algeria. In 1995 a suicide bomber dressed as a priest attempted to assassinate Pope John Paul II in Manila.

Suicide attacks by Palestinians began after the First Intifada but were not regular events; however, many more took place during the Second (al-Aqsa) Intifada. The first Palestinian suicide bombing occurred in April 1994 in the West Bank. It killed 8 Israelis and was carried out to avenge the deaths of 25 Muslims who had been praying in the Ibrahimi Mosque when they were killed by Israeli settler Baruch Goldstein. Hamas explained that its basic policy was only to attack Israeli soldiers, but if Palestinian civilians were slaughtered in deliberate attacks, then it would break that policy. There were 198 known suicide-bombing attacks in Israel and Palestine between 1994 and July 2002, which killed 120 people. The bombers died in 136 of those attacks. Because many of the bombers were intercepted and/or the attacks otherwise failed, the numbers of casualties are far lower than in the numerous suicide attacks carried out in Iraq since 2003. Attacks increased after the beginning of the Second Intifada in September 2000. Although suicide bombings comprised only a small percentage of actual attacks launched by Palestinians against Israelis, they accounted for perhaps half the Israelis killed between

2000 and 2002. In 2003 there were 26 attacks killing 144, but in 2004, 15 attacks and 55 dead. In 2005 Hamas ordered a cease-fire, which was, however, not binding on the other groups that had engaged in attacks: the Abu Ali Mustafa Brigades of the Popular Front for the Liberation of Palestine, Islamic Jihad, and the al-Aqsa Martyrs Brigades. During 2005 there were 7 attacks killing 23, and then in 2006 only 2 attacks.

Many of the suicide attackers in Lebanon in the 1980s were Christians; Palestinian suicide bombers have been presumed to be Muslims, although there are many Christians in the Palestinian national movement. A Greek Orthodox religious figure, Archimandrite Theosios Hanna, supported *fida'iyin n shahids* (fighter martyrs) in several speeches. Other Christian leaders have explained the attacks as a desperate response to a brutal military occupation. It is obvious from the Tamil, Japanese, or anarchist violence that the motivation is primarily nationalist, and in fact Islam strictly forbids suicide and engaging recklessly in jihad so as to obtain martyrdom. According to classical doctrine, there are set rules regarding who may participate in jihad, and these exclude children, those with dependants, and also, traditionally, women. The main religious justification is that under circumstances of military occupation, jihad is required of Muslims. In Islam, there is a difference between an individual and a collectively incumbent religious duty. Religious authorities who decry the linkage of Islam with suicide and the killing of innocent people try to convince their audiences that the greater jihad, the striving to be a good Muslim in every possible aspect of life, can substitute for jihad as armed struggle, or that if armed struggle is necessary, it should not involve attacks of this type. Among

convocations of clerics who have met on this issue, most acknowledge that jihad is licit for Palestinians, and some believe it is licit in Iraq, although many object to suicide attacks. In 20 books of recantation of violent jihad, the leaders of the Gamaat Islamiya have provided powerful arguments against violence employed for the right reason (in their view) but with the wrong methods, or timing. Not all religious authorities take this position, of course, and unfortunately the televised footage or videos of suicide bombers serve as a recruiting tool for others.

For most Muslims, suicide is anathema. Many would-be suicide bombers are motivated by the desire to combat social injustice; others find irresistible the temptation of martyrdom with its promise of rewards in paradise. Martyrdom has its own history in early Islam, and it is believed that martyrs are cleansed of their sins and that they will have special power to intercede on behalf of their relatives and close friends on the Day of Judgment. The families of suicide bombers are often extremely proud of their loved ones and praise them publicly as heroes. Some Palestinian suicide bombers received financial support from the Iraqi government, and in this way were able to provide for their dependants. Suicide bombers also believe that they will be remembered as popular heroes.

Would-be Palestinian suicide bombers have often used the argument that all Israelis serve in the military, at least as reserves, and therefore are combatants and not really civilians. In Iraq, the suicide attacks since the coalition invasion of 2003 were initially directed against coalition forces, but then turned to Iraqi citizens working for the government, police, or military, and also to ordinary civilians. In addition, groups such as al-Qa'ida fi Bilad al-Rafhidayn (al-Qaeda in Mesopotamia) have targeted

Shia civilians, declaring them to be "renegades" or apostates and therefore subject to death. The attacks spiked in 2005. In 2003 there were 25 suicide bombings; in 2004, 140; in 2005, 478; in 2006, 300; in 2007, more than 200 suicide bombings; in 2008, more than 115 suicide bombings. Although far fewer, there were a number of costly suicide bombings in the spring of 2009.

Suicide bombings were also employed by insurgents in Afghanistan, although here there were not as many casualties, most probably because the Taliban have chosen to target military personnel or politicians, rather than civilians, and because the planning for them is often poor. Large numbers of civilian casualties have resulted from certain attacks, as in the Baghlan in 2007, where the target was a politician and 70 people died, or when a local militia leader was targeted at a dogfight in Kandahar in February 2008, and 80 people died.

There are differing attitudes in the various states where suicide attacks have occurred. While most all people fear such attacks, many citizens support the notion of armed resistance. Since al-Qaeda and groups similar to it have been active, counterterrorist agencies, police, and gendarmeries around the world have been focusing on ways to prevent suicide bombings.

Suicide bombings are part of asymmetric warfare. Advantages for any violent radical group employing this tactic are that no escape need be arranged for the bombers and that they are not expected to live to reveal information. Also, the materials for the explosive devices are inexpensive.

Al Qaedist tactics have created a new *fiqh al-jihad*, or rules of jihad, that are somewhat different from the past. For example, in a collective jihad, women, children, and parents of dependant children, or the children of the elderly, were not to volunteer for jihad, but in the five-year period when such attacks were most prevalent in Israel and in the last several years in Iraq, bombers have come from both genders, although most were men. It is a common assumption that suicide bombers are drawn from the poor and desperate, but a careful study of most suicide terrorist acts shows this is untrue; the bombers were, rather, the ideologically committed of different backgrounds. On occasion, Afghani and Iraqi authorities have claimed that mentally impaired people have been induced to be bombers, but this must be only a small number. Sometimes those who were recruited to such actions were chosen for their psychological predispositions not to suicide but to suggestibility, and were prevented, if possible, from contacting their families once their mission was set, so as not to give any hint of their intent. In the case of Palestinian suicide bombers, those attackers who authorities said were traceable to Hamas and Islamic Jihad were persons with no major family responsibilities and who were over the age of 18. In some cases, recruiters sought individuals who could speak Hebrew well.

Understandably, suicide bombings are enormously upsetting to potential civilian victims. Suicide bombers turn up when they are least expected as their victims go about their daily business, and victims and bystanders are taken completely by surprise. The victims are often civilians, and children make up a sizable percentage of those killed. Because the bomber has no concern for his or her own life, it is difficult to prevent such attacks. In Israel and in Iraq, many individuals and businesses have hired security guards who are specially trained to spot potential bombers. Airport and general transport security has now been increased, worldwide.

Amy Hackney Blackwell and Sherifa Zuhur

See also: al-Qaeda in Iraq; Iraqi Insurgency; Jihad

Further Reading

Aboul-Enein, Youssef H., and Sherifa Zuhur. *Islamic Rulings on Warfare.* Carlisle Barracks, PA: Strategic Studies Institute, 2004.

Friedman, Lauri S. *What Motivates Suicide Bombers?* Farmington Hills, MI: Greenhaven, 2004.

Khosrokhavar, Farhad. *Suicide Bombers: Allah's New Martyrs.* Translated by David Macey. London: Pluto, 2005.

Rosenthal, Franz. "On Suicide in Islam." *Journal of the American Oriental Society* 66 (1946): 239–259.

Skaine, Rosemarie. *Female Suicide Bombers.* Jefferson, NC: McFarland, 2006.

Sunni Islam

Largest of the two predominant branches of Islam. Approximately 85 percent of Muslims worldwide are adherents of Sunni Islam, although the exact proportions of the two branches are disputed. Muslims themselves seldom used the word "Sunni" prior to the 2003 invasion of Iraq and subsequent occupation or the Islamic Revolution in Iran. It derives from a medieval Arabic phrase, *ahl al-sunnah wa al-jama'a*, meaning those who live according to the Prophet's model, unified in a community. In the early period, this term did not refer to all Muslims but rather to those who were engaged in Islamic scholarship and learning. The *sunnah*, or way, of the Prophet Muhammad refers to his tradition, or practice, of Islam during his 23 years of life following the initial revelation of Allah's words to him. However, "sunnah" generally referred to any tradition of the ancient Arabs.

It is mostly in the West that Muslims are differentiated as Sunnis or Shia. If asked, a Muslim may instead identify himself by a school of Islamic law or jurisprudence, such as the Hanafi school, which was the official legal doctrine of the Ottoman Empire, or of a particular movement. Since the most recent Islamic revival (*sahwa islamiyya*) began in the 1970s, the term *sunniyyun* (plural of *sunni* used interchangeably with *Islamiyyun*) has acquired the meaning of a very devout Muslim, or a *salafi*.

In contrast with the more institutionalized clerics, courts, and systems of Sunni Muslim learning, Sufi Islam is a mystical movement within Islam, the goal of which is the spiritual development of the individual. Sufis seek out personal guides (*shaykh* or *pir*) and are organized into brotherhoods (*tariqat*). There are Shia as well as Sunni Sufi orders. Sufism can be highly ascetic, while mainstream Islam is not. In contemporary times, sometimes even official clerics are also Sufis; however, the Salafists oppose Sufism.

Sunni Muslims do not adhere to the doctrine of the imams, as do several sects of Shia Muslims (excluding the Zaydiyya). In the past, they generally judged the validity of the caliph (the temporal political and military leader) or the caliphate (Islamic government) itself by his or its adherence to the faith and the order and harmony that he or it maintained. In contrast with the Shia, Sunni Muslims believe that Abu Bakr, Umar, and Uthman—the first three Rashidun caliphs following Muhammad—were legitimate successors of Muhammad and that they are of equal standing with the fourth caliph, Ali, Muhammad's son-in-law. Ali became the fourth caliph in 656 CE after the murder of Caliph Uthman and was himself assassinated in 661. However, there were other Muslims, not Ali's supporters, who also opposed the Umayyads, so the political divisions over leadership were complex.

It was not a requirement that the political and religious leadership in Sunni Islam trace its lineage through Ali, although the requirements of a caliph as defined by the scholar Abu al-Hasan Ali Ibn Muhammad Ibn Habib al-Mawardi (972–1058) indicated that he must be of the Prophet Muhammad's Quraysh tribe, male, not physically impaired, and pious. Any link to the Ahl al-Bayt, the immediate family members of the Prophet was, however, highly regarded. The caliphs lost their real authority in 1055. They retained an element of religious authority only in name, as the caliph was mentioned in the Friday prayers. With the Mongol sack of Baghdad in 1258, the caliphs lost all power. For Sunni Muslims, other political leaders were acceptable, though they were supposed to uphold Islamic law. When the Ottoman sultans years later declared themselves to be caliphs in order to wage jihad, other Muslims questioned their religious claim. By the 20th century some Muslims understood the caliphate as an ideal structure but one that could be replaced by other forms of authority. Others supported attempts to restore the caliphate.

In the absence of the caliphate, Muslim politics continued under the precept that other rulers, sultans, or emirs would rule to the best of their ability in accordance with the Sharia (Islamic law) and uphold the *hisba*, the principle of "commanding the good and forbidding the evil," a key principle in Islam. Clerics, or *ulama* (those who possess *'ilm*, religious knowledge), were to be consulted by the ruler, issue fatawa, and help to guide the believers.

To justify Islamic rule the Ottomans, who were Sunni Muslims, later governed under a particular theory called the circle of equity, in which mutual responsibilities were to provide equity, security, and justice. In the 20th century both Sunni and Shia politicized Islamic movements have argued for a more intensely Islamic government. The Muslim Brotherhood, Hamas, Hezbullah, the Gamaat Islamiya, and al-Qaeda have all taken this position. These groups draw on very important arguments about governance and the state that have developed in Islamic history. The Muslim Brotherhood relinquished jihad as armed struggle and sought to change society through *dawa*, a program involving recruitment, education, and social support. Hezbollah and Hamas argue for both armed struggle and *dawa*. Islamic Jihad (in Egypt), Gamaat Islamiya, and al-Qaeda all argue that the groups who only conducted *dawa* are not supporting Muslims, that jihad as armed struggle is necessary. However, the Gamaat Islamiya and Egyptian Islamic Jihad (in Egypt, excluding those members who joined al-Qaeda) recanted their use of jihad beginning in 1997 and reached a truce with the Egyptian government in 1999.

In general, individual interpretations of Islamic law by scholars may vary. There is no pope or central authority in Sunni Islam. In Sunni Islam, unlike Shia Islam, there is no *marjaiyya*, or formal policy of choosing a cleric as a "source of emulation." However, there are today many very popular Sunni clerics and preachers whose followers are loyal to their various positions.

The Sunni legal schools employ a principle of lawmaking known as *ijma*, or consensus, that is not employed by the Shia legal schools. However, there are differences in the legal definitions of that consensus. Additionally, a Sunni Muslim could resort to a cleric of one school to obtain a ruling, or fatwa, and is generally expected to adhere to the commonly acknowledged features of his own school. But Muslims may also seek advice from other clerics or authorities, and advice columns in newspapers and on the Internet provide differing opinions, sometimes based on the positions of other legal schools.

Muslims believe that the Qur'an is the literal word of God delivered in Arabic by the angel Gabriel to Muhammad over a period of 23 years. Any desecration of the Qur'an is therefore a desecration of the very words of Allah. Although the Qur'an is the final statement of Allah to humanity, when it does not offer explicit advice on a particular matter, a Muslim may appeal to a jurist to look to the Prophet's *sunnah*, as recorded in the *ahadith*, or collected materials concerning the tradition, behavior, practices, and sayings of the Prophet. They may also use *qiyas*, or a type of analogy, in determining the licitness of any action, or behavior, or the principle of *ijma*.

The *hadith* are always introduced by listing the chain of their transmitters. Ideally, the first transmitter of the text was a companion (*sahabah*) of Muhammad. An important companion was Abu Bakr, also known as "The Most Truthful" (*al-Siddiq*), the first caliph. The next companions in level of importance are the next two caliphs, Umar and Uthman. The Shia reject the *hadith* transmitted by those they call Unjust Companions, who repudiated the leadership of Ali abi Talib. Although these three are important companions, there are ten who are thought to warrant paradise. A much longer list of *sahabah* exist because Sunnis consider anyone who knew or even saw Muhammad, accepted his teachings, and died as a Muslim to be a companion. Early Sunni scholars identified these companions, wrote their biographies, and listed them in various reference texts. This identification was essential because their testimonies and

their reputation for veracity affirm and determine the content of the *hadith* and, therefore, the *sunnah*.

There are many collections of these original oral traditions, but they are graded according to their soundness with six respected collections, two of which—that of Muslim and Bukhari—are considered most reliable. However, many Muslims repeat and believe in *hadith* that are not necessarily the most sound, and since the reform movement of the 19th century, some Muslims believe that the *hadith* brought many unwanted innovations or, conversely, too much imitation of tradition (*taqlid*) into Islam. Shia Islamic law generally uses *hadith* that pertain to Muhammad as told to members of Ali's family. These variations lead to some differences in Sunni Islamic law and Shia Islamic law.

Muslims must practice their faith through demonstrated religious rituals and obligations. Many sources speak of five religious practices or duties, often referred to as the Five Pillars. The first pillar is called bearing witness (*shahadah*) and is the recitation of the creed or confession of faith, called the Testimony of Faith: "There is no God, but Allah; and Muhammad is His prophet." The *shahadah* is also uttered as part of the Muslim call (*adhan*) to prayer and is part of the Tashahud, which follows each set of two prayer sequences, when they are recited at least five times daily (at different times two, three, or four sequences are the minimum required). The second pillar is prayer (*salat*), performed at least five times a day (dawn, noon, midafternoon, sunset, and evening). Muslims purify themselves before prayer by washing their hands, face, mouth, nose, ears, and feet. During prayer, all Muslims face Mecca. The third pillar is fasting (*sawm*) during the daylight hours for all of the month of Ramadan, the ninth month of the Islamic lunar calendar. This fasting means that no food or beverages are consumed and that there is no smoking or sexual intercourse. Those who are sick are excused from fasting and make up their fast. Other days of fasting may be observed, but it is obligatory during Ramadan.

The fourth pillar is almsgiving, effectively a tax (*zakat*) of 2.5 percent calculated on one's income and assets. But unlike a tax, it is supposed to be voluntary. It is used for the community's poor, the promotion of Islam, and the maintenance of the mosque and other religious institutions. The fifth pillar is the required pilgrimage (*hajj*) once in a lifetime to the holy city of Mecca, as commanded in the Qur'an in surah XXII, al-Hajj, 22–33.

The responsibility for performing these duties falls on the individual, but stricter Muslims and Muslim governments hold that it is the duty of the state to command the good and thus to enforce their performance. There are other strictures as well. For example, Muslims must not drink alcohol, not simply as a forbidden substance but because it clouds alertness and judgment and makes it impossible to pray. Pork is forbidden, as are games of chance. Many Muslim women believe that covering their heads is a required individual duty, but others do not. Modest behavior is, however, required of both men and women.

Many Westerners know little about Islam, with the exception of the Five Pillars. Yet ethical behavior is very important to Islamic belief, including the commitment to social justice, as in protection of the weak and aid to the poor and socially disadvantaged. Islam seeks to promote an ethical life lived within a community. It is more difficult in many ways to be a good Muslim while fulfilling one's obligations to family and community than to live as a hermit, and the

Prophet Muhammad is said to have promoted marriage and discouraged celibacy or an extreme ascetic lifestyle. Many of the rules regarding relations between men and women, which non-Muslims find very strict and hard to understand, are indeed intended to provide a moral and ethical grounding for the community.

Muslims are concerned with *iman*, or faith, as well as acts of submission (*islam*) and rightful intentions (*ihsan*), and many religio-philosophical principles guide them. The most basic aspect of Islam is belief in Allah and the Oneness (*tawhid*) of Allah. This monotheism is expressed in many ways. Muslims believe in the prophets and believe that they brought important messages to mankind, but Muhammad is considered the Seal of Prophecy, or the last prophet. Nonetheless, Jesus, Moses, Abraham, and others are revered. However, Muslims believe that some Jews did not heed the word of God in his divine message to them. Muslims, who believe that Jesus was only a prophet, also argue that Christians wrongly recognize Christ as Father and Divine Spirit. The doctrine of the Trinity violates the idea of the Oneness of Allah.

Muslims recognize the scriptures as revelations of Allah. Allah was the creator, but he did not simply create the world and humankind and leave humanity to fend for itself. Rather, Allah provided revelations for the guidance of men. The Qur'an is the transcending revelation of Allah that cannot be contradicted by any other revelations of Allah. Still, Muslims recognize other revelations, which include the Jewish and Christian holy scriptures, as well as the Zoroastrian texts.

Muslims believe in the angels (*malaika*), who are the servants of Allah. Angels were not given the free will that Allah granted to humans. Their duties include recording all human deeds, ensouling the fetus at 120 days of gestation (although some Islamic scholars believe ensoulment occurs on the 40th or 80th day), watching over and caring for creation, gathering souls at death, and much more.

All Muslims also believe in the Day of Judgment and in the Resurrection (*qiyama*), when Allah will return to judge all of humanity, Muslim and non-Muslim, including the dead. After the Resurrection, every human is held accountable for his or her deeds. The deeds of each individual are judged by Allah and weighed on a scale. If the good outweighs the evil, then the individual gains entrance into Paradise. If the evil outweighs the good, the individual spends eternity in Hell.

In the pre-Islamic era, referred to as the *jahiliyya* or time of barbarity, people believed entirely in preordination. Islam rejects this passivity because people possess free will and can thus choose to do good or evil and are held accountable for their decisions. At the same time, it is difficult to retain faith in the face of tragedy, poverty, or disaster. The Muslim belief in the omnipotence of God, his transcendence and simultaneous immanence, is meant to solace the believer.

The application of reason, in the form of Hellenic philosophical arguments to theology, philosophy, and the sciences, was prominent in the Golden Age of Islam. Reacting to the philosophers and those who used logical reasoning (*kalam*) were Traditionists, the scholars who focused on *hadith* to determine the *sunnah* and rejected the methodology of logical reasoning.

Multiple Sunni traditions, or schools of law and theology, arose over time. Not all survive today. These schools share the basic theology described above and assert the primacy of the Qur'anic revelation, but there are notable differences.

Sunni Islamic law is based on the Qur'an and the *sunnah*, as nuanced by the particular *hadith* collector and his interpretation. Different scholars using different assumptions, reasoning, hermeneutics (guiding interpretive principles), and source materials arrived at different applications of Islamic law, which were organized into schools known as *madhahib*. Muslims assert that Sharia never changes but that the understanding and application of it into jurisprudence (*fiqh*) does change, since jurisprudence is carried out by human beings. Muslims generally seek to avoid illict innovation (*bidah*), but many "innovations" have to be considered. Thus, the Qur'an predates the telegraph. Thus, the application of *fiqh* to adjudicate the use of the telegraph was a matter of interpretation. In addition to the usual sources of law, jurists took into account *maslaha*, public benefit or the common good, in considering new technology.

There are four surviving major schools of law in Sunni Islam. The various schools predominate in different regions. These dominant Sunni schools of law are Hanbali, Hanafi, Maliki, and Shafi, and all use the Qur'an as their primary source.

Hanbali law is the strictest tradition and was practiced by Muslims in Saudi Arabia, Qatar, Syria, Palestine, and elsewhere; with the growth of Salafism and neoSalafism, it has expanded. It was founded by Ahmad ibn Hanbal and is the dominant tradition on the Arabian Peninsula, although it has adherents in Iraq, Syria, Jerusalem, and Egypt as well.

The Hanafi *madhhab* may be the largest school. It was founded by Abu Hanifa and encompasses 30 percent of Sunnis. Its adherents are mainly in Turkey, Central Asia, the Balkans, Iraq, Afghanistan, Pakistan, India,

Bangladesh, lower Egypt, and in former states of the Soviet Union. Both the Mongol Empire and the Ottoman Empire promoted the Hanafi tradition. When the Ottoman sultan Selim the Grim (1512–1520) captured Palestine, he imposed Hanafi law on the region. The official judicial traditions and systems in contemporary Syria, Jordan, and Palestine are derived from the Hanafi tradition.

The Maliki school has approximately 15 percent of Sunnis as adherents. It was founded by Malik ibn Anas and has adherents in North Africa and West Africa, particularly upper Egypt, Algeria, Tunisia, Morocco, Mauritania, and Libya, as well as in the Sudan, Kuwait, Dubai, and Abu Dhabi. The Maliki school derives its *fiqh* through consensus more than do any of the other traditions. The Maliki system of lawmaking is built on the Qur'an and the *hadith*, supplemented by an interpretation of *ijma* (consensus), as being the consensus or agreed opinion of the People of Medina, and analogy (*qiyas*). In addition, Malik considered the statements of the Prophet's companions and referred to the public good (*maslahah*), customary law (*urf*), common practice (*adat*), and several other legal principles.

The Shafi school was founded by Muhammad ibn Idris al-Shafi and has adherents in the southern Arabian Peninsula, the Hijaz, Palestine, Indonesia, Malaysia, Thailand, Cambodia, parts of India, the Philippines, Sudan, Ethiopia, Somalia, North Yemen, Kurdistan, Sri Lanka, and lower Egypt. The Shafi school utilizes the *usul al-fiqh* (roots of lawmaking) in a way that places *ijma* ahead of analogy.

Historically, there were many Sunni schools and trends in theology. Among the important or well-known trends were the Mutazila, whose doctrine was abandoned, and the Ashariyyah, Maturidiyyah, and Salafism (which has at least two versions).

The Mutazila school was established in Iraq by Wasil bin Ata (699–749). Abbasid caliph al-Mamun (813–827) made Mutazila theology the state religion and persecuted all dissenters. At the time, Muslims had debated the uncreatedness versus the created (manmade) nature of the Qur'an and many other theological questions. Mutazilites rejected the doctrine of the uncreated Qur'an, but with their downfall Muslims accepted precisely that doctrine. The Mutazila's name came from their intermediate position on the question of sin: they asserted that Muslims who commit grave sins and die without repentance cannot be treated as nonbelievers, but judgment must be withheld until the resurrection. The Mutazilites rejected anthropomorphic interpretations of God. For instance, the phrase "hand of God" might refer symbolically to God's power to the Mutazila, whereas their opponents would insist it meant the actual hand of God.

The Ashariyyah school was founded by Abu al-Hasan al-Ashari (873–935) and became the dominant Sunni theology in that era. It emphasizes divine revelation and stresses the understanding of that revelation through the application of human reasoning.

The Maturidiyyah was founded by Abu Mansur al-Maturidi (d. 944). Maturidis believe that the existence of Allah as understood in Islam can be derived through reason alone and that such is true of major concepts of good and evil, legal and illegal.

Salafism, a reform movement in Islam, actually developed in two different contexts in 18th-century Arabia and in 19th-century Egypt and Ottoman Empire. The 19th-century to early 20th-century reformers Jamal al-Din al-Afghani, Muhammad

Abduh, Qasim Amin, and Rashid Rida initiated a discussion about the decline of the Muslim world and the reforms it should carry out to overcome the negative influence of Western colonialism and imperialism. While Afghani looked for an Islamic ruler who would stand up to the West and believed that Pan-Islam could solve the problem, Muhammad Abduh, an Egyptian jurist, recommended reform of Islamic education and the methodology of Islamic law in which blind imitation of the past would cease. He thought that Sunni Muslims should consider a return to *ijtihad* (a Shia methodology of lawmaking) to meet contemporary requirements, and he wanted Western sciences introduced into the educational curriculum. Qasim Amin argued for an end to enforced marriages, female seclusion, and lack of education for women, while Rashid Rida pursued a somewhat stricter and more Islamist approach to the proper way of life for Muslims.

Earlier, Muhammad abd al-Wahhab in Arabia promoted a strict monotheism, which he claimed would cleanse Islam of many syncretic traditions that constituted *shirk*, or polytheism. This tradition is referred to by his enemies as Wahhabism, which is the general term used today in the West. The *muwahiddun*, or Unitarians as they call themselves, or Wahhabists who fought as warriors for the Saud tribe, were known as the Ikhwan (brethren). In general, the muwahiddun are considered Salafis, because they wanted to cleanse Islamic practice and society of un-Islamic accretions and innovations (bida) that had arisen through cultural synthesis. However, this cleansing is a matter of gradation, so not all Wahhabis, as the West calls them, are either violent purists or ardent Salafists. The Wahhabis adhere to the Hanbali school of law, although some modern Salafis speak of rejecting all legal tradition and utilizing only the Qur'an and the sunnah. The Salafis were anti-Ottoman, anti-Shia, and anti-Sufi, and opposed such practices as Sufi ceremonies and visiting tombs, even at Mecca. These Salafis called for jihad in its active form with which they, in alliance with the Saud family, drove out first the Ottomans and then, in a later historical period, the Rashids and the Hashimites.

Terrorist and al-Qaeda leader Osama bin Laden is a neo-Salafi and a Wahhabi. He believes that the Saudi Arabian royal family does not strictly uphold Wahhabi or Salafi values and should be militantly opposed for its alliance with the West. Other Salafis have been part of the resistance to U.S. occupation and the new Iraqi government in post-2003 Iraq.

Some Salafis consider the Shia to be renegades (this refers to a specific denigrating legal epithet given them during the civil wars in Islamic history) or apostates, apostasy being a capital crime in Islam. The Shia had come to fear and hate the Wahhabis because of their raids on Shia areas historically, but this animosity is not true of all Sunnis and Shia who, in general, lived peacefully alongside each other in prewar Iraq. Some charge that the United States and Israel, as well as certain Arab countries, are heightening fears in the region of a Shia crescent of influence, running from Iran to the Shia of Iraq and the Gulf States, and then to the Shia of Lebanon. Such discourse could create more problems among Muslims in the region. Therefore, King Abdullah of Saudi Arabia has spoken out against sectarian discord. Elsewhere leaders such as at al-Azhar try to represent the Jafari *madhhab* as a legitimate legal school of Islam.

Richard M. Edwards and Sherifa Zuhur

See also: Jihad; Salafism; Sharia; Shia Islam

Further Reading

Ahmed, Akbar S. *Islam Today: A Short Introduction to the Muslim World*. Rev. ed. London: I. B. Tauris, 1999.

Armstrong, Karen. *Islam: A Short History*. New York: Modern Library, 2002.

Esposito, John L. *The Oxford History of Islam*. New York: Oxford University Press, 2000.

Esposito, John L. *What Everyone Needs to Know about Islam*. New York: Oxford University Press, 2002.

Fuller, Graham E., and Rend Rahim Francke. *The Arab Shi'a: The Forgotten Muslims*. Hampshire, UK: Palgrave Macmillan, 2001.

Gregorian, Vartan. *Islam: A Mosaic, Not a Monolith*. Baltimore: Brookings Institute Press, 2004.

Sachiko, Muratam, and William C. Chittick. *The Vision of Islam*. New York: Paragon House, 1994.

Salamah, Ahmad Abdullah. *Shia and Sunni Perspective on Islam: An Objective Comparison of the Shia and Sunni Doctrines Based on the Holy Quran and Hadith*. Jedda, Saudi Arabia: Abul-Qasim Publication House, 1991.

Sunni Triangle

Region of Iraq, populated largely by Sunni Muslims, which has been at the epicenter of the Iraqi insurgency during the Iraq War, which began in 2003. The Sunni Triangle begins near Baghdad then extends west to Ramadi and north to Tikrit. Each side of the triangle is roughly 125 miles long. This region, which lies generally northwest of the capital city of Baghdad, is densely populated. Tikrit, the birthplace of former Iraqi president Saddam Hussein, has been one of the epicenters of the insurgency since 2003. Also lying within the triangle are the cities of Mosul, Fallujah, Samarra, and Baqubah, all of which have been heavily involved in the insurgency. Hussein's strong tribal and familial connections to the area have traditionally made it the strongest base of support for his regime, and many of his advisers, confidantes, and military commanders hailed from the area.

The term "Sunni Triangle" did not enter the popular lexicon until 2003, after a *New York Times* story that ran on June 10 used it to describe the area in which the growing insurgency was based. The Sunni Triangle witnessed several major offensives conducted by coalition forces designed to flush out and neutralize Iraqi insurgents. The first was Operation RED DAWN, launched in December 2003. Its goal was the capture of the deposed President Hussein. On December 13, 2003, Hussein was found alive and captured in ad-Dawr, a small village not far from his hometown of Tikrit. Hussein's apprehension was a significant public relations and morale boost for coalition forces occupying Iraq.

On April 4, 2004, coalition forces implemented Operation VIGILANT RESOLVE, an attempt to capture control of Fallujah from insurgent forces. The operation precipitated the First Battle of Fallujah, which lasted until May 1, 2004. U.S. forces were unsuccessful in their endeavor, and they sustained 27 killed in the fighting. The prematurely terminated operation proved a public relations nightmare for the United States, as it drove home the notion that its forces were now waging a dangerous and increasingly ineffective counterinsurgency.

During the Second Battle of Fallujah (November 7–December 23, 2004), U.S. forces, working in concert with Iraqi forces, were successful in wresting control of the city from the insurgents. At the time, the

An Iraqi insurgent aims his rocket propelled grenade launcher at U.S. forces on March 26, 2004, during intensive fighting in the town of Fallujah in the so-called Sunni Triangle, where support for Saddam Hussein was strong and rebels often carried out attacks against American forces. Witnesses said heavy gunfire and explosions were heard when marines moved into the center of the city. (AP Photo)

Pentagon termed the vicious combat at Fallujah the worst urban fighting in which American forces had been involved since the January to March 1968 Battle of Hue, during the Tet Offensive of the Vietnam War. The victory in Fallujah was costly, however. U.S. forces suffered 95 killed; Iraqi forces reported 11 killed. At least 1,350 insurgents died in fighting, while another 1,500 were taken captive.

During November 8–16, 2004, American and allied Iraqi Security Forces fought Iraqi insurgents in the Battle of Mosul. It was designed to coincide with the Second Battle of Fallujah. U.S.-led forces were only partly successful in seizing control of Mosul, as a number of insurgents remained in the western third of the city, from which they engaged in hit-and-run tactics. Despite the capture of Fallujah and other counterinsurgency operations, the Sunni Triangle remained among the most dangerous regions of Iraq for U.S. and allied forces throughout the conflict.

Paul G. Pierpaoli Jr.

See also: Fallujah, First Battle of; Fallujah, Second Battle of

Further Reading

Buzzell, Colby. *My War: Killing Time in Iraq.* New York: Putnam, 2005.

Keegan, John. *The Iraq War: The Military Offensive, from Victory in 21 Days to the Insurgent Aftermath.* New York: Vintage, 2005.

Ricks, Thomas E. *Fiasco: The American Military Adventure in Iraq.* New York: Penguin, 2006.

Supreme Iraqi Islamic Council

Shia resistance group founded in 1982 and a powerful political party in post-2003 Iraq. The Supreme Iraqi Islamic Council (SIIC) was created and known for decades as the Supreme Council for the Islamic Revolution in Iraq (SCIRI). It is an Islamist-oriented organization whose goal has been the creation of an Islamic-based regime in Iraq. The group advocates a decentralized Iraqi government and the establishment of an autonomous zone reserved for Shiites in the south of Iraq. The party's name was changed in 2007 to remove the term "Islamic revolution" from the party's official title. This move also seemed to signal a concern on the part of the SIIC to eschew the advocacy of civil and sectarian violence in Iraq, and to draw more Iraqis into its ranks.

The SCIRI was formed in 1982, during the Iran-Iraq War (1980–1988). At that time the Islamic Dawa Party, Iraq's principal Islamist group, was severely repressed by the Saddam Hussein regime. The SCIRI was formed as a party in exile in Iran, with the backing of the Iranian regime, and contrasted with the Islamic Dawa Party, many of whose members left Iran because they did not wish to fight Iraqis in the Iran-Iraq War. Muhammad Baqir al-Hakim, a member of one of Iraq's most prominent Shia clerical families, came to lead the group. Upon the creation of the party, Hakim made it clear that the primary and immediate goal of the organization was to overthrow Hussein's Baathist regime and to establish an Islamic state in Iraq, along the lines of the regime in Iran. But the SCIRI also became an umbrella organization, allowing other Shia groups to ally with it.

The SCIRI espoused the belief that, ideally, an Islamist regime must be controlled by Islamic scholars (*ulema*), the system that is in operation in Iran. Other Shia Islamist groups, however, did not subscribe to that framework, believing instead that the government should be guided by the whole of the Muslim community (*ummah*). Until the fall of the Hussein regime in 2003, the SCIRI operated largely in exile and along the fringes of Iraqi politics.

That all changed after the Anglo-American–led invasion of Iraq in March 2003, which ousted Hussein from power. Working in tandem with other Shia groups, the SCIRI moved to solidify its base and influence in a nation that had been dominated for many years by the Sunnis. Taking its cues from Islamist organizations in other countries, especially the Muslim Brotherhood and Hamas, the SCIRI gained many adherents by providing humanitarian aid and basic services to displaced and poor Shia Iraqis. The United States became closer to SCIRI than to any of the other Shia parties, for despite its Islamism, the group was well organized, promised to control other Shia militias, and had English-speaking leaders, whom the Americans preferred to Ibrahim al-Jafari of the Islamic Dawa Party. However, other American and British officials have sometimes viewed the party with a weary eye, as the SIIC is likely receiving financial support and, allegedly, weapons from Iran. In an attempt to make itself more credible, the party has soft-pedaled its devotion to revolution and the imposition of an Islamic state in Iraq since the 2003 invasion. Instead, it has stated its commitment to democratic processes and has demonstrated a willingness to cooperate with rival political parties.

Not surprisingly, the SIIC's power base is located in the center and south of Iraq. It competes with other Shia parties, particularly Fadhila in the city of Basra, which has a heavily Shia population. The party maintains an armed militia, known as the Badr Brigades. It is believed that these forces contain from 5,000 to 10,000 well-armed men, the weapons of which have come largely from the Iranians. Badr's headquarters are located in Baghdad.

The party suffered a setback in August 2003 when its leader, Ayatollah Hakim, was killed in Najaf in a car bombing. It has been posited that al-Qaeda in Iraq was behind the murder. Hakim's brother, Abd al-Aziz al-Hakim, then took control of the organization. He died in a Tehran hospital in August 2009 of lung cancer and was succeeded by his son, Ammar al-Hakim.

Currently the SIIC retains the most seats of any Iraqi political group in the Council of Representatives. In January 2005 it joined forces with the United Iraqi Alliance and captured six of the eight Shia-majority governorates and garnered 40 percent of the votes in Baghdad. Numerous SIIC members have held both official and unofficial positions with the Iraqi government. Hakim was a member of the Iraqi Governing Council, created by the United States, and served as that body's president briefly in late 2003. Hakim has adeptly walked a political tightrope and managed to maintain relatively cordial relations with the United States. Indeed, he has met with numerous high-level U.S. officials, including Secretary of Defense Donald Rumsfeld, and had a one-on-one meeting with President George W. Bush at the White House in December 2006. Nevertheless, SIIC's control of the southern Iraqi governorates has come under fire for alleged corruption and the misdeeds of its Badr organization.

Paul G. Pierpaoli Jr.

See also: Badr Organization; Hakim, Abd al-Aziz al-; Mahdi Army; Sadr, Muqtada al-; Shia Islam

Further Reading

Nasr, Vali. *The Shia Revival: How Conflicts within Islam Will Shape the Future.* New York: Norton, 2006.

Packer, George. *The Assassins' Gate: America in Iraq.* New York: Farrar, Straus and Giroux, 2005.

Stansfield, Gareth. *Iraq: People, History, Politics.* Cambridge: Polity, 2007.

Surge, U.S. Troop Deployment, Iraq War

The term "troop surge" refers to the early January 2007 decision by the George W. Bush administration to deploy approximately 20,000–30,000 additional American troops to Iraq to arrest insurgent-inspired violence. Those insurgents included both al-Qaeda terrorists and rival Sunni and Shiite sectarian militias. U.S. Army general David Petraeus, commander of U.S. forces in Iraq, is credited with the surge strategy. The impetus for the troop surge was the November 2006 U.S. midterm election, in which the Republican Party lost control of both houses of Congress, largely because of growing public opposition to the Iraq War and dismay with the level of casualties among U.S. soldiers.

With the Democrats having made opposition to the Iraq War the central issue of the 2006 election and calling for a withdrawal of U.S. troops from Iraq, Bush announced a change in strategy to reduce violence and improve security in Iraq. This followed the resignation of Secretary of Defense Donald Rumsfeld, a key architect of the Iraq War, in December 2006. Referring to a "new way forward" in a televised national speech on January 10, 2007, the president announced a plan to secure the capital city, Baghdad, from both al-Qaeda and sectarian militias, and rid Anbar Province (stretching west from Baghdad to the Syrian and Jordanian borders) of al-Qaeda fighters. Approximately 16,000 additional U.S. troops were deployed to secure Baghdad, and another 4,000 troops were sent to Anbar Province.

By June 15, 2007, with these additional troops in place, the surge began in earnest. Instead of simply launching raids against al-Qaeda and sectarian militias, U.S. and Iraqi forces in Baghdad established posts within neighborhoods controlled by these groups. In Anbar Province, because of public outrage sparked by al-Qaeda's murdering of hundreds of Iraqi Muslims, Sunni tribes severed their ties with al-Qaeda and aligned themselves with the Iraqi government and the U.S. military. In so doing, these tribes formed militias ("Sons of Iraq"), comprising some 103,000 men, many of them former insurgents and terrorists, armed and paid by the United States to defend their communities against al-Qaeda. Although this proved effective in rooting out al-Qaeda insurgents in the short term, in the long run these militias will have to be reintegrated into either the Iraqi military or police forces, or find gainful employment elsewhere, in order for them to remain loyal to the Iraqi government.

The surge strategy emerged from the belated recognition that Iraqi security forces were as yet unable to provide security without significant American assistance and support, and that the number of U.S. troops had to be increased to effectively stamp out the insurgency. It was also recognized that to defeat an insurgency, military forces must take up residence and maintain a physical presence within the areas infested by insurgents because, in the words of General Petraeus, "you can't commute to this fight; you must

live among the people." Accordingly, the surge increased U.S. troop strength in Baghdad and Anbar Province, the two most violent regions of Iraq, not only to clear but also to hold territory, thus reinforcing Iraqi military and police presence. U.S. troops were also to assist Iraqi forces as they established security. The downside of this strategy was that it prolonged the foreign military presence in the country, which is what had provoked the insurgents and thus gave them cause to continue resistance.

Since early 2007, with continued American military assistance, particularly in the form of logistics and air support, Iraqi forces have demonstrated increasing competence and skill in battling insurgents and providing security. In addition, Iraqi prime minister Nuri al-Maliki, a leader of the Islamic Dawa Party, showed a willingness to confront militias, including Shia militias, as evinced by Iraqi military operations in the cities of Basra, Baghdad, and Ninawa. Also, Muqtada al-Sadr, the leader of the powerful Shiite Mahdi Army, agreed not to confront the Iraqi government and U.S. military, and has maintained that promise since mid-June 2007. In both Baghdad and Anbar Province, al-Qaeda was seriously weakened, but unfortunately its signature tactic of inflicting mass casualties through car bombs targeting Shiites, including Shiite mosques, had resumed again in 2009. Coalition efforts in these two areas forced the group to flee to the northern city of Mosul and the surrounding province of Nineveh, as well as to the religiously mixed province of Diyala. Iraqi and U.S. forces then battled al-Qaeda in these new areas. Nonetheless, the situation remained volatile, with al-Qaeda still a dangerous threat and the possibility that any one of the factors that had contributed to the military gains under the surge could be reversed and produce an increase in violence.

The results of the troop surge could be seen in the statistical decline in both Iraqi and U.S. casualties. According to a June 2008 Pentagon report, violence in Iraq dropped between 40 and 80 percent from presurge levels, while the number of violent incidents fell to their lowest point in more than four years. In addition, fewer U.S. troops were killed in May 2008, when 19 died (compared to 126 in May 2007), than in any other month since the invasion of Iraq in March 2003; 29 U.S. troops were killed in June 2008 compared to 101 in June 2007. The Iraqi Body Count, a group that keeps a tally of Iraqi casualties from media reports, noted that 712 Iraqi civilian deaths occurred in June 2008, less than a third of the average during the summer of 2007.

Expanding revenues from the export of Iraqi oil and continued growth in the Iraqi economy (4 percent in 2007) also contributed to a decline in violence in the country, as unemployment dropped. The June 2008 Pentagon report, however, warned that security gains could not be preserved without continued progress in economic development and reconstruction; increasing government services, such as electricity (currently available for a national daily average of only 14.9 hours, including just 13 hours in Baghdad); health care, water, and sewage treatment; and national political reconciliation among Iraq's rival religious and political groups. An important step in political reconciliation was taken with the passage of a long-awaited and needed Amnesty Law on February 26, 2008, for Iraqis accused or convicted of crimes of terrorism. In addition, Iraq's largest Sunni Arab bloc, the Iraqi Accord Front, prepared to rejoin Prime Minister Maliki's cabinet after a yearlong boycott protesting the government's alleged policies of excluding and marginalizing Sunnis. The inclusion of Sunnis into Iraq's government was cited by both the United States and Iraq as a major factor in bringing about national unity. Sunni Arabs had a great deal of power during Saddam Hussein's regime, but became marginalized after he was toppled in 2003. Since then, the Iraqi government has been dominated by Shiites and Kurds.

Despite these developments, however, it was acknowledged that the Iraqi government remained corrupt and inefficient, and that it lacked sufficiently qualified personnel to effectively govern and execute policy and programs.

The surge also entered presidential politics in the United States. In the summer of 2008, Republican candidate John McCain made much of his advocacy of, and support for, the surge. He sought to make the troop surge a major issue in the campaign, attacking his Democratic opponent Barack Obama for his opposition to it. Obama pointed out that it was not just the increase in troop strength but also the reconciliation of the Sunni tribes that had contributed to the decrease in violence. He also noted that McCain had supported the earlier Bush policies that had not worked, whereas he (Obama) had opposed the war from the beginning.

In sum, the surge proved to be successful, but as Petraeus remarked, "we can't kill ourselves out of this endeavor." Ultimately, it is only the Iraqi government that can build a stable, secure, prosperous, and united nation.

Stefan Brooks

See also: al-Qaeda in Iraq; Anbar Awakening; Iraqi Insurgency; Iraq Study Group; Petraeus, David Howell

Further Reading

Engel, Richard. *War Journal: My Five Years in Iraq*. New York: Simon and Schuster, 2008.

Galbraith, Peter. *The End of Iraq: How American Incompetence Created a War without End*. New York: Simon and Schuster, 2007.

Isikoff, Michael, and David Corn. *Hubris: The Inside Story of Spin, Scandal, and the Selling of the Iraq War*. New York: Three Rivers/Random House, 2007.

T

T-62 Main Battle Tank

Soviet-designed main battle tank (MBT). The weaknesses of previous Soviet tank designs indicated that a newer vehicle with better armor and firepower was needed to defeat the latest tanks being developed in the West. Thus the T-62 was fielded in 1961 as the replacement for the T-54/55 series tanks. In essence, it was little more than a marginal upgrade and in a number of ways was not much of an improvement over its predecessor. The primary innovation in the T-62 was in its main gun, being a smoothbore 115-millimeter (mm) capable of firing fin-stabilized sabot armor defeating and high-explosive antitank (HEAT) ammunition.

Because of the inclusion of the 115-mm gun, the ammunition became extremely bulky and difficult to handle. This caused Soviet engineers to develop a unique gunnery system for the tank. When the main gun was fired, the shell casing, instead of clattering to the floor as in most tanks of that time and thus becoming a hazard to the loader, would slide from the breech into a cradle. The gun would elevate automatically while the cradle would rock back to mechanically eject the casing through a small port in the top rear of the turret. This created a few interesting problems. The elevating of the gun took the gunner off of his target, forcing the commander to maintain acquisition instead of searching for other targets. When the casing was ejected, the commander pressed a detent on his controls, and the gun would realign back to the original target location. Of course, this assumed that neither the T-62 nor the enemy tank had since moved. This could cause serious problems in any tank-on-tank engagement.

The T-62's most vexing problems were automotive, and these would become almost legendary. Many Middle Eastern countries were not pleased with the T-62's performance and thus continued to use the older T-55 as their MBT until a better MBT was available. The T-62's engine tended to overheat in hot climates, and in desert operations this was a serious problem. It was not uncommon to see T-62 crews operating in combat with the rear deck doors open to allow better cooling of the power plant, which of course made the engine vulnerable to small-arms fire. Moreover, when the tank was turned violently, especially in loose sand, the sprockets tended to throw the track on the inside of the turn. This was a major problem, as violent turns to disrupt the aim of enemy gunners are one means of protection during combat.

Despite its problems, the T-62 was exported to nations including Egypt, Syria, and Iraq. The T-62 saw its most extensive combat service in the October 1973 Yom Kippur (Ramadan) War, in which 300 T-62s spearheaded Syria's attempts to exploit its early success in the Golan Heights. However, the problems of the T-62, noticeable in training, became even more acute in combat service, and thus it has never lived up to its advertised potential. When the 1991 Persian Gulf War began,

U.S. soldiers inspect an Iraqi T-62 main battle tank destroyed near Ali al-Salem Air Base during Operation DESERT STORM. (Defense Visual Information Center)

Iraq still possessed 1,000 T-62s in its inventory, with most of them deployed in the Republican Guard divisions. As most of those units avoided combat, the T-62 saw little action.

However, some did see action, for one regular Iraqi Army division, the 10th Armored, had some T-62s assigned to its 17th Armored Brigade. While this brigade saw limited action, a few Iraqi battalions with T-62s saw more extensive action, such as the battalion defending at Objective Minden, a bit of lonely desert just west of the Iraqi-Kuwaiti border. These tanks, along with a host of other armored vehicles, were attacked by American AH-64 Apache helicopters from the 4th Battalion, 229th Aviation Regiment, during the night of February 26, 1991, causing many of the crews to simply abandon their undamaged vehicles, which were later captured intact by coalition forces. Another T-62 battalion was probably

attached to the Tawakalna Division when it was deployed to delay the coalition advance through the desert late on February 26. This force initially delayed the advance of elements of the U.S. VII Corps but was eventually overrun. The actual number of T-62s lost was probably only around 250, but precise numbers are unknown.

The next time the T-62 saw combat action was during the U.S.-led invasion of Iraq War (2003–) in 2003. Unlike in the Persian Gulf War, many actions in the Iraq War have been small unit-level affairs, with Iraqi commanders displaying significant difficulty in massing their forces for offensive action. Early in the campaign, a platoon of American M1-A1 Abrams tanks from B Company, 1–64 Armor, probing in the darkness toward Objective Liberty southwest of Nasiriyah encountered dug-in T-62s that lit up their thermal imagine sights. In a matter of two minutes the Abrams tanks had destroyed four T-62s and several other armored vehicles.

However, few T-62s were actually encountered, as American combat reports attest. For example, on April 3, 2003, the 2nd Brigade Combat Team, 3rd Infantry Division, reported destroying 33 T-72 and 19 T-55s but only 2 T-62s. Another element of the division, this time Task Force 2–69 Armor, engaged and destroyed several T-62s at Objective Custer, located at the northwest corner of Baghdad. Otherwise, few if any other T-62s were engaged or knocked out during the 40-plus days of heavy combat in Iraq. The dearth of combat service for the T-62 is indicative of the problems encountered when using this MBT. And while some Middle Eastern nations continue to deploy upgraded T-62s, their numbers are dwindling as they are being steadily replaced by the more effective T-72 or even by the older but more reliable and now upgraded T-55s. At one point in time the T-62 had a brief opportunity for enduring glory, that being during the Syrian drive into the Golan Heights in 1973. However, since then the tank has woefully underperformed.

The specification for the T-62A are: Armament: one 115-mm U5-TS smoothbore main gun with rate of fire of three to five rounds per minute, one 12.7-mm machine gun, one coaxial 7.62-mm machine gun Ammunition main gun: 40 rounds Armor: Turret front, 242-mm at 0 degrees; hull front, upper, 102-mm at 60 degrees.

Crew: 4; Weight: 39.37 tons; Length: 21 feet 9 inches; Width: 10 feet 10 inches; Height: 7 feet 10 inches; Engine: V-12 diesel, 580 horsepower; Speed: Road, 31 mph Range: 280 miles.

Russell G. Rodgers

See also: Iraq, Army; Iraqi Freedom, Operation

Further Reading

Bourque, Stephen A. *Jayhawk! The VII Corps in the Persian Gulf War.* Washington, DC: Department of the Army, 2002.

Fontenot, Gregory et al. *On Point: The United States Army in Iraqi Freedom.* Annapolis, MD: Naval Institute Press, 2005.

Foss, Christopher, ed. *Jane's Armour and Artillery, 2007–2008.* Coulsdon Surrey, UK: Jane's Information Group, 2007.

Gordon, Michael R., and General Bernard E. Trainor. *The Generals' War: The Inside Story of the Conflict in the Gulf.* New York: Little, Brown, 1995.

Hull, Andrew W., David R. Markov, and Steven J. Zaloga. *Soviet/Russian Armor and Artillery Design Practices, 1945 to Present.* Darlington, MD: Darlington Publications, 1999.

Milsom, John. *Russian Tanks, 1900–1970.* New York: Galahad Books, 1970.

Scales, Robert H. *Certain Victory: The U.S. Army in the Gulf War.* Washington, DC: Brassey's, 1994.

T-72 Main Battle Tank

Soviet-designed main battle tank (MBT). Competitive designs to replace the T-55 and T-62 resulted in the development of two new tank designs by the mid-1960s. These tanks, the T-64 and T-72, caused a considerable stir in Western defense establishments. The simpler and less expensive design of the two, the T-72, became the Soviets' export tank of choice.

The T-72 took some radical departures from previous Soviet tank designs. The crew was reduced to three, with the loader being replaced with a mechanical system. This autoloader caused considerable problems during initial testing, but those issues were soon resolved. Once developed, the autoloader delivered a rate of fire of up to 10 rounds per minute for the new 125-millimeter (mm) smoothbore main gun. Ammunition for the main gun was stowed in a revolving basket on the turret floor and included fin-stabilized sabot, high-explosive antitank (HEAT), and standard high-explosive rounds.

The T-72 was also an automotive improvement over previous Soviet tanks. And while armor protection was still somewhat conventional, the improved power plant allowed more armor to be used, with up 600-mm of armor for the hull front. The T-72 saw its combat debut in Southern Lebanon during the Israeli offensive known as Operation Peace For Galilee, launched in June 1982. Iraq also used the T-72 to good effect during the Iran-Iraq War (1980–1988). However, it was during the 1991 Persian Gulf War and the U.S.-led invasion of Iraq (2003) that the T-72 saw some of its most extensive tank-on-tank action.

During the Persian Gulf War, Iraq had approximately 1,000 T-72s, of which about 300 were the newer T-72M with thicker armor. These were mostly grouped in the Republican Guard divisions that were placed in operational reserve in northern Kuwait. As coalition forces plunged through the Iraqi defenses, the Iraqi Army began to pull out of Kuwait, and several Republican Guard divisions were detailed to provide a screen to the west of Kuwait to delay the advancing U.S. VII Corps. The Tawakalna Mechanized Division, supplied with 280 T-72s, occupied a poorly prepared screen over a 30-mile area when it was probed by American forces on February 29, 1991.

In several successive battles, including the now-famous one at 73 Easting on February 26, most of the Tawakalna Division's T-72s were destroyed. In one particular engagement, the 1st Armored Division's 1st Battalion, 37th Armor, shot up 24 T-72s with a loss of only 4 M1-A1 tanks, damaged by friendly fire. The Tawakalna's tankers did show some ability and courage in the fight, such as keeping their engines off to reduce thermal signatures and waiting for the American tanks to move through their positions to engage them in the flank. In one instance, a T-72 was able to knock out an M1-A1 and injure two of its crew at a range of 1,000 yards with a well-placed flank shot in the turret ring. However, better training and communications, not to mention numbers (the Tawakalna was outnumbered four to one), were clearly on the side of the American forces, allowing them to better coordinate their assets in a combined-arms fight.

The second major engagement involved T-72s of the Iraqi Medina Armored Division at a place later dubbed Medina Ridge on February 27. This Iraqi division had moved into hastily prepared positions just west of the Rumaila oil fields to protect a large Iraqi logistics center there. Elements of their 2nd Brigade were preparing lunch when they were surprised by the 2nd Brigade of the U.S. 1st Armored Division. Visibility was limited to 1,500 yards, but the M1-A1s' thermal sights allowed the Americans to spot the surprised Iraqis beyond this range. Crews from Lieutenant Colonel Steve Whitcomb's 2nd Battalion, 70th Armor, and Lieutenant Colonel William Feyk's 4th Battalion, 70th Armor, began to shoot up T-72s as if they were on a gunnery range, even as the Iraqis attempted to return fire by shooting at the M1-A1s' muzzle blasts. Some T-72s were destroyed as far off as 4,200 yards. In just over one hour, the Iraqi armored brigade had been destroyed, with more than 50 hulks of burning T-72s littering the desert. In many instances, the turrets had been blown off by the detonation of the ammunition on the turret floor caused by the incendiary splash of the American depleted uranium sabot rounds, dubbed "silver bullets" by the tankers. The total number of T-72s lost during Operation DESERT STORM was probably no more than 150, but the exact number is unknown.

The next serious engagement for the T-72 occurred in the Iraq War, but this time most were used in small groups rather than in larger formations, as in the Persian Gulf War. One tank-on-tank action occurred on April 3–4, 2003, when elements of the 3rd Infantry Division's 2nd Brigade Combat Team (BCT) were hit by a counterattack of the Medina Armored Division's 10th Armored Brigade just south of Baghdad at what Americans called Objective Saints. The Iraqis led with a company of T-72s, followed by mounted infantry. When three of the tanks were destroyed, killing the Iraqi brigade commander, the remainder of the brigade withdrew only to attempt a flanking maneuver, whereby American Abrams and Bradleys bagged another 15 T-72s and a number of infantry carriers. The next day the 2nd BCT destroyed an additional 17 T-72s.

On April 3, 2003, troopers of the 3rd Squadron, 7th Cavalry, prepared to cover the flank of the 1st BCT near Objective Montgomery. What occurred later that day was probably the only large-scale T-72 counterattack mounted by the Iraqis during the war. A battalion-sized element from the Hammurabi Division was spotted by aerial reconnaissance, and the troopers moved out with their tanks to engage them. The Iraqi tankers had positioned themselves behind a berm to spring an ambush but were spotted there and were quickly engaged. In rapid succession the American tankers shot up the Iraqi T-72s, and in 15 minutes 20 hulks were burning at the top of the berm. No precise number of T-72s lost has been released,

but the number destroyed during the drive to Baghdad was probably about 200.

Despite its performance in the Persian Gulf War and the Iraq War, the T-72 is overall a very good tank, but it has faired poorly when matched against combat forces with better-trained crews, more sophisticated communications, and massive logistical support.

Specifications of the T-72 M/S Shilden Export are:

Armament: one 125-mm 2A46 main gun with automatic loader, rate of fire of eight rounds per minute; one 12.7-mm NSVT machine gun; one 7.62-mm coaxial machine gun Ammunition main gun: 45 rounds Armor: Turret Front, 280-mm at 0 degrees; hull front, upper, 600-mm equivalent.

Crew: 3; weight: 43.8 tons; length: 22 feet 10 inches; width: 11 feet 9 inches with skirts; height: 7 feet 2 inches; engine: V-12 multifuel, 840 horsepower at 2,000 rounds per minute; road speed, 37 mph; range: 285 miles and 342 miles with long-range fuel tanks.

Russell G. Rodgers

See also: Iraqi, Army; IRAQI FREEDOM, Operation

Further Reading

Bourque, Stephen A. *Jayhawk! The VII Corps in the Persian Gulf War.* Washington, DC: Department of the Army, 2002.

Fontenot, Gregory et al. *On Point: The United States Army in Iraqi Freedom.* Annapolis, MD: Naval Institute Press, 2005.

Foss, Christopher, ed. *Jane's Armour and Artillery, 2007–2008.* Coulsdon Surrey, UK: Jane's Information Group, 2007.

Gordon, Michael R., and General Bernard E. Trainor. *The Generals' War: The Inside Story of the Conflict in the Gulf.* New York: Little, Brown, 1995.

Hull, Andrew W., David R. Markov, and Steven J. Zaloga. *Soviet/Russian Armor and Artillery Design Practices, 1945 to*

Present. Darlington, MD: Darlington Publications, 1999.

Scales, Robert H. *Certain Victory: The U.S. Army in the Gulf War*. Washington, DC: Brassey's, 1994.

Zaloga, Steven. *T-72: Soviet Main Battle Tank*. Hong Kong: Concord Publications, 1989.

Terrorism

There is no settled definition of the word "terrorism." Most scholars and defense analysts believe that terrorism is a tactic, rather than a philosophy or set ideology. History has shown that groups may employ terrorism at some times and not at others. There is an active debate about whether "terrorism" is the appropriate term solely for violence by nonstate entities, or whether state terrorism must also be included. Some consider terrorism to be acts or threats of violence, directed against noncombatants, to shock or achieve a change in a political status quo by indirect means. However, others label some actions against military or governmental personnel to be terrorist in nature when they do not comply with international law. Still others write about terrorism as a pathology wherein violence is the motivating force and not merely a means to an end. This approach is problematic as it could apply to individual pathological acts of violence as in recent cases of school shootings in Western countries. Terrorism may be employed for a wide variety of ideological, religious, or economic reasons.

Terrorism is also a tool in asymmetric conflict and a force magnifier. The impact of a small number of individuals committing terrorist actions can be huge, and even a large paramilitary or military force may seem ineffective in combating it, particularly if success is measured by the complete eradication of such incidents.

Numerous academic and governmental experts recognize the arguments over what constitutes terrorism and thus do not employ the term. Certainly there has been reaction to the U.S. government's application of the term in the Global War on Terror. "Violent extremism" has been used for many years in place of "Islamic terrorism" in the Muslim world and has begun to be used in the West in the last few years. Here, the focus is on the use, or relinquishment, of violence, rather than the movement employing it.

Some analysts date modern terrorism to the Russian anarchist organization Narodnaya Volya (People's Will) of the 19th century, which attempted, through assassinations, to overthrow the czarist regime. Their methods were adopted by anarchists throughout the world, and the decades leading up to World War I were marked by frequent assassinations, including that of U.S. president William McKinley in 1901. The assassinations of the Austrian archduke Franz Ferdinand and his wife, Sophie, in Sarajevo in June 1914 sparked the outbreak of World War I.

Terrorist activities occurred in the Middle East prior to World War I, but in most cases the group responsible for terrorist activities was either a state-controlled force that claimed to be acting in the interests of state security or engaged in war, or a militia or force fighting against the state or another organization. Examples include the genocide perpetrated by Turkish authorities against the Armenians and subsequent actions in recent years by Kurds against Turks in Turkey. Yet atrocities committed by Israeli forces in 1948 against Palestinians have often been excused as legitimate acts of war.

In numerous instances colonial powers have been confronted by indigenous peoples employing asymmetric warfare tactics, and both have resorted to terrorism. For instance, in the conflict between Algerian nationalist groups and the French government and military, both sides engaged in acts of terrorism. The nationalist Front de Liberation Nationale (National Liberation Front, FLN) bombed crowded civilian locations frequented by Westerners as well as Algerians, and the French bombed residences in the Arab-inhabited *casbah* of Algiers and resorted to the torture of suspects in retaliation.

Terrorism by both Arabs and Jews against each other and by Jewish forces against the British mandate power occurred in Palestine in the 1930s. Following Israel's creation in 1948, Palestinian groups, some supported by neighboring Arab governments, began to launch military attacks against Israel. After Israel's victory in the 1967 Six-Day War and the rise of the popular movement in the refugee camps, Palestinian groups organized a wave of terrorist activities from 1969 to 1973. The political leadership of the movement then determined that these tactics brought too heavy an Israeli response and were detrimental to their cause, although they had served a purpose in focusing world attention on the plight of the Palestinians. In these same years, radical left-wing organizations in the United States such as the Weatherman and the Red Army in Europe and beyond (Japan) also engaged in acts of terrorism. Terrorism continued to be a major aspect of the Israeli-Palestinian confrontation and the inability to conclude an Arab-Israeli peace treaty but also as a response to Israeli military actions employing collective punishment against Palestinians or Palestinian communities.

Terrorist actions also appeared in Saudi Arabia. After the 1991 Persian Gulf War extremists began preaching against U.S. military forces in Saudi Arabia, claiming that it was unconscionable for the Saudi government to allow Christian forces to determine the political responses of the Saudi government toward other Muslim governments and to operate from the peninsula where the holy cities of Mecca and Medina are located. Their objection was chiefly regarding the presence of Western military forces; however, Saudi Arabia has long been home to a large expatriate community in its oil industry, and some extremists objected to their presence on Saudi soil as well.

On November 13, 1993, the Office of the Program Manager/Saudi Arabian National Guard (OPM/SANG) was badly damaged by a car bomb. Four Saudi nationals confessed and were executed on May 31, 1996. According to their confessions, they were veterans of jihads in Afghanistan, Bosnia, and Chechnya; they claimed that the Saudi rulers were apostates; and they were inspired by Islamic law to commit the attacks.

One month later the Khobar Towers in Dhahran, Saudi Arabia, were destroyed by a truck bomb, killing 19 U.S. servicemen in a plot carried out by Saudi Hezbollah. In 1996 and again in 1998, al-Qaeda leader Osama bin Laden announced a fatwa declaring that Muslims should attack U.S. personnel and interests around the world, drive U.S. forces from Saudi Arabia, remove the Saudi royal family and other apostate Arab regimes from power, and liberate Palestine. Of these goals, the most vital, and yet most unattainable, for bin Ladin was the removal of the Saudi royal family, and in fact his campaign against the United States is based on his analysis of U.S. government support for the Saudi royal family's hold on power. Bin Laden moved to various locations—Pakistan, Afghanistan, the Sudan, and then back again to Afghanistan—to plan his campaign.

The current War on Terror began with Operation ENDURING FREEDOM in Afghanistan, a month after the devastating September 11 attacks on the United States carried out by al-Qaeda. Objectives of the operation included removing the Taliban from power, destroying al-Qaeda's training camps, and killing or capturing its operatives. In 2002, the Taliban was partially defeated, but many al-Qaeda and Taliban members escaped and new recruits soon appeared, drawn from Afghanistan and the religiously conservative northwest region of Pakistan. These groups continue to attack North Atlantic Treaty Organization (NATO) troops, Afghan government officials, and civilians. Suicide bombings, never before utilized in Afghanistan, became a regular occurrence. Taliban and al-Qaeda operatives (including bin Laden) operated with relative freedom in the northwest reaches of Pakistan and could easily slip back across the border into Afghanistan.

In 2003, Operation Iraqi Freedom spearheaded by the United States removed Saddam Hussein and his regime from power and liberated Iraq. However, more than 40 different groups of Sunni Muslims as well some Shiite militias opposed and began to fight the coalition forces. These included such groups as al-Qaeda in Mesopotamia, Ansar al-Islam, and others. They engaged in regular fighting but also used terrorist attacks, mainly suicide bombings, against U.S., coalition, and Iraqi forces and civilians in attempts to destabilize the country so that they might drive the United States and its allies from Iraq and take power.

Between 2003 and 2005 more than 500 suicide car bombings and vest attacks occurred. Targets included refineries, electrical stations, police stations, open-air markets, and even mosques. The insurgents' intent was to undermine the public's confidence that the government would ever be able to provide essential services and security. However, in 2006, Sunni sheikhs, with strong financial incentives from both Saudi Arabia and the coalition, formed alliances to fight against al-Qaeda in Mesopotamia and other violent Islamist groups. This strategy accompanied the Western insistence on a coalition troop surge that began in early 2007. Yet acts of terrorism increased in the spring of 2009 and targeted the sheikhs who had cooperated with the coalition forces. Other acts of terrorism with suicide and truck bombings continue to plague Afghanistan and now, increasingly, Pakistan as well.

Donald Redmond Dunne and
Elliot Paul Chodoff

See also: al-Qaeda in Iraq; Iraqi Insurgency; Mahdi Army

Further Reading

Crenshaw, Martha, ed. *Terrorism in Context.* University Park: Pennsylvania State University Press, 1995.

Dershowitz, Alan. *The Case for Israel.* New York: Wiley, 2003.

Gettleman, Marvin, and Stuart Schaar, eds. *The Middle East and Islamic World Reader.* New York: Grove, 2003.

Gunaratna, Rohan. *Inside Al Qaeda: Global Network of Terror.* New York: Berkley Publishing Group, 2003.

Harel, Amos, and Avi Issacharoff. *34 Days: Israel, Hezbollah and the War in Lebanon.* New York: Palgrave Macmillan, 2008.

Hoffman, Bruce. *Inside Terrorism.* New York: Columbia University Press, 2006.

Mockaitis, Thomas R. *The "New" Terrorism: Myths and Reality.* Westport, CT: Praeger 2007.

Tigris and Euphrates Valley

An area of the Fertile Crescent largely occupied by present-day Iraq and referred to, in English, as the "cradle of civilization" because it was the birthplace of the world's earliest cultures. It is known in Arabic as *al-bilad al-rafhidhayn* ("land of the two rivers"; i.e., Mesopotamia). From the times of the Sumerians and Babylonians to the present, both the Tigris and the Euphrates Rivers have been dammed to control flooding and harnessed for irrigation and hydro-electric power. For more than six millennia, they have been essential to the environmental, economic, and political makeup of the Persian Gulf region.

The Tigris River (Nahr al-Dijlah), the second largest river in Southwestern Asia, is 1,180 miles long; it arises in the Taurus Mountains of eastern Turkey, flows through Turkey and Syria, and joins the Euphrates River in southern Iraq at Qurna. The two rivers then form the Shatt al-Arab waterway, which empties into the Persian Gulf. By the time it reaches the Shatt al-Arab, 70–80 percent of the flow of the Tigris River has been diverted. Because the Tigris has been prone to flooding, which inundates large areas and collapses levees, both the Turkish and Iraqi governments have built dams and a diversion channel to control the problem.

The Euphrates (Nahr al-Furat), the longest river in Southwestern Asia at 1,730 miles, also has its origins in the highland regions of eastern Turkey, where its two major tributaries, the Murat and the Kara Su rivers, join. It flows through deep canyons and narrow gorges to Syria and, after joining with two more tributaries, it enters Iraq, where it joins with the Tigris. The river annually floods, caused by snow melting in the mountains of northeastern Turkey. The Euphrates, Greek for "fertilizing" or "fruitful," is one of the four rivers that Westerners believe flowed from the Garden of Eden, as detailed in the biblical book Genesis. It provided the water that led to the flowering of the Sumerian civilization

in the fourth millennium BCE, and its river valley formed the heartland for the later empires of Babylonia and Assyria. For centuries the river separated the Roman and Persian Empires. As the crossroads for trade between Egypt, India, and China, the Tigris-Euphrates River Valley has distinct geographical and political implications. The region has been subject to numerous invasions and controversies over the use of its waterways.

The valley's ecosystem of marshlands formed over thousands of years, but after Iraqi dictator Saddam Hussein's rise to power in the late 1970s, the ecology of the Tigris-Euphrates river system and salt marshes suffered greatly. It is estimated that up to 90 percent of the marshes and 60 percent of the wetlands were destroyed by Iraqi government policies. In the 1990s, Hussein's government water-control projects drained the marsh areas to gain military access to the region and to drive out the rebellious native Marsh Arabs, leaving only about 10,000 people. Dykes and dams were built that diverted the waters of the Tigris and Euphrates around the marshes, causing the vegetation and water that fed the surrounding soil and many of the native wildlife and their habitats to disappear. The drainage policy was reversed by the new Iraqi government following the 2003 Anglo-American–led invasion of Iraq, and roughly half of the marshes have now been restored, but whether they will fully recover is uncertain.

Controversy over water rights and use of the rivers remains. Since 1990, Turkey's Southeastern Anatolia Development Project has built 22 dams and 19 power plants. The Turkish government hopes that by the end of its development on the two rivers nearly 2 million hectares of land will be irrigated. Syria in 1993 completed the Tabaqah

(Euphrates) Dam, to form a reservoir for irrigating cotton, but it and other dams have diverted much-needed water to Iraq. Building dams was not a priority during Hussein's regime, but Iraq now has seven dams in operation. Iraq is now concerned that construction of huge hydroelectric plants and dams along the two rivers by both Turkey and Syria will affect the social and economic stability of the region.

Gary Lee Kerley

See also: IRAQI FREEDOM, Operation

Further Reading

Maxwell, Gavin. *People of the Reeds*. New York: Harper, 1957.

Metz, Helen Chapin, ed. *Iraq: A Country Study*. Washington, DC: Headquarters, Department of the Army, 1990.

Nicholson, Emma, and Peter Clark. *The Iraqi Marshlands: A Human and Environmental Study*. London: Politico's Publishing, 2002.

Thesiger, Wilfred. *The Marsh Arabs*. 2nd rev. ed. London: HarperCollins, 1985.

Tikrit

City in north-central Iraq, known primarily as the birthplace of Iraqi dictator Saddam Hussein and also as a center of the Iraqi resistance that began after the Anglo-American–led invasion of Iraq in 2003. The city is also the home of one of Hussein's many elaborate presidential palaces, known popularly by Iraqis as the Birthday Palace. Tikrit is located approximately 90 miles north-northwest of Baghdad along the Tigris River. It serves as the administrative seat of Salahuddin Province. In 2002, prior to the Iraq War, it had a population of 550,000 people. Because of the war and the prolonged insurgency that has been centered in and around Tikrit, the city has lost a significant amount of its population, but the actual size of the exodus is not now known.

Tikrit is an old city; the first written references to it occurred in the early seventh century CE. In its earliest known history, it was known as Tagrit. The great 12th-century Muslim military leader Saladin (Salah-al din Yusuf ibn Ayyâb) was born in Tikrit. He fought Crusader forces under King Richard I of England to a standstill and captured Jerusalem in 1187. In September 1917, during World War I, Tikrit was overrun by British forces in the course of an offensive against the forces of the Ottoman Empire. A somewhat nondescript city, Tikrit gained great importance after Saddam Hussein's rise to power in the late 1970s, as he was born there on April 28, 1937. Hussein remained fiercely loyal to his Tikriti tribe (Al bu Nasir), centered in and around Tikrit, and many of his top advisers and government administrators came from that city. Hussein believed that he could trust only those from his own family or tribe. For the same reason, many of the commanders in Hussein's vaunted Iraqi Republican Guard also came from Tikrit.

Most coalition commanders believed that Hussein would seek refuge in Tikrit during an invasion of Iraq, so the city became the scene of great military concentration as soon as the Iraq War began in March 2003. Tikrit came under almost immediate and heavy aerial bombardment designed to flush out Hussein, his followers, and elements of the Republican Guard who might have sought a safe haven in the city. In April 2003, a contingent of several thousand U.S. marines and coalition forces descended on the city, accompanied by more than 300 armored vehicles, to secure it and search for any Hussein hold-outs. The city was taken with almost no resistance, but Hussein was nowhere to be found. Nevertheless, once Hussein had left Baghdad, presumably

A UH-60 Black Hawk helicopter flies past one of Saddam Hussein's former palaces in Tikrit, Iraq. (U.S. Department of Defense)

just before the invasion of Iraq began, he is believed to have fled to the vicinity of Tikrit, where he was sheltered and hidden by supporters and relatives. On December 13, 2003, U.S. forces found Hussein hidden in a small, underground bunker in a small town just outside Tikrit.

The Iraqi insurgency, meanwhile, has heavily involved Tikrit, located in the northern part of what has been called the Sunni Triangle. It has provided many insurgent fighters and has been the scene of numerous bombings and ambushes against coalition troops. By 2007, Tikrit had been partially pacified, and the U.S. Army, working with Iraqi officials, has begun to institute economic reforms in the area designed to improve education and increase job opportunities. A textile mill, the profits from which

will help fund a vocational school, was already up and running by the end of 2007.

Paul G. Pierpaoli Jr.

See also: Hussein, Saddam

Further Reading

Aburish, Said K. *Saddam Hussein: The Politics of Revenge.* New York: Bloomsbury, 2000.

Tripp, Charles. *A History of Iraq.* Cambridge: Cambridge University Press, 2007.

Topography, Kuwait and Iraq

Kuwait, which encompasses just 6,969 square miles (a bit smaller than the state of New Jersey), is a Middle Eastern nation that lies in the northwestern corner of the

Arabian Peninsula. It borders Saudi Arabia to the south, Iraq to the west and north, and the Persian Gulf to the east. Despite its small size, it boasts a 120-mile sea coast and has nine off-shore islands, including Bubiyan, the largest island, which encompasses 333.2 square miles.

Kuwait is essentially flat desert, which slopes gradually down from the extreme west of Shigaya and Salmi (the highest areas of the nation, about 950 feet above sea level), east to the Persian Gulf. Between west and east are a series of shallow valleys and very low hills, including Kura al-Maru, Liyah, Shagat al-Jleeb, and Afris. The southeastern portion of the country is entirely flat, with the notable exception of Ahmadi Hill, which is approximately 450 feet above sea level. A desert region that receives very little rainfall, Kuwait has no mountains and is the only nation in the world that does not have any natural lakes, reservoirs, or rivers. Fresh water is a precious commodity and is supplied mainly via limited underground supplies, neighboring countries, and, increasingly, by large desalinization plants along the coast. Because of Kuwait's relatively flat topography and lack of surface water or mountains, the area has traditionally been a crossroads for nomads and a gathering place in which to do business and conduct trade. That same topography, however, makes the small nation vulnerable to invasion, such as the Iraqi invasion of Kuwait in August 1990.

There are approximately 2.4 million people living in Kuwait, the vast majority of whom live in and around the coastal capital at Kuwait City. Less than 1 percent of Kuwait's landmass is used for agriculture, as the region's torrid climate and lack of rainfall render permanent agricultural pursuits very difficult. Because of lack of vegetation and a lack of rainfall, Kuwait is subject to raging sandstorms, especially in June and July, when high temperatures average 107°F to 114°F in most of the country.

Kuwait is home to the world's fifth-largest known petroleum reserve, which dominates the economy. Eighty percent of the government's revenue is derived from oil sales, which make up nearly 95 percent of the country's exports. During the 1991 Persian Gulf War, when Iraqi forces set ablaze hundreds of Kuwaiti oil wells as they retreated into Iraq, they unleashed an environmental catastrophe. Soot and huge lakes of oil rendered a sizable portion of southern and southeastern Kuwait virtually uninhabitable. Even today, more than 5 percent of Kuwait's landmass is covered by a semiliquified asphaltlike coating, rendering it virtually impossible to traverse.

With a landmass of 169,234 square miles (slightly larger than California) and a population of 29.3 million, Iraq is far more varied topographically than its neighbor Kuwait. It boasts a number of large cities, and the population is far more evenly distributed than that of Kuwait. Iraq occupies the northwestern portion of the Zagros mountain range, the eastern edge of the Syrian Desert, and the northwestern part of the Arabian Desert. It is bordered by Kuwait to the south, Saudi Arabia to the south and west, Syria to the northwest, Turkey to the north, and Iran to the east. Nearly land-locked, Iraq's only access to the Persian Gulf is in the far southeastern part of the country, near the Iranian and Kuwait border. The Shatt al-Arab Waterway, on the Iraqi-Iranian border, is also a key access point to the Persian Gulf.

Mainly a desert climatologically, Iraq nevertheless has varied weather and seasons. It has several large surface water supplies, including lakes and reservoirs. Its two main river systems are the Tigris and Euphrates, which bifurcate the country roughly in the middle and parallel each other. Between the two rivers is rich, fertile, arable land in which many of Iraq's farming activities take place. The far northern part of Iraq is quite mountainous, especially near the Turkish and Iranian borders. Steppes and highland yield to mountain ranges as high as 13,000 feet above sea level. Agriculture is possible here at the lower elevations, and rainfall tends to be highest in this region. In the south and southeast, near the delta of the Tigris and Euphrates rivers, the land is punctuated by large marshes, which Iraqi president Saddam Hussein attempted to eradicate in the late 1980s and early 1990s. The vast deserts in the south and southwest of the country are relatively flat and feature a classic desert environment, with scarce rainfall, torrid summers, and brief, cool (and sometimes rainy) winters. Located in the central part of Iraq, Baghdad, the capital, has a population of about 7 million people and has a modified desert climate; summers are long and blisteringly hot, but the winters are cooler and wetter than those in the southern desert regions.

The most sparsely populated areas of Iraq are in the southern and southwestern deserts, where pastoral nomadic tribes chiefly reside. About 12 percent of Iraq's landmass in currently taken up by agriculture. The nation is home to the word's second-largest known oil reserves (behind only Saudi Arabia), although it is estimated that there remains a vast amount of oil in Iraq that has not been tapped. Other natural resources are notably absent in any significant amounts in Iraq. Except in the northeast, Iraq is subject to periodic, seasonal sandstorms that can reduce visibility to less than a tenth of a mile. In the planning for Operations DESERT STORM and IRAQI FREEDOM, U.S. military planners had to take into account the possibility of such storms. Both invasions were set for late winter and early spring to avoid the intense heat of Iraqi summers.

Paul G. Pierpaoli Jr.

See also: IRAQI FREEDOM, Operation

Further Reading

Marr, Phebe. *The Modern History of Iraq.* 2nd ed. Boulder, CO: Westview, 2003.

Rodgers, Mary, ed. *Iraq in Pictures: Visual Geography Series.* Minneapolis: Lerner Publications, 1990.

Torture of Prisoners

Torture is generally defined as the deliberate infliction of pain, whether physical or psychological, on a victim or a prisoner for a variety of purposes. In wartime torture has historically been most commonly used as an interrogation technique to extract intelligence information from prisoners of war (POWs) in a rapid fashion. Otherwise, it has been used as a punishment and method of dehumanization. This has been particularly true in the various recent Middle Eastern wars. Torture has also been routinely employed to achieve propaganda advantage, as in securing confessions or testimonials denouncing the policies of their own government.

Torture is banned by international law as a fundamental violation of human rights, whether inflicted on enemies or one's own population. It is specifically banned by the Third and Fourth Geneva Conventions (1929 and 1949), as well as the United Nations (UN) Convention against Torture (1987). Torture nonetheless remains a disturbingly common aspect of contemporary conflicts, and not only in the Middle East. Beyond wartime, the United Nations Convention against Torture regards capital punishment as well as many of the sanctioned legal punishments in

Iran, Saudi Arabia, Libya, Pakistan, and under the Taliban to be torture.

Torture was long an established part of judicial procedure to extract confessions and was regularly employed, for example, during the Spanish Inquisition. Only in the past two centuries have there been concerted efforts to ban torture and establish penalties for its use.

There is an ongoing debate over what constitutes torture by nations that do not conform to international standards. Some nations have regularly employed drugs to extract information from prisoners and interrogators have routinely used sleep deprivation, enforced positions, light and sound bombardment, harassment, beatings, waterboarding, removal of teeth and fingernails, confinement in extremely small spaces, severe cold, and electric shocks to secure what they seek. In the United States, some police departments and law enforcement agencies had, even prior to September 11, 2001, assaulted detainees.

Amnesty International reported that more than 150 nations routinely employed torture in the period 1997–2000. Clearly, it remains a prominent human rights issue into the 21st century.

In the Middle East, a region that contains numerous totalitarian regimes as well as religious strife, torture has played a role in internal security, warfare, and struggles between political movements. Israel has long used assault, sleep deprivation, enforced bodily positions, electric shock (more recently forbidden), and other "coercive interrogation" methods when questioning suspected Palestinian terrorists. Although the Israeli Supreme Court ruled that all torture was illegal, allegations of degrading and inhuman treatment of Palestinian detainees continue to be leveled against Israeli authorities. Likewise, the

government of Saudi Arabia claims that torture is against Islamic law, but there is ample evidence that the Saudi regime continues to employ torture, particularly against domestic prisoners. In addition, the punishments of lashing, beheading, and amputation are considered torture by the United Nations (UN), but Saudi Arabia does not accept this position. Similar evidence of the routine use of torture in interrogations of suspects has been documented in Egypt, Iran, Iraq, Jordan, Lebanon, and Syria.

During the Israeli-Arab War of 1948–1949, the 1967 Six-Day War, and the 1973 Yom Kippur (Ramadan) War, each side accused the other of torturing POWs. There is strong evidence that prisoners were subjected to physical beatings and other forms of punishment to discover useful information and that many were killed. During the Iran-Iraq War (1980–1988), both belligerents were accused of torturing prisoners. Sometimes, the torture was designed to elicit information for tactical use on the battlefield; more often, however, the torture was for purely sadistic reasons, to punish an enemy.

In the 1991 Persian Gulf War (Operation DESERT STORM), captured coalition pilots were paraded before international news cameras showing signs of physical injuries. Upon their release, American pilots reported that they had been beaten by their Iraqi captors, who demanded that they renounce their religious beliefs in favor of Islam and that they sign statements admitting to war crimes.

During the U.S.-led Global War on Terror (from 2001), American military forces have been repeatedly accused of torturing suspected terrorists to obtain information about planned attacks on U.S. targets. In particular, human rights advocates have accused U.S. authorities of employing inhumane and degrading treatment against detainees at the Guantánamo Bay Naval Base in Cuba. This included severe beatings, waterboarding, sleep deprivation, and sensory deprivation. The detainees also claimed that they received threats of bodily harm and were humiliated sexually and forced to remain in uncomfortable positions for prolonged periods. Despite international condemnation, the United States has refused to release the majority of the prisoners held at Guantánamo Bay, has yet to charge them with a particular crime, and has not opened the facility to international observers or the media. After his administration took office in January 2009, President Barack Obama directed that the Guantánamo Bay facility be closed within a year. However, as of April 2013 it remains open, although it houses fewer than 200 inmates.

In 2003, after the U.S.-led Operation IRAQI FREEDOM began, allegations of torture perpetrated by U.S. military personnel began to surface. These first concerned the infamous Abu Ghraib prison in Baghdad. Abu Ghraib had served as a major detention facility under the dictatorship of Saddam Hussein, and unspeakable offenses had been committed there against opponents of the regime and other prisoners. After U.S. forces took Baghdad in April 2003, they began using the prison to hold suspected terrorists and members of the Iraqi military. In April 2004 the prison came to the public's attention when photographs of naked prisoners, some hooded and attached to electrical wires, were published in a variety of media sources. An internal U.S. Army investigation determined that some guard personnel, led by Army Specialist Charles Graner, had instigated the mistreatment of prisoners without official sanction. A number of the individuals were charged and brought to trial. Others, such as those in authority, saw their military careers ended because of the scandal.

By mid-2005 there was mounting evidence that the United States had indeed engaged in torture in Afghanistan, Iraq, and Guantánamo, and rumors circulated concerning torture at the secret detention facilities believed to be in Jordan, Morocco, Eastern Europe, and elsewhere. This prompted a public outcry as well as protests from Human Rights Watch, Amnesty International, and even the UN. On December 30, 2005, President George W. Bush signed legislation passed by Congress that banned the torture of detainees, although critics pointed out that the president can still approve such tactics by using his broad powers as commander in chief. The law was enacted after an acrimonious fight between the Bush administration and many members of Congress, at the time controlled by his own Republican Party.

On June 12, 2008, the U.S. Supreme Court dealt the Bush administration a severe blow when it declared that suspected terrorist detainees at Guantánamo Bay may petition U.S. civilian courts to release them. The *Boumediene v. Bush* case essentially gave enemy combatants the right to file a writ of habeas corpus in a U.S. court. Just a few weeks later, on June 23, a Federal appeals court struck down the Bush administration's classification of detainees at Guantánamo as "enemy combatants." Many argued for the closing of the Guantánamo detention facility, including some within the Bush administration, and the decision to do this by the Obama administration received the endorsement of the commander of the U.S. Central Command (CENTCOM), General David Petraeus. The disposition of the prisoners at Guantánamo remains the principal stumbling block. Thus, some claim that the Yemeni prisoners, who constitute a large number of those held there, should not be returned to Yemen. The concern is that an indigenous movement linked to al-Qaeda is known to be active there.

Paul Joseph Springer

See also: Abu Ghraib; Guantánamo Bay Detainment Camp

Further Reading

Danner, Mark. *Torture and Truth: America, Abu Ghraib, and the War on Terror.* New York: New York Review Books, 2004.

Friedman, Lori, ed. *How Should the United States Treat Prisoners in the War on Terror?* Farmington Hills, MI: Greenhaven, 2005.

Hersh, Seymour. *Chain of Command: The Road from 9/11 to Abu Ghraib.* New York: HarperCollins, 2004.

Human Rights Watch. *Torture and Ill-Treatment: Israel's Interrogation of Palestinians from the Occupied Territories.* New York: Human Rights Watch, 1994.

Human Rights Watch. *Behind Closed Doors: Torture and Detention in Egypt.* New York: Human Rights Watch, 1992.

Meeropol, Rachel, and Reed Brody. *America's Disappeared: Secret Imprisonment, Detainees, and the "War on Terror."* New York: Seven Stories, 2005.

Sampson, William. *Confessions of an Innocent Man: Torture and Survival in a Saudi Prison.* Toronto: McClelland and Stewart, 2005.

Zabecki, David T. "Torture: Lessons from Vietnam and Past Wars." *Vietnam* (October 2008): 32–35.

U

Umm Qasr

Iraqi port city located on the Faw (Fao) peninsula in the southern part of the country. The city sits astride the Khawr Abd Allah estuary, which leads directly into the Persian Gulf. Umm Qasr is separated from Kuwait by a small inlet. Until the 1991 Persian Gulf War, when it was destroyed, a bridge spanned the inlet, linking the two nations.

Umm Qasr is strategically important because it is one of the Iraqis' few access points to deep water. Over the last half century its importance has only increased as successive Iraqi regimes sought to invest in it as an alternative to the Shatt al-Arab waterway, which borders on Iran, Iraq's perennial adversary.

Over the centuries, Umm Qasr has mainly been a fishing enclave, but it has also served military purposes. In 325 BCE, Alexander the Great landed there when he undertook the conquest of Mesopotamia. During the World War II years the city was used as a port in which American Lend-Lease supplies were dropped as they made their way to the Soviet Union. In early 1950 Iraqi king Faisal II invested heavily in Umm Qasr to rebuild and modernize its port facilities. After Faisal was overthrown in 1958, the new Iraqi government created a naval base at Umm Qasr; the city remained the chief headquarters for the Iraqi Navy until the 2003 invasion of Iraq.

In 1961 Iraqi leader Abd al-Karim Qasim accelerated the port city's development in an effort to end Iraqi reliance on the Shatt al-Arab waterway. By 1967 the city's new port facilities, including a new rail line that linked Umm Qasr with Baghdad and Basra, were completed. The new port had been constructed largely by a consortium of companies from Lebanon, West Germany, and Sweden.

Umm Qasr came under attack during the Iran-Iraq War (1980–1988), but the port itself never fell into Iranian hands, even though the Faw peninsula was largely occupied in 1986. The Iranians were not dislodged until 1988. Umm Qasr was at the center of Iraqi-Kuwaiti tensions that led to war in 1990. Both nations claimed sovereignty over the inlet that provides access to the port, and disputes over control of two nearby islands also fed Iraqi and Kuwaiti mutual ill will. Umm Qasr was bombed heavily during Operation DESERT STORM in 1991, and after the conflict Kuwait gained control over the access inlet. The Iraqi government refused to recognize the change, however.

Between 1992 and 2003 Iraqi dictator Saddam Hussein further built up the port at Umm Qasr and redirected much oceangoing commerce to it. This was done to punish the port city of Basra, which had been at the epicenter of antigovernment rebellions that followed the Persian Gulf War. By early 2003 Umm Qasr had an estimated permanent population of some 40,000 people.

During the 2003 Anglo-American–led invasion of Iraq (Operation IRAQI FREEDOM), coalition forces targeted Umm Qasr as one of their first and primary targets. Between March 21 and March 25, 2003, British Royal Marines, the U.S. 15th Marine Expeditionary Unit, and Polish GROM (Operational Mobile

Reaction Group) fought against an unexpectedly stout Iraqi resistance in and around Umm Qasr. The port was finally secured on March 25, and thereafter coalition forces used it as a transshipment point for vast amounts of humanitarian aid to the Iraqi people after the fall of Hussein's regime.

Paul G. Pierpaoli Jr.

See also: IRAQI FREEDOM, Operation; Umm Qasr, Battle of

Further Reading

Keegan, John. *The Iraq War: The Military Offensive, from Victory in 21 Days to the Insurgent Aftermath.* New York: Vintage, 2005.

Tripp, Charles. *A History of Iraq.* Cambridge: Cambridge University Press, 2007.

Umm Qasr, Battle of

First military engagement of the 2003 Iraq War (Operation IRAQI FREEDOM). The Battle of Umm Qasr unfolded in and around the Iraqi port city of Umm Qasr, located in the southern part of the country on the Faw (Fao) peninsula, from March 21 to 25, 2003. The port at Umm Qasr, which is Iraq's only deep-water port, is very close to Kuwait; indeed, only a small inlet separates the two nations.

Taking control of Umm Qasr was one of the coalition's first military objectives during the opening days of Operation IRAQI FREEDOM. American and British commanders knew that seizing the city and port would deny the Iraqis any way of challenging the naval blockade. More importantly, they also hoped to secure the port as the base for a large humanitarian mission, whereby tons of food, medicine, clothing, and other supplies would be moved into Iraq once Iraqi president Saddam Hussein's regime had been toppled.

The Umm Qasr offensive, which involved the 15th U.S. Marine Expeditionary Unit, British Royal Marines, and integrated units from Poland's Operational Mobile Reaction

U.S. marines fighting in Umm Qasr, Iraq, on March 23, 2003. (U.S. Department of Defense)

Group (GROM), moved toward Umm Qasr overland from Kuwait and through the very southern edge of Iraq. The operation began on March 21, 2003. Coalition forces were confident that the port and surrounding city could be taken quickly and with little resistance. As a convoy of about 20 coalition vehicles lumbered toward Umm Qasr, the Iraqis peppered it with small-arms fire. They then opened up with mortar fire, taking the allies by surprise. The Americans called in British artillery support from northern Kuwait, not far from the border. While some shells hit Iraqi positions, others fell perilously close to U.S. Marine Corps units, which were forced into a hasty withdrawal. After regrouping, the coalition forces called for M-1A1 Abrams tanks, which then punched through Iraqi defensive positions.

Many of the Iraqi defenders were members of Hussein's elite Republican Guard, who resorted to guerrilla-style tactics to keep coalition forces off balance. Some were disguised in civilian clothing and would hold up white flags. When coalition forces approached, they would scurry into foxholes and bunkers, and open fire. The Iraqi resistance at Umm Qasr was unexpectedly stout, and some critics have claimed that coalition forces took the Iraqi threat too lightly and were thus ill prepared for a protracted fight there.

After more determined fighting on the part of the Iraqis, coalition forces made use of Bradley fighting vehicles and intended on calling in Cobra attack helicopters to help root out resistance in and near the port. The Bradleys arrived, but the Cobras did not, as there had been insufficient time to organize a mission. On March 25 the port was declared free of Iraqi opposition, but sporadic and pitched fighting continued to occur in the old city of Umm Qasr.

Not until the first few days in April had all of Umm Qasr been pacified. Meanwhile, coalition minesweepers, U.S. Navy SEALS, and even trained dolphins began the laborious task of clearing the port waters and approaches of mines. Navy personnel made an unsettling discovery when they found a number of Iraqi civilian boats rigged with mines and explosive devices, making the minesweeping operation all the more difficult. The first ship to make it into port was the British RFA (Royal Fleet Auxiliary) *Sir Gallahad*.

The Battle of Umm Qasr gave pause to many coalition commanders and strategists who had believed that securing the port city would be a quick and easy affair. Fortunately, subsequent operations went more or less according to plan, but the battle proved that no operation, however well planned, can proceed successfully without proper intelligence and preparation.

Paul G. Pierpaoli Jr.

See also: Iraqi Freedom, Operation; SEAL Teams; Umm Qasr

Further Reading

Gordon, Michael R., and General Bernard E. Trainor. *Cobra II: The Inside Story of the Invasion and Occupation of Iraq.* New York: Pantheon, 2006.

Keegan, John. *The Iraq War: The Military Offensive, from Victory in 21 Days to the Insurgent Aftermath.* New York: Vintage, 2005.

United Kingdom, Air Force, Iraq War

The United Kingdom's Royal Air Force (RAF) played a significant role during Operation Telic (the British contribution to Operation Iraqi Freedom). Commanded by Air Vice Marshal Glenn Torpy, Royal Air

Force composite squadrons in Iraq included elements from squadrons based at RAF Marham, RAF Leeming, RAF Leuchars, RAF Coltishall, RAF Cottesmore, RAF Waddington, RAF Benson, RAF Brize Norton, RAF Lyneham, RAF Kinloss, and RAF Odiham. These squadrons operated Panavia Tornado F3, Panavia Tornado GR4, Sepecat Jaguar, and Boeing/British Aerospace AV-8B Harrier II combat aircraft; McDonnell Douglas/Boeing C-17 Globamaster II and Lockheed C-130 Hercules transport aircraft; and Vickers-Armstrong VC-10 aerial tankers. Helicopters operated by the RAF included the Boeing CH-47 Chinook heavy transport, the Aérospatiale Puma medium-lift transport, and the Westland Lynx attack helicopter. Finally, the RAF deployed the RAF Regiment to protect its air stations in the Gulf region. In all, of the 46,000 British troops to participate in the initial stages of Operation TELIC, 8,100 served in the Royal Air Force.

In comparison to the 1991 Persian Gulf War, during which a sustained air campaign of 34 days preceded the ground offensive, the plan for Operation IRAQI FREEDOM was a simultaneous launch of ground and air attacks. Popularly known by the completely inadequate misnomer of "shock and awe," the aim of these attacks was for the American and British air forces to blitz Iraq with precision weapons from the air to destroy key leadership, command-and-control, and military targets, while ground forces raced to Baghdad to topple the government.

The campaign began just after 1:00 a.m. on March 20, 2003, when the American air commander Lieutenant General Michael "Buzz" Moseley launched a pair of Lockheed F-117 Nighthawk stealth bombers to attack a target in Baghdad's downtown area, where Iraqi president Saddam Hussein and his sons, Uday and Qusay, were purportedly meeting.

Following this initial attack, throughout the day of March 20, through the night of March 20–21, and throughout the day of March 21, air efforts focused on aiding allied troops who had by this time crossed into Iraq.

On the night of March 21–22 the full fury of the allied bombing campaign was launched. In all, 1,500 British and American missions were flown that night, 700 of which were by strike aircraft, and approximately 1,000 targets were hit. This firepower was augmented by the coalition naval component; British and American vessels at sea also launched 500 cruise missiles before dawn on March 22. Yet throughout these first two days and nights of the campaign, commanders placed several restrictions on bombing targets. The bridges across the Tigris and Euphrates were not destroyed, as these would be needed by the rapid advance of American and British troops. Likewise, much of the Iraqi communications infrastructure was left untouched because allied war leaders needed Iraqi troops to receive word that their political leadership had fallen. Finally, the electricity grid sustained little damage out of fear that destroying it would make postwar stability and recovery harder to accomplish. On the night of March 22–23 British and American aircraft flew 800 strike sorties, followed by an additional 1,500–2,000 sorties over the next 48 hours. On March 25 a *shamal* blew in, causing a fierce sandstorm that lasted for three days, yet still the air attacks continued unabated, with sorties rising to 2,000 in each 24-hour period.

Over this time, the attacks shifted from preplanned targets to targets of opportunity, particularly against Iraqi ground forces deployed in the defense of Baghdad. By April 4, 85 percent of all allied air attacks were focused on Iraqi ground units. The fall of Baghdad and the end of the conventional war in Iraq followed shortly thereafter. On April 8 the Iraqi Republican Guard units defending the city dispersed into smaller units, and by April 11 all Iraqi forces within the environs of Baghdad had been eliminated. In total, from March 20 to April 12 the British and American air forces flew 36,275 sorties, of which 14,050 were strike sorties. The RAF lost no aircraft to enemy fire or suffered any casualties from Iraqi guns. Tragically, however, one RAF Tornado was shot down by an American Patriot missile in a friendly fire incident, killing both crew members. Only a small number of RAF personnel and equipment remained in Iraq after mid-June 2003.

Benjamin John Grob-Fitzgibbon

See also: IRAQI FREEDOM, Operation

Further Reading

Keegan, John. *The Iraq War: The Military Offensive, from Victory in 21 Days to the Insurgent Aftermath.* New York: Vintage, 2005.

Murray, Williamson, and Robert H. Scales Jr. *The Iraq War: A Military History.* Cambridge, MA: Belknap, 2005.

United Kingdom, Army, Iraq War

The British Army was the second-largest force contributor, behind the U.S. Army, to the anti–Saddam Hussein coalition during the 2003 Iraq War (2003–2009). The British military operation during the Iraq War was code-named Operation TELIC. The British Army began deploying units to the region in anticipation of the conflict in January 2003, ultimately deploying some 26,000 soldiers for the invasion of Iraq. The British ground force was centered on the 1st Armoured Division, which included the 7th Armored

Brigade, the 16th Air Assault Brigade, and the 102st Logistics Brigade in addition to various infantry, artillery, medical, and support units. The division was commanded by Major General Robin Brims. Royal Air Force air marshal Brian Burridge was the British national contingent commander, and British Army major general Peter Wall was his chief of staff.

The British forces were placed under the operational control of the U.S. I Marine Expeditionary Force (I MEF). The I MEF was the eastern column of the two-prong coalition advance into Iraq. Once the ground invasion began on March 22, the main elements of the I MEF advanced toward Baghdad, while the British forces, along

A member of a British army sniper team of the 42nd Royal Highland Regiment (Black Watch), Basra, Iraq, in September 2004. (U.S. Department of Defense)

with most of the Australian and Polish troops, undertook operations in the southeastern portion of Iraq, including first the capture of the Faw (Fao) peninsula and the strategic port of Umm Qasr in an operation in support of Special Air Service (SAS) units and Royal Marine commandos. The division then advanced and captured the airport outside of Basra, Iraq's second-largest city, four days after the start of the invasion.

After instituting a loose blockade, on April 6 British forces launched a three-prong attack on Basra itself and captured the city after meeting light resistance. By the end of the day British forces had secured their main objectives. In an effort to minimize looting and lawlessness, officers conducted a series of negotiations with local and tribal leaders to craft an interim security agreement for Basra.

The British then assumed command of the Multi-National Force Southeast, which included their own ground units as well as contributions from a range of other states. The force endeavored to maintain security for the region around Basra in the face of a growing insurgency. As a result of the frequency of roadside bombings and mine damage, Britain purchased and deployed new armored patrol vehicles and personnel carriers.

The British also participated in the coalition program to train Iraqi security personnel, including more than 22,000 police officers. British forces served as advisers to Iraqi units through transition teams, which remained with the national troops during security operations. Meanwhile, the British Ministry of Defense began to withdraw its own forces from Iraq. By May 2003 British Army forces had been reduced to 18,000. A series of rotations replaced the British 1st Armoured Division with the British 3rd Infantry Division in July 2003. Through 2004 and 2005 the British Army maintained about 8,500 troops in Iraq but began to reduce its force presence over the next several years, so that by the end of 2008 only about 4,100 troops remained. On April 30, 2009, British prime minister Gordon Brown announced the end of British combat operations in Iraq and a phased withdrawal of the remaining British forces there. By July 28, 2009, all remaining British troops had left Iraq and been redeployed to Kuwait after the Iraqi government rejected a request to extend their mission in a training capacity.

In 2005 additional troops were deployed to provide security for Iraqi national elections. Also in 2005, the British began to transfer control over basic training for military recruits to the Iraqi National Army, and British forces began to turn over military facilities to their Iraqi counterparts. Through 2006, additional provinces were turned over to Iraqi security forces.

British forces conducted a number of exercises with Iraqi forces, including Operation SINBAD from September 2006 to March of 2007. SINBAD was designed to provide security to more than 550 infrastructure projects in Basra and to dislodge antigovernment militias in the region. British troops have also participated in operations outside of their area of responsibility, such as Operation FARDH AL QANOON in which two battalions served alongside Iraqi forces in security sweeps in Baghdad.

In 2007 British forces withdrew from their last major post within Basra, creating a security vacuum that led to renewed fighting between Shiite militias. An offensive by the Iraqi Army to displace the militias failed. Nonetheless, the transfer of control meant that all four southern provinces within the scope of operations of the British had been handed over to the Iraqis.

British participation in the Iraq War was controversial among the public, who increasingly supported the withdrawal of forces after 2003. In December 2008 British prime minister Gordon Brown announced that the majority of British troops would be withdrawn from Iraq through 2009, leaving only approximately 400 troops who would continue to participate in training missions. During Britain's involvement in Iraq, 179 military personnel had been killed, and 3,598 had been wounded or injured.

Tom Lansford

See also: Basra; IRAQI FREEDOM, Operation; IRAQI FREEDOM, Operation, Coalition Ground Forces

Further Reading

Cockburn, Patrick. *The Occupation: War and Resistance in Iraq.* New York: Verso, 2007.

Keegan, John. *The Iraq War: The Military Offensive, from Victory in 21 Days to the Insurgent Aftermath.* New York: Vintage, 2005.

Murray, Williamson, and Robert H. Scales Jr. *The Iraq War: A Military History.* Cambridge, MA: Belknap, 2005.

United Kingdom, Marines, Iraq War

The United Kingdom's Royal Marines played a vital role during Operation TELIC (the British contribution to Operation IRAQI FREEDOM). Royal Marine forces in Iraq included the Headquarters 3 Commando Brigade, the 40th Commando, the 42th Commando, the United Kingdom Landing Force Command Support Group, the Commando Logistic Regiment Royal Marines, the 29th Commando Regiment Royal Artillery, the 539th Assault Squadron Royal Marines, the 9th Assault Squadron

Royal Marines, the 59th Independent Commando Squadron Royal Engineers, and the 131st Independent Commando Squadron Royal Engineers (Volunteers). Elements of the following units were also present in Iraq: the 45th Commando, the Headquarters Commando United Kingdom Amphibious Forces, the 20th Commando Battery Royal Artillery, the Fleet Protection Group Royal Marines, the 4th Assault Squadron Royal Marines, the Royal Marines Band Service, and the Royal Marines Reserve City of London, Scotland, Bristol, Mersey-side and Tyne. Finally, the following units served as attachments with the Royal Marines during Operation TELIC: C Squadron, the Queen's Dragoon Guards; C Squadron, the Royal Scots Dragoon Guards; and 18th Squadron Royal Air Force.

British forces engaged in Operation TELIC, including Royal Navy, British Army, Royal Marines, and Royal Air Force, numbered some 46,000 troops, of whom 4,000 were Royal Marines. The British ground component, including the Royal Marines, was contained within the 1st Armoured Division, which was comprised of the 7th Armoured Brigade (the famed "Desert Rats" of the Persian Gulf War), the 16th Air Assault Brigade, and the 3rd Commando Brigade Royal Marines, the latter of which had the U.S. Marine Corps' 15th Marine Expeditionary Unit attached to it. Led by Brigadier Jim Dutton, the 3rd Commando Brigade was tasked with spearheading an amphibious assault on the Faw (Fao) peninsula in southern Iraq, securing the port of Umm Qasr, and assisting in the seizure of the Basra, Iraq's second-largest city.

The amphibious landing of the 3rd Commando Brigade on the Faw peninsula was the most ambitious operation undertaken by the Royal Marines since the 1982 Falklands War, complicated by the fact that unlike in the Falklands, the landing would be opposed. The first Royal Marines to enter Iraq, spearheaded by Bravo Company, 40th Commando, left Kuwait by helicopter on the night of March 20, 2003, landing on the Faw peninsula less than an hour later. They were soon joined by the remaining companies of 40 Commando, and were supported by artillery fire from British and American units stationed on Kuwait's Bubiyan Island, as well as from three British frigates and one Australian frigate positioned in the Persian Gulf. In addition, the 40th Commando fired more than 5,000 mortar rounds in the initial assault to help secure its positions. The 40th Commando's immediate purpose was to secure the southern Iraqi oil fields and oil infrastructure to prevent Iraqi forces from setting them alight, as they had done in the 1991 Persian Gulf War. While the 40th Commando was engaged in this task, the 42nd Commando was airlifted to positions north of 40th Commando to form a block that would prevent any Iraqi forces from moving south to engage the 40th Commando.

Following the successful seizure of the oil fields, the 40th Commando moved to secure the Iraqi banks of the Shatt al-Arab waterway, which flows along the border with Iran. The 42nd Commando moved into the port city of Umm Qasr seized earlier by U.S. marines, which they soon opened up to vital humanitarian aid. By March 30 each of these tasks had been completed. The entirety of the 40th Commando— together with L Company, 42nd Commando; C Squadron, the Queen's Dragoon Guards; and C Squadron, the Royal Scots Dragoon Guards—then embarked on Operation JAMES, a 19-hour battle involving both Lynx attack helicopters and Challenger II main battle tanks whose purpose was to secure the town of Abu al Khasib on the approach to Basra.

From there the Royal Marines moved into Basra itself, seizing control of Iraqi dictator Saddam Hussein's summer palace. By April 6, just over two weeks after the first marines of the 40th Commando had landed on Iraqi territory, Basra had fallen. The Royal Marines had succeeded in their task, taking and holding the 60-mile coastline of the Faw peninsula and opening up the port and cities of Umm Qasr, Abu al-Khasib, and Basra. Following these operations, the 3rd Commando Brigade left Iraq in June 2003. As of December 2008, there had been 12 rotations of British forces in Iraq (Operations TELIC II through TELIC XIII). The Royal Marines, however, played no great role in these deployments, in large part having deployed to Afghanistan instead. All British troops had departed Iraq by the end of July 2009. In all, the Royal Marines suffered 11 fatalities during the period of British involvement in Iraq.

Benjamin John Grob-Fitzgibbon

See also: Basra; IRAQI FREEDOM, Operation; Umm Qasr

Further Reading

Fox, Robert. *Iraq Campaign, 2003: Royal Navy and Royal Marines*. London: Agenda Publishing, 2003.

Keegan, John. *The Iraq War: The Military Offensive, from Victory in 21 Days to the Insurgent Aftermath*. New York: Vintage, 2005.

Murray, Williamson, and Robert H. Scales Jr. *The Iraq War: A Military History*. Cambridge, MA: Belknap, 2005.

UN Monitoring, Verification and Inspection Commission

United Nations (UN) weapons-inspection regime created by UN Security Council Resolution 1284, passed on December 17,

1999. The United Nations Monitoring, Verification and Inspection Commission (UNMOVIC) took up the work of the previously disbanded United Nations Special Commission (UNSCOM), which had been tasked with verifying Iraq's compliance with post–Persian Gulf War agreements mandating the destruction of all Iraqi weapons of mass destruction (WMD). More specifically, UNMOVIC's mandate was to ensure the identification and destruction of any biological, chemical, and nuclear weapons as well as missiles with a range greater than approximately 100 miles.

UN secretary-general Kofi Annan named Swedish diplomat Hans Blix to head UNMOVIC as executive chairman. Blix, who had been chairman of International Atomic Energy Agency (IAEA) from 1981 to 1997, served with UNMOVIC from March 1, 2000, to June 30, 2002. In addition to Blix, the UN appointed 16 individuals who helped Blix conduct inspections and compile verification facts.

Unlike UNSCOM, its predecessor agency, all of UNMOVIC's inspectors and employees were UN employees. This was done to quell concerns that the inspections were politically motivated or being unduly influenced by individual nation-states. The staff included scientists, analysts, engineers, operational planners, and, of course, seasoned weapons inspectors. Headquartered in New York City, UNMOVIC was divided into four operational segments: training and technical support, information, planning and operations, and analysis and assessment. Every three months the executive chairman was obliged to present a report to the UN Security Council on UNMOVIC's findings and actions in Iraq.

As it turned out, UNMOVIC proved to be as controversial as UNSCOM. Although Blix chided Iraqi president Saddam

Hussein's government for playing "cat-and-mouse" games in regard to its cooperation with UN weapons inspectors, Blix's reports to the Security Council concluded that UNMOVIC had not found any illicit WMD in Iraq. This ran counter to the George W. Bush administration's claims, however, which asserted that Iraq did indeed have WMD. Before long the United States concluded that UNMOVIC was ineffectual and had not revealed findings of WMD to stave off an invasion of Iraq.

On November 8, 2002, the UN Security Council passed Resolution 1441, which essentially allowed Iraq one final opportunity to cooperate fully and unconditionally with weapons inspectors and to explain contradictions in its verification process. UNMOVIC inspectors returned to Iraq that same month but were unable to unearth any credible evidence of illicit WMD programs in Iraq. The Bush administration dismissed UNMOVIC's reports, alleging that it had evidence of WMD in Iraq and that UNMOVIC was being pressured by the UN and the international community not to divulge evidence of WMD in order to avoid a showdown with the Iraqis.

On the eve of the Anglo-American–led invasion of Iraq in March 2003, UNMOVIC evacuated the country, still claiming that Iraq had disarmed appropriately. UNMOVIC continued to operate in those areas it was able to influence thereafter, but after the invasion its actions were largely completed. UNMOVIC's mandate lapsed on June 29, 2007, per UN Security Council Resolution 1762.

Many in the UN and the international community did not support the March 2003 invasion of Iraq. They further believed that the United States and Great Britain had purposely tried to sabotage and discredit UNMOVIC to help justify the war against Iraq. Blix was absolutely furious over the contretemps, and in a February 2004 report to the Security Council he admitted that Iraq should have been more forthcoming with weapons inspectors since 1991 but also maintained that UNSCOM and UNMOVIC had accomplished the task of ridding Iraq of WMD. That same month during a television interview in Great Britain, Blix pointedly asserted that the United States and Britain had purposely overemphasized the threat of Iraqi WMD to justify their invasion. In the end no WMD have been located in Iraq, even after years of searching by perhaps thousands of members of the occupation forces in Iraq.

Blix claims that the United States so mistrusted him that his home and office were bugged.

Paul G. Pierpaoli Jr.

See also: Blix, Hans; UN Security Council Resolution 1284; UN Special Commission; Weapons of Mass Destruction

Further Reading

Blix, Hans. *Disarming Iraq.* New York: Pantheon, 2004.

Butler, Richard. *The Greatest Threat: Iraq, Weapons of Mass Destruction and the Growing Crisis in Global Security.* New York: PublicAffairs, 2000.

Byman, Daniel. "After the Storm: U.S. Policy toward Iraq since 1991." *Political Science Quarterly* 115(4) (2000–2001): 493–516.

UN Security Council Resolution 1284

Resolution adopted by the United Nations (UN) Security Council on December 17, 1999. Resolution 1284 established the UN Monitoring, Verification, and Inspection Commission (UNMOVIC), reaffirmed the mission of the International Atomic Energy

Agency (IAEA), and charged both with overseeing Iraqi compliance with previous Security Council resolutions, most notably 687, which had gone into effect on April 3, 1991. Although not all Security Council members endorsed the final draft of Resolution 1284, the council generally recognized the need for a resolution of its kind in light of the fact that UN inspections had been inactive in Iraq for a year, after having been withdrawn because of Iraqi intransigence.

UNMOVIC, which replaced the UN Special Commission (UNSCOM) created by Resolution 687, was specifically tasked with monitoring Iraq's compliance with the restrictions enumerated in paragraphs 8 through 10 of that same resolution. Therein the Iraqi government was informed of the necessity to destroy, remove, or render harmless its biological and chemical weapons and related matériel, as well as any ballistic missiles capable of traveling more than 100 miles. Paragraphs 12 through 13 of Resolution 687 further outlined the requirements for Iraq to shut down its nuclear weapons program under observation of the IAEA; Resolution 1284 reiterated the agency's role in this regard.

At the time Resolution 1284 was approved, the Security Council was composed of delegates from Argentina, Bahrain, Brazil, Canada, Gabon, Gambia, Malaysia, Namibia, the Netherlands, Slovenia, and the five permanent member states (People's Republic of China [PRC], France, the Russian Federation, the United Kingdom, and the United States). Eleven nations voted in favor of the resolution while four abstained (France, China, the Russian Federation, and Malaysia).

The Chinese government's misgivings over the final draft of the resolution revolved around two issues. First, it believed the resolution did not adequately provide incentives to encourage Iraqi compliance by specifying the process through which UN sanctions would be suspended. Second, it asserted that a consensus had not been reached by the council members, which might therefore undermine UNMOVIC's authority. China underscored the second matter to emphasize its disapproval of the actions of certain council members, particularly the United States and Great Britain, who had ostensibly undertaken unilateral military action in Iraq (Operation DESERT FOX in 1998) and who had imposed a no-fly zone in Iraq without council approval. Echoing similar sentiments concerning illicit unilateral maneuvers, Russia chose to abstain, rather than veto, the draft resolution. It did so because only some of its former objections had been addressed. Thus while Russia gave its limited approval, it nevertheless warned that it would not stand idly by if attempts were made to impose the resolution with force. France was concerned with the ambiguity surrounding the process by which sanctions would first be suspended and then lifted.

Jason Robert Tatlock

See also: UN Monitoring, Verification and Inspection Commission; UN Special Commission; Weapons of Mass Destruction

Further Reading

Bennis, Phyllis. "And They Called It Peace: U.S. Policy on Iraq." *Middle East Report* 215 (2000): 4–7.

Murphy, Sean D. "Contemporary Practice of the United States Relating to International Law." *American Journal of International Law* 94, no. 1 (2000): 102–39.

UN Special Commission

Organization established pursuant to United Nations (UN) Security Council Resolution 687, adopted on April 3, 1991. The United Nations Special Commission (UNSCOM) was tasked with overseeing, together with the International Atomic Energy Agency (IAEA), the inspection of Iraqi weapons programs to ensure compliance with UN resolutions calling for the dismantling of that nation's weapons of mass destruction (WMD). Although the IAEA and UNSCOM cooperated in fulfilling their individual mandates, the IAEA was specifically responsible for investigating Iraq's nuclear capabilities, while UNSCOM was responsible for biological, chemical, and long-range missile armaments. Swedish diplomat Rolf Ekéus headed UNSCOM from 1991 to 1997, while Richard Butler headed it from 1997 to 1999. UNSCOM was disbanded in 1999 and replaced by the United Nations Monitoring, Verification and Inspection Commission (UNMOVIC) under the authority of Resolution 1284, adopted on December 17, 1999.

UNMOVIC was authorized in an attempt to reinvigorate the UN monitoring program with the goal of achieving Iraq's full compliance with Security Council demands. The need for a new approach was evident, for not only were weapons inspections stalled for a year (since 1998), but UNSCOM was widely perceived as biased and ineffectual, as was made evident at the meeting in which Resolution 1284 was adopted. At that time, the Chinese delegation intimated that any entity replacing the "infamous" UNSCOM must, unlike UNSCOM, operate with objectivity, impartiality, transparency, and accountability. Indeed, for the Russian Federation, the military force used by the United Kingdom and the United States against Iraq in December 1998 (Operation DESERT FOX) was both unilaterally conceived and erroneously justified by citing an inaccurate report given by Executive Chairman Butler, which had suggested that Iraq had not fully cooperated with weapons inspectors. China, moreover, went so far as to entertain the possibility that Butler had been complicit in preparing inaccurate reports that could then be utilized in an attempt to rationalize the use of force. In rebutting such allegations of impropriety, specifically as put forth by Russia in addressing the Security Council on December 16, 1998, Butler was later to argue that his conclusions about Iraqi noncompliance in his December 15 report were inescapable.

A significant difference between UNSCOM and UNMOVIC was that the organizational structure of the new investigative unit would have greater accountability and less room for unilateral movement by the executive chairperson. Butler would find these modifications problematic, but ostensibly they made UNMOVIC less susceptible to political manipulation. Certain of the key changes stipulated that the UN secretary-general would have direct charge of the commission; the appointed chairperson would require Security Council approval before assuming the post; a college of commissioners, made up of politicians rather than weapons experts, would be consulted prior to the implementation of significant policy alterations; and all personnel would be UN employees.

To be sure, UNSCOM fell victim to political infighting and global power politics, which the Iraqis were all too eager to exploit. Charges were leveled on more than one occasion—by Iraq and other UN nations—that UNSCOM was being undermined by sabotage aimed at destroying the regime of Iraqi dictator Saddam Hussein. Hussein specifically charged that the U.S. Central Intelligence Agency (CIA) had infiltrated UNSCOM, which was his justification for denying UNSCOM personnel access to certain government facilities, including the Baath Party headquarters in Baghdad.

UNSCOM was not terribly popular inside the UN either. In December 1998 Butler declared the Iraqi regime uncooperative, which triggered Operation DESERT FOX (December 16–19, 1998), a punitive bombing raid against Iraqi military targets carried out by U.S. and British naval and air assets. UNSCOM remained virtually nonoperational until December 1999, when UNMOVIC was formed.

Despite its controversial nature, UNSCOM accomplished much in its eight-year tenure. Of note was its ability to quickly implement an unprecedented weapons inspection and disarmament program when nothing of its kind had existed before. Within two months of its inception, UNSCOM had already begun inspections and was quite successful in overseeing the destruction of much illicit weapons material and equipment. Examples of the demolition of Iraq biological, chemical, and long-range missile programs over-seen by UNSCOM included the destruction of 48 missiles, together with 20 tons of illicit fuel and 56 stationary missile launch sites; the eradication of 38,537 chemical munitions and chemical weapons agents totaling 690 tons; and the dismantling of the Hakam biological weapons plant and equipment from similar facilities at Manal and Safah. Hakam especially was a significant facility where such deadly biological agents as anthrax and botulinum toxin had been produced.

Immediately following the adoption of Resolution 1284 in 1999 and the consequent conclusion of the mandate of UNSCOM, the American delegation at the Security Council highlighted the important accomplishments of executive chairmen Ekéus and Butler. The former was lauded for his work in building UNSCOM from scratch; the latter was credited with sustaining UNSCOM's mission in the face of an increasingly uncooperative Iraq. What is more, both men played a key role in uncovering previously unknown weapons programs, which included biological weapons and a program to produce VX gas

Jason Robert Tatlock

See also: Blix, Hans; UN Monitoring, Verification and Inspection Commission; UN Security Council Resolution 1284; Weapons of Mass Destruction

Further Reading

Butler, Richard. *The Greatest Threat: Iraq, Weapons of Mass Destruction and the Growing Crisis in Global Security.* New York: PublicAffairs, 2000.

Byman, Daniel. "After the Storm: U.S. Policy toward Iraq since 1991." *Political Science Quarterly* 115, no. 4 (2000–2001): 493–516.

UN Weapons Inspectors

Following the Persian Gulf War of 1991, the United Nations (UN) Security Council authorized a team of weapons inspectors to rid Iraq of all its weapons of mass destruction (WMD), which included biological and chemical weapons as well as all materials related to nuclear weapons development. As a condition for the cessation of hostilities against Iraq in the Persian Gulf War (Operation DESERT STORM) following the coalition forces' liberation of Kuwait, the UN Security Council passed Resolution 687 on April 3, 1991. This called for the creation of the United Nations Special Commission (UNSCOM) to inspect and disarm Iraq's WMD as well as all its missiles with a range greater than 90 miles.

From 1991 to 1999 UNSCOM was charged with enforcing UN Resolution 687. In 1999 a successor to UNSCOM came into being. It was known as the United Nations Monitoring, Verification and Inspection Commission (UNMOVIC) and was in Iraq from December 2002 to March 2003. Although Iraq repeatedly sought to conceal the extent of its WMD program and also resisted cooperating fully with UNSCOM by, for example, denying inspectors access to certain sites, UNSCOM nevertheless engaged in significant disarmament activities. However, the sheer size of the country of Iraq, the technically complex nature of disarmament, and repeated Iraqi deception and resistance to UNSCOM efforts make it hard to know precisely the extent of success. For its part, Iraq accused UNSCOM of spying and of being a puppet of the United States and Israel.

In late 1998 UNSCOM withdrew from Iraq in the face of renewed Iraqi resistance and imminent punitive American and British air strikes in December. For the next four years, there were no weapons inspectors operating inside Iraq. This, of course, prompted concerns that Iraqi dictator Saddam Hussein had secretly renewed his WMD program.

Beginning in 2002, U.S. president George W. Bush demanded that Iraq comply with UN resolutions and disarm once and for all or face an invasion. On November 8, 2002, UN Security Council Resolution 1441 declared that Iraq was in violation of Resolution 687. It denounced Iraq's "omissions or false statements" with respect to its WMD stockpiles and offered Iraq "a final opportunity to comply with its disarmament obligations." In December 2002 in the face of an imminent American and British invasion of Iraq, Hussein agreed to allow UN weapons inspectors back into the country; however, they were withdrawn in March 2003 just before the beginning of the Iraq invasion (Operation IRAQI FREEDOM) on March 20, 2003.

The head of UNMOVIC, Hans Blix, a Swedish diplomat, reported to the UN on March 7, 2003, that Iraq had not provided sufficient documentary evidence to account for its WMD stockpiles and missiles. He expressed doubt as to whether Iraq had fully agreed to disarm. Unlike the United States, Britain, and Spain, however, a majority of members of the Security Council, including France, China, and Russia, opposed any resolution authorizing an attack or invasion of Iraq on this basis. The Americans, supported by Britain and Spain, denied that any additional UN resolution was necessary to authorize the use of force against Iraq. Indeed, they cited UN Security Council Resolution 686 of November 29, 1990, which authorized any UN member to use "all necessary means" to "restore international peace and security to the Persian Gulf Region." The three nations also pointed out that the Iraqis had violated 16 UN resolutions and in 12 years had failed to disarm. Based on the October 11, 2002, authorization by the U.S. Congress to use force against Iraq, the United States, along with Britain, commenced Operation IRAQI FREEDOM on March 20, 2003.

In the aftermath of the invasion, the Iraqi Survey Group was unable to find any WMD. Several reasons have been advanced for this. The most obvious explanation is that Iraq had ceased its program sometime before 2003. Indeed, one of Saddam Hussein's sons-in-law, Hussein Kamal, who had charge of Iraq's WMD program, made this claim repeatedly and with extensive detail upon defecting to Jordan in 1995, but U.S. and British intelligence agents doubted his veracity even though he, unlike other defectors, did not make efforts to secure personal financial gain. Indeed, he returned to Iraq and was killed. Upon being captured in December 2004, Saddam Hussein apparently also told American interrogators that Iraq no longer had WMD. U.S. officials also considered the veracity of his comments problematic.

Other explanations for the absence of WMD rest on sheer speculation and have never been verified but remain popular in certain political circles. For example, although no evidence exists to prove this claim, some critics of Operation IRAQI FREEDOM claim that the Bush administration knew Iraq had halted its WMD program but lied to the American people to justify the invasion and regime change. Other critics of the war, mostly Democrats but some Republicans as well (most of whom had voted for the war), have since argued that Bush was misled by faulty intelligence, which was driven by the need to provide evidence to support the war rather than by a balanced appraisal of the true situation on the ground. They have concluded that the Bush administration presented only that evidence that supported its own conclusions. The U.S. Senate Intelligence Committee issued two reports in 2004 and 2006 documenting Bush administration intelligence failures regarding Iraq.

Finally, some observers believe that Iraq hid its remaining WMD stockpiles or shipped them to Iran and/or Syria. It is highly unlikely that Iraq would ever ship such stockpiles to Iran. Although no conclusive evidence has been put forth to support this claim, its supporters cite the fact that Russian truck convoys left Iraq for Syria and other countries as coalition forces invaded. Those who support this theory also make the claim that Russia was assisting Hussein's WMD program development.

Stefan Brooks

See also: UN Monitoring, Verification and Inspection Commission; UN Security Council

Resolution 1284; UN Special Commission; Weapons of Mass Destruction

Further Reading

Blix, Hans. *Disarming Iraq.* New York: Pantheon, 2004.

Butler, Richard. *The Greatest Threat: Iraq, Weapons of Mass Destruction and the Growing Crisis in Global Security.* New York: PublicAffairs, 2000.

Pearson, Graham S. *The UNSCOM Saga: Chemical and Biological Weapons Non-Proliferation.* New York: Palgrave Macmillan, 2000.

Ritter, Scott. *Endgame: Solving the Iraqi Crisis.* New York: Simon and Schuster, 2002.

Trevan, Tim. *Saddam's Secrets: The Hunt for Iraq's Weapons.* New York: HarperCollins, 1999.

Whitney, Craig. *The WMD Mirage: Iraq's Decade of Deception and America's False Premise for War.* New York: PublicAffairs, 2005.

U.S. Agency for International Development, Iraq

Principal U.S. governmental organization that supervises and distributes American foreign aid to Iraq, which began in 2003 shortly after Operation IRAQI FREEDOM overthrew the Saddam Hussein regime. The genesis of the U.S. Agency for International Development (USAID) may be found in the 1947 Marshall Plan and President Harry S. Truman's 1949 Point Four Program. Both of those programs systematized U.S. foreign assistance in the post–World War II era.

The U.S. Congress created the Agency for International Development with the passage of the 1961 Foreign Assistance Act. The act mandated the establishment of an umbrella organization for U.S. foreign economic assistance, which led to the creation of the USAID on November 3, 1963. Since then, the USAID has distributed hundreds

A Kurdish farmer tends his crops in northern Iraq in 2007. USAID workers helped to form a farmers association with the aim of giving farmers ownership of their land. (U.S. Agency for International Development)

of billions of dollars of aid around the world and has served as a unifying organization that brings together almost all U.S. financial, technical, and economic development programs under one broad banner.

Over the years, the USAID has weathered periodic reform initiatives and considerable criticism that it is a bureaucratic leviathan that wastes money that could be channeled to other purposes. Nevertheless, it continues on, more than 45 years after its creation, as the premier U.S. foreign assistance agency. The USAID receives its guidance from the U.S. secretary of state, whose job it is to ensure that USAID's aims and programs are consonant with American foreign policy goals and mandates established by the U.S. Congress.

The postwar reconstruction of Iraq, a primary mandate for the USAID, represents the single largest U.S. foreign aid initiative since the Marshall Plan. Among the USAID's chief missions in Iraq are economic reconstruction and growth, the reinvigoration of health care and educational systems, the support of democratic institutions, the provisioning of humanitarian aid to homeless and displaced persons, and the rebuilding and upgrading of critical infrastructure, to include sewage treatment plants, electrical generation facilities, and water treatment systems. All of these activities are meant to foster representative democracy, internal security, and economic independence. Clearly, the ongoing Iraqi insurgency has made it quite difficult for USAID to achieve its goals; the continuing presence of large numbers of U.S. and coalition troops in the country has also been a challenge for USAID officials.

USAID workers have been working with former Iraqi government officials, retraining them and readying them to take over various governmental functions. They have also been working with provincial and municipal government officials in an attempt to ensure that basic services are met at the local and regional level. USAID is also working closely with the Central Bank of Iraq and the Ministry of Finance, helping them implement effective budgetary and cost-tracking measures.

From 2003 to 2006, USAID added 1,292 megawatts of electricity to Iraq's electric grid, bringing electrical service to hundreds of thousands of people. USAID has also rebuilt or expanded 19 water treatment plants, bringing potable water to 3.1 million Iraqis who heretofore had no access to clean water. USAID improvements to sewage treatment facilities have brought modern sewage service to at least 5.1 million Iraqis. In health care, USAID has also provided many improvements. In 2005 alone, almost 98 percent of all Iraqi children were vaccinated against childhood diseases. In education, USAID has built, rebuilt, or refurbished thousands of schools and has developed programs to ensure that all Iraqis have access to educational institutions, from elementary level to university. In cities and towns hard hit by fighting, USAID is working in tandem with other international agencies and multinational corporations to revitalize local economies.

In 2007, USAID spent $1.959 billion on all programs in Iraq; in 2009 the budget was substantially less, closer to $1.49 billion. The amount of USAID funds spent in Iraq since 2003 is approaching $10 billion; the United States spent $13.5 billion (albeit in 1950 dollars) on the Marshall Plan (1947–1952), which helped reconstruct all of Western Europe. Currently, there are no plans to dismantle USAID in Iraq, and so considerably more money will likely be spent in the years to come. Clearly, the continuing insurgency in Iraq has hampered

USAID efforts to reconstruct the country, and it is anyone's guess how much money has been wasted trying to rebuild a nation that remains at war with itself.

Paul G. Pierpaoli Jr.

See also: IRAQI FREEDOM, Operation

Further Reading

Agresto, John. *Mugged by Reality: The Liberation of Iraq and the Failure of Good Intentions.* New York: Encounter Books, 2007.

Glantz, Aaron. *How America Lost Iraq.* New York: Jeremy P. Tarcher, 2005.

Stephenson, James. *Losing the Golden Hour: An Insider's View of Iraq's Reconstruction.* Dulles, VA: Potomac Books, 2007.

U.S. Air Force, Iraq War

The participation of the United States Air Force (USAF) in the Iraq War, designated Operation IRAQI FREEDOM, begun on March 20, 2003. The USAF has provided logistical, strategic, and tactical air support for U.S. and coalition forces since the beginning of the conflict. The USAF utilized the Combined Air Operations Center (CAOC), which U.S. forces had established at the beginning of the Afghanistan War, dubbed Operation ENDURING FREEDOM, in 2001. The CAOC, originally stationed in Saudi Arabia and moved to Qatar in 2003, monitors and controls all air operations in Operation ENDURING FREEDOM and Operation IRAQI FREEDOM. Moreover, the CAOC provides intelligence and relays target information to airborne aircraft. During the first five months of Operation IRAQI FREEDOM, Lieutenant General T. Michael Moseley served as commander, U.S. Central Command Air Forces (CENTAF), giving him command of all air forces under the U.S. Central Command (CENTCOM).

Much of the air force's efforts on the first two days of Operation IRAQI FREEDOM focused on ground support for forces moving into Iraq from Kuwait. In addition, the USAF bombed command and control targets (communication sites, artillery, surface-to-air missile sites, air-defense command centers, air traffic control facilities, and airfields) throughout Iraq. From late March 21 through March 22, USAF aircraft also heavily bombed the Iraqi capital of Baghdad. The initial bombing campaign, referred to as shock and awe, was aimed at ousting Iraqi president Saddam Hussein's Baath regime from power. Yet, the Iraqi government did not submit to the initial air assault. U.S. CENTCOM and U.S. CENTAF deemed many Iraqi command and control targets off limits for fear of civilian casualties, and so air strikes had limited initial effectiveness in toppling Hussein.

By early April, USAF aircraft had begun to focus more on close air support for U.S. ground forces making their way toward Baghdad, demolishing any infantry, gun and artillery emplacements, tanks, and armored vehicles that hindered the coalition advance. Simultaneously, the USAF continued to provide strategic air support in and around Baghdad, which fell to coalition forces on April 9–10, 2003. Soon after the end of the conventional aspect of Operation IRAQI FREEDOM, which was marked by the capture of Baghdad, Iraqi insurgents quickly organized, thus hindering the coalition's ability to create and maintain security in the country. The return of sovereignty to the new Iraqi government in June 2004 prompted a shift in air force strategy toward one that emphasized counterinsurgency and security.

From August 2003 to February 2006, Lieutenant General Walter E. Buchanan III served as commander of U.S. CENTAF, thus placing him in control of the air force component of the counterinsurgency in Iraq. The USAF increased its employment of unmanned aircraft for intelligence, surveillance, and reconnaissance missions, during which the remote-controlled drones searched for insurgent activity in Iraq. Moreover, the air force increased the number of "on call" close air support missions, during which aircraft remain airborne and wait for orders to strike a target near the respective area of responsibility. The Iraqi insurgents have thrived on quick, covert tactics, and the "on call" aircraft offer a timely response to often unexpected attacks on American and coalition ground forces or Iraqi civilians.

In late 2003 U.S. CENTCOM established the Multinational Security Transition Command–Iraq (MSTC-I) to develop Iraqi security personnel. Two years after the establishment of MSTC I, the USAF assumed responsibility of training and developing the Iraqi Air Force (IAF), a task still being carried out. In early 2009 newly elected U.S. president Barack Obama announced plans to draw down American forces in Iraq, heightening the need to quickly train Iraqi military and security personnel.

In February 2006 Lieutenant General Gary L. North assumed command of U.S. CENTAF (changed to USAFCENT [U.S. Air Forces Central] in March 2008). While tasked with continuing to provide close air support for U.S. and allied forces and bolstering the IAF, U.S. airmen have seen an increase of security positions on the ground. Throughout the war, the USAF has always provided base defense, but beginning in 2006, U.S. airmen have also provided convoy protection.

As the Iraqi insurgency persisted throughout 2006, President George W. Bush announced in early 2007 that U.S. forces would see a troop surge of additional soldiers and marines to Iraq. Thus, throughout 2007 and 2008 the USAF tripled the number of airmen that performed ground support duties for the U.S. Army and Marine Corps. In addition to convoy security, USAF personnel performed explosives forensic analysis and police duties in Iraqi cities. Yet the increase in grounded airmen did not translate to a decrease in air support. The year of the surge resulted in the most close air support sorties flown since the start of the insurgency in 2003. Moreover, the USAF has persisted throughout the conflict in bombing insurgent strongholds and safe houses, bomb-making facilities, and weapons stockpiles.

U.S. CENTCOM officials reported a decrease in insurgent activity in 2008 after the surge took hold. The addition of U.S. forces pushed the insurgents into open areas, offering easier targets for USAF aircraft, which explains another reason for the increase in close air support sorties in 2007. Throughout 2008 and early 2009, Iraqi ground forces have conducted operations with help from coalition airpower, including the USAF.

The USAF has utilized a vast array of aircraft during Operation IRAQI FREEDOM. As of April 1, 2008, the Air Force had flown nearly 353,000 sorties in support of Operation IRAQI FREEDOM. As of early 2009, the USAF reported 48 deaths in Operation IRAQI FREEDOM.

Early 2009 saw 27,558 USAF personnel serving in Iraq and Afghanistan. From the beginning of the Global War on Terror in September 2001 to the end of 2009, the USAF has deployed a total of 347,080 personnel to Iraq and Afghanistan.

John Southard

See also: IRAQI FREEDOM, Operation; IRAQI FREEDOM, Operation, Air Campaign

Further Reading

Boyne, Walter J. *Beyond the Wild Blue: A History of the U.S. Air Force, 1947–2007.*

2nd ed. New York: Thomas Dunne Books, 2007.

Cassidy, Robert. *Counterinsurgency and the Global War on Terror: Military Culture and Irregular War.* Palo Alto, CA: Stanford University Press, 2008.

Donnelly, Thomas. *Operation Iraqi Freedom: A Strategic Assessment.* Washington, DC: AEI Press, 2004.

Murray, Williamson, and Robert H. Scales Jr. *The Iraq War: A Military History.* Cambridge, MA: Belknap, 2005.

Thaler, David E., Theodore W. Karasik, Dalia Dassa Kaye, Jennifer D. P. Moroney, Frederic Wehrey, Obaid Younossi, Farhana Ali, and Robert A. Guffey. *Future U.S. Security Relationships with Iraq and Afghanistan: U.S. Air Force Roles.* Santa Monica, CA: RAND Corporation, 2008.

U.S. Army, Iraq War

In the Iraq War (2003–2011), the U.S. Army deployed more personnel and matériel than any of the other U.S. armed services or those of its allies within the coalition. The ground forces involved were smaller than what most military commanders recommended, however, considerably increasing the risks if the coalition encountered unexpected obstacles. Since 2001 the all-volunteer U.S. Army typically had numbered some 500,000 active-duty soldiers in 10 divisions, with another 500,000 in the Army National Guard and the U.S. Army Reserve. With decreases in army strength since the end of the Vietnam War, and particularly since the end of the Cold War in 1991, reservists and National Guardsmen had taken on a greater role. Army ground forces were organized as follows: divisions of some 20,000 personnel each; brigades of up to 4,000 individuals each; battalions (800), companies (200), and platoons (30).

U.S. Army general Tommy Franks, commander of U.S. Central Command (CENTCOM), had overall command of U.S. and coalition forces during the invasions of both Afghanistan and Iraq. Following Franks in command of U.S. forces in Iraq have been U.S. Army generals Ricardo Sanchez (June 2003–2004), George W. Casey (2004–2007), David Petraeus (2007–2008), and Raymond Odierno (2008–2012).

Overall commander of the land component (U.S. Army, U.S. Marine Corps, and coalition forces) in the March–April 2003 invasion of Iraq was U.S. Army lieutenant general David McKiernan, commander of the Third U.S. Army/U.S. Army Forces Central Command. Total army strength in the invasion force was some 55,000 men formed into V Corps in Kuwait, under Lieutenant General William Scott Wallace. He controlled two divisions, part of a third, and a fourth on its way. Engineer (to include bridge-builders), supply, and other units were available to be attached to the combat forces as required. The logistics element included some 2,500 trucks that would support the units moving north into Iraq toward Baghdad.

The lead element of V Corps was the 3rd Infantry Division (Mechanized). Known as the "Rock of the Marne," the 3rd Division was commanded by Major General Buford C. Blount III and numbered some 18,000–20,000 men. Its major offensive element consisted of some 170 Abrams tanks and 200 Bradley Fighting Vehicles, with close air support from Apache Long Bow tank-killing helicopters and Black Hawk transport helicopters. It also had a brigade-sized artillery unit. The 3rd Infantry Division led the invasion of Iraq from Kuwait. Its mission was to drive north from Kuwait to the west of the Euphrates River and the I Marine Expeditionary Force.

After the invasion started, the 3rd Infantry Division was joined by the 101st Airborne Division and a brigade of the 82nd Airborne Division, which had the mission of securing objectives short of the Iraqi capital of Baghdad. The 101st Airborne Division, known as the "Screaming Eagles," numbered about 20,000 men and was the army's only air assault division. Commanded by Major General David Petraeus and organized as light infantry, it deployed 275 helicopters.

The 2nd Brigade Combat Team of the 82nd Airborne Division, known as the "Falcon Brigade," numbered about 4,000 paratroopers commanded by Colonel Arnold Neil Gordon-Bray. Its mission and that of the 101st was to provide security to bases and supply routes on the way to Baghdad.

The 173rd Airborne Brigade, based in Vicenza, Italy, parachuted into northern Iraq on March 26. Commanded by Colonel William C. Mayville, its mission was to tie down Iraqi troops there and prevent them from reinforcing to the south, as well as to secure the Kurdish areas there, especially Kirkuk and Mosul. To accomplish this, the 173rd conducted a combat jump (Operation NORTHERN DELAY) to secure Bashur Airfield in northern Iraq. Once this was accomplished, McDonnell Douglas C-17 Globemaster aircraft carried out history's first combat air landing of main battle tanks. Troops of the Special Operations Command, comprising the 75th Ranger Regiment, the 5th Special Forces Group, and the 160th Special Operations Aviation Regiment, were to secure key bridges and operate in the Iraqi desert to cut routes to Syria and occupy areas that might be suitable for the firing of Scud missiles.

Only as the invasion came to an end did the 4th Infantry Division, which had been scheduled to invade northern Iraq from Turkey but had failed to receive permission from the Turkish government for this plan, begin arriving in Kuwait. Commanded by Major General Raymond L. Odierno, it possessed the most up-to-date equipment. The 4th Infantry Division was the army's first digitized division, with its commanders able to track the movement of its vehicles on the battlefield. The fact that it had only begun its movement to Kuwait by March 19, 2003, probably served to mislead Iraqi leader Saddam Hussein into believing that the invasion was still some time off.

Army casualties in the fighting reflect their larger proportionality of personnel in Iraq. As of January 3, 2009, a total of 4,212 Americans had died in Operation IRAQI FREEDOM, with 3,394 of these combat related. Most of the American casualties IRAQI FREEDOM occurred after the end of the initial invasion of Iraq and the toppling of the Hussein regime at the end of April 2003. The army accounted for 2,455 of those deaths and another 604 from nonhostile deaths, equaling 3,059 of 4,212. The army's total wounded was 21,354 out of a U.S. total of 30,934. Of the army's wounded, 7,139 required medical air transport, signifying serious wounds. In 2009 the army was preparing to refocus its efforts in Afghanistan while slowly drawing down in Iraq.

Dylan A. Cyr and Spencer C. Tucker

See also: Franks, Tommy Ray; IRAQI FREEDOM, Operation; IRAQI FREEDOM, Operation, Ground Campaign; McKiernan, David Deglan

Further Reading

Atkinson, Rick. *In the Company of Soldiers: A Chronicle of Combat.* New York: Henry Holt, 2005.

Gerrard, Howard. *U.S. Army Soldier: Baghdad 2003–04 (Warrior).* Oxford: Osprey, 2007.

Keegan, John. *The Iraq War: The Military Offensive, from Victory in 21 Days to the Insurgent Aftermath.* New York: Vintage, 2005.

Murray, Williamson, and Robert H. Scales Jr. *The Iraq War: A Military History.* Cambridge, MA: Belknap, 2005.

Neville, Leigh. *Special Operations Forces in Iraq (Elite).* Oxford: Osprey, 2008.

Zinsmeister, Karl. *Boots on the Ground: A Month with the 82nd Airborne in the Battle for Iraq.* New York: St. Martin's, 2004.

U.S. Coast Guard, Iraq War

From the very outset of Middle Eastern operations, the U.S. Coast Guard's training and experience in these and other maritime activities played an important part in Operation IRAQI FREEDOM. Late in 2002, coast guard headquarters alerted various units in the service's Pacific Area (PACAREA) and Atlantic Area (LANTAREA) for possible deployment to the Middle East. From November 2002 through January 2003, these units began activation activities for an expected deployment in early 2003. In January IRAQI FREEDOM, PACAREA's first major units deployed to the Persian Gulf, including the high-endurance cutter *Boutwell* (WHEC-719) and the oceangoing buoy tender *Walnut* (WLB-205). Their responsibilities included maritime interdiction operations (MIO), and the *Walnut*, in conjunction with members of the Coast Guard's National Strike Force, would lead possible oil-spill containment operations.

LANTAREA provided many units of its own, sending the high-endurance cutter *Dallas* (WHEC-716) to the Mediterranean to support and escort Military Sealift Command shipping and coalition battle groups in that theater of operations. It also sent four 110-foot patrol boats (WPBs) to Italy with support personnel and termed their base of operations Patrol Forces Mediterranean (PATFORMED) and sent a set of four WPBs to the Persian Gulf with a Bahrain-based command called Patrol Forces Southwest Asia (PATFORSWA).

The service also activated Port Security Units (PSUs) and law enforcement boarding teams (LEDETs), which had each proven successful in the 1991 Persian Gulf War. LANTAREA sent PSU 309 (Port Clinton, Ohio) to Italy to support PATFORMED while PACAREA sent PSU 311 (San Pedro, California) and PSU 313 (Tacoma, Washington) to Kuwait to protect the Kuwait Naval Base and the port of Shuaiba, respectively. LEDET personnel initially served on board the WPBs and then switched to navy patrol craft to perform MIO operations.

At 8:00 p.m. on March 19, 2003, coalition forces launched IRAQI FREEDOM. By the time hostilities commenced, all coast guard units were manned and ready. On March 20 personnel from PSU 311 and PSU 313 helped secure Iraq's offshore oil terminals. On March 21 littoral combat operations began and the 110-foot *Adak* served picket duty farther north than any other coalition unit along the Khor Abd Allah waterway. The *Adak* captured the first Iraqi maritime prisoners of the war, whose patrol boat had been destroyed upstream. On that same day the *Adak* participated in the capture of two Iraqi tugs and a mine-laying barge.

Once initial naval operations ceased, coast guard units began securing port facilities and waterways for the shipment of humanitarian aid to Iraq. On March 24, PSU 311 personnel deployed to the Iraqi port of Umm Qasr, and four days later the 110-foot *Wrangell* led the first humanitarian aid shipment to that port facility. In addition to their primary mission of boarding vessels in the northern Persian Gulf, Coast Guard LEDET teams secured the Iraqi shoreline from caches of weapons and munitions. Buoy tender *Walnut*, the original mission of which included environmental protection from sabotaged oil facilities, surveyed and completely restored aids to navigation markers for the shipping lanes leading to Iraq's ports.

On May 1, President George W. Bush declared an end to formal combat operations in Iraq; however, within a year the Coast Guard suffered its first and only casualty of IRAQI FREEDOM. On April 24, 2004, terrorists navigated three small vessels armed with high explosives toward Iraq's offshore oil terminals. During this attack, the navy patrol craft *Firebolt* intercepted one of the suspicious watercraft, and members of LEDET 403 and navy crewmen proceeded toward the suspicious vessel in a rigid-hull inflatable boat (RHIB). Terrorists on board the small vessel detonated their explosive cargo as the RHIB approached, overturning the boat and killing LEDET member Nathan Bruckenthal and two navy personnel. Bruckenthal was the first Coast Guardsman killed in combat since the Vietnam War, and he received full military honors in funeral services at Arlington National Cemetery.

During Operation IRAQI FREEDOM, the Coast Guard performed the same vital functions that have long represented its core missions, such as in-shore patrol, MIO operations, and port security operations. The PSUs performed their port security duties efficiently despite the fact that their units were split up between three separate port facilities and two oil terminals. The WPBs operated for many hours without maintenance in waters too shallow for any major navy assets and served as the coalition fleet's workhorses in boarding, escort, and force protection duties. The personnel of PATFORMED and PSU 309 demonstrated that Coast Guard units could serve in areas that lacked any form of Coast Guard

infrastructure. PATFORSWA performed its support mission effectively even though the Coast Guard had never established such a support detachment. Fortunately, *Walnut* never had to employ its oil spill capability, but it proved indispensable for MIO operations and aids to navigation (ATON) work on the Khor Abd Allah waterway. The *Dallas* and *Boutwell* provided logistical support and force protection and MIO operations with their boarding teams.

William H. Thiesen

See also: IRAQI FREEDOM, Operation, Coalition Naval Forces

Further Reading

Schneller, Robert J., Jr. *Anchor of Resolve: A History of U.S. Naval Forces Central Command/Fifth Fleet*. Washington, DC: Naval Historical Center, 2007.

Seeger, Eric, ed. *The United States Coast Guard: The Shield of Freedom, 2005*. Tampa, FL: Government Group Services, 2005.

Tripsas, Basil, Patrick Roth, and Renee Fye. *Coast Guard Operations during Operation Iraqi Freedom*. Alexandria, VA: CNA Corporation, 2004.

U.S. Middle East Policy, 1945 to Present

Before World War II American involvement in the Middle East was limited. World War II, however, encouraged nationalist forces in the Middle East, thereby weakening the British and French imperial position there. It also brought an enhanced American economic and military presence in the region, as the United States stationed troops in Iran and in 1945 acquired long-term air base rights at Dhahran, Saudi Arabia. By the time the war ended, the American government sought continuing control of the region's strategically vital oil resources. These ambitions sometimes provoked friction and tensions between the United States and its Western allies, Britain and France, two imperial powers in decline that often resented growing American economic and military might. Even more significantly, these ambitions quickly brought the United States into conflict with the Soviet Union, and the Middle East was soon perceived as an important theater of Cold War rivalry.

From the late 1940s onward, successive American and Soviet governments competed not just to control Middle Eastern petroleum resources but also to gain international support and ideological loyalty from the patchwork of predominantly Muslim states across the area stretching from North Africa, Arabia, and the Persian Gulf to Afghanistan and Pakistan. As a rule, relatively conservative monarchical or authoritarian regimes leaned toward the United States, while radical nationalist governments tended to align themselves with the Soviets. U.S. support for the creation of the Jewish state of Israel in 1948 and increasingly close ties between those two countries further complicated American relations with Arab states throughout the region, most of whom deeply resented the existence of Israel.

The erosion of the position of European powers in the Middle East led both American and Soviet officials to seek to expand their own influence in the region. One of the earliest Cold War crises erupted over Iran. In 1941 the British and Russians had overthrown that country's Nazi-oriented monarch, Shah Reza Pahlavi I, and jointly occupied Iran, seeking to deny its oil resources to Germany and to safeguard supply routes to the Soviet Union. Both countries pledged that their forces would leave Iran within six months of the ending of hostilities in World War II.

In the autumn of 1945 Soviet officials backed separatist forces in establishing an independent Soviet Socialist Republic in Iran's northern province of Azerbaijan and encouraged a similar separatist movement in Kurdistan, setting up a puppet state there in early 1946. American and British forces withdrew on schedule in early 1946, but the Soviets announced their intention of retaining at least some troops in the north of the country, precipitating one of the earliest crises of the developing Cold War. The United States used the forum of the new United Nations (UN) organization to endorse Iranian demands for complete Soviet withdrawal.

After complicated maneuverings between Iranian politicians and Soviet representatives, the Soviets withdrew their forces in exchange for promised oil concessions in northern Iran. With the backing of American advisers, in late 1946 Iranian prime minister Qavam es-Sultanah, who had in the interim successfully negotiated with the United States a substantial package of military, economic, and cultural support, reneged on this bargain, and shortly afterward Iranian forces successfully overturned the Azerbaijani and Kurdish republics.

This episode contributed to growing American distrust of Soviet designs on the Middle East. Simultaneous Soviet demands that the Turkish government accord the Soviet Union special rights over the Dardanelles Straits, which was the only passage for Russian naval and commercial vessels from the Black Sea to the Mediterranean, further confirmed such suspicions. American officials encouraged the Turkish government to refuse these Soviet demands and reinforced their stance by dispatching an American naval squadron to the Mediterranean.

In early 1947 the British government announced that economic difficulties meant that it could no longer continue to provide military or financial assistance to the governments of Greece, then fighting a communist insurgency, and Turkey, raising the specter that Soviet power might move in to fill the vacuum left by Britain's departure. This crisis became the occasion for President Harry S. Truman to announce in February 1947 what became known as the Truman Doctrine, a wide-ranging pledge that the United States would provide assistance to any state threatened by internal or external communist subversion. The geographical proximity of Greece and Turkey to shipping routes along which much Middle Eastern oil was transported alarmed policy makers in Washington and encouraged the United States to provide aid. Both Greece and Turkey subsequently received extensive economic assistance under the Marshall Plan, announced later in 1947. In 1952 the two states simultaneously became members of the North Atlantic Treaty Organization (NATO), tying them firmly into western defensive alliances.

The American quest for reliable and stable long-term allies in the Middle East itself proved more problematic. One added complication was American support for Israel, which became heavily dependent on American aid, both governmental and private. President Truman's personal inclinations were largely responsible for American endorsement of the new state, a policy that, for strategic and diplomatic reasons, the State Department and the Defense Department both attacked. Most Arab states, whether conservative or radical, fiercely opposed Israel's very existence. Israel's military success in gaining and retaining previously Arab territories in several brief but bitter and hard-fought wars (1948–1949, 1956, 1967, 1973) only deepened Arab resentment. Hostility toward Israel was widespread and intense in Arab countries, Turkey, and Iran, making it difficult and even

personally hazardous for Middle Eastern leaders to moderate their stance and seek compromise with Israel.

In 1981, for example, a cell of a radical Islamist group assassinated President Anwar Sadat of Egypt, who with strong encouragement from U.S. president Jimmy Carter had negotiated a peace agreement with Israel two years earlier. Repeated American and other outside efforts to broker a final and permanent peace settlement and modus vivendi between Israel and its Arab opponents, including Palestinians from territories seized by Israel in the recurrent Arab-Israeli conflicts, became almost standard fixtures of the late 20th- and early 21st-centuries international diplomatic arena but were at best only partially successful. Almost invariably, they fell victim to extremist forces on both sides. Although a Palestinian state eventually came into existence on lands Israeli forces had taken in the various wars, throughout the first decade of the 21st centuries several key issues still remained unresolved, provoking bitter divisions among Israelis, Palestinians, and the broader Arab community.

The two countries that became the strategic linchpins of American alliance policy in the Middle East were Saudi Arabia and Iran, which together with Iraq possessed the bulk of the region's oil reserves. Under Saudi pressure, in 1950 ARAMCO (Arabian-American Oil Company) renegotiated its royalty agreement with the Saudi government so that each party received 50 percent of the profits. In 1951, Saudi Arabia signed a mutual defense agreement with the United States, and from then on a permanent American Military Training Mission was based in the kingdom. Saudi governments upgraded their military forces and placed lucrative armaments orders with American defense companies, goods they paid for with the proceeds of oil sales. In return for loyal support from the conservative Arab kingdom, for decades U.S. governments consistently overlooked the absence of democracy and disregard for international human rights standards that characterized the Saudi regime. The strong ties that the United States developed with this and other authoritarian Middle Eastern governments meant that the Americans were often perceived as representing illiberal forces opposing change and as the successors to European imperialists.

Such views were reinforced by the close American relationship with another monarchical regime, that of Iran. In 1951, the Iranian government announced its intention of nationalizing the Anglo-Iranian Oil Company; the British, who controlled the refineries, withdrew their technicians and blockaded all exports of Iranian oil, provoking severe economic difficulties within Iran. The government headed by Prime Minister Mohammad Mossadegh stood firm, and eventually, after an abortive attempt to replace him by the young shah, Reza Pahlavi II, declared a national emergency and took control of the Iranian military. In alliance with radical Muslims and the nationalist, leftist Tudeh Party, in 1952 Mossadegh implemented nationalist reforms, especially in agriculture, and broke diplomatic relations with the United Kingdom. Britain turned to the United States for assistance, characterizing Mossadegh as a radical who was turning toward communism and steering Iran into the Soviet orbit.

The administration of Republican president Dwight D. Eisenhower, which took office in January 1953, proved sympathetic to the British and authorized the Central Intelligence Agency (CIA) to spend up to $1 million removing Mossadegh. CIA agents in Tehran spread rumors and disinformation and in some cases acted as agents provocateurs. Economic problems intensified, and Mossadegh suspended parliament and extended his emergency powers. The CIA sought to persuade the indecisive young shah to dismiss Mossadegh, while Mossadegh urged the monarch to leave the country. Eventually, in 1953, the shah dismissed Mossadegh, but the latter refused to step down from office, and the shah took refuge in Italy. Major promonarchy and antimonarchy protests were held throughout the country, as Iranians of all political stripes assumed that before long Mossadegh would declare Iran a republic and himself head of state.

Promonarchy forces, heavily funded by the CIA, gained the upper hand, however, and Iranian tanks and troops entered Tehran and besieged the prime minister's residence until Mossadegh surrendered. He was subsequently placed under house arrest, then put on trial for treason and sentenced to three years in prison. General Fazlollah Zahedi, one of the military leaders who arrested Mossadegh, became prime minister, and the shah resumed power.

From then until the shah's overthrow in 1979, he would be a key U.S. ally in the Middle East. The shah soon reached an agreement with the British and Americans, under whose terms the foreign oil companies still made substantial profits and large amounts of Iranian oil once more flowed to world markets. These revenues, together with several billions of dollars in American military and economic assistance, enabled the shah to modernize his country and make it a strong military state. The 1953 coup also represented the first occasion when the CIA was instrumental in successfully ousting another government. The success of this undertaking subsequently emboldened CIA director Allen W. Dulles and other agency officials to try to orchestrate comparable operations against several other foreign governments U.S. leaders found unpalatable—in Guatemala, Cuba, the Dominican Republic, and Chile.

In addition to its Iranian alliance, the United States attempted to persuade other Middle Eastern states to collaborate against potential Soviet expansionism. In 1955 American diplomats encouraged the establishment of the Baghdad Pact, a grouping of Turkey, Iran, Iraq, Pakistan, and Britain, which established a military liaison with the United States. The objective was to erect a bastion of anticommunist states along the Soviet Union's southwestern frontier. The alliance was originally known as the Middle Eastern Treaty Organization (METO). After Iraq, the only Arab member, withdrew in 1958 in the aftermath of a revolution led by the leftist and Moscow-oriented Baath Party, the United States joined as a full member and the grouping became the Central Treaty Organization (CENTO). The organization proved largely ineffective in preventing the spread of Soviet influence in the Middle East. During the 1960s and 1970s, the Soviet Union simply bypassed the CENTO states to develop close military and economic ties with Egypt, Syria, Iraq, Yemen, Somalia, and Libya, establishing bases in Egypt, Somalia, and Yemen.

Although the United States sought to portray its own policies as representing a break with the earlier Western imperialism many Arab nationalists deeply resented, these efforts were not particularly successful. American dealings with Egypt during the 1950s demonstrated that, even when the U.S. government tried to dissociate itself from European colonialism, its policies often proved unconvincing and failed to win over skeptical opponents. In 1952

Gamal Abdel Nasser, a young military officer, became president of Egypt. He was determined to reverse decades of Western-inflicted humiliation in the Arab world and to overthrow Israel. In 1955 Nasser sought and obtained arms for this purpose from the Soviet bloc, whereupon the United States withdrew promised economic assistance for a major hydroelectric project, the Aswan Dam. Nasser then announced his intention to nationalize the Suez Canal, then still under British and French control, and to use canal revenues to finance the dam project.

Against American advice, in October 1956 the British, French, and Israelis jointly attacked Egypt, defeating its army, whereupon Nasser blocked the canal. The British, French, and Israelis thought a major Egyptian military setback would cause the Egyptian population to rise up and overthrow President Nasser. Fearing a major oil crisis, permanent Middle Eastern instability, and the further strengthening of both radical nationalism and Soviet influence, Eisenhower demanded that the invaders withdraw their forces, threatening to cease financial support for the beleaguered British currency should they refuse to do so. The crisis left Nasser more popular than ever before not only in Egypt but also in the broader Arab world and the Third World.

During the Suez crisis, the Soviet Union also threatened to use nuclear weapons against the invaders unless they withdrew. Fearing that this move presaged enhanced Soviet interest in the region, in January 1957 Eisenhower sought congressional authority both to increase economic and military aid to anti-Soviet Middle Eastern states and to deploy American military forces in the region if necessary to oppose overt armed aggression from any nation controlled by international communism. Arab states immediately condemned the Eisenhower Doctrine. Under its auspices the United States intervened in both Lebanon and Jordan in 1958. The negative responses by the United States to the Arabist trend in the Middle East and U.S. interventions convinced some that the United States was a conservative power wedded to the status quo. Throughout the 1960s the military-based republican governments in the Middle East tended to turn to the Soviet Union or the Eastern bloc for assistance.

In June 1967 a swift preemptive strike by Israel destroyed the Egyptian Air Force on the ground and initiated a new Arab-Israeli War, which ended in a stunning Israeli victory. The outcome was seen as a terrible defeat by the entire Arab world, and it created a new wave of misery for the Palestinians of the West Bank and Gaza, who now passed under direct Israeli military rule. The war demonstrated conclusively to the Arab world the unshakeable U.S. support for Israel over the interests of the Palestinians.

The 1967 Arab defeat had far-reaching effects. It encouraged the growth of radical movements who were opposed to the existing Arab governments and willing to engage in acts of terrorism and airline hijackings outside the region. It also discouraged moderate support for state-led Arabism. U.S. Middle East policy makers did not appear to appreciate the profound malaise in the region over the 1967 defeat.

From the early 1970s onward, the United States was forced to respond to dramatic changes in the configuration of power in the Middle East. In October 1973, Egypt, Syria, and Iraq launched a surprise attack on Israel. By the second week, Israeli forces had largely reversed early Arab successes, leaving Israel's military supplies heavily depleted. The U.S. government resupplied Israel, a move the Arab states deeply resented. In response, Arab members of the Organization of Petroleum Exporting Countries (OPEC), led by Saudi Arabia, cut back on oil production, quickly leading oil prices to quadruple. These policies stoked gathering inflation throughout the Western world, contributing to a major economic downturn that lasted throughout the 1970s. American inability to persuade OPEC, several of whose members were U.S. clients or allies, to moderate its policies contributed to a growing sense that American power was in decline. During the 1960s and 1970s, moreover, Arab states largely obtained control of their own oil industries, either, as with Saudi Arabia, through negotiations with American and other foreign firms or, where more radical states such as Libya or Iraq were concerned, through outright seizure and nationalization.

Developments in the late 1970s greatly disturbed the stability of overall U.S. strategy in the Middle East. A key American ally lost power, the shah of Iran, while Soviet military policies in Afghanistan and the Horn of Africa seemed to herald a menacing expansion of Soviet power in the region. Although Mohammad Reza Shah Pahlavi had tried to modernize his country, his authoritarian policies, persecution of opponents, and the social disruptions caused by his reforms eventually alienated many Iranians and were among the reasons why in late 1978 and early 1979 a large-scale Islamic revolution ended his rule and changed the entire basis of the government in Iran. In a surprising action, radical Iranian students stormed the U.S. embassy in Tehran on November 4, 1979, to protest past American support for the ousted shah, especially his admission to the United States for medical treatment. They captured 52 Americans and held them hostage. In April 1980 U.S. military forces mounted an ineffectual rescue attempt in which eight American servicemen died. The entire episode was widely regarded as a major national humiliation for the United States. The hostage crisis was not ended until the inauguration of Republican president Ronald Reagan in January 1981, when the Iranians released the hostages in return for a previously negotiated agreement that the U.S. government would unfreeze blocked Iranian economic assets.

In November 1979, another American ally was shaken when 500 armed Islamic fundamentalists seized the Grand Mosque of Mecca. They had hoped to capture King Khalid and his officials, who were supposed to have been at prayer, but instead many others were taken hostage. The incident showed that religious militancy was not confined to Iran, for the hostage takers led by Juhayman al-Utaybi refused to give up. Blood could not be shed in the Grand Mosque, but eventually a fatwa was issued that permitted the use of force. The official tally from the incident was 255 dead and another 560 injured before the Grand Mosque was secured.

In Afghanistan, meanwhile, in late December 1979 a Soviet-backed palace coup replaced one leftist president with another. Soviet ground forces and paratroopers promptly entered the country, the beginning of a decade-long war in which 15,000 Soviet troops and almost 1 million Afghans died. In addition, since 1977 many thousands of Soviet and Cuban troops had been stationed in Ethiopia, supporting that nation in a war with neighboring Somalia over the disputed Ogaden territory. Top American officials interpreted these developments as evidence of a systematic effort to enhance Soviet influence in territories bordering the Middle East and to take advantage of the regional destabilization caused by recent

events in Iran. These developments, together with skyrocketing oil prices and high inflation and unemployment, contributed to a growing sense of malaise and American impotence in international affairs.

President Jimmy Carter responded by proclaiming in his January 1980 State of the Union address that "business as usual" with the Soviet Union was no longer possible and that the United States would take all measures necessary to defend the Persian Gulf. The president moved to reinstitute containment policies, demanded annual 5 percent increases in military spending, proposed that young American men be compelled to register for a potential draft, and moved to create a Persian Gulf rapid deployment force. He also called for energy policies that would make the United States less dependent on foreign oil. Carter's speech, which effectively reiterated the 1957 Eisenhower Doctrine, also marked a definite break with his earlier efforts toward Soviet-American détente and disarmament, inaugurating several years of deep ideological and strategic antagonism between the two superpowers.

Throughout the 1980s the Carter and Reagan administrations provided substantial financial support and equipment for the Afghan mujahideen, a collection of Islamist resistance groups that conducted guerrilla warfare against occupying Soviet forces. The United States also offered neighboring Pakistan funding, logistical backing, and personnel to establish and run military training camps for the mujahideen. Pakistani special forces quietly took part in the war, and their British and American counterparts were also believed to be quietly involved. The war proved a lengthy, expensive, and ultimately unwinnable morass for the Soviet Union. In 1985 a new Soviet president, Mikhail Gorbachev, came to power. Gorbachev quickly moved to initiate new policies intended to moderate decades of Cold War hostilities and bring about rapprochement with Western powers. He removed Soviet forces from the Horn of Africa. In March 1988 he also announced that all Soviet forces would be withdrawn from Afghanistan within 12 months. Although Soviet forces left Afghanistan on schedule, bitter civil war continued in Afghanistan. In the later 1990s, the country fell under the control of the radical Islamic Taliban, which allowed it to become a haven for anti-Western Muslim terrorist groups.

Following the 1979 Islamic Revolution in Iran and ensuing U.S. embassy hostage crisis, relations between the United States and Islamic Iran remained hostile. The American government imposed an embargo on all commercial and financial dealings with Iran by U.S. citizens; air traffic was suspended; and most other contacts entirely or largely halted. In September 1980, President Saddam Hussein of Iraq began a major war against neighboring Iran, seeking to settle long-standing border disputes between the two states and to make Iraq the regional hegemon. The war soon stalemated, and for several years the two countries were bogged down in bloody stalemate. During this conflict, the United States leaned toward Iraq, and Hussein was able to purchase military supplies from the United States and other Western powers. In 1982 the United States normalized diplomatic relations with Iraq, which had been broken ever since the 1967 Arab-Israeli War. In 1987 and 1988, American naval forces in the Persian Gulf, deployed there in an effort to protect oil tankers from attack by either belligerent, skirmished repeatedly with Iranian vessels. In July 1988 an American cruiser, the *Vincennes*, shot down an Iranian passenger jet,

killing 290, an incident for which the U.S. government later paid Iran almost $132 million in compensation but never apologized.

American policy was nonetheless not entirely consistent. Officials in the Reagan administration, which had publicly stated that it would not pay any ransom to secure the return of American hostages, secretly offered to sell Iran badly needed weaponry. Any monies received were to be used to support operations by American-backed antigovernment Contra guerrillas in El Salvador, thereby evading a ban the U.S. Congress had recently imposed on the use of any American government funds for this purpose. The release of American hostages would also constitute part of the purchase price. After these dealings became public in late 1986, Reagan administration officials defended them on the grounds that their contacts and negotiations with relatively moderate Iranian officials had increased the probability that more conciliatory and less anti-American political forces would eventually come to power in Iran. The Iran-Contra scandal, as it became known, was nonetheless a major political embarrassment for the Reagan administration, casting doubt on its good faith and competence as well as its stated hard-line attitude on terrorism.

The Iran-Iraq War finally ended in 1988 with no decisive victory on either side. Both countries suffered heavy losses of manpower in a war each found economically debilitating and destructive. Believing that this step would not encounter serious opposition, in August 1990 Saddam Hussein sent his forces into, and annexed, neighboring Kuwait, a small, wealthy, and oil-rich state allied with the United States. Hussein's action alarmed other rich but militarily weak Arab states nearby, notably Saudi Arabia. This was the first major international crisis since the proclamation earlier that year of the ending of the Cold War between the Soviet Union and the United States. U.S. president George H. W. Bush was instrumental in forging an international coalition, including the NATO powers, Saudi Arabia, and Japan, committed to expelling Iraqi forces from Kuwait and in winning a UN resolution authorizing such action. Hussein attempted to win support from other Arab states by proclaiming his intention of attacking Israel should coalition forces invade, but only the Palestine Liberation Organization (PLO) supported his efforts. Launched in January 1991, Operation DESERT STORM ended quickly and successfully as Hussein's troops were swiftly driven from Kuwait and pushed back into Iraqi territory.

Bush and his advisers soon decided to halt the invasion of Iraq, however, as they did not wish to deal with the challenges that overthrowing Hussein was likely to bring in its train, and they therefore left the weakened dictator in power but subject to confining UN sanctions and restrictions. Although the United States directly encouraged separatist Kurds in northern Iraq and Shiite Muslims in the south to rise up against Hussein's regime, they received no support from coalition forces, and Hussein's military brutally suppressed the revolts, using poison gas against the Kurds and killing tens of thousands of rebels.

Addressing Congress shortly after the Persian Gulf War had ended, a triumphant Bush promised aid to the Middle East. He then proclaimed that the ending of the Cold War had made it possible for the UN to function as its founders had originally intended, so that there was a very real prospect of a new world order, one in which freedom and respect for human rights would find a home among all nations. Critics charged that Bush envisaged that the United States would use its unrivaled military and economic might to dominate the new world order in its own interests. During the 1990s, the principal focus of U.S. international policy was economic, as the American government concentrated on what was termed globalization, liberalizing trade and investment practices and promoting the spread of free market norms.

President William (Bill) Clinton made energetic although only partially successful efforts to reach a permanent resolution of the Palestinian-Israeli impasse, but otherwise, the Middle East attracted only sporadic attention. Despite criticism from humanitarian organizations, throughout the 1990s UN sanctions on significant trade with Iraq remained in place, although a program whereby Iraqi oil was exchanged for food was eventually initiated. British and American warplanes bombed potential military targets and enforced no-fly zones in southern and northern Iraq, permitting the Kurds there to enjoy virtual autonomy.

With the ending of the Cold War, the overarching principle of American foreign policy could no longer, as in the past four decades, be the containment of communism. The Reagan administration saw a new enemy in radical Islam.

Harvard University political scientist Samuel P. Huntington claimed global conflict was inevitable. Basing his ideas on those of historian Bernard Lewis, he suggested that international fault lines would now correspond with differing belief and value systems, such as the Western Judeo-Christian tradition, Islam, and Confucianism, and that major clashes among these civilizations must be anticipated. Many unfamiliar with the Middle East belatedly seized on Huntington's thesis following the events of September 11, 2001.

An Islamic revival had, meanwhile, shaken the Arab world, fueled in part by the shock of the defeat at the hands of Israel in 1967 but also driven by the failure of nationalist non-Islamist movements. The Islamic Revolution in Iran in 1979 was simultaneously Islamist and nationalist. The new Iranian leader, Ayatollah Ruhollah Khomeini, was hostile to the United States because he and many other Iranians feared that the United States might intervene to reverse the revolution. Certainly the U.S. government opposed the concept of an Islamic government, characterizing it as a medieval theocracy. In Afghanistan, however, throughout the 1980s equally conservative Muslim mujahideen guerrilla forces battling the Russian occupiers received substantial American economic and military aid, which came to an end once the Soviets had left.

During the 1990s, Islamic rebels battled Russian rule in Chechnya, but partly due to the failure to reach a comprehensive Israeli-Palestinian settlement, something many Muslims believed was primarily due to American bias toward Israel, militant Islamic antagonism focused increasingly on the United States. As the Soviet-Afghanistan War wound down in the late 1980s, certain Islamic mujahideen groups involved in that conflict founded a new organization known as al-Qaeda; its objective was to continue the jihad, or holy war, on other fronts. The most prominent figure in this group, Osama bin Laden, who came from a wealthy Saudi family, used his own financial resources to support its undertakings and could also tap heavily into other Arab sources of funds.

Official Saudi support for American operations during the 1991 Persian Gulf War deeply angered bin Laden, who deployed his organization not just against the United States but also against the Saudi government and other Middle Eastern nations, including Egypt, who were close American associates.

Bin Laden issued public proclamations, or fatwa, demanding the expulsion of all foreign troops from Islamic lands and the overthrow of Middle Eastern governments that acquiesced in their presence. Al-Qaeda personnel, expelled from Saudi Arabia, found refuge first in Sudan and then in Afghanistan, where a radical Islamic regime, the Taliban, took power in 1996. During the 1990s al-Qaeda claimed responsibility for several terrorist assaults on prominent American targets at home and overseas, including a 1993 truck bomb attack on the World Trade Center in New York; simultaneous 1998 car bombings of U.S. embassies in Kenya, Nairobi, and Dar es Salaam, Tanzania; and a 2000 suicide attack on the American destroyer USS *Cole* in Yemen. In response, the Clinton administration declared al-Qaeda a terrorist organization, and in summer 1998 reacted to the embassy bombings with air strikes on al-Qaeda training camps in Sudan and Afghanistan.

In January 2001, President George W. Bush, eldest son of the president who had launched the first Gulf War, took office. In the areas of diplomacy and defense, Bush appointed numerous top officials associated with a predominantly Republican think tank venture, the New American Century project. Many of these individuals, including Bush's influential vice president, Richard B. Cheney, a former secretary of defense, believed that the United States had been mistaken in not overthrowing Saddam Hussein in 1991 and had publicly called on Clinton, Bush's predecessor, to drive the Iraqi president from power. They argued that Hussein, who in 1998 expelled UN inspectors charged with monitoring his weapons programs, was determined to regain regional hegemony by developing chemical, biological, and nuclear weapons of mass destruction (WMD). Since these ambitions posed a long-term threat to U.S. strategic interests, New American Century affiliates argued that their country would be morally and legally justified in taking preemptive action to overthrow him and preclude this potential danger.

The Bush administration also sought to prevent Iran from developing nuclear weapons, an ambition clearly cherished by the Iranian government, which, though now rather more secular in character than during most of the 1980s and 1990s, was nonetheless decidedly anti-American. Initially, the Bush administration accorded combating international terrorism a much lower priority.

The events of September 11, 2001, when two dozen Arab Islamic extremists associated with al-Qaeda hijacked four American airliners and used these to launch suicide attacks on the World Trade Center towers in New York and the Pentagon in Washington, D.C., brought a dramatic change, as the president publicly declared an expansive Global War on Terror. Al-Qaeda claimed responsibility for the attacks, in which almost 3,000 civilians died, giving the American public a novel sense of vulnerability to terrorist threats. Bush called on the Taliban government of Afghanistan, which had provided bases and training camps for thousands of al-Qaeda operatives, to surrender bin Laden and his top advisers, but Mullah Mohammed Omar, the Afghan leader, refused as this would violate tribal and Islamic ethics. In October 2001, the United States and Britain, in collaboration with the forces of anti-Taliban Afghan Northern Alliances warlords, began military hostilities against Afghanistan. By the end of the year they had overthrown the Taliban government and driven al-Qaeda into the rugged mountains of the Afghan-Pakistan border, although coalition forces failed to capture bin Laden.

Afghan representatives subsequently held a traditional Loya Jirga assembly, which chose a Pashtun aristocrat, Hamid Karzai, as Afghanistan's new president. The new leader publicly committed his country to democracy and sought to implement wide-ranging social and economic reforms. Militarily, his regime nonetheless remained heavily dependent on British and American troops, and its authority did not extend far beyond Kabul, the Afghan capital. In 2006 a resurgence by Taliban forces threatened to destabilize the country, a development that many observers blamed on the failure of the U.S. government to concentrate on winning complete victory in Afghanistan. As the last year of Bush's presidential term began, the situation in Afghanistan remained precarious, with many expecting further Taliban territorial gains. One plausible explanation for the diversion of American resources from Afghanistan was the eagerness of the Bush administration at all costs to return to its earlier agenda and launch a second war against Iraq, which began in 2003.

Throughout 2002 Bush administration officials made the case that Iraq represented the greatest and most pressing international threat to American interests, making it vital to overthrow Saddam Hussein before he could inflict long-term strategic damage on the United States. In his January 2002 State of the Union address, the president proclaimed that the three most dangerous external enemies for the United States were Iraq, Iran, and North Korea, who, he declared, constituted an "axis of evil." With support from British prime minister Tony Blair but over strong opposition from such long-term European allies of the United States as France and Germany, and to great skepticism from Russia and China, the Bush administration pressured the UN Security Council to endorse resolutions stating that Iraqi weapons programs had equipped that country with formidable armaments whose possession put it in breach of earlier UN demands and constituted ample justification for an outside invasion designed to topple Hussein's government. UN weapons inspectors failed to unearth any quantities of such weaponry and many foreign governments doubted whether Iraq actually held appreciable stockpiles of banned armaments. Subsequent revelations suggested that Bush and his top advisers, together with their British counterparts, doctored intelligence reports to make it appear that Iraq had acquired far more in the way of stored weapons and production capabilities than was really the case. Supporters of an invasion, notably Vice President Cheney, also claimed that close ties existed between al-Qaeda and other terrorist organizations and Hussein, alleging that the Iraqi president had in some way been involved in the September 11, 2001, attacks. No information tied the Iraqi president to these attacks and al-Qaeda links were at best tenuous.

Ignoring all internal and external protests and misgivings, the Bush administration eventually proclaimed its determination to move unilaterally against Iraq even if it proved impossible to obtain a UN resolution specifically authorizing this undertaking.

Leading American supporters of war within the administration, notably Paul Wolfowitz, deputy secretary of defense, believed in addition that an invasion of Iraq would give the United States an ideal opportunity to remake the entire Middle East. From this perspective, war against Iraq came to seem almost a magic bullet, an exercise in transformational diplomacy that would recast the whole region. They argued that, by removing Hussein and replacing him with a democratic government, one

that would bring Iraq the benefits of peace, prosperity, and economic development, the United States would encourage the contagious democratization of all the remaining Middle East. The belief was that the creation of a progressive, stable, flourishing, and affluent Iraq would so impress other states in the region that they would, practically automatically, seek to establish similar governmental systems themselves, almost painlessly inaugurating a benign era of American-led peaceable economic growth and forward-looking social development throughout the Middle East.

On March 20, 2003, an American-led allied coalition force, to which the British contributed by far the second most sizable contingent, launched a full-scale invasion of Iraq. Military victory was quickly attained, as coalition forces took Baghdad and other major Iraqi cities and toppled statues of Hussein. Major looting and disorder marred the allied triumph, an early indication that coalition forces might have more trouble maintaining civil control than they did winning battles. On May 1, 2003, Bush declared an end to major combat, standing on an American aircraft carrier deck before a banner declaring, "Mission Accomplished." In December 2003, American forces finally captured Hussein, who eventually stood trial and was executed three years later.

U.S. officials soon discovered, however, that it was far easier to overthrow Hussein's government than to restore peace, order, and stability to Iraq, let alone to establish a democratic government capable of exercising authority and acceptable to all parties in Iraq. Deep ethnic, religious, and political fissures divided the country. While Hussein's regime had been largely secular in outlook, his rule had relied primarily on the country's Sunni Muslim element, while the majority of the Iraq population, who were Shia Muslims, had been largely excluded from power. In addition, the Kurds of the north sought autonomy, if not outright independence, and had no wish to be controlled by a government based in Baghdad, the Iraqi capital. In mid-2003 occupying forces disbanded the largely Sunni armed forces, so that by default much power on the ground was exercised by various militia groupings, predominantly Shiite but also Sunni organizations. For several years, large areas of Iraq were in a state of virtual civil war, characterized by suicide bombing attacks against military, civilian, and religious targets, murders, kidnappings, and torture. No foreigners, whether soldiers or civilians, could count on being personally secure, nor could any Iraqis, even in the supposedly most protected areas of Baghdad.

The toll of Iraqi dead and injured was exponentially higher than the casualty figures for the coalition forces, but even those continued to rise inexorably, belying official U.S. claims of success. Only 138 U.S. soldiers were killed in Iraq before Bush declared the end of major combat; by the end of 2009, the dead numbered 4,370.

What was supposed to be a splendid little war, bringing maximum results at minimum costs, swiftly metamorphosed into a grim quagmire, and it became ever more unclear how the United States could extricate itself from this entanglement. A brief moment of optimism after December 2005, when elections were held in Iraq under the political constitution accepted earlier that year, quickly dissipated, as it became clear that members of most ethnic groups had voted for candidates from their own groups and Iraq remained bitterly politically divided, with no genuine consensus emerging among the competing parties. Violence escalated, and the government of Prime Minister Nuri al-Maliki was widely perceived as lacking the strength and authority to control and pacify the country.

Bush administration officials alleged that al-Qaeda units had infiltrated into Iraq and charged the Syrian and Iranian governments with supporting Shiite militia forces within Iraq in an effort to promote their own political influence in the country. As casualties continued to rise, with no convincing exit strategy in sight, popular support for the war fell dramatically among the American public and politicians, and in the November 2006 midterm elections George W. Bush's Republican Party lost control of both houses of Congress.

Media revelations, illustrated with dramatic photographs and video footage, that American soldiers had savagely abused Iraqi captives held in Abu Ghraib prison and other facilities, circulated widely around the world, discrediting the Bush administration's claims that the Iraqi intervention was designed to uphold human rights and other liberal principles. Throughout the Arab and Muslim world, distrust and antagonism toward the United States soared dramatically. More broadly, the tactics the U.S. government embraced in pursuit of the Global War on Terror inflicted enormous damage on the country's international reputation.

Massive antiwar demonstrations occurred across Europe and in much of Asia. Even states that had been allies of the United States began to reconsider their support for the war. Several nations that had initially been part of the American-led international coalition and that had intervened in Iraq withdrew or reduced their forces. In Spain, the new government that won elections in March 2004, shortly after 191 Spaniards died and almost 2,000 were injured in terrorist bombings of train stations in Madrid, quickly announced that all Spanish troops would leave Iraq. The Labour politician Gordon Brown, who replaced the strongly prowar Tony Blair as British prime minister in July 2007, likewise embarked on a program of gradual British troop withdrawals.

By then, the U.S. government had announced a new strategy in Iraq. In December 2006, an independent bipartisan commission headed by James A. Baker III, former secretary of state during the first Iraq war, issued a report urging that the United States should seek to stabilize the situation in Iraq. Its recommendations included increasing temporarily American military forces in Iraq, allowing Iraqi civilian and military officials and forces to take increasing responsibility for running the country themselves, providing greater aid for training and equipment that would enhance their ability to do so, leaving occupying forces only in support roles, and working in collaboration with the UN, the European Union, and other regional governments, including those of Saudi Arabia, Iran, and Syria, to restore and maintain order in Iraq. The Baker Report also urged a renewed effort to bring about a permanent Palestinian-Israeli peace settlement, a recommendation that Bush and Secretary of State Condoleezza Rice sought to implement in late 2007 and early 2008.

The Bush administration did announce a troop surge in January 2007, and by the end of that year the military situation in Iraq had immensely improved, as moderate Shiite and Sunni forces began to gain some authority, so that full-scale civil war seemed less probable. In general, violence and suicide bombings had decreased by late 2008 but unfortunately resumed in the spring of 2009. The situation improved throughout 2010 and 2011. President Barak Obama vowed to remove remaining combat troops by the end of 2011. Although the al-Maliki government wished to have at least some forces remain, he failed to reach a status of forces agreement with the United States, and the last troops left in December 2011.

Close cooperation with Iran, the region's most substantial Shiite Muslim power, whose relative strength was much enhanced by the weakening of neighboring Iraq and Afghanistan, its former rivals and counterweights, proved more problematic. Ever since taking office, Bush administration officials had sought to prevent Iran from developing nuclear weapons but had only succeeded in obtaining ambiguous commitments from Iranian president Mahmoud Ahmadinejad. In July 2007, the U.S. Congress passed resolutions condemning covert Iranian military involvement in Iraq, authorizing the use of American force against Iran if deemed necessary to halt its nuclear program. Such strained relations rather precluded close Iranian cooperation with the United States and its allies over Iraq. U.S. ambassador to Iraq Zalmay Khalilzad (2005–2007) encouraged communication between Iraq and Iran, for he believed that the two neighbors could deal productively with such issues at border disputes and pilgrim traffic to Islam's holy cities. Afghan president Hamid Karzai has also said that his government is seeking a positive relationship with Iran, and he has requested that the United States not involve Afghanistan in its anti-Iran policies.

As the American presidential elections approached ever closer in 2008, Middle Eastern policy was in flux. The situation was yet further complicated in the last days of December 2007 by the assassination of former Pakistani prime minister Benazir Bhutto, who recently returned to her country after a decade of exile to contest impending democratic elections there. In Pakistan, a military government headed by former army chief President Pervez Musharraf had held power since 1999. After September 11, 2001, the U.S. government had dropped its earlier objections to Musharraf's authoritarian regime, and Pakistan had become a leading ally in the Global War on Terror, especially with U.S. efforts to extirpate al-Qaeda and its leaders.

Militant Muslim elements nonetheless enjoyed substantial political influence in much of Pakistan and were believed to be responsible possibly with the connivance of some Pakistani security officials for Bhutto's death. Following her assassination, riots and disorder convulsed much of Pakistan, bringing fears that a major American ally and regional strategic partner was itself in serious jeopardy of destabilization. Soaring oil prices added still another twist, since a large proportion of the world's petroleum reserves were located in the Middle East. In January 2008 Bush appealed to Saudi Arabia to use its influence in OPEC to reduce the cost of oil, but the response of Saudi officials was unenthusiastic.

As top U.S. politicians competed for the Republican and Democratic presidential nominations in 2008, their preferred strategies for approaching the Middle Eastern situation and especially the still-continuing American occupation of both Iraq and Afghanistan remained somewhat vague and unspecific. Most American presidential candidates stated that they sought the withdrawal of most if not all American troops from Iraq and Afghanistan but that they would endeavor to accomplish this objective while leaving governments friendly to the United States in power in those countries, so as to safeguard American interests there.

The Barack Obama administration announced in early 2009 that it would send thousands of additional troops to Afghanistan, an indication that U.S. and NATO operations in that country would intensify in the near future. The situation in Iraq has greatly stabilized, but the Obama administration admits that even when most U.S. forces are eventually withdrawn, a residual force of several thousand will remain indefinitely.

Priscilla Roberts

See also: Bush, George Walker; Bush Doctrine; Hussein, Saddam; Iraqi Freedom, Operation

Further Reading

Brands, H. W. *Into the Labyrinth: The United States and the Middle East 1945–1993*. New York: McGraw-Hill, 1994.

Cooley, John K. *Payback: America's Long War in the Middle East*. Washington, DC: Brassey's, 1991.

Goode, James F. *The United States and Iran: In the Shadow of Musaddiq*. New York: St. Martin's, 1997.

Hart, Parker T. *Saudi Arabia and the United States: Birth of a Security Partnership*. Bloomington: Indiana University Press, 1998.

Knights, Michael. *Cradle of Conflict: Iraq and the Birth of Modern U.S. Military*. Annapolis, MD: Naval Institute Press, 2005.

Lesch, David W. *The Middle East and the United States: A Historical and Political Reassessment*. New York: Perseus, 2006.

Painter, David S. *Oil and the American Century: The Political Economy of the U.S. Foreign Oil Policy, 1941–1954*. Baltimore: Johns Hopkins University Press, 1986.

Salt, Jeremy. *The Unmaking of the Middle East: A History of Western Disorder in Arab Lands*. Berkeley: University of California Press, 2008.

Yergin, Daniel. *The Prize: The Epic Quest for Oil, Money, and Power*. New York: Simon and Schuster, 1993.

U.S. National Elections of 2004

The 2004 U.S. national elections selected a president and vice president as well as members of both the U.S. House of Representatives and the Senate. In large measure, the elections were seen as a litmus test for the incumbent George W. Bush administration and its handling of foreign and national security policy, particularly the Global War on Terror and the Iraq War, which had begun in March 2003. The Democratic field of potential nominees going into the 2004 primaries was unusually large. The contenders included former senator Carol Mosely Braun; retired general Wesley Clark; former governor Howard Dean; Senator John Edwards; former house minority leader Dick Gephardt; Senator Bob Graham; Senator John Kerry; Representative Dennis Kucinich; Senator Joseph Lieberman; and the Reverend Al Sharpton. Bush was not seriously challenged for the Republican Party nomination, so he remained the presumptive nominee during the entire campaign. Bush also decided to retain sitting vice president Dick Cheney as his running mate.

Former Vermont governor Howard Dean was an early favorite and front-runner, and his scathing denunciation of the 2003 Iraq invasion and the botched postwar occupation effort was the centerpiece of his campaign. He also ran as a populist, which gave him plenty of ammunition to attack the Bush administration's economic policies and its failure to alleviate serious problems in the American health insurance system. Dean, however, was perhaps too strident and too leftist for mainstream Democrats, and he faired poorly in the January 2004 Iowa caucus, finishing a distant third, behind Kerry (the winner) and Edwards (a close runner-up). As the primaries progressed into the late winter and early spring, the many Democratic hopefuls systematically dropped out of the race as Kerry won an impressive string of state primaries. By March, Kerry, a U.S. senator from Massachusetts, had all but sewn up his party's nomination.

In early July Kerry chose North Carolina senator John Edwards as his vice presidential running mate. Edwards had been a challenger for the presidential nomination and was a highly photogenic politician, although his experience in politics was relatively short-lived. The Democratic Convention went off without a glitch in Boston later in the month, and the two men emerged to begin their campaign against the Bush-Cheney ticket. It would prove to be a difficult fight.

Kerry's main election platform included opposition to the Iraq War, health care concerns, an uneven economy, and the evaporation of well-paying jobs in the United States. Kerry also accused the Bush administration of having tarnished the image of the United States abroad by its flawed rationale for war in Iraq and its prosecution of the Global War on Terror in the aftermath of the September 11, 2001, terror attacks. Bush, meanwhile, capitalized on his handling of the post–September 11 environment, arguing that his policies had kept the nation safe, the proof of which could be found in the fact that no other terrorist attacks had occurred since then. He strongly defended his decision to go to war in Iraq and claimed that getting rid of Iraqi dictator Saddam Hussein was an important component of the Global War on Terror. Both implicitly and explicitly, the Bush camp suggested that a United States under a Kerry presidency would be less safe both at home and abroad. Because the economy at that point was still relatively sound, Bush and Cheney defended their economic policies, which had included large tax cuts for wealthy Americans and soaring budget deficits.

Kerry and Edwards attempted to use the growing unpopularity of the Iraq War and Bush's sagging popularity to whip up antiwar sentiment, but they were never entirely successful. The war at that point was still supported by a majority of Americans, and the Republicans tried to turn the tables by suggesting that the nation should not change presidents in the midst of a war, especially when the alternative was portrayed as indecisive. The Bush campaign labeled Kerry as a "flip-flopper" and used the senator's own words against him, particularly Kerry's bizarre backpedal that claimed he had been "for the war before [he] was against it." The Bush campaign used character assassination and innuendo to try to convince voters that Kerry could not be trusted with issues such as national security and foreign policy. The Kerry campaign was sometimes slow to react to such attacks, and its responses were not entirely effective.

A series of damaging television ads that began running in the late summer of 2004 also hurt Kerry's campaign. Sponsored by a conservative group known as the Swift Boat Veterans for Truth, the ads were an attempt to denigrate Kerry's Vietnam War experience and cast serious doubt on his character and fitness to serve as president. The Bush campaign claimed that it had nothing to do with the ads, but it did nothing to disclaim them, either. Kerry did not respond quickly or forcefully enough to them, which made him appear weak and indecisive. By late September, the Republicans and other Kerry detractors had done a credible job of portraying him as an effete Massachusetts liberal who was not in the mainstream of U.S. politics.

Kerry scored well in the first presidential debate held on September 30, 2004. He came across as articulate, knowledgeable, likable, and decisive. Bush, on the other hand, who could never be accused of eloquence, came across as sullen, defensive, testy, and out of touch. His periodic scowls and body language did little to help his poor performance. Bush fared better in the last two debates, however.

In the end the nation was spared a repeat of the contentious outcome of the 2000 election, when Bush eked out a close but clear win in both the popular vote and the Electoral College. Bush captured 50.7 percent of the popular vote to Kerry's 48.3 percent. The Bush-Cheney ticket garnered 286 electoral votes, while Kerry-Edwards captured 251. In the House of Representatives, the Republicans picked up three additional seats, while the Democrats lost two. In the Senate, the Republicans picked up four new seats, and the Democrats lost four.

Just two years later, in the midterm 2006 congressional elections, however, the Republicans lost control of both houses of Congress. And by 2007, President Bush's approval rating dropped into the low 30 percent range, a rating only slightly higher than the lowest approval ratings notched by presidents Harry Truman (22 percent in 1952), Richard Nixon (24 percent in 1974), and Jimmy Carter (28 percent in 1979). Clearly, support of the Iraq War and the general direction of U.S. foreign and domestic policy slipped badly in the months after the 2004 elections.

Paul G. Pierpaoli Jr.

See also: Bush, George Walker; Kerry, John

Further Reading

O'Connor, Karen J., and Larry J. Sabato. *Essentials of American Government:*

Continuity and Change, 2004 Election Update. 6th ed. New York: Longman, 2005.

Sabato, Larry J. *Divided States of America: The Slash and Burn Politics of the 2004 Presidential Election.* New York: Longman, 2005.

Thomas, Evan. *Election 2004: How Bush Won and What You can Expect for the Future.* New York: PublicAffairs, 2005.

U.S. National Elections of 2008

The 2008 U.S. national elections built on the previous momentum of the Democratic Party, which had swept the off-year 2006 legislative elections by gaining control of both houses of Congress. The November 4, 2008, elections resulted in more Democratic seats gained in Congress and, more important, saw the election of Democrats Barack Obama and Joseph Biden to the presidency and vice presidency, respectively. Obama was the first African American to achieve the nation's highest office and was the first Democrat to sit in the White House since President Bill Clinton (1993–2001). The election was certainly one of the most important in U.S. political history, for not only did it shatter racial barriers, but it also resoundingly repudiated the Republican Party and witnessed massive voter turnout, especially among young voters, who cast their ballots overwhelmingly for the Obama/Biden ticket. Only the passage of time would tell the true magnitude of the election, but many pundits had already begun to speak of a fundamental realignment of political power in America, akin to those seen in 1896, 1932, and 1980.

Obama won the presidency by a comfortable margin over his Republican opponent, Senator John S. McCain III. He captured 52.9 percent of the popular vote compared to McCain's 45.7 percent. Obama's margin of victory in the Electoral College was even more impressive: 365 votes to McCain's 173. Obama carried every northeastern state from Minnesota and Iowa in the west to Maine and Virginia in the east. He also carried North Carolina and Florida in the South, two states that had recently trended Republican in presidential contests. In the far west, Obama carried California, Oregon, Washington, Nevada, Colorado, and New Mexico. McCain did well in the Deep South and in the sparsely populated states of the Plains and the West.

In Congress, Democrats increased their majorities in both the House and Senate. Republicans lost 21 seats, and the Democrats gained an equal number. This resulted in a total of 251 seats for the Democrats and 178 seats for the Republicans, giving the Democrats a 76-seat advantage. In the Senate, the Democrats increased their seats by 8, giving them 59 (including 2 independents who caucused with the Democrats). The Republicans lost 8 seats, holding just 41 after the elections. This gave the Democrats an 18-seat majority.

It is clear that many congressional Democrats rode into power on Obama's coattails, because public opinion polls just prior to the elections showed widespread and deep voter disapproval of Congress, which had been controlled by the Democrats since January 2007. Thus, the Democratic gains may well have had more to do with President George W. Bush's unpopularity and Obama's wide appeal than voter interest in Democratic congressional candidates per se.

Obama ran a masterful, nearly flawless campaign. It was tightly organized, almost always on message, and remarkably free of gaffes and slipups. But it was Obama's awe-inspiring money raising that made the biggest difference. His campaign managers harnessed the power of the Internet in ways that McCain never could. Most of the money raised was through small, individual, online contributions. When the election was over, Obama had heavily outspent his opponent and had raised more money than any political candidate in U.S. history.

Most lauded Obama's choice in August 2008 of longtime Democratic senator Joe Biden to be his running mate. Biden had run for the Democratic presidential nomination but had failed to garner sufficient support and had dropped out and thrown his support to Obama. In the Senate since the 1970s, Biden had much experience in Washington, knew the ins and outs of Congress, and filled in Obama's acknowledged lack of experience in foreign and military affairs.

McCain, who had become the presumptive nominee of his party well before Obama had secured his party's nomination, was also a Senate stalwart, having served in that capacity since 1987. A naval officer and Vietnam War hero, he had spent more than seven years as a prisoner of war (POW) and had endured significant torture. Few questioned his foreign policy or military bona fides, but his consistent support of the Iraq War hurt his chances among the many Americans who opposed the war. McCain's campaign was not well managed; it could not stay focused on key topics for very long, and McCain and others in his campaign were prone to verbal and political gaffes. His choice of the mostly unknown Sarah Palin as his vice presidential running mate likely handicapped his campaign, although it did garner intense media coverage, which up until Palin's nomination was dominated by the Obama candidacy. Palin's performance in news interviews dealing with her knowledge of foreign policy was comical. She projected no solid policy message other than the far-right Republican

values that alienated many Americans. Vice presidents may stay in the background, but with an older presidential candidate in John McCain, whose age and health were issues, Palin seemed more of a liability than an asset.

It is a noteworthy fact that as late as June or July 2008, both candidates had been focusing largely on the Iraq War, the Global War on Terror, the Afghan War, and other national security and foreign policy imperatives. All those subjects were seen as McCain strong suits. That began to change, quickly, in August and September. The U.S. economy began to deteriorate at a dizzying pace in the late summer and early fall, precipitated by an ongoing housing crisis, an emergent subprime mortgage fiasco, and a string of spectacular bank and investment house failures. The George W. Bush administration moved haltingly and clumsily to steady the economy but to little avail. Even a massive government stimulus package failed to stop the slide. As the stock market swooned, unemployment skyrocketed, and housing prices collapsed, many Americans were convinced that neither McCain nor the Republicans could be trusted to make things right. The economic crisis played into Obama's hands, and within weeks the campaign was focused not on the Iraq War or national security but on economic security. This helped both the Democratic Party at large and the Obama campaign in particular.

Obama's rise to power can be viewed as a combination of the novelty of his message, appeal to youth, sustained opposition to many of George W. Bush's foreign and domestic policies, obviously keen intellect and masterful speaking, and well-organized campaign, as well as the precipitous decline of the U.S. economy.

Obama had his work cut out for him for when he assumed office in 2009, the economy continued to move steadily downward. Ironically, an orderly withdrawal of U.S. forces from Iraq and shifting of emphasis to Afghanistan, which had been one of his early pledges, seemed comparatively easy compared to the intractable economic problems facing the nation.

Paul G. Pierpaoli Jr.

See also: Bush, George Walker; Obama, Barack Hussein, II; McCain, John Sidney, III

Further Reading

Ifell, Gwen. *Breakthrough: Politics and Rage in the Age of Obama*. New York: Doubleday, 2009.

Todd, Chick, and Sledon Gawiser. *How Barack Obama Won*. New York: Vintage, 2009.

USA Today Editors. *America Speaks: The Historic 2008 Election*. Chicago: Triumph Books/Random House, 2008.

U.S. Navy, Iraq War

Nearly uncontested by the Iraqi Navy, U.S. sea power functioned in a variety of roles in support of the ground offensive during Operation IRAQI FREEDOM. U.S. naval operations amply demonstrated the impact of enhanced interservice coordination and technological advancements made since the 1991 Persian Gulf War.

The U.S. Navy deployed five carrier battle groups headed by the *Theodore Roosevelt* (CVN-71), *Harry S. Truman* (CVN-75), *Kitty Hawk* (CV-63), *Abraham Lincoln* (CVN-72), and *Constellation* (CV-64) and three amphibious ready groups to join coalition forces that executed Operation IRAQI FREEDOM during March and April 2003. The *Nimitz* (CVN-68) battle group was already en route for a normal deployment as the Pentagon prepared for war. In total 63,000

sailors, 83,000 marines, 84 warships, and nearly 800 navy and marine aircraft participated in the conflict under the direction of Vice Admiral Timothy Keating of the U.S. Central Command (CENTCOM).

As hostilities commenced, Navy SEALS, in conjunction with British and Polish commandoes, seized Iraq's offshore oil platforms and key pumping stations. Mine-clearing operations, including the use of trained dolphins, opened the Khor Abd Allah waterway far enough to reach the port of Umm Qasr, which would prove critical in the distribution of humanitarian aid. Iraqi forces were unable to inflict any casualties through mines, suicide boats, or antiship missiles.

On the night of March 21, 2003, in keeping with the completely misguided plans to shock and awe the enemy with U.S. firepower, surface vessels and submarines fired nearly 400 Tomahawk cruise missiles into Iraq, targeting command and communications centers principally. By the end of the following month, more than 800 Tomahawks had been fired by U.S. naval assets. Los Angeles–class attack submarines supplied one-third of those strikes, in a display of their growing versatility in the post–Cold War era. With an independent, inertially guided navigation system and a range of up to 1,500 miles, the Tomahawk was an ideal weapon, providing excellent first-strike capability against radar and command and control facilities.

During the war, naval airpower reflected a revolution in efficiency and capability as navy and marine aircraft registered more than 13,000 sorties during March–April 2003. Practically all ordnance delivered was precision-guided, which has not been the case during Operation DESERT STORM. Indeed, nearly all naval aircraft could deploy inertial- and satellite-guided all-weather bombs with 2,000-pound payloads known as Joint Direct Attack Munitions (JDAMs). As with the other services, the Navy benefited from the growing use of unmanned aerial vehicles (UAVs) to downlink real-time video surveillance for targeting data.

Operations were further enhanced by the digitization of the air tasking order (ATO), which had previously been physically delivered to carriers to specify mission assignments. The Grumman EA-6B Prowler carried augmented self-protection jamming pods to facilitate its electronic warfare mission. The newest version of the McDonnell Douglas (now Boeing) F/A-18 Super Hornet was also available for combat use. Other navy and marine aircraft in theater included the Grumman F-14 Tomcat, Sikorsky CH-53 Sea Stallion, Boeing CH-46 Sea Knight, Grumman E-2C Hawkeye, McDonnell Douglas AV-8B Harrier, Sikorsky HH-60H Seahawk, and the Lockheed S-3 Viking.

Surface warfare operations also improved, thanks to the addition of a highly versatile platform. The Arleigh Burke–class of guided missile destroyers joined the Ticonderoga-class of cruisers in featuring the Aegis weapons system to upgrade the navy's long-range strike capability and air defense network. Their phased array radars provided rapid threat prioritization and the ability to track up to 100 targets simultaneously.

Spared much of a naval threat, maritime personnel in some cases performed beyond their typical parameters. For example, navy explosive ordnance disposal teams helped clear improvised explosive devices (IEDs) from Iraqi roadsides. The P-3 Orion patrol aircraft, long a mainstay of antisubmarine operations against the former Soviet Union, performed surveillance and intelligence gathering above Iraq.

As of the end of April 2003 there were 4 navy combat and noncombat deaths and 65 marine fatalities. Although the navy performed its missions admirably, planners noted several lessons learned in anticipating future conflicts. For instance, while carriers can substitute for air bases in regions where the United States has little forward presence, future designs will have to accommodate more planes and higher sortie rates. Also, several aircraft classes, including the F-14, EA-6B, E-2C, and S-3, are aging and/or have strenuous maintenance requirements. In addition, some sort of arsenal ship with long-range missile strike capability could obviate the need for slower bombers, such as the North American/Rockwell/ Boeing B-1B Lancer and Boeing B-52 Stratofortress, which could be vulnerable against an adversary with a more capable military.

Jeffrey D. Bass

See also: Iraqi Freedom, Operation, Coalition Naval Forces

Further Reading

Cordesman, Anthony H. *The Iraq War: Strategy, Tactics, and Military Lessons.* Westport, CT: Praeger, 2003.

Keegan, John. *The Iraq War: The Military Offensive, from Victory in 21 Days to the Insurgent Aftermath.* New York: Vintage, 2005.

Murray, Williamson, and Robert H. Scales Jr. *The Iraq War: A Military History.* Cambridge, MA: Belknap, 2005.

U.S. Special Operations Command

Unified command responsible for the conduct of all unconventional warfare missions undertaken by the U.S. military. U.S. Special Operations Command (USSOCOM) was activated on June 1,

1987, and is headquartered at MacDill Air Force Base, Florida. It is one of the 10 unified commands in the U.S. military structure.

USSOCOM was established in response to the failure of Operation EAGLE CLAW, the 1980 attempt to free Americans taken hostage from the U.S. embassy in Tehran by Iranian revolutionaries. The preparations for and execution of EAGLE CLAW were impeded by serious problems with cross-service command and control, coordination, funding, and training. Action analysis of the failed operation led to the establishment of the Special Operations Advisory panel and the 1st Special Operations Command in 1982. In 1983, further movement to consolidate Special Operations Forces (SOF) was led by Senator Barry Goldwater (R-Ariz.). By 1984 the U.S. Congress created the Joint Special Operations Agency, but it had no operational control. Later in 1984 Senator Sam Nunn (D-Ga.), Senator William Cohen (R-Maine), and Representative Dan Daniel (D-Va.) convinced Congress to take a more active role.

Over the next two years Congress studied the uses and funding of SOF. Senators Nunn and Cohen introduced a bill calling for a joint military operation for SOF and an office within the Department of Defense to oversee it. This organization was to be commanded by a four-star general. The Nunn-Cohen Act was signed into law in October 1986. With the dissolution of the U.S. Readiness Command, USSOCOM was created and approved for operations by President Ronald Reagan on April 13, 1987.

The first commander in chief special operations command (USCINCSOC) was General James J. Lindsay, who served from 1987 to 1990. He was followed by General Carl W. Stiner (1990–1993), General Wayne A. Downing (1993–1996), General Henry H. Shelton (1996–1997), General Peter J.

Schoomaker (1997–2000), General Charles R. Holland (2000–2003), General Bryan D. Brown (2003–2007), and Admiral Eric T. Olsen (2007–present).

USSOCOM draws its manpower from all branches of the U.S. Armed Forces. Its two original members were the U.S. Army and the U.S. Navy. Army elements include the 75th Ranger Regiment, U.S. Army Special Forces, 160th Special Operations Aviation Regiment, 4th Psychological Operations Group (Airborne), 95th Civil Affairs Battalion (Airborne), and Special Operations Support Command (Airborne). Navy elements include SEALs, Special Warfare Combatant-Craft Crewman, and Seal Delivery Vehicle Teams. The U.S. Air Force special operations units came under USSOCOM in 1990, including the 1st Special Operations Wing, the 27th Special Operations Wing, the 352nd Special Operations Group, the 353rd Special Operations Group, the 919th Special Operations Wing (U.S. Air Force Reserve), and the 193rd Special Operations Wing (Air National Guard). In 2005, the Pentagon authorized the addition of U.S. Marine Corps elements to USSOCOM, which included the Marine Special Operations Battalion, Marine Special Operations Advisory Group, and Marine Special Operations Support Group.

To handle highly classified missions requiring swift action, possible hostage rescue, and counterterrorism, USSOCOM also contains the Joint Special Operations Command consisting of 1st Special Forces Operational Detachment–Delta, Naval Special Warfare Development Group, Intelligence Support Activity, and 24th Special Tactics Squadron. Each service maintains its own command and training regime.

Since its inception, USSOCOM has played a major role in U.S. military actions.

It provided forces for the safe navigation of the Persian Gulf (Operation EARNEST WILL) and the capture of Panamanian president Manuel Noriega (Operation JUST CAUSE). As world attention shifted more to the Middle East, USSOCOM again was asked to lead the way. For Operation DESERT STORM, SOF led the invasion of Iraq with strategic intelligence and by locating Scud missile sites. In the Global War on Terror, SOF and USSOCOM have won more battles, ranging from overthrowing the Taliban in Afghanistan to leading the search for al-Qaeda leader Osama bin Laden, to providing counterterrorism operations in Iraq.

Shawn Livingston

See also: SEAL Teams

Further Reading

Brown, Bryan D. Dugg. "U.S. Special Operations Command: Meeting the Challenges of the 21st Century." *Joint Force Quarterly* 40 (2006): 38–43.

Clancy, Tom, Carl Stiner, and Tony Koltz. *Shadow Warriors: Inside the Special Forces*. New York: Berkley Books, 2003.

United States Special Operations Command History: 20 (1987–2007) Proven in the Past, Vigilant Today, Prepared for the Future. MacDill Air Force Base, FL: U.S. Special Operations Command, 2007.

Zimmerman, Dwight Jon, and John Gresham. *Beyond Hell and Back: How America's Special Operations Forces Became the World's Greatest Fighting Unit*. New York: St. Martin's, 2007.

V

Vehicles, Unarmored

Unarmored vehicles have played a major role in the transport of troops and in other logistical functions since the introduction of the internal combustion engine in the years before the beginning of World War I. The nations involved in the 1991 Persian Gulf War, the 2001 invasion of Afghanistan, and the 2003 Iraq War employed a range of such vehicles. Many models were slightly modified versions of vehicles available on the commercial market, while others were designed and purpose-built to military specifications.

Unarmored military vehicles were divided into five broad categories. First, all countries used some form of light reconnaissance vehicle based loosely on the four-wheel drive U.S. Jeep. These scout vehicles were capable of high speed and could carry four to six soldiers or a small amount of cargo. They could also be armed with machine guns or light antitank or antiaircraft weapons. Second, there were light cargo trucks, which typically had the capacity to carry up to 2.5 tons cross-country or twice that load on improved roads. These were often six-wheeled and had the ability to carry either troops or cargo. Third, there were medium cargo trucks that had the ability to move up to 5 tons and were usually six-to-eight wheeled. Fourth, there were the heavy cargo trucks, which could handle more than 7 tons, and carry tanks and other armored and tracked vehicles. Heavy trucks were typically six-to-10 wheeled. Fifth, and

finally, there was a range of specialized vehicles that included ambulances, amphibious vehicles, water carriers, and communications vehicles.

Like other nations in the Middle East, Iraq utilized the UAZ 69 (also commonly known as the GAZ 69), the popular Russian version of the venerable U.S. Jeep. The UAZ 69 was a four-wheel drive vehicle that came in several models, including a 1.25-ton version for light cargo. It performed well off road and in the region's desert terrain. Iraq utilized a variety of foreign-made transport and supply trucks. Many of these were customized to adapt to the heat and harsh climate of the area. However, Iraq did not have the variety of specialized unarmored vehicles that Western countries typically possessed. When Iraqi forces over-ran Kuwait in August 1990, they captured a number of Kuwaiti vehicles, including the British-made Cargocat. The 1.5-ton vehicle was specifically designed for the desert, and Iraqi forces confiscated scores for their use.

During the Persian Gulf War, coalition air superiority allowed the U.S.-led allies to effectively target and destroy much of Iraq's transport capability. Approximately half of Iraq's unarmored military vehicles were destroyed during the war. After the Persian Gulf War, sanctions prevented Iraq from acquiring new vehicles or parts for their existing fleet. Consequently, the military's transport arm was seriously eroded as soldiers were forced to cannibalize vehicles for replacement parts. The result was that

Iraq's transport arm had limited capabilities prior to the Iraq War, and those assets were degraded quickly once combat began as trucks and other vehicles were targeted by coalition aircraft, drones, and ground units. Once the Saddam Hussein regime fell in April 2003, Iraqi insurgents increasingly utilized civilian vehicles, especially four-wheel drive pickup trucks, to conduct quick attacks on coalition forces. However, the vehicles proved vulnerable to ground fire and were easy to track; insurgents therefore shifted tactics by using roadside bombs and other improvised explosive devices (IEDs).

The Taliban initially used a broad assortment of unarmored vehicles, including Soviet-era trucks and civilian vehicles pressed into military service, often with improvised armaments. During Operation ENDURING FREEDOM, allied aircraft and ground units were able to effectively destroy most of the Taliban's ground transport. Unmanned aerial drones were increasingly deployed after the fall of the Taliban in December 2001 to monitor vehicle traffic and to undertake attacks. By the 2003 winter campaigns motorcycles had become an increasingly important vehicle for the Taliban and other insurgents concurrent with the change in tactics related to increased terrorist strikes, including bombings and targeted assassinations.

The United States and its allies employed general-purpose and highly specialized vehicles in both Iraq and Afghanistan. At the heavy end of the spectrum were vehicles such as the U.S. M-1070 Heavy Equipment Transport System (HETS). This behemoth weighed more than 41,000 tons and with its trailer could handle a payload of 140,000 pounds, including hauling the M-1 Abrams main battle tank.

In addition to general cargo and transport trucks, the United States employed the High-Mobility Multi-Purpose Wheeled Vehicle (commonly known as the Humvee or Hummer). These four-wheel drive vehicles were much larger than the M-151 model Jeeps they replaced. They had a 2.5-ton load capacity, could carry up to eight troops in addition to a two-person crew, and had a range of 300 miles. Humvees could be armed with several weapons systems, including light or heavy machine guns, antitank and antiaircraft missiles, and small howitzers. They could also be lightly armored. Humvees had excellent climbing capabilities, and they could traverse grades of more than 25 degrees and ford water more than two feet deep. They also proved quite reliable in the desert. The United States eventually deployed more than a dozen different Humvee models. During the Persian Gulf War, the United States used approximately 20,000 Humvees, and in the Iraq War, it deployed more than 10,000 of them, making the Humvee the most widely used U.S. vehicle in both conflicts.

The British version of the Humvee was the Land Rover 90 or the 110 (later succeeded by the Defender and then the "Snatch" Land Rover, which was lightly armored). The Land Rovers came in a variety of models, and like the Humvee could be armed and configured to undertake a variety of roles. The smaller wheelbase of some of the Land Rovers made them better suited to urban combat, especially during the Iraq War and the Iraqi insurgency (some U.S. units, including special operations forces, used the Land Rovers instead of the Humvees).

While the Humvees, Land Rovers, and other unarmored vehicles performed well in the initial phases of combat in both Iraq wars and in Afghanistan, the increasing use of IEDs revealed substantial problems with the vehicles. Insurgents in Afghanistan and Iraq quickly realized that the unarmored vehicles were vulnerable to mines, IEDs, and shoulder-fired rocket-propelled grenade (RPG) launchers. Unarmored transport and supply vehicles were particularly vulnerable to mines and IEDs, but, because of their extensive use, Humvees and other light vehicles were the most common targets of insurgent attacks.

Through 2008, more than 1,500 Humvees had been destroyed or seriously damaged in Afghanistan and Iraq, with more than 400 U.S. service personnel killed in the attacks (almost 10 percent of total casualties). Among the British in Afghanistan and Iraq, casualties from attacks on Land Rovers accounted for one-eighth of total casualties. Land Rovers had less off-road capability than their U.S. counterparts, especially in the mountainous terrain of Afghanistan, and this forced them to remain on roads more frequently.

The U.S. and British governments were criticized for reacting too slowly to improve the armor and other protection afforded troops in light vehicles. In 2004, coalition allies in both theaters began to increase the protection in unarmored vehicles. Many troops improvised, adding ad hoc light armor to their vehicles by welding plates on the exterior or by attaching Kevlar vests to the surface areas of the Humvee. Such modifications seriously eroded the capabilities of the vehicles, as the engines and suspensions were not designed for the extra weight. The United States began reinforcing Humvees in theater with the FRAG Kit 5, which added additional armor to the door and floors of the vehicles with minimal performance sacrifices. Meanwhile, the Department of Defense dramatically increased its purchases and deployments of lightly armored versions of the Humvees, ordering an additional 2,000 of the armored models. The lightly armored Humvees weighed about 1,000 pounds more than their older counterparts and required a more powerful engine (and at $180,000 each, cost about twice as much as the unarmored versions). These vehicles could withstand a small mine or IED up to about 12 pounds and provided marginally effective protection against small-arms fire. They were still extremely vulnerable to RPGs and larger mines or IEDs. Furthermore, insurgents began to use particularly powerful bombs with shaped charges that were dubbed explosively formed penetrators (EFPs), which could easily destroy lightly armored Humvees.

Concurrent with the effort to increase armor, U.S. defense officials also increased the deployment of anti-IED devices. Most of these systems involved electronic radio-frequency jammers to prevent the detonation of IEDs. In 2007 IED use peaked, with more than 2,800 devices either detonated by insurgents or discovered by coalition forces in Iraq. The United States and its allies in Afghanistan and Iraq have also begun to deploy more armored vehicles with capabilities similar to those of reconnaissance and light cargo or transport vehicles. Meanwhile, the United States has plans to upgrade and eventually replace the Humvee.

Tom Lansford

See also: IRAQI FREEDOM, Operation, Ground Campaign; U.S. Army, Iraq War

Further Reading

Bhatia, Michael, and Mark Sedra. *Afghanistan, Arms and Conflict: Armed Groups, Disarmament and Security in a Post-War Society.* New York: Routledge, 2008.

Cockburn, Patrick. *The Occupation: War and Resistance in Iraq.* New York: Verso, 2007.

Keegan, John. *The Iraq War: The Military Offensive, from Victory in 21 Days to the Insurgent Aftermath.* New York: Vintage, 2005.

Lacey, Jim. *Take Down: The 3rd Infantry's Twenty-One Day Assault on Baghdad.* Annapolis, MD: Naval Institute Press, 2007.

Murray, Williamson, and Robert H. Scales Jr. *The Iraq War: A Military History.* Cambridge, MA: Belknap, 2005.

Zucchino, David. *Thunder Run: The Armored Strike to Capture Baghdad.* New York: Grove, 2004.

Viking Hammer, Operation

Part of the March 2003 Anglo-American–led invasion of Iraq (Operation Iraqi Freedom), Operation Viking Hammer was an offensive waged from March 28 to March 30, 2003, in northern Iraq by anti–Saddam Hussein Kurds with the assistance of coalition special operations forces, against the Islamic terrorist group Ansar al-Islam.

The original planning for Operation Iraqi Freedom had called for a northern front, but when the Turkish government denied the coalition the use of its territory, planners had to shift strategy. Instead, they hoped to utilize pro-American militias of the Kurdish Regional Government. The latter was dominated by two groups, the Patriotic Union of Kurdistan (PUK), led by Jalal Talabani, and the Kurdistan Democratic Party (KDP), led by Masoud Barzani. The PUK's Peshmerga militias were the largest and best trained of the Kurdish forces.

In the months prior to the invasion, the United States had inserted special operations forces to train and coordinate with the Kurds. Coalition planners believed that a Kurdish military campaign would keep Iraqi units tied down in the northern regions of the country and therefore render them unavailable to fight the two main prongs of the invading forces, which would advance from the south. To support the Kurds, the coalition planned to deploy additional special operations forces. Later, airborne units would be dropped in to fight alongside the Peshmerga and KDP fighters in attacks on Iraqi targets, including the important cities of Mosul and Kirkuk. The plan was a bold endeavor that asked a small number of special operations forces, airborne troops, and Kurdish fighters to accomplish the same goals as 60,000 U.S. ground troops, namely tying down 13 Iraqi divisions.

The Kurds were apprehensive that they would be vulnerable to attacks by Islamic terrorist groups located along the border with Iran if they deployed their forces to the south. Viking Hammer was designed essentially to neutralize the threat to the Kurdish heartland. Viking Hammer and subsequent offensives were also an effort by the United States to demonstrate the country's commitment to the Kurds and ensure support from the Kurdish Regional Government in a postwar Iraq. However, the United States was concurrently trying to avoid further straining relations with Turkey, which faced an ongoing Kurdish separatist insurgency. Consequently, the United States chose not to supply the Peshmerga with extensive weaponry for fear that some might be used against Turkish forces.

Before the Peshmerga could engage the Iraqi forces, they had to first secure their own territory and suppress Ansar al-Islam, a Kurdish Sunni Islamist group. Ansar al-Islam was originally formed in 2001 by Islamist Kurdish factions. The group was dominated by Kurds who had fought against the Soviets in Afghanistan. Led by Mullah Krekar, Ansar al-Islam sought to impose a strict version of Sharia (Islamic law) on towns near the border with Iran, including Halabja, Biyara, and Tawela. It also worked with other smaller Islamist groups against the Kurdish Regional Government and was blamed for a number of terrorist attacks against rival Kurdish groups. Ansar al-Islam had approximately 500–600 fighters and controlled more than 100 square miles of territory. Its allies in the other small Islamist groups provided an additional 100–300 fighters to Ansar al-Islam. U.S. defense officials were especially concerned about Ansar al-Islam because of intelligence that the group was harboring senior al-Qaeda figures, information which was unfounded. The Peshmerga and KDP militias in Viking Hammer numbered approximately 7,000 troops of varying quality with an assortment of mainly Soviet-era weaponry, including mortars, some artillery, and a limited number of armored vehicles. Most were armed with AK-47s and had about 150–200 rounds apiece. Many lacked uniforms, boots, or helmets and instead wore tennis shoes and red scarves. However, the Kurds were highly motivated, and U.S. special operations forces provided the heavy firepower (including mortars, grenade launchers, and machine guns) and also had charge of communications between units. Most importantly, the U.S. personnel were able to coordinate ground support from coalition aircraft and cruise missiles.

There were approximately 600 U.S. soldiers from the 10th Special Forces Group with the PUK and KDP, organized into 12-member teams. U.S. colonel Charlie Cleveland was the operational commander of the covert U.S. troops. The special operations forces had previously staged in Romania and been given the code name Task Force Viking (which led, in turn, to the offensive's title, Viking Hammer). In Viking Hammer, the Kurdish offensive was led by 40 soldiers of the 3rd Battalion of the 10th Special Forces Group, commanded by Lieutenant Colonel Ken Tovo. Tovo divided his men into split teams; each 6-member group

worked with a Kurdish unit of 150–800 troops.

Ansar al-Islam and its allies had constructed a series of complexes on mountains and hilltops overlooking the valleys near Halabja, Iraq. The Kurds were apprehensive that any attack would leave them vulnerable to mortar and machine gun fire from the heights. U.S. personnel scouted the positions and pretargeted them for air strikes. On March 21, 2003, 64 cruise missiles hit Ansar al-Islam bunkers in a three-hour period. The pro-U.S. Kurds were impressed by the precision and power of the attack. About 100 members of the radical Islamic Group of Kurdistan, an ally of Ansar al-Islam, were killed in the strikes, and the remainder of the group surrendered the following morning. Another small Islamic group also surrendered before the main offensive commenced.

On March 28, the U.S.-Kurdish force began its attack at 6:00 a.m. The allies were divided into four groups, each led by a special forces team. The Ansar al-Islam fighters proved to be a tough and experienced foe, for they had the routes into the mountains covered with mortars, would fire a limited number of rounds, and then would move in an effort to avoid being targeted by U.S. spotters. Peshmerga artillery and mortars provided the opening salvos from the coalition forces. When the advance encountered its first organized resistance, air strikes were called in and two U.S. McDonnell Douglas/Boeing Navy F-18s dropped precision-guided 500-pound bombs on the Iraqi position. By 9:00 a.m., the Kurds had captured Gulp, the first significant village. Coalition forces found various weapons, including explosive suicide vests and bomb-making materials. The four teams had to assault and capture a series of bunkers and complexes under mortar fire and incoming rounds from

Katyusha rockets. Slowly, they moved into the mountains, using the heavy weapons and sniper fire of the special operations forces to engage enemy positions. The mountainous terrain impeded the ability of the U.S. troops to radio for air strikes, and the coalition forces had to rely on their own weapons and capabilities. U.S. snipers proved especially effective because of their long-range capabilities. By the afternoon, the combined forces had taken the strategic town of Sagrat, which had served as the headquarters of the senior Ansar al-Islam leaders. Around 5:00 p.m., the U.S. forces were able to regain radio contact and arrange air strikes on enemy positions. Once again, 500-pound precision-guided bombs were used.

Over the next two days, the U.S.-Kurdish force continued its advance. Much of the fighting involved attacks on enemy cave complexes. The coalition forces endeavored unsuccessfully to use tear gas to force the fighters from the caves. When that tactic failed, the U.S. forces used grenades and antitank missiles to destroy the cave bunkers. The Peshmerga forces did not have equipment to engage in night fighting, which limited the ability of the coalition forces to pursue Ansar al-Islam fighters. After the first day of combat, increasing numbers of the Islamic fighters were fleeing across the border into Iran. The Iranians reportedly disarmed the fighters but did not detain them. Some were forcibly returned across the border.

The U.S. forces were able to collect a considerable amount of intelligence on Ansar al-Islam and its links with al-Qaeda. In addition, the coalition forces found that almost half of the fighters killed or captured were foreign born and had come to Iraq to train for terrorist missions. On March 29, a U.S. team explored a suspected chemical weapons manufacturing and training facility in Sagrat. The team discovered instructions on the manufacture of chemical weapons; they also found chemical suits and traces of the highly toxic ricin.

Sporadic fighting continued until March 30, the day VIKING HAMMER officially ended. During the operation, 3 Peshmerga soldiers were killed and 23 were wounded. No U.S. personnel were killed or seriously wounded. Approximately 150–250 Ansar al-Islam fighters were killed, in addition to the 100 killed among the Islamic Group of Kurdistan. After VIKING HAMMER, the Kurdish forces moved south as part of the broader coalition northern offensive against the regular Iraqi Army. Ansar al-Islam reemerged after the fall of Saddam Hussein as one of the numerous groups in the anti-U.S. insurgency.

Tom Lansford

See also: IRAQI FREEDOM, Operation; Kirkuk; Kurds; Mosul

Further Reading

Gunter, Michael M. *The Kurds Ascending: The Evolving Solution to the Kurdish Problem in Iraq and Turkey.* New York: Palgrave Macmillan, 2008.

McKiernan, Kevin. *The Kurds: A People in Search of Their Homeland.* New York: St. Martin's, 2006.

O'Leary, Brendan, John McGarry, and Khaled Salih, eds. *The Future of Kurdistan in Iraq.* Philadelphia: University of Pennsylvania Press, 2005.

Tucker, Mike. *Among Warriors in Iraq.* New York: Lyons, 2005.

Yildiz, Kerim, and Tom Blass. *The Kurds in Iraq: The Past, Present and Future.* London: Pluto, 2004.

War Correspondents

The history of news reporters covering combat operations dates back at least to the Crimean War (1853–1856) waged by Great Britain, France, and Turkey against Imperial Russia. William Howard Russell, who covered that war for the *Times* (London), is generally considered the world's first war correspondent. Since that time, correspondents have covered virtually every major conflict throughout the world. During the 20th century, war correspondents brought the realities of combat "up close and personal" to readers and viewers in their respective countries in major wars such as World War I, World War II, the Korean War, and the Vietnam War, and in countless lesser conflicts throughout the world. Yet, inevitably, the presence of civilian reporters on the battlefield creates an unavoidable tension between the correspondents, whose only job is to report the facts as they witness them, and the military officers and government officials whose principal duty is to win the war they are fighting. Increasingly, this tension centers on the degree of access to the wars' combat zones that governments grant to war correspondents. While reporters—driven by deadlines and the need to produce ratings-garnering headlines—consistently demand unrestricted free access, government officials and military officers seek to keep war correspondents' access limited to what they judge as "reasonable." The recent wars in the Middle East serve as prime examples of this issue.

In the modern Middle East, three recent or ongoing conflicts—the 1991 Persian Gulf War, the Afghanistan War (October 7, 2001–present), and the Iraq War (March 20, 2003–present)—have led to dramatic developments in the history of war correspondence. These include the growing prominence of media giants such as Cable News Network (CNN), MSNBC, and Fox News; news briefings by high-ranking military officers; news pools attached to military units; and journalists embedded with fighting forces. All of these developments have exposed news media to accusations of government and corporate control, however. An attempt to counter this alleged censorship has led to a proliferation of chiefly Internet-based alternative news sites. Moreover, the rising casualty rates among journalists in Afghanistan and particularly Iraq have highlighted the inherent risks of war correspondence. No longer viewed as neutral observers, journalists are increasingly targeted for their alleged political or sectarian affiliations.

The roots of increasing governmental and military control over journalistic reporting go back to the Vietnam War, the Falklands War, and the U.S. invasions of Grenada (1983) and Panama (1989). U.S. supporters of the Vietnam War and many Vietnam War combat veterans alleged that negative journalistic reports were largely responsible for the erosion of American support for the war, in particular, coverage of the 1968

NBC News correspondent David Bloom reports from Iraq in this undated television image. Bloom died during the Iraq War while serving as an embedded reporter. (AP Photo)

Tet Offensive. The general lack of the largely Saigon-based Vietnam War reporters' "up front" credibility and the perception of inaccurate reporting during Tet and the Vietnam War in general resulted in virtually an entire generation of military officers distrusting the media's accuracy and even their motives. This distrust of media methods, accuracy, and motives has had a profound impact on U.S. government attitudes and policies regarding reporters' access to combat operations when they are in progress. When many of the Vietnam-generation military officers assumed high command in the Persian Gulf War and the Afghanistan and Iraq conflicts, their perception of past media bias greatly influenced the U.S. decision to forego a policy of unrestricted access for journalists in the later conflicts in the Middle East.

During the 1982 Falklands War, the British government sought to control press coverage. British governmental and military officials assigned no more than 29 correspondents and photographers to pools that accompanied the Falklands invasion force. Various reporters later complained of direct censorship. Following the British cue, American government and military officials largely excluded the media from Operation Urgent Fury, the 1983 invasion of Grenada. The 15 reporters finally allowed on Grenada found their movements severely curtailed. Similarly, Operation Just Cause, the 1989 invasion of Panama to overthrow President Manuel Noriega, deployed a select pool of journalists who complained that they were barely briefed and kept well away from military action.

Persian Gulf War

Although U.S. government and military officials aimed at creating more transparency during the Persian Gulf War, the inevitable accusations of censorship and disinformation abounded because the government did not permit reporters unrestricted access. Following governmental cues, the American media demonized Iraqi president Saddam Hussein, some echoing president George H. W. Bush's characterization of him as a "new Hitler" and representing the war as inevitable. Opposition to the war, which at any rate was slight and disorganized, was mainly ignored except for a few high-profile incidents. Although Iraqi forces committed sufficient outrages during their occupation of Kuwait to fill numerous news reports, charges of propaganda were raised when it was discovered that many of these were Kuwaiti public relations fabrications —such as reports of Iraqi soldiers throwing Kuwaiti babies out of incubators.

Seventeen members of the national media pool arrived in Saudi Arabia on August 13, 1990, well before Operation DESERT STORM was launched on January 17, 1991, and they were closely monitored during Operation DESERT SHIELD. Headed by Michael Sherman, six government public affairs officers were to handle Persian Gulf media. These officials set up the main military briefing rooms and television studios in Dhahran and Riyadh, Saudi Arabia, and organized "media response teams," a pool system whose members were sometimes permitted to accompany select military units. An intense competition among journalists ensued, but reporters were largely denied access to actual combat. A number of disgruntled journalists affiliated with small media organizations filed a legal brief, claiming that the pool system violated their First Amendment right of free expression. The war ended, however, before courts ruled on the matter.

Those who tried to work outside the pool had little success. Some rented hotel rooms in Saudi Arabia and attended daily military briefings, where such well-prepared military spokespersons as coalition commander General H. Norman Schwarzkopf provided carefully selected information. Meanwhile, General Colin L. Powell, chairman of the Joint Chiefs of Staff, and other Defense Department officials provided daily briefings to reporters at the Pentagon. Pool members, however, largely failed to challenge the data they were given before, during, and immediately after the conflict.

So-called unilaterals or freelancers also found their movements hampered. By mid-February 1991, some 20 had been detained or threatened with detention. Similarly, television correspondents Peter Arnett of CNN, John Simpson of the BBC, and Brent Sadler of Independent Television News (ITN) evoked criticism for reporting the first stage of the war from Baghdad. Their vivid film of initial air attacks garnered high viewer ratings and helped fuel the soaring popularity of major news networks. Nevertheless, U.S. government officials objected to the correspondents' presence in an enemy capital. In particular, reports of the bombing of a deep military command and control bunker in the Amariyah district of Baghdad—the upper levels of which were also being used as a civilian air raid shelter—which killed 408 civilians, deeply embarrassed coalition officials and provided the Saddam Hussein regime with useful propaganda.

Prompted by governmental and military spokespersons and backed by correspondents from major news media, a sanitized version of combat emerged from coverage of the Persian Gulf War. Critics cited the U.S. government's portrayals of the success of weapons systems such as smart bombs, Tomahawk cruise missiles, and the Patriot antimissile system as grossly exaggerated, charges generally confirmed by postwar analysis. Criticism was far from limited to weapons systems, however. Charges abounded that unrestricted free press access had prevented reporters from independently verifying official information that was provided regarding the extent of U.S. friendly fire casualties, the true number of Iraqi military and civilian deaths resulting from coalition ground and air combat actions, and the amount of oil pollution caused by coalition bombing (versus that caused by Iraqi sabotage). Barry Zorthian's statement to the National Press Club on March 19, 1991, may well summarize the judgment of many war correspondents who felt shut out by Department of Defense press restrictions during the Persian Gulf War: "The Gulf War is over and the press lost."

Afghanistan War

As in the Persian Gulf War, war correspondents in the ongoing conflict in Afghanistan, which began as Operation ENDURING FREEDOM on October 7, 2001, have been targeted by appeals to patriotism and national security. For instance, shortly after the war began, major U.S. networks agreed to have any statements from al-Qaeda leader Osama bin Laden screened and edited by the U.S. government. The Arab-language television network Al Jazeera soon was targeted for broadcasting a release from bin Laden on the eve of the first air strike on Afghanistan. On November 13, 2001, Al Jazeera's office in Kabul was struck by a U.S. missile, which officials claimed was intended to hit a well-known al-Qaeda facility. A second attack, again claimed to be mistaken, targeted Al Jazeera's Baghdad office on April 8, 2003, killing a reporter and wounding a cameraman.

From the outset of Operation ENDURING FREEDOM, U.S. defense secretary Donald Rumsfeld warned the media to expect little Pentagon cooperation. When the aerial bombardment began on October 7, 2001, no Western journalists were within the three-quarters of the country controlled by the Taliban, for reporters had gathered in Pakistan and territory held by the anti-Taliban Northern Alliance. By November 10, seven journalists had been killed as they spread out to areas abandoned by the Taliban, whose forces had earlier arrested Sunday Express (London) reporter Yvonne Ridley on September 28. Several months later, the Pentagon unveiled plans to establish three Coalition Press Information Centers, in Mazar-e Sharif, Bagram, and Qandahar Airport. Staff members would be charged with helping journalists get photographs and interviews. Still, Assistant Secretary of Defense Victoria Clarke encouraged journalists to remain in Bahrain for the best access to war coverage. These procedures led to questions about how much uncensored news was reaching Western readers and viewers. As early as 2002, for instance, Daily Mirror (London) correspondent John Pilger claimed that about 5,000 civilian deaths had resulted from bombing raids in Afghanistan, almost double the toll of the September 11, 2001, terrorist attacks on New York.

Yet, the dangers of reporters' unrestricted access to war zones have been clearly shown in Afghanistan. Faced with problems of access, an inhospitable terrain, language barriers, and the danger of ambush, journalists complain that they face a hidden war in Afghanistan. Particularly in the south of the country, correspondents have encountered difficulties in hiring local "fixers" willing to risk Taliban retribution. On March 4, 2007, for instance, Taliban forces abducted *La Repubblica* (Rome) reporter Daniele Mastrogiacomo along with Afghan journalist Ajmal Nakshbandi and their driver, Sayed Agha, in Helmand Province. While Mastrogiacomo was later released in a prisoner exchange, both Afghans were beheaded. This incident followed the killing of two German *Deutsche Welle* (Berlin) journalists in October 2006.

New restrictions imposed in 2006, whereby media outlets were told not to publish interviews and reports critical of Afghani president Hamid Karzai's foreign policy or the U.S.-led coalition forces, have led to further protests of curtailment of press freedom.

Iraq War

Operation IRAQI FREEDOM, an ongoing conflict that began with the invasion of Iraq on March 20, 2003, accomplished a new twist in the pool system that had been practiced in the Persian Gulf War and, to some extent, in Afghanistan. At the commencement of the campaign, such major news syndicates as CNN had announced huge budgets for war coverage, planning to devote 24 hours a day to the conflict. However, much to the disappointment of reporters demanding unrestricted free access to combat operations, the Department of Defense chose only to use reporters embedded with combat units. "Embeds" would receive basic training and accompany their assigned units through combat. Embeds were allowed to report what they wished so long as they revealed no information that the enemy could use.

While supporters saw the embed system as restoring "up front" credibility to reporters, whom they had perceived as being aloof and unsympathetic to the real problems faced by troops engaged in waging war, critics of the embed system claimed that it resulted in a loss of objectivity among correspondents—who soon discovered that they identified with troops in their assigned units. A few correspondents, such as CNN's Christiane Amanpour (who became a media celebrity through her reporting of the Persian Gulf War and Bosnian conflict), objected to the restrictions, but she was warned that she had to abide by the rules.

More than in the 1991 Persian Gulf War, journalists found that dry, colorless government media briefings offered them little material to produce the dramatic headlines that garner top ratings in the highly competitive news business. Moreover, international television viewers have increasingly become the media giants' target audience, and correspondents often found their reports hampered by syndicate expectations. Yet, despite the claims that access was unduly restricted, war correspondents were instrumental in exposing such incidents as Abu Ghraib prisoner abuse, the overhyped Jessica Lynch "rescue" operation, and the extent of Iraqi civilian casualties due to coalition bombing, such as during the Second Battle of Fallujah in November 2004.

In short, the war in Iraq suggests that correspondents, unlike during the Persian Gulf War, became more critical, a mood that reflects and even fuels the growing public opposition to the war. Statistics also suggest that Iraq is now the world's most dangerous location for journalists. The conservative estimates of the Committee to Protect Journalists indicate that violence in Iraq claimed the lives of 32 journalists in 2006, the highest number that the organization has recorded to date. Between 2003 and the end of 2008, the Committee to

Protect Journalists reported that 136 journalists died in Iraq, while 56 additional media workers (nonjournalists) died. The conflicts in Kuwait, Afghanistan, and Iraq reveal that war correspondence is becoming an increasingly risky enterprise, whether "pooled," "embedded," or acting independently.

Anna M. Wittmann

See also: Iraqi Freedom, Operation; Iraqi Insurgency

Further Reading

Allan, Stuart, and Barbie Zelizer, eds. *Reporting War: Journalism in Wartime*. New York: Routledge, 2004.

Allen, Tim, and Jean Seaton, eds. *The Media of Conflict: War Reporting and Representation of Ethnic Violence*. London: Zed Books, 1999.

Feinstein, Antony. *Dangerous Lives: War and the Men and Women Who Report It*. Toronto: Thomas Allen, 2003.

Fisk, Robert. *The Great War for Civilization: The Conquest of the Middle East*. New York: Vintage Books, 2007.

Knightley, Phillip. *The First Casualty: The War Correspondent as Hero and Myth-Maker from the Crimea to Iraq*. Baltimore: Johns Hopkins University Press, 2004.

McLaughlin, Greg. *The War Correspondent*. London: Pluto, 2002.

Tumber, Howard, and Frank Webster. *Journalists under Fire: Information War and Journalistic Practices*. London: Sage, 2006.

War Powers Act

Joint resolution of the U.S. Congress, enacted on November 7, 1973. The War Powers Act limits the authority of the president to deploy U.S. troops and/or wage war without the express consent of Congress. It has influenced nearly every major American military deployment in the Middle East since its passing. The act became law over then president Richard M. Nixon's veto following the withdrawal of U.S. combat forces from the Republic of Vietnam (South Vietnam) during the Vietnam War. It was designed to ensure that the president and Congress would share responsibility in making decisions that might lead the United States into a war. Its passage was prompted by the highly unpopular Vietnam War, during which both the Lyndon Johnson and Richard Nixon administrations enmeshed the United States in a major war while bypassing the constitutional provision that grants Congress the power to declare war (Article I, Section 8).

Under the War Powers Act, the president is required to notify and consult with Congress prior to deploying U.S. troops into hostile situations and to consult regularly with Congress once troops have been deployed. If within 60 days of introducing troops Congress has not declared war or approved of the military deployment, the president must withdraw the troops unless he certifies to Congress an "unavoidable military necessity" that requires an additional 30 days to remove the troops. Although every president, Democrat and Republican, has claimed the War Powers Act to be an unconstitutional violation of the president's authority as commander in chief, presidents have nevertheless been careful to notify Congress of their decision to deploy U.S. forces.

According to the Congressional Research Service, since the passage of the War Powers Resolution in 1973, U.S. presidents have submitted over 100 such reports to Congress. On April 24, 1980, following the failed attempt to rescue American hostages in Iran, President Jimmy Carter submitted a report to Congress. Some members of Congress objected to Carter's failure to consult with Congress before executing the operation. Carter, however, claimed that because the mission depended on complete secrecy, consultation was not possible; moreover, the White House argued that a rescue operation did not constitute an act of aggression or force.

On September 29, 1983, Congress invoked the resolution to authorize the deployment of U.S. Marines to Lebanon for 18 months as part of a United Nations (UN) peacekeeping mission there. On April 14, 1986, President Ronald W. Reagan ordered air strikes on Libya for its involvement in a terrorist bombing in a West Berlin discotheque that killed two U.S. soldiers. Reagan informed Congress of the attack, but because the operation was short-lived, the question of congressional approval was essentially moot.

In January 1991 President George H. W. Bush secured congressional authorization to use force to compel Iraq to withdraw from Kuwait per a UN mandate. After the end of the Persian Gulf War on February 28, 1991, the War Powers Act again became a potential issue regarding the situation in the Middle East. President William J. Clinton launched several air attacks against Iraqi targets in an effort to compel Iraqi dictator Saddam Hussein's compliance with UN resolutions. In 1998 Clinton also ordered cruise-missile attacks on targets in Afghanistan and Sudan in retaliation for two deadly bombings involving U.S. embassies, likely carried out by al-Qaeda. However, because of the brief and secretive nature of the operations, Clinton did not invoke the War Powers Act.

Following the September 11, 2001, terrorist attacks on the United States, President George W. Bush secured congressional authorization a week later to use whatever force necessary against those responsible for the attacks. Based on this authorization, in October 2001 the U.S. attacked and invaded Afghanistan to overthrow the Taliban regime that had given Osama bin Laden and al-Qaeda sanctuary.

In 2002 the Bush administration sought another congressional approval to wage a potential war against Iraq to compel it to cooperate with the UN resolution that had called for the disarming of Iraq and the declaration of all weapons of mass destruction (WMD). On October 16, 2002, Bush signed into law the joint congressional resolution, which enjoyed wide bipartisan support, empowering him to wage war against the regime of Iraqi dictator Saddam Hussein. The October 2002 authorization of military force against Iraq obviated presidential compliance with the War Powers Act.

Although Congress authorized the use of force against Iraq, the March 2003 invasion of Iraq and subsequent war and insurgency there has called into question not only the effectiveness of the War Powers Act, but also—and more importantly—Congress's role in foreign policy and decisions involving war. The failure to find any weapons of mass destruction, the principal reason cited by Bush for the invasion of Iraq, has led critics of the war to question not only the president's responsibility to both Congress and the public, but also the role of Congress in declaring war and, specifically, as the War Powers Act intended, checking or overseeing the president's war-making powers.

Regardless of which administration holds the White House, tension over the exercise of war powers undoubtedly will continue between the executive and legislative branches of government. Presidents, Democrat and Republican, will still seek to implement U.S. foreign policy through the unrestricted use of all elements of national power—economic, political, and military—while

Congress, through its legislative powers, will continue to exercise its vital role of providing the necessary "checks and balances" to ensure that executive branch power does not become "unrestricted." Given the volatile situation in the Middle East, the region will likely continue to be the focal point for future confrontations between presidents and Congress over war powers.

Stefan Brooks

See also: Bush, George Walker; IRAQI FREEDOM, Operation

Further Reading

Bobbit, Phillip. "War Powers: An Essay on John Hart Ely's *War and Responsibility: Constitutional Lessons of Vietnam and Its Aftermath.*" *Michigan Law Quarterly* 92, no. 6 (May 1994): 1364–1400.

Irons, Peter. *War Powers: How the Imperial Presidency Hijacked the Constitution.* New York: Metropolitan Books, 2005.

Yoo, John. *The Powers of War and Peace: The Constitution and Foreign Affairs after 9/11.* Chicago: University of Chicago Press, 2005.

Weapons of Mass Destruction

Weapons of mass destruction (WMD) are biological, chemical, and nuclear weapons capable of inflicting mass casualties. Use of these weapons is viewed as not only immoral, but also contrary to international law and the laws of war because WMD have the ability to kill indiscriminately large numbers of human beings and inflict extensive damage to buildings beyond combatants or military assets. During the Cold War, fears about nuclear weapons and their use were commonplace. Nevertheless, these weapons were under tight control, and neither side dared employ them for fear of the total destruction that a retaliatory strike would bring. With the end of the Cold War, however, nuclear proliferation has become a significant problem, and the likelihood of a rogue state or terrorist group attaining WMD, including nuclear weapons, has increased substantially.

During the Iran-Iraq War (1980–1988), Iraq employed chemical weapons against Iranian troops, something Iraqi dictator Saddam Hussein publicly admitted to in December 2006 during his trial for war crimes. It remains in dispute whether Iran employed them as well. In 1988, as part of an operation to suppress a revolt by Iraqi Kurds, the Hussein government unleashed a chemical attack on the northern Iraqi town of Halabja, killing at least 5,000 people in the first recorded event of such weapons being used against civilians since the Japanese use of chemical weapons against the Chinese during the Second Sino-Japanese War (1937–1945).

Since the terror attacks of September 11, 2001, the fear of and danger posed by WMD have increased significantly, owing to the desire of terrorist groups such as al-Qaeda and their affiliates to acquire and employ such weapons against the United States and other countries. The September 11 terrorist attacks on the United States and the 2004 Madrid and 2005 London bombings clearly demonstrated the ability and willingness of al-Qaeda to engage in terrorism to inflict mass casualties, leaving no doubt about the organization's willingness to use WMD in future terrorist attacks. Al-Qaeda is believed to have been responsible for a series of terrorist attacks in March and April 2006 in Iraq, in which chlorine gas killed dozens and sickened hundreds.

Because of the instability and recurrence of war and conflict in the Middle East, the presence of WMD has only heightened the

UN weapons inspectors stand at the base of Iraq's "supergun" in 1991. Under the terms ending the Persian Gulf War, Iraqi president Saddam Hussein agreed to allow UN inspection of facilities and the dismantling of weapons of mass destruction. By 1998, the Iraqi leader had expelled the inspectors. (Corel)

arms race between Arab states and Israel, and also between Arab states themselves. Egypt, Syria, Algeria, and Iran are all believed to have significant stockpiles of biological and chemical weapons. In 2003, seeking to normalize relations with the United States and Europe and end its international isolation and reputation as a sponsor of terrorism, Libya announced that it was abandoning its WMD programs. Observers have suggested that President George W. Bush's decision to invade Iraq in 2003, ostensibly to rid it of WMD, along with Libya's failure to end its isolation and convince the United Nations (UN) to lift its sanctions, prompted this change of behavior.

Syria is believed to possess extensive chemical weapons stockpiles and delivery systems, and to have been seeking to develop a similarly robust biological weapons program. Egypt was the first country in the Middle East to develop chemical weapons, which may have been prompted, at least in part, by Israel's construction of a nuclear reactor in 1958. The size of Egypt's chemical weapons arsenal is thought to be perhaps as extensive as Iraq's prior to the 1991 Persian Gulf War, although the end of hostilities between Egypt and Israel since the 1978 Camp David Accords may have obviated the need for maintaining the same quantities of such weapons.

In 1993, as part of the Arab campaign against Israel's nuclear weapons program, Egypt and Syria (along with Iraq) refused to sign the Chemical Weapons Convention (CWC), which bans the acquisition, development, stockpiling, transfer, retention, and use of chemical weapons. These states also refused to sign the Biological Weapons

Convention (BWC) of 1975, which prohibits the development, production, acquisition, transfer, retention, stockpiling, and use of biological and toxin weapons. Iraq later signed the BWC, and it signed the CWC after Hussein's ouster. The extent of Egypt's biological weapons program is unknown, but it clearly has the ability to develop such weapons if it already does not have weaponized stockpiles.

With respect to nuclear weapons, Israel is believed to possess as many as 100 nuclear warheads, although the Israeli government has never publicly confirmed possessing such weapons. On December 12, 2006, Israeli prime minister Ehud Olmert admitted in an interview that Israel possessed nuclear weapons, only to be contradicted the next day by a government spokesman, who denied that Olmert had made such an admission. In the meantime, Israel has refused to sign the Nuclear Non-Proliferation Treaty (NPT) and has not allowed UN International Atomic Energy Agency (IAEA) inspectors access to its suspected nuclear sites.

Israel has repeatedly shown its willingness to use force to maintain its suspected Middle East nuclear monopoly and deny any Arab state the ability to acquire or develop nuclear weapons. In 1981 the Israeli air force destroyed an Iraqi nuclear reactor site under construction at Osiraq, Iraq. In September 2007 Israeli warplanes carried out an attack against a suspected nuclear facility in Syria. Iran is currently enriching uranium for what it claims are peaceful purposes, but the United States and much of Western Europe have accused Iran of aspiring to build nuclear weapons. That state's refusal to cooperate with the IAEA led the United Nations to impose sanctions on Iran in December 2006 and March 2007 as punishment for its defiance of the United Nations. Since then the West has pressed for more sanctions, but its efforts have met resistance from such nations as Russia and the People's Republic of China.

Of particular international concern in 2009 were Pakistan in southern Asia and the Democratic People's Republic of Korea (DPRK, North Korea) in East Asia. Pakistan successfully conducted underground nuclear tests in May 1998 and is believed to possess a number of atomic bombs. Abdul Qadeer Kahn, widely regarded as the chief scientist in the development of Pakistan's atomic bomb, confessed in January 2004 to having been involved in a clandestine network of nuclear proliferation from Pakistan to Libya, Iran, and North Korea (which in October 2006 successfully conducted an underground nuclear test). Pakistani president General Pervez Musharraf then announced that he had pardoned Kahn, who is regarded by many Pakistanis as a national hero, despite the fact that the technology transfer is thought to have made possible North Korea's acquisition of the atomic bomb.

In the spring of 2009, however, major fighting erupted between Pakistani government forces and the Taliban, who controlled the Swat Valley in the northwestern part of the country. The stability of Pakistan and the security of its nuclear arsenal appeared in question.

Stefan Brooks

See also: UN Monitoring, Verification and Inspection Commission; UN Security Council Resolution 1284; UN Special Commission; UN Weapons Inspectors

Further Reading

Hamel-Green, Michael. *Regional Initiatives on Nuclear- and WMD-Free Zones: Cooperative Approaches to Arms Control and Non-proliferation.* New York: United Nations Publication, 2006.

Katona, Peter et al. *Countering Terrorism and WMD: Creating a Global Counter-Terrorism Network*. New York: Routledge, 2006.

Mauroni, Albert. *Where Are the WMD? The Reality of Chem-Bio Threats on the Home Front and on the Battlefield*. Annapolis, MD: Naval Institute Press, 2006.

Schneider, Barry. *Avoiding the Abyss: Progress, Shortfalls, and the Way Ahead in Combating the WMD Threat*. Westport, CT: Praeger, 2006.

Wilson, Joseph Carter, IV

U.S. diplomat, career foreign service officer, and a central figure in the Valerie Plame Wilson incident, which dogged the George W. Bush administration for several years after the launching of the Iraq War. Joseph Carter Wilson IV was born in Bridgeport, Connecticut, on November 5, 1949, to a prosperous family and grew up in both Europe and California. He graduated from the University of California–Santa Barbara in 1971 with an undergraduate degree in history. After working for a time as a carpenter, he pursued graduate studies in public administration and entered the Foreign Service in 1976.

From 1976 to 1998, Wilson held a series of increasingly important diplomatic posts, both in Washington and abroad. Many of his postings were in Africa, where he earned a reputation as an earnest, well-informed diplomat who was easy to work with. During this time, Wilson, who hailed from a staunchly conservative Republican family, began to make connections with several influential Democratic legislators. Although he worked to distance himself from partisan politics as a diplomatic officer, during 1985 and 1986 he was a congressional fellow first for Democratic senator Al Gore and then for Democratic representative Tom Foley. These assignments gained him important connections within the Democratic Party hierarchy.

From 1988 to 1991, Wilson was stationed in Baghdad, Iraq, where he served as the deputy chief of mission to U.S. ambassador of Iraq April Glaspie. This placed him in the center of the crisis that resulted from the Iraqi invasion and occupation of Kuwait, which began on August 2, 1990. He was reportedly the last U.S. diplomat to have met with Iraqi president Saddam Hussein before the 1991 Persian Gulf War began in January 1991. Wilson told Hussein in no uncertain terms that he had to quit Kuwait immediately or face military consequences. Hussein scoffed at Wilson's demand and subsequently sent him a letter in which he threatened to murder anyone harboring "foreigners" in Iraq. Wilson then publicly castigated Hussein for his threat, a rare move for a diplomat. As the war approached, Wilson provided refuge for more than 100 Americans at the U.S. embassy in Baghdad and was largely responsible for the orderly and safe evacuation of several thousand Americans from Iraq. President George H. W. Bush lauded Wilson's actions, calling him a "true American hero."

After holding several ambassadorial posts, Wilson served as the political adviser to the commander in chief of U.S. Forces, Europe (EUCOM), in Stuttgart, Germany, from 1995 to 1997. From 1997 to 1998 he served as special assistant to President Bill Clinton and senior director of African affairs for the National Security Council (NSC).

Wilson retired from government service in 1998 and began his own international consulting and management firm, JC Wilson International Ventures. He also began actively supporting numerous national Democratic lawmakers, including

Senator Ted Kennedy and Representative Charles Rangel.

Because of his lengthy diplomatic career, past dealings with Saddam Hussein, and expertise in African affairs, the Central Intelligence Agency sent Wilson on a clandestine mission to Niger in February 2002. His task was to ascertain the accuracy of reports that Saddam Hussein had attempted to purchase "yellowcake uranium" (enriched uranium) from Niger, which had become a key accusation of the George W. Bush administration as it built its case for war with Iraq. Wilson returned and concluded in a report to the Bush administration that it was "highly doubtful" that Iraq ever attempted to buy yellowcake uranium in Niger. Information showed that documents used to build this case against Iraq were forged. However, in Bush's 2003 State of the Union Address, the president claimed that British reports (now presumed erroneous) indicated that Hussein had recently attempted to purchase "significant" quantities of uranium in Africa. This was a significant part of the American case for war against Iraq.

Outraged by the Bush administration's clear repudiation of his report and chagrined by the rush to war with Iraq, which had begun in March 2003, Wilson wrote a controversial op-ed piece for the *New York Times* that was published on July 6, 2003. Titled "What I Didn't Find in Africa," Wilson's article clearly spelled out the case for faulty intelligence on Iraq and castigated the Bush White House for exaggerating the Iraqi threat. The article also spelled out the general outlines of his 2002 trip to Niger. The following week, conservative columnist Robert Novak, in an attempt to discredit Wilson's article, revealed that Wilson's wife, Valerie Plame Wilson, was a covert CIA officer.

Novak's revelation precipitated an avalanche of accusations and recriminations, including Wilson's claim that the outing of his wife—an ethics violation as well as illegal—was part of an elaborate White House plan to discredit him and take the focus off of the faulty intelligence that had led to war. The revelation led to a federal investigation by the Justice Department, which convened a grand jury. Several of Bush's top aides, including Karl Rove, came within the investigation's crosshairs, as did those of Vice President Dick Cheney. Ultimately, in March 2007 I. Lewis "Scooter" Libby, Cheney's chief of staff, was found guilty of numerous offenses, including lying under oath and obstruction of justice. Bush commuted Libby's sentence, but the entire affair sullied the White House and added more fodder to the antiwar lobby's fire. No one else was implicated in the leak scandal, although it is likely that others besides Libby were involved.

Wilson and his wife, Valerie, brought a civil suit against Cheney, Rove, Libby, and several others, but the case was dismissed on jurisdictional grounds. In 2004 Wilson published a popular if incendiary book titled *The Politics of Truth*, which expanded his side of the story in the Valerie Plame Wilson incident and excoriated the Bush administration for its conduct in the lead-up to, and during, the Iraq War. The book raised the stakes in the Washington blame game and only added to the increasingly shrill and bitter recriminations surrounding the war in Iraq. Wilson continues to speak out against the war and to criticize the Bush administration.

Paul G. Pierpaoli Jr.

See also: Central Intelligence Agency; Cheney, Richard Bruce; Libby, I. Lewis; Weapons of Mass Destruction; Wilson, Valerie Plame

Further Reading

Ricks, Thomas E. *Fiasco: The American Military Adventure in Iraq.* New York: Penguin, 2006.

Wilson, Joseph. *The Politics of Truth: Inside the Lies That Led to War and Betrayed My Wife's CIA Identity.* New York: Carroll and Graf, 2004.

Wilson, Valerie Plame

Central Intelligence Agency (CIA) covert officer whose identity was leaked to the press in 2003, precipitating the long and contentious Valerie Plame Wilson incident. Valerie Elise Plame was born on April 19, 1963, in Anchorage, Alaska, the daughter of a career U.S. Air Force officer. She graduated from Pennsylvania State University in 1985 and began her career with the CIA that same year as a new trainee. Because of the clandestine nature of the CIA and Plame's work, few details of her 20-year career with the agency are known. What is known is that she worked in various posts, usually with a dual role: a public position and a covert one in which she concentrated on weapons proliferation and counterproliferation activities. The CIA sponsored her graduate studies, which resulted in a master's degree from the London School of Economics in 1991 and another master's degree from the College of Europe (Belgium) that same year.

Plame met Ambassador Joseph C. Wilson IV at a party in Washington, DC, in 1997. The following year they were married. At the time of their courtship, Wilson was working in the West Wing as special assistant to President Bill Clinton and senior director of African affairs for the National Security Council (NSC). Wilson retired from government service in 1998 and

Former Central Intelligence Agency operative Valerie Plame Wilson, shown here with her husband, former ambassador Joseph Wilson, on April 29, 2006, in Washington, D.C. Plame's identity and status as an undercover operative for the CIA were leaked to the media after her husband publicly criticized the George W. Bush administration's rationale for going to war with Iraq in 2003. (AP/Wide World Photos)

began his own international management and consulting company.

In February 2002 the George W. Bush administration and the CIA sent Wilson on a mission to Niger, where he was to ascertain the accuracy of reports that Iraq had attempted to purchase enriched (yellowcake) uranium from that nation. Wilson was well placed to do this given his extensive experience dealing with Saddam Hussein in the late 1980s and early 1990s. Upon Wilson's return, he stated in a report that there was no credible evidence that any Iraqi official tried to engage Niger in a scheme that would have resulted in the transfer of enriched uranium to Iraq. Nevertheless, the Bush administration continued to press this claim, and it was specifically mentioned in President Bush's 2003 State of the Union address. The Niger-Iraq connection was used as a major pretext for the war against Iraq, which commenced in March 2003.

Outraged by the Bush administration's continuing claims concerning the Niger-Iraq connection, Wilson wrote an op-ed piece that appeared in the *New York Times* on July 6, 2003. The article revealed his trip to Niger the year before and laid bare the administration's theory on the validity of the reports coming from Niger. He also asserted that the White House had knowingly exaggerated the Iraqi threat so as to legitimize its pretext for the Iraq War. Predictably, Wilson's article exercised the Bush administration and, if Wilson and Plame Wilson's allegations are true, triggered a deliberate attempt to discredit and sabotage them both, a plan that involved the West Wing and the staffs of both Bush and Vice President Dick Cheney.

On July 14, 2003, the syndicated conservative newspaper columnist Robert Novak wrote an article to counter Wilson's letter. In the *Washington Post*, Novak revealed that Wilson's wife was a CIA operative whose job was to work on issues of weapons proliferation and weapons of mass destruction (WMD). That revelation, which presumably came from someone high up in the Bush administration, caused an instant sensation, as it is illegal for a government official to knowingly reveal the identity of a covert CIA officer. Besides sparking an acrimonious political atmosphere between Republicans and Democrats, and between supporters of the war and antiwar activists, the revelation about Plame Wilson's identity triggered a federal investigation in the Department of Justice. The Wilsons immediately alleged that the leak was a purposeful attempt to retaliate against Ambassador Wilson for his op-ed piece.

After a tortuous investigation, a federal grand jury indicted Cheney's chief of staff, I. Lewis "Scooter" Libby, on several charges, including lying under oath and obstruction of justice. He was found guilty in March 2007, but Bush quickly commuted his sentence. No other Bush administrations officials were indicted or convicted in the Plame Wilson incident, but the investigation left a dark cloud over the White House during a time in which the Iraq War was going very badly. Interestingly, no one was actually indicted or convicted for having perpetrated the leak in the first place, although it has to be assumed that someone within the Bush administration, with top-secret clearance, did so. Some Bush supporters claim that Plame Wilson's clandestine activities were already known in Washington and that Wilson's op-ed piece was politically motivated and designed to discredit the president.

Wilson and Plame Wilson later brought a civil suit against those who were thought to be directly involved in the leak, including Cheney himself, but the case was denied on jurisdictional grounds. That case is now on appeal. Plame Wilson left the CIA in December 2005. She caused a stir in 2006 when it was reported that she was about to receive $2.5 million for her memoir. That figure, however, has never been verified by her or her publisher. Her detractors asserted that she was using the incident for personal gain. Others, however, argued that she had a right to tell her side of the story and that it might shed more light on the case. Plame Wilson encountered some difficulty with the CIA, which insisted that certain passages in her manuscript be rewritten before the book could be published. In October 2007

Plame Wilson's book was finally released with the title *Fair Game: My Life as a Spy, My Betrayal by the White House*. Despite the tantalizing title, the book did not shed any significant new light on the Plame Wilson incident. Plame Wilson then embarked on a major speaking tour, promoting her book and relaying her side of the story.

Paul G. Pierpaoli Jr.

See also: Central Intelligence Agency; Cheney, Richard Bruce; Libby, I. Lewis; Weapons of Mass Destruction; Wilson, Joseph Carter, IV

Further Reading

Plame Wilson, Valerie. *Fair Game: My Life as a Spy, My Betrayal by the White House*. New York: Simon and Schuster, 2007.

Ricks, Thomas E. *Fiasco: The American Military Adventure in Iraq*. New York: Penguin, 2006.

Wilson, Joseph. *The Politics of Truth: Inside the Lies That Led to War and Betrayed My Wife's CIA Identity*. New York: Carroll and Graf, 2004.

Wolfowitz, Paul Dundes

Neoconservative academic, U.S. assistant secretary of state for East Asian and Pacific affairs (1982–1986), and deputy secretary of defense (2001–2005). Wolfowitz was the chief architect of the Bush Doctrine that advocated preemptive strikes against potential threats to U.S. interests. Wolfowitz first proposed preemptive strikes against Iraq during the Ronald Reagan administration (1981–1989) and strongly advocated the 2003 Iraq War. Paul Wolfowitz was born in Ithaca, New York, on December 22, 1943. He graduated from Cornell University in 1965. He earned a doctorate in political science from the University of Chicago in 1972. His dissertation focused on the potential for nuclear proliferation in the Middle East.

Wolfowitz taught political science at Yale University from 1970 to 1972 and became an aide in U.S. Democratic senator Henry "Scoop" M. Jackson's 1972 and 1976 presidential campaigns. Wolfowitz began working in the U.S. Arms Control and Disarmament Agency (ACDA) in 1972 and studied policies related to the SALT I strategic arms limitation talks and the Henry Kissinger/Richard Nixon policy of détente. George H. W. Bush, then director of the Central Intelligence Agency (CIA), formed a committee to which Wolfowitz, in his continuing capacity at the ACDA, was assigned as a member of a team that discredited both détente and SALT II. This work brought Wolfowitz's ideas to the attention of U.S. secretary of defense Donald Rumsfeld and Governor Ronald Reagan of California.

In 1977 Wolfowitz became deputy assistant secretary of defense for regional programs in the Jimmy Carter administration and continued to develop his theory that the best way to prevent nuclear war was to stop conventional war. It was also during this time that Wolfowitz became convinced that the highly petroleum-dependent West was extremely vulnerable to disruptions in Persian Gulf oil. In studying the issue, Wolfowitz envisioned the possibility that Iraq might one day threaten Kuwait and/or Saudi Arabia, a scenario that was realized when Iraqi president Saddam Hussein ordered the invasion and annexation of Kuwait in August 1990. Wolfowitz determined that the United States had to be able to quickly project force into the region. His studies formed the rationale for the creation of the U.S. Central Command (CENT-COM), an organization responsible for the U.S. Rapid Deployment Forces that proved so important to the successful prosecution of the 1991 Persian Gulf War and the 2003 Iraq War.

Wolfowitz left the Defense Department in 1980 for a visiting professorship at the Paul H. Nitze School of Advanced International Studies (SAIS) at Johns Hopkins University. He reentered public service in 1981, becoming the director of policy planning for the State Department, where he was tasked with conceptualizing President Reagan's long-term foreign policy. Wolfowitz's distrust of Hussein resurfaced when Wolfowitz disagreed with the administration's policy of covertly supporting Iraq in the Iran-Iraq War (1980–1988). He also disagreed with the administration's sale of Airborne Warning and Control System (AWACS) aircraft to Saudi Arabia and its incipient dialogue with the Palestine Liberation Organization (PLO).

U.S. secretary of state George P. Shultz appointed Wolfowitz assistant secretary for East Asian and Pacific affairs in 1982, and in that capacity Wolfowitz urged the Reagan administration to support democracy in the Philippines. Wolfowitz believed that a healthy democracy was the best defense against communism or totalitarianism, a view that would again be reflected as part of the rationale for the 2003 Iraq War. He then served as U.S. ambassador to the Republic of Indonesia (1986–1989).

President George H. W. Bush named Wolfowitz undersecretary of defense for policy (1989–1993). In this post, Wolfowitz was responsible for U.S. military strategy in the post–Cold War era and reported to Defense Secretary Richard (Dick) Cheney. Wolfowitz disagreed with the decision not to overthrow Hussein in the 1991 Persian Gulf War (Operation DESERT STORM). Wolfowitz saw the decision as poor strategy, believing that this task would then have to be undertaken in the future. He also saw it

as a betrayal of the Iraqi Shiites and Kurds, whom the United States had encouraged to revolt and then largely abandoned.

Wolfowitz left public service during the William J. Clinton presidency, returning to Johns Hopkins as dean of the SAIS from 1993 to 2001. He did not forgo politics, however, and in 1997 became a charter member of the Project for a New American Century (PNAC), a neoconservative think tank. Fellow charter members included Donald Rumsfeld, Dick Cheney, and Richard Perle. In 1998 Wolfowitz signed an open PNAC letter to Clinton urging a policy shift away from containing Iraq to a preemptive attack against Iraq. Wolfowitz later joined a group that advised the 2000 Republican Party presidential candidate George W. Bush on foreign policy matters.

Wolfowitz became U.S. deputy secretary of defense in 2001 and served in that capacity until 2005. It was in this capacity that he urged Bush to mount a preemptive strike on Iraq following the September 11, 2001, terrorist attacks. This idea of preemptive strikes against potential threats, which Wolfowitz had first conceived during the Reagan era, came to be known as the Bush Doctrine. An American- and British-led military coalition invaded Iraq in March 2003, asserting in part that Iraq's alleged weapons of mass destruction (WMD) were an imminent threat worthy of preemptive intervention. As the war dragged on and settled into a bloody stalemate and no WMD were found in Iraq, Wolfowitz and his neoconservative cohorts were gradually shunted aside. Bush subsequently nominated Wolfowitz to be the 10th president of the World Bank Group, and he assumed the post on June 1, 2005.

Wolfowitz's tenure at the World Bank was almost immediately controversial, the result of several appointments he made that smacked of cronyism. His apparent romantic involvement with Shaha Riza, a Tunisian-born Middle East specialist employed as a communications director by the World Bank, raised many eyebrows. The relationship clearly violated World Bank guidelines that forbade relationships between supervisors and subordinates. Later investigations found that Wolfowitz had sought and received pay increases for Riza that ran counter to World Bank guidelines. By the spring of 2007 the World Bank's board of executives had begun to pressure Wolfowitz to resign. After weeks of resisting such pressure, he finally agreed to step down on May 17, effective June 30. Wolfowitz is currently a visiting fellow at the American Enterprise Institute. He is also involved in a number of international organizations and continues to serve as a consultant for the State Department.

Richard M. Edwards

See also: Bush, George Walker; Feith, Douglas; Neoconservatism; Rumsfeld, Donald Henry

Further Reading

Crane, Les, ed. *Wolfowitz on Point*. Philadelphia: Pavilion, 2003.

Mann, James. *Rise of the Vulcans: The History of Bush's War Cabinet*. New York: Viking, 2004.

Woodward, Robert Upshur

American journalist, acclaimed investigative reporter, and chronicler of the George W. Bush administration following the September 11, 2001, terror attacks on the United States. Robert (Bob) Upshur Woodward was born in Geneva, Illinois, on March 26, 1943, but spent his childhood in nearby Wheaton, Illinois. He graduated from Yale University in 1965 and was commissioned a lieutenant in the U.S. Navy. He left the navy in 1970.

Instead of attending law school as his father wished, Woodward went to work as a reporter for the *Montgomery* [Alabama] *Sentinel* before moving on to the much more prestigious *Washington Post* in 1971. The investigative work by Woodward and fellow *Washington Post* reporter Carl Bernstein on the June 1972 Watergate break-in ultimately led to revelations about President Richard M. Nixon's use of slush funds, obstruction of justice, and various dirty tricks that resulted in congressional investigations and the president's resignation in August 1974.

The Watergate Scandal made Woodward a household name and one of the most sought-after investigative reporters in the nation. He and Bernstein later wrote *All the President's Men*, which was made into a movie starring Robert Redford and Dustin Hoffman, and *The Final Days*, which covered their Watergate reporting. Woodward's work on the Watergate story garnered him a Pulitzer Prize. In 1979 the *Washington Post* promoted him to assistant managing editor of the Metro section, and in 1982 he became assistant managing editor for investigative news. Woodward received a second Pulitzer Prize for his reporting on the attacks of September 11, 2001, and their aftermath.

Woodward's books are written in the voice of an omniscient narrator and are compiled from in-depth research, but they rely most heavily on extensive interviews with crucial principals. Most often the subjects of these works have a natural interest in cooperating with Woodward. Without their input they are more likely to be portrayed poorly in the product. All of Woodward's books have received criticism from some commentators, who usually point to inconsistencies or contest the factuality of the interviews.

Woodward's *The Commanders* (1991) covered the George H. W. Bush administration's

Robert Woodward, who with fellow reporter Carl Bernstein, broke the story of the Watergate scandal that forced President Richard Nixon from office. Woodward, shown here on May 7, 1973, has written a series of well-received books on the development of the George W. Bush administration's Iraq policy. (AP/Wide World Photos)

handling of the December 1989 to January 1990 Panama invasion and the Persian Gulf War of 1991. In *The Agenda* (1994), Woodward examined the passing of President Bill Clinton's first budget. In *The Choice* (1996), Woodward covered the 1996 presidential election. In *Shadow* (1999), he examined how the legacy of Watergate has affected how five presidents have dealt with scandal since 1974. In *Maestro* (2000), he analyzed the Federal Reserve Board; its chairman, Alan Greenspan; and the American economy. In 2005 following the death of Marc Felt, the anonymous source "Deep Throat" from Watergate, Woodward and Bernstein wrote *Secret Man*, providing new revelations about their Watergate experience.

Woodward has also written four books on the George W. Bush administration

following the terrorist attacks of September 11, 2001: *Bush at War* (2002), *Plan of Attack* (2004), *State of Denial* (2006), and *The War Within: A Secret White House History, 2006–2008* (2008). Woodward received criticism for his alleged excessive friendliness with Bush and his agenda after the publication of both *Bush at War* and *Plan of Attack*. The third and fourth books, however, were far more critical of the Bush administration and its failings in the Iraq War. All of the books illustrate well the divisions within the White House and the Pentagon, and the manner in which decisions were made within the Bush administration.

Woodward's *Plan of Attack* chronicles the Bush administration's reaction to September 11, the opening salvos in the Global War on Terror, and the planning and implementation of Operation Enduring Freedom, which saw U.S. and coalition forces topple the Taliban regime in Afghanistan. *Plan of Attack*, on the other hand, takes a more controversial slant by examining how, when, and why Bush decided to go to war against Iraq in 2003 and remove Saddam Hussein from power. Woodward's main contention is that the Bush administration had planned on regime change in Iraq just weeks after the September 11, 2001, attacks, even though there was no evidence linking Hussein to these. In *State of Denial*, the journalist chronicled the many missteps, mistakes, and gaffes that turned the 2003 war in Iraq into an embarrassing quagmire. The book also showed how many members of the administration were in denial about their role in the debacle and refused to see the seriousness of the situation. The book came out less than a month before the November 2006 congressional elections, which swept the Republicans from power in both houses and brought about the forced resignation of Secretary of Defense Donald Rumsfeld.

In 2008 Woodward published *The War Within*, his fourth book on the Bush presidency. Woodward's conclusions were damning, claiming that Bush was detached from reality vis-à-vis the Iraq War and that he had left management of the conflict to his generals. Bush's troop surge strategy was purportedly postponed until after the 2006 midterm elections because the president did not want to hamper the Republicans' chances at the voting booth.

Woodward is such a part of the Washington establishment that it is sometimes difficult to say to what extent his interpretations are affected by conventional wisdom, as he is one of the primary shapers of conventional wisdom. Certainly, his painstaking interviews and investigative research have fully established his credentials as one of today's most keen and insightful observers regarding the formation of presidential policy.

Michael K. Beauchamp and
Paul G. Pierpaoli Jr.

See also: Bush, George Walker; Iraqi Freedom, Operation; War Correspondents

Further Reading

Shephard, Alicia P. *Woodward and Bernstein: Life in the Shadow of Watergate*. Indianapolis: Wiley, 2006.

Woodward, Bob. *Bush at War*. New York: Simon and Schuster, 2002.

Woodward, Bob. *Plan of Attack*. New York: Simon and Schuster, 2004.

Woodward, Bob. *State of Denial: Bush at War, Part III*. New York: Simon and Schuster, 2006.

Woodward, Bob. *The War Within: A Secret White House History, 2006–2008*. New York: Simon and Schuster, 2008.

Z

Zawahiri, Ayman al-

Former leader of the Egyptian organization Islamic Jihad, and second-in-command of the terrorist al-Qaeda organization. Born in Cairo, Egypt, on June 19, 1951, to a family of doctors and scholars (his father was a pharmacologist and chemistry professor), Ayman al-Zawahiri joined the Muslim Brotherhood at age 14. Soon he became an Islamist militant. Following the execution by the Egyptian government of Islamist thinker Sayyid Qutb in 1966, Zawahiri established with several of his schoolmates an underground cell with the aim of overthrowing the Egyptian government. Zawahiri vowed "to put Qutb's vision into action." His cell eventually merged with others to form the Egyptian Islamic Jihad.

A good student, al-Zawahiri received an undergraduate degree in 1974 from Cairo University. He served as a surgeon in the Egyptian Army for three years. He completed a master's degree in surgery in 1978 and set up a clinic. That same year he married.

In the late 1970s Islamic Jihad became active and came under attack by the Egyptian state security forces. After the arrest and torture of many of its members by the Egyptian security services, certain army members of the Islamic Jihad, including Lieutenant Khalid Islambouli, assassinated Anwar Sadat on October 8, 1981, and then carried out actions intended to bring down the government. This attempt failed in the face of security forces and army opposition. Zawahiri and hundreds of members of Islamic Jihad and the Gamaat Islamiya, an umbrella group, were jailed as coconspirators in the assassination of Sadat. After serving three years in prison, Zawahiri and many of his coconspirators were released in 1984.

Zawahiri subsequently went to Peshawar, Pakistan, and there joined the Maktab al-Khidmat (Jihad Service Bureau), under the leadership of Dr. Abdullah Azzam and supported by Saudi financier Osama bin Laden. By the time of the final Soviet withdrawal from Afghanistan in 1989, bin Laden had broken with his mentor Azzam over the nature of the jihad. The rift that developed between the two men was ideologically motivated. Bin Laden and Zawahiri wanted to export the jihad worldwide beyond Afghanistan and Palestine, and Azzam, who dissented from this plan, was killed.

In the early 1990s Zawahiri and bin Laden traveled first to Egypt and later to Sudan, where they established training camps at the behest of Sudanese leader and Islamist thinker Hassan al-Turabi. Zawahiri merged Islamic Jihad with bin Laden's al-Qaeda organization after issuing a joint fatwa on February 23, 1998. Zawahiri was subsequently instrumental in planning the bombing of the U.S. embassies in Nairobi and Dar es Salaam in 1998 as well as the attacks on September 11, 2001. Following the U.S. invasion of Afghanistan in October 2001, Zawahiri went into hiding, releasing videos and speeches periodically to incite others to engage in the jihad against the United

States. He also published *Knights under the Prophet's Banner* (December 2001), which outlined al-Qaeda's ideology.

After the March 2003 Anglo-American–led invasion of Iraq, Zawahiri's speeches and writings took on an apocalyptic tone. In a July 2005 letter he framed the jihad in Afghanistan as a vanguard for the ultimate establishment of an Islamic state in the Levant, Egypt, Iraq, and neighboring states on the Arabian Peninsula; multiple public statements by Zawahiri have since repeated this point. In his video response to Pope Benedict XVI's remarks on Islam in September 2006, Zawahiri called Benedict a "charlatan" because of his remarks on Islam. However, the term used by Zawahiri to refer to the pope as a "charlatan and deceiver" was the theological term *al-Dajjal*. In Islamic theology and tradition, *al-Dajjal* refers to the Antichrist, who will return just prior to the Day of Judgment. Zawahiri is known to have been influenced by the Saudi thinker Safar al-Hawali's book *The Day of Wrath*, which predicted that the world would end in 2012.

While the Terrorism Center at the U.S. Military Academy, West Point, is careful to note that the impact of Zawahiri's ideology is considered "totally insignificant," among most Islamist thinkers he still remains a potent figure in the Muslim world. Although his precise whereabouts are unknown, Zawahiri is believed to be living in the mountainous region along the Pakistan-Afghanistan border.

Ojan Aryanfard

See also: Terrorism

Further Reading

Gunaratna, Rohan. *Inside Al Qaeda: Global Network of Terror.* New York: Berkley Publishing Group, 2003.

Haddad, Yvonne, and Jane Smith. *The Islamic Understanding of Death and Resurrection.* Oxford: Oxford University Press, 2002.

Rabasa, Angel. *Beyond al-Qaeda: Part 1, The Global Jihadist Movement* and *Beyond al-Qaeda; Part 2, The Outer Rings of the Terrorist Universe.* Santa Monica, CA: RAND Corporation, 2006.

Zinni, Anthony Charles

U.S. Marine Corps general, commander of U.S. Central Command (CENTCOM), and special envoy for the United States to Israel and the Palestinian National Authority (PNA). Anthony Charles Zinni was born to Italian immigrant parents in Philadelphia, Pennsylvania, on September 17, 1943. In 1965 he graduated from Villanova University with a degree in economics and was commissioned in the U.S. Marine Corps. In 1967 he served in Vietnam as an infantry battalion adviser to a South Vietnamese marine unit. In 1970 he returned to Vietnam as an infantry company commander. He was seriously wounded that November and was medically evacuated. Thereafter Zinni held a variety of command, administrative, and teaching positions, including at the Marine Corps Command and Staff College at Quantico, Virginia.

In 1991 as a brigadier general Zinni was the chief of staff and deputy commanding general of the Combined Joint Task Force (CJTF) for Operation Provide Comfort, the Kurdish relief effort in Turkey and Iraq. In 1992 and 1993 he was the director of operations for Operation Restore Hope in Somalia. As a lieutenant general, he commanded the I Marine Expeditionary Force (I MEF) from 1994 to 1996. In September 1996, as a full general, he became deputy commanding general of the CENTCOM, the U.S. military combatant

Marine Corps general Anthony Zinni, commander of the U.S. Central Command between 1997 and 2000, shown briefing reporters at the Pentagon on December 21, 1998, on his assessment of Operation DESERT FOX, a four-day bombing campaign of Iraq. (U.S. Department of Defense)

command responsible for most of the Middle East. He served as commanding general of CENTCOM from August 1997 until his retirement from the military in September 2000.

Upon leaving the military, Zinni participated in a number of different diplomatic initiatives. In late 2001, at the request of his old friend Colin L. Powell, then secretary of state, Zinni became the special envoy for the United States to Israel and the PNA.

Zinni arrived in Israel on November 25, 2001. He conducted several negotiating sessions with Prime Minister Ariel Sharon and PNA president Yasser Arafat individually but never with the two together. On December 12 the Palestinian suicide bombing of a bus near the settlement of Emmanuel effectively cut off all dialogue between the two sides. Zinni returned to the United States on December 17.

Zinni made his second short trip to the region from January 3 to 7, 2002. While he was conducting a meeting with Arafat, the Israelis intercepted and captured an illegal Palestinian arms ship in the Red Sea. The *Karine A* was carrying some 50 tons of weapons ordered by the PNA from Iran, a direct violation of the Oslo Accords.

Zinni returned to the region for the last time on March 12, 2002. While he believed that he was starting to make some headway, on March 27 a Palestinian suicide bomber struck a Passover Seder being held at an Israeli hotel. The Israelis launched a massive military retaliation against the Palestinians and severed all ties with Arafat. Zinni departed the region on April 15.

Although Zinni resigned his position as a special envoy, he continued to serve as an unofficial consultant. On August 5, 2003, he spent several hours in Washington, DC, briefing Major General David T. Zabecki, incoming senior security adviser of the newly established U.S. Coordinating and Monitoring Mission. In an address Zinni gave at Harvard's Kennedy School of Government on December 8, 2004, he stressed that resuming the peace process between Israel and the Palestinians was the single most important step the United States could take to restore its stature in the world. But interestingly enough, he noted that it would be a mistake to assign more high-profile special envoys to the mission. He favored the presence of professional negotiators.

Following his retirement from the military, Zinni held visiting appointments at several U.S. universities and in May 2005 became the president of international operations for MCI Industries.

An initial supporter of the George W. Bush administration and its foreign policy, Zinni quickly became one of the highest-profile military critics of the war in Iraq after he retired from CENTCOM. Distinguishing Afghanistan from Iraq, Zinni continued to believe that the invasion of Afghanistan to oust the Taliban regime and deprive al-Qaeda of its operating base was the right thing to do. Iraq was a totally different case. Although Saddam Hussein was a regional nuisance, Zinni believed his regime was totally contained and was no real strategic threat. Zinni was also certain that the case for weapons of mass destruction (WMD) was vastly overstated, remembering well the intelligence picture he had monitored daily while at CENTCOM.

While Zinni was still at CENTCOM in early 1999 immediately following the air strikes of Operation DESERT FOX, intelligence indicators and diplomatic reporting painted a picture of Hussein's regime as badly shaken and destabilized. In anticipation of the possible requirement for CENTCOM to have to lead an occupation of Iraq should Hussein fall, Zinni ordered the preparation of a comprehensive operations plan (OPLAN). Code-named DESERT CROSSING, it called for a robust civilian occupation authority with offices in each of Iraq's 18 provinces. The DESERT CROSSING plan was a dramatic contrast to what eventually played out under the anemic Coalition Provisional Authority, which for almost the first year of its existence had little presence outside Baghdad.

During the run-up to the invasion of Iraq, Zinni became increasingly concerned about the quality of the planning, especially the posthostilities phase. Queries to old contacts still at CENTCOM confirmed that OPLAN DESERT CROSSING had all but been forgotten. Zinni came to believe that the United States was being plunged headlong into an unnecessary war by political ideologues who had no understanding of the region. True to the promise he made to himself when he was wounded in Vietnam, Zinni became one of the first senior American figures to speak out against what he saw as "lack of planning, underestimating the task, and buying into a flawed strategy." Zinni soon found himself one of the most influential critics of the Bush administration's handling of the war in Iraq. In 2008 Zinni joined the teaching faculty at Duke University's Sanford Institute of Public Policy.

David T. Zabecki

See also: DESERT CROSSING, OPLAN; IRAQI FREEDOM, Operation

Further Reading

Clancy, Tom, with Anthony Zinni and Tony Kolz. *Battle Ready.* New York: Putnam, 2004.

Leverett, Flynt, ed. *The Road Ahead: Middle East Policy in the Bush Administration's Second Term.* Washington, DC: Brookings Institution, 2005.

Zinni, Anthony, and Tony Koltz. *The Battle for Peace: A Frontline Vision of America's Power and Purpose.* London: Palgrave Macmillan, 2006.

Chronology

1920	Creation of Iraq by the United Kingdom with approval of the League of Nations.	**1995**	Oil for Food Program Begins.
1932	Iraq gains independence from Britain.	**1998**	Saddam Hussein ends cooperation with UN weapons inspectors in October; U.S. bombs Iraqi weapons facilities in December.
1979	Saddam Hussein becomes president of Iraq and then establishes dictatorship.	**1998**	In a letter to President Clinton, neoconservatives call upon the president to remove Saddam from power. Many who sign it will serve in the Bush administration.
1980–1988	Iran-Iraq War; the U.S. backs Iraq, supplying it with weapons.		
1990	Saddam Hussein invades Iraq on August 2.	**2000**	In presidential debate with Vice President Al Gore, Texas governor George W. Bush criticizes the Clinton administration for not removing Saddam Hussein from power. Bush goes on to win the fall election.
1991	U.S.-led coalition expels Saddam from Kuwait in Gulf War; following lengthy air campaign the ground war lasts fewer than 100 hours and ends in defeat of Iraqi forces on February 28. The United Nation (UN) later establishes a safe haven for the Kurds in northern Iraq. Iraq forced to admit UN weapons inspectors.	**2001**	September 11 attacks followed by invasion of Afghanistan.
		September 2002	President Bush makes the case for war to the UN based upon assertion that Iraq possessed weapons of mass destruction (WMD).
1992	No-fly zone established over Southern Iraq in August.		

October 2002	Congress approves war with Iraq.
November 2002	Weapons inspectors allowed back into Iraq.
March 7, 2003	The United States with support from the United Kingdom and Spain submits a resolution calling for authorization to remove Saddam Hussein by force. The resolution fails to gain sufficient support, and the United States withdraws it on March 17.
March 18, 2003	The United States announces that it has formed a coalition of 30 countries willing to participate in a war with Iraq, although not all provide military forces. The United States and the United Kingdom will provide most of the troops.
March 19, 2003	President Bush addresses the American people to announce the start of Operation IRAQI FREEDOM.
March 21, 2003	Intense air campaign dubbed "shock and awe" begins.
April 8, 2003	U.S. forces take Baghdad.
May 1, 2003	President Bush lands on the aircraft carrier USS *Abraham Lincoln* and declares "mission accomplished" and end to conventional hostilities.
May 11, 2003	L. Paul ("Jerry") Bremer becomes head of the

	Coalition Provisional Authority (CPA).
May 16, 2003	Bremer promulgates Coalition Provisional Authority (CPA) General Order No. 1: De-Ba'athification of Iraqi Society, which removes all former Baath party members above a certain level from government offices exacerbating already severe unemployment.
May 22, 2003	UN formally lifts sanctions against Iraq.
May 23, 2003	Bremer promulgates CPA General Order No. 2: Dissolution of Entities, disbanding the Iraqi military without pay and further aggregating unemployment and contributing to the bitterness that fueled the insurgency.
July 13, 2003	Iraqi Interim Governing Council holds its first meeting.
July 22, 2003	Saddam Hussein's two sons, Uday and Qusay, are killed in a gun battle with coalition forces.
August 7, 2003	Jordanian Embassy bombing indicates growing insurgency.
August 15, 2003	UN Security Council resolution 1500 creates UN Assistance Mission in Iraq.
August 19, 2003	UN headquarters bombing kills Special Envoy Sergio Vera di Milo.

August 29, 2003	Najaf bombing kills 124, including Shia cleric Ayatollah Mohammed Baqr al-Hakim.	**August 5–27, 2004**	Battle of Najaf; coalition forces combat Sadr's militias.
October 27, 2003	Baghdad bombings signal start of Ramadan Offensive.	**November 7–17, 2004**	U.S. forces launch Operation PHANTOM FURY (Second Battle of Fallujah) to regain control of the city.
December 13, 2003	Saddam Hussein captured by U.S. forces in Tikrit.	**November 8–16, 2004**	Battle of Mosul.
December 31, 2003	U.S. military fatalities for the year total 486.[1]	**December 21, 2004**	Suicide bomber infiltrates forward operating base in Marez, killing 16 Americans and six others.
March 2, 2004	Golden Mosque bombed in Karbala.		
March 8, 2004	Iraqi provisional constitution signed.	**December 31, 2004**	U.S. military fatalities for the year total 849.
March 31, 2004	Ambush of four Blackwater contractors in Fallujah. Desire to retaliate leads White House to launch First Battle of Fallujah.	**January 30, 2005**	National elections for the Iraqi Legislative Council give the United Iraqi Alliance Party a majority, with Kurdish Alliance coming in second.
April 4, 2004	Shia uprising led by Muqtada al-Sadr begins; fighting will last until August.	**February 8, 2005**	Hillah car bombing kills 127 people in deadliest single attack to date.
April 18, 2004	Photos of Abu Ghraib prisoner abuse scandal become public, sparking major controversy for U.S. forces.	**March 16, 2005**	Iraqi National Assembly meets for the first time.
April 18, 2004	Spain announces that it will withdraw its 1,300 troops from Iraq.	**March 29, 2005**	Approximately 40,000 Iraqi troops supported by U.S. forces launch Operation LIGHTENING against the insurgents in Baghdad, the largest operation by the new Iraqi armed forces to date.
June 1, 2004	Iraqi Interim Government assumes power.		
June 8, 2004	UN Security Council Resolution 1546 transfers power from CPA to the Interim Government.	**April 6, 2005**	Jalal Talabani (Kurd) elected president of Iraq.
		May 8, 2005	Battle of a-Qaim.

---

[1]Annual casualty figures from http://www.icasualties.org/Iraq/index.aspx, accessed January 20, 2012.

July 19, 2005	Musayyib bombing.		Iraqi Accord Front with just over 15 percent.
August 1–4, 2005	Battle of Haditha.	December 31, 2005	U.S. military fatalities for the year total 846.
September 2005	Anbar Awakening Council formed.	February 22, 2006	al-Askari Mosque bombing.
September 1, 2005	Battle of Tal Afar.	April 24, 2006	Hamdania incident.
September 14, 2005	Baghdad bombings kill 160 and injure 500 in deadliest day of violence in the capital.	May 20, 2006	Regular Iraqi government replaces transitional government.
September 19, 2005	Basra prison incident.	June 7, 2006	Abu Musab al-Zarqawi, leader of al-Qaeda in Iraq, killed in bombing raid by U.S. forces.
September 29, 2005	Balad bombing.	July 25, 2006	Operation RIVER FALCON launched.
October 15, 2005	Iraqi constitution approved by referendum.	July 27, 2006	International Compact with Iraq, a combined venture among the government of Iraq, the UN, and the World Bank to promote develop-ment, launched.
October 24, 2005	Bombing of Palestine and Sheraton Ishtar hotels in Bhagdad.		
November 5, 2005	Operation STEEL CURTAIN.	October 19, 2006	Battle of Amarah.
November 18, 2005	Khanaqin bombings.	November 23, 2006	Sadr City bombings.
November 19, 2005	Haditha incident: U.S. soldiers kill 24 people, including 15 civilians, in Haditha, allegedly in retaliation for the death of a soldier from their unit.	December 6, 2006	*Report of the Iraq Study Group.*
		December 25, 2006	Start of Diyala campaign.
December 15, 2005	Iraqi legislative elections result in United Iraqi alli-ance garnering just over 41 percent of the vote followed by the Democratic Patriotic Alliance of Kurdistan with almost 23 percent, and the	December 30, 2006	Saddam Hussein executed.
		December 31, 2006	U.S. military fatalities for the year total 822. UN report claims 34,000 Iraqis died violently during 2006.

January 10, 2007	President Bush announces surge strategy, increasing combat troops in Iraq by approximately 20,000, increasing to a peak of 170,000 by October, to recoup deteriorating situation.
January 11, 2007	Iranian Liaison Office in Arbil raided by U.S. forces.
January 20, 2007	Insurgents raid Karbala provincial headquarters, capturing and killing five U.S. Soldiers.
January 28, 2007	Second Battle of Najaf.
February 3, 2007	Baghdad Market bombing.
February 27, 2007	Insurgents besiege British base in Basra.
March 6, 2007	al-Hillah bombings.
March 23, 2007	Iranians seize 15 British personnel in international waters.
March 27, 2007	Tal Afar bombing.
March 27, 2007	Iraq government approves a draft law allowing former Baath party members to resume posts from which they had been removed by the CPA.
April 6, 2007	Operation BLACK EAGLE launched against Mahdi Army.
April 18, 2007	Baghdad bombings.
April 23, 2007	Mosul massacre.
May 1, 2007	President Bush vetoes congressional bill that would have required the beginning of U.S. troop withdrawals by October 1, 2007.
June 13, 2007	al-Askari Mosque bombing.
June 16, 2007	Coalition forces launch Operation PHANTOM THUNDER.
July 16, 2007	Kirkuk bombings.
July 17, 2007	Amirli truck bombing.
July 26, 2007	Baghdad Market bombing.
August 14, 2007	Yazidi community bombings kill nearly 800 people.
August 15, 2007	Coalition forces launch Operation PHANTOM STRIKE against al-Qaeda in Iraq; operation will last until January 2008.
September 16, 2007	Blackwater incident in which contractors kill 17 Iraqi civilians in Baghdad.
December 17, 2007	British forces formally hand over control of Basra to the Iraqi government.
December 31, 2007	U.S. military fatalities for the year total 904.
January 8, 2008	Coalition forces launch Operation PHANTOM PHOENIX.
January 18, 2008	Day of Ashura fighting.

January 23, 2008	Beginning of Ninawa Campaign.
February 21, 2008	Turkish forces make an incursion into northern Iraq in pursuit of PKK (Kurdistan Workers Party) personnel.
March 24, 2008	U.S. military fatalities in Iraq reach 4,000.
March 25, 2008	Battle of Basra begins.
June 10, 2008	General David Petraeus becomes commander of U.S. Central Command.
July 29, 2008	Operation AUGURS OF PROSPERITY begins.
November 17, 2008	United States and Iraq sign Status of Forces agreement under which the United States agrees to withdraw its combat forces from Iraqi cities by June 30, 2009 and all remaining units by December 31, 2011.
January 31, 2009	Iraqi Governate elections to local councils in 14 of 18 provinces saw Nuri al-Maliki's State of Law coalition win 126 of 440 contested seats.
July 25, 2009	Legislative elections in Kurdish region of Iraq give Barham Salih's list the majority of seats and make

	him prime minister of Iraqi Kurdistan.
August 19, 2009	Bombings in Baghdad kill 101 people.
October 25, 2009	Bombings in Baghdad kill 155 people.
December 8, 2009	Bombings in Baghdad kill 127 people.
March 7, 2010	Parliamentary elections give Iyad Allawi's party a plurality of votes, but Nuri al-Maliki, who finishes second, remains prime minister by forming a coalition with the National Iraqi Alliance, which came in third.
August 18, 2010	Formal end to U.S. operations as last U.S. combat troops depart for Kuwait, with the remaining units scheduled to leave by the end of 2011.
October 22, 2010	Wikileaks releases thousands of classified documents, some containing embarrassing revelations about the war.
December 15, 2011	Official end to war as remaining U.S. forces leave Iraq after failure to reach a status of forces agreement that would have allowed some troops to remain.

Select Bibliography

Agresto, John. *Mugged by Reality: The Liberation of Iraq and the Failure of Good Intentions*. New York: Encounter Books, 2007.

Ajami, Fouad. *The Arab Predicament*. New York: Cambridge University Press, 1981.

Ajami, Fouad. *The Foreigner's Gift: The Americans, the Arabs, and the Iraqis in Iraq*. New York: Free Press, 2008.

Alfonsi, Christian. *Circle in the Sand: Why We Went Back to Iraq*. New York: Doubleday, 2006.

Allawi, Ali A. *The Occupation of Iraq: Winning the War, Losing the Peace*. New Haven, CT: Yale University Press, 2007.

Anderson, Jon Lee. *The Fall of Baghdad*. New York: Penguin, 2004.

An-Na'im, Abdullahi Ahmed. *Islam and the Secular State: Negotiating the Future of Shari'a*. Cambridge, MA: Harvard University Press, 2008.

"Ansar al-Islam in Iraqi Kurdistan." Human Rights Watch Backgrounder, www.hrw.org/legacy/backgrounder/mena/ansarbk020503.htm.

Associated Press. "In Motley Array of Iraqi Foes, Why Does U.S. Spotlight al-Qaida?" *International Herald Tribune*, June 8, 2007.

Atkinson, Rick. *In the Company of Soldiers: A Chronicle of Combat*. New York: Henry Holt, 2004.

Bahmanyar, Mir. *Shadow Warriors: A History of the US Army Rangers*. Oxford: Osprey Publishing, 2006.

Baker, James A. III, and Lee H. Hamilton, co-chairs, *Report of the Iraq Study Group*. New York: Vintage Books, 2006.

Bensahel, Nora. *After Saddam: Prewar Planning and the Occupation of Iraq*. Santa Monica, CA: RAND Arroyo Center, 2008.

Bergen, Peter I. *The Osama bin Laden I Know: An Oral History of al Qaeda's Leader*. New York: Free Press, 2006.

Biddle, Stephen. "Victory Misunderstood: What the Gulf War Tells Us about the Future of Conflict." *International Security* 21, no. 2 (Fall 1996): 139–79.

Blackwell, James A. "Professionalism and Army Doctrine: A Losing Battle?" In *The Future of the Army Profession*, edited by Don M. Snider and Lloyd J. Matthews, 325–48. Boston: McGraw-Hill, 2005.

Blake, Bernard, ed. *Jane's Weapons Systems, 1988–89 (Jane's Land-Based Air Defence)*. London: Jane's, 1988.

Bodansky, Yossef. *The Secret History of the Iraq War*. New York: Regan Books, 2004.

Bonin, John A. *U.S. Army Forces Central Command in Afghanistan and the Arabian Gulf during Operation ENDURING FREEDOM: 11 September 2001–11 March 2003*. Carlisle, PA: Army Heritage Center Foundation, 2003.

Bourque, Stephen A. "Hundred-Hour Thunderbolt: Armor in the Gulf War." In *Camp Colt to Desert Storm: The History of U.S. Armored Forces*, edited by George F. Hofmann and Donn A. Starry, 497–530.

Lexington: University Press of Kentucky, 1999.

Bowden, Mark. *Guests of the Ayatollah: The First Battle in America's War with Militant Islam.* New York: Atlantic Monthly, 2007.

Bowman, Steven R. *Iraq: U.S. Military Operations* [Electronic Resource]. Washington, DC: Library of Congress, Congressional Research Service, 2006.

Boyne, Walter J. *Beyond the Wild Blue: A History of the United States Air Force, 1947–2007.* 2nd ed. New York: Thomas Dunne Books, 2007.

Boyne, Walter J. *Operation Iraqi Freedom: What Went Right, What went Wrong, and Why.* New York: Forge, 2003.

Bragg, Rick. *I Am a Soldier, Too: The Jessica Lynch Story.* New York: Vintage, 2003.

Bremer, L. Paul, III. *My Year in Iraq: The Struggle to Build a Future of Hope.* New York: Simon and Schuster, 2006.

Brisard, Jean-Charles, in collaboration with Damien Martinez. *Zarqawi: The New Face of al-Qaeda.* New York: Other Press, 2005.

Brockwell, The Lord Butler of. *The Review of Intelligence on Weapons of Mass Destruction.* London: Stationery Office, 2004.

Bulliet, Richard W. *Islam: The View from the Edge.* New York: Columbia University Press, 1994.

Burns, John, and Melissa Rubin. "U.S. Arming Sunnis in Iraq to Battle Old Qaeda Allies." *New York Times,* June 11, 2007.

Burton, Brian, and John Nagl. "Learning as We Go: The US Army Adapts to Counterinsurgency in Iraq, July 2004–December 2006." *Small Wars and Insurgencies* 19, no. 3 (2008): 303–27.

Carothers, Thomas and Marina Ottaway, eds. *Uncharted Journey: Promoting Democracy in the Middle East.* Washington, DC: Carnegie Endowment for International Peace, 2005.

Cassidy, Robert. *Counterinsurgency and the Global War on Terror: Military Culture and Irregular War.* Palo Alto, CA: Stanford University Press, 2008.

Catherwood, Christopher. *Churchill's Folly: How Winston Churchill Created Modern Iraq.* New York: Carroll and Graf Publishers, 2004.

Cavaleri, David. *Easier Said Than Done: Making the Transition between Combat Operations and Stability Operations.* Ft. Leavenworth, KS: Combat Studies Institute Press, 2005.

Chandrasekaran, Rajiv. *Imperial Life in the Emerald City: Inside Iraq's Green Zone.* New York: Knopf, 2006.

Chehab, Zaki. *Iraq Ablaze: Inside the Insurgency.* New York: I. B. Tauris, 2006.

Chiarell, Peter, Patrick Michaelis, and Geoffrey Norman. "Armor in Urban Terrain: The Critical Enabler." *Armor* (June–October 2004): 7–9.

Cleveland, William L. *A History of the Modern Middle East.* 3rd ed. Boulder, CO: Westview, 2004.

Cockburn, Andrew, and Patrick Cockburn. *Out of the Ashes: The Resurrection of Saddam Hussein.* New York: Harper Collins, 1999.

Cockburn, Patrick. *Muqtada: Muqtada al-Sadr, the Shia Revival, and the Struggle for Iraq.* New York: Scribner, 2008.

Cockburn, Patrick. *The Occupation: War and Resistance in Iraq.* New York: Verso, 2007.

Congressional Research Service, Report to Congress. *Iraq: Post-Saddam Governance and Security, September 6, 2007.* Washington, DC: U.S. Government Printing Office, 2007.

Cook, David. *Understanding Jihad.* Berkeley: University of California Press, 2005.

Coopersmith, Nechemia, and Shraga Simmons. *Iraqi Security Forces: A Strategy for Success.* Westport, CT: Praeger Security International, 2005.

Coopersmith, Nechemia, and Shraga Simmons. *The Iraq War: Strategy, Tactics, and Military Lessons.* Washington, DC: CSIS Press, 2003.

Cordesman, Anthony H. *The Iraq War: Strategy, Tactics, and Military Lessons.* Westport, CT: Praeger, 2003.

Cordesman, Anthony H., and Jose Ramos. "Sadr and the Mahdi Army: Evolution, Capabilities, and a New Direction." Washington, DC: Center for Strategic and International Studies, August 4, 2008.

Coughlin, Con. *Saddam: King of Terror.* New York: Gale, 2003.

Daalder, Ivo H., Nicole Gnesotto, and Philip H. Gordon. *Crescent of Crisis: U.S.-European Strategy for the Greater Middle East.* Washington, DC: Brookings, 2006.

Danner, Mark. *Torture and Truth: America, Abu Ghraib, and the War on Terror.* New York: New York Review Books, 2004.

Deflem, Mathieu, and Suzanne Sutphin. "Policing Post-War Iraq: Insurgency, Civilian Police, and the Reconstruction of Society." *Sociological Focus* 39, no. 4 (November 2006), 265–83.

DeLong, Michael, and Noah Lukeman. *Inside CentCom: The Unvarnished Truth about the Wars in Afghanistan and Iraq.* Washington, DC: Regnery, 2004.

DeRosa, John P. J. "Platoons of Action: An Armor Task Force's Response to Full-Spectrum Operations in Iraq." *Armor* (November–December 2005): 7–12.

DeYoung, Karen. *Soldier: The Life of Colin Powell.* New York: Knopf, 2006.

Diamond, Larry. *Squandered Victory: The American Occupation and the Bungled Effort to Bring Democracy to Iraq.* New York: Times Books, 2005.

DiMarco, Louis A. *Traditions, Changes and Challenges: Military Operations and the Middle Eastern City.* Ft. Leavenworth, KS: Combat Studies Institute Press, 2004.

Donnelly, Thomas. *Operation Iraqi Freedom: A Strategic Assessment.* Washington, DC: AEI Press, 2004.

Dreyfus, Robert. *Devil's Game: How the United States Helped Unleash Fundamentalist Islam.* New York: Metropolitan Books, 2005.

Drogin, Bob. *Curveball: Spies, Lies, and the Con Man Who Caused a War.* New York: Random House, 2007.

Eland, Ivan. *Partitioning for Peace: An Exit Strategy for Iraq.* Oakland, CA: Independent Institute, 2008.

Enderlin, Charles. *The Lost Years: Radical Islam, Intifada, and Wars in the Middle East, 2001–2006.* New York: Handsel Books, 2007.

Engbrecht, Shawn. *America's Covert Warriors: Inside the World of Private Military Contractors.* Dulles, VA: Potomac Books, 2010.

Engel, Richard. *War Journal: My Five Years in Iraq.* New York: Simon and Schuster, 2008.

Esposito, John L. *The Islamic Threat: Myth or Reality?* New York: Oxford University Press, 1992.

Fawn, Rick, and Raymond Hinnebusche, eds. *The Iraq War: Causes and Consequences.* Boulder, CO: Lynne Rienner, 2006.

Feldman, Noah. *The Fall and Rise of the Islamic State.* Princeton: Princeton University Press, 2008.

Fontenot, Gregory, E. J. Degen, and David Tohn. *On Point: The United States Army in Operation Iraqi Freedom.* Annapolis, MD: Naval Institute Press, 2005.

Francona, Rick. *Ally to Adversary: An Eyewitness Account of Iraq's Fall from Grace.* Annapolis, MD: Naval Institute Press, 1999.

Franks, Tommy, with Malcolm McConnell. *American Soldier.* New York: Regan Books, 2004.

Frederick, Jim. *Black Hearts: One Platoon's Descent into Madness in Iraq's Triangle of Death.* New York: Harmony Books, 2010.

Fuller, Graham E., and Rend Rahim Francke. *The Arab Shi'a: The Forgotten Muslims.* New York: St. Martin's, 2000.

Furnish, Timothy R. *Holiest Wars: Islamic Mahdis, Their Jihads, and Osama Bin Laden.* Westport, CT: Greenwood, 2006.

Gaddis, John Lewis. *Surprise, Security and the American Experience.* Cambridge, MA: Harvard University Press, 2005.

Galbraith, Peter. *The End of Iraq: How American Incompetence Created a War without*

End. New York: Simon and Schuster, 2006.

Gander, Terry J. *Anti-Tank Weapons*. Marlborough, UK: Crowood, 2000.

Gander, Terry J. *The Bazooka: Hand-Held Hollow-Charge Anti-Tank Weapons*. London: PRC Publishing, 1998.

General Accounting Office. *Operation Desert Storm: Evaluation of the Air War; Report to Congress*. Washington, DC: U.S. Government Printing Office, 1996.

Gerrard, Howard. *U.S. Army Soldier: Baghdad 2003–04 (Warrior)*. Oxford: Osprey, 2007.

Gordon, Michael R., and Bernard R. Trainor. *Cobra II: The Inside Story of the Invasion and Occupation of Iraq*. New York: Pantheon Books, 2006.

Gordon, Philip, and Jeremy Shapiro. *Allies at War: America, Europe, and the Crisis over Iraq*. New York: McGraw-Hill, 2004.

Graham, Bradley. *By His Own Rules: The Ambitions, Successes, and Ultimate Failures of Donald Rumsfeld*. New York: Public Affairs, 2009.

Graham-Brown, Sarah. *Sanctioning Saddam: The Politics of Intervention in Iraq*. London: I. B. Tauris, 1999.

Grau, Lester W. "Guerrillas, Terrorists, and Intelligence Analysts." *Military Review* (July–August 2004): 42–49.

Graveline, Christopher, and Michael Clemens. *The Secrets of Abu Ghraib Revealed*. Dulles, VA: Potomac Books, 2010.

Greenberg, Karen J., and Joshua L. Dratel, eds. *The Torture Papers: The Road to Abu Ghraib*. Cambridge: Cambridge University Press, 2005.

Haass, Richard. *The Opportunity: America's Moment to Alter History's Course*. New York: Public Affairs, 2006.

Haass, Richard. *War of Necessity, War of Choice: A Memoir of Two Iraq Wars*. New York: Simon and Schuster, 2009.

Hadar, Leon T. *Sandstorm: Policy Failure in the Middle East*. New York: Palgrave Macmillan, 2005.

Hafez, Mohammed. *Suicide Bombers in Iraq: The Strategy and Ideology of Martyrdom*. Washington, DC: United States Institute of Peace Press, 2007.

Hallion, Richard P. *Storm over Iraq: Air Power and the Gulf War*. Washington, DC: Smithsonian Institution Press, 1997.

Hammer, Joshua. "Samara Rises." *Smithsonian* 39, no. 10 (January 2009): 28–37.

Hanson, Victor Davis. *Between War and Peace: Lessons from Afghanistan to Iraq*. New York: Random House, 2004.

Hashim, Ahmed S. *Insurgency and Counterinsurgency in Iraq*. Ithaca, NY: Cornell University Press, 2006.

Herring, Eric, and Glen Rangwala. *Iraq in Fragments: The Occupation and Its Legacy*. Ithaca, NY: Cornell University Press, 2006.

Holmes, Tony. *US Navy Hornet Units in Operation Iraqi Freedom*. 2 vols. Botley, Oxford, UK: Osprey, 2004–2005.

International Crisis Group. *Middle East Report Number 55: Iraq's Muqtada al-Sadr: Spoiler or Stabiliser?* Washington, DC: International Crisis Group, July 11, 2006.

Isikoff, Michael, and David Corn. *Hubris: The Inside Story of Spin, Scandal, and the Selling of the Iraq War*. New York: Crown Publishers, 2006.

Johnson, David E., M. Wade Markel, and Brian Shannon. *The 2008 Battle of Sadr City*. Santa Monica, CA: RAND Corporation, 2011.

Kagan, Frederick. *Finding the Target: The Transformation of American Military Policy*. New York: Encounter, 2006.

Karsh, Efraim. *Saddam Hussein: A Political Biography*. New York: Grove/Atlantic, 2002.

Karsh, Efraim, and Inari Karsh. *Empires of the Sand: The Struggle for Mastery of the Middle East, 1789–1923*. Cambridge, MA: Harvard University Press, 1999.

Katzman, Kenneth. "Iran's Activities and Influence in Iraq." *CRS Report for Congress*, January 24, 2008.

Keegan, John. *The Iraq War: The Military Offensive, from Victory in 21 Days to the Insurgent Aftermath*. New York: Vintage, 2005.

Kepel, Gilles. *Beyond Terror and Martyrdom: The Future of the Middle East*. Cambridge, MA: Harvard University Press, 2008.

Khalidi, Rashid. *Resurrecting Empire: Western Footprints and America's Perilous Path in the Middle East*. Boston: Beacon, 2004.

Kilcullen, David. *The Accidental Guerrilla: Fighting Small Wars in the Midst of a Big One*. New York: Oxford University Press, 2009.

Knights, Michael. *Cradle of Conflict: Iraq and the Birth of the Modern U.S. Military*. Annapolis, MD: Naval Institute Press, 2005.

Lambeth, Benjamin S. *American Carrier Air Power at the Dawn of a New Century*. Santa Monica, CA: RAND Corporation, 2005.

Larson, Eric V. et al. *Assessing Irregular Warfare: A Framework for Intelligence Analysis*. Santa Monica, CA: RAND Arroyo Center, 2008.

Lesch, David W. *The Middle East and the United States: A Historical and Political Reassessment*. New York: Perseus, 2006.

Livingston, Gary. *An Nasiriyah: The Fight for the Bridges*. Top Sail Beach, NC: Caisson Press, 2004.

Lowry, Richard, with Howard Gerrard. *US Marines in Iraq: Operation Iraqi Freedom, 2003*. Oxford: Osprey, 2006.

Lubin, Andrew. "Ramadi: From the Caliphate to Capitalism." *Proceedings* 134 (April 2008): 54–61.

Lynch, Kristin. *Supporting Air and Space Expeditionary Forces: Lessons from Operation Iraqi Freedom*. Washington, DC: RAND Corporation, 2004.

MacGregor, Douglas. *Warrior's Rage: The Great Tank Battle of 73 Easting*. Annapolis, MD: Naval Institute Press, 2009.

Mackey, Sandra. *The Reckoning: Iraq and the Legacy of Saddam Hussein*. New York: Norton, 2002.

McCary, John A. "The Anbar Awakening: An Alliance of Incentives." *Washington Quarterly* 32 (January 2009): 43–59.

Metz, Steven. *Learning from Iraq: Counterinsurgency in American Strategy*. Carlisle, PA: Strategic Studies Institute, 2007.

Miller, Richard F. *A Carrier at War: On Board the USS* Kitty Hawk *in the Iraq War*. Washington, DC: Potomac Books, 2003.

Mingst, Karen A., and Margaret P. Karns. *United Nations in the Twenty-First Century*. 3rd ed. Boulder, CO: Westview, 2006.

Mockaitis, Thomas R. *Iraq and the Challenge of Counterinsurgency*. Westport, CT: Praeger, 2007.

Mockaitis, Thomas R. *The Iraq War: A Documentary and Reference Guide*. Santa Barbara, CA: ABC-CLIO/Greenwood, 2011.

Moore, Rebecca R. *NATO's New Mission: Projecting Stability in a Post–Cold War Era*. Westport, CT: Praeger Security International, 2007.

Moroney, Jennifer D. P., Frederic Wehrey, Obaid Younossi, Farhana Ali, and Robert A. Guffey. *Future U.S. Security Relationships with Iraq and Afghanistan: U.S. Air Force Roles*. Santa Monica, CA: RAND, 2008.

Munthe, Turi, ed. *The Saddam Hussein Reader*. New York: Thunder's Mouth Press, 2002.

Murray, Williamson, and Robert H. Scales Jr. *The Iraq War*. Cambridge, MA: Belknap/Harvard University Press, 2003.

Musharraf, Pervez. *In the Line of Fire: A Memoir*. New York: Simon and Schuster, 2006.

Myers, Richard B., and Malcolm McConnell. *Eyes on the Horizon: Serving on the Front Lines of National Security*. Riverside, NJ: Threshold Editions, 2009.

Nakash, Yitzhak. *Reaching for Power: The Shi'a in the Modern Arab World*. Princeton, NJ: Princeton University Press, 2006.

Nasr, Vali. *The Shia Revival: How Conflicts within Islam Will Shape the Future*. New York: Norton, 2006.

Naveh, Shimon. *In Pursuit of Military Excellence: The Evolution of Operational Theory*. London: Frank Cass, 1997.

Neville, Leigh. *Special Operations Forces in Iraq (Elite)*. Oxford: Osprey, 2008.

O'Leary, Brendan, John McGarry, and Khaled Salih. *The Future of Kurdistan in Iraq*. Philadelphia: University of Pennsylvania Press, 2005.

Packer, George. *The Assassins' Gate: Americans in Iraq*. New York: Farrar, Straus and Giroux, 2007.

Parrish, Robert D., and N. A. Andreacchio. *Schwarzkopf: An Insider's View of the Commander and His Victory*. New York: Bantam, 1991.

Pelletiere, Stephen. *Losing Iraq: Insurgency and Politics*. Westport, CT: Praeger Security International, 2007.

Perito, Robert M. *Special Report: The Iraq Federal Police: U.S. Police Building under Fire*. Washington, DC: United States Institute of Peace, October 2011.

Perry, Walter L., and John Gordon IV. *Analytical Support to Intelligence in Counterinsurgencies*. Santa Monica, CA: RAND Corporation, 2008.

Phillips, David L. *Losing Iraq: Inside the Postwar Reconstruction Fiasco*. Boulder, CO: Westview, 2005.

Pintak, Lawrence. *Reflections in a Bloodshot Lens: America, Islam, and the War of Ideas*. Ann Arbor: University of Michigan Press, 2006.

Plame, Valerie. *Fair Game: My Life as a Spy, My Betrayal by the White House*. New York: Simon and Schuster, 2007.

Polk, William R. *Understanding Iraq: The Whole Sweep of Iraqi History, From Genghis Khan's Mongols to the Ottoman Turks to the British Mandate to the American Occupation*. New York: HarperCollins, 2005.

Pollack, Kenneth M. *A Path out of the Desert: A Grand Strategy for America in the Middle East*. New York: Random House, 2008.

Pollack, Kenneth M. *The Threatening Storm: The Case for Invading Iraq*. New York: Random House, 2002.

Potter, Lawrence G., and Gary G. Sick. *Iran, Iraq, and the Legacies of War*. New York: Palgrave Macmillan, 2004.

Powell, Colin, with Joseph E. Persico. *My American Journey*. New York: Ballantine, 2003.

Purdum, Todd S., and the staff of the *New York Times*. *A Time of Our Choosing: America's War in Iraq*. New York: Times Books/Henry Holt, 2003.

Rahimi, Babak. "The Future of Moqtada al-Sadr's New Jaysh al-Mahdi." *CTC Sentinel* 2, no. 1 (January 2009).

Ramadan, Tariq. *Western Muslims and the Future of Islam*. New York: Oxford University Press, 2004.

Record, Jeffrey. *Wanting War: Why the Bush Administration Invaded Iraq*. Dulles, VA: Potomac Books, 2009.

Reuter, Christoph. *My Life Is a Weapon: A Modern History of Suicide Bombing*. Princeton, NJ: Princeton University Press, 2004.

Ricks, Thomas E. *Fiasco: The American Military Adventure in Iraq*. New York: Penguin, 2006.

Ricks, Thomas E. *The Gamble: General David Petraeus and the American Military Adventure in Iraq*. New York: Penguin, 2009.

Ripley, Tim. *Air War Iraq*. Barnsley, UK: Pen and Sword, 2004.

Ripley, Tim. *Tank Warfare*. Drexel Hill, PA: Casemate, 2003.

Robinson, Linda. *Tell Me How This Ends: General David Petraeus and the Search for a Way Out of Iraq*. New York: Public Affairs, 2007.

Romjue, John L. *From Active Defense to Air-Land Battle: The Development of Army Doctrine, 1973–1982*. Fort Monroe, VA: United States Army Training and Doctrine Command, 1984.

Sanchez, Ricardo S., with Donald T. Phillips. *Wiser in Battle: A Soldier's Story*. New York: Harper, 2008.

Scales, Robert H. *Certain Victory: The U.S. Army in the Gulf War*. Washington, DC: Brassey's, 1994.

Schwarz, Anthony J. "Iraq's Militias: The True Threat to Coalition Success in Iraq." *Parameters* (Spring 2007): 55–71.

Sciolino, Elaine. *The Outlaw State: Saddam Hussein's Quest for Power and the Gulf Crisis.* New York: Wiley, 1991.

Shadid, Anthony. *Night Draws Near: Iraq's People in the Shadow of America's War.* New York: Henry Holt, 2004.

Shaffer, Brenda. *The Limits of Culture: Islam and Foreign Policy.* Cambridge, MA: MIT Press, 2006.

Simon, Reeva Spector, and Eleanor H. Tejirian, eds. *The Creation of Iraq, 1914–1921.* New York: Columbia University Press, 2004.

Simpson, John. *The Wars against Saddam: Taking the Hard Road to Baghdad.* New York: Macmillan, 2003.

Smith, Niel, and Sean MacFarland. "Anbar Awakens: The Tipping Point." *Military Review* (March–April 2008): 41–52.

Stansfield, Gareth R. V. *Iraqi Kurdistan: Political Development and Emergent Democracy.* New York: Routledge, 2003.

Strasser, Steven, ed. *The Abu Ghraib Investigations: The Official Independent Panel and Pentagon Reports on the Shocking Prisoner Abuse in Iraq.* New York: Public Affairs, 2004.

Swain, Richard M. "AirLand Battle." In *Camp Colt to Desert Storm: The History of U.S. Armored Forces*, edited by George F. Hofmann and Donn A. Starry, 360–402. Lexington: University Press of Kentucky, 1999.

Teamey, Kyle, and Jonathan Sweet. "Organizing Intelligence for Counterinsurgency." *Military Review* (September–October 2006): 24–29.

Thaler, David E., Theodore W. Karasik, Dalia Dassa Kaye, Jennifer D. P. Moroney, Frederic Wehrey, Obaid Younossi, Farhana Ali, and Robert A. Guffey. *Future U.S. Security Relationships with Iraq and Afghanistan: U.S. Air Force Roles.* Santa Monica, CA: RAND, 2008.

Tibi, Bassam. *The Challenge of Fundamentalism: Political Islam and the New World Disorder.* Berkeley: University of California Press, 1998.

Tucker, Terry. "Heavy Armor: The Core of Urban Combat." *Armor* (May–June 2005): 4, 49.

Von Zielbauer, Paul. "G.I. Gets 100 Years for Rape and Killing in Iraq." *New York Times*, August 5, 2007, http://www.nytimes.com/2007/08/05/us/05abuse.html (accessed March 10, 2010).

Weeks, John S. *Men against Tanks: A History of Anti-Tank Warfare.* New York: Mason/Charter, 1975.

West, Bing. *The Strongest Tribe: War, Politics, and the Endgame in Iraq.* New York: Random House, 2007.

West, Bing, and Ray L. Smith. *The March Up: Taking Baghdad with the 1st Marine Division.* New York: Bantam, 2003.

Williams, Garland H. *Engineering Peace: The Military Role in Postconflict Reconstruction.* Washington, DC: United States Institute of Peace, 2005.

Williams, M. J. *NATO, Security and Risk Management, From Kosovo to Kandahar.* Milton Park, UK: Routledge, 2008.

Wilson, Joseph. *The Politics of Truth: Inside the Lies That Led to War and Betrayed My Wife's CIA Identity.* New York: Carroll and Graf, 2004.

Wingate, Brian. *Saddam Hussein: The Rise and Fall of a Dictator.* New York: Rosen, 2004.

Wong, Edward. "The Reach of War: Violence, Militants Show the Beheading of 3 Kurdish Hostages." *New York Times*, March 22, 2009.

Woodward, Bob. *Plan of Attack.* New York: Simon and Schuster, 2004.

Woodward, Bob. *State of Denial: Bush at War, Part III.* New York: Simon and Schuster, 2006.

Woodward, Bob. *The War Within: A Secret White House History, 2006–2008.* New York: Simon and Schuster, 2008.

Worth, Robert. "Blast Destroys Shrine in Iraq, Setting Off Sectarian Fury." *New York Times*, February 22, 2008. http://www.nytimes.com/2006/02/22/international/

middleeast/22cnd-iraq.html (accessed March 19, 2012).

Wright, Donald P., and Timothy R. Reese. *On Point II: Transition to the New Campaign. The United States Army in Operation IRAQI FREEDOM, May 2003– January 2005.* Ft. Leavenworth, KS: Combat Studies Institute Press, 2008.

Zabecki, David T., and Bruce Condell, eds. and trans. *Truppenführung: On the German Art of War.* Boulder, CO: Lynne Rienner, 2001.

Zinsmeister, Karl. *Boots on the Ground: A Month with the 82nd Airborne in the Battle for Iraq.* New York: St. Martin's Paperbacks, 2004.

Zinsmeister, Karl. *Dawn Over Baghdad: How the U. S. Military Is Using Bullets and Ballots to Remake Iraq.* New York: Encounter Books, 2004.

Contributors

Rebecca Adelman
Assistant Professor
University of Maryland-Baltimore County

Kristian P. Alexander
Associate Instructor
University of Utah

Christopher Paul Anzalone
Independent Scholar

James Arnold
Independent Scholar

Ojan Aryanfard
Independent Scholar

Stephen E. Atkins
Adjunct Professor of History
Texas A&M University

Ralph Martin Baker
Independent Scholar

Matthew Basler
Assistant Professor
U.S. Air Force Academy

Jeffrey D. Bass
Assistant Professor of History
Quinnipiac University

Robert F. Baumann
Professor of History
U.S. Army Command and General Staff
College

Michael K. Beauchamp
Visiting Assistant Professor
Texas A&M University

Robert Berschinski
Independent Scholar

Amy Hackney Blackwell
Independent Scholar

James C. Bradford
Professor of History
Texas A&M University

Ron Briley
Assistant Headmaster
Sandia Preparatory School

Jessica Britt
Independent Scholar

Stefan Brooks
Assistant Professor of Political
Science
Lindsey Wilson College

Gates Brown
Management and Program Analyst at
Financial Management Services
Department of the Treasury

Jeffery A. Charlston
Associate Professor
University of Maryland University College

Elliot Paul Chodoff
University of Haifa, Israel

Lawrence Cline
Associate Professor of Intelligence Studies
American Military University
Adjunct Instructor, Center for Civil-Military
Relations
Naval Postgraduate School

Dylan A. Cyr
Sessional Instructor, History
University of Waterloo

Marcel A. Derosier
Independent Scholar

Christopher Dietrich
Assistant Professor of History
Fordham University

Scott R. DiMarco
Director of Library and Information
Resources
Mansfield University of Pennsylvania

Paul William Doerr
Associate Professor
Acadia University, Canada

Michael Doidge
Independent Scholar

Donald Redmond Dunne
Colonel, U.S. Army

Richard M. Edwards
Senior Lecturer
University of Wisconsin Colleges

Shawn Fisher
Instructor of History and Social Sciences
Harding University, Arkansas

Benjamin D. Forest
Major, Air Command and Staff College

William E. Fork
Independent Scholar

Elun A. Gabriel
Associate Professor of European History
St. Lawrence University

Benjamin John Grob-Fitzgibbon
Assistant Professor of History
University of Arkansas

Michael R. Hall
Associate Professor of History
Armstrong Atlantic State University

William P. Head
Historian/Chief, WR-ALC Office
of History
U.S. Air Force

Arthur M. Holst
Master of Public Administration
Program Faculty
Widener University

Charles Francis Howlett
Associate Professor
Molloy College

Robert B. Kane
Adjunct Professor of History
Troy University

Gary Lee Kerley
North Hall High School
Gainesville, Georgia

Chen Kertcher
School of History
Tel Aviv University

John T. Kuehn
Associate Professor
U.S. Army Command and General
Staff College

Tom Lansford
Dean, Gulf Coast
University Southern Mississippi

Alison Lawlor
Independent Scholar

Mark F. Leep
Independent Scholar

Keith A. Leitich
Independent Scholar

Shawn Livingston
Public Service Librarian
University of Kentucky

Robert W. Malick
Adjunct Professor of History
Harrisburg Area Community College

Jerome V. Martin
Command Historian
U.S. Strategic Command

Mitchell McNaylor
Independent Scholar

Herbert F. Merrick
Independent Scholar

Thomas R. Mockaitis
Professor of History
DePaul University

Kirsty Anne Montgomery
Independent Scholar

Jerry D. Morelock
Colonel, U.S. Army, Retired
Editor in Chief, *Armchair
General* Magazine

Gregory W. Morgan
Independent Scholar

Lisa Marie Mundey
Assistant Professor
University of St. Thomas

Keith Murphy
Associate Dean
Fort Valley State University

Charlene T. Overturf
Adjunct Faculty
Armstrong Atlantic State University

James D. Perry
Independent Scholar

Paul G. Pierpaoli Jr.
Fellow
Military History, ABC-CLIO, Inc.

Peter J. Rainow
Independent Scholar

Priscilla Roberts
Associate Professor of History,
School of Humanities
Honorary Director,
Centre of American Studies
University of Hong Kong

Russell G. Rodgers
Staff Historian
U.S. Army

Karl Lee Rubis
University of Kansas

Carl Schuster
Captain, U.S. Navy, Retired
Visiting Assistant Professor of History
Hawaii Pacific University

Larry Schweikart
Independent Scholar

Jeff Seiken
Independent Scholar

John Sigler
Rear Admiral, U.S. Navy, Retired

George L. Simpson Jr.
Professor of History
High Point University

Ranjit Singh
Assistant Professor of Political Science and
International Affairs
University of Mary Washington

John Southard
Visiting Lecturer
Georgia State University

Daniel E. Spector
Independent Scholar

Paul Joseph Springer
Assistant Professor
United States Military Academy

Melissa Stallings
Independent Scholar

Kenneth Szmed Jr.
Independent Scholar

Jason Robert Tatlock
Assistant Professor of History
Armstrong Atlantic State University

Randy Jack Taylor
Librarian
Howard Payne University

William H. Thiesen
Independent Scholar

Spencer C. Tucker
Senior Fellow
Military History, ABC-CLIO, Inc.

Richard B. Verrone
Affiliated Scholar
Texas Tech University

Tim J. Watts
Subject Librarian
Kansas State University

Adam P. Wilson
Lecturer in History
University of Tennessee, Martin

Anna M. Wittmann
Instructor in English
University of Alberta

David T. Zabecki
Major General, U.S. Army, Retired

Sherifa Zuhur
Visiting Professor of National
Security Affairs
Regional Strategy and Planning Department
Strategic Studies Institute
U.S. Army War College

Index

Page numbers in **bold** indicate main entries in the encyclopedia.